A Texas Portfolio DISCARDED

ISBN 0-201-86125-9

3 4 5 6 7 8 9 10 - DO - 95 94

Communicate Choose one
of the captions from one of the
state symbols that you see on
pages 2-3. Research the subject that you choose and give
an oral report to the class.

Overview

Texas is the second largest state in the United
States. Because of its size, the Lone Star State is like
many states in one. Ecologists have divided Texas into
ten regions, based on its many kinds of vegetation. As
you will see, each region has its own plants, animals,
and endangered species.

Nearly every county in Texas uses some form of irrigation to grow crops. Most irrigating is done with
underground water. Thus, the subject of underground
water—its uses and its conservation—is an important
one in the state. Crops such as cotton, rice, wheat, and
grain sorghum grow well in Texas. The state is also
known for its cattle, horses, hogs, and poultry. Genetic
breeding has produced heartier breeds of animals and
healthier varieties of plants.

The land in Texas has undergone many changes in
the last hundred years as cities and farms have spread
over the prairies. Prairie land has been used for different purposes over the years as people's needs have
changed. However, as wildlife habitats are threatened,
the shrinking prairie has resulted in more endangered
species of plants and animals. But Texas is still home to
hundreds of exotic plants, animals, and fish.

As industrial and agricultural growth has threatened
the environment, concerned Texans throughout the
state are working to protect and improve the environment. Highway beautification programs begun in the

State Motto Friendship
Texas takes its name from the
Indian word *tejas*, which means
"friends" or "allies."

State Flower Bluebonnet
Growing throughout the state
of Texas, the bluebonnet has
purplish-blue flowers with a
white or yellow center.

State Fish Guadalupe Bass
The Guadalupe bass is found in
the clear, spring-fed waters in
the Hill Country. It is a member
of the black bass family.

State Tree Pecan
The pecan tree can reach a
height of 30 m and can provide
excellent shade. The tree yields
the popular pecan nut.

1930's continue today as highways are planted with grasses, trees, and wildflowers. Anyone in Texas can help restore and maintain the state's nine forests by planting a seedling provided by the Texas Forest Service. Ecologists are also bringing back from the edge of extinction such birds as the golden-cheeked warbler and Attwater's prairie chicken.

Texas is southeast of the Rocky Mountains and bordered by the Gulf of Mexico. As a result of its geographical location, Texas experiences floods, hurricanes, and tornadoes. The state has seen some of the worst storms in the United States, including the Great Galveston Storm of 1900.

The word *oil* has long been associated with Texas. Texas supplies almost one-third of the oil used in the United States. Because oil is a fossil fuel, it is a nonrenewable resource. Thus, Texas is exploring renewable energy sources that will not threaten the ecosystem. The state is also a pioneer in the technology being developed to clean up oil spills that occur offshore.

Finally, technological advances in many areas take place in Texas. For example, the state has one of only four supercolliders in the world. The superconducting cyclotron, as the device is called, is used to do nuclear research. This research results in better health care and improvements in industry. In fact, people who have never even heard of the cyclotron can benefit from it. As you read this Texas Portfolio, you will learn more about Texas and all that the state has to offer.

State Flag Lone Star
The state flag adopted in 1839 is red, white, and blue standing for bravery, strength, and loyalty. The Lone Star is the symbol of Texas.

State Bird Mockingbird
The official state bird, the mockingbird has a gray coat with an ash-white breast. The mockingbird is well known for its exact imitations of the notes of other birds.

State Gem Texas Blue Topaz
The Texas blue topaz is a hard mineral ranging in color from clear to light blue. Most of these gems are found in the Edwards Plateau region.

State Shell Lightning Whelk
The lightning whelk is found along the Gulf Coast. The body of the shell has wavy, brown stripes.

State Grass Sideoats Grama
Found throughout Texas, sideoats grama is a native prairie grass. It provides food for both livestock and birds. When full grown, it stands 80 cm tall.

Panorama of Texas

Texas boasts a unique variety of landscapes in its 691,030 square kilometers. Rangeland, farmland, desert, plains, rolling hills, mountains, and coastlines make Texas one of the richest states in the nation in terms of landforms.

Ecologists have divided Texas into ten regions based on the different kinds of vegetation found across the state. As you can see from the map on page 5, vegetation ranges from oak trees to sagebrush depending on climate. Of course, animal life also varies from region to region with the kind of vegetation available for food. These regions show you that Texas is like many states in one.

TEN REGIONS OF TEXAS

1 Piney Woods

2 Gulf Prairies and Marshes

3 Post Oak Savannah

4 Blackland Prairies

5 Cross-Timbers and Prairies

6 South Texas Plains

7 Edwards Plateau

8 Rolling Plains

9 High Plains

10 Trans-Pecos

High Plains
Landform: Short grasslands that have become farmland
Temperature: 9°C to 38°C
Rainfall: 30 cm to 51 cm
Vegetation: Sideoats grama, buffalograss, sagebrush, mesquite
Animals: Quail, mourning dove, mule deer, turkey, exotic aoudad sheep, prairie dog, sand-dune sagebrush lizard, antelope

Trans-Pecos
Landform: Desert and mountain ranges
Temperature: 2°C to 36°C
Rainfall: 20 cm to 51 cm
Vegetation: Peyote, creosotebush, catclaw, tarbush, pinyon-oak-juniper woodlands
Animals: Mule deer, antelope, dove, quail, mountain lion, pupfish, Colima warbler, mosquito fish, western mastiff bat

Edwards Plateau
Landform: Rolling terrain dotted with springs, rivers, and streams
Temperature: 6°C to 34°C
Rainfall: 38 cm to 84 cm
Vegetation: Live oak, post oak, mesquite, juniper, sage, pricklypear, basin bellflower, Texas snowbells, Edwards Plateau cornsalad, Texas wild rice
Animals: Axis deer, sika deer, fallow deer, white-tailed deer, Guadalupe bass, antelope, blind catfish, cave salamanders, black-capped vireo, golden-cheeked warbler, bald eagle

South Texas Plains
Landform: Open grassland that has become a thorn forest with subtropical trees and shrubs
Temperature: 4°C to 35°C
Rainfall: 46 cm to 89 cm
Vegetation: Texas persimmon, mesquite, live oak, pricklypear
Animals: Quail, white-tailed deer, wild hogs, javelina, turkey, bobcat, mountain lion, ocelot, Berlandier's tortoise, gray wolf, giant toad

Post Oak Savannah
Landform: Open grassland that has been cultivated
Temperature: 0°C to 37°C
Rainfall: 76 cm to 114 cm
Vegetation: Post oak, blackjack oak, yaupon, Navasota ladies' tresses orchid
Animals: Deer, quail, squirrel, armadillo

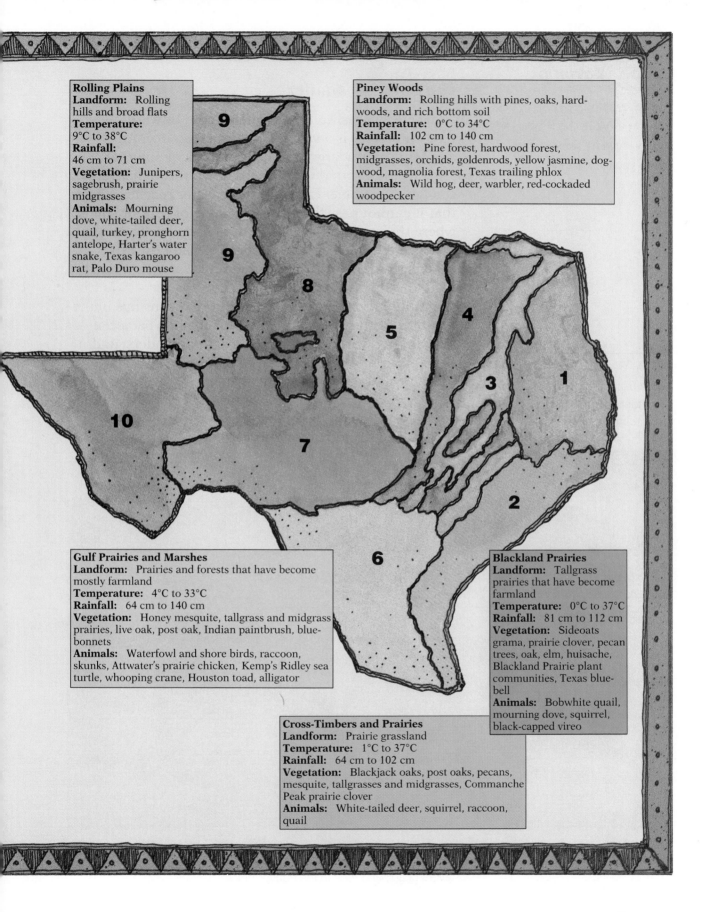

Rolling Plains
Landform: Rolling hills and broad flats
Temperature: 9°C to 38°C
Rainfall: 46 cm to 71 cm
Vegetation: Junipers, sagebrush, prairie midgrasses
Animals: Mourning dove, white-tailed deer, quail, turkey, pronghorn antelope, Harter's water snake, Texas kangaroo rat, Palo Duro mouse

Piney Woods
Landform: Rolling hills with pines, oaks, hardwoods, and rich bottom soil
Temperature: 0°C to 34°C
Rainfall: 102 cm to 140 cm
Vegetation: Pine forest, hardwood forest, midgrasses, orchids, goldenrods, yellow jasmine, dogwood, magnolia forest, Texas trailing phlox
Animals: Wild hog, deer, warbler, red-cockaded woodpecker

Gulf Prairies and Marshes
Landform: Prairies and forests that have become mostly farmland
Temperature: 4°C to 33°C
Rainfall: 64 cm to 140 cm
Vegetation: Honey mesquite, tallgrass and midgrass prairies, live oak, post oak, Indian paintbrush, bluebonnets
Animals: Waterfowl and shore birds, raccoon, skunks, Attwater's prairie chicken, Kemp's Ridley sea turtle, whooping crane, Houston toad, alligator

Blackland Prairies
Landform: Tallgrass prairies that have become farmland
Temperature: 0°C to 37°C
Rainfall: 81 cm to 112 cm
Vegetation: Sideoats grama, prairie clover, pecan trees, oak, elm, huisache, Blackland Prairie plant communities, Texas bluebell
Animals: Bobwhite quail, mourning dove, squirrel, black-capped vireo

Cross-Timbers and Prairies
Landform: Prairie grassland
Temperature: 1°C to 37°C
Rainfall: 64 cm to 102 cm
Vegetation: Blackjack oaks, post oaks, pecans, mesquite, tallgrasses and midgrasses, Commanche Peak prairie clover
Animals: White-tailed deer, squirrel, raccoon, quail

Underground Water

The Edwards Aquifer

The Edwards Aquifer, located in the Edwards Plateau region, is a valuable natural resource. An aquifer is an underground layer of rock or soil that contains water. Ground water seeps down through layers of soil and limestone. Eventually, the water reaches a layer that it cannot pass through. This layer of rock or soil is where the water collects to form the aquifer. The water comes out of the earth from springs. The Edwards Aquifer contains twice the amount of water contained in all the surface reservoirs in Texas.

About forty different species of organisms live in the aquifer's depths. Aquifer organisms include bacteria, shrimp, flat worms, snails, beetles, salamanders, and catfish. Because they have been living in total darkness for thousands of years, many aquifer organisms are blind and colorless. Blind shrimp, blind catfish, and the colorless salamander are just some of the organisms that make an aquifer environment unique.

This blind and colorless salamander has adapted to its environment. ▼

▲ Rainwater falling on the Edwards Plateau filters down through layers of soil and rock to the aquifer below.

Irrigation

Irrigation is the process of bringing water to otherwise dry land. Land is irrigated to make it suitable for growing plants and crops. Irrigation allows farmers to grow such crops as wheat, cotton, and rice. The water used for irrigation in Texas comes from rivers, lakes, and aquifers. But most of the state's irrigated land receives water pumped from underground wells.

There are three major irrigation methods--surface irrigation, sprinklers, and subsurface irrigation. With the surface method, the water travels to the crop by flowing over the land's surface. With the sprinkler method, water is thrown over a large circular field by a revolving sprinkler. Subsurface irrigation uses underground pipes to bring water directly to plant roots.

▲ This man and his son are irrigating a cornfield using a surface irrigation method. Water runs through the field in ditches or furrows.

Consider This

Who Should Own Underground Water?

Should landowners continue to own the water that is located beneath their land or should the state own and regulate the use of underground water? If, for example, the Edwards or Ogallala Aquifer were declared an underground river, this would enable the state to control use of the water as well as to meter and charge for it. This poses obvious economic advantages to the state.

Consider Some Issues
Water ownership concerns Texas landowners all over the state. But it especially worries small, independent farmers such as Stanley Miller, shown in the photo. Miller farms 450 acres (182.1 hectares) of irrigated cotton, corn, soybeans, and grain sorghum. He and his family live on the land they farm. They drink from the same water source used to water their crops. Miller is against state ownership and regulation first because of the cost to farmers. Second, Miller feels that private ownership of underground water promotes conservation.

Think About It Farmers are particularly aware that water is a precious resource. They know that their land would be worthless without it. Thus, farmers have a personal stake in using water wisely.

Debate It Who do you think should own and control underground water? Have a class debate and state the reasons behind your opinion.

Agriculture in Texas

Agriculture is the business of food production. Food is literally the sun's energy turned into products such as bread, milk, cereal, and hamburger. Agriculture is one of the most important industries in Texas. Farms and ranches have taken advantage of modern technology in the areas of crop and livestock management to increase productivity. In crop production, irrigation is an important factor. Nearly every county uses some form of irrigation. Herbicides and pesticides are used for weed and insect control. Genetic engineering and selective breeding have greatly increased cattle and poultry production. Major Texas crops include cotton, feed crops, food grains, vegetables, oil crops, fruits, and nuts. Texas livestock includes beef cattle, dairy cows, hogs, chickens, horses, and sheep.

A Typical Texas Farm

Irrigation systems bring water to dry farmland. Texans farm many acres of irrigated land.

In most years since 1880, Texas has led all states in cotton production.

Windmills are used on farms to pump water and to drive electric generators for lighting.

Texas farmers raise fine saddle and race horses, cow ponies, polo ponies, and work horses.

Many Texas farmers keep dairy herds for milk, butter, and cheese production.

Beef cattle are one of Texas' largest sources of agricultural income.

Cotton

Cotton is the major fiber crop grown in the United States. Since 1880, Texas has led all states in cotton production in most years. Cotton is a warm-season annual crop. It requires a growing season of 180 to 240 frost-free days to mature. The bolls, which contain the cotton fibers, begin to form as the flowers die. It is the boll that is harvested. After the bolls are picked, the lint, or fiber, and seeds are separated. The lint can be spun into yarn, and the seeds can be made into cottonseed oil.

Grain Sorghum

Texas is a leading state in the production of grain sorghum. In its early stages, the sorghum plant looks like corn. But sorghum develops thick, solid stems with large seed-bearing heads. Genetic plant research has been done to develop high-yielding hybrid varieties of sorghum. These varieties are also resistent to insects and disease. Sorghum is often called the "camel crop" because it grows well under hot, dry conditions.

Wheat

Wheat is the most important grain crop grown in the world. It is also one of the most important crops grown in Texas. Wheat is a grass-type plant. Each plant has three main parts: the head, the stem, and the roots. Each head contains about fifty kernels. The most useful part of the wheat kernel is the endosperm. This is the part that is made into white flour. A popular variety of wheat in Texas is red winter wheat. It is used to make bread, pies, cakes, and cookies.

All parts of the cotton plant can be used to make products for both people and animals. ▶

◀ Sorghum is a grain crop used for feeding livestock.

▲ Scientists are always working to develop new varieties of wheat that will resist cold, disease, and insects and give farmers a greater yield.

Rice

Rice is a cereal grass grown on the coastal prairies of Texas. The rice plant grows 60 to 180 cm tall. At the top of the highest stalk is the head or panicle. Each panicle bears 60 to 150 flowers, or spikelets. It is the spikelet that forms the grain of rice. A grain of rice has a loose, rough outer shell, or hull. The kernel within the hull is surrounded by a series of brownish skins called bran coats. These contain most of the vitamins and minerals. The bran coats stick tightly to the kernel, which is the part you eat.

◀ The quarter horse is often used on ranches to herd and sort cattle.

The ostrich could become a common sight on some Texas farms. ▶

▲ The Longhorn has been associated with Texas since the 1800's. It is a well-known beef-producing animal.

Hogs

Hogs rank with cattle, dairy, and poultry products as one of the main sources of farm income in the United States. Texas farmers raise such breeds as the Duroc and Hampshire because both are known for their fine lean meat and large litters. Interestingly, Texas also has herds of wild hogs, which come from farm hogs that escaped and became wild again.

Poultry

Ducks, chickens, geese, and turkeys are a common sight on the many small farms in Texas. These birds have always been raised for their meat and their eggs. But recently in Texas, a very different kind of bird is being raised on farms—the ostrich. This large, long-necked bird provides meat, pretty feathers, and hide that is softer than cowhide but just as tough for boots and handbags.

Quarter Horses

Texas ranks nationally as a leading state in the raising of horses. One of the most popular breeds is the quarter horse. The quarter horse was named for its ability to race at high speed for up to a quarter of a mile. Because of their intelligence and sure-footedness, quarter horses are used for cutting, or sorting out, cattle. They are used for racing, jumping, and trail riding.

Texas Longhorn Cattle

In the 1800's, there were more than four million Longhorns in Texas. But by 1900, the Longhorn had almost been wiped out. Cattle drives had thinned the herds to dangerously low levels. Fortunately, the Texas Longhorn is once again grazing on cattle ranches around the state. Longhorn cows have unusually long horns and a horn spread that can span 1.21 m. Longhorns are not solid in color but are a combination of white with red, black, or brown. The Longhorn continues to be prized for its meat, which is low in fat compared with that of other breeds.

Biotechnology

The word *biotechnology* joins the words *biology* and *technology*. Biotechnology refers to how biology has been applied to solve real-life problems and to improve plants and animals. Genetic breeding is an example of biotechnology. Genetic breeding results in new and healthier breeds of plants and animals. Plants and animals are bred to resist such things as disease, insects, and extreme temperatures.

Biotechnology is involved in the manufacturing of food and household products. Biotechnologists have participated in AIDS research and in the discovery of drugs used to treat AIDS patients. These scientists also study how to convert plant material, or biomass, into useable fuel. Many of the problems that modern society faces will be solved with the help of biotechnology.

Genetic Breeding

Genetics is the study of inherited traits. Scientists have used genetics to improve different varieties of plants and animals. Researchers also study the results when crossbreeding occurs in the wild. When two species share the same habitat, animals in the wild will sometimes crossbreed. This has been the case with the Texas red wolf and the coyote, which has resulted in a red wolf with the features of a coyote.

In the area of crop production, biotechnological research has produced a new variety of corn. It is higher in protein than the original varieties. This new corn is used for livestock feed, or fodder. The advantage to the livestock owner is that less fodder is needed for the animals because of its greater protein content.

An example of successful crossbreeding of cattle occurred in the South Texas Plains region in the 1930's. At that time, the King Ranch crossbred a Brahman bull with a Shorthorn cow to produce a new breed of cattle called Santa Gertrudis. Santa Gertrudis cattle are about five-eighths Shorthorn and three-eighths Brahman. This was the first distinct breed of cattle produced in the United States. The Santa Gertrudis breed is more resistant to disease and insects than some other breeds. The cattle are also well adapted to hot climates and noted for their good beef production.

▲ The Santa Gertrudis breed of cattle (*top*) is the result of mating Brahman bulls (*middle*) with Shorthorn cows (*bottom*). Santa Gertrudis cattle are an example of genetic breeding.

The Disappearing Prairie

Every region in Texas has undergone change as industry and agriculture have claimed more land. Open prairie land has been especially affected as people's needs have changed. Prairie land has been used differently by different people since the 1800's. The following diagram charts the history of prairie land as it has changed over time in many sections of the state.

1. In the early 1800's, tallgrass prairies covered much of the state.
2. Elk, bison, deer, and wolves roamed the tallgrass prairies.
3. Prairie land increasingly changed to farm land.When large-scale oil production began in Texas in 1901, oil wells sprang up on the prairies.
4. Where farmland was allowed to return to its nat ural state, shorter grasses appeared. In some areas, mesquite and cactus grew and coyotes and rattlesnakes thrived.
5. Wildfires, sometimes sparked by lightning, raced across the prairies burning out the underbrush.
6. After the fires, new grasses would spring up.
7. Ranchers use these grasses by allowing their cattle to graze on the land.

Skills WorkOut

Make a Model Illustrate the disappearing prairies and the changes that have occurred in the land from the early 1800's to the present. Use a time line to illustrate changes in land use, vegetation, animals, and habitats.

1

2

3

4

5

6

7

Skills WarmUp

Predict   Select a species of plant or animal. Predict what would happen to that plant or animal if there were no conservation laws. What effect would this have on the ecosystem?

Plants and Animals of Texas

Plants

Because of its diverse climates, Texas contains a great variety of vegetation. The state has about 600 different kinds of grasses alone. Some of the more common grasses are sideoats grama, Bermuda grass, indiangrass, big and little bluestem, and buffalograss. Texas also has more than 100 varieties of native cactus. Some of the more colorful or interesting cacti include the green-flowered torch, claret cup, yucca, Texas rainbow, and prickly pear.

Sideoats grama is the state grass of Texas. It grows in more types of soil than any other native grass in the state. Sideoats grama provides food for both wildlife and livestock. It has been an important factor in the development of Texas rangeland. Sideoats grama is a warm-season perennial grass. Its leaf blade is from 3 to 7 mm wide. At the end of each stem there are between 40 and 80 seed clusters.

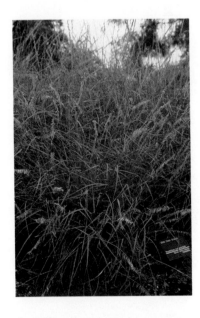

▲ Sideoats grama is a grass that provides food for livestock and rangeland animals. At certain times of the growing season, the many seeds dry up and are eaten and scattered by birds.

▲ Bermuda grass grows in fields and in places where few other plants thrive. It sends up stems from long runners that branch on the ground.

The cactus is a good example of a plant that has adapted to the dry, desert-like conditions in some parts of the state. The plant is unique in that it has a shallow root system that enables it to absorb the maximum amount of available water. The xylem, or woody tissue of the root system, carries the water from the ground to storage cells. The cells absorb and hold the water for later use. The storage cells allow the cactus to swell or shrink depending on the amount of water available. Sharp spines arranged in rows around the plant serve to reflect heat away from the plant. The body of the cactus is covered with a thick waxy coat that keeps the plant from drying out in the heat. Many cacti produce beautiful and colorful flowers.

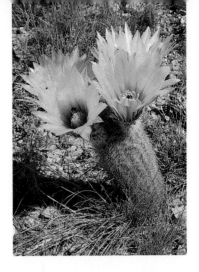

▲ In most plants, food for the plant is made in the leaves, and the leaves also give off moisture. In the cactus, most of the leaves have disappeared so the plant can hold its moisture. This cactus is called a rainbow cactus.

The claret cup cactus was named for its bright red, or claret-colored, flowers. ▶

▲ The giant dagger yucca is found in Texas only in Big Bend National Park.

▲ The prickly pear is a type of cactus with prickly fruit that is shaped somewhat like pears. The fruit grows on the edge of the flat leaf-like joints.

Animals

Texas is home to a variety of wildlife. Mule deer, wild sheep, pronghorn antelope, bobcats, raccoons, prairie dogs, and foxes roam the High Plains region. The hardy armadillo, the state mascot, lives in plentiful numbers in the brushlands. Turkeys, white-tailed deer, and beavers now thrive in East Texas because of restocking programs run by the state wildlife service.

Thanks to conservation practices begun in the 1960's, a quarter of a million alligators now live in the Gulf marshes. The Kemp's Ridley sea turtle, which is

The only kind of armadillo in the United States is the nine-banded armadillo. Its shell consists of nine narrow bands of armor that slide over one another when the armadillo moves. ▼

Mule deer got their name because their large ears look like those of mules. This male, or buck, has large, full-grown antlers. ▼

▲ Wild turkeys, such as this one, live in small flocks in wooded areas. They eat nuts, seeds, insects, berries, and other small fruits.

Alligators like to lie in the sun during the day and hunt for food at night. Female alligators lay eggs in grassy nests. ▶

another endangered animal, also lives in the Gulf marshes. The turtle's eggs are now being hatched in labs in Galveston, and tiny sea turtles are being returned to the Gulf.

The bald eagle, our national bird, nests along the Gulf of Mexico from August to March. The whooping crane and the sandhill crane can also be found along the coast. Because they are endangered, whooping cranes are tagged with radio transmitters so that scientists can learn more about their migration patterns. As conservation efforts continue, Texas will no doubt remain famous for the diversity of its animal life.

The Kemp's Ridley turtle is an endangered species. Conservationists are placing the eggs of protected turtles in the sand on "safe" beaches. They hope that the eggs will hatch and that these turtles will return to the safe places in which they hatched. ▼

The whooping crane's loud whoop can be heard over great distances. ▼

▲ Aoudad, or wild, sheep live in the High Plains region.

Bald eagles can have wing spans of up to 2 m. ▼

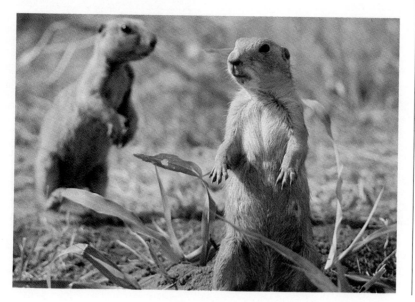

◀ The prairie dog is a member of the squirrel family. It got its name because its shrill bark sounds like the bark of a dog.

Classify Divide into groups of four or five. Create a poster that illustrates the food chain of a saltwater or freshwater ecosystem.

Marine Life

Saltwater Fish

The coastline of Texas stretches 591 km along the Gulf of Mexico. About 500 different species of saltwater fish live in the waters off the Texas coast. Thus, it is not surprising that commercial fishing represents a two billion dollar industry in the state. Shrimp, crab, oyster, red drum, trout, and flounder are some of the most popular seafood and fishes harvested in Texas. They live in a variety of habitats, such as estuaries, bays, natural reefs, and the open waters of the Gulf of Mexico.

Particularly rich habitats exist around off-shore oil rigs in the Gulf. The rigs are covered with the algae, snails, and crustaceans on which many fish feed. New marine research and conservation practices help to ensure that all these habitats will continue to support rich marine life.

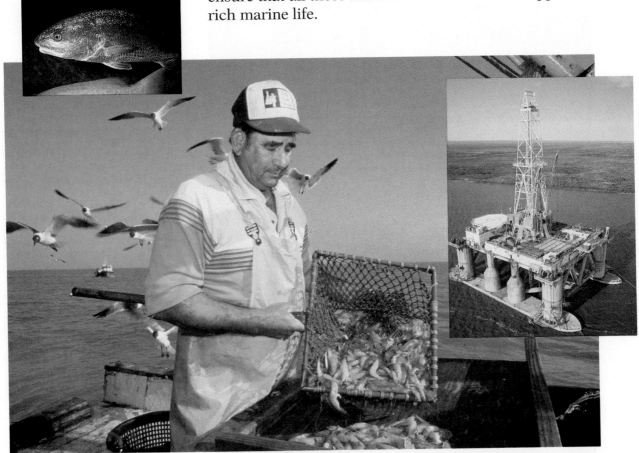

▲ Shrimp and the red drum are common saltwater catches off the coast of Texas. The red drum (*left*) has now adapted to freshwater lakes and reservoirs in the state. Oil rigs in the Gulf of Mexico (*right*) have become rich habitats for fish that feed on the crustaceans that cling to the underwater structure.

Freshwater Fish

There are about 247 species of freshwater fish in Texas. Freshwater sport fishing is big business in Texas. About 1.6 million people fish for recreation in the state. Creeks, rivers, lakes, reservoirs, and stock ponds yield such favorite freshwater fish as bass, crappie, and catfish. Striped bass, the largest member of the bass family, live in Lake Whitney in the Cross-Timbers and Prairies region of the state. Guadalupe black bass, the state fish, is found only in the Guadalupe, Llano, and Colorado Rivers in the Edwards Plateau region.

Recently, the Texas Parks and Wildlife Department introduced some saltwater fish, such as red drum, into freshwater lakes and reservoirs. This has been done to increase fish numbers and provide a variety of species in each location. Such management practices should guarantee healthy fish populations for years to come.

A wide variety of freshwater fish, such as the Guadalupe bass (*left*), crappie (*right*) and catfish (*bottom*) thrive in the rivers, lakes, and streams around the state. ▼

Skills WarmUp

Classify List 20 different kinds of flowers and trees with which you are familiar. Now divide them into groups based on their similarities and differences. Make a collage to illustrate your classification system.

Improving the Environment

Highway Beautification

As you travel along Texas highways in the spring, you see many colorful wildflowers such as bluebonnets, Indian paintbrushes, and buttercups growing on hillsides. Trees and shrubs also add to the natural beauty. Although this vegetation is native to Texas, the highways were not always so beautiful. What you see now is the result of the efforts of the Texas Highway Department and the involvement of dedicated people like Lady Bird Johnson, wife of late President Lyndon Johnson.

Highway beautification programs actually began in 1930. They continue today as one percent of highway construction funds are set aside just for landscaping. Schools, civic groups, and other organizations have also become involved by adopting sections of roadways to landscape and maintain. Texans are proud of their highways and have united in a campaign to keep them clean. The message to motorists is expressed by the campaign's slogan: "Don't Mess with Texas."

▲ Lady Bird Johnson has played a major role in planting Texas highways with trees and wildflowers. These before (*inset*) and after photographs show how the look of a Texas highway was changed by wildflowers. ▶

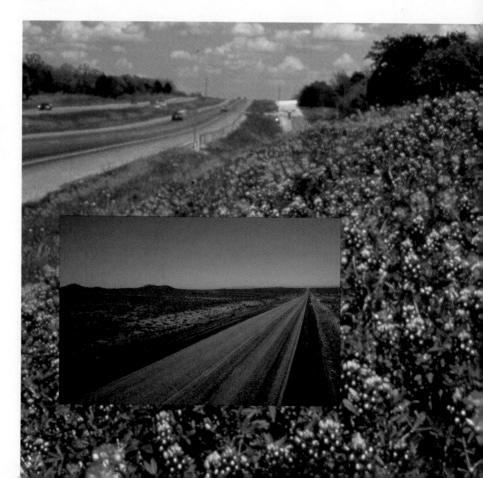

Replanting Texas Forests

Texas boasts four national forests and five state forests. In fact, forest area in Texas is larger than the states of Massachusetts, Connecticut, New Hampshire, Rhode Island, and Vermont combined. The trees, shrubs, and plants in these forests provide food, shelter, and protection for many species of birds and animals. Forest vegetation also helps to improve the quality of the lakes and streams that are home to the various forms of aquatic life that are native to Texas.

The Texas Forest Service provides information on maintaining and restoring the forests. It also provides seedlings to individual conservationists interested in forest replanting. Most of these seedlings are raised from genetically improved seeds. The loblolly pine, live oak, cottonwood, and slash pine are just some of the varieties of trees that people can choose to plant. Keeping the forests alive for future generations is a responsibility that Texans have gladly accepted.

▲ People can plant slash pine seedlings that will grow to look like these trees.

Consider This

Can One Person Make a Difference?

Walter Chapman is just one Texan who believes in giving back to the land more than he has taken from it. Chapman's hobby is planting and growing pecan trees. Pecan nuts are first planted in barrels, where they are nurtured for one year. Seedlings are then transplanted to the orchard. Within six years, the trees are bearing pecans.

Consider Some Issues
One person can burn down a forest by tossing a match. One person can seriously threaten an endangered species of animal by illegally hunting it. Or, one person can take a vacant city lot and plant a flower or vegetable garden that the whole community can enjoy.

Think About It   Pecan trees contribute to the environment by bearing edible nuts. The trees also help prevent soil erosion, return nutrients to the soil, and keep bird and animal life on the land. What other benefits do you think could result from Chapman's work?

Write About It   Write a paper on why you think one person can make a difference to the environment. Include examples of people who have contributed something positive to the environment. Or, include examples of what you think people could do to help improve the environment.

Protecting Endangered Species

Protecting endangered plants and animals is a major concern in Texas. Beautiful plants, such as the Navasota ladies' tresses orchid, have been threatened by industry. Birds, such as the golden-cheeked warbler and the Attwater's prairie chicken, have become endangered as their habitats have shrunk. Research is now being done on these plants and animals to ensure that they will continue to exist.

Navasota Ladies' Tresses Orchid   The Navasota ladies' tresses orchid is 20 cm to 37.5 cm tall and has small, cream-colored flowers. The plants grow along the wooded branches of the Brazos and Navasota Rivers in the Post Oak Savannah region. A number of these orchids were in danger recently because they were growing over an active vein of coal. A mining company wanted to begin mining in the area. Botanists, or people who study plants, were brought in to count the orchids in the proposed work area. Since there were too many endangered plants there, the mining site was moved. If only a few plants had been growing in the area, they would have been transplanted before work began.

Golden-Cheeked Warbler   The golden-cheeked warbler's habitat in the Edwards Plateau region consists of live oak, shinnery oak, cedar, and mesquite as well as a variety of grasses. As trees have been cut down to make way for cities, farms, and industries, the warbler's habitat has been dangerously reduced.

Currently, ecologists are trying to determine how many of these birds are left in the region. But counting is difficult because the birds are small and secretive. The females and their cedar bark nests are well hidden up in hardwood trees. The easiest way for ecologists to count golden-cheeked warblers is to wait for breeding season. At that time, the male warblers sit high in the treetops and sing. Ecologists take advantage of this pattern of behavior by listening for the warbler's song and counting each song as a bird.

Attwater's Prairie Chicken   The Attwater's prairie chicken was identified as an endangered species in

▲ The Navasota ladies' tresses orchid was thought to have disappeared. But now, the orchid is a protected species and is making a comeback in Texas.

▲ The Edwards Plateau region, the golden-cheeked warbler's natural habitat, has become densely populated. The spread of cities and farms has threatened this bird with extinction.

1967. In the 1940's, the coastal prairies were home to about 7,000 of these birds. Now there are fewer than 500 left. The Attwater's prairie chicken's habitat has shrunk. Rice and cotton farming and overgrazing have almost destroyed the bird's home.

In order to save the bird, the Attwater's Prairie Chicken Refuge was established in 1972. Here, ecologists study pictures of the land taken from space by satellites. They can determine how the land has changed over the years, where habitats have been lost, and what replaced them. In addition, foundations in Texas such as the Gulf Coastal Prairies Foundation are contributing to study and breeding programs.

Recently, Attwater's prairie chicken eggs hatched in captivity. If such breeding programs work, Attwater's prairie chickens will be given to zoos around the state. Eventually, there may be enough birds for conservationists to begin releasing them into the wild.

▲ The Attwater's prairie chicken is one of the most endangered game birds in the United States.

Career Corner *Ecologist*

Who Will Save Endangered Species?

As a youngster, Fred Smeins spent most of his time outdoors. He had no idea that he would grow up to be a scientist. In college, the sciences fascinated Smeins. He majored in biology, got a master's degree in botany and plant ecology, and a Ph.D. in plant and animal ecology. He worked his way through college by working outdoors. This was an education in itself as he learned about animals, their habitats, and the plants they eat.

Dr. Smeins is currently a Professor of Ecology in Rangeland Ecology Management at Texas A & M University. Not only does he teach but he is also involved in the research of endangered species such as the Attwater's prairie chicken.

Smeins is studying the habitat of the Attwater's prairie chicken, which is in the Gulf Prairies and Marshes region. His research involves examining the land and native vegetation that once supported this bird. Smeins' goal is to reintroduce the Attwater's prairie chicken on some of the large ranches. Hopefully, living conditions on the ranches will allow the birds to breed and thrive.

If you would like to help save endangered species of animals, you can prepare by taking classes in biology and ecology. You could get first-hand experience with plants and animals by volunteering as a field research assistant to an ecologist. For a career as an ecologist, field experience is very important.

▲ Flooding occurs when rivers and streams overflow their banks during storms, and run-off water is more than saturated ground can absorb.

Strong winds from hurricanes can uproot trees, blow roofs off houses, and destroy buildings. Hurricanes also cause heavy rains, high tides, and flooding. ▶

Natural Disasters

Floods

Intense thunderstorms with long periods of hard rain are common in Texas. During one of these storms, from 50 to more than 100 mm of rain can fall in less than a half hour. Flash floods often result when saturated ground cannot absorb any more rainwater. In addition, rivers, streams, and lakes overflow their banks, adding to the run off. During intense thunderstorms in May 1990, for example, the Brazos River overflowed its banks. At the same time, the Trinity and Red Rivers overflowed their banks. Because of the severe flooding, over fifty counties in Texas had to be declared disaster areas. This flood was one of the worst in Texas history. Damage to livestock, agricultural equipment, land, and other property cost the state over one billion dollars.

Hurricanes

Hurricanes, violent wind and rain storms, often hit the Gulf coast. A hurricane develops in four stages. A hurricane begins as a small disturbance of air over the ocean in a tropical area. This disturbance is classified only as a tropical depression as long as wind speeds remain below 43 km/h. As the winds increase to 117 km/h, the storm is classified as a tropical storm. At this stage, the winds are swirling in a circle around a calm region, or eye. When the winds increase to speeds over 119 km/h, the storm is classified as a hurricane. The strongest winds of a hurricane rotate around the eye. The rotation of the winds is the result of the earth's rotation on its axis.

Some of the worst hurricanes to hit the Texas Gulf coast have had winds in excess of 280 km/h. The most destructive hurricane in the history of the United States hit Galveston, Texas, on September 8, 1900. The Great Galveston Storm, as it was called, claimed 6,000 lives and damaged every structure in Galveston.

Tornadoes

A tornado is a very violent, funnel-shaped windstorm. No one knows exactly what causes tornadoes. But scientists do know that they form within thunderheads under certain conditions. First, there must be a layer of warm, humid air close to the ground. Above this there must be a layer of cold, dry air. The layer of cold air keeps the warm air from rising. If a cold front then comes in, it lifts the warm humid air, trapping it between the two layers of colder air. Some of the warm air breaks through the upper layer and rushes upward. More air follows, forming the well-known funnel shape of a tornado.

Because Texas is southeast of the Rocky Mountains and bordered by the Gulf of Mexico, air currents from both directions often collide over the state. An estimated average of 118 tornadoes touch down in Texas each year. One of the largest twisters to ever touch down in Texas occurred on May 11, 1970, in Lubbock. It destroyed a quarter of Lubbock. Property damage totaled one hundred and thirty-five million dollars.

◄ Tornadoes are dark, funnel-shaped columns of rotating air.

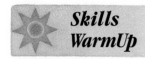
Texas Energy Resources

Energy is needed for powering cars, heating homes, running factories, and generating electricity. Texas utilizes such available energy resources as fossil fuels; nuclear energy; and solar, wind, and water power. Oil, coal, and natural gas are called fossil fuels because they formed millions of years ago from decayed animals and plants. Fossil fuels must be conserved because they are considered nonrenewable resources.

Wind and water power and nuclear energy are also used to generate electricity. Nuclear reactors are now being used in many parts of the world to supply nuclear power. Solar energy is energy from the sun that is converted into electricity. All of these are considered renewable resources. Therefore, they are being explored as the energy sources of the future.

Oil

Texas contains large reserves of oil deep within the earth. In fact, the state provides 28% of the oil used in the United States. When oil wells are drilled into the earth's crust, scientists learn more about the rich geological history of Texas.

The oil that is being used today began to form 350 million years ago. As plants and animals died in prehistoric times, their remains settled on muddy ocean floors. There, bacteria caused the plant and animal matter to decay. Sand and mud, called sediments, then built up over the decaying matter. The weight of the sediments pressing down on the remains formed hard layers of rock called sedimentary rock. The combination of bacteria, heat, and pressure changed the plant and animal remains into oil and natural gas. Over millions of years, more layers of sedimentary rock trapped the oil and gas in vast underground pools. These are the oil reserves that are being tapped today.

However, underground oil supplies will not last forever. The process of oil formation takes millions of years. In addition, the conditions that first formed oil have changed. Scientists are not certain that oil is still being formed today. Therefore, oil is considered a nonrenewable resource and must be used wisely.

▲ Oil is a fossil fuel formed from the remains of plants and animals over millions of years. Wells like this one tap oil reserves deep within the earth.

Oil-Eating Bacteria

Accidents involving supertankers have dumped millions of liters of oil into the Gulf of Mexico. These oil spills are ecological disasters for Texas. Many kilometers of coastline are affected. Living things along the shore become coated with oil and die. Oil floating on top of the water blocks out the sunlight needed by ocean plants for photosynthesis. The amount of oxygen in the water is seriously reduced by oil spills. Fish and other marine life can die from lack of oxygen. The long-term effects of an oil spill are severe and last for decades.

When an oil spill occurs, clean-up measures must begin within four to six hours. An experimental clean-up method is currently being tested in Texas. This method involves oil-eating microbes. These tiny organisms are prepared in a lab where scientists create them by splicing genes of bacteria. The microbes are designed to digest oil when sprayed onto oily water. They help speed up the natural biodegradation, or breaking down, process.

However, there are some problems with the oil-eating microbes. First, these bacteria cannot survive very long in the water. Also, wave action and the density of some spills limit their success. In addition, the microbes themselves need oxygen and so can reduce the oxygen supply to the marine life they are designed to save. There is still much research to be done in the area of cleaning up oil spills. But scientists and environmentalists are now working together to solve the problem.

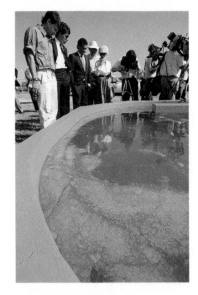

▲ These people are watching experimental oil-eating bacteria break down and consume particles of oil in a vat.

Oil spills in the waters off the Texas coast seriously threaten the ecology of the oceans and the shoreline. ▼

Skills WarmUp

Observe Study the modern devices around you for one week. Choose one device or machine that you think has changed or saved people's lives. Give an oral report to the class explaining your opinion.

Advances in Technology

Superconducting Cyclotron

At the Cyclotron Institute at Texas A & M University, nuclear research is being done with a machine called the superconducting cyclotron. There are only four of these devices in the world today. The cyclotron contains 40 km of wire that conducts electricity with no resistance. The wire is kept at a temperature of only four degrees Kelvin above absolute zero.

The electricity going through the wire acts with magnets to create a magnetic field. A beam of ionized particles is then released into the magnetic field where they gain energy and speed. Next, the particles are, in effect, shot at a target in a kind of nuclear explosion. Scientists can then "read" the target. What they see tells them something about the behavior of ionized particles. This knowledge can be applied in the fields of industry and medicine. For example, the cyclotron is now being used to treat some forms of cancer.

You can see the 40 km of wire that conducts electricity in the cyclotron. The beam of ionized particles in the cyclotron is made up of protons and neutrons, which are the charged particles in the nucleus of an atom. ▶

Treating Cancer with the Cyclotron

The cyclotron is currently being used as a tool in the treatment of cancer. The cyclotron produces beams of protons and neutrons. These are the charged particles in an atom's nucleus. The first step in the treatment of cancer is to determine the location of the tumor in the body. This is often done through ultrasound, which is a nonradioactive imaging technique. Ultrasound uses high-frequency sound waves to form pictures of the interior of the body. By looking at the pictures, doctors can find the tumor. The ultrasonic image can also help doctors determine the exact size of the tumor.

After a tumor has been located in a patient's body, the tumor can be targeted for the cyclotron. A beam from the cyclotron can be aimed directly at that target. Cyclotron treatment is most effective when the tumor is small and the cancer has not spread to other parts of the body. The cyclotron is also being used in the treatment of skin cancer on the head and neck. Unlike radiation, beams of neutrons and protons can destroy a tumor without harming the healthy tissue around it. Thus, although most people have never heard of the cyclotron, it is a machine that can save lives.

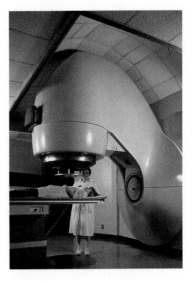

▲ This person is undergoing painless cancer treatment with a type of cyclotron.

Career Corner   Nuclear Physicist

Who Operates the Cyclotron?

Dr. Don May is the Chief Accelerator Physicist at the Cyclotron Institute at Texas A & M University. His job is to operate the huge cyclotron efficiently and safely. Dr. May decides how fast a beam of ionized particles should be. He must make his decision based on the kind of experiment being done. He also calculates how a beam changes as its speed changes inside the cyclotron. He must be alert to dangers and record data accurately.

Dr. May is delighted when visitors come to see the cyclotron when the machine is not in use. However, visitors are cautioned about the magnetic field that is present in the research area. The field can affect watches, magnetic credit cards, and pacemakers in people with heart conditions.

Nuclear physicists are involved with pure research and high technology. To become a nuclear physicist, you must be good in science and math. You would have to study chemistry and physics in college. You might gain experience in the field by working as an assistant in a lab. But for jobs as important as Dr. May's, graduate studies in nuclear physics are a must.

Portfolio Review

Check Your Knowledge

Choose the answer that best completes each sentence.

1. An aquifer is an underground layer of rock or soil that contains (oil, gas, water, clay).

2. The most important grain crop grown in the world is (rice, corn, sorghum, wheat).

3. Botanists are scientists who study (animals, plants, land, water).

4. A good example of a plant that has adapted to desert-like conditions is (sideoats grama, Bermuda grass, rice, cactus).

5. The King Ranch developed a breed of cattle called (Longhorn, Brahman, Shorthorn, Santa Gertrudis).

Determine whether each statement is true or false. Write *true* if it is true. If it is false, change the underlined word(s) to make the statement true.

6. The <u>mockingbird</u> has the ability to imitate the sounds of other birds.

7. Cotton, a <u>cool</u> season annual crop, requires from 180 to 240 frost-free days to mature.

8. The most important part of the wheat kernel is the <u>endosperm</u>, which is used in making flour.

9. The wire that conducts electricity through the superconducting cyclotron must be kept at a very <u>warm</u> temperature in order for it to operate properly.

10. The Edwards Aquifer contains <u>three times</u> the amount of water contained in all the surface reservoirs in Texas.

Check Your Understanding

Apply the concepts you have learned to answer each question.

1. Draw and label the different parts of a grain of rice.

2. Explain how the quarter horse got its name and describe how this horse is used.

3. Why are oil, coal, and natural gas called fossil fuels?

4. Explain how a hurricane develops in four stages.

5. **Data Bank**   Use the information on pages 4 and 5 to answer the following questions.

   a. Which region has more desert and mountain ranges than any other region?

   b. Which region is home to the endangered golden-cheeked warbler?

   c. Which region has changed from grassland to thorn forest?

6. **Application**   Much forest land has been cleared for farmland and other uses. After the trees were cut down, heavy rain resulted in a flash flood. What will happen to the soil now that the trees have been removed?

7. **Critical Thinking**   In the Edwards Plateau region of Texas, the top layer of soil is not very deep. This area of the state is subject to alternating periods of flooding and drought. What will happen to the soil if farmers and ranchers continue to remove native grasses? What will happen to the wildlife in the Edwards Plateau region if the grasses disappear?

Develop Your Skills

Use the skills you have developed in this portfolio to complete each activity.

1. **Interpret Data**   The diagram below shows the arrangement of a pecan orchard. The first row contains trees that are from one to six years old. The second row contains trees that are seven, the third row eight, and so on.

   a. What is the average yield of pecans for a tree that is seven years old?

   b. What is the average yield of pecans for each tree in row 3?

   Row

1	2	3	4	5

   Key
   ● = pecan tree

Age	Average Yield/Year
1-6	0
7	15
8	30
10	60
15	100

2. **Make Graphs**   Compare the average temperatures of the ten regions of Texas. Show the information on a bar graph. Then take an average of the rainfall of each region and show this information on a line graph. Compare the information on both graphs and explain the relationship between rainfall and temperature.

3. **Design an Experiment**   Once clean water is polluted, it is no longer safe to use. This water must be cleaned before it is safe to use again. But this process is difficult and costly. Devise an experiment to show how polluted water could be cleaned easily and inexpensively. Describe the problem, materials, procedure, expected observations, and conclusions.

Make Connections

1. **Link the Concepts**   Below is a concept map showing how some of the main concepts in *A Texas Portfolio* link together. Only part of the map is filled in. Finish the map, using words and ideas that you have learned in this portfolio.

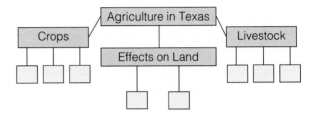

2. **Science and Social Studies** Governments in countries around the world have begun conservation practices to save endangered species of animals. Investigate what countries have done to save at least three different kinds of birds, fish, or animals. Identify the country involved, the endangered species being protected, and the steps taken to save the species from extinction.

3. **Science and You**   The development and use of pesticides has helped to increase crop yields. However, there are environmental risks associated with the use of pesticides. Write a report on the pros and cons of using pesticides.

4. **Science and Math**   Research two different genetically bred plants or animals. State what fraction of each original parent is present in the product. For example, Santa Gertrudis cattle are 3/8 Brahman and 5/8 Shorthorn.

Texas and You

Apply the concepts you have learned and the skills you have developed in this portfolio to complete each activity.

1. **Science and Art**   Design a symbol of your own to represent some other important building, plant, animal, or object that stands for Texas in your own mind.

2. **Science and Writing**   Now that you have read *A Texas Portfolio*, write your own one-page Overview describing the state. Be sure to include descriptions of plants, animals, crops, and natural resources that you feel are important to Texas.

3. **Make a Model**   Design your own irrigation system. Create either a model or a detailed drawing to show how your system would work.

4. Use magazines and newspapers to cut out drawings or photographs of Texas livestock. Make a poster showing hogs, poultry, horses, cattle, or a combination of these. Identify each picture you use.

5. **Science and Writing**   Choose an endangered bird or animal discussed in this portfolio, such as the Kemp's Ridley turtle, Attwater's prairie chicken, or golden-cheeked warbler. Write a brief conservation message to the state from the creature's point of view.

6. **Science and You**   Choose one of the natural disasters discussed on pages 24 and 25. Make a scrapbook showing the history of either floods, hurricanes, or tornadoes in your part of the state. List the disasters, and include pictures from magazines and newspapers to illustrate the incidents.

Explore Texas

Use the knowledge you have gained in this portfolio and appropriate outside resources to do the following research projects.

1. **Science and Technology**   Explore the subject of biotechnology. Write a paper explaining what biotechnology is and how it is being used to solve problems in agriculture, industry, and medicine.

2. **Research**   Find out more about desert plants and animals in Texas. Research living things in the Trans-Pecos region of the state. List and describe at least three plants and three animals that live in the dessert.

3. Make a list of ten saltwater fish and ten freshwater fish associated with Texas. Choose one fish from each category and write a detailed description of it and its habitat.

4. **Compare and Contrast**   Compare renewable and nonrenewable energy resources. Discuss the different forms of each, how they are used to generate power, and why one form may be better than another.

5. **Research**   Research a major oil spill that has occurred in the last ten years in the Gulf of Mexico. Find out how the spill happened, what happened to the ecology as a result of the accident, and how the spill was cleaned up.

6. **Research**   Research the superconducting cyclotron. Besides being used to treat cancer, how else is the cyclotron used? What industrial uses might it have? Write a report describing major uses of the device that might affect large numbers of people.

Addison-Wesley

Science Insights
Exploring Living Things

Authors

Michael DiSpezio, M.A.
Science Consultant
North Falmouth, Massachusetts

Marilyn Linner-Luebe, M.S.
Former Science Teacher
Fulton High School,
Fulton, Illinois

Marylin Lisowski, Ph.D.
Professor of Education
Eastern Illinois University
Charleston, Illinois

Bobbie Sparks, M.A.
K–12 Science Consultant
Harris County Department
  of Education
Houston, Texas

Gerald Skoog, Ed.D.
Professor and Chairperson
Curriculum and Instruction
Texas Tech University
Lubbock, Texas

⟁ *Addison-Wesley Publishing Company*

Menlo Park, California • Reading, Massachusetts • New York
Don Mills, Ontario • Wokingham, England • Amsterdam • Bonn
Paris • Milan • Madrid • Sydney • Singapore • Tokyo
Seoul • Taipei • Mexico City • San Juan

Content Reviewers

Antonia Adamiak
Biology Teacher
West Windsor-Plainsboro High School
Princeton Junction, New Jersey

Catherine K. Carlson
Science Department Chairperson
Parkhill Junior High School
Richardson, Texas

Charles Chinn
Science Teacher
Mortons Gap School
Mortons Gap, Kentucky

Barbara J. Cornelius
Sixth Grade Science Teacher
Russell Middle School
Winder, Georgia

Elaine Gima
Biology Teacher
Narbonne High School
Harbor City, California

Karel Lilly
Science Department Chairperson
Foshay Junior High School
Los Angeles, California

Richard White
Science Department Chairperson
Austin Community Academy
Chicago, Illinois

Multicultural Reviewers

William Bray
Stanford University
Stanford, California

Gloriane Hirata
San Jose Unified School District
San Jose, California

Joseph A. Jefferson
Ronald McNair School
East Palo Alto, California

Martha Luna
McKinley Middle School
Redwood City, California

Peggy P. Moore
Garnet Robertson Intermediate
Daly City, California

Steven Oshita
Crocker Middle School
Burlingame, California

Modesto Tamez
Exploratorium
San Francisco, California

Front cover photographs: Telegraph/FPG International (Earth); Jeff Foott/Bruce Coleman Inc. (honeycomb); Rod Planck/Tom Stack & Associates (bee); Telegraph/ FPG International (integrated chip wafer); Gareth Hopson for Addison-Wesley (geode).

Back cover photographs: Jeff Foott/Bruce Coleman Inc. (honeycomb); Rod Planck/ Tom Stack & Associates (bee).

ISBN 0–201–25728–9

4 5 6 7 8 9 10—DO—97 96 95 94

Contents

Unit 1
Exploring the
Sciences

page 1

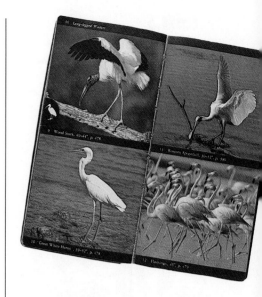

Unit 4
Simple Organisms

page192

Unit 8
Ecology

page 534

Activities and Features

ScienceInsights

Discovering is part of the fun...

Preview

Find out the **main topics** in each unit by reading the chapter titles.

Discover

Explore a **resource section** and **develop your skills** by answering the Data Bank questions.

Unit 8
Ecology

Chapters

25 Organisms and Their Environment
26 Interactions Among Organisms
27 Climate and Biomes
28 Humans and the Environment

Data Bank

Use the information on pages 624 to 631 to answer the following questions about topics explored in this unit.

Estimating

By approximately how many British Thermal Units did the United States increase its oil usage between 1940 and 1980?

Comparing

Which continent is more densely populated, Asia or Europe?

Predicting

What type of fuel do you think will be used the most in the United States in the year 2050?

Interpreting Data

What two types of forests would you most likely find at similar altitudes?

Tallest Tree Species

| California redwood 113 m | Douglas fir 93 m | Noble fir 85 m | Giant sequoia 84 m | Ponderosa pine 72 m | Cedar 67 m | Sitka spruce 66 m |

Explore

A **Data Bank** resource section filled with fun and interesting graphs, charts, and facts.

Oxygen Requirements for Activities

Activity	Oxygen used per hour (L)
Baseball	70
Basketball	90
Bicycling	55
Dancing	100
Football	110

Crustaceans 3%
Arachnids 7%
Centipedes and millipedes 1%
Others 1%
Insects 88%

Chapter 16 Invertebrates II

Chapter Sections

16.1 Mollusks
16.2 Arthropods
16.3 Insects
16.4 Echinoderms

What do you see?

❝ I see a parade of colors flashing. It seems like a kind of wing—more like a butterfly's or dragonfly's wing. The colors are green, yellow, red, blue, and blue-green with black spots all over. It seems like some sort of wing because you can see the scales a little bit. You can almost see the shape of the wing, too. ❞

Erik Gomez
Clifton Middle School
Houston, Texas

To find out more about the photograph, look on page 342. As you read this chapter, you will learn about many different kinds of invertebrates.

320

Preview

Use the **Chapter Outline** as a study guide. Read the **Objectives** to help you understand your learning goals.

Explore

Science is more than words. **Skills exploration** is an easy and fun way to develop skills that lead to success.

▼

16.1 Mollusks

Objectives

▶ **Describe** the characteristics of mollusks.
▶ **Compare** mollusks to other invertebrates.
▶ **Describe** the features of each class of mollusks.
▶ **Make inferences** about geologic history based on mollusk fossils.

 Skills WarmUp

Classify Study ten seashells. Look at the shells closely with a hand lens. Classify the shells into two groups based on one property. What property did you use? What are some other properties that you could use to divide the shells into two groups?

How fast do you move when you're getting ready for school in the morning? Do you move at a "snail's pace"? When your teacher asks you a question in class, do you just "clam up"? These expressions describe human behavior, but they also tell you something about snails and clams. Snails and clams are invertebrates called **mollusks** (MAHL uhsks). All mollusks have soft bodies, and many are covered by hard shells.

Characteristics of Mollusks

Mollusks live mostly in the ocean, but some can be found in freshwater habitats. A number of mollusks have also adapted to life on land. Snails and slugs are common in damp places in your backyard.

There are more than 100,000 species of mollusks. They range in size from tiny snails only a few millimeters across to the 20-m-long giant squid.

No matter what their shape or size, all mollusks ... body plan. Like the bodies of ... ans ... ns ... area ... al ... ns. ... plan ... mollusks for ... ly parts are ... In many mol... e shell.

Figure 16.1 ▲
This oyster (top) and squid (bottom) may look very different, but they are both mollusks.

Chapter 16 Invertebrates II **321**

Challenge

Do the **Check and Explain** questions to check your understanding.

◀

 Science and Technology
Fiber Optics! Television! Surgery!

Imagine a surgeon performing knee surgery through a tiny incision, or cut, in your knee. With advances in medicine and fiber optics technology, many joint operations are performed just this way. It is called arthroscopic (AR throh SKAHP ihk) surgery.

Arthroscopic surgery is usually performed on knee, shoulder, elbow, and hip joints. Many athletes have arthroscopic surgery to help prolong their sports careers. The technique uses a straight, tubelike instrument called an arthroscope. It contains lenses and bundles of optical fibers. The lenses magnify, and the optical fibers transmit light.

During arthroscopic surgery, the arthroscope is put into a small incision. The surgeon can look through the arthroscope and see what the problem is. An image is also transmitted to a television monitor. Through a second incision, the surgeon can correct the problem by using special small instruments. The image on the monitor helps surgeons see what they are doing.

Because the incisions are so small, there is little tissue damage and little discomfort. Therefore, people heal quickly, and often can be released from the hospital on the same day as their surgery.

Check and Explain

1. Look at the skeleton on page 394. What are the scientific names for the breastbone, hipbone, wrist bones, and upper arm bone? Classify each bone.
2. Describe how each freely-movable joint mo...
3. **Infer** How is the sk...

Figure 19.6 ▲
What are some advantages to arthroscopic surgery?

Exploring is understanding...

Explore

Photographs, diagrams, and colorful illustrations help you **discover** and **explore** the world of science.

Beneath the waxy cuticle, the epidermis covers the upper and lower surfaces of a leaf.

Mesophyll is moist spongy tissue inside the leaf. It contains cells that photosynthesize and a system of veins.

Leaf Adaptations The shapes and sizes of leaves vary, depending on their environment. Plants in shady forests have large leaves to capture light. Plants in dry environments have small, thick, wax-coated leaves to prevent drying.

Figure 14.8
Leaf Structure ▼

Stomates are openings in the lower epidermis.

A vein has xylem, phloem, and supporting tissue. Water and minerals enter a leaf through the xylem. Glucose made in the leaf exits through the phloem.

14   Flowering Plants   279

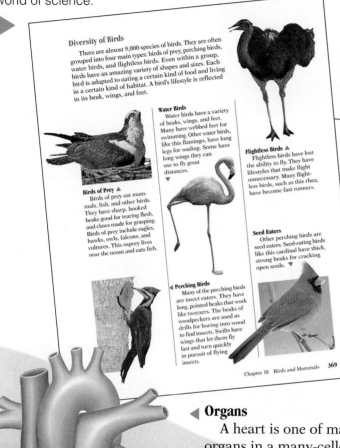

Diversity of Birds

There are almost 9,000 species of birds. They are often grouped into four main types: birds of prey, perching birds, water birds, and flightless birds. Even within a group, birds have an amazing variety of shapes and sizes. Each bird is adapted to eating a certain kind of food and living in a certain kind of habitat. A bird's lifestyle is reflected in its beak, wings, and feet.

Water Birds
Water birds have a variety of beaks, wings, and feet. Many have webbed feet for swimming. Other water birds, like this flamingo, have long legs for wading. Some have long wings they can use to fly great distances. ▼

Birds of Prey ▲
Birds of prey eat mammals, fish, and other birds. They have sharp, hooked beaks good for tearing flesh, and claws made for grasping. Birds of prey include eagles, hawks, owls, falcons, and vultures. This osprey lives near the ocean and eats fish.

Flightless Birds ▲
Flightless birds have lost the ability to fly. They have lifestyles that make flight unnecessary. Many flightless birds, such as this rhea, have become fast runners.

Seed Eaters
Other perching birds are seed eaters. Seed-eating birds like this cardinal have thick, strong beaks for cracking open seeds. ▼

Perching Birds
Many of the perching birds are insect eaters. They have long, pointed beaks that work like tweezers. The beaks of woodpeckers are used as drills for boring into wood to find insects. Swifts have wings that let them fly fast and turn quickly in pursuit of flying insects.

Chapter 18   Birds and Mammals   369

◀ Organs

A heart is one of many organs in a many-celled animal such as a dog or a human. The heart is mostly made up of cardiac muscle tissue. It also contains nerve and connective tissues. Muscle, nerve, and connective tissues work together to pump blood through the heart and body.

Connect

It's easier to learn **new ideas** and **concepts** when they're closely connected to the photographs and illustrations.

Discover

Learn skills and how science is everywhere by doing the **Activities** and **SkillBuilders**

Activity 28 How does acid rain affect plants?

Skills Observe; Hypothesize; Control Variables

Task 1 Prelab Prep
1. Collect the following items: water, distilled vinegar, graduated cylinder, pH paper, 4 small pots or paper cups, potting soil, 2 leaves each from 3 deciduous trees or shrubs, eyedropper, radish and bean seeds.
2. Make an acidic water solution by mixing 50 mL of vinegar with 150 mL of water in a graduated cylinder. The solution should have a pH of 4.0. Test it.
3. Fill four pots or cups three-quarters full of potting soil.
4. Make the following labels: *Radish—Normal pH, Radish—Acidic pH, Bean—Normal pH,* and *Bean—Acidic pH.* Attach one label to each pot.
5. For each pair of deciduous leaves, label one *Normal pH* and the other *Acidic pH.*

Task 2 Data Record
On a separate sheet of paper, copy Table 28.1. Use it to record your data and include dates.

Table 28.1 Effects of Acid on Vegetables

	Observations
Radish—Normal pH	
Radish—Acidic pH	
Bean—Normal pH	
Bean—Acidic pH	
Leaf A—Normal pH	
Leaf A—Acidic pH	
Leaf B—Normal pH	
Leaf B—Acidic pH	
Leaf C—Normal pH	
Leaf C—Acidic pH	

Task 3 Procedure
1. Place a few drops of normal water on the surfaces of the de_____ leaves labeled *Normal pH.* Place _____ water on the lea_____
2. Set aside these _____ Continue with the _____ Record your ob_____
3. Plant 5 radish s_____ 5 bean seeds i_____
4. Wet the soil of _____ or the acidic w_____
5. Set aside thes_____ tions and rec_____
6. Observe and _____ surfaces of t_____

Task 4 Analysi_____
1. Identify the _____
2. What effect _____ have on the _____
3. What effec_____ have on th_____
4. Were ther_____ and grow_____

Task 5 Conc_____
Write a short sum_____ affected seed growth and leaf appearanc_____

Everyday Application
What is the pH of the soil in your yard or on the school grounds? Mix some soil with water and test it with the pH paper. Find out which plants like slightly acidic soil and which do not. Which plants will grow best in your soil?

Extension
Collect water samples from several sites in the area of your school. Test the pH of _____

SkillBuilder *Making a Model*

Geologic Time Scale

The geologic time scale spans about 4,600 million years and is divided into eras. Fossils that show life forms are associated with each era. A model that shows the relative length of time in each era can help you to understand how the length of each era is different.

Collect a metric ruler, a meter stick, 4 different colored pencils, transparent tape, 1.5 m of adding-machine tape, or narrow strips of paper taped together. Copy the table below and complete the third column, using the scale of 1 cm for each 100 million years.

1. Measure out the correct amount of tape for each era. Label each era and color it a different color.
2. Use the information on pages 158–159 and the Data Bank on page 630 to draw or write in examples of life during each era.

3. Which era has the most new life forms?
4. Which era is the longest? Why is this era so much longer than the others?
5. How many times longer is the Precambrian era than the Paleozoic?
6. Does it make sense to divide the Precambrian era into two eras? If so, where would you draw the dividing line?

Geologic Time Scale

Era	Length of Time (millions of years)	Tape Length (cm)
Precambrian	3,960	
Paleozoic	395	
Mesozoic	180	
Cenozoic	66	

Connect

Learn how past discoveries have led to today's science **theories laws**, and **technologies**

Historical Notebook

Solving the Mystery of the Elements

Ancient peoples of many cultures recognized that some substances could not be broken down into simpler substances. In India, a book written around 1000 B.C. listed 5 "elements": earth, water, air, space, and light. By 300 B.C., people in China believed there were 5 elements—water, fire, wood, metal, and earth—constantly changing into one another. The ancient Greeks knew of 12 of the actual elements known today. However, they were not recognized as elements.

In the 1700s, experiments by a French chemist named Anton Lavoisier gave the co_____ cept of the *chemical* element a working defi_____ tion. Lavoisier listed 33 elements. However, these were not true elements.

After chemical elements were defined, s_____ tists began to recognize that materials suc_____ gold, tin, and iron were elements. In the p_____ years, many new elements have been _____

ELEMENTS

☉ Hydrogen		⊕ Strontian	46
⊖ Azote	5	⊕ Barytes	68
● Carbon	54	① Iron	50
② Oxygen	7	② Zinc	56

Explore

Apply **decision-making skills** to real-world problems.

Consider This

Should Protection of Coral Reefs Come First?

The kind of climate reef corals need to grow is also the kind of climate humans like to live in. On Key Largo, an island off the coast of Florida, developers want to build a new community called Port Bougainville. Environmentalists, however, say that building the community would endanger nearby coral reefs.

into the sea.

Coral reefs are home to an amazing array of living things, and they protect shores from erosion by waves. For these reasons and others, some people argue that reefs should be protected by limiting what humans can do in the areas around them.

Others c_____

Consider Some Issues Scie_____ tists believe t_____ is damaging _____ wide. People _____ polluting the oc_____ sewage, by an_____ the reefs, and b_____ and digging on _____

Connect

Explore real-world opportunities in a wide variety of **careers**

Career Corner *Virologist*

Who Finds Out Which Viruses Cause Disease?

The word was in from San Diego. Schools were closed, and many people were forced to stay home from work. As everyone at the Centers for Disease Control in Atlanta, Georgia, had been expecting, a new virus was spreading. It had reached San Diego and was causing a flu epidemic. The virus had been identified in Asia and probably arrived on a naval ship.

Virologists have a major role in trying to keep epidemics like _____ der control. In this

those most likely to become very ill from the disease.

Virologists often grow viruses in human tissue cultures. They observe what the virus does to find out if it causes disease, and if so, how. Many virologists use an electron microscope to help them see the viruses they study.

Virologists sometimes provide information to the general public about how a viral disease is transmitted. They are _____

agricultural animals and plants. They help prevent epidemics among sheep and cattle as well as in many crops.

If you would like to become _____

Writing is understanding...

Review

Read the **Chapter Summary** and **Chapter Vocabulary**

Chapter 13 Review

Concept Summary

13.1 Characteristics of Nonflowering Plants
- Bryophytes, mosses, and ferns are examples of nonflowering plants.
- Nonflowering plants evolved specialized tissues and organs that enabled them to live on land.
- The plant life cycle has a sexual gametophyte stage and nonsexual sporophyte stage.

13.2 Bryophytes
- Bryophytes grow only in moist environments. The gametophyte is the largest and longest-lived part of their life cycle.
- Mosses have small leaflike structures arranged in a spiral on a short stalk. They have rhizoids.
- Liverworts have flat leaflike or lobed

structures that make up the main part of their bodies. Hornworts are close relatives of liverworts.

13.3 Nonflowering Vascular Plants
- Ferns are nonflowering vascular plants with true roots, stems, and leaves. The sporophyte is the largest and longest-lived part of their life cycle.
- Horsetails have jointed stems and leaves arranged in whorls.
- Club mosses have club-shaped spore cases at the tips of their stems.
- Gymnosperms are nonflowering vascular plants that produce seeds.
- Pollen makes it possible for gymnosperms to survive and reproduce away from damp environments.

Chapter Vocabulary

gametophyte (13.1)	moss (13.2)	liverwort (13.2)	conifer (13.3)
sporophyte (13.1)	rhizoid (13.2)	pollen (13.3)	pollination (13.3)
spore (13.1)			

Check Your Vocabulary

Use the vocabulary words above to complete the following sentences correctly.

1. The _____ stage in the plant life cycle reproduces sexually.
2. Nonsexual reproductive cells with a protective covering are called _____.
3. _____ have needle-shaped leaves and seeds produced in cones.
4. Bryophytes have rootlike structures called _____.
5. Gymnosperms' sperm cells are packaged inside grains of _____.
6. The _____ stage of a plant reproduces nonsexually with spores.
7. When pollen reaches the female gametophyte, _____ occurs.

8. A bryophyte with green leaflike structures arranged in a spiral on a short stalk is called a _____.
9. The body of a _____ is divided into rounded sections, or lobes.

Explain the difference between the words in each pair.

10. Spore, seed
11. Rhizoid, root
12. Pollen, sperm

Write Your Vocabulary

Write sentences using each vocabulary word above. Show that you know what each word means.

Chapter 13 Nonflowering Plants **267**

Chapter 13 Review

Check Your Knowledge

Answer the following in complete sentences.

1. Why do the cells of bryophytes not dry out in the air?
2. How do club mosses, horsetails, and ferns transport water from the roots to the above-ground parts of the plant?

... club moss

... like when the ... peared on the ... ame for the ... that time?

... s.

... from mosses?

... mon living

... fern is just part ... the name for ... the other part?

... tement is true ... e. If it is false, ... to make the

... oss life cycle, ... te male and

... must adapt to ... oil and rain.

... they devel- ... es to carry

... at the tips ... are spore

... when dino- ... ferns had ... ant life.

...nts

Check Your Understanding

Apply the concepts you have learned to answer each question.

1. How is the life cycle of a fern different from the life cycle of a moss?
2. **Compare and Contrast** All land plants have a way to disperse their offspring, which means to scatter them over a large area. In what stage of its life cycle can a fern disperse offspring? In what stage does this occur in a gymnosperm? How do nonflowering plants compare in their methods of dispersal?
3. Are club mosses really mosses? Explain why or why not.
4. **Mystery Photo** The photograph on page 252 is a close-up view of a fern. The yellow clumps are sori on the underside of the leaf. They contain spores. These spores are an important part of the fern's reproductive cycle. What happens if a spore lands in moist, shaded soil?
5. Gymnosperm sperm cells do not have flagella for swimming. How do they travel instead? What advantage do they have over sperm cells that must swim?
6. Describe how pollination occurs in the life cycle of a pine tree.
7. **Extension** Which process is simpler: making paper from trees or from recycled paper? Why?
8. **Compare and Contrast** How do nonflowering plants differ from many-celled algae? How are they similar?
9. Why can a redwood tree grow as tall as 100 m high? Describe the adaptation that allows plants to grow far above the soil.

Develop Your Skills

Use the skills you have developed in this chapter to complete each activity.

1. **Interpret Data** Bracken fern spreads quickly in cleared areas as its rhizomes grow outward and make new plants. The map below shows where bracken fern grew in a certain field at the beginning of 1989. It also shows the edge of bracken fern growth at the beginning of each following year...

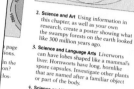

Make Connections

1. **Link the Concepts** Below is a concept map showing how some of the main concepts in this chapter link together. Only part of the map is filled in. Finish the map, using words and ideas you find in the chapter.

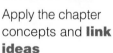

2. **Science and Art** Using information in this chapter, as well as your own research, create a poster showing what the swampy forests on the earth looked like 300 million years ago.

3. **Science and Language Arts** Liverworts can have lobes shaped like a mammal's liver. Hornworts have long, hornlike spore capsules. Investigate other plants that are named after a familiar object or part of the body.

4. **Science and You** Pollen makes gymnosperm reproduction possible. It also makes many people sneeze. Research pollen allergies. How does pollen affect allergic people?

Chapter 13 Nonflowering Plants **269**

Connect ▲

Apply the chapter concepts and **link ideas**

Challenge ▲

Try the questions to **check your understanding** Sharpen your **critical-thinking skills**

Connect

Read the literature selections to find out how **science connects** to other subjects. ▼

Science and Literature Connection

Yosaku marched up and down the neat rows of radishes and cabbages and beans. He was proud as a warrior inspecting his soldiers. . . .

Between two cabbage stalks stretched a spider-web, and in the center sat a handsome spider. Its body, dark as polished teak, was striped with gray that shone like silver in the sunlight.

"Greetings," said Yosaku politely. "You honor me by visiting my garden." He stepped back, so as not to disturb his guest. His heel struck something much too soft for a cabbage, far too thick for a bean.

"Ssssssss!" A huge and ugly snake slipped over his sandal.

"Ava!" exclaimed Yosaku, waving his hoe. The snake's tongue darted in and out of its mouth, its bright, cold eye fixed upon the spider. The spider froze, as if tied in its own ropes.

"Off with your head!" Yosaku shouted at the snake.

But as he brought down his hoe, the handle caught and ripped the full sleeve of his kimono. Yosaku missed, and the snake slithered away. The spider ran down from its web and disappeared among the cabbages.

Yosaku looked at his torn sleeve. The kimono was beyond mending and he ... ... for Yosaku was poor.

"The Cloud Spinner"

The following Japanese folk tale is adapted from the story "The Spider Weaver" in Japanese Children's Favorite Stories

ears were playing tricks.

"Honorable Mr. Yosaku!" Yosaku tied his old kimono tight and padded to the door. There stood a young girl. Her robe was of rich black silk stitched with rows of silver thread. Yosaku blinked. Perhaps his eyes tricked him, too.

The girl bowed low. "You are in need of new kimono?"

Yosaku stared down at the girl's dark glossy head. She reminded him of something, but he was too sleepy to remember what. "So I am," he answered.

She looked up at him and smiled shyly. "If you will allow, I would be pleased to weave new cloth for kimono."

Yosaku, astounded by such a grand offering, slid the door wide. "You are welcome in my house."

rhythm of the loom. When he awoke in the morning, there were seven new kimono, neatly laid out next to his mat.

Yosaku rubbed his eyes. "How can this be?" He ran to the weaving room. "Already you made new kimono for every day of the week!"

"Do not question, Honorable Yosaku." The girl looked modestly down at her hands. "And please do not come into this room while I work."

Yosaku bobbed his head. "It shall be as you wish," he agreed. . . .

Yosaku asked nothing, not even the girl's name, but his curiosity was growing even greater than the stack of kimono in his cupboard. So, at the week's end, he tip-

toed to the window of the weaving room. Slowly, softly he slid back the ricepaper screen. In the center of the room sat his visitor at the newly strung loom. Only it was not the young girl. It was a giant spider!

"Aaaah!" Yosaku clapped his hand over his mouth. . . .

She was swallowing great mouthfuls of cotton and spinning it out as finished thread. No wonder the girl was not hungry!

Yosaku watched as all eight of the spider's legs, working together, wove the thread into cloth. . . .

Yosaku crept away from the window. He had come close to spoiling the spider-girl's secret. But he had an idea of his own.

Skills in Science

Reading Skills in Science

1. **Evaluate Sources** This folk tale contains scientific accuracies as well as inaccuracies. Identify three of each.

2. **Predict** During the course of the tale, the reader is given clues regarding the identity of the girl. Reread the selection and identify these clues.

Writing Skills in Science

1. **Predict** Write an ending to the tale describing Yosaku's idea and what ...

Activities

Classify List the physical traits of the spider in this tale. Use your list and reference tools to identify a particular species to which the spider might belong.

Communicate In a library, research types of spider webs and the reasons for the differences in structure. Use string or yarn to create a model of one type of web.

Where to Read More

Someone Saw a Spider by Shirley Climo. New York: Crowell, 1985. Contains the complete text of "The Cloud Spinner" and other spider facts and folk tales.

Concept Mapping...

Reading a science textbook is not like reading a magazine or a story. You usually don't have to work hard to understand a story. You probably won't remember it for a long time, either. But when you read science, you are reading to learn something new. You will need to think about what you read. You will also need to remember as much as you can. You may just *read* a story, but you will need to *study* your textbook.

Build a Concept Map

One way to help you study and remember what you have learned is to organize the information in the chapter visually. You can do this by making concept maps. In a concept map, the main ideas are identified by a word or phrase enclosed in a box. When these boxes are linked together, you can better understand the meanings of the ideas by seeing how the concepts are connected to one another. To build a concept map, follow the steps below.

Identify

1. Identify the concepts to be mapped. They may come from a short section of your book, directions from an activity, or a vocabulary list. List the concepts on a separate sheet of paper or on small cards.

Decide

2. Decide which concept is the main idea. Look for ways to classify the remaining concepts. You may want to list or rank the concepts from the most general to the most specific. For example, look at the concept map shown above. Notice that "body regions" is general, and then "head," "thorax," and "abdomen" are more specific concepts.

Organize

3. Place the most general concept at the top of your map. Link that concept to the other concepts. Draw a circle or square around each concept.

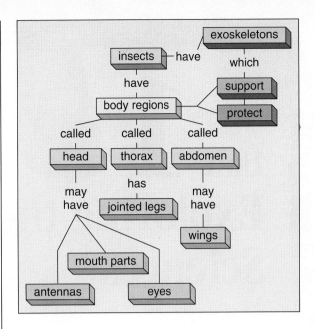

Choose

4. Pick linking words for your map that identify relationships between the concepts. Linking words should not be the concepts themselves. Label all lines with linking words that explain how each pair of concepts relate to each other.

Create

5. Start making your map by branching one or two general concepts from your main concept. Add other, more specific, concepts to the general ones as you progress. Try to branch out. Add two or more concepts to each concept already on the map.

Connect

6. Make cross-links between two concepts that are already on the map. Label all cross-links with words that explain how the concepts are related. Use arrows to show the direction of the relationship.

As you build a concept map, you are doing two things. First, you are automatically reviewing what you already know. Second, you are learning more. Once you have a completed map, you can use it to study and test yourself. You will often find that several different maps can be made from the same group of concepts.

Unit 1
Exploring the Sciences

Chapters

Data Bank

Use the information on pages 624 to 631 to answer the following questions about topics explored in this unit.

Reading a Diagram

Which is larger, an atom or a molecule?

Comparing

Which planet is closest to the sun? Which planet is farthest from the sun?

Making a Graph

Make a bar graph to compare how many kilometers each planet is from the sun.

Calculating

How much larger is Jupiter than Earth?

Scientists work in laboratories and in the field, such as on ocean liners and in rain forests. They use many skills, techniques, and tools in their work. What tool is the scientist using in the photograph?

1

Chapter **1**

Studying Science

What do you see?

66I think the picture is pollen. These objects are smaller than a grain of salt. This was taken from under a microscope. I am highly allergic to this, so it would make me sneeze and I'll be miserable.**99**

Mike Scian
Schulyer-Colfax
Middle School
Wayne, New Jersey

To find out about the photograph, look on page 28. As you read this chapter, you will learn the methods that scientists use to gain knowledge about the world you live in.

1.1 Science Skills and Methods

Objectives

▶ **Identify** and **use** science skills.

▶ **Describe** a controlled experiment.

▶ **Describe** a scientific method.

▶ **Distinguish** between theory and law.

▶ **Make a model** of a safety symbol.

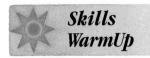
What is science? If you looked up the word *science* in a dictionary, you would read many different definitions. In these definitions, you probably would read several key words again and again. Most likely, these key words would be *knowledge, skills, systemized,* and *experiment*. You may not know what systemized means. *Systemized* means "planned in an orderly way." Science is a way of gathering and organizing information about the natural world and universe. The knowledge was acquired by observing, experimenting, or studying information in an orderly way.

Science Skills

When scientists study, observe, and experiment, they gather information, or **data**. While they work, scientists use many skills. Sometimes these skills are called science process skills. As you read about these skills, you will discover a kind of secret. These skills are not some mysterious or hard way to do something. You may not realize it, but you use many of these skills every day.

Observe The most direct way of gaining knowledge about something in nature is to observe it. When you observe, you use one or more of your senses to get information about your surroundings. Your senses are sight, touch, taste, smell, and hearing. Your ability to observe can be extended through the use of tools, such as microscopes, thermometers, and rulers. Look at Figure 1.1. Write as many observations as you can about it. Which sense did you use most often?

Figure 1.1 ▲
You can make observations about the color, shape, and design of these traffic signs.

Figure 1.2 ▲
What can you infer would be written on these signs?

Infer When you infer, or make an inference, you suggest a possible explanation for an observation. You often can make more than one inference to explain the same observation. Look at Figure 1.2. You probably can infer several things about the drawings. For example, one inference could be that they represent traffic signs. Most likely, you also could infer that one of the drawings represents a stop sign because of its color and eight-sided shape. The shape and color help you infer its meaning without reading the word STOP on it.

Estimate When you estimate, you make careful guesses. Estimating skills are used to gather information when exact measurements are not needed or when they would be impossible or too time-consuming to get. You learn to make estimates about many things. You estimate speed, distance, size, time, and so on.

Measure When you need exact and careful information about an observation, you measure. Measurements describe the amount of an observation. Measurements include both a number and a unit. The number of things in a group, the size of an object, the speed of a car or an airplane, your height and weight—all of these are forms of measurement.

Predict When you predict, you state what you think might happen in the future. Predictions are based on past experiences and observations. Therefore, you can give the how-and-why something might occur. Knowing why a prediction is right or wrong is important.

Figure 1.3 ▲
Estimate the number of blocks ▶ in the cube and the number of flowers in the photograph. Count the number of blocks and flowers for a more exact measurement. Compare your numbers.

Classify   When you classify, you group things based on how they are alike. You may be able to group things in many different ways. Some ways to group things are by size, color, shape, texture, or any other characteristic. In science, rocks are classified by how they are formed. Living things, or organisms, are classified into groups that share common ancestors. Organisms that have common ancestors have similar characteristics.

Hypothesize   When you state a hypothesis (hy PAHTH uh sihs), you suggest an answer to a problem. Your answer is based on information that you know. Think of a hypothesis as an explanation or an idea that states why something may always occur. Once you state a hypothesis, you can test your hypothesis by observing, studying, or experimenting. Your observations, research, or the results of experiments should support your hypothesis. If not, you need to look at your hypothesis again and state a new one.

Record and Organize   Scientists must keep careful records of their observations. During activities and investigations, you, too, will record observations, measurements, predictions, and so on. Often you will want to organize the data you collect in some way. There are a number of ways you can record and organize data. Some ways are tables or charts, graphs, and diagrams.

Analyze   Once data have been recorded and organized, you need to analyze the data. When you analyze data, you study the data to look for trends or patterns. You are looking to see if your data support your hypothesis, prediction, or inference.

Skills WorkOut

Interpret Data   Examine a page from a phone book. How are these data organized? Can you uncover any pattern between name, address, and phone number? Why aren't the entries made according to numerical order of the phone numbers?

Safety Skills

Just as safety is important in everyday life, safety is important in your science classroom. When working in a laboratory, you should always follow these general safety guidelines.

▶ Do not chew gum, eat, or drink in the laboratory.

▶ Read through the activity before you start. Reread each procedure before you follow it.

▶ Clean up your laboratory work area after you complete each activity.

Study the safety symbols and guidelines in Table 1.1. By following these guidelines, you can help make the science laboratory a safe place.

Table 1.1 Laboratory Safety

 Plant Safety
▶ Use caution when collecting or handling plants.
▶ Do not eat or taste any unfamiliar plant or plant parts.
▶ If you are allergic to pollen, do not work with plants or plant parts without a gauze face mask.

 Eye Safety
▶ Wear your laboratory safety goggles when you are working with chemicals, open flame, or any substances that may be harmful to your eyes.
▶ Know how to use the emergency eyewash system. If chemicals get into your eyes, flush them out with plenty of water. Inform your teacher.

 Heating Safety
▶ Turn off heat sources when they are not in use.
▶ Point test tubes away from others when heating substances in them.
▶ Use the proper procedures when lighting a Bunsen burner.
▶ To avoid burns, do not handle heated glassware or materials directly. Use tongs, test-tube holders, or heat-resistant gloves or mitts.

 Clothing Protection
▶ Wear your laboratory apron. It will help protect your clothing from stains or damage.

 Poison
▶ Do not mix any chemicals unless directed to do so in a procedure or by your teacher.
▶ Inform your teacher immediately if you spill chemicals or get any chemicals on your skin or in your eyes.
▶ Never taste any chemicals or substances unless directed to do so by your teacher.
▶ Keep your hands away from your face when working with chemicals.

 Animal Safety
▶ Handle live animals with care. If you are bitten or scratched by an animal, inform your teacher.
▶ Do not bring wild animals into the classroom.
▶ Do not cause pain, discomfort, or injury to an animal. Be sure any animals kept for observations are given the proper food, water, and living space.
▶ Wear gloves when handling live animals. Always wash your hands with soap and water after handling live animals.

 Fire Safety
▶ Tie back long hair when working near an open flame. Confine loose clothing.
▶ Do not reach across an open flame.
▶ Know the location and proper use of fire blankets and fire extinguishers.

 Glassware Safety
▶ Check glassware for chips or cracks. Broken, cracked, or chipped glassware should be disposed of properly.
▶ Do not force glass tubing into rubber stoppers. Follow your teacher's instructions.
▶ Clean all glassware and air dry them.

 Electrical Safety
▶ Use care when using electrical equipment.
▶ Check all electrical equipment for worn cords or loose plugs before using them.
▶ Keep your work area dry.
▶ Do not overload electric circuits.

 Sharp Objects
▶ Be careful when using knives, scalpels, or scissors.
▶ Always cut in the direction away from your body.
▶ Inform your teacher immediately if you or your partner is cut.

Experiments

What's the best way to find out about something? If you said, ask questions, you're on the right track. In your everyday life, you ask many questions to find out information. Science enables you to ask questions and then find the answers to your questions. One of the best ways to find answers in science is to experiment.

What do scientists do when they experiment? What would you do? If you said that you would carefully plan a series of activities, steps, or procedures, you would be off to a good start. Experiments must be planned and designed to:

▶ Observe how something behaves.

▶ Investigate an observation.

▶ Test an idea, prediction, hypothesis, or even an inference.

▶ Find an answer to a question.

When you plan and design an experiment, you should be sure that the experiment can be repeated. It must be able to be repeated exactly as you did it. Often, experiments need to be repeated by other people or even by you to make sure the data and conclusions are accurate. Repeating an experiment also ensures that all people doing the experiment will have the same hypothesis.

Most experiments are **controlled experiments**. In a controlled experiment, there are two test groups—the experimental group and the control group. The control group is a standard by which any change can be measured. In the experimental group, all factors are kept the same as in the control group except one.

In a controlled experiment, the factors that are kept the same are **constants**. The factor that is changed by the person doing the experiment is the **variable**. Study Figure 1.5, which shows a controlled experiment.

Figure 1.5   A Controlled Experiment ▼

Hypothesis: Adding plant food extends the time that cut flowers stay fresh.

The same kind of flower was placed in each vase.

Notice that the number of petals on each flower is the same.

Each vase contains an equal amount of distilled water.

Control Group

Both vases received the same amount of sunlight. The water temperatures were the same in both vases.

An equal amount of plant food was added to the two vases in the experimental group.

Experimental Group

After three days, the tulips in the control group wilt and begin to lose petals. The tulips in the experimental group stay fresh for one week. Do the observations support the hypothesis? Write a conclusion.

Methods of Science

Is there one method of approaching a problem, an experiment, or an issue? The answer is yes and no. You may have heard the phrase *scientific method* used to describe the way scientists find out about the natural world. Modern scientific method is the systemized testing of ideas, hypotheses, predictions, and inferences about the natural world. Scientific method also involves a lot of communication. Scientists constantly exchange ideas and information.

Scientific method is not a set of steps to follow like those in a cookbook recipe. Instead, there are many different ways to study, investigate, and think about scientific problems.

Read Figures 1.6 and 1.7. They show a model for designing and planning an experiment and a model for decision making. They will help you in life and as you do the activities in this book.

Figure 1.6   Designing and Planning an Experiment ▼

State the Problem
What do you want to find out? State the problem as a question.

Hypothesize or Predict
What do you think may happen? What information from past experiences or observations are you using to state your hypothesis or make your prediction?

Plan Your Experiment
Do you need a control? If so, what is the variable? What are the constants? Write a step-by-step procedure that another person could easily follow. Your experiment must be able to be repeated exactly the way you did it.

Gather Data
How will you gather your data? Will you observe, estimate, or measure? Any other ways?

Record and Organize Data
How will you record and organize your data? Will you use tables and graphs? Will you include diagrams and drawings?

Analyze Data
Do you see any trends or patterns in the data? Do the data support your hypothesis or prediction? Do you need more information?

Conclude
State your conclusion based on your data. Your data should either support your conclusion or lead you to another hypothesis. Have any new questions or problems come up?

Figure 1.7 Decision Making

Think About It
Do you clearly understand the issue? State the issue in your own words. What are the different points of view about the issue?

Write About It
Research information about the issue. Find information about each point of view. Remember that most issues have at least two points of view.

Organize It
Organize the information so that you can see what information supports the different points of view.

Analyze and Evaluate It
Evaluate the points of view. What solutions and reasons are given for each point of view? What are the possible results of each point of view?

Conclude
Write a conclusion that expresses your opinion. Be sure that you support your conclusion with data.

Decide About It
Do you need more information? If so, complete more research.

From Facts to Laws

In science, no matter what is stated, the statement is always backed by observations, studies, tests, and experiments. Even science facts! In science, a fact is an agreement made by qualified scientists about many observations of the same thing.

If new observations are made, science facts can even be changed. Take the shape of the earth as an example. For much of recorded history, the earth was considered to be flat. It was a "fact of the times." Today, of course, everyone knows that the earth is more or less a sphere. Actually, the earth is slightly flattened at the poles and bulges a little at the equator.

When scientists want to interpret facts, they state a theory. In science, a theory is not used in the same way that a detective states a theory about a crime. A scientific theory is an idea that has been tested again and again. It is based on many separate, but related, hypotheses that have been repeatedly tested. A theory explains why and how something happens. A theory, in turn, may be stated as a scientific law. If the hypotheses of a theory are tested over and over and all the observations support the theory, a scientific law may be stated.

Just because a theory or law is stated does not mean it can't be changed. Scientific theories and laws evolve. As new hypotheses are tested, theories are often redefined.

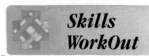
Models in Science

Have you ever seen a model train set? Or a model car, ship, or building? A model is a way to represent something. A model train, car, ship, or building looks just like the actual object. These models are small copies that are built to scale. That is, there is a mathematical ratio between the dimensions of the model and the real object. For example, the scale for a building may be 1 centimeter to 2 meters, meaning each centimeter on the model will equal 2 meters on the real building.

There are many types of models. Some models are drawn on paper, such as diagrams and building blueprints. Maps are also models. Maps do not look like the object they represent. For example, a city street map does not look like real city streets. Yet the map is very useful. Some models are mental models. In a mental model, you imagine what something would look like if you could observe it.

Career Corner

What Careers Use Scientific Skills and Knowledge?

Careers that use scientific skills and knowledge are many and varied. They may range from artists to physicists.

Table 1.2 lists several branches of science and three careers that use scientific skills and knowledge related to each branch. Notice that knowledge about different sciences is needed for some careers.

Each branch of science includes a large body of knowledge. Many of these branches have even smaller, specialized branches. For example, anatomy is a branch of biology.

Table 1.2 Careers in Science

Branch	Study	Careers
Anatomy	Structure and parts of living things	PE teacher, physician, physical therapist
Chemistry	Makeup of substances and the changes that substances undergo	Chef, food scientist, chemical machinist
Biology	All living things	Soil scientist, public health educator, medical illustrator
Meteorology	Weather and the earth's atmosphere	Air pollution technician, air traffic controller, weather reporter
Mechanics	Movement of objects and the action of forces on objects	Automobile designer, architect, underwater photographer
Physics	Properties, changes, and the interaction of matter and energy	Artist, electrician, materials scientist

Scientists, engineers, architects, and certain businessmen and businesswomen are just a few people who use models in their work. They use models as plans from which real objects can be built. Models are also used to help people understand things that may not or could not be observed directly.

Science and Technology
Safety in a Symbol

A tanker truck overturns on a highway. A clear liquid spills across the road. Within minutes, the highway patrol has closed the road, and an emergency response crew has arrived. The crew looks at the side of the tanker and sees a sign with a symbol and an identification number. A quick call is made to the Chemical Transportation Emergency Center (CHEMTREC).

At CHEMTREC, the number is used to identify the substance and tell the emergency response crew the proper emergency procedures to use. CHEMTREC provides information about any health hazards, risks of fire or explosion, and cleanup procedures. With this information, spills can be handled quickly and efficiently, with few risks to people or the environment.

You have probably seen these symbols on tanker trucks. Each hazardous material is identified by a special shape, color, and identification number. For example, tanker trucks that transport gasoline will have the safety symbol for a flammable liquid. Gasoline is represented by its identification number. International safety symbols such as those used by CHEMTREC can greatly reduce chances of injury to people and harm to the environment.

Figure 1.8 ▲
CHEMTREC hazard symbols are recognized internationally.

Check and Explain

1. Name three science process skills, and explain how you used them today.

2. What are the two groups in a controlled experiment?

3. **Apply** What procedure would you use to decide if a rain forest should be cut down for farmland?

4. **Make a Model** Design a safety symbol to use in your home.

1.2 Measuring with Scientific Units

Objectives

▶ **Identify** SI base units and prefixes.

▶ **Compare** density, mass, and volume.

▶ **Measure** common objects using SI units.

Did you know that you get shorter during the day? While you are up and moving around, gravity pulls you toward the earth. Your body becomes more compact than it was earlier in the day. So by the end of the day, you are slightly shorter. Scientists discovered this by taking and comparing height measurements.

When something is measured, you describe it in terms of numbers and units. The system of measurement used throughout most of the world today is the *Système internationale d'unitès,* or SI. This system was developed in France in 1791 and was revised and modernized in 1960. You may have heard it called the metric system. The name comes from its base unit of length, the meter.

Base units in SI, or metric units, are shown in Table 1.3. You are most likely to use the units for length, mass, time, and temperature. SI is easy to use. Unlike other systems of measurement, SI units are based on multiples of ten. SI uses prefixes, such as *kilo-* or *centi-,* to indicate how many times a unit should be multiplied or divided by ten. These prefixes are shown in Table 1.4.

Table 1.3   SI Units

Measure	Unit/Symbol
Length	Meter/m
Mass	Gram/g
Area	Square meter/m^2
Volume	Liter/L, cubic centimeter/cm^3
Temperature	Degrees Celsius/°C
Time	Second/s

Table 1.4   Prefixes used in SI

Measurement	Unit	Symbol
kilo	1,000	k
hecto-	100	h
deca-	10	da
deci-	1/10	d
centi-	1/100	c
milli-	1/1000	m
micro-	1/1,000,000	μ

Multiples of ten make conversion between units very simple. You simply move the decimal point. For instance, 130 centimeters equals 1.3 meters. Think of it in terms of U.S. money: $1.00 = 100 pennies or 10 dimes. These are base 10 measurements. A centimeter is 1/100 of a meter, and a kilogram is 1,000 grams.

Length

The basic SI unit of length is the **meter** (m). A meter is about the distance from the floor to the knob of a door. Chances are that the SI measuring tool that you'll be using in class is a 1-meter-long ruler called a meter stick.

A meter stick is divided up into smaller units. A meter stick, a tape measure, or any other measuring device with a scale marked in equal divisions makes it possible for you to make exact measurements. A scale helps you find out how many units there are as you measure, without having to count them one by one.

The SI units of length are the kilometer (km), the meter, the centimeter (cm), and the millimeter (mm). Use whichever unit is most appropriate for the length you are measuring. The meter stick is marked in units called centimeters. A centimeter is 1/100 of a meter. Your little finger is about 1 centimeter across. As you can see in Figure 1.9, each centimeter is divided into ten smaller units called millimeters. A dime is about 1 millimeter thick.

Figure 1.9 ▼
You will measure many distances that are less than 1 meter. The numbers on this metric ruler represent centimeters.

Volume

Take a deep breath. As your lungs fill with air, you can feel your chest expand. The change in lung size can be measured in terms of **volume**. Volume is the amount of space that something occupies. As your lungs expand, they occupy more space.

Because the SI base unit of length is the meter, the unit of volume is the **cubic meter**, or m³. A cubic meter is the space occupied by a cube: 1 m × 1 m × 1 m. This unit of volume is used to measure large quantities, such as the volume of concrete in a building. In your science activities, you are more likely to use the cubic centimeter (cm³).

You are probably most familiar with the metric unit of volume, the **liter** (L). Soft drinks often come in 1-liter or 2-liter containers. A smaller unit of volume is the milliliter (mL). There are about 20 drops of water in each milliliter.

In your science class, you will probably use a graduated cylinder to measure liquid volumes. As you can see in Figure 1.10, the cylinder is marked in milliliters. Notice that liquids in a graduated cylinder have a curved surface. The liquid rises slightly up the sides of the container and dips slightly in the center. That dip in the surface of the liquid is called the *meniscus*. Find the meniscus in Figure 1.10. To measure the volume of liquid accurately, you read the level of the liquid at the *lowest point* of the meniscus. The best way to do this is to look at the surface of the liquid at eye level.

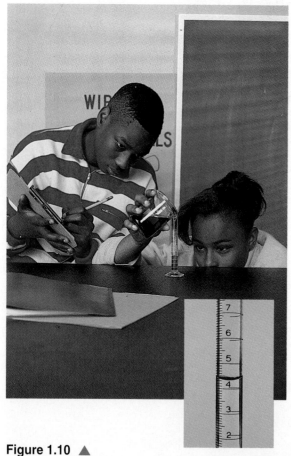

Figure 1.10 ▲
You can measure liquid volume with a graduated cylinder. To read, place your eye at the surface level of the liquid.

Mass and Weight

Did you know that things are slightly lighter when weighed at the equator than at the poles? That's because an object's weight depends on the force of gravity. At the equator, gravity is measurably less, so things are lighter.

Because weight measurements depend on where they are taken, weight can be unreliable for scientific use. That is why scientists use a measurement called **mass**. Mass is the amount of matter that an object contains. Your body's mass consists of your bones, teeth, hair, skin, muscles, organs, and all the other things of which your body is made. Since it does not depend on gravity, an object's mass always remains the same, no matter where the measurement is taken.

The basic unit of mass is the **kilogram** (kg). In the laboratory, however, scientists often use a much smaller unit called the gram (g). The cap of a pen has a mass of about 1 gram. For even smaller measurements, scientists use a milligram (mg). How many milligrams are equal to one gram?

You will use a balance to determine an object's mass. A balance lets you compare an unknown mass with a known mass. Look at the double-pan balance in Figure 1.11. When the arm of the balance is even, the two masses are equal.

Density

Take a piece of aluminum foil and crumple it into a ball. Then take some clay and make a ball the same size. Hold the two balls in your hands. Compare them. Which feels heavier? Though they are the same size, the clay ball will feel heavier than the aluminum one. The clay ball is denser.

Every substance has its own characteristic **density**. Density is the measure of how much matter is packed into a given volume. In mathematical terms:

$$density = mass/volume$$

Scientists often measure density in grams of matter per cubic centimeter (g/cm^3). Lead has a density of about 11 g/cm^3. This means that for every cubic centimeter of lead, there are about 11 grams of matter. Balsa wood has a density of about 0.1 g/cm^3. This means that every cubic centimeter of balsa wood contains about 0.1 grams of matter. Which is the more dense, lead or balsa wood?

In addition to helping identify a substance, an object's density determines if the material will float or sink. The density of everything is compared to the density of pure water. Materials with densities greater than that of pure water (1 gm/cm^3) always sink. Materials with densities less than that of water always float. How will an object with the same density as water behave? Will lead float or sink in water? If a cubic centimeter of balsa wood is placed in water, will it float or sink?

◀ **Figure 1.11**

The kilogram is the basic unit for mass in the metric system. What unit would you use to measure the mass of five paper clips?

Figure 1.12 ▲
On the Celsius scale, water freezes at 0°C and boils at 100°C.

Temperature

You've probably had your temperature taken when you were sick. Chances are that your body temperature was above 98.6 degrees Fahrenheit (F), which is what it is when you are healthy. Scientists, however, do not use Fahrenheit temperature readings. Instead, they measure temperature using the Celsius scale. In fact, most of the countries of the world use Celsius as their temperature scale. On this scale, your body temperature is about 37 degrees Celsius, or 37°C.

In your classroom, you probably will use a Celsius thermometer to measure temperature. A thermometer is a thin glass tube filled with a colored liquid. As the liquid heats up, it expands and moves up the tube. As the liquid cools, it moves down the tube. The sides of this tube are marked in degrees Celsius. Two important reference marks on the Celsius scale are the freezing point (0°C) and the boiling point (100°C) of water.

SkillBuilder *Measuring*

Average Mass

The mass of a small object such as a rubber band is hard to measure directly. To get its mass, you need to determine the rubber band's average mass. First, you can count out 100 rubber bands. Then measure the total mass of the rubber bands. Divide the total mass by 100. This method gives an average mass for the rubber bands and assumes that individual masses do not vary much.

Use the method above to estimate and measure the masses of some common objects.

1. Estimate the mass of each of the following:

    a. a rubber band

    b. a small paper clip

    c. a piece of notebook paper

2. Record your estimates in a data table similar to the one shown.

3. Count out 10 of each object in step 1. Measure the mass. Divide this by 10. Record this measurement in your table.

4. Count out 100 of each object in step 1. Measure the mass. Divide this by 100. Record this measurement in your table.

How accurate were your estimates? Did the average masses vary as your sampling size increased?

Object	Estimate	Average Measurement	
		10	100

Time

The basic SI unit of time is the second. In your classroom, you will use a watch with a second hand to measure time. As you know, other units such as the minute, hour, day, and year are not based on the number ten. There are 60 seconds in a minute, 60 minutes in an hour, 24 hours in a day, and 365 1/4 days in a year. This system of measuring time is used everywhere in the world. In science, however, the prefix *milli-* is used with the unit second for some short time measurements.

Science and You *Settling Cereals*

Have you ever opened a sealed cereal box to discover that the box wasn't full? Did this make you wonder what happened to the contents? Perhaps there was some mistake during packaging. You may find the answer to your questions by examining the package. Somewhere on the box you're likely to come across this statement: "Contents measured by weight, not by volume."

At the packaging plant, the boxes were filled with unbroken cereal. The amount of cereal added to each box was determined by the cereal's weight, not by the amount of space the cereal took up. Therefore, although the box might contain the right amount of cereal, it may not appear full.

During shipping, cereal flakes often crumble and settle to the bottom of the package. This settling compacts the cereal, making the box appear less than full. So when you open the sealed box, it appears as if you didn't get what you paid for . . . but you did. The cereal's weight hasn't changed at all!

Figure 1.13 ▲
Cereals and crackers are sold by weight, not by volume.

Check and Explain

1. Why do you use SI units in science?

2. Why is mass a more reliable measure than weight?

3. **Predict** Aluminum has a density of 2.7g/cm³. Will a block of aluminum sink or float?

4. **Measure** Find the following objects in your classroom: an object 5 cm long, an object with a mass of about 10 g, an object at least 2 m tall.

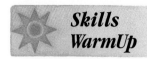
1.3 Graphing

Objectives

▶ **Identify** types of graphs.

▶ **Explain** the use of variables on line graphs.

▶ **Classify** the type of graph needed to show specific kinds of data.

What is a graph? A graph is basically a picture of data. It shows numerical data as a diagram. Think of a graph as a picture of a table of data. You've probably seen many different graphs in newspapers and magazines, and on television news reports. Many businesses also use graphs. Graphs are useful tools for presenting information.

Kinds of Graphs

There are three kinds of graphs: circle, bar, and line graphs. No matter which kind of graph you look at, all graphs let you compare numerical data. Each kind of graph, however, shows the data in a different way.

Circle Graphs Think about a pie cut into pieces, and you have a mental model of a circle graph. A circle graph is a divided circle. It shows how a part or share of something relates to the whole value. You can see what fraction, percentage, share, or proportion each part represents.

Look at the circle graph in Figure 1.14, which shows how much of our trash consists of paper and paper products. You can even compare two groups very easily. Compare the percentage of metal trash and yard waste.

Bar Graphs Just like its name describes, a bar graph has bars. The bars help you compare things. You can compare measurements—such as weight, height, and length—of the sizes of things. Bar graphs also let you compare amounts, quantities, and changes.

Look at the bar graph in Figure 1.15. It shows the shortest and longest lengths of four North American

Components in Trash

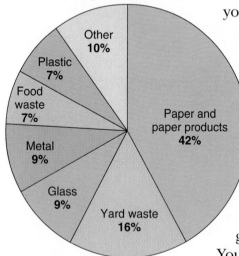

Figure 1.14 ▲
What type of waste makes up most trash? Which wastes make up equal percentages of trash?

snakes. You can see very easily which snake is the longest and which is the shortest.

Notice that the bar graph is drawn on graph paper. On the left side of the graph, there is a scale showing length in centimeters. These data are plotted on the vertical line, called the *y*-axis. Each bar is labeled on the horizontal line, called the *x*-axis. On this graph, the labels are letters keyed to the names of the snakes.

When you build a bar graph, you need to choose the scale by looking at the highest and lowest numbers in your data. On this graph, the scale ranges from 0 to 140 cm. Notice that the scale is higher than the longest snake. Also, the numbered divisions are in equal amounts of 20 cm. All bar graphs have a scale and equal divisions.

Line Graphs Line graphs let you plot several different forms of data. They also show changes. Line graphs can help you answer if-then questions. They help you see patterns or trends in data. Unlike bar graphs and circle graphs, you can also plot several different sets of data on one line graph and easily make comparisons. Figure 1.16 shows a line graph that has been drawn based on certain statistics. In this case, the population growth of the United States is measured. Notice that the population size (responding variable) is being measured every 20 years (manipulated variable).

The manipulated variables are the *x*-values. The years plotted are on the *x*-axis. The responding variable (the one that changes when the year is changed) is displayed on the *y*-axis.

Look at Figure 1.16. For the year 1880, a dot is placed at 50 million. The dot is placed directly across

Minimum and Maximum Lengths of Some Snakes

Key
- A Southern copperhead
- B Eastern cottonmouth
- C Northern water snake
- D Eastern coral snake

Figure 1.15 ▲
Which snake has the longest maximum length? The shortest?

Figure 1.16
On a graph, what point is the origin? ▼

United States Population Growth

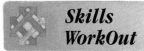
from the *y*-value and directly above the *x*-value. What was the population of the United States in 1920?

When all the values are presented as points on the graph, a line is drawn connecting all the points. Notice that the line shows a change and a trend. The rapid increase in the United States population is shown. You can even see that between certain years, the population grew much more rapidly than between other years. Predict what the population of the United States will be in 2020.

Science and Technology
Just a Touch of a Key

Until a few years ago, all graphs in print were drawn by hand. A graphic artist went through the same steps as you just did to produce a graph. Every time a mistake was made, it had to be erased. If the page contained too many errors, it was thrown away. As you might imagine, this could be a long and tiresome task.

Today most graphic artists have a new and powerful graph maker, the computer. All the computer needs is a graph-making program and some data, and Presto! It generates a perfect, customized graph. In fact, all the graphs in this book were made on a computer.

By taking advantage of a computer's power, complex graphing is just a keystroke away. The final graph can even be produced in several colors. In addition, the computer can calculate the exact shades needed to create the illusion of three dimensions.

Check and Explain

1. Name the three kinds of graphs.

2. On a line graph, which variable depends on the other?

3. **Analyze** The average temperatures of five cities are given in degrees Celsius: –5, 5, 15, 25, and 18. What scale would you use on a bar graph? What would be the equal divisions?

4. **Classify** Choose the kind of graph you would use if you wanted to show how many blue herons lived in a wetlands in 1970, 1975, 1980, 1985, 1990, and 1995.

1.4 Microscopes and Lasers

Objectives

▶ **Distinguish** between convex and concave lenses.

▶ **Describe** the parts of a compound microscope.

▶ **Compare** compound microscopes and electron microscopes.

▶ **Infer** why scientists use microscopes in their work.

⬡ **Skills WarmUp**

Observe   Use a hand lens to look at things around you. Look at your hand, your desk, notebook paper, a piece of hair, and other things. Make drawings of three of the things you observe. How does a hand lens change the objects you view?

There are many living things all around you that you can't see. How can you find out if these things exist? As scientists have done for many years, you can view many small living things and parts of living things by using a **microscope**. A microscope is a tool that makes things appear larger than they really are. In a microscope, light and lenses combine to bring objects into view.

Light and Lenses

The sun is the main source of light energy. Other sources of light are electric light bulbs and flames. Without light, you would not be able to see anything. Most things that you see are visible because they reflect light from other sources.

When light strikes an object, several things can happen. Some materials allow light to pass through them in straight lines. In other materials, light passes through in straight lines, but it is diffused in different directions. You can't see through these objects. In fact, most objects don't allow light to pass through them.

When light passes through glass, it bends. It bends again when light leaves the glass. The bending, or refraction, of light is caused by the difference in the speed of light in the glass and in the air. You can see how light refracts in Figure 1.17.

If glass is formed into certain shapes, it can be used to bend light. The glass can make things appear smaller, larger, closer, or farther away. A piece of glass that can bend light in some way to make an object look smaller, larger, closer, or farther away is a **lens**. There are two main types of lenses: convex lenses and concave lenses.

Figure 1.17 ▲
When light rays pass from air into water or glass, they bend. Notice how the straws appear bent in this glass of water.

Convex lens

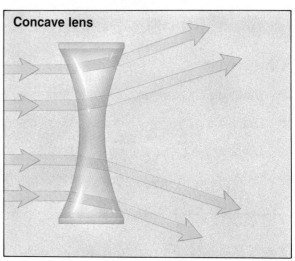

Concave lens

Figure 1.18 ▲
What happens when light rays strike a convex lens? What happens when light rays strike a concave lens?

Convex Lenses Convex lenses are used as magnifying lenses. They are thin on the edges and thick in the center. Look at Figure 1.18. To form images, convex lenses bring light rays together at the center of the lens. This is the thickest part of the lens. The point at which the light rays converge is the focal point.

You may be interested to know that your eyes have convex lenses in them. They are different from the hard lenses used in microscopes. Your eyes are soft, flexible lenses. With their flexibility, the muscles in your eyes can easily change the shape of the lens in each eye. The change in shape focuses light onto the back of your eye. This allows you to clearly see images of objects both near and far away.

Concave Lenses Concave lenses are thin in the center and thick on the edges. Look at Figure 1.18. Notice that concave lenses are different from convex lenses because concave lenses spread light rays out. Concave lenses are often used with convex lenses to form very sharp images.

Compound Microscopes

A microscope uses light and lenses to produce an enlarged image of an object. A simple microscope, such as a hand lens, has only one lens. A microscope with two or more lenses is called a compound microscope.

Look at the compound microscope in Figure 1.19. It has three lenses. One lens is located at the top of the viewing tube. This lens is the ocular lens. It is located in the eyepiece. The other two lenses are located in the revolving nosepiece. These are the objective lenses. By turning the nosepiece, you can view objects under either high power or low power.

By multiplying the power of the ocular lens by the power of the objective lens, you can calculate the total magnification power of the microscope. For example, if the eyepiece is 10x and the objective is 43x, the total magnification is 430x.

**Figure 1.19
Compound Microscope**

Coarse focus
Controls movement of body tube, used only to bring the image into view.

Fine focus
Controls movement of body tube, used to sharply focus the image.

Arm
Supports the body tube.

Eyepiece
Contains the ocular lens. You look through the eyepiece.

Body tube
Holds the system of lenses.

Revolving nosepiece
Contains the objective lenses and can be rotated.

High-power
Objective lens

Low-power
Objective lens

Stage clips
Holds microscope slides in place.

Stage
Platform that holds slides.

Diaphragm
Controls the amount of light reflected through the hole in the stage.

Light source
Collects and directs light up through the hole in the stage and through the object being viewed.

Base
Supports the microscope.

Electron Microscopes

You use a compound microscope to view objects that are magnified under 1,000x. Scientists, however, can view objects that are magnified one million times or more by using electron microscopes. Electron microscopes use tiny particles called electrons to produce enlarged images of objects.

The first type of electron microscope was developed in the 1930s. It was called a transmission electron microscope, or TEM, for short. Within a TEM, a beam of electrons is aimed at a specially prepared object. Magnets focus and direct the beam. Electrons passing through the object strike photographic film. When the film is developed, it contains a magnified image of the object.

The scanning electron microscope, or SEM, is another type of high-magnification microscope. Within an SEM, electrons are bounced off the surface of a prepared object. By recording the reflection of this beam, scientists obtain a three-dimensional view of the magnified object.

Lasers

Lasers are tools that produce a very narrow, intense beam of light. Lasers are often used by surgeons as a type of scalpel. Surgeons can use them for surgery that requires work on small, delicate body parts, such as the eye. Lasers are also used to remove cancer cells from the body.

Lasers are not only used for surgery. Welders use them to cut cloth and harden metals. You may even go to a grocery store that uses laser cash registers. These registers add up items that are marked with special codes.

Figure 1.20 ▲
A false-color TEM of cells in human tissue (top). A human hair seen through an SEM (bottom).

Figure 1.21 ▶
Lasers are used in many areas, including medicine, communication, and manufacturing.

Science and Technology
Optical Instruments

A microscope is an optical instrument. An optical instrument uses mirrors or lenses to produce images. Cameras, telescopes, and binoculars are three other optical instruments that you may have used.

A camera is similar to your eyes. Both your eyes and a camera allow light to enter through a lens. However, a camera lens may be made up of several separate lenses. The image produced by a camera lens falls on photographic film that contains chemical substances that are sensitive to light.

Have you ever used a telescope to view the night sky? With a telescope, you can view objects that are very far away. Telescopes have mirrors and lenses that produce enlarged images of distant objects.

A very powerful telescope is called a refracting telescope. In a refracting telescope, a series of lenses is used to focus and magnify light from distant objects. The larger the lenses used in a refracting telescope, the greater the light-gathering power. One of the most powerful refracting telescopes is at the Yerkes Observatory in Wisconsin. This telescope has a light-gathering power that is about 40,000 times greater than the light-gathering power of the human eye!

A reflecting telescope is even more powerful than a refracting telescope. A reflecting telescope uses a mirror instead of a lens as the objective. Because they can be built larger than refracting telescopes, reflecting telescopes have greater light-gathering power.

Figure 1.22 ▲
The Lick Observatory in California has both refracting and reflecting telescopes. In the foreground, you can see one of their reflecting telescopes.

Check and Explain

1. How is a convex lens different from a concave lens?

2. Where are the lenses located in a compound microscope?

3. **Compare** How is an electron microscope different from a compound microscope?

4. **Infer** State at least four ways that you think microscopes can help scientists in their work.

Activity 1 *How do you prepare a wet mount slide?*

Skills Observe; Collect Data; Infer

Task 1 Prelab Prep
1. Collect the following items: unruled paper, scissors, dropper, water, slides, cover-slips, Elodea leaf, newspaper, tweezers.
2. Carefully carry a microscope to your work area.

Task 2 Data Record
1. On one sheet of paper write, *Wet Mount of Letter "e"* at the top. On another sheet write, *Wet Mount of Elodea Leaf.*
2. Divide each sheet in half lengthwise. Label the upper portion *Low Power* and the lower portion *High Power.*

Task 3 Procedure
1. Use the scissors to cut out the lowercase letter "e" from the newspaper.
2. Use the dropper to place a drop of water on the center of a slide. Use the tweezers to place the letter "e," face-up, in the water drop. Add another drop of water to the slide.
3. As shown below, touch one edge of the coverslip to the water. Allow the water to spread out along this edge, then slowly lower the coverslip over the drop. Keep the "e" somewhat in the center. Be careful not to trap any air bubbles.

4. Move the low-power objective into place. Use the coarse adjustment to raise the body tube about 5 cm above the stage. Secure the "e" slide on the stage using stage clips.
5. Lower the objective so that it is about 2 mm above the coverslip.
6. Look through the eyepiece and adjust the mirror so the "e" is illuminated. **CAUTION! Do not aim the mirror directly at the sun. Direct sunlight can injure your eyes.**
7. Use the coarse focus to raise the body tube. Once you see an image, switch to fine focus. When you have the "e" in focus, draw what you see. Label the drawing *low power*.
8. Carefully click the high-power objective into place. When in high power, use only the fine focus knob. Once you have the "e" in focus, draw what you see. Label the drawing *high power*.
9. Repeat steps 2–8, using a small section of Elodea leaf instead of the letter "e."

Task 4 Analysis
1. How does viewing the letter "e" through the microscope change the appearance of the "e"?
2. What happens to the images when you switch from low power to high power?
3. How does viewing the "e" differ from viewing the leaf?

Task 5 Conclusion
Explain how a compound microscope helps you study both nonliving things and living things.

Extension

Use the wet mount technique to make slides of a human hair. Then view the slides under a microscope. Describe what you see.

Chapter 1 Review

Concept Summary

1.1 Science Skills and Methods
▶ Scientists use many skills; they observe, infer, estimate, measure, predict, classify, hypothesize, record, organize, and analyze.
▶ Scientists perform experiments to gather data about nature.
▶ Scientific facts, theories, and laws may change.
▶ Scientists use models to represent the parts of nature they study.

1.2 Measuring with Scientific Units
▶ Scientists measure length, volume, mass, density, temperature, and time with standard SI units.
▶ Mass is the amount of matter an object contains; it is not the same as weight.

▶ Density is a measure of mass per unit volume.

1.3 Graphing
▶ Circle graphs show how the parts of something make up a whole.
▶ Bar graphs compare one aspect of several different things.
▶ Line graphs show data defined by two variables.

1.4 Microscopes and Lasers
▶ Because they bend light, lenses are used in microscopes to make things appear larger.
▶ Electron microscopes can magnify objects more than one million times.
▶ Lasers are used by surgeons as a kind of scalpel.

Chapter Vocabulary

data (1.1)
controlled experiment (1.1)
constant (1.1)
variable (1.1)

meter (1.2)
volume (1.2)
cubic meter (1.2)
liter (1.2)

mass (1.2)
kilogram (1.2)
density (1.2)

microscope (1.4)
lens (1.4)

Check Your Vocabulary

Use the vocabulary words above to complete the following sentences correctly.

1. An object's _____ is measured as g/cm³.
2. The basic SI unit for length is the _____.
3. An object too small to be seen can be studied with a _____.
4. In an experiment, a _____ is a factor that is kept the same.
5. The SI unit often used to measure the volume of large containers is the _____.
6. An SI unit for volume based on the meter is the _____.
7. An object's _____ is a measurement of how much matter it contains.

8. In a _____, there are two test groups.
9. The information gathered by scientists is called _____.
10. A piece of glass shaped to bend light is a _____.
11. An SI unit for mass is the _____.
12. In an experiment, a _____ is a factor that is changed.
13. Liters are used to measure _____.

Write Your Vocabulary

Write sentences using each vocabulary word above. Show that you know what each word means.

Chapter 1 Review

Check Your Knowledge

Answer the following in complete sentences.

1. What two parts must be included in all measurements?

2. What should you wear when working in the laboratory?

3. What is a controlled experiment?

4. Why is a circle graph often called a pie graph?

5. What is one reason a scientist might make a model?

6. Name two SI units used to measure volume.

7. Why do scientists measure mass instead of weight?

8. What is a microscope used for?

Determine whether each statement is true or false. Write *true* if it is true. If it is false, change the underlined word(s) to make the statement true.

9. <u>Concave</u> lenses magnify images.

10. <u>Line</u> graphs have an *x*-axis and a *y*-axis.

11. To measure the volume in a graduated cylinder, you read the level of the <u>highest point</u> of the meniscus.

12. Scientific facts <u>never</u> change.

13. SI units are based on multiples of <u>100</u>.

14. An <u>electron microscope</u> is used to magnify objects over one million times.

Check Your Understanding

Apply the concepts you have learned to answer each question.

1. **Application** What kind of graph—circle, bar, or line—would you use to show each of the following kinds of data?

   a. The heights of the members of your family.

   b. The amount of time taken up by commercials and regular programming during an average prime-time television hour.

   c. Your height on your birthday each year for the past 10 years.

   d. The number of teachers in your school who teach science.

2. What SI unit would you use to measure each of the following?

   a. The volume of water in a pond.

   b. The width of a flower.

   c. The temperature of the ocean.

   d. The density of ocean water.

3. What should you do if you get a chemical in your eyes during a laboratory activity?

4. **Mystery Photo** The photo on page 2 shows grains of ragweed pollen magnified many times. What kind of microscope do you think was used to make this image? Why might scientists find it useful to see this kind of detail on grains of pollen?

5. Which is the greater length, 1.5 m or 150 mm? Which is the larger volume, 1 m³ or 1 L?

6. A compound microscope has a 10x ocular and objectives of 21x, 46x, and 74x. What are its possible magnifications?

Develop Your Skills

Use the skills you have developed in this chapter to complete each activity.

1. **Interpret Data** The circle graph below shows the makeup of a raccoon's diet over a two-week period. The amounts of each kind of food were measured in grams.

   a. What portion of the raccoon's food is made up of animals?

   b. The amount of frogs and salamanders in the raccoon's diet is how many times greater than the amount of fish?

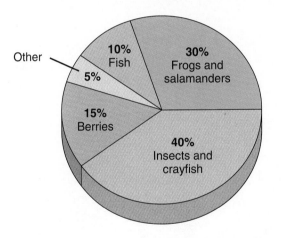

2. **Data Bank** Use the information on page 631 to answer the following questions.

   a. How long is the King cobra? Convert its length to centimeters.

   b. How long is the Komodo dragon? Convert its length to millimeters.

3. **Infer** Make an inference based on each of the following observations.

   a. A wet dog walks away from a pond.

   b. Your mailbox is empty.

   c. Your friend has a sunburn.

   d. You have a substitute teacher today.

Make Connections

1. **Link the Concepts** Below is a concept map showing how some of the main concepts in this chapter link together. Only parts of the map are filled in. Copy the map. Using words and ideas from the chapter, complete the map.

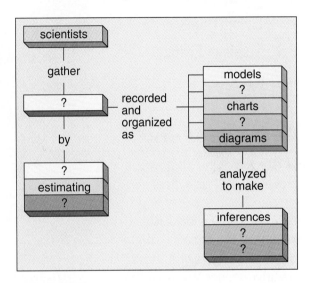

2. **Science and Living** Choose one of the science process skills and describe how you could use it to benefit your daily life.

3. **Science and Technology** Electron microscopes can magnify objects many more times than can light microscopes, but they cannot be used to study living organisms or living cells. Research ways in which high-power light microscopes can provide clear images of living cells at very high magnifications.

4. **Science and History** Many of the modern methods of science are based on the ideas or work of scientists who lived many centuries ago. Find out the names of some important scientists who lived before the 1800s. Choose one and write a report about his or her contributions to science.

Chapter 2

The Earth and Living Things

What do you see?

66 I think that the photograph is of the west coast. I can see the San Francisco Bay and the mountains. It looks like it was taken from space. The colors like the browns and greens represent the elevation of mountains, valleys, and flat land. 99

Garrett Lamb
Arundel Elementary School
San Carlos, California

To find out more about the photograph, look on page 48. As you read this chapter, you will learn more about why the earth is unique.

2.1 The Living Planet

Objectives

▶ **Define** the earth's biosphere.

▶ **Explain** why the earth is a unique planet.

▶ **Explain** the importance of the earth's land, water, and atmosphere to living things.

▶ **Design** a circle graph comparing the distribution of land and water on earth.

Skills WarmUp

Compare Use a globe. Turn the globe so that the South Pole faces you. Draw the areas of land and water. Now turn the globe so that the North Pole is in front of you. Draw the areas of land and water. Compare the two drawings. Is the amount of land and water on each half of the earth equal? Which half— south or north—has more water? More land?

Make a list of all the places where you think living things are found. You probably named places on land, in water, and in the air. Living things can be found nearly everywhere on the earth, even in the most unlikely places. For example, several kinds of worms live so deep in the ocean that sunlight can't reach them. Most penguins live in icy Antarctica. Some kinds of lizards can even survive in the hottest deserts.

All living things exist at or near the earth's surface in a life-supporting zone called the **biosphere**. What sort of place can support life? Living things need sunlight, water, matter, and air. In the biosphere, the land, water, and air satisfy the needs of all living things.

The Third Planet

The earth is located 150 million km from the sun. The earth is part of a system of planets and other objects in space that orbit, or revolve around, the sun. This system is called the solar system. Look at Table 2.1. Of the nine planets in the solar system, the earth is the third planet from the sun and the fifth largest planet.

The earth is unique in the solar system because it is the only planet where life is known to exist. Water is found on the earth as a liquid, a solid, and a gas—unique among the planets. However, because of the earth's distance from the sun, most of the earth's water is in a liquid state. Water is needed to support life. The other planets are either closer to the sun and too hot, or farther from the sun and too cold.

Table 2.1   The Nine Planets

Position from Sun	Diameter (km)
Mercury	4,878
Venus	12,012
Earth	12,756
Mars	6,787
Jupiter	142,984
Saturn	120,536
Uranus	51,118
Neptune	49,660
Pluto	2,400

Communicate Pretend you are in charge of collecting ten photographs to be placed in a space probe headed for distant galaxies. What photographs would you select that would best describe the earth? Explain your choices.

**Figure 2.1
Earth's Continents
and Oceans**

North America This is the only continent to have every kind of climate—from the dry cold of the Arctic to the wet heat of the tropics. The abundant animal and plant life varies with the climate.

South America The greatest variety of animals on any continent live in the rivers, swamps, and tropical rain forests of South America. In fact, one-fourth of all the known kinds of mammals live in these rain forests.

Antarctica Only mosses and a few small insects can live on this ice-buried continent. However, many kinds of animals, such as fish, krill, penguins, seals, whales, and flying birds, live in the sur-rounding ocean.

Unlike the much larger outer planets, which are mostly gas, the earth is mostly solid. You know this solid part as land. Land provides some of the substances needed for life. It also provides a surface on which life could develop. Surrounding the land is air. The air contains the water vapor and gases also needed to support life.

Earth's Waters The most abundant substance on the earth is water. Most of the earth's water is salty and exists in the world ocean. Only 3 percent of all the earth's water is fresh. Rivers, ponds, streams, and most lakes and swampy wetlands are bodies of fresh water.

Look at the map in Figure 2.1. Notice that there is really one big body of water—the world ocean. Geographers divide the world ocean into five major oceans. Find the Pacific, Atlantic, Indian, Antarctic, and Arctic oceans on the map in Figure 2.1.

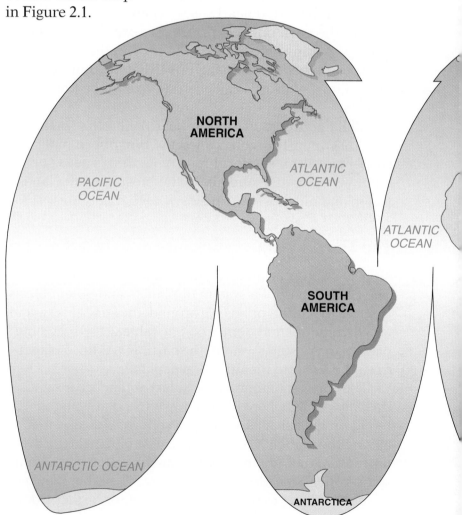

Of the five oceans, the Pacific is the largest and deepest. Smaller bodies of salt water in the world are seas.

The oceans and bodies of fresh water contain an amazing variety of living things. Large ocean kelp and freshwater algae provide food and shelter for some fishes. Certain animals, such as fishes, snails, and turtles, make their homes in either fresh water or ocean water. Water life ranges in size from tiny microscopic bacteria to the blue whale—the largest living animal.

Earth's Landmasses   As shown in Figure 2.1, only a little of the earth's surface is actually land. The relationship is about 28 percent land to 72 percent water. The large landmasses on the earth are called continents. Geographers define continents as very large landmasses that are surrounded, or nearly surrounded, by salt water. Table 2.2 names the seven continents.

Table 2.2
The Earth's Continents

Africa
Antarctica
Asia
Australia
Europe
North America
South America

Europe   Vast forests in Europe have been cut down to make way for cities and farms. Most of Europe's wildlife live in areas difficult for people to reach, or in special preserves or zoos.

Africa   The world's largest desert, the Sahara, stretches across Northern Africa. Much of the continent is grassland—home for hyenas, elephants, giraffes, lions, and zebras.

Asia   Asia is the largest continent. Camels, cobras, reindeer, the Giant Panda, yaks, Siberian tigers, bamboo, kudzu, beech trees, and ginkgos live in Asia.

Australia   Most of Australia is dry grassland—home to many unique animals, such as kangaroos, kookaburras, wallaroos, and emu.

Many different kinds of living things make their homes on the earth's continents. Some animals, such as snakes, live on every continent except Antarctica. The same is true of some plants. Mosses are found on every continent, including Antarctica. Some animals and plants only live naturally on one continent. For example, koalas are unique to Australia. The cacao (kuh KAY oh) bean from which chocolate is made, grows on several continents but only in areas close to the equator.

Earth's Atmosphere   The earth is surrounded by an envelope of gases called the **atmosphere**. The atmosphere extends 700 km above the surface of the earth. It is constantly moving in complex, but regular, patterns. The interactions between the atmosphere, ocean, and land determine the weather and climate on the earth.

Look at Table 2.3. The atmosphere is a mixture of different kinds of gases. Notice that nitrogen is the most abundant gas in air. The next most abundant gas is oxygen. Name two other gases that make up air.

All living things need the gases in the atmosphere. For example, animals and plants use the oxygen in air with sugars to carry on certain processes. These processes provide the animals and plants with energy. Besides oxygen, plants use carbon dioxide to make fuel for growth. In the oceans, living things use the atmospheric gases dissolved in the ocean water.

Table 2.3   **The Gases in Air**

Nitrogen	78%
Oxygen	21%
Argon, carbon dioxide, neon, helium, krypton, hydrogen, xenon, and ozone	1%

Science and Technology   *Infrared Sensors*

Look at Figure 2.2. It is a picture of the Monterey area in California taken from a satellite called LANDSAT I. Scientists call getting information about things at a great distance, or things one can't touch, *remote sensing*. Satellites orbiting in space are remote sensors. Instruments on board satellites provide scientists with information about the earth.

To take the photograph in Figure 2.2, the LANDSAT I satellite used heat, or infrared, sensors. All objects—even your chair, this book, and your body—give off infrared waves. As an object gets hotter, it gives off more and more infrared waves. Infrared waves are like light, but they can't be seen by the human eye. Though invisible, these waves may be detected and measured. Just as your eye can detect a yellow object as different from a

Figure 2.2 ▲

In this LANDSAT I satellite photograph, the planted areas are red and the unplanted areas are blue.

blue one, infrared sensors can detect temperature changes. Especially helpful for scientists is the ability of infrared to detect many things from far away.

One specific use of infrared sensors helps scientists survey croplands and forests. Remote sensing by infrared photography provides pictures showing ground heat as shades of red and blue. Areas with thick plant life appear red; areas with thin plant life appear blue or white. By observing an area over time, scientists can detect changes in the amount of plant life in the area. Scientists can use the information to identify areas of frost damage or plant loss in tropical rain forests.

Infrared sensors can also be used to identify soil and rock types, to map natural features, to detect pollution and water flowing from rivers into oceans, and to study clouds and the ocean. The information scientists learn from remote sensors can help us use and preserve the land, air, and water on the earth.

Check and Explain

1. Define biosphere.

2. Why is the earth a unique planet?

3. **Predict** How do you think life on the earth would be affected if the earth were farther away from the sun? Explain your answer.

4. **Graph** Design a circle graph that shows the distribution of land and water on the earth. Label and title your graph.

Classify Write the words
Living, *Dead*, and *Nonliving*
at the top of a piece of paper.
Then place each of the following
items in the correct column: pear,
candle, shirt, radio, sunflower,
baseball, owl, strand of hair, oak
tree, snow, shark, bicycle.

2.2 Characteristics of Living Things

Objectives

▶ **Distinguish** between living and nonliving things.

▶ **List** and **describe** the characteristics of living things.

▶ **Make a model** that shows your understanding of an organism's adaptations.

L ook at Figure 2.3. Can you tell the living things from the nonliving things? Make a list of the living things and a list of the nonliving things. Then compare your lists to those of a classmate. Explain to your classmate how you decided which things were living.

You probably thought correctly that the rocks and water were nonliving things, but how could you tell? When you classified the living and nonliving things, you needed to identify common characteristics among the objects. Making a list of the common characteristics of living things is not as easy as it might sound. In fact, scientists still debate about the basic characteristics of life and nonlife. However, there do seem to be some generally accepted characteristics that are common to all living things. All living things:

▶ are made of one or more cells.

▶ obtain and use energy.

▶ grow and develop.

▶ respond to their environment.

▶ reproduce.

▶ are adapted to their environment.

Some nonliving things may have *some* of these six characteristics, but not *all* of them. For example, an icicle may seem to grow, but an icicle is not living. A car gets and uses energy, but it is not living—gasoline needs to be pumped into a car. A robot may move or even speak, but it is not living.

Figure 2.3 ▲
Tide pools contain many living things that can be seen at low tide.

Cells

All organisms are made of one or more **cells**, and every cell comes from another cell. A cell is the basic unit of a living thing that can perform all the processes associated with life. A chemist might call a cell a chemical factory. A cell provides all the conditions needed for the chemical reactions of living things.

Cells vary in type and function. A single cell can be an entire living organism. Most of the animals and plants you are familiar with, such as cats and trees, are made of many cells. These organisms may contain thousands, millions, even billions of cells. Most cells, even those of the blue whale, are microscopic in size. The small cell size allows the necessary exchange of materials between the cell and its environment.

Nonliving things are not made of cells. Cells are found in nonliving matter only if that matter was once alive and is now dead. Wood, for example, is made of cells of the once-living tree it came from.

Figure 2.5 ▲
What is the energy source for the berries? For the mouse?

Figure 2.4 ▲
This piece of wood is no longer living. How can you tell it was once part of a living thing?

Energy

Think of all the things you may do in a day. Run down a hill. Eat an apple. Read this book. Or sleep. You would not be able to do these things without energy. Energy is the ability to make things move or change.

Living things get energy from their environment, or surroundings. They use that energy to grow, develop, and reproduce. All organisms need energy to build the substances that make up their cells. Plants get their energy from sunlight. Animals and humans get energy from the food they eat.

For life to be maintained, a balance must exist between an organism's energy-producing processes and its energy-using processes. The constant balancing of these two systems within an organism is called **metabolism**. Examples of metabolic processes in living things include breaking down foods, building body parts, transporting materials, and removing wastes.

Stimulus and Response

How do you react when you hear a sudden loud noise? Most likely, you jump. When this happens, you are reacting to a stimulus in your environment. A **stimulus** is a change that occurs in the environment. Sound is a stimulus. Other stimuli include light, pressure, odors, and temperature changes. Reaction to a stimulus is called a **response**.

Growth and Development

All living things grow. Sometimes growth simply means getting larger—not changing. But that is not always the case. A coconut, when it sprouts, produces roots, a trunk, and leaves that continue to grow for years. As it grows, the palm tree takes in substances from the air and soil to make living tissue. After the palm tree stops getting larger, it continues to add new material to replace existing parts that wear out.

A balloon, on the other hand, may seem to "grow" if you blow it up. But a balloon grows bigger only if someone adds more air inside it. A balloon may

Figure 2.6 ▶
The decreasing number of daylight hours in the fall stimulate monarch butterflies to fly to their wintering grounds where they "sleep" until the seasons change.

change only if someone stretches it or twists it. A balloon won't grow bigger by just laying on a table.

As some organisms grow, most go through a cycle of change called development. Think of a caterpillar developing into a butterfly, or a small seed blossoming into a flower. Organisms grow and develop at different rates. Humans grow to adulthood in about 18 years. Some tadpoles, however, grow and become frogs in a few weeks. Some insects actually reach their adult stage in one day.

Reproduction

All organisms can reproduce. The process by which organisms produce more organisms like themselves is called **reproduction**. Although all living things can reproduce, reproduction is not essential for the survival of an individual organism. However, because all individual organisms eventually die, reproduction is necessary if a group of similar organisms is to survive.

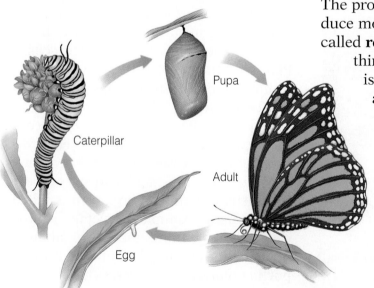

Pupa

Caterpillar

Adult

Egg

◀ **Figure 2.7**
During its lifetime, a butterfly grows and develops. As it develops, its appearance changes.

Adadaptation

Touch each of your fingertips with your thumb. Then pick up a pen or pencil and look at your hand. You can do these actions because of the joint in your thumb. This joint is an example of an **adaptation**. An adaptation is a characteristic that enables an organism to live and reproduce successfully in its environment.

All organisms must be adapted to their enviroments to survive. For example, rattlesnakes can live in the desert. Triggerfish can survive in coral reefs. Beavers can live in forest ponds. Examples of adaptations in a beaver are shown in Figure 2.8. Look at the beaver's legs and tail. A beaver's powerful hind legs help it drag heavy loads. The flat tail serves as a rudder for swimming. These adaptations help the beaver build a home of log and mud. A beaver also has sharp teeth. The shape of its teeth helps in cutting down trees. Name some other adaptations that help a beaver survive.

Figure 2.8
Some adaptations help the beaver build its home. Others help the beaver get food, protect itself, and keep warm.

Historical Notebook

Disproving Spontaneous Generation

People have not always known that living things come from other living things. Hundreds of years ago, people thought that living things came from nonliving matter. They based this idea on their observations. For example, people sometimes saw maggots suddenly appearing on rotting meat, or mice suddenly appearing in a pile of rags. This idea, called spontaneous generation, was put to the test in the 1600s by Francisco Redi, an Italian physician.

Redi designed a controlled experiment to test the idea that maggots came from rotting meat.

He put some meat into three sets of jars. One set of jars was left open. Another set of jars was sealed. The third set of jars was covered with mesh screen.

Redi thought that if spontaneous generation was possible, maggots would appear on the meat in the sealed jars. Redi's experiment and the results are shown below.

1. Observe the results of Redi's experiment shown below. Write down your observations.

2. What did Redi's experiments prove?

Science and You *Goose Bumps*

Have you ever stepped out of a shower or bath and discovered tiny bumps on your skin? Have you noticed those same bumps when you are outside in cold weather? If so, then you have observed an adaptation called *goose bumps*.

A goose bump is caused by the contraction of a muscle located around a hair. Flex your arm. When you do this, you are contracting your upper arm muscle. The contracting muscle causes a bulge in your arm. When you are exposed to chilly air, tiny muscles in your cold skin begin to contract. These muscle contractions cause tiny bulges. Your skin gets a bumpy look, and your hairs stand on end.

Goose bumps are a helpful adaptation for animals with fur. When an animal's hairs stand on end, air is added in the fur. The hairs help hold this layer of air in place. The hair and air keep the cold air away from the animal's body. The thicker the fur, the less cold air will touch the animal's skin. This helps keep the animal's body temperature at a normal level. You don't have fur, but you do have thick hair on your head. Goose bumps on your head help keep your head warm. Look at Figure 2.9. How do goose bumps help birds?

Besides cold temperature, fear is also a stimulus for goose bumps. A scared animal with its hair on end looks larger and stronger to its enemy. This response is not very useful to you because most of your body hairs are short and sparse.

Figure 2.9 ▲
During cold weather the stimulus of the cold causes a bird's feathers to puff out. This helps keep in body heat, just like human goose bumps do.

Check and Explain

1. What is a cell?

2. List and describe six characteristics of all living things.

3. **Reason and Conclude** Why is a dog a living thing? Why is a car a nonliving thing? Explain your answers by discussing the characteristics of living things.

4. **Make a Model** Draw and color an imaginary animal in a jungle environment. What colors would best protect the animal in this kind of environment? Explain your choice of colors.

2.3 Needs of Living Things

Objectives

▶ **Describe** the needs of living things.

▶ **Identify** the sun as a primary source of energy.

▶ **Predict** what would happen to an organism if its needs were not met in its environment.

Skills WarmUp

Make a Graph Make a list of the five most important things you need to stay alive. Rank them in order of their importance. Then find out what your classmates wrote. Make a bar graph showing the class results.

If you were to travel in space, what things would you need to survive? You probably answered air, food, and water. These are some of the things you and other living things need to live. The earth may be described as a huge "spaceship." It is the only planet in the solar system with the right environment to support the needs of millions of different kinds of organisms.

Six Common Needs

All organisms must interact with their environment to survive. There are many different environments in the biosphere. Yet each different environment provides the energy, food, water, air, proper temperature, and living space that the organisms living there need.

Energy All living things need energy. Where does this energy come from? Directly or indirectly, the sun is the main energy source for most organisms. For example, all plants use the sun's energy to make sugars and starches. Plants use these nutrients to fuel their growth. Animals, however, get their energy by eating plants or other animals.

Food All organisms need some type of food or nutrients. Food keeps the life processes going within cells. Growth and transport are processes fueled by food. Different kinds of organisms eat different kinds of food. Some organisms, such as deer, eat only plants. Some animals eat only other animals. Other animals eat both plants and animals. Some organisms do not eat their food. Plants absorb their nutrients from the soil. Some worms deep in the ocean absorb nutrients from the ocean water.

Figure 2.10 ▲
This frog gets its energy by eating other animals, such as insects and even other frogs.

Figure 2.11 A Pond

The sun is the main source of energy for all living things.

Water Water is a very important need of living things. Humans need water so much that you could live longer without food than without water. In fact, you can live about one or two months without food, but only about one week without water. Your body mass is about 70 percent water. This is true of most organisms.

Besides making up most of the body mass, water has two other important functions. Water is needed to dissolve and transport substances in an organism. Nutrients and wastes can be dissolved in water. Once dissolved, these substances can be transported throughout the organism's body. In animals, blood transports wastes and nutrients. Blood is mostly water. Instead of blood, trees have watery sap.

Temperature Outside temperature and internal temperature are important to living things. Few organisms can live in environments where temperatures are either extremely hot or extremely cold. Most organisms need to live within certain temperature ranges.

Freshwater plants and animals need very little water. They have special adaptations to keep too much water from entering their systems.

Oxygen and other atmospheric gases enter the surface water.

Algae, reeds, pondweed, lily pads, and duckweed compete for a place in the sun at the pond's surface.

The soil on the pond's bottom contains nutrients that are absorbed by plant roots for growth.

Temperature is also important to organisms because they need to maintain a proper body temperature to carry out metabolism. The ability of an organism to keep conditions inside its body the same, even though conditions in the environment may change, is called **homeostasis**.

Animals that can maintain a stable body temperature regardless of their surroundings are called **endothermic**. Birds, dogs, and humans are endothermic. Some animals, such as fishes, frogs, and turtles, can't regulate their body temperatures. As the outside temperature changes, so do their internal temperatures. These animals are **ectothermic**. They depend on heat energy from the sun for warmth.

Gas Exchange All living things must exchange gases with their environment. Land animals and plants get oxygen from the air. Organisms that live in water get oxygen that is dissolved in the water.

Skills WorkOut

Analyze You use water every day in many different ways. It is important to your general well-being. Identify the different ways that you use water. Why is each way important? Rank the ways you use water from the most important to the least important. Then write a brief essay explaining why you ranked the first use and the last use in the positions you did.

Duckweed fronds are food for snails and insect larvae.

The pond provides living space for all the pond's organisms. A male stickleback makes a nest on the pond floor and tries to attract a female to mate.

Turtles must lie in the sun to raise their body temperatures so they can become active enough to hunt for food.

Carbon dioxide is also important to living things. When you breathe out, you release carbon dioxide. Plants use carbon dioxide to make sugars. During this process, they also release oxygen into the air. Plants also release carbon dioxide as a waste product.

Living Space   All organisms need living space. This space may provide food or shelter. The space may have sunlight or be dark. All living things compete for the earth's limited space. The struggle among living things to get the proper amount of water, food, and energy in a living space is called **competition**.

There are many ways in which living things compete for their space, or territory. Some birds, for example, use sounds to keep other animals away from their territory. Plants, too, compete for living space. Without sunlight or water, small plants may die in the shadow of larger plants.

Consider This

Should Animals Be Kept in Zoos?

There are zoos all over the world where exotic animals are kept for the public to visit. Zoos offer an opportunity for people to see and experience animal life from other parts of the world.

Zoo experiences educate people about the variety and needs of animals. However, zoo animals live in confinement and under conditions that differ greatly from their natural environments.

Consider Some Issues   Animals that are kept in zoos are well cared for and protected from danger. They receive highly nutritious diets and special medical care.

Some zoos breed endangered animals. Zoo breeding programs may help save animal populations from extinction.

In many parts of the world, prime animal habitat is being taken over for human settlement. Saving habitat is important for the survival of endangered animals.

Removing wild animals from their natural habitat and confining them in zoos for people to view may be cruel and unfair to the animals.

International trade in wild animals may involve abusing these animals.

Think About It   What might happen to some wild animal populations in 20 years if zoos didn't exist? How could you be affected by the changes that might result?

Write About It   Write a report stating your position for or against keeping animals in zoos. Include your reasons for choosing that position.

Science and Technology *Salty Waters*

Beware: Deadly Water! This warning describes most of the earth's water because most of it is in oceans. Ocean water contains salts, minerals, and elements. Many kinds of living things cannot drink or live in ocean water.

Humans need some salts, especially sodium chloride, which you know as table salt. In fact, a certain amount of salt is needed in your diet for your body to function properly. Ocean water, however, contains about seven times the amount of salts that your body can withstand. People could not survive if they drank only salt water.

For centuries, people have looked for ways to remove salt from ocean water. Today salt is removed through a process called *desalination* (dee sal ih NAY shun). Most modern desalting plants use a method called flash distillation. During this process, ocean water boils or "flashes" to form steam, leaving the salt behind. When the salt-free vapor cools, it changes back into water. Once the salt has been removed and the water is purified, it is drinkable.

In some parts of the world, desalting plants are a major source of fresh water. In the desert countries of the Middle East, such as Saudi Arabia and Kuwait, desalting plants produce millions of liters of fresh water each day. Although there are some desalting plants in the United States, few places use desalting because it is a costly process.

Figure 2.12 ▲
The Yuma desalination plant desalts about 275 million liters of water each day. Desalination is one way to lower the amount of salts in some river water. It also makes ocean water drinkable.

Check and Explain

1. What are four needs of living things?

2. What is the main source of energy for most living things?

3. **Apply** What needs may be met with the following things: a bird's nest, a scuba diving tank, pond water, a rock in shade, a sunflower seed?

4. **Predict** Several kinds of organisms share the pond environment shown on pages 42–43. Choose one of the organisms. Describe how it would be affected if its numbers increased in this environment.

Activity 2   *How does temperature affect mold growth?*

Skills   Measure; Observe; Infer; Analyze

Task 1   Prelab Prep

1. Collect the following items: 4 self-lock bags with labels, pen, Celsius thermometer, a slice of bread, plastic knife, hand lens, metric ruler.
2. Number the labels from 1 to 4 and date each one.
3. On the first label write *Freezer*. Label the remaining bags *Refrigerator*, *Closed Box*, and *Control*.

Task 2   Data Record

1. On a separate sheet of paper, draw a data table for each location like the one shown below. You should have four separate data tables.
2. In the data tables, record all your observations about the color(s), size, and amount of any mold you see.

Task 3   Procedure

1. Measure the temperature at each location: inside a freezer, inside a refrigerator, inside a closed box in a warm location, and wherever you regularly store bread. *Note: Be sure the regular storage place is dark.* The control is your regular storage place for bread.
2. Cut the slice of bread into four equal sections. Put one section of bread in each bag.
3. Place each bag in its location.
4. Each day for five days, examine the bread for mold growth. Use the hand lens and ruler.

CAUTION! Do not remove the bread from the bag. After recording your observations, return the bag to its place.

Task 4   Analysis

1. Identify the variable in this activity.
2. At which location(s) did mold grow on the bread?
3. What was the temperature of the first location to have mold growing on the bread?
4. What were the temperature and location of the bread with the most mold? The least mold?
5. At what temperature and location did mold grow the fastest? The slowest?

Task 5   Conclusion

Write a short paragraph explaining how temperature affects the rate of mold growth on bread.

Everyday Application

Suppose you bought a month's supply of bread for lunches. Explain why the temperature of the place where you stored the bread might be important.

Extension

Develop a hypothesis about the effect of moisture on the growth of mold on bread. Write your procedures and test your hypothesis. Be sure to include a control in your experiment.

Table 2.4   Mold Growth

Date	Time	Temperature (°C)	Location (Number)	Condition of Bread

Chapter 2 Review

Concept Summary

2.1 The Living Planet
▶ The biosphere is the zone of water, land, and air that supports all life on earth.
▶ The world ocean is divided into the Pacific, Atlantic, Indian, Antarctic, and Arctic oceans.
▶ The landmasses on earth are divided into continents, which are the homes to many living things.
▶ The atmosphere that surrounds the earth contains a combination of nitrogen, oxygen, and various other gases.

2.2 Characteristics of Living Things
▶ Living things carry on certain life processes that nonliving things cannot.

▶ The cell is the basic unit of a living thing that can perform life processes.
▶ The processes of living things include movement, metabolism, growth and development, response, reproduction, and adaptation.

2.3 Needs of Living Things
▶ Living things need energy, food, water, proper temperature, air, and living space to survive in their environments.
▶ The sun is the primary source of energy for most living things.
▶ Endothermic animals maintain stable internal body temperatures. Ectothermic animals cannot regulate their body temperatures.

Chapter Vocabulary

biosphere (2.1)	metabolism (2.2)	reproduction (2.2)	endothermic (2.3)
atmosphere (2.1)	stimulus (2.2)	adaptation (2.2)	ectothermic (2.3)
cell (2.2)	response (2.2)	homeostasis (2.3)	competition (2.3)

Check Your Vocabulary

Use the vocabulary words above to complete the following sentences correctly.

1. A ____ is a change in the environment that produces a response.
2. The ____ is an envelope of gases that surrounds the earth.
3. Animals that maintain stable body temperatures are ____ .
4. A ____ is the basic unit of a living thing that can perform all the life processes.
5. All of the chemical changes that happen in an organism are called ____ .
6. The thin zone on the earth that supports all life is called the ____ .
7. An organism's ability to keep its body conditions the same although environmental conditions change is ____ .

8. An ____ is a characteristic that enables an organism to survive and reproduce in its environment.
9. The struggle between living things for available living space is called ____ .
10. Reacting to a stimulus in the environment is called a ____ .
11. Animals that cannot regulate their body temperatures are called ____ .
12. The process by which living things produce more organisms like themselves is ____ .

Write Your Vocabulary

Write two or more paragraphs using five of the vocabulary words. Show that you know what each word means.

Chapter 2 *Review*

Check Your Knowledge

Answer each of the following in complete sentences.

1. List the six common needs of all living things.

2. What is an ectothermic animal?

3. What parts of the earth's surface make up the biosphere?

4. How could you tell a nonliving thing from a living thing?

5. Give an example of an adaptation in a beaver that helps it to survive.

6. Why is the sun important to all living things?

7. Name three things that living things compete for in their living space.

8. Give an example of a metabolic process.

9. What is one function water has for living organisms?

Choose the answer that best completes each sentence.

10. Plants get energy from (sunlight, trees, people, leaves).

11. All living organisms are made of (leaves, sunlight, blood, cells).

12. To move or change, organisms need (water, matter, competition, energy).

13. Breaking down food, building body parts, and transporting materials are all processes in (metabolism, reproduction, adaptation, responding).

14. As organisms grow, they also may change or (breathe, develop, eat, compete).

15. The most common gas in the atmosphere is (oxygen, nitrogen, helium, water).

Check Your Understanding

Apply the concepts you have learned to answer each question.

1. Write an example of a stimulus. Give a response to the stimulus you chose.

2. List the unique features of the earth.

3. Draw an animal or plant. Explain how this living thing meets its needs for survival.

4. Choose a living organism and discuss how it successfully competes for its living space.

5. **Mystery Photo** The infrared photograph of the San Francisco Bay Area and the Central Valley in California on page 30 was taken by a satellite. "Warm" areas are red; "cool" areas are blue. Why do forests and farmland look red? Why do towns look blue? Predict what your community would look like from an infrared satellite photograph. Draw a satellite picture of your community.

6. **Application** Is a pumpkin seed living or nonliving? Explain your answer.

7. **Critical Thinking** Make a table listing the six common needs of living things. In the table, describe how the needs are met for a snake and a polar bear. Using the information in your table, write a paragraph comparing and contrasting how the needs are met for these two animals.

8. **Application** You read in a magazine that plants respond to the stimulus of music by growing larger. Design an experiment to test the magazine's claim. Be sure to include a control. What is the hypothesis of your experiment? What is the variable?

Develop Your Skills

Use the skills you have developed to complete each activity.

1. **Interpret Data** The graph below shows the changing population of the arctic hare and the arctic fox over time.

   a. Describe what happens to the hare and fox population over time.

   b. What might be the cause for the hare population change?

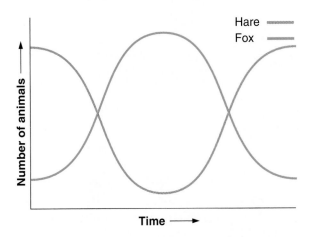

2. **Data Bank** Use the information on page 624 to answer the following questions.

   a. Which planets have oxygen?

   b. Which planet is the most like the earth in size?

3. **Make a Graph** Use the information contained in Table 2.3 on page 34 to make a circle graph showing the different kinds of gases in air. Remember to title your graph.

4. **Communicate** Choose a living or a nonliving thing. Have students in the class ask three questions from the list of characteristics for living things to determine whether your choice is alive or not.

Make Connections

1. **Link the Concepts** Below is a concept map showing how some of the main concepts in this chapter link together. Only parts of the map are filled in. Copy the map. Using words and ideas from the chapter, complete the map.

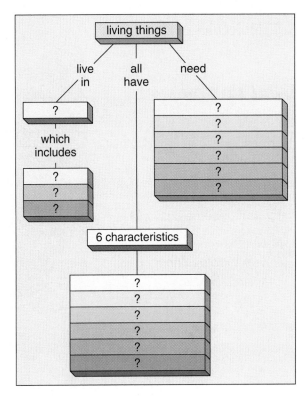

2. **Science and Society** Suppose a factory were built on the edge of a wilderness park in your home town. Plan a mock town meeting to discuss the impact of this factory on the plants and animals in the park. Divide the class into three groups for the mock meeting: factory owners, forest rangers, and community citizens.

3. **Science and Art** Draw or paint a picture of an environment such as a beach or a forest. On a separate piece of paper, draw a picture of an animal that could live in your environment.

Chapter 3

The Chemistry of Living Things

What do you see?

66I think the picture shows duck feathers. Duck feathers have a special oil on them. This makes the water bead so that the duck will not absorb water and become heavy.99

Katie Eskra
Haven Middle School
Evanston, Illinois

To find out about the photograph, look on page 68.
As you read this chapter, you will learn about matter and its importance to living things.

3.1 Matter

Objectives

▶ **Distinguish** between atoms and molecules.

▶ **Distinguish** between elements and compounds.

▶ **Interpret** the parts of a chemical formula.

▶ **Graph** the proportions of elements in the human body.

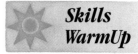
What do you have in common with a glass of water, a star, and a balloon filled with air? Like you, these things are made up of **matter**. Matter is anything that takes up space and has *mass*. Mass is the amount of matter in an object. The mass of an object is not the same as the space it takes up. A balloon filled with water has a greater mass than the same balloon filled with air.

Look around you. Everything is made of matter, including the book you are reading and the chair you are sitting in. Even your own body is made of matter. In fact, the entire universe is made of matter.

Physical Properties of Matter

How would you describe a pencil? It may be the color yellow. When you touch the pencil, it probably has a smooth texture. A pencil is also long, thin, and hard. Color, texture, shape, and hardness are some of the *physical properties*, or characteristics, of matter. Physical properties can be observed or measured without changing the makeup of a substance. Mass, volume, and density are three other physical properties of matter.

Physical properties help you identify kinds of matter. For example, each different kind of matter has a different *density*. You can see this if you fill a jar with the same amount of water and oil. Oil is less dense than water, so the oil will float on top of the water. All substances that are less dense than water float on top of water. All substances that are denser than water sink in water. Before you can decide what a substance is, you need to know several of its properties.

Figure 3.1 ▲
You can see many kinds of matter in the photograph. Describe the physical properties of two substances that you see.

Table 3.1
The Particle Theory of Matter

All matter is made of very tiny particles.
There are spaces between particles.
All the particles in a substance are the same; different substances are made of different particles.
Forceful attractions draw particles together; the attractions may be strong or weak.
The particles move at all times; as particles gain energy, they move faster.

Phases of Matter

All matter is made of tiny particles. You cannot see these particles. Scientists, however, have carried out many experiments in which they have observed the behavior of particles in matter. To explain their observations, scientists have developed the *particle theory of matter*. Read Table 3.1, which lists these observations. What causes particles to move faster?

The particle theory of matter helps explain the differences among the *phases* of matter. Phase is a property that scientists can use to classify matter. Solids, liquids, and gases are the three phases of matter.

Solids   Your pencil, book, and chair are all solids. Solids have a definite shape and a definite volume. Because the particles in a solid are very close together, the solid keeps its shape. However, the particles in a solid vibrate back and forth. They are held in fixed positions by strong forces.

Liquids   A liquid has a definite volume, but it does not have a definite shape. The particles of a liquid move around freely. If you pour a liter of water into different containers, the water always takes the shape of the containers. The volume of the water, however, stays the same. A liter of water will not fit into a half-liter bottle.

Gases   A gas has no definite shape or volume. The particles of a gas move constantly and rapidly in all directions. They are much farther apart than the particles in solids or liquids. A gas fills all the available space in a container. You can see this by pumping air into a tire or a balloon.

Figure 3.2

Matter can exist as a solid, liquid, or gas. ▼

Solid

Liquid

Gas

Figure 3.3 Different Models of Atoms

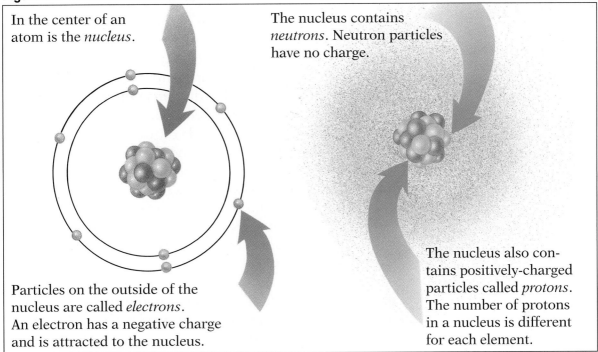

In the center of an atom is the *nucleus*.

The nucleus contains *neutrons*. Neutron particles have no charge.

Particles on the outside of the nucleus are called *electrons*. An electron has a negative charge and is attracted to the nucleus.

The nucleus also contains positively-charged particles called *protons*. The number of protons in a nucleus is different for each element.

Elements and Atoms

All forms of matter are made of one or more basic substances called **elements**. There are 91 known elements in nature. Elements cannot be changed into simpler substances by any chemical process or by heating.

Elements exist in nature as solids, liquids, or gases. Most elements are solids at room temperature. Iron, silver, gold, lead, and carbon are examples of solids. Some elements exist as gases. Oxygen, hydrogen, nitrogen, and helium are examples. These elements are present in the earth's atmosphere. However, you do not see or smell them because they are odorless, colorless gases. Only two elements exist as liquids at room temperature. They are mercury and bromine. Because they are very poisonous, mercury and bromine are normally found only in chemical laboratories.

The building blocks of elements are **atoms**. Each element is made of only one kind of atom. Each kind of atom has specific properties that make it different from every other kind of atom. An oxygen atom is different from a tin atom, helium atom, carbon atom, and so on.

Each atom is made up of different particles called *subatomic particles*. Study the models of an oxygen atom in Figure 3.3. What are the three main parts of an atom?

Compounds and Molecules

A substance that is made of more than one kind of element is called a **compound**. In a compound, elements are chemically combined. For example, oxygen and hydrogen are elements. At room temperature, they are both gases. When oxygen and hydrogen combine chemically, they form water. Water is a compound.

Most compounds are made of **molecules**. They are the smallest part of a compound that have all the properties of the compound. A molecule is made of two or more atoms chemically bonded together.

The elements that make up a compound are always present in the same proportions. Each molecule of water consists of two atoms of hydrogen and one atom of oxygen. Each molecule of carbon dioxide consists of one atom of carbon and two atoms of oxygen.

A compound cannot be separated into the elements that form it except through a chemical reaction. For example, water can be separated into oxygen and hydrogen by passing an electric current through it. Electric energy breaks the chemical bonds that hold the molecule together.

Figure 3.4   Molecule of Water

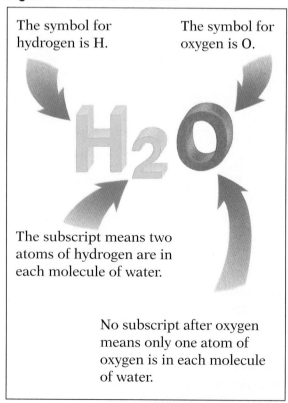

The symbol for hydrogen is H.

The symbol for oxygen is O.

The subscript means two atoms of hydrogen are in each molecule of water.

No subscript after oxygen means only one atom of oxygen is in each molecule of water.

Figure 3.5   Molecule of Carbon Dioxide

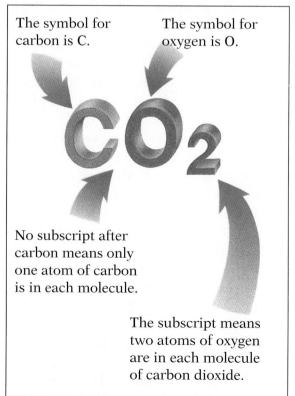

The symbol for carbon is C.

The symbol for oxygen is O.

No subscript after carbon means only one atom of carbon is in each molecule.

The subscript means two atoms of oxygen are in each molecule of carbon dioxide.

Chemical Symbols and Formulas

Chemists all over the world use a kind of shorthand to name elements and compounds. Every element is represented by a **chemical symbol**. A chemical symbol is represented by either a capital letter or a capital letter and a small letter. Table 3.2 shows some elements and their symbols. What is the chemical symbol for iron?

Combinations of symbols are used to represent compounds. These symbols are called **chemical formulas**. Look at Figure 3.5. What is the chemical formula for carbon dioxide?

Sometimes a formula represents a molecule of an element, not a compound. For example, the symbol for nitrogen is N. Nitrogen, however, occurs naturally as a molecule containing two atoms of nitrogen bonded together. Nitrogen is a *diatomic molecule*. Therefore, the formula for a molecule of nitrogen is N_2.

Look at the formulas in Figures 3.4–3.6. Each symbol in a chemical formula represents an element. The numbers written below the line in a chemical formula are *subscripts*. A subscript indicates the number of atoms in the molecule. If there is only one atom of an element in a molecule, no subscript follows the symbol for the element. If there is more than one atom of an element in the molecule, the symbol is followed by a subscript.

Table 3.2
Common Elements

Name	Symbol
Aluminum	Al
Calcium	Ca
Carbon	C
Chlorine	Cl
Copper	Cu
Gold	Au
Helium	He
Hydrogen	H
Iron	Fe
Nitrogen	N
Oxygen	O
Sodium	Na
Zinc	Zn

Figure 3.6   Molecule of Sucrose (table sugar)

What element does the C represent?

What element does the O represent?

What does the subscript after the O mean?

What does the subscript after the C mean?

How many elements are present in the sucrose molecule?

What is the total number of atoms in a molecule of sucrose?

Solving the Mystery of the Elements

Ancient peoples of many cultures recognized that some substances could not be broken down into simpler substances. In India, a book written around 1000 B.C. listed 5 "elements": earth, water, air, space, and light. By 300 B.C., people in China believed there were 5 elements—water, fire, wood, metal, and earth—constantly changing into one another. The ancient Greeks knew of 12 of the actual elements known today. However, they were not recognized as elements.

In the 1700s, experiments by a French chemist named Anton Lavoisier gave the concept of the *chemical* element a working definition. Lavoisier listed 33 elements. However, 7 of these were not true elements.

After chemical elements were defined, scientists began to recognize that materials such as gold, tin, and iron were elements. In the past 200 years, many new elements have been

ELEMENTS

⊙ Hydrogen	1	⊕ Strontian	46
⊖ Azote	5	✴ Barytes	68
⬤ Carbon	5	Ⓘ Iron	50
◯ Oxygen	7	Ⓩ Zinc	56

discovered. Today chemists can even change some of the elements into new ones.

1. Why do you think it was important for scientists to define chemical elements?

2. **Research** Find out who discovered radium, hydrogen, and oxygen. Write a report about the discovery of one of these elements.

Science and You
Here an Element, There an Element

Did you know that your body contains some of the same elements as the earth's crust and a squash? Table 3.3 on page 57 shows the main elements in the human body, the earth's crust, and a squash. Notice that oxygen is the most abundant element in all three. What other elements are common to all three?

Look at the tables listing the main elements in the human body and the squash. Why do you think oxygen and hydrogen are two of the most abundant elements? If you guessed that it has something to do with water, you are right. All living things need water to carry out life processes. Notice that carbon is also abundant. It is the basis of important molecules that both you and plants need to carry out life processes.

Most living things contain the same elements in similar proportions. A table listing the elements in the body of a

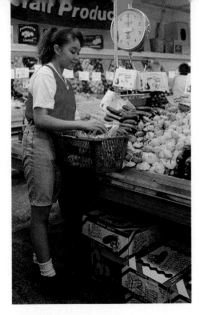

Figure 3.7 ▲
What three main elements does your body have in common with summer squash?

Figure 3.8 ▲
Rocks are combinations of minerals, and most minerals are made of more than one element.

Table 3.3

Human Body	%
Oxygen	65
Carbon	18
Hydrogen	10
Nitrogen	3
Calcium	2
Phosphorus	1.1
Potassium	0.35
Sulfur	0.25
Chlorine	0.15
Sodium	0.15
Iodine	0.1
Trace Elements	under 0.1

Earth's Crust	%
Oxygen	46.6
Silicon	27.7
Aluminum	8.1
Iron	5.0
Calcium	3.6
Sodium	2.8
Potassium	2.6
Magnesium	2.1
Other	1.5

Squash	%
Oxygen	85
Hydrogen	10.7
Carbon	3.3
Potassium	0.34
Nitrogen	0.16
Phosphorus	0.05
Calcium	0.02
Magnesium	0.01
Iron	0.008

cat or a giant squid would be very similar to a table listing the elements in the human body.

Look at the table listing the elements in the earth's crust. Some of the elements, such as aluminum, iron, and magnesium, are metals. Your body also contains metals, but they are in very small amounts. Magnesium and iron are examples. They are part of a group called *trace elements*.

Notice that oxygen makes up nearly 50 percent of the total mass of the earth's crust. The value for oxygen does not include oxygen in the atmosphere. Oxygen combines with other elements to form many solid rock materials.

Check and Explain

1. How does an atom differ from a molecule?

2. The chemical formula for calcium carbonate, or lime, is $CaCO_3$. What elements make up $CaCO_3$? How many atoms are in one molecule of $CaCO_3$?

3. **Infer** Rust is a substance that forms when iron combines with oxygen. Is rust an element or a compound?

4. **Make a Graph** Make a circle graph showing the proportions of elements found in the human body.

3.2 Changes in Matter

Objectives

▶ **Explain** how water changes phases.

▶ **Distinguish** between physical and chemical changes.

▶ **Describe** the main parts of a chemical equation.

▶ **Interpret** what happens during a chemical reaction.

Matter changes in many ways. You know, for example, that water can change from a liquid to a solid. Ice is frozen water. Some of its properties are very different from those of liquid water. But is it still water? The answer is yes. You probably have seen wood burn. Is it still wood after burning? The answer is no. Eventually a burning piece of wood changes into ashes, soot, water vapor, and other gases.

Physical Changes

Matter can exist as solids, liquids, or gases. On the earth, water is a substance that exists naturally in all three phases. Energy causes water to change from one phase to another. For example, when heat energy is added to ice, the ice changes to liquid water. As more heat is added, water will eventually change to water vapor. Water vapor is a gas.

When water changes from one phase to another, it undergoes a *physical change*. A physical change is one in which some of the physical properties of a substance change, but the identity of the substance remains the same. If you cut a piece of wood in half, you get two pieces of wood. The identity of the wood does not change. It is still wood. If you bend a wire hanger, it changes the hanger's shape, but the metal does not change into something else.

Mixtures Sometimes a physical change occurs when substances combine. A mixture is two or more substances that do not combine chemically. A mixture can exist as a solid, liquid, or gas. For example, the atmosphere is made of a mixture of different gases. The gases may mix

Figure 3.9 ▲
Faces have been carved into Mount Rushmore. Though the shape of the mountain changed, the granite did not.

in the atmosphere, but they keep their separate chemical properties. Soil is made of a mixture of different solids such as clay and rock particles.

Solutions If you have ever tasted sea water, you know that it is very salty. Salt water is an example of a solution. A solution is a type of mixture in which one substance is evenly mixed with another substance. When salt is added to water, the taste of the water changes and the salt becomes invisible. However, neither the makeup of the water nor the salt has changed. The water is still water. The salt is still salt. In sea water, particles of water are evenly mixed with different kinds of salt.

Chemical Changes

When wood burns, it undergoes a *chemical change*. The wood is changed into many different substances. In a chemical change, the chemical identity of a substance is changed. Chemical changes occur in both living and nonliving things. Some examples of chemical changes are plants making sugars and starches for growth; the changing color of leaves; or cooking food.

During a chemical change, a chemical reaction takes place. When a chemical reaction occurs, new substances are produced. One common chemical reaction takes place when iron atoms combine with oxygen atoms to produce iron oxide, or rust. Rust is a new substance that has different properties than iron. For example, rust is a different color than iron.

Skills WorkOut

Observe Mixtures can sometimes be separated out. To see how this happens, you need a magnet, some sugar, a bowl, and some iron filings. Find two ways to separate the substances in the mixture. How can you tell that you have made a mixture?

Figure 3.10 ▲
Burning trees produce heat, light, ash, and gases. It is a chemical change because you can't get the trees back by mixing the products together. What chemical changes are happening to
◀ these cars?

59

Chemical Reactions and Equations

Chemists represent chemical reactions by writing **chemical equations**. In a chemical equation, symbols represent elements and formulas represent compounds. Look at Figure 3.11. It shows the chemical equation for the formation of carbon dioxide from carbon and oxygen.

Figure 3.11
Formation of Carbon Dioxide

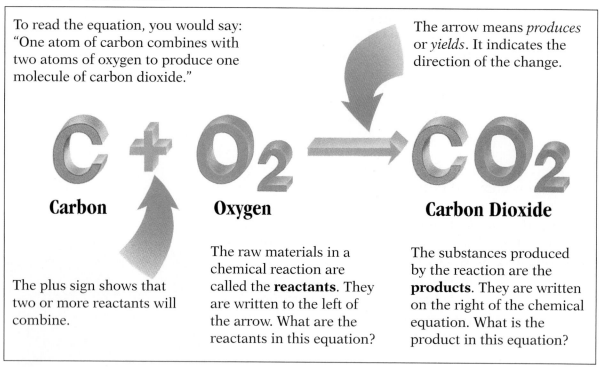

To read the equation, you would say: "One atom of carbon combines with two atoms of oxygen to produce one molecule of carbon dioxide."

The arrow means *produces* or *yields*. It indicates the direction of the change.

Carbon

Oxygen

Carbon Dioxide

The plus sign shows that two or more reactants will combine.

The raw materials in a chemical reaction are called the **reactants**. They are written to the left of the arrow. What are the reactants in this equation?

The substances produced by the reaction are the **products**. They are written on the right of the chemical equation. What is the product in this equation?

Balanced Chemical Equations

Look at the following chemical equation for the formation of water from hydrogen and oxygen:

$$H_2 + O_2 \rightarrow H_2O$$

In this equation, you can identify the atoms and molecules in the reaction. Notice, however, that two oxygen atoms are on the left side of the arrow but only one is on the right. One oxygen atom has disappeared.

Scientists have shown that atoms do not disappear during chemical reactions. Matter cannot be created or destroyed. To correct the equation, you must *balance* it. You balance a chemical equation by placing numbers called *coefficients* in front of chemical formulas. A coefficient is a number that shows how many molecules or atoms of a substance are involved in the reaction. The number of atoms of each element must be the same on both sides of a chemical equation.

To balance the equation, first place a coefficient before the product. You need to show that two atoms of oxygen are on each side of the equation. So write a 2 before the product:

$$H_2 + O_2 \rightarrow 2H_2O$$

Now the oxygen atoms are balanced, but the hydrogen atoms are not. There are four hydrogen atoms on the right and only two on the left. Write a 2 before the H on the left side of the equation:

$$2H_2 + O_2 \rightarrow 2H_2O$$

The left side of the equation now has four atoms of hydrogen and two atoms of oxygen. The same number of atoms are on the right side. To read this equation, you would say: "Two hydrogen molecules react with one oxygen molecule to produce two water molecules."

SkillBuilder *Interpreting Data*

Chemical Equation Balancing Act

A balanced chemical equation has the same number of atoms of each element on both sides of the equation. Try balancing the following equations.

1. Write each equation shown. Leave space below each equation in case you need to balance it.

2. Count the atoms that represent the reactants in the equation. Then count the atoms that represent the products. If the number of atoms in the reactants and product(s) are not equal, you need to balance the equation.

3. For the unbalanced equations, add a coefficient in front of a formula or symbol so the number of atoms of that element is equal on each side of the equation. Continue this process until you have balanced the atoms of each element.

4. Check your balancing act by counting the atoms of each element on both sides of the equation.

Equations

$$P + O_2 \rightarrow P_4O_{10}$$

$$N_2 + O_2 \rightarrow NO$$

$$BaCl_2 + H_2SO_4 \rightarrow BaSO_4 + HCl$$

$$Li + Cl_2 \rightarrow LiCl$$

$$2K + Cl_2 \rightarrow 2KCl$$

$$Mg + N_2 \rightarrow Mg_3N_2$$

1. What does a coefficient represent?

2. Why must chemical equations be balanced?

Using references, write two balanced equations. Then change the equations so that they are unbalanced. Exchange the unbalanced equations with a partner. See if you can balance them.

Science and Technology
Practical Polymers

Figure 3.12 ▲

Plastics can be rubbery, stringy, clear, opaque, hard, or flexible. Which of these characteristics are useful in computers?

How many different plastic products can you name? Plastics are one of many types of *synthetic polymers*. They are formed from chemical reactions. In these types of reactions, thousands of small molecules are joined into long chains. Polymers are giant molecules. Each polymer is a compound with its own chemical properties and structure. Polymers form a variety of materials—from the material that makes up hard football helmets, to the material that makes up squeezable catsup bottles, to the material for plastic wrap.

Polymers are important substances in many ways. In the plastics industry alone, there are more than 45 different polymers in use today. These plastics are used in telephones, pipes, toothbrushes, toys, compact discs, and other items. In addition to plastics, synthetic polymers are used to make many of the fabrics for clothes that you wear. Nylon, rayon, and dacron are examples. Polymers are also used to build artificial hearts, knees, and other body parts. Even computers would not exist without polymers. The keyboard and data storage disks are both plastic or plastic coated. The microchip is embedded in plastic.

At one time, cars were made mostly of steel. Today most cars have plastic door trims, hoods, and fenders. In the future, cars will contain even more plastic parts. One day you may ride in a car made almost entirely of plastic, including the engine!

Check and Explain

1. Explain how water changes from a solid to a liquid.

2. What are the reactants and products in a chemical equation?

3. **Reason by Analogy** A lump of sugar burns. Is this an example of a physical change or a chemical change? Explain why.

4. **Communicate** In your own words, describe what the following chemical reaction for hydrogen peroxide means: $H_2 + O_2 \rightarrow H_2O_2$.

Activity 3 *What happens during a chemical reaction?*

Skills Observe; Measure; Graph; Infer

Task 1   Prelab Prep
1. Collect the following items: ruler, pencil, paper, graph paper, spoon, powdered bleach, water, small jar, Celsius thermometer.
2. Fill the jar three-quarters full with water.

Task 2   Data Record
1. On a separate sheet of paper, copy Table 3.4. Number up to 10 minutes.
2. Record your observations in the data table.
3. After your table is complete, graph your data. Use your ruler and graph paper to draw the line graph shown below. Add your data points. Remember to title your graph.

Task 3   Procedure
1. Add one teaspoon of bleach to the jar of water. **CAUTION! Wear gloves, a laboratory apron, and goggles when using bleach**.
2. Stir the mixture with the spoon. Observe the mixture as you stir.
3. Put the thermometer into the liquid.

Table 3.4   Temperature Change

Time (Minutes)	Temperature (°C)	Observations
1		
2		
3		
4		
5		
6		

4. Observe the thermometer every minute for ten minutes. Record the temperature at each observation in your data table.

Task 4   Analysis
1. What happened when you added bleach to the water?
2. What does the rising temperature indicate?
3. When did the temperature stop rising?
4. Why did the temperature stop rising?

Task 5   Conclusion
Write a short paragraph explaining why this activity is an example of a chemical reaction. Did the activity require energy? Explain.

Everyday Application
Household bleach contains a chemical called sodium hypochlorite. This chemical contains oxygen that easily combines with dyes to form a colorless compound. The combination of oxygen and dyes causes colors to fade. Select ten items from your closet. Check the labels for washing instructions. Classify your clothes into two groups: those that can be washed with bleach and those that can't. What else do the clothes in each group have in common?

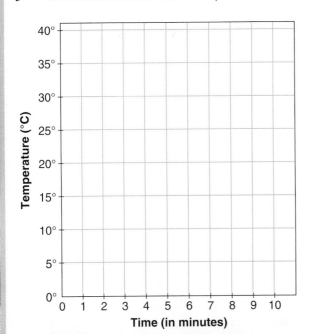

3.3 Molecules of Life

Objectives

▶ **Define** and describe carbohydrates, lipids, and proteins.

▶ **Explain** why nucleic acids are important to the cell.

▶ **Infer** whether certain compounds are organic or inorganic.

If you could see the molecules that make up your body, you would notice something similar about them. Each molecule would be made of long, twisting chains of carbon atoms. Carbon is the basis for all life on earth. In all living things, carbon atoms form many kinds of bonds that make up many molecules.

Organic Compounds

In all living things, carbon compounds are present. Carbon compounds that occur naturally in the bodies, the products, and the remains of living things are called **organic compounds**. Living things also contain **inorganic compounds**. Most inorganic compounds do not contain carbon. Water and minerals are the main inorganic compounds in living things.

Three groups of organic compounds are especially important to living things. These three groups are carbohydrates, proteins, and lipids. Most of the life processes use one or more of these groups of compounds.

Proteins Proteins are complex molecules. They are made of long chains of **amino acids**. Amino acids are simple molecules that contain carbon, oxygen, hydrogen, and nitrogen. The specific amino acids and their arrangement determine the shape of the protein.

Your cells use proteins to build and repair body parts. Proteins also help speed up chemical reactions and protect the body from disease. No single protein serves all of these functions. The human body contains more than 100,000 different types of protein molecules, each with its own function.

Figure 3.13 ▲
An octopus' skin can change color because of organic compounds called pigments.

Carbohydrates Carbohydrates are organic compounds that most living things use to store energy. Each carbohydrate molecule is made up of oxygen, hydrogen, and carbon atoms.

Starches and sugars are the two classes of carbohydrates. Sugars are simple carbohydrate molecules. Starches are complex carbohydrate molecules consisting of many sugars linked together. In living things, sugars and starches are broken down into **simple sugars**. Simple sugars, such as glucose, are then transported to all the cells in the body. In the cells, simple sugars provide fuel for energy.

Carbohydrates are found in many of the foods that you eat, such as potatoes, bread, rice, pasta, and bananas.

Lipids Lipids are a group of organic compounds that contain carbon, hydrogen, and oxygen. Lipids are placed in one group because they share one physical property. They do not mix with water.

Fats, oils, and waxes are three types of lipids. Foods that contain lipids include butter, vegetable oil, and animal fats.

Your body uses lipids for energy storage, drawing on them when carbohydrates are not available. A specific amount of lipids provides more than twice as much energy as the same amount of carbohydrates. In your body, lipids are broken down into simpler molecules and transported to cells.

Nucleic Acids Carbohydrates and proteins combine in living cells to form **nucleic acids**. Nucleic acids control all the activities of a cell. They also carry the instructions that enable organisms to reproduce.

There are two types of nucleic acids in living cells, DNA and RNA. DNA directs a cell to perform all of its processes. RNA copies these directions and takes them to the parts of the cell where they are carried out.

Figure 3.14 Organic Compounds in a Tostada

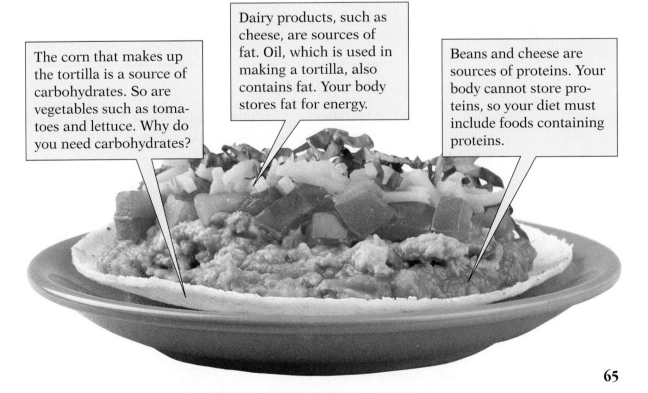

The corn that makes up the tortilla is a source of carbohydrates. So are vegetables such as tomatoes and lettuce. Why do you need carbohydrates?

Dairy products, such as cheese, are sources of fat. Oil, which is used in making a tortilla, also contains fat. Your body stores fat for energy.

Beans and cheese are sources of proteins. Your body cannot store proteins, so your diet must include foods containing proteins.

Hypothesize Cut part of a
cucumber into slices as thin as
you can make them. Place the
slices on a plate near a sunny
window. Observe and record
what happens for several days.
What conclusion can you draw
about the chemical composition
of living things?

Science and You *Proper Proteins*

Your body needs 20 different amino acids to
build all its proteins. Your cells, however, can only manufacture 12 of them. The other eight, called *essential
amino acids*, must be obtained from proteins in the foods
you eat.

Most animal proteins, such as fish, meat, poultry,
and eggs, contain all eight of the essential amino acids
in the proper proportions. Animal proteins are called
complete proteins. Most plants lack one or more of the
essential elements. Plant proteins are called *incomplete
proteins*. You can, however, get all the essential animo
acids from plants alone by combining certain types of
plant foods, such as beans and grain. A meal of beans
and rice gives you the same protein value as a meal of
steak and eggs.

The key to obtaining essential amino acids from plants
is how you combine them in your diet. For example,
beans supply you with a certain amino acid that is missing in corn. Corn, on the other hand, contains an essential amino acid that is not present in beans. Thus, a meal
of corn and beans will provide you with all the essential
amino acids that your body requires.

A lack of essential amino acids in your diet can be
very dangerous to your health. It can lead to protein
deficiency. Some of the symptoms of protein deficiency
include lowered energy, stunted growth, and lowered
resistance to disease.

Check and Explain

1. What are organic compounds? Name and describe
   three types of organic compounds.

2. Why are nucleic acids important to living things?

3. **Predict** What might happen if you did not eat
   enough foods high in carbohydrates?

4. **Infer** Decide if the following substances contain
   carbon compounds. Explain your conclusions.

   a. water   d. table salt

   b. catsup   e. sand

   c. apple   f. butter

Chapter 3 Review

Concept Summary

3.1 Matter

▶ All things are made of matter. Matter is anything that takes up space and has shape.

▶ Matter exists as solid, liquid, or gas. Solids have definite volume and shape. Liquids have definite volume but not shape. Gases have neither definite volume nor definite shape.

▶ All matter is made of elements. The building blocks of elements are atoms.

▶ Two or more elements joined together form a compound. A molecule is the smallest part of a compound.

3.2 Changes in Matter

▶ A physical change is a change in a substance's physical properties but not its chemical identity. A chemical change forms a new substance.

▶ Chemical equations show how raw materials react to form products.

3.3 Molecules of Life

▶ Organic compounds, such as proteins, carbohydrates, and lipids, contain carbon and occur naturally in living things.

▶ The human body contains many proteins, each with a specific function such as building or repairing body parts or speeding up chemical reactions.

▶ Living things use carbohydrates such as starches and sugars to store energy.

▶ Lipids are used for energy storage when carbohydrates are not available.

▶ The two types of nucleic acids, DNA and RNA, control cell activity and contain instructions for cell reproduction.

Chapter Vocabulary

matter (3.1)	molecule (3.1)	reactant (3.2)	amino acid (3.3)
element (3.1)	chemical symbol (3.1)	product (3.2)	simple sugar (3.3)
atom (3.1)	chemical formula (3.1)	organic compound (3.3)	nucleic acid (3.3)
compound (3.1)	chemical equation (3.2)	inorganic compound (3.3)	

Check Your Vocabulary

Use the vocabulary words above to complete the following sentences correctly.

1. Long chains of ____ make proteins.

2. Anything that takes up space and has mass is ____ .

3. Cell activities in living things are controlled by ____ .

4. A chemical reaction can be represented by a ____ .

5. In living things, carbohydrates are broken down into ____ for fuel.

6. A substance that is made up of more than one kind of element is called a ____ .

7. The raw materials in a chemical reaction are called ____ .

Explain the difference between the words in each pair.

1. chemical symbol, chemical formula

2. mixture, solution

3. reactant, product

4. organic compound, inorganic compound

5. atom, molecule

6. element, compound

7. amino acids, nucleic acids

Chapter 3 Review

Check Your Knowledge

Answer each of the following in complete sentences.

1. What form of matter has definite volume but not definite shape?
2. Starches and sugars are examples of what type of organic compound?
3. How many types of atoms can be contained in an element?
4. What happens during a chemical change?
5. How does your body use proteins?
6. Name the three phases of matter.
7. Give an example of a physical change.
8. What is the difference between organic compounds and inorganic compounds?
9. What is matter?
10. How do chemists represent elements?

Determine whether each statement is true or false. Write *true* if it is true. If it is false, change the underlined term so that the sentence is true.

11. A <u>chemical change</u> affects a substance's characteristics but does not change its identity.
12. Molecules are made of atoms and are the building blocks of <u>elements</u>.
13. Organic compounds include <u>proteins</u>, carbohydrates, and lipids.
14. In chemical equations, chemical formulas represent <u>compounds</u>.
15. A <u>physical</u> change occurs when ice melts.
16. You balance a chemical equation by placing <u>letters</u> called coefficients in front of the chemical formulas.

Check Your Understanding

Apply the concepts you have learned to answer each question.

1. Sometimes a thin, cloudy coating will form on an aluminum surface such as an aluminum pot or pan. A chemical reaction takes place between oxygen in the air and the aluminum to produce the coating, aluminum oxide. The equation for this reaction is written below.

$$4Al + 3O_2 \rightarrow 2Al_2O_3$$

Identify the following in the equation:

   a. reactants
   b. product
   c. coefficients
   d. molecule
   e. compounds
   f. elements
   g. chemical symbols
   h. chemical formulas

2. **Classify** Identify each of the following as a physical or chemical change.

   a. Ice melting into water
   b. Drink mix dissolving in water
   c. Gasoline burning in a car's engine
   d. Hydrogen and oxygen forming water
   e. The breakdown of lipids for energy

3. **Predict** What would happen if you regularly ate large quantities of fatty foods and used up very little energy? How would your body respond if you ate less food than you needed for the energy you use? Explain your answers.

4. **Mystery Photo** The photograph on page 50 shows beads of water on pheasant feathers. Water does not penetrate the feathers; instead, it rolls off. Feathers are waterproof. Review the pages on organic compounds and look for references to water. What might help bird feathers repel water? How?

Develop Your Skills

1. **Data Bank** Use the information on page 624 to answer the following questions.

   a. What gases exist in the atmosphere of Mars?

   b. Which gases on Mars are elements? Compounds?

   c. How is Mars' atmosphere like Earth's?

2. The equation below shows the chemical breakdown of glucose, a simple sugar.

   $$C_6H_{12}O_6 + 6O_2 \rightarrow 6CO_2 + 6H_2O$$

   a. How many molecules of oxygen are needed to break down each molecule of glucose?

   b. In the reactants, how many atoms of oxygen are there? Atoms of carbon? Atoms of hydrogen?

   c. In the products, how many atoms of oxygen are there? Atoms of carbon? Atoms of hydrogen?

3. **Interpret Data** The graph below shows temperature changes for water.

   a. At which point(s) on the graph would water be in a solid phase?

   b. A liquid phase?

   c. A gas phase?

   d. Is the phase change of water a chemical or a physical change?

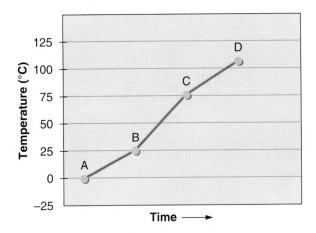

Make Connections

1. **Link the Concepts** Draw a concept map showing how the concepts below link together. Add terms to connect, or link, the concepts.

   atoms   inorganic
   elements   compounds
   molecules   carbohydrates
   compounds   lipids
   organic   proteins
   compounds   carbon
         matter

2. **Science and Technology** Many items that people use every day are made of synthetic polymers. One drawback to synthetic polymers is that they decompose very slowly, causing waste problems. Find out more about synthetic polymers at the library. What are some positive and negative effects of polymer use? Should people limit the amount of objects made with polymers? Write a paragraph in which you state and defend your position. Include suggestions to limit polymers' negative effects.

3. **Science and P.E.** The energy your body uses to grow, play, and carry out basic functions comes from the food you eat. This energy is measured in calories. Use a book on health to find out how many calories you use during a half hour of the following activities.

   a. playing tennis   d. running
   b. playing basketball   e. biking
   c. walking slowly   f. sleeping

4. **Science and You** Make a list of ten physical changes you experience daily. Make a list of ten chemical changes you experience daily. Compare your list of changes with that of a classmate.

Science and Literature Connection

It was mostly because of my father that I was in Africa that fateful summer. I had won a prize for what now seems like a fairly dopey little high school science project on gorilla communication. But Max acted as if I had invented the wheel. He rewarded me by arranging for me to work for the summer with none other than Dr. Charlotte Wingate. . . .

Like Jane Goodall and Dian Fossey and the other primate researchers, Charlotte had come to Africa to observe apes in the wild. She had been there for two years—long enough to locate a small troop of western lowland gorillas. She was hoping to get some new information on this very rare and endangered species of gorilla, studying them with no attempt to tame them or train them or interact with them in any way. I, on the other hand, was dying to communicate with them. I would have liked to find out more about their "language" and even to try to reach them with mine. But Charlotte had laid out the ground rules during my first five minutes in camp. Trying to get friendly with the gorillas was a no-no. I was there to assist her work and to learn, not to do my own thing. . . .

[During a walk one morning] I sat down to rest and drink the can of soda I'd brought along. By this time it had stopped raining, but I was damp and sticky. My back was itching. I rubbed it against the back of a tree. Felt good. In the middle of my ecstatic back-scratching [a gorilla we called] Naomi appeared.

She came into view as she always did. Quietly, without fanfare. Suddenly she was at my side.

The Gorilla Signs Love

The following excerpt is from the book The Gorilla Signs Love *by Barbara Brenner*

"Hi, baby." It was out before I remembered. No talking.

Naomi squatted next to me, seeming content just to be there. I took another swig of soda. When I glanced over at her I saw that she was watching this operation with great attention.

It occurred to me that she might like some soda. But I did not ask her. I was honoring Charlotte's no-talk rule. . . .

I sat and drank. I made up my mind that if this gorilla really wanted some soda, she was going to have to ask for it.

Impossible? Not for Naomi. All at once she turned those lively brown eyes in my direction. After she'd caught my eye, she gave me the "gimme" sign. . . . Still I waited. It was then she raised her hand to her lips in a perfect imitation of my drinking.

My whole body turned shaky with excitement. . . .

All of Charlotte's rules went out of my head.

"Yes, you want a drink. Sure you do. Okay. Here." I handed Naomi the can of soda. I would have given her anything.

"Drink," I said. As I said it I gave her the official Ameslan (American Sign Language) sign for it—a clenched fist and a thumb to the mouth. It was very close to what Naomi had done on her own.

She took the can and put it to her lips. She drank. Then she handed the can back to me.

Here was my chance to test whether she understood the sign.

"Drink," I said, making the sign again.

She ignored me completely. She reached out and popped a leaf into her mouth. It was as if the drinking sequence had never occurred. . . .

"Drink," I said again to my new friend, making the sign once more.

Still Naomi ignored me. I persisted. Finally she did something so clever that I had to laugh.

She leaned over, gently took the can of soda from my hand and shook it. She was showing me that it was empty.

"Love"   "Drink"

Skills in Science

Reading Skills in Science

1. **Find Context Clues** How old is the narrator? Where did her encounter with Naomi take place? Who is Max?

2. **Infer** Why did Charlotte insist that members of the team not get friendly with the gorillas? Did this rule ensure that there wouldn't be any communication between the humans and the gorillas?

Writing Skills in Science

1. **Detect the Writer's Mood** Imagine you are the narrator of this story. Write a letter to Max describing your experience with Naomi.

2. **Uncover Assumptions** Anthropomorphism is the attributing of human motivation or behavior to animals. Describe some ways the narrator anthropomorphizes Naomi.

Activities

Communicate Visit the school or local library to learn more about American Sign Language. Practice communicating with a partner using Ameslan.

Collect Data The author mentions that the lowland gorilla is an endangered species. Research population estimates of this species as well as steps taken to protect it.

Where to Read More

As Dead As a Dodo by Peter Mayle. Boston: Godine, 1982. Beautiful illustrations accompany the narrative describing sixteen vanished species.

Gorillas in the Mist by Dian Fossey. Boston: Houghton Mifflin, 1983. Famed primate researcher Dian Fossey describes her experience studying gorillas in their natural environment.

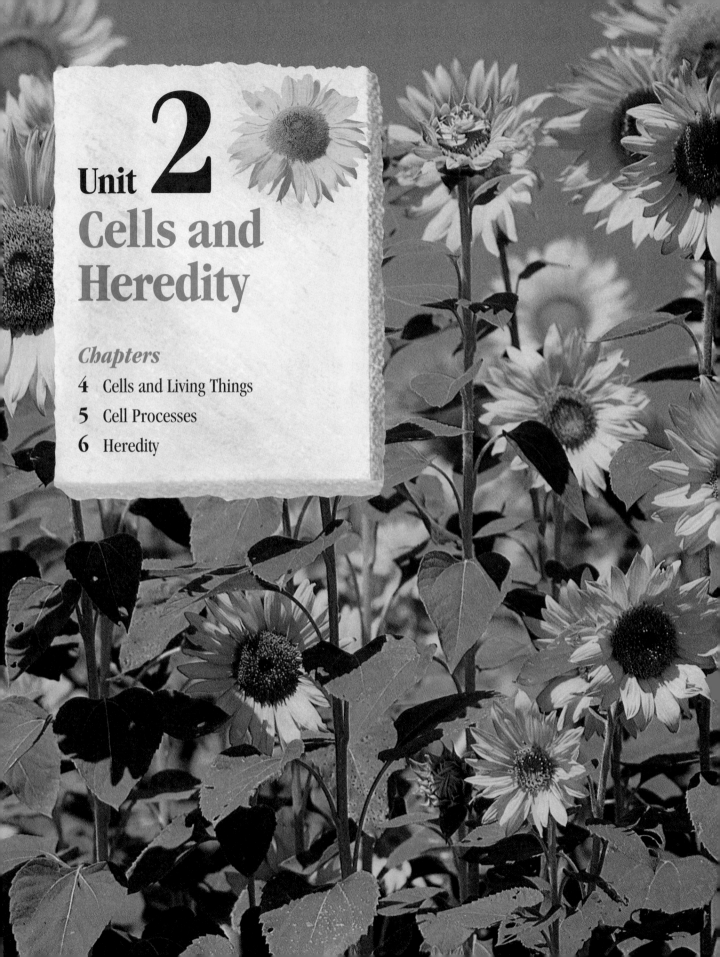

Unit 2
Cells and Heredity

Chapters

Data Bank

Use the information on pages 624 to 631 to answer the following questions about topics explored in this unit.

Interpreting Data

Which lives longer, a red blood cell or a skin cell?

Comparing

Which is larger, an animal cell or a frog egg?

Classifying

What things can only be seen with an electron microscope? What can only be seen with a light microscope? What can be seen with both a light and an electron microscope?

The photograph to the left is of sunflowers in an Illinois field. What characteristics do the sunflowers have in common? Do you see any differences among the sunflowers? If so, what are they?

Chapter 4

Cells and Living Things

What do you see?

"This picture looks like a group of cells. It looks like there are cell walls. The nucleus is glistening or there is light shining through the nucleus. They may be animal cells. The cells look like they have been dyed red."

Christa Haynes
Summitt Middle School
Edmond, Oklahoma

To find out about the photograph, look on page 90. As you read this chapter, you will learn about different cells and the important life processes they perform.

4.1 The Cell Theory

Objectives

▶ **Describe** the historical development of the cell theory.

▶ **State** the major ideas of the cell theory.

▶ **Make analogies** between everyday objects and cells.

Classify All things can be classified as either living, once living, or nonliving. Classify each of these things as living, once living, or nonliving: an autumn leaf, a cotton shirt, a tulip, a steel beam, a car, a dog, string beans, and a cow. How do you know what things are living?

Each brick in a brick house is a unit of structure for the house. In living things, the basic unit of structure is the **cell**. All living things or things that were once living are made up of one or more cells. Though you can see the bricks in a brick house, most cells are hard to see with the unaided eye. The cell is also the basic unit of function in all living things. Each cell carries out all life processes.

Development of the Cell Theory

Ideas about cells are taken for granted by most life scientists today. However, 350 years ago, no one even guessed that living things were made of units so small they couldn't be seen.

The first steps in developing modern ideas about cells were made in the late 1600s. In 1675, a Dutch shopkeeper named Anton van Leeuwenhoek (LAY vehn hook) looked at pond water through a simple microscope. He observed what he called "animalcules," or what are known today as single-celled organisms. Without knowing it, van Leeuwenhoek was probably the first person to see living cells.

Around the same time, Robert Hooke, an English scientist and inventor, used a crude compound microscope to look at a very thin slice of cork. Hooke observed that the cork was made up of "a great many little boxes." Hooke called these boxes *cells,* which comes from a Latin word meaning "little rooms." Hooke's name stuck. However, Hooke was not looking at living cells. He was actually looking at the walls of dead plant cells.

Almost 200 years passed before the importance of Hooke's and van Leeuwenhoek's observations was fully

Figure 4.1 ▲
Robert Hooke made this drawing of cork cells using a compound microscope that he built.

understood. During that time, new and better microscopes were developed. In the 1830s, a German botanist named Matthias Schleiden noticed that all the plants he observed under a microscope seemed to be made of tiny units. In 1838, he stated that all plants were made up of similar units, or cells.

Other scientists began to discover that cells were not only found in plants, but in other living things as well. Another German scientist, Theodor Schwann, observed animal tissue and stated that cells were the building blocks of both plants *and* animals. Schwann also pointed out many similarities between plant and animal cells. He noted that there were many different kinds of cells, each with a different function.

In 1858, German physician Rudolf Virchow made an important conclusion about the cells Schleiden and Schwann had seen in all living things. Virchow stated that cells are produced only by other living cells.

Historical Notebook

Looking at Lenses

Magnifying lenses have been used for more than 3,000 years. However, Anton van Leeuwenhoek was the first to use the type of glass lenses that are used today. Van Leeuwenhoek ground his own lenses as a hobby and made his own simple microscopes. These microscopes used only one lens, not multiple lenses as in compound microscopes. He viewed many things with his simple microscopes, including pond microorganisms and even the scum on his teeth. Some of his lenses could magnify up to 270 times.

Robert Hooke was one of the first inventors to successfully use a compound microscope by combining two or more lenses. He placed two lenses in a metal tube, one on each end. The photograph on the right shows a copy of Hooke's microscope. Although Hooke's microscope could magnify more than 100x, it was difficult to observe many details of living cells.

In the early 1800s, better glass-making methods produced lenses that revealed more details in a cell. Since that time, microscope designers have constructed some microscopes that can even show a three-dimensional view of a cell.

1. Why was Hooke's microscope an important development?

2. **Write** Imagine what it would be like to be one of the first people to discover cells through your own microscope. Write a description of your discovery. Remember that you do not yet know what a cell is.

These ideas about the cell have been put together into a set of statements called the **cell theory**. The cell theory states that

▶ All living things are made up of one or more cells.

▶ Cells are the basic units of structure and function in living things.

▶ All cells come only from other living cells.

Science and Technology *Even a Closer Look*

Since the time of van Leeuwenhoek, one of the greatest challenges for scientists has been to find a way to clearly view the parts of a cell. Another challenge has been to observe a living cell without killing it.

In a compound-light microscope, many cell parts appear larger, but not always more detailed. Details of a cell's structure are best seen in a transmission electron microscope, or TEM. A TEM can magnify an object up to a million times. However, a TEM uses beams of high-speed electrons. The beams create a vacuum. No living cells can survive in this vacuum. TEMs, therefore, can't be used to observe living cells.

In their search for a more detailed view of living cells, scientists are developing new, improved microscopes. At Cornell University, researchers have developed a microscope called the *superoptical microscope.* Lenses aren't used in a superoptical microscope. Instead, light is conducted through optical fibers in a tube. The light travels along the optical fibers to devices that produce a picture on a large screen. It's almost like watching living cells on television!

Figure 4.2 ▲

Superoptical microscopes do not damage the cells or cell parts being viewed. Scientists can use these microscopes to study living cells.

Check and Explain

1. Which scientist gave us the name "cell"?

2. What are the three parts of the cell theory?

3. **Reason and Conclude** Why is a cell considered the smallest thing that can be called living?

4. **Make Analogies** The beginning of this section describes cells as being similar to bricks in a building. What other things are like cells? Make a list. For each item, explain how it is similar to a cell.

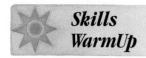
4.2 Parts of a Cell

Objectives

▶ **Describe** the structure of a cell.

▶ **Explain** the functions of a cell's organelles.

▶ **Compare** and **contrast** plant and animal cells.

▶ **Construct a table** that shows an understanding of cell functions and structure.

I magine a small town or city. What are some of its parts? There are roads, factories, schools, and houses. There are power lines and telephone lines. Many different people work in the town, supplying needed services to the town and to surrounding areas. Each person has a special job to do. Each building has a special use. All the people, services, buildings, and other structures work together to make the town function properly.

A cell is like a small town or city. The different parts of a cell have special jobs. Each part helps the cell carry out its life processes. Each part helps to keep the cell working properly. Just as the parts of a town must work together, the parts of a cell also must work together to live.

Figure 4.3 ▲
The plant cells (left) and animal cells (right) look different, but they have many similar structures.

Figure 4.4   Plant Cell

Cell wall

Cell membrane

Golgi body

Nuclear membrane

Nucleus

Ribosome

Endoplasmic reticulum

Cytoplasm

Mitochondrion

Vacuole

Chloroplast

Cell Membrane

On a map, the boundaries of each town are marked with a heavy line. Driving from town to town, you see signs that show the edge of one town and the beginning of the next.

All cells have boundaries, too. Look at the plant cell in Figure 4.4 and find the **cell membrane**. A cell membrane is a thin structure that surrounds both plant and animal cells. It is mostly made up of proteins and lipids.

The cell membrane has several functions. It protects the inside of the cell by separating the cell from its surroundings. Cell membranes also support the cell and give it shape.

The most important job of the cell membrane is controlling what enters and leaves the cell. All things that a cell needs, such as water and nutrients, enter through the cell membrane. Waste products exit through the cell membrane. The cell membrane controls this traffic. It prevents

harmful substances from entering and keeps useful substances inside.

In this way, the cell maintains a stable internal environment even though conditions outside the cell may change. The ability of a cell to maintain a stable internal environment is called homeostasis (hoh mee oh STAY sihs). The cell membrane is the part of the cell that makes homeostasis possible.

Cell Wall

Plant cells have an additional structure outside the cell membrane called the **cell wall**. The cell wall is one of the characteristics that separates plant cells from animal cells.

The cell wall is stiff. It provides support and protection for the cell, allowing the plant to grow upright. The cell wall is partly made up of fibers of cellulose (SEHL yoo lohs). Cellulose is a complex compound formed from sugar molecules.

Nucleus

In a town, the mayor and city council make important decisions about the workings of the town. They govern the town. In a cell, the **nucleus** governs the cell. The nucleus is the control center for most of the cell's activities. It also controls cell reproduction.

Recall that molecules called nucleic acids carry instructions for cell processes and reproduction. These molecules are stored in the nucleus. They are what the nucleus uses to control the workings of the cell.

The instructions carried on nucleic acid are formed by a type of chemical code. This code tells the other parts of the cell how to perform their functions. Different parts of the DNA's code are turned "on" or "off" to control cell processes.

Most cells have a nucleus surrounded by a membrane called the nuclear membrane. It separates the nucleus from the rest of the cell. Bacteria and blue-green bacteria have a nuclear area. This area is not surrounded by a membrane. In cells with a nuclear membrane, the membrane controls the substances that enter and leave the nucleus.

You can see the nucleus of a cell with a compound microscope. It is easy to identify. The nucleus is usually round or oval shaped, and near the middle of a cell. The nucleus also appears darker than the rest of a cell. Find the nucleus in Figure 4.5.

Figure 4.5 Animal Cell

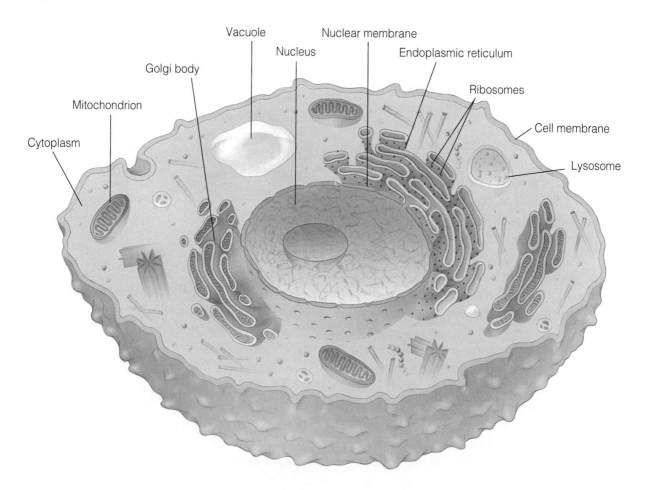

Cytoplasm

Most of the cell's processes take place in the **cytoplasm**. The cytoplasm is all the living material in a cell except the nucleus. The prefix *cyto-* means "of the cell." *Plasm* comes from the Greek word meaning "something molded." The cytoplasm is a jellylike substance that contains many different chemical compounds. Just like other living things, most of the cytoplasm is water. In fact, it is about 80 percent water. The nucleus and other special tiny parts called **organelles** float in the cytoplasm. Each organelle in a cell has a special form and function. Organelles carry out life processes such as releasing energy, making proteins, and storing food and water.

Although the nucleus controls the growth of a cell, most of the materials needed for growth are made in the cytoplasm. The cytoplasm expels waste materials through the cell membrane. In addition, the organelles in the cytoplasm carry out their functions here.

Career Corner   Health Technician

Who Tests Your Blood?

Have you ever had your blood tested? If you have, you may not realize that a health technician, not a doctor, tests your blood. The health technician performs a number of different tests on the blood, such as finding the number of blood cells, typing your blood, and checking for unusual chemicals. These tests will tell a doctor whether or not your blood is healthy.

Health technicians perform almost everything that needs to be done in a lab. The actual job the technician does depends on the type of lab he or she works in. For example, *biological technicians* conduct research, such as studying and analyzing cells and microscopic organisms, to help biologists develop cures for human diseases. The technician shown in the photograph is an *optical technician*. Optical technicians make eyeglasses and contact lenses. And the technician at your doctor's office is a *medical-laboratory technician.* These technicians not only look at your blood, they also do such things as prepare solutions, keep records of tests, and clean and sterilize equipment.

If you are interested in being a health technician, you will need two years of training after high school. You may also need some college courses in math and science. Some special skills are learned on the job or through apprenticeships.

Organelles

The organelles in a cell are like the different services in a town. In a town, each service provides a special job. Trash is collected and removed from the town. Communication is provided by the telephone company. The electric and gas company supplies energy to all the buildings in the town. In a cell, each organelle has a special job to do. Together, the organelles keep the cell working properly.

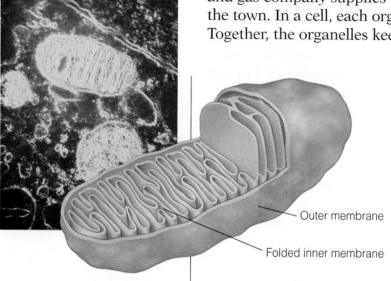

Outer membrane

Folded inner membrane

Mitochondria ▲

The structures that are the powerhouses of the cell are the mitochondria (myt uh KAHN dree uh). You can compare the mitochondria to a power plant in a town. Both structures provide energy. Mitochondria release the energy stored in food. This energy can then be used by the cell to carry out its life processes.

Ribosomes

The tiny, round dark organelles in a cell are ribosomes. Some ribosomes are attached to the endoplasmic reticulum. Others float freely in the cytoplasm. Ribosomes are the protein factories of cells. They assemble proteins, which the cell uses for growth, repair, and control. ▶

Endoplasmic Reticulum

A town has roads and highways. A cell has the endoplasmic (ehn duh PLAZ mihk) reticulum (rih TIHK yuh luhm), or ER, for short. The ER is made up of membranes. The membranes fold into a network of tubes and canals that run throughout the cytoplasm. Just as the roads and highways of a town are used to transport materials from one place to another, the ER transports materials throughout a cell.

▼

Ribosomes

Golgi Bodies ▶

Both animal and plant cells have Golgi (GOHL jee) bodies. Golgi bodies look like stacks of flattened sacs. You can think of a Golgi body as a center of manufacturing and shipping within the cell. Materials that are transported by the endoplasmic reticulum usually stop first at Golgi bodies, where they are altered or stored before moving to other parts of a cell.

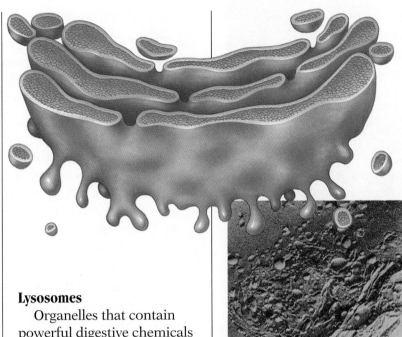

Lysosomes

Organelles that contain powerful digestive chemicals for breaking down large food molecules into smaller food molecules are called lysosomes. Lysosomes also break down waste products and old cell parts. You can think of them as the "garbage collectors" of the cell. These small, baglike structures are found in animals and a few plants.

Vacuoles

The fluid-filled sacs that float in the cytoplasm are called vacuoles (VAK yoo ohls). Vacuoles store water and food materials. They also store wastes and help the cell get rid of the wastes. Both animal and plant cells have vacuoles.

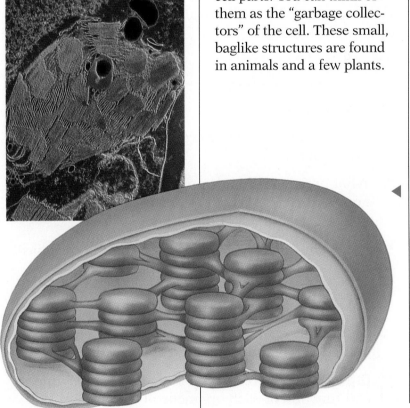

Chloroplasts

Plant cells have green, oval-shaped organelles called **chloroplasts**. Plants are the only organisms that have these structures. The chloroplast contains a compound called **chlorophyll**. Chlorophyll traps energy from the sun to make glucose. Chlorophyll also gives the chloroplast its green color.

Figure 4.6 ▲

Artificial skin combined with living skin cells from a patient's own body can be used to help burn patients recover. This type of "bandage" helps prevent scars from forming.

Science and Technology *A Living Bandage*

If you have ever burned your skin, you know that it is very painful. Serious burns can also be very dangerous. To prevent infection and help speed up healing, physicians may cover serious burns with a special bandage. Unlike the bandages you use at home, this bandage is made of living skin cells!

The "skin" that forms the bandage closely resembles human skin. However, it is actually a manufactured combination of living human skin cells and proteins from cows. The skin cells are grown in a laboratory from a small portion of healthy skin. This process is known as *culturing,* or growing, cells.

To grow skin cells in the laboratory, scientists must provide the cells with the same environment as a normal skin cell. In the human body, blood provides skin cells with food, oxygen, special chemicals, and a way to remove wastes. In the laboratory, portions of healthy skin are removed from the body and placed in germ-free bags. These bags are filled with nutrients and chemicals. Like blood, this mixture meets the needs of the cells so that they can grow and reproduce.

When enough cells have grown and reproduced, they are removed from the bags. Doctors use the cultured skin cells in surgery. The cells are also used to test new drugs and surgical techniques.

Check and Explain

1. Name and describe five organelles found in the cytoplasm.

2. What organelles could you find in lettuce cells but not mouse cells? What organelles could you find in mouse cells but not lettuce cells?

3. **Reason by Analogy**   Match the cell part to the object that shows the best analogy. Explain.

   a. Endoplasmic reticulum   Skin
   b. Vacuole   Nut shell
   c. Cell wall   Storage warehouse
   d. Cell membrane   Highway

4. **Organize Data**   Create a table that gives the name and function of each organelle of the cell.

Activity 4 *How do animal cells and plant cells differ?*

Skills Observe; Compare and Contrast; Make a Model; Interpret Data

Task 1 Prelab Prep
1. Before beginning the activity, make sure your work area is clean. Be sure to wear a lab apron.
2. Collect the following items: distilled water, dropper, 2 slides, tweezers, elodea plant, coverslips, microscope, flat toothpick, iodine solution, 3 sheets of paper.

Task 2 Data Record
1. On a separate sheet of paper, draw the data table shown. Record your observations in the data table.
2. Label a second sheet of paper *Elodea Cell*. Label a third sheet of paper *Cheek Cell*. You will draw models of the observed cells on these sheets.

Task 3 Procedure
1. Place a drop of water in the center of a clean slide. **CAUTION! Slides and coverslips have sharp edges.**
2. Use tweezers to remove a small leaf from the elodea plant. Place the leaf in the drop of water. Place a coverslip over the leaf.
3. Observe the elodea leaf through the microscope under low power. Make notes of what you see.
4. Observe the elodea under high power. Record what parts of the cells you see in the data table. Then draw a single cell and label the different parts you have identified.
5. Using the blunt end of a toothpick, gently scrape some cells from the inside of your cheek.
6. Smear the cheek cells onto a clean slide. Add a drop of water and a coverslip.
7. Observe the cheek cells under low and high power. Record your observations.
8. Remove the slide and lift up one edge of the coverslip. Add a drop of iodine solution.

Replace the coverslip. **CAUTION! Iodine can stain skin and clothes.**
9. Observe the cheek cells under low power and high power. Record what parts of the cells you see in the data table. Then draw a single cell and label the different parts you have identified.

Task 4 Analysis
1. What structures did you see in both the elodea cells and the cheek cells?
2. What structures did you see only in the elodea cells? What structures did you see only in the cheek cells?
3. What structures of the cheek cells could you observe after adding iodine?

Task 5 Conclusion
Write a short paragraph explaining the similarities and differences between the elodea cells and the cheek cells. Based on your observations, how do plant cells differ from animal cells?

Extension

Collect some pond or aquarium water. Make slides using drops of water, and see how many organisms and cell structures you can identify. Draw your observations on a chart.

Table 4.1 Parts of Cells

Organelle	Elodea Cell	Cheek Cell
Cell membrane		
Cell wall		
Cytoplasm		
Nucleus		
Vacuole		
Chloroplasts		

4.3 Organization of Living Things

Objectives

▶ **Identify** tissues, organs, and systems in an organism.

▶ **Explain** how organs work together in systems.

▶ **Classify** the organs, tissues, and systems in an organism.

Y ou are a many-celled organism because your body is made up of more than one cell. In fact, the human body is made up of billions of cells. However, many organisms, such as amebas, have only one cell. They are single-celled organisms. To see most single-celled organisms, you need a microscope.

A many-celled organism carries out more complex activities than a single-celled organism. For example, you can walk, swim, run, jump, and throw. An ameba, however, can only swim. In a many-celled organism, cells are organized to work together. There are five main levels of organization: cells, tissues, organs, organ systems, and the organism.

Cells

In many-celled organisms, cells perform many different functions. The cells in your muscles work together so that you can move. Muscle cells, however, do not work alone. For example, muscle cells contract only when impulses from nerve cells set them into action. The muscle cells shown here are found in the heart. ▼

Cells, Tissues, and Organs

Most many-celled organisms have cells that are *specialized;* that is, there are different types of cells that do different kinds of work. Each group of specialized cells is organized into **tissues**. Each kind of tissue performs a certain function.

◀ **Tissues**
Muscle cells make up three different kinds of muscle tissue in the human body: smooth, skeletal, and cardiac. The cardiac muscle tissue shown here is found only in the heart.

In many organisms, tissues are organized into groups called **organs**. An organ is a group of tissues that work together to perform special functions. Both plants and animals have tissues and organs.

Organ Systems

A group of organs that work together make up an organ system. Some organisms, such as sponges, have no organ systems. Some organisms, such as jellyfish, have a few organ systems. And very complex organisms, such as dogs and humans, have ten organ systems.

Organisms

The highest level of cell organization is the organism. All organisms carry out life processes. In some organisms, such as humans, the different organ systems work together to keep the organism alive. One organ system, called the respiratory system, enables you to breathe. Your muscular and skeletal systems enable you to support, protect, and move your body. Your digestive system enables you to release the energy and nutrients your body needs to work properly.

Organ Systems

The heart, blood, and a network of blood vessels make up the human circulatory system. You also have nine other organ systems:

- skeletal
- muscular
- skin
- endocrine
- reproductive
- digestive
- respiratory
- excretory
- nervous

▼

◀ **Organs**

A heart is one of many organs in a many-celled animal such as a dog or a human. The heart is mostly made up of cardiac muscle tissue. It also contains nerve and connective tissues. Muscle, nerve, and connective tissues work together to pump blood through the heart and body.

Science and Technology *Pacemakers*

Each day your heart beats about 100,000 times! With each beat, the heart contracts, pumping blood throughout your body. This continuous supply of circulating blood keeps you alive.

To work efficiently, the muscle tissues of the heart must work together. The coordination of these tissues is controlled by another tissue that produces an electric signal. When the muscle cells detect the electric signal, they tighten, or contract, in unison.

For some people, the tissue that produces the electric signal does not work properly. When this happens, the muscle tissues in the heart may not work together. The heartbeat slows down or becomes uneven. This, in turn, may decrease the amount of blood circulating through the body.

If a person's heartbeat is too slow or uneven, it can be regulated by a pacemaker. A pacemaker is an electronic device that keeps blood circulating properly. Pacemakers are made of a battery, a miniature timing device, and a set of wires. They send electric signals to the muscle cells to tell them when to contract.

Pacemakers are placed inside a person's body. The wires are attached to the heart. At regular intervals, electrical energy is sent from the battery through the wire to the heart. This electric "jolt" stimulates the heart muscles, causing them to contract at the same time.

Figure 4.7 ▲
What kind of energy does a pacemaker and your heart tissue use to contract your heart muscles?

Check and Explain

1. List at least one example of each of the following: cell, tissue, organ, organ system, and organism.

2. Describe the difference between a cardiac muscle cell, cardiac muscle tissue, and the heart.

3. **Reason and Conclude** Can a single-celled organism contain tissue? Explain.

4. **Classify** Classify the following as a tissue, organ, or system:

   a. Brain, spinal cord, and nerves
   b. Heart
   c. Group of muscle cells

Chapter 4 Review

Concept Summary

4.1 The Cell Theory

▶ The cell theory states that all living things are made of cells. Cells form the structure and function of living things, and cells only come from other living cells.

▶ The cell theory was developed through the work of several scientists including van Leeuwenhoek, Hooke, Schleiden, Schwann, and Virchow.

4.2 Parts of a Cell

▶ Cells are made of different parts that work together to meet the needs of the cell.

▶ The outer cell layer is called the cell membrane. It controls what enters and leaves the cell.

▶ The nucleus controls the cell's activities and stores the information needed for reproduction.

▶ Cytoplasm is the gel-like substance inside the cell that makes up the cell material.

▶ Organelles are the small structures inside of a cell that carry on life processes such as releasing energy, making proteins, and storing food and water.

▶ Chloroplasts and cell walls are found only in plant cells.

4.3 Organization of Living Things

▶ Multicellular organisms have specialized cells to perform different functions.

▶ Cells of similar structure and function join together to form tissues. Groups of tissues make up organs, and groups of organs working together make up organ systems.

▶ An organism, the highest level of cell organization, can carry out all life processes.

Chapter Vocabulary

cell (4.1)	cell wall (4.2)	organelle (4.2)	tissue (4.3)
cell theory (4.1)	nucleus (4.2)	chloroplast (4.2)	organ (4.3)
cell membrane (4.2)	cytoplasm (4.2)	chlorophyll (4.2)	

Check Your Vocabulary

Use the vocabulary words above to complete the following sentences.

1. A cell's activities, including reproduction, are controlled by the cell's _____ .

2. In plants, sun energy is converted to food by the compound _____ .

3. Specialized cells organized to perform a certain function are called _____ .

4. A plant cell differs from an animal cell because it has a _____ outside the cell membrane.

5. The living material in the cell, excluding the nucleus, is called _____ .

6. A set of statements called the _____ describe the basic concepts about cells.

7. A group of tissues that works together to perform a special function is called an _____ .

8. The thin outer covering, or the _____ , controls what enters and exits cells.

9. The tiny, special parts of a cell that carry out life processes are called _____ .

10. The basic unit of structure and function for all living things is the _____ .

11. The chlorophyll in a _____ gives a plant its green color.

Write Your Vocabulary

Write sentences using each vocabulary word above. Show that you know what each word means.

Chapter 4 Review

Check Your Knowledge

Answer the following in complete sentences.

1. List the statements in the cell theory.

2. What is one purpose of the cell membrane?

3. Where in a cell is cellulose located?

4. List two organelles and their functions.

5. How did cells get their names?

6. Explain the statement "cells are specialized."

Choose the answer that best completes each sentence.

7. The first person to observe living cells was probably (Schleiden, Schwann, Hooke, van Leeuwenhoek).

8. The (cell membrane, lysosome, nuclear membrane, cellulose) protects, supports, and gives shape to cells.

9. The cell powerhouses are the (Golgi bodies, lysosomes, mitochondria, vacuoles).

10. Your heart is an example of an (organ system, organ, organism, organization).

11. Digestive chemicals in (chloroplasts, ribosomes, lysosomes, chlorophyll) break down food, wastes, and old cell parts.

12. The unit of structure for living things is the (organism, tissue, plant, cell).

13. The cell's control center is the (brain, cytoplasm, nucleus, scientist).

14. To grow skin cells in a laboratory, scientists must provide the cells with the same (chloroplasts, environment, hair, light) as a normal skin cell.

15. The cell theory states cells come only from (living cells, pond water, nonliving cells, cork).

Check Your Understanding

Apply the concepts you have learned to answer each question.

1. If animal cells contained chlorophyll, how would animal life be different?

2. The suffix -elle means "small" or "tiny" in Latin. Using this information, write a definition for organelle.

3. Describe how cells, tissues, organs, and organ systems are related.

4. Describe how the parts of a cell are like a city or town. Identify what parts of a town are similar to several cell organelles.

5. **Mystery Photo** The photograph on page 74 shows the bone tissue of a human thigh bone. The white spaces are channels that contain nerves or blood vessels for living bone cells. The black dots are cells in the bone matrix. Bone cells produce hard layers between one another. Fibers grow between the cells and hold them together. In what organ system would this tissue be found?

6. **Reason and Conclude** Which kind of cell would you expect to have more mitochondria, a muscle cell or a fat storage cell?

7. **Classify** What makes the skin an organ, rather than a tissue or organ system?

8. **Apply** How would the cell theory be affected if scientists could make living cells from carbon, oxygen, and other elements found on earth?

9. **Compare and Contrast** Compare the labels on Figure 4.4 and Figure 4.5. What do they tell you about the structures of these cells?

Develop Your Skills

Use the skills you have developed in this chapter to complete each activity.

1. **Observe** Look at the cell picture below to answer the following questions.

   a. Is this a plant or animal cell? How can you tell?

   b. How many mitochrondria are in the cell?

   c. Is there a vacuole?

2. **Design an Experiment** Imagine you are Anton van Leeuwenhoek looking at small moving objects in your microscope. Design an experiment to determine whether these things are living or non-living. Make sure you change only one variable.

3. **Data Bank** Use the information on page 625 to answer the following questions.

   a. Which is larger, a mitochondrion or a ribosome?

   b. Which needs a light microscope to be seen, a plant cell or a virus?

Make Connections

1. **Link the Concepts** Below is a concept map showing how some of the main concepts in this chapter link together. Only parts of the map are filled in. Copy the map. Using words and ideas from the chapter, complete the map.

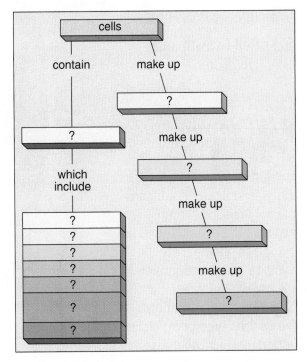

2. **Science and Language Arts** Write a children's story about the cell and its parts. Give personalities to the cell organelles. Tell the function of each organelle as part of your story. Try reading your story to a child to see if your information is clear and exciting.

3. **Science and Technology** Scientists can culture many different kinds of human cells. Choose two types of human cells. Research in your library how these cells are cultured and for what purpose.

4. **Science and Social Studies** Draw a time line that shows the events that led to the cell theory.

Chapter 5

Cell Processes

What do you see?

"I see a figure-8 shaped, lined, green structure. I think that this structure is a chloroplast. I think this because it appears to be submerged in cytoplasm inside a cell. I think it's green because of the chlorophyll inside. Chloroplasts are what give plants their green color. It is important because it aids the plant in photosynthesis, which makes the plant grow."

Andrea Winn
Austin Academy
Garland, Texas

To find out about the photograph, look on page 108. As you read this chapter, you will learn more about cells and their life processes.

5.1 Movement of Substances

Objectives

▶ **Describe** the role of the cell membrane in moving substances into and out of cells.

▶ **Explain** what it means for the cell membrane to be selectively permeable.

▶ **Distinguish** between diffusion and osmosis.

▶ **Infer** how the process of osmosis affects the cells of living things.

Skills WarmUp

Classify Make two lists. On one list, include the things you transport into your bedroom each day. On the other list, include the things you transport out of your bedroom each day.

I magine what would happen to cities if all roads, railroads, and airports suddenly shut down. There would be no way to transport materials from one place to another. Food, clothing, medicine, or other resources could not be brought into cities. Garbage could not be carried out of cities. If all lines of transport were blocked, cities would stop functioning. Like a city, your body also needs to transport materials. Your cells must take in needed materials, such as nutrients, water, and oxygen. Your cells must also get rid of wastes.

Diffusion

Look at Figure 5.1. What happens to the hot water when the tea bag is placed in the cup? Tea from the leaves moves out of the bag and into the surrounding water, flavoring it and coloring it brown. Movement of the tea throughout the water is explained by a process called **diffusion** (dih FYOO zhuhn). Diffusion is the movement of a substance from an area of high concentration to an area of low concentration. In the water, tea moves from high concentration in the bag to areas of lower concentration in the water. Eventually, tea spreads evenly throughout the water.

Water diffuses freely through the cell membrane in the same way that tea diffuses through a cup of water. Water surrounds most cells in your body, and all your cells contain water. Many substances vital to cells are dissolved in water. Cells, therefore, are affected by the diffusion of substances that are dissolved in water.

Figure 5.1 ▲
Tea leaves diffuse in a cup of hot water.

Osmosis

The diffusion of water across the cell membrane is called **osmosis** (ahz MOH sihs). Osmosis and diffusion are types of passive transport. During passive transport, materials move freely through the cell membrane because they do not require energy.

Like any other substance, water tends to move from high to low concentration. Water containing dissolved substances has a lower concentration of water than pure water. What would happen, then, if an animal cell were placed in pure water? The inside of an animal cell contains many dissolved substances. Therefore, the water concentration in the cell would be less than the water concentration outside the cell. So the water from the outside would diffuse through the membrane into the cell. The cell would swell and might even burst. Your body cells are like the animal cells. To prevent your cells from bursting, your body fluids have the same concentration of dissolved substances that your cells have.

SkillBuilder *Interpreting Data*

Diffusion Rate and Temperature

When you put a package of drink mix in water, you usually stir it to spread the mix evenly through the water. But if you didn't stir it, eventually the drink mix would spread through the water on its own, by diffusion. The water temperature can affect the diffusion rate of a substance.

The graph shows the rate at which drink mix diffuses through water at different temperatures. Study the graph, then answer the following questions:

1. At what temperature did the drink mix take the least amount of time to diffuse?

2. At what temperature was the diffusion rate the slowest?

3. What can you conclude about the effect of water temperature on the rate of diffusion?

4. For maximum diffusion in a short amount of time, what water temperature would be best for mixing the drink mix completely?

In one or two sentences, explain the methods you would use to make a packaged drink mix diffuse quickly.

Cell Membranes and Transport

Everything that moves into or out of a cell must pass through the cell membrane. The membrane is the key to how cells control the movement of life substances.

Certain substances diffuse freely into or out of cells. For these substances, the membrane is *permeable* (PUR mee uh buhl). For example, if the concentration of oxygen is lower inside a cell, oxygen will diffuse into the cell.

For many other substances, the cell membrane is a barrier. They cannot pass freely through the membrane, even if the substances are more concentrated on one side of the membrane than on the other side. For these substances, the membrane is *impermeable*.

Because a cell membrane is impermeable to some materials and permeable to others, it is described as *selectively permeable*. This characteristic of a cell membrane is explained by its structure. Look at the model of a cell membrane in Figure 5.2. Notice that the cell membrane is made up of two layers of lipid molecules. The lipid molecules slip past each other to form tiny gaps. Water and other small molecules can easily enter or leave the cell through these gaps. But many larger molecules can't fit through the tiny gaps.

How, then, do larger molecules like sugars and amino acids get into a cell? Larger molecules move through the cell membrane using special particles of protein embedded in the cell membrane. You can see these particles of protein in the model of the cell membrane in Figure 5.2. The protein molecules, or "carriers," actually carry larger molecules from one side of the membrane to the other. Carrier molecules are specialized to do certain jobs. Each carrier molecule allows the movement of only one type of molecule across a cell membrane.

Figure 5.2
A Model of a Cell Membrane

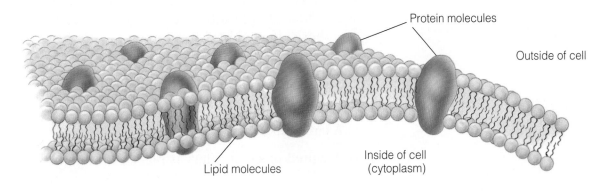

Protein molecules

Outside of cell

Lipid molecules

Inside of cell
(cytoplasm)

Active Transport

Many substances that can move freely through the membrane must be kept at a higher concentration on one side of the cell membrane than on the other. In order to move a substance to a more concentrated area, a cell uses active transport. Active transport requires energy. The large particles of protein in the cell membrane are involved in active transport.

 ### Science and Technology
Freezing Body Organs

How can human tissue be frozen and not be destroyed? The answer to this question is important for preserving transplant organs. Cryobiology is the study of freezing living things without harming them.

Recall that freezing causes water to expand and that cell contents are mostly water. When the water in a cell freezes, ice crystals damage the cell. Some techniques that reduce the water content also upset the balance of vital substances in the cell. Cryobiologists have developed a technique for preserving thin samples of tissue. Animal tissue is cooled rapidly to a very low temperature, and water is diffused from the cells. The dry tissue is then warmed to room temperature. Cryobiologists are trying to perfect this process for making large organs usable for transplants.

Figure 5.3 ▲
Cryobiologists study the effects of cold on living things. What happens to human cells when they are frozen?

Check and Explain

1. Why is the cell membrane selectively permeable?

2. In what way is a vegetable strainer like a selectively permeable membrane? In what way is it not?

3. **Reason and Conclude**   A tea bag is placed in hot water. Identify the substances affected by osmosis and those affected by diffusion.

4. **Infer**   What happens to the cells of the organisms in the following situations? Explain how the process of osmosis affects the cells.

   a. A cat drinks salty water.

   b. A wilted piece of celery is placed in water.

5.2 Energy Processes

Objectives

▶ **Explain** how plants store energy through photosynthesis.

▶ **Describe** how plants release energy during cell respiration.

▶ **Compare** photosynthesis and respiration.

▶ **Predict** if photosynthesis will take place.

Organisms get the energy they need to carry out their life processes from the chemical bonds in food. For example, when you eat a tuna fish sandwich, your body uses the energy that was stored in the cells of the tuna. The tuna obtained this energy by eating smaller fishes. The smaller fishes, in turn, may have fed on microscopic organisms or plants that lived in the ocean.

All animals depend on other organisms to obtain energy. Plants, however, do not depend on other organisms for energy. Plants get energy by a process called **photosynthesis** (foh toh SIHN theh sihs).

Photosynthesis

The word *photosynthesis* means "putting together with light." During photosynthesis, plants use the energy in sunlight and materials from air and water to join molecules of water and carbon dioxide. These materials make glucose, a simple sugar.

Photosynthesis takes place in the chloroplasts of a plant's cells. It occurs in two stages. During the first stage, energy from sunlight is absorbed by chlorophyll. Chlorophyll is a green pigment in the chloroplasts of a plant's cells. The light energy trapped by chlorophyll is used to split molecules of water (H_2O) into molecules of hydrogen (H_2) and oxygen (O_2). Some of the oxygen is a waste product that is released through tiny openings in the plant's leaves. The hydrogen remains in the chloroplasts.

During the second stage of photosynthesis, hydrogen combines with carbon dioxide (CO_2) to produce glucose ($C_6H_{12}O_6$). This completes the sugar-making process.

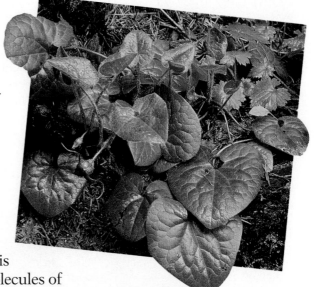

Figure 5.4 ▲
Chlorophyll gives this wild ginger plant its green color. Chlorophyll traps light energy from the sun for photosynthesis. Where in the plant cell is chlorophyll found?

Combined, the two stages of photosynthesis result in a chemical reaction described by the following equation:

$$6CO_2 \ + \ 6H_2O \ + \ \text{Light Energy} \rightarrow C_6H_{12}O_6 \ + \ 6O_2$$

Carbon dioxide   Water   Glucose   Oxygen

Reactants   **Products**

Sunlight provides the energy needed for the reaction to take place. The reactants, shown on the left side of the arrow, are carbon dioxide and water. These are the materials plants need to make glucose. Plants get carbon dioxide from air, and water from air and soil. The products, shown on the right side of the arrow, are glucose and oxygen.

During photosynthesis, light energy is changed, or converted, into chemical energy. This chemical energy is stored in sugar or starch in the plant's leaves and seeds. Major stages of photosynthesis are shown in Figure 5.5.

Figure 5.5   Photosynthesis

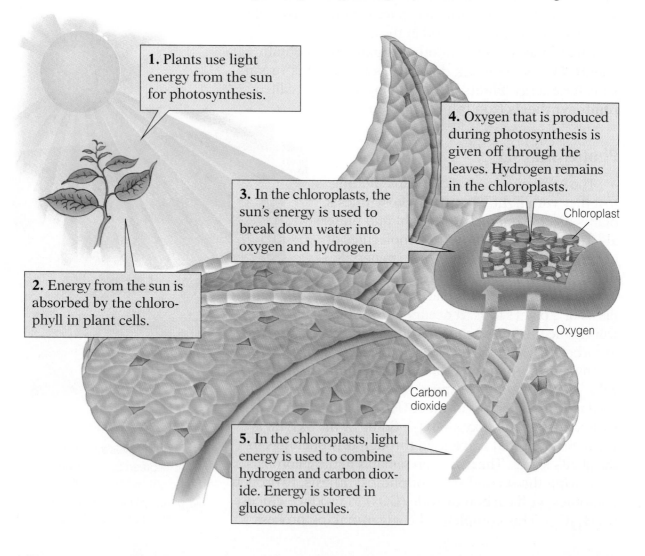

1. Plants use light energy from the sun for photosynthesis.

2. Energy from the sun is absorbed by the chlorophyll in plant cells.

3. In the chloroplasts, the sun's energy is used to break down water into oxygen and hydrogen.

4. Oxygen that is produced during photosynthesis is given off through the leaves. Hydrogen remains in the chloroplasts.

Chloroplast

Oxygen

Carbon dioxide

5. In the chloroplasts, light energy is used to combine hydrogen and carbon dioxide. Energy is stored in glucose molecules.

Respiration

The cells of both plants and animals use the chemical energy stored in glucose. However, before any cell can use this energy, the glucose molecules must break apart. Cells combine glucose with oxygen in order to break down glucose into simpler substances. This process, called **respiration**, releases the stored energy of glucose.

During respiration, glucose breaks down into water and carbon dioxide and releases energy. The energy is carried throughout the organism by a compound called ATP. The chemical reaction for respiration is

$$C_6H_{12}O_6 + 6O_2 \rightarrow 6CO_2 + 6H_2O + \text{Energy (ATP)}$$

Glucose · · · · · · Oxygen · · Carbon dioxide · · · Water

What are the products of this chemical reaction? What are the reactants? How does this reaction compare with the reaction for photosynthesis?

Like photosynthesis, respiration takes place inside the cell. Respiration begins in the cytoplasm. Enzymes break down carbohydrates into glucose. Glucose breaks down to form acids, carbon dioxide, and two molecules of ATP. The acids break down further in the mitochondria of the cell. Here, oxygen joins with the acids to produce carbon dioxide and water. Many molecules of ATP are also released. ATP carries energy throughout the organism. The processes of photosynthesis and respiration are compared in Table 5.1.

Table 5.1   Photosynthesis versus Respiration

Photosynthesis	Respiration
Uses water (H_2O)	Gives off water (H_2O)
Uses carbon dioxide (CO_2)	Gives off carbon dioxide (CO_2)
Makes glucose ($C_6H_{12}O_6$)	Breaks down glucose ($C_6H_{12}O_6$)
Gives off oxygen (O_2)	Uses oxygen (O_2)
Requires light	Occurs all the time; does not need light
Takes in light energy	Releases energy (ATP) stored in glucose ($C_6H_{12}O_6$)
Occurs only in cells with chlorophyll: cells of plants and some bacteria and protists	Occurs in cells of most organisms

Skills WorkOut

Observe   Place a freshly picked leaf in water. Wait 30 minutes. While the leaf is still under water, observe the surface of the leaf. What forms on the leaf? Why?

Skills WorkOut

Classify List the vegetables and fruits you ate during the last three days. Divide the list into four columns: green, nongreen, sweet, and nonsweet. Identify the foods that contain chlorophyll. Identify those that contain glucose.

Fermentation

Respiration happens only if oxygen is present. When the cells do not have enough oxygen to carry out respiration, another energy-releasing process may take place. This process is called **fermentation**.

During both respiration and fermentation, glucose breaks down to form carbon dioxide and an acid. In respiration, the acid is broken down further in the presence of oxygen to make carbon dioxide, water, and many molecules of ATP. When no oxygen is present, fermentation occurs. The acid is broken down further to produce carbon dioxide, either alcohol or lactic acid, and a small amount of ATP.

The production of either lactic acid or alcohol is determined by the type of cell. For example, your muscle cells may produce lactic acid if oxygen is not present. The cells of certain fungi and bacteria produce lactic acid used in making yogurt and cheese. Yeast cells ferment during bread baking to produce alcohol.

Career Corner *Bread Baker*

Who Bakes the Bread for Your Sandwiches?

Without understanding the fermentation process, the ancient Egyptians discovered that adding yeast to flour causes bread to rise. Bakers all over the world have carried on the practice for centuries.

Most bakers use only the basic ingredients in bread: yeast, flour, water, and salt. They knead and "set" the dough, then let it rise for 3 to 16 hours at a temperature around 29°C. The yeast causes the small amount of sugar in the flour to ferment. As the sugar breaks down, alcohol and carbon dioxide are released into the dough. Flour has an elastic substance, called gluten, that traps bubbles of carbon dioxide in the bread. As the bubbles expand, the dough rises.

A final burst of fermentation, called "oven spring," occurs during baking. The heat kills the yeast and evaporates the alcohol in the dough. Without yeast fermentation, the bread you eat would be flat and hard instead of fluffy and soft.

Baking bread requires special skills. Bakers must know the right balance of ingredients. They must be able to judge when dough has been kneaded to the right consistency. A good loaf of bread is allowed to rise

and bake at just the right time. Bakers receive on-the-job training and often learn skills from more experienced bakers. You can also learn to be a commercial baker through courses offered in community colleges or vocational schools.

Science and You *Chemistry of Sore Muscles*

Have you ever had a muscle cramp during or after exercise? What do you think caused it? You probably never knew that the pain you felt was caused by fermentation!

In your cells, glucose is constantly combining with oxygen to provide your body with the energy it needs. When you run, swim, or do other forms of exercise, the muscle cells doing the work need an extra supply of oxygen to carry out respiration. However, even though you are breathing hard, you may not be taking in as much oxygen as your tired muscles need.

Fortunately, your muscle cells store energy in the form of a carbohydrate called glycogen. When your cells do not have enough oxygen to carry out respiration, glycogen breaks down through the fermentation process. In this process, the glycogen changes into glucose, and then into carbon dioxide and lactic acid, releasing ATP.

If you breathe deeply after exercise, more oxygen is available to your muscle cells. Respiration then continues. Normally, the lactic acid produced by fermentation changes back into glucose or glycogen in your cells. However, the lactic acid formed through fermentation can accumulate in your muscle cells. If too much lactic acid builds up, it can cause a painful cramp or sore muscles.

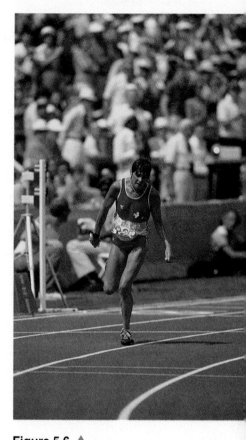

Figure 5.6 ▲
When you don't get enough oxygen to muscles during exercise, muscle cells begin to produce energy by lactic acid fermentation. This runner will need to breathe deeply and walk after she finishes her race to avoid cramps and sore muscles.

Check and Explain

1. What three things are required for photosynthesis to occur?

2. Explain how the meaning of the word *photosynthesis* is related to the process.

3. **Compare** How do the products and reactants in photosynthesis compare to those in respiration?

4. **Predict** Which of these situations meet all three requirements for photosynthesis to occur?

   a. A house plant in a well-lighted room at midnight

   b. Sprouting seedlings in an open field on a sunny day

   c. A lawn during a severe drought

   d. A cornfield on an evening with no moonlight

Activity 5   How does light affect plant growth?

Skills

Observe; Infer; Control Variables

Task 1   Prelab Prep

1. Collect the following items: 2 labels, 2 pots, 6 small plants of the same species and similar in size, measuring cup.
2. Number the labels *1* and *2* and date each one.
3. Find suitable locations for the plants: a place in the sunlight and a place in darkness.

Task 2   Data Record

1. Write a different location on each label:
   1. Sunlight   2. Darkness.
2. Copy the data table below onto a separate sheet of paper.
3. Use the data table to record your observations about the appearance of the plants in each pot.

Table 5.2   Plant Data

Date	Pot Number	Observation
	1 Sun	
	2 Dark	
	1 Sun	
	2 Dark	
	1 Sun	
	2 Dark	
	1 Sun	
	2 Dark	
	1 Sun	
	2 Dark	
	1 Sun	
	2 Dark	

Task 3   Procedure

1. Label each pot. Put three plants in each one. Place the pots in their locations.
2. Water the plants according to the needs of their species. Use the measuring cup to make sure all the plants get the same amount of water.
3. Record the appearance of the plants in each pot on the data table every other day. Do not remove the plants from their locations.

Task 4   Analysis

1. Identify the variable in this activity.
2. Which plants changed the most during the time you observed them? Which plants changed the least?
3. What were the light needs of the plants you used? Check the seed package or pot label on your plants.
4. What concept from this chapter relates to the change you observed in the plants?
5. What conclusion can you draw from the changes in the appearance of the plants? Explain.
6. Can you think of any other cause(s) that might have contributed to the effect you observed?

Task 5   Conclusion

Write a short paragraph explaining how sunlight affected the plants. Explain why.

Everyday Application

What happens to plants if they are not placed near sunlight? Explain why it is important to grow plants in the right locations. Then describe some different ways that you could bring unhealthy plants back to life.

Extension

Develop a hypothesis about the effect of different amounts of sunlight on plants. Write your procedures and test your hypothesis.

5.3 Cell Growth and Division

Objectives

▶ **Explain** how cell division affects living things.

▶ **Explain** the role of mitosis in cell division.

▶ **Describe** the various phases of mitosis.

▶ **Make models** of the phases of mitosis.

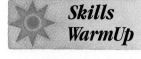
The cells that make up your body are constantly changing. For example, cells change when different substances enter and leave the cell. The size and number of cells you have also changes constantly. Individual cells get larger or they divide and make new cells. In an adult human, as many as 25 million new cells are made every second. Most new cells replace damaged or dead cells.

Cell Division

Your body makes new cells during a process called *cell division*. When cell division takes place, two identical cells are produced. In single-celled organisms, cell division results in the formation of two new organisms. In many-celled organisms, cell division increases the number of cells making up the organism. Because of cell division, a many-celled organism can grow and develop from a single cell, the fertilized egg. As the cells increase in number, the organism grows.

Figure 5.7 shows the cycle of cell growth and division. A cell may take a few hours or a few days to complete one cycle. Most of a cell's life is spent in a phase of growth and development called interphase. During interphase, the amount of DNA in the nucleus is doubled. To form a complete new cell, both the nucleus and the cytoplasm must divide. The amount of time it takes a cell to divide depends on the type of cell, the temperature, and the nutrients in the cell. The process by which a cell nucleus divides into two identical nuclei is called **mitosis** (my TOH sis). As you can see in Figure 5.7, the process of mitosis occurs in several phases.

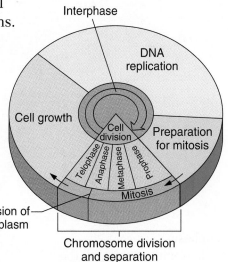

Figure 5.7 ▲
During a cell cycle, a cell grows, prepares for division, and divides into two identical cells, each of which begins the cycle anew.

Phases of Mitosis Recall that the nucleus controls all the activities of the cell. More specifically, the threadlike strands called **chromosomes** (KROH muh ZOHMZ), located in the nucleus, control cell activity. Chromosomes also carry the genetic material that passes the traits of parents to their offspring.

Look at Figure 5.8. It shows the cycle of growth and division that takes place in animal cells. Notice that the cycle starts with interphase and continues through the four phases of mitosis.

**Figure 5.8
Animal Cell Cycle**

Telophase

When the chromosomes reach opposite ends of the cell, the spindle breaks up into proteins. A nuclear membrane forms around each set of single chromosomes. Two identical nuclei now exist. A furrow forms at the center of the cell membrane. The furrow deepens and divides the cell completely.

Anaphase

The spindle fibers pull the chromatids apart, separating each one from its duplicate. Each chromosome moves to opposite sides of the cell. The cell now has two identical sets of single chromosomes.

Interphase

During this phase, the cell makes enough proteins, enzymes, mitochondria, and other substances for two cells. In the cytoplasm, structures called *centrioles* duplicate to form two pairs. In the nucleus, each chromosome forms an exact copy of itself, or replicates. These spread through the nucleus in threadlike strands.

Chromatid

Metaphase

The centromeres of the chromatid pairs are lined up in the center of the cell. Each individual chromatid is attached to a spindle fiber.

Centriole

Prophase ▲

The chromosomes, now called chromatids, form short, thick rods and pair up in the center of the nucleus. A centromere connects the two halves of each double chromatid. In the cytoplasm, a fibrous structure, called the spindle, forms between the centriole pairs. The centrioles move to opposite sides of the cell, and the nuclear membrane breaks apart.

Spindle fibers

Figure 5.9 ▲
The cells at the tip of this corn root are in various stages of their cell cycles. The cell in anaphase has a cell plate beginning to form across the middle of the cell.

Mitosis in Plants Cell division differs slightly in plants and animals. In plant cells, spindle fibers don't attach to centrioles during mitosis. The rigid plant cell wall does not form a furrow in the middle as the animal cell membrane does. Instead, a structure made of liquid-filled pouches called the cell plate forms across the middle of the dividing cell. As this plate grows, its edges fuse with the old wall to divide the cell into two. Each half of the cell then forms its own cell wall. When the cell walls are complete, the newly formed cells take on nutrients and increase in size.

Science and Society
Cell Division out of Control

Have you ever wondered what cancer is? Think about how the nucleus controls the cell and tells it when to stop dividing. Scientific research shows that cancer develops when cells divide at a faster-than-normal rate. These fast-dividing cells are abnormal. They may have unusual chromosomes. Parts of the cell may be missing or out of place. The cell surface is altered. Cancer cells can invade tissue in different parts of the body.

For years, doctors treated all cancers by removing the cancerous tissue. Through research, radiation and chemotherapy were found to be useful tools for treating cancer. Scientists have identified many *agents* that may contribute to cancer in humans. Among these are excess exposure to certain chemicals, ultraviolet radiation, and cigarette smoke. However, the best cure for cancer would be learning what triggers cancerous growth in the first place.

Check and Explain

1. How can cell division affect a single-celled organism? A many-celled organism?

2. What are the four phases of mitosis?

3. **Find Causes** Why is it important for the nuclear membrane to break apart?

4. **Make a Model** Draw the telophase of a plant cell and the telophase of an animal cell. Show clearly how this phase differs in plants and animals.

Chapter 5 Review

Concept Summary

5.1 Movement of Substances

▶ Cell membranes regulate the passage of materials in and out of the cell.

▶ Some substances, like oxygen and water, diffuse freely through the cell membrane by osmosis.

▶ Large molecules, like sugars and amino acids, must pass through the membrane with carrier proteins.

▶ A cell membrane is selectively permeable because it is impermeable to some materials and permeable to others.

5.2 Energy Processes

▶ During photosynthesis, light energy is used to change carbon dioxide and water into glucose and oxygen.

▶ During respiration, oxygen is combined with glucose to release carbon dioxide, water, and ATP.

▶ Fermentation is an energy-releasing process that produces carbon dioxide, alcohol or lactic acid, and ATP.

5.3 Cell Growth and Division

▶ All cells have a cycle of growth and division.

▶ The period of growth and development in a cell is called interphase. During interphase, the cell doubles in size.

▶ The cell's nucleus and cytoplasm divide during mitosis. Mitosis has four phases: prophase, metaphase, anaphase, and telophase.

Chapter Vocabulary

diffusion (5.1)	photosynthesis (5.2)	fermentation (5.2)	chromosome (5.3)
osmosis (5.1)	respiration (5.2)	mitosis (5.3)	

Check Your Vocabulary

Use the vocabulary words above to complete the following sentences correctly.

1. The process of breaking down glucose with oxygen is called ____ .

2. The diffusion of water across the cell membrane is called ____ .

3. The process by which plants convert light energy to chemical energy is ____ .

4. Movement of a substance from a high concentration to a low concentration is ____ .

5. A cell divides into two identical nuclei during ____ .

6. Respiration releases more ATP energy from glucose than ____ does.

7. Cell activity is controlled by ____ in a cell's nucleus.

Identify the word or term in each group that does not belong. Explain why it does not belong.

8. Photosynthesis, respiration, fermentation

9. Osmosis, diffusion, mitosis

10. Chromosome, mitosis, fermentation

11. Mitochondria, centromere, chromatid

12. Carbon dioxide, water, spindle fiber

13. Mitochondria, mitosis, respiration

14. Fermentation, chlorophyll, photosynthesis

15. Interphase, anaphase, telophase

Write Your Vocabulary

Write sentences using each vocabulary word above. Show that you know what each word means.

Chapter 5 Review

Check Your Knowledge

Answer the following in complete sentences.

1. What are the phases of mitosis?

2. What are the reactants of respiration?

3. How does diffusion differ from osmosis?

4. What makes the structure of a cell membrane selectively permeable?

5. List the products of fermentation.

6. What is the function of a cell plate?

7. Give the overall equations for photosynthesis and respiration.

8. Name two substances that diffuse freely across a cell membrane.

9. During what phase of mitosis does the cell divide into two new cells?

Determine whether each statement is true or false. Write *true* if it is true. If it is false, change the underlined term to make the statement true.

10. For substances that diffuse freely in and out of cells, the membrane is <u>permeable</u>.

11. The <u>chloroplasts</u> capture light energy from the sun.

12. Respiration can only happen if oxygen is <u>absent</u>.

13. Plants get carbon dioxide from <u>soil</u>.

14. Everything that passes in or out of a cell must move through the <u>centrioles</u>.

15. Cell division occurs during <u>interphase</u>.

16. In a cell membrane, <u>protein</u> molecules carry sugars into the cell.

17. Respiration begins in the cytoplasm of a cell and ends in the <u>mitochondria</u>.

18. During anaphase, spindle fibers pull the <u>cytoplasm</u> apart.

Check Your Understanding

Apply the concepts you have learned to answer each question.

1. What is the difference between a permeable membrane and an impermeable membrane?

2. How could each of the following affect photosynthesis in a plant:

   a. Cloudy weather

   b. Lack of water

   c. Nighttime

3. Describe how mitosis differs in plants and animals.

4. **Mystery Photo** The photo on page 92 shows a chloroplast in the leaf of a pea plant. The large white object in the cell is a white starch body, a product of photosynthesis.

   a. Why do plants use photosynthesis?

   b. What is the role of the chloroplasts during photosynthesis?

5. **Make a Model** Draw a picture of a plant cell cycle. Be sure to label each stage as well as the cell parts. Clearly show what is happening in the cell at each stage.

6. **Apply** Give an example of diffusion in your everyday life.

7. Describe how large molecules like sugars and amino acids get into a cell.

8. **Make a Table** Make a table comparing photosynthesis, respiration, and fermentation in the following areas: raw materials, products, energy, location.

9. Explain why the mitochondria are sometimes called the "power houses" of a cell.

Develop Your Skills

Use the skills you have developed to complete each activity.

1. **Interpret Data** The drawing below shows two substances in water. A membrane divides the water in half.

   a. Is the membrane permeable to substance 1? Substance 2? How do you know?

   b. In which direction will substance 1 flow? Why?

   c. In which direction will substance 2 flow? Why?

   d. Is this an example of diffusion or osmosis? Explain.

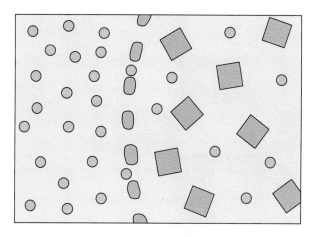

○ Substance 1   ▢ Substance 2

2. **Data Bank** Use the information on page 626 to answer the following questions.

   a. Which body cell has the longest cell life? Shortest cell life?

   b. Which cells live at least one week?

3. **Predict** Suppose you put 30 beans in a jar and then covered the beans with water. Then you marked the water level on the jar with a pen. What would happen to the water level in the jar? Explain.

Make Connections

1. **Link the Concepts** Below is a concept map showing how some of the main concepts in this chapter link together. Only parts of the map are filled in. Copy the map. Using words and ideas from the chapter, complete the map.

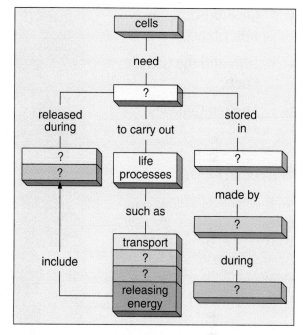

2. **Science and Technology** Throughout history people have used the process of fermentation to make certain kinds of food. Research the use of fermentation in a particular food process, such as cheese or yogurt making.

3. **Science and Language Arts** Research the story of how the steps in mitosis were discovered. Write a short story of the discovery for a magazine.

4. **Science and You** Make bread or cake following a recipe that uses yeast. Watch for signs of fermentation. How do you know that fermentation is occurring? Why do you not taste the alcohol in bread or cake made with yeast?

Chapter 6 Heredity

What do you see?

66 The photo is a close-up of some corn. The corn was bred to have different colors. Some people think that it looks pretty. They put it in a display, usually in the fall. 99

Jennette Piry
Mason Middle School
St. Louis, Missouri

To find out about the photograph, look on page 132. As you read the chapter, you will learn more about how characteristics are passed from generation to generation.

6.1 Basic Principles of Heredity

Objectives

▶ **Describe** the work of Gregor Mendel.

▶ **Distinguish** between dominant and recessive genes.

▶ **Explain** the difference between phenotype and genotype.

▶ **Predict** the results of a simple genetic cross using a Punnett square.

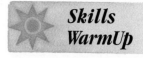
How would you describe yourself so you could be found in a crowd? What characteristics help to identify you? Notice the many differences among the people in the crowd shown in Figure 6.1. The people have different skin color and hair color. Their noses and ears are shaped differently. These are just a few characteristics, called traits, that make each person unique. All living things are identified by their traits.

Where did your traits come from? You inherited each trait from your parents. The passing of traits from parents to offspring is called **heredity**. The genetic material of your parents combined to form a genetic code that determines all your traits.

Mendel's Experiments

In the 1860s, an Austrian monk named Gregor Mendel made the first detailed investigation of how traits are inherited. Mendel studied the heredity of pea plants he grew in the monastery garden. The conclusions he reached in his research form the foundation of **genetics**, the study of inheritance.

Pea plants were ideal for Mendel's study because they were easy to grow. More importantly, peas have several traits that occur in just two easy-to-recognize forms. For example, the plants are either tall or short, and the seeds are either green or yellow. The structure of pea flowers was also important because Mendel could control the pollination of each plant. He could either let a pea plant pollinate itself, or he could cross-pollinate one pea plant

Figure 6.1 ▲
Each of these people has a unique set of traits determined by his or her heredity.

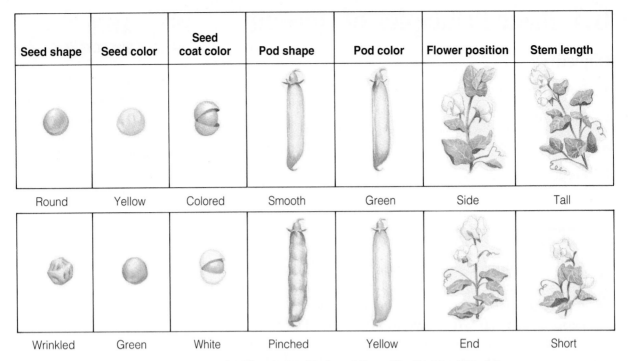

Seed shape	Seed color	Seed coat color	Pod shape	Pod color	Flower position	Stem length
Round	Yellow	Colored	Smooth	Green	Side	Tall
Wrinkled	Green	White	Pinched	Yellow	End	Short

▲ **Figure 6.2 Traits of Peas Studied by Mendel**

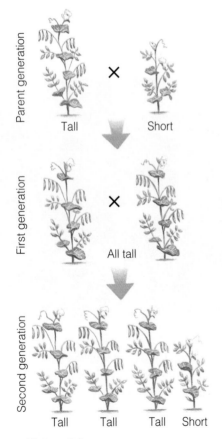

Parent generation

Tall × Short

First generation

All tall ×

Second generation

Tall Tall Tall Short

Figure 6.3 ▲

What trait was hidden in the first generation of offspring?

with another. By crossing two different plants, Mendel was able to see how the traits of two parents showed up in the offspring.

Look at Figure 6.2. Mendel studied the inheritance of seven different traits. To start, he made sure that he had pea varieties in which each of these traits stayed the same, generation after generation. For example, he grew tall plants that produced only tall plants. Mendel called such plants pure-breeding, or pure. When the pure plants were self-pollinated, they produced only offspring like themselves.

Mendel began his experiments by studying the stem length of peas. He took pure tall plants and crossed them with each other. Like self-pollinated pure tall plants, they produced only tall plants. He crossed pure short plants. Just as he expected, the pure short plants produced only plants with a stem length like their own.

Next, Mendel crossed a pure short plant and a pure tall plant. This time, the results were a surprise. All the seeds that came from crossing pure tall and pure short plants grew into tall plants. However, when these tall offspring crossed with each other, the next generation had both tall and short plants! The trait for shortness disappeared in the first generation, but it reappeared in the second. This experiment is shown in Figure 6.3.

Patterns of Inheritance

Mendel tried similar crosses with other traits and found the same pattern. In each case, crossing plants with different pure traits produced offspring with only one of the traits. The other trait was somehow hidden. When these offspring were crossed with each other, the hidden trait showed up in some of their offspring.

Mendel came up with an important hypothesis that fit these observations. He decided that a trait is determined by a pair of "factors." When two pea plants are crossed, he concluded, each parent must contribute *just one* factor to each offspring. In this way, a pair of factors passes to the offspring. Mendel also decided that a factor could be either strong or weak. When a strong factor and a weak factor paired, the strong one determined the trait in the offspring. Only when two weak factors paired could a weak factor express its trait.

Dominant and Recessive Genes   Today Mendel's factors are called **genes**. A gene is a unit of genetic material that determines a trait. As Mendel discovered, many genes exist in two forms. The strong form Mendel described is called a **dominant** gene. The weak form is called a **recessive** gene. In peas the gene for tallness is dominant and the gene for shortness is recessive.

Genotypes and Phenotypes   One of Mendel's important findings was that the traits a plant expressed differed from the factors, or genes, the plant inherited. Either two tall genes *or* a tall gene and a short gene could produce a tall plant. The trait that an organism actually shows is called the **phenotype** (FEE noh TYP). The gene combination that determines the phenotype is called the **genotype** (JEHN oh TYP). When a genotype is a combination of a dominant and a recessive gene, it is called a **hybrid**.

Genotypes are written with letter symbols. A capital letter is used for the dominant gene. The same letter in lowercase is used for the recessive gene. For example, T is a symbol for tallness, and t for shortness. The symbols TT, tt, and Tt represent the three different genotypes for stem length found in pea plants. Which two genotypes produce tall plants? Which is the hybrid genotype? The genotypes of the peas in Mendel's cross are shown in Figure 6.4.

Skills WorkOut

Infer   A guinea pig with white fur is born to parents with black fur. However, in guinea pigs, black fur is the dominant trait over white fur. Explain how this could have happened.

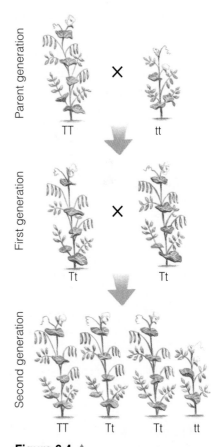

Parent generation

TT   ×   tt

First generation

Tt   ×   Tt

Second generation

TT   Tt   Tt   tt

Figure 6.4 ▲
Compare the genotypes of these pea plants to their phenotypes.

Inherited Genes

What happens when genes combine as shown in Figure 6.4? Remember that a parent passes on only one of its paired genes to each offspring. The pair of genes must separate. Gene separation occurs during the formation of sex cells, which are called **gametes** (GAM eets). In peas, the gametes are either pollen grains or unfertilized seeds, called ovules.

Look at Figure 6.5. The squares on the left stand for two of the offspring produced by Mendel's cross of a pure tall plant and a pure short plant. Notice that in both, one of the genes is T and the other is t. When each of these plants produces gametes, half the gametes will get the T gene. The other half will get the t gene. The diagram shows the two kinds of gametes produced by each parent.

When pollen from one parent fertilizes ovules from the other, the gametes join in pairs. Four different combinations of

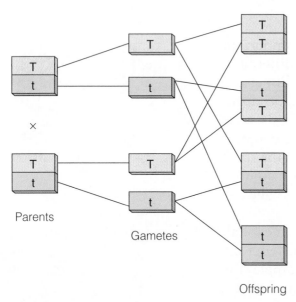

Parents

Gametes

Offspring

Figure 6.5 ▲
Each offspring gets a different combination of genes from the two parents. You can see in this cross that only one out of four offspring will have the tt genotype.

the T and t genes are possible. One combination, for example, is a T from the first parent and a T from the second parent. Another combination is a T from the first parent and a t from the second parent. What are the other combinations shown in Figure 6.5? Check to see that these are the same genotypes as the plants in the second generation in Figure 6.4.

The gametes join with each other randomly. In other words, each combination has an equal chance of occurring. An ovule containing a T, for example, has a 50-50 chance of being fertilized by a pollen grain containing a T or one containing a t.

Principles of Genetics

Mendel's work became the basis for the principles of genetics. Since Mendel's time, the work of many other scientists has also helped establish these principles. The first two principles summarize what you just learned.

▶ The traits of an organism pass from the parents to the offspring.

▶ Gene pairs determine traits.

▶ Organisms inherit genes in pairs. One gene comes from the gamete of each parent.

▶ Two members of a gene-pair separate, or segregate, at random. Half the gametes carry one of the genes and half carry the other gene.

▶ Genes are dominant or recessive. When paired, a dominant gene hides the effect of a recessive gene.

▶ The gene for a particular trait segregates independently of the genes for other traits. That is, genes do not segregate together.

Punnett Squares

An easy way to predict the genetic results of a cross between two organisms is to draw a diagram called a Punnett square. Notice that the Punnett square in Figure 6.6 has four boxes. Each box contains one of the possible combinations of genes for one trait inherited from the parents.

In this Punnett square, both parents are hybrid plants (Tt). When they cross, the result is that one out of four offspring is genotype TT. Two out of four are Tt. What is the other possible genotype?

Punnett squares can help you predict the numbers of different phenotypes produced by a certain cross. For the cross in Figure 6.6, three out of four boxes, or 75 percent, contain genotypes that result in tall plants. Therefore, about 75 percent of the offspring from this cross will grow to be tall. How can you tell that 25 percent will be short?

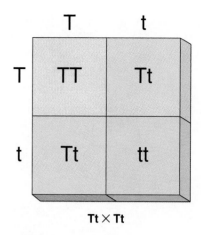

Tt × Tt

Figure 6.6 ▲
The letters on the left and top margins of a Punnett square stand for the genotypes of the two parents.

SkillBuilder Predicting

Punnett Squares

In dogs, dark hair (D) is dominant over light hair (d). What would happen if a dog that breeds pure for dark hair mates with a dog that breeds pure for light hair? What are the possible phenotypes of the offspring? You can use a Punnett square to answer these questions.

You begin by setting up the Punnett square as shown here. The letters on the left represent the possible genes in the sex cells of the dark-haired parent, and the letters on the top show the possible genes in the sex cells of the other parent. Copy this Punnett square on a separate sheet of paper and fill in the genotypes of the offspring.

1. What genotype will all the offspring have? What phenotype is this?

2. Make another Punnett square to show a cross of two of these offspring. What are the possible genotypes that result from this cross?

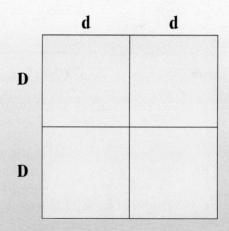

3. For each puppy produced by this second cross, what are the chances that it will have light hair?

4. If a litter of eight puppies is produced, how many are likely to have dark hair?

5. Explain how Punnett squares can be used to predict the results of genetic crosses.

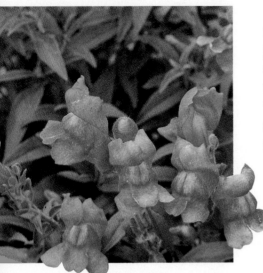

Incomplete Dominance

Many genes in plants and animals behave differently than the ones Mendel studied in peas. In one common pattern, two genes in a pair are different, but neither is dominant over the other. When the different genes pair together, they produce a trait somewhere between the traits of the two parents. For example, a cross between a red-flowered snapdragon and a white-flowered snapdragon produces offspring with pink flowers.

Genes that interact in this way show what is called **incomplete dominance**.

Figure 6.7 ▲
This snapdragon is the offspring of a red parent and a white parent.

Science and You *Your Multigene Traits*

Many inherited human traits are not as simple as stem length and seed color in peas. More than one gene determines these traits, so they are called multigene traits. None of the genes is dominant or recessive, but each gene contributes to the trait. Many different combinatons of these genes are possible. As a result, there is a wide range in these traits. For example, humans are not either tall or short. They are any height within a certain range. Another example is skin color. Three or four possible genes control skin color. A person's skin color varies from very light to very dark.

Check and Explain

1. What is the difference between a dominant gene and a recessive gene?

2. If the gene for round seeds in peas (R) is dominant, and the gene for wrinkled seeds (r) is recessive, what would be the phenotype of the following genotypes? RR, Rr, rr.

3. **Find Causes** Are green pods or yellow pods dominant in pea plants? Explain how you could find out.

4. **Predict** In dogs, short hair is dominant and long hair is recessive. Complete a Punnett square to show the results of a cross between a shorthaired dog with a genotype of Ss and a longhaired dog with a genotype of ss. What genotypes are possible? What phenotypes are possible?

6.2 Chromosomes and Inheritance

Objectives

▶ **Describe** the process and results of meiosis.

▶ **Explain** how sex is determined in humans.

▶ **Explain** why some traits are sex-linked.

▶ **Infer** the genotype of colorblind parents.

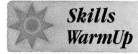
Suppose you wanted to see a gene. Where would you look? If you looked inside a cell's nucleus at the right time, you would see dense structures like the ones in Figure 6.8. These structures are called chromosomes.

Each of the chromosomes you see in Figure 6.8 is made of many genes. One gene is a very small segment of a chromosome. There may be as many as 50,000 genes on one human chromosome.

Chromosome Facts

Mendel discovered the principles of inheritance without knowing about chromosomes. His principles, however, related directly to the way chromosomes behave. Around the time of Mendel's death in 1884, the development of high-power microscopes enabled scientists to see and study chromosomes. They soon realized that chromosomes were the physical basis of inheritance.

Chromosomes normally occur in pairs because the offspring inherits one chromosome from each parent. Both chromosomes in a pair have the same appearance and length, and both contain the same types of genes. Consequently, genes also occur in pairs. Whatever its characteristic number of chromosomes, an organism has the same number of chromosomes in all of its body cells.

Every species of living things has a certain number of chromosome pairs in its cells. An organism's size or complexity doesn't determine this number. Table 6.1 shows the number of chromosome pairs for various organisms.

Table 6.1
Normal Chromosome Number

Species	Pairs of Chromosomes
Cat	19
Dog	39
Goldfish	47
Horse	32
Human	23
Onion	8
Potato	44

Figure 6.8 ▲
Human Chromosomes

Meiosis

Recall that each sex cell, or gamete, contributes one gene to the offspring. For each chromosome from a pair to end up in a different sex cell, the chromosome pairs must separate.

The formation of gametes involves a special kind of cell division called **meiosis** (my OH sihs). The process of meiosis produces gametes with one set of unpaired chromosomes. Follow the process of meiosis in Figure 6.9. It shows what happens in an organism with three pairs of chromosomes in its body cells.

1. The chromosomes in the parent cell condense and arrange themselves. The two chromosomes in each pair are shaded differently to make them easier to follow. Each contains different forms of the same genes.

2. Meiosis begins when the three pairs of chromosomes in the parent cell are all copied.
▼

3. The cell then divides into two new cells, just as in mitosis. Each cell has a complete set of three chromosome pairs. Notice that these new pairs are different from the pairs of chromosomes in the parent cell.
▼

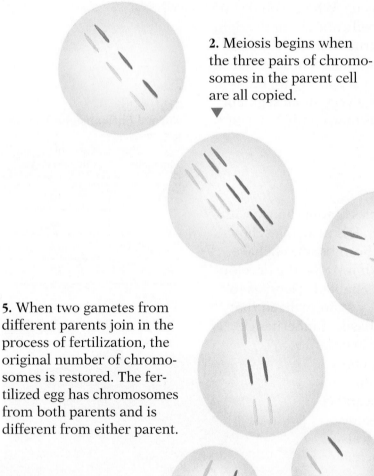

5. When two gametes from different parents join in the process of fertilization, the original number of chromosomes is restored. The fertilized egg has chromosomes from both parents and is different from either parent.

▲

4. The two new cells each divide again to produce four cells. Each of the four has just three unpaired chromosomes, or half the total number of the original parent cell. These four cells are all gametes. Notice that they contain two different combinations of chromosomes.

Figure 6.9
The Process of Meiosis

Sex Determination

The 23 pairs of chromosomes in a human cell are shown in Figure 6.10. Notice that the chromosomes in each of the first 22 pairs are alike. The chromosomes in pair 23, however, are not alike. The longer one is called an **X chromosome**, and the shorter one is a **Y chromosome**. These are the sex chromosomes. The combination of sex chromosomes you have in your body cells determines your sex. Females have two X chromosomes. Males have one X and one Y chromosome.

Since a female has only X chromosomes, her egg cells, or ova, all contain an X chromosome. Consequently both males and females inherit an X chromosome from their mother. Male sex cells, or sperm, carry either an X or a Y chromosome. If a sperm containing a Y chromosome fertilizes the ovum, the baby will be a boy. If the sperm has an X chromosome, the baby will be a girl. The father's sperm, therefore, determines the sex of a child.

Figure 6.10 ▲
Are these the chromosomes of a male or a female?

Sex-Linked Traits

Some genes not related to sex traits are also carried on the X chromosome. In males, traits for the genes carried on the X chromosome that do not match genes on the Y chromosome are always expressed in the offspring. These traits are called sex-linked traits because the genes for them are on the sex chromosome.

A common sex-linked trait is colorblindness. The genes needed to distinguish red from green are on the X chromosome. A female with one defective and one normal X chromosome has normal color vision. However, if a male is missing these genes on his X chromosome, he is colorblind. There are no genes for normal color vision on the Y chromosome to cover for the defective X chromosome.

One way of tracing a trait through generations of offspring is to make a pedigree chart. Figure 6.11 is a pedigree showing how colorblindness was inherited in one family. A horizontal line joining a circle and a square means the couple had children.

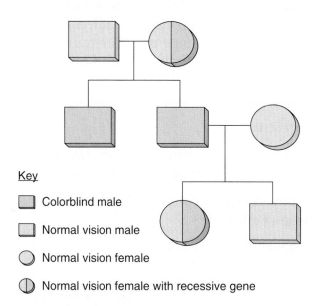

<u>Key</u>

▪ Colorblind male

▫ Normal vision male

◯ Normal vision female

◐ Normal vision female with recessive gene

Figure 6.11 ▲
A pedigree shows how traits are inherited.

Figure 6.12 ▲

Find the extra chromosome in the karyotype (left). People with Down's syndrome can often live normal lives (right).

Science and Technology *Karyotypes*

The photograph of the 23 pairs of human chromosomes in Figure 6.12 is a karyotype. Karyotypes aid in counting and identifying chromosomes. Sometimes there are extra or missing chromosomes. Chromosomes are visible only in dividing cells. To make a karyotype, dividing cells are stained with a dye and then photographed. The individual chromosome pairs are cut out and organized by length on a sheet of paper. Extra or missing chromosomes are then noted.

The karyotype in Figure 6.12 shows an extra number 21 chromosome. This causes a condition called Down's syndrome. This extra chromosome prevents normal development of the eyes, mouth, hands, and brain.

Check and Explain

1. Horses have 32 pairs of chromosomes in their body cells. How many chromosomes are in their sex cells?

2. In humans, how do the chromosomes of a male differ from those of a female?

3. **Reason and Conclude** Why is red-green colorblindness called a sex-linked trait?

4. **Infer** Colorblind females are rare, but they do exist. A colorblind female's parents must have what genotypes?

Activity 6 *How do you make a model of gene inheritance?*

Skills Model; Collect Data; Interpret Data; Infer

Task 1 Prelab Prep

1. Collect 4 strips of paper, each 10 cm long and 2 cm wide.
2. Fold the strips lengthwise. Each strip of paper represents a chromosome carrying a gene pair for one characteristic. One side of a "chromosome" carries one gene, and the other side carries the other gene. Number the strips 1 through 4. Write your initials on each strip.
3. For each of the four characteristics in Table 6.2, select a genotype. You should end up with four different genotypes, such as LL, cc, Dd, and XX.
4. On one side of your first chromosome, write one letter of your chosen earlobe genotype. On the other side, write the other letter. For example, if your genotype is Ll, one side should have a L and the other side a l.
5. Repeat step 4 three times to label the genes of the other three chromosomes.
6. Work with a partner identified by your teacher. Each pair should consist of a male and a female. Your partner should have made up his or her own set of chromosomes.

Task 2 Data Record

1. On a separate sheet of paper, make a chart with a row for each characteristic. Make a column for you and your partner and three columns to represent offspring.
2. Use the chart to record the genotypes and phenotypes of you and your partner, and the results of your chromosome pairing.

Task 3 Procedure

1. At the same time as your partner, take your chromosome number 1, hold it above the floor or table, and drop it. Note the genes that face up on each chromosome. Together they are the gene pair that determine whether a child has free or attached earlobes. Record the genotype and phenotype for this characteristic on your chart.
2. Repeat step 1 with the other three chromosomes.
3. Repeat the pairing process twice to determine the genotypes and phenotypes for a second and third child.

Task 4 Analysis

1. How were the three children alike and different?
2. What were the chances of the child being a female each time? If the first child was a female, what were the chances that the second child would be a female?

Task 5 Conclusion

Use the results of this activity to explain why inheritance is a matter of chance. Is Mendel's conclusion that one trait could be passed on to offspring independently of another trait supported? Explain.

Extension

Add the trait for colorblindness to the X chromosome of the male and to one of the X chromosomes of the female. Repeat the experiment.

Table 6.2 Characteristics

Chromosome	Phenotype	Genotype
1	Free earlobes Attached earlobes	LL or Ll ll
2	Curly hair Straight hair	CC or Cc cc
3	Dimples No dimples	DD or Dd dd
4	Female Male	XX XY

Infer Can you fold your tongue?
Are your earlobes attached?
Infer by the number of people
in your class who answer yes to
each of these questions which
traits are dominant and which
are recessive.

6.3 DNA and the Genetic Code

Objectives

▶ **Describe** the kind of information carried by a gene.

▶ **Describe** the structure of DNA.

▶ **Explain** how DNA replication takes place.

▶ **Communicate** how mutations can be both harmful
and helpful.

L ook closely at the words you are reading right now. Why do they make sense to you? Could you read this page if the words were out of order? Words are a code that you know. The code is your language. Each word transmits information to you. If the words or letters were in a different order, they would make no sense or have a different meaning.

In a similar way, the genes in the cells of your body contain a code called the genetic code. The genetic code is the basis of heredity. Like a language, the genetic code transmits information. A gene is very much like a long sentence in the "language" of heredity.

The Genetic Code

How do you think a gene carries information? How does it tell an organism to have dark hair or to be tall? The language of heredity is a chemical language. A gene is actually a set of instructions for assembling a protein. The genetic code tells a cell how to put together a particular protein piece by piece. But what do proteins have to do with an organism's traits?

Proteins are very important to cells. They perform a variety of tasks depending on their structure. Proteins form most of the cell's substance. They are a part of every cell process. They carry other substances or messages to organs or tissues. Some make hair or skin a certain color. Others stimulate the body to grow longer bones. Still others make it possible for your eyes to distinguish red and green. Proteins have a role in creating all the traits of an individual organism. Thus, by carrying a code for assembling proteins, genes determine traits.

▲ A DNA molecule is shaped like a long ladder twisted into a spiral. Study the model of the DNA molecule above. The uprights of the ladder are alternating sugar and phosphate groups. The rungs of the ladder are nitrogen bases joined in pairs. There are four different nitrogen bases: adenine (A), guanine (G), cytosine (C), and thymine (T). The four bases fit together to make base pairs. A always makes a base pair with T. G always makes a base pair with C. The genetic code is set by the order of nitrogen bases in the DNA.

DNA

Genes are made of a substance called deoxyribonucleic (dee AHKS uh RY boh noo KLAY ihk) acid, which is commonly referred to as DNA. Genes carry coded information due to the special properties of DNA. The way DNA is put together, or its structure, forms a code that is "read" by other parts of a cell. Also, DNA makes identical copies of itself. These properties make it possible for DNA to carry all the information an organism needs to live and reproduce.

A DNA molecule "unzips" to form two strands, as shown below. Notice that as the molecule unzips, the base pairs separate. Each single strand of DNA then picks up bases present in the cell's cytoplasm. In this way, two complete molecules of DNA are created. Notice that each new DNA molecule has the same order of base pairs as the original. This copying process is called **replication**.
▼

Protein   DNA

▲ A gene is a particular sequence of base pairs. When a cell "reads" the genetic code of a gene, it uses an unzipped segment of DNA. Each group of three bases on one of the strands is like a word in the genetic code. The sequence A-C-T means something different from T-C-A. Each of these "words" is one genetic instruction, coding for a particular amino acid.

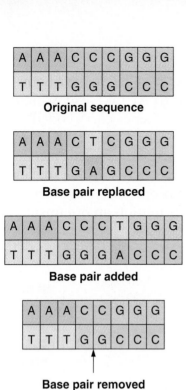

Original sequence

| A | A | A | C | C | C | G | G | G |

| T | T | T | G | G | G | C | C | C |

Base pair replaced

| A | A | A | C | T | C | G | G | G |

| T | T | T | G | A | G | C | C | C |

Base pair added

| A | A | A | C | C | C | T | G | G | G |

| T | T | T | G | G | G | A | C | C | C |

Base pair removed

| A | A | A | C | C | G | G | G |

| T | T | T | G | G | C | C | C |

Figure 6.13 ▲

How does each of these errors change the DNA sequence?

Mutations

When you copy from the blackboard, sometimes you may make mistakes. In a similar way, mistakes occur when DNA and chromosomes replicate. Look at Figure 6.13 to see some common mistakes in replication. Changes in the DNA sequence may cause a different protein to be made.

Another kind of mistake results in larger changes in the hereditary material. Whole pieces of chromosomes may be left out or added when cells divide. A change in DNA or the chromosomes is called a **mutation**. Mutations occur in both body cells and sex cells. Only mutations in sex cells pass on to offspring.

Most mutations are not harmful. A mutation in a body cell might cause that cell to die but have no effect on the body. Sometimes mutations in the sex cells are useful for the species. For example, a mutation could change the size of a food plant or the number of seeds it produces. Some mutations are harmful. Gene mutations in humans may cause as many as 4,000 different diseases and disorders. Some mutations in body cells are known to cause cancer. Some mutations in sex cells can cause birth defects.

Chemical Mutagens

Substances and conditions that increase the chance of mutations are called mutagens. Mutagens can affect DNA and change the genetic code. Mutagens are everywhere in the environment. They are found in some chemicals used for killing insects and in some chemical wastes from factories. Small amounts of these chemicals may get into the air, food, and drinking water. The chemicals in cigaratte smoke are common mutagens.

The sun, some kinds of rocks, and nuclear materials all give off radiation that can increase the rate of mutations. Many devices that run on electricity, such as televisions and computer screens, also give off radiation. In 1986, the explosion of a nuclear power plant at Chernobyl in the Ukraine exposed many people in Eastern Europe to radiation. Nuclear bomb explosions in the 1940s and 1950s increased the level of radiation in the soil and atmosphere in some areas. Prolonged exposure and high doses of mutagens cause genetic changes that may result in cancer.

Inherited Diseases

Many diseases are caused by the effects of inherited genes. In most cases, there is only a small difference between the DNA sequence in the defective gene and a normal one. This difference is enough to cause serious and often fatal diseases. These disease-causing genes are the result of a mutation that occurred long ago. They pass from one generation to the next.

Recessive genes cause most inherited diseases. A person with one of the genes is a carrier. A person with two genes has the disease. Cystic fibrosis is the most common genetic disease of this type in the United States. About one child in every 2,000 is born with cystic fibrosis. The disease causes thick mucus that clogs the airways of the lungs. Bacteria grow on this mucus and destroy the lungs. In 1989, scientists found the gene that causes cystic fibrosis on chromosome 7.

A recessive gene also causes sickle-cell anemia. In people with sickle-cell anemia, most of the red blood cells stiffen and become an odd shape. These diseased cells carry less oxygen than normal cells. The disease is most common among African Americans. About 1 in 500 have sickle-cell anemia and eventually die from it.

Dominant genes cause a few inherited diseases. The most common disease of this type is Huntington's disease. This disease usually strikes people between the ages of 35 and 45. Other kinds of disorders are listed in Table 6.3.

Skills WorkOut

Make a Model Use colored buttons, plastic paper clips, or candies to make a segment of DNA. Use the following code: red = A, green = T, brown = G, yellow = C. Make the following strand of DNA: T-C-C-G-T-A-T-T-T-G-G-T-T-G-G. Make this a double strand using the base-pairing rules: T pairs with A; C pairs with G. Next, model a mutation by remaking the strand with two errors.

Table 6.3   Inherited Disorders in Humans

Disorder	Description	Cause
Albinism	Inability to produce pigment in some or all organs, resulting in abnormally light skin, hair, and eye color	Recessive gene
Achondroplasia (form of dwarfism)	Condition in which person is far below normal size and lacks ability to grow normally	Dominant gene
Huntington's Disease	Progressive loss of muscle control and mental abilities, occurring from about age 35 to 45	Dominant gene
Phenylketonuria (PKU)	Mental retardation (unless treated during infancy) resulting from buildup of phenylalanine, an amino acid in proteins	Recessive gene
Tay-Sachs Disease	Brain cells do not function normally, resulting in progressive loss of motor skills and mental abilities, blindness, and seizures; babies born with Tay-Sachs disease live only for a few years	Recessive gene

Figure 6.14 ▲
How much time do you spend out in the sun? Why is too much sun harmful?

Science and You *Sunburn and DNA Damage*

How many times have you gotten sunburned when you were only in the sun for "a little while"? Ultraviolet radiation given off by the sun burned your skin. Skin damage from ultraviolet, or UV, radiation builds up over a long period of time. UV radiation can damage the DNA in skin cells. Such damage can cause premature aging. With time, UV radiation can cause different forms of skin cancer in some people.

Dark skin has some protection against sunburn and UV radiation. For this reason, skin cancers are rare among people who have large amounts of melanin, such as Africans. However, too much exposure to direct sunlight can damage the skin of all humans.

The health risks posed by exposure to UV radiation increase as the ozone layer thins. Ozone is a gas in the upper atmosphere that filters out most of the UV radiation from the sun. Some kinds of commercial chemicals released into the air destroy the ozone layer.

Sunscreen and sunblock lotions give protection from UV radiation. The sun protection factor, or SPF, is a number on the label that tells you how much UV radiation is blocked out. An SPF of 10 means that a person using this sunscreen receives the same amount of UV radiation in 10 hours that she would receive in 1 hour without the sunscreen. Sunscreens with an SPF of 15 or higher offer the best protection from UV radiation.

UV radiation comes from the sun in two slightly different energy levels, called UVA and UVB. The best sunscreens block out both kinds.

Check and Explain

1. In what form does a gene carry information?

2. If a DNA molecule is "unzipped" and one strand has the code T-A-A-G-G-C, what is the code of the other strand?

3. **Predict** How would heredity in humans be different if all the genes were on two chromosomes?

4. **Communicate** What is a mutation? Explain how some mutations can be harmful, while others are helpful. Give examples.

6.4 Applied Genetics

Objectives

▶ **Explain** how selective breeding has been used to modify the traits of plants and animals.

▶ **Identify** four useful applications of selective breeding.

▶ **Describe** how DNA is changed by genetic engineering.

▶ **Predict** how genetic engineering could be useful.

Skills WarmUp

Communicate If you could invent a perfect apple to eat, what would you do? Describe your perfect apple and how you would go about growing such an apple.

How many different breeds of dogs can you name? What characteristics make one breed different from another? In Figure 6.15, you can see two examples of the different sizes and shapes of dogs.

Even though they are different, all dogs belong to the same species. Dogs can breed with each other because they all have 78 chromosomes. Many different breeds of dogs were developed deliberately over the last 12,000 years. Dog breeders chose individual dogs with desired traits and mated them.

Knowledge of how traits pass from parents to offspring is used to develop desirable traits in other organisms as well. People breed cows that produce more milk, horses that run faster, trees that produce more fruit, and flowers of a certain color.

Selective Breeding

The process of choosing and mating organisms with desired traits is called selective breeding. Most of the plant and animal products you eat are probably the result of selective breeding. Chickens, for example, have been selectively bred to lay more eggs. As a result, the best laying hens today can lay an average of 250 eggs per year. Seventy years ago, the average per year was only 120.

How would you bring out this kind of desirable trait in an organism? Say you had a flock of 100 chickens. You might use the 10 best-laying hens to parent the next generation. You would then select the best layers from their offspring to produce another generation. The ongoing process of breeding the chickens that lay the most eggs has increased egg production more than twofold.

Figure 6.15 ▲
Notice the very different bodies, legs, and ears of these two dogs.

Better Grain for More People

How many kinds of bread can you buy in a market? Wheat, rye, potato, and corn are just a few kinds you might choose. The grain in each kind of bread originated centuries ago in different parts of the world. For example, people ate corn in Mexico and South America 10,000 years ago. Rye originated in the Middle East and was used as grain in Ancient Rome. Wheat was grown in Asia and Europe as early as 4,000 B.C.

People soon began using methods to cross-breed, or hybridize, many different grains. These methods became especially common in the 1800s. They led to the development of plants that resist disease and produce enough grain to feed large numbers of people.

Today cross-breeding techniques are especially useful to people in developing countries, such as India and Brazil. In certain areas of these countries, populations are large, and soil is poor

in nutrients. In the 1970s, scientists developed a grain called triticale. It is a crossbreed of wheat and rye. Triticale has the protein quality of rye, and it can grow in poor soil.

1. What is the advantage of using cross-breeding methods to develop new grains?

2. **Research** Find out what countries grow and use triticale. How much triticale is grown each year?

Figure 6.16 ▲

Genetic engineers transferred a firefly gene to this plant. Notice how the plant now "glows" in the dark.

Genetic Engineering

Using selective breeding, it may take a long time to develop a special trait in an organism. Selective breeding slowly changes particular genes. However, since 1975, scientists have developed an entirely new way of changing the traits of organisms. They actually take genes from one kind of organism and place them in another. This process is called genetic engineering.

Through genetic engineering, scientists can produce organisms with traits that are not possible through selective breeding. Genetic engineers have made fish grow fatter with genes taken from rats. They have developed tobacco plants that produce chemicals normally made by organs in the human body. Genetic engineers have also produced plants that are resistant to frost. They've even produced crops, such as potatoes, that make their own insect repellent. The possibility of custom-designed life forms is almost endless.

Recombinant DNA   Normally the DNA from two different kinds of organisms could never combine. When genetic engineers move genes from organism to organism, they create new DNA. This new DNA is called recombinant DNA.

For recombinant DNA to change an organism's traits, it must be in every cell of the organism's body. For this reason, the DNA in single-celled organisms, such as bacteria, is the easiest to change. The bacterium passes on to its offspring any change made in its DNA.

Look at Figure 6.17. It shows how a human gene is added to the genetic material of a bacterium. The small ring inside the bacterium is a piece of DNA that many bacteria have in addition to their larger chromosome. It is called a plasmid. Using special enzymes, the plasmid is split open. A human gene is then "spliced" into the plasmid and the ends rejoined.

Bacteria as Chemical Factories   The gene added to the bacterium in Figure 6.17 carries instructions for producing a human protein. As the bacterium and its offspring carry on their life processes, they produce this human protein.

One human gene that genetic engineers have spliced into bacteria is the gene for the hormone insulin. Insulin is normally made by the pancreas. The pancreas of a person with diabetes cannot make insulin. Diabetics can live normal lives, however, by taking the insulin made by genetically altered bacteria. Engineered bacteria produce many other useful substances, such as human growth hormone, a protein to treat anemia, and a substance that may help fight cancer.

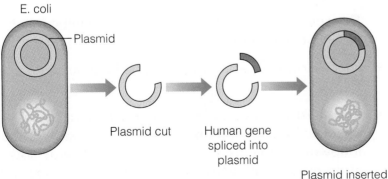

E. coli

Plasmid

Plasmid cut

Human gene spliced into plasmid

Plasmid inserted into E. coli

◀ **Figure 6.17**
The genetically-engineered bacterium will faithfully replicate the human gene in its plasmid. All of its offspring will carry out the instructions in the new gene.

Science and Technology
The Human Genome Project

Together all the genes of a species make up its *genome*. The human genome has 50,000 to 100,000 genes. In 1988, scientists began a project that would "read" the entire library of genetic information contained in the human genome. The project includes scientists from all over the world and will cost $3 billion or more. Scientists expect to complete the project around the year 2005.

The data from this project will be used to make a map of each chromosome. To give you an idea of how complicated this is, imagine creating a map that shows every building on every street in every city and town in the United States! To start, scientists must cut the chromosomes into smaller and smaller pieces to study them.

Using computers, people in hundreds of laboratories then store and track all the accumulated information. Scientists will also use special sequencing machines to determine the sequence of base pairs in DNA.

The chromosome maps will show the location of genes that cause diseases such as cancer and heart disease. Genes that protect some humans from certain diseases may also be found. Once these human genes are mapped, it may be possible to detect and remove disease-causing genes. The human genome project, therefore, offers the possibility of curing many inherited diseases.

Figure 6.18 ▲

A computer helps tell scientists the order of base pairs on a short piece of human DNA.

Check and Explain

1. Explain how breeders get the most desirable traits in dogs.

2. How do genetic engineers change the genetic material on a chromosome?

3. **Infer** How does selective breeding help farmers? Explain.

4. **Hypothesize** Describe how genetic engineering and/or selective breeding might be used to solve each of the following problems: lack of a human hormone; low grain production; food plants destroyed by a specific disease; poor wool quality in a herd of sheep.

Chapter 6 Review

Concept Summary

6.1 Basic Principles of Heredity
▶ Every living thing is identified by its traits.
▶ Individual traits are determined by genes, which are either dominant or recessive. A recessive gene is masked by a dominant gene.
▶ Offspring receive one gene from each parent.

6.2 Chromosomes and Inheritance
▶ Genes are located on the chromosomes.
▶ A sex cell containing one set of single chromosomes is formed during meiosis.
▶ The X and Y chromosomes determine sex in humans.
▶ Sex-linked traits can occur in males because the Y chromosome cannot make up for the effects of genes on the X chromosome.

6.3 DNA and the Genetic Code
▶ All the information an organism needs to live and reproduce is carried by DNA.
▶ The sequence of the base pairs in DNA makes up instructions for assembling proteins.
▶ DNA can make copies of itself through the process of replication.

6.4 Applied Genetics
▶ Selective breeding can bring out desired traits in a species.
▶ Genetic engineering is the insertion of a gene from one species into the DNA of another.

Chapter Vocabulary

heredity (6.1)	recessive (6.1)	gamete (6.1)	Y chromosome (6.2)
genetics (6.1)	phenotype (6.1)	incomplete dominance (6.1)	replication (6.3)
gene (6.1)	genotype (6.1)	meiosis (6.2)	mutation (6.3)
dominant (6.1)	hybrid (6.1)	X chromosome (6.2)	

Check Your Vocabulary

Use the vocabulary words above to complete the following sentences correctly.

1. The first work in ____ was done by Gregor Mendel with pea plants.

2. A ____ is a unit of DNA inherited by an organism.

3. A ____ gene is masked if it is paired with a dominant gene.

4. A ____ is the gene combination for a single trait.

5. Of the two sex chromosomes, the ____ has fewer genes.

6. A duplicate DNA molecule forms during ____ .

7. A female has two ____ .

8. The trait that shows in an organism is its ____ .

9. A ____ gene is always expressed.

10. During ____ , cells are formed with one set of unpaired chromosomes.

11. When each parent breeds pure for a different trait, the offspring is called a ____ .

12. A ____ causes a change in the DNA of a cell.

13. A trait somewhere between two others is a result of ____ .

14. A sex cell is called a ____ .

15. ____ is the passing of traits from parent to offspring.

Chapter 6 Review

Check Your Knowledge

Answer the following in complete sentences.

1. When pure-breeding plants are self-pollinated, what will be the genotype of their offspring?

2. What does the genetic code do?

3. What is produced during meiosis?

4. What set of human chromosomes is not always identical?

5. What kind of cells are most commonly used in genetic engineering? Why?

6. What is incomplete dominance? Give an example.

7. When is a mutation harmful? When is a mutation helpful? Give examples of both.

Choose the answer that best completes each sentence.

8. The results of a genetic cross can be predicted by using a (puzzle, line graph, set of equations, Punnett square).

9. Of the four nitrogen bases, adenine always pairs with (guanine, cytosine, thymine, protein).

10. The number of chromosomes in a many-celled organism is always (odd, large, greater than 20, even).

11. A gene is a set of instructions for assembling a (protein, chromosome, trait, genotype).

12. Meiosis produces gametes with (one, two, three, four) set(s) of unpaired chromosomes.

13. A combination of a dominant and recessive trait is a (phenotype, genotype, hybrid, factor).

Check Your Understanding

Apply the concepts you have learned to answer each question.

1. What is the difference between mutations in sex cells and mutations in body cells?

2. **Infer** Just as some people have an extra twenty-first chromosome, others have an extra sex chromosome. What do you think would be the gender of someone with two X chromosomes and a Y?

3. Explain what happens to the chromosomes in a cell during meiosis.

4. How is it possible for a person to carry a genetic disease without actually having it?

5. **Predict** Use a Punnett square to show the results of a cross between two parents, each with one dominant gene for curly hair.

6. **Mystery Photo** The photograph on page 110 shows an ear of ornamental corn. This kind of corn has been selectively bred to have kernels with different colors. If you looked at two ears of this kind of corn, do you think the color patterns would be exactly the same? Why or why not?

7. A boy's father is not colorblind. Is it possible for the boy to be colorblind?

8. **Application** Many scientists are concerned that genetic engineering may be dangerous. What do you think they worry about happening?

9. **Extension** Why do dog breeders want to know the pedigrees of all their animals as far back as possible?

Develop Your Skills

Use the skills you have developed in this chapter to complete each activity.

1. **Interpret Data** The pedigree below shows the inheritance of a trait called achondroplasia in a certain family. Achondroplasia is a form of dwarfism. It is rare, but the gene that causes it is dominant. Blue symbols in the pedigree indicate individuals with achondroplasia. Squares stand for males and circles for females.

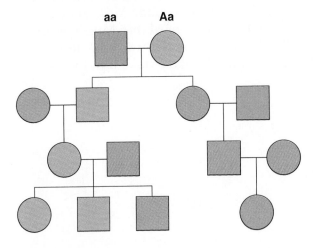

a. What is the genotype of the achondroplasic son in the first generation?

b. If the average–height daughter in the third generation marries an average–height man, can they have any achondroplasic children?

2. **Data Bank** Use the information on page 624 to answer the following questions.

a. When Mendel crossed a pure yellow-seeded pea with a pure green-seeded pea, what seed color did all the offspring have?

b. When the offspring of this cross were crossed with each other, how many yellow-seeded plants resulted? How many green-seeded plants?

Make Connections

1. **Link the Concepts** Draw a concept map showing how the concepts below link together. Add terms to connect, or link, the concepts.

genes	genetic code
cytosine	mutation
chromosomes	proteins
adenine	DNA
nitrogen bases	thymine
guanine	

2. **Science and Math** How is the chance of a human baby being a boy or girl similar to the chance of a tossed coin landing heads or tails? Use a coin toss to explain why there is a 50-50 chance of the baby being a girl.

3. **Science and You** Do a survey of the eye colors of the people in your class. Graph the results. What is the most common eye color? What can you infer about the genes that determine eye color?

4. **Science and Society** Write a paragraph discussing the problems a colorblind person might have when buying clothes, crossing the street, using makeup, or painting a picture. What could be done to solve these problems?

5. **Science and Technology** Find out what genetically engineered organisms have been produced recently. Describe what their added genes are meant to do.

6. **Science and Math** Recall that there are four nitrogen bases and that a group of three bases, called a triplet, forms a code for a certain amino acid. Determine the number of possible triplet codes.

Science and Literature Connection

The Plant People

The following excerpt is from the book The Plant People *by Dale Carlson*

Sam bent over a microscope in the school lab. He was examining a piece of Nancy Ward's skin. She hadn't minded when he cut her. She didn't mind anything, now.

"It's impossible," said Sam.

They'd all seen some terrible things. But this was a nightmare!

Mike put his eye to the microscope. Then he straightened up.

"I think I know." Mike's voice trembled.

"What?" asked Sam.

"There's been a change." Mike breathed deeply. When he spoke again, his voice was steady. "A change in the cells. Some are still human. Others look like plant cells."

"Look like?" said Sam. "They are the cells of a plant!"

Mike broke down. "How can skin change like that?!" he cried.

"I don't know," said Sam in defeat. "I just don't know enough about science, Mike. I can tell you what's happening. But I can't tell why or how. . . ."

Mike left the school. He had to phone Carson City. Every day he telephoned. "We'll send someone down" the police kept promising. But they seemed in no hurry.

People wandered the streets. More than usual, Mike thought. They seemed to be looking for something. They stopped at the sight of growing things. . . .

[Mike] felt a hand grip his arm. It was Larry Borden, [a classmate]. Mike saw that Larry's skin was really bad. He didn't, or couldn't talk. But he seemed to want something. And he made Mike understand. He looked hard into Mike's eyes. Then, Larry pointed toward the desert. Larry wanted Mike to take him there. . . .

They rode out of town. In the desert, Larry began to breathe harder. He was excited. . . . Like a sleepwalker, he moved slowly. He stopped at a cactus. Before Mike could get to him, Larry plunged his hand into the thorns.

[In an instant, Mike] was by Larry's side. He wanted to help Larry deal with the pain from the thorns. But there was no pain. On Larry's face there was nothing but pleasure.

It seemed impossible. But how could anything be impossible? Mike knew exactly what he had seen. It was called osmosis. Larry had taken food into his body through his skin!

Now Mike knew why nobody had been eating. . . . They couldn't eat food through their mouths. . . . But why had Larry needed to go out to the desert? Why not eat in his own backyard? Was there some human feeling left in him? Mike would never know. Larry Borden no longer talked.

Back in town, a terrible sight waited for Mike. The people were reaching for leaves. They were grasping for whole plants. And not just with their hands. With every part of their bodies! They ate, touching their skins to the food.

Skills in Science

Reading Skills in Science

1. **Classify** How would you best classify this text: fiction, science-fiction, or nonfiction? Give evidence for your response.

2. **Find Context Clues** What observations did Mike make that led him to conclude that Larry and other members of the town had begun to take on plantlike traits?

3. **Find the Main Idea** What was it that Larry needed Mike to do? Quote the sentence containing this information.

Writing Skills in Science

1. **Compare and Contrast** Describe the two kinds of cells in Nancy Ward's skin that Mike observed through the microscope.

2. **If . . . Then Arguments** How would your life be different if the cells in your body underwent the same type of change as Larry's body cells?

Activities

Evaluate Sources Compare the author's description of osmosis with the discussion of it in your textbook. Does the author of this story describe osmosis accurately?

Experiment Design an activity using thin slices of cucumber and salt water to illustrate the process of osmosis.

Predict Suppose Mike had not taken Larry out to the desert. Design a skit to show what might have happened to Larry.

Where to Read More

Cactus, the All-American Plant by Anita Holmes. Four Winds, 1982. This book examines the Sonoran cacti, provides tips for raising the plants, and includes recipes for cooking with cactus!

Cactus by Cynthia Overbeck. Lerner, 1982. A detailed study of the parts of a cactus plant and how the organism is adapted to its unique environment.

Unit 3
Evolution and Classification

Chapters

Data Bank

Use the information on pages 624 to 631 to answer the following questions about topics explored in this unit.

Classifying

What is the species name of a dog? What is the species name of a polar bear?

Interpreting Data

What epochs make up the Cenozoic era? Which of these epochs is most recent?

Observing

In what ways are all the animals on the chart related on page 628? Describe some physical characteristics that these animals have in common.

Reading a Table

During which period in the earth's history did the first mammals appear? When did dinosaurs die out?

The photograph to the left is of crabs on rocks in the Galápagos Islands. What other kinds of organisms might you find on these islands?

Chapter 7

Diversity of Living Things

What do you see?

"I see a grayish-green bug. It's on a tree, maybe a redwood. The bug looks like a piece of mold. It might use this technique for camouflage. It has four long, skinny legs and two short, big legs. The tail looks like an old samurai helmet, and the head looks like a rectangle with a circle on each short side. It has two short antennas, also."

Joshua Wragg
Whitford School
Beaverton, Oregon

To find out about the photograph, look on page 154. As you read the chapter, you will learn more about the variety of living things.

7.1 Diversity and Adaptation

Objectives

▶ **Define** and **explain** the term *adaptation*.

▶ **Explain** why different organisms living in the same habitat may have similar adaptations.

▶ **Infer** how organisms use their senses to adapt to their environment.

What makes one kind of organism different from another? Look at the birds in Figure 7.1. How are the ostrich and hummingbird different? You can see that each bird has a beak, wings, and feet, but each body part is a different size and shape. These structural differences in their body parts not only make them look different from one another, but they are also used differently.

In every living thing, the body structure is important to survival. The hummingbird's wings, for example, allow it to hover at a flower while it sucks nectar with its long, narrow beak. The ostrich's long, powerful legs allow it to run at fast speeds. Every kind of organism is unique because of its special characteristics and how it uses them to live.

Adaptations

A characteristic, structure, or behavior that helps an organism live is an **adaptation**. Adaptations help organisms get food, protect themselves, move, reproduce, and carry on life processes. The sharp teeth and claws of a tiger are an adaptation for catching and eating prey. A chameleon's long, sticky tongue is an adaptation for catching insects. The joints of your legs are an adaptation for walking.

An organism's adaptations help it survive in a particular **habitat**. A habitat is the area or place where an organism lives. With its adaptations, an organism is adapted to its habitat. The emperor penguin, for example, has adaptations that help it live successfully in an extremely cold climate, where other birds, such as robins and sparrows, could not live.

Figure 7.1 ▲
How are the hummingbird's adaptations different from the ostrich's?

Diversity of Adaptations

As you may know, many different habitats exist on the earth. Each habitat has a variety of organisms that live there in different ways. This variety of life is called **diversity**.

Below you can see some examples of the many adaptations that living things have. As you look at each organism, imagine the kind of habitat in which it lives. Think about how the organism uses all its adaptations to survive in that habitat.

▲ Coconuts, which are the seeds of one kind of palm tree, can float from island to island because of their thick, airy husks.

The long, broad wings of a turkey vulture help it glide and soar without using large amounts of energy. ▼

▲ Jackrabbits living in the desert have long ears that provide a large body surface for giving off extra heat.

Bats can move freely in darkness by sending out sound waves. When the sound waves hit an object, they echo back to the bat's large ears. ▼

▲ The powerful front legs and half-meter-long tongue of the anteater help it get into the hard mounds of termites.

▲ Dandelion seeds are carried on the wind by an umbrellalike structure. Dandelions can spread over large areas.

Patterns of Adaptations

Many adaptations are found in more than one kind of organism. Similar adaptations occur in organisms for two main reasons.

Organisms in the Same Habitat In order to survive the same kinds of conditions, organisms need similar adaptations. For example, animals living in cold areas tend to have rounded bodies with short limbs and small ears. Can you name some animals that fit this description? These body shapes expose the least amount of body surface to the cold environment and help conserve body heat.

Look at Figure 7.2. Notice the similarities in the two plants. Plants that live in very hot, dry areas have similar adaptations. Most have thick, small, hairy leaves or no leaves at all. Since plants lose water through their leaves, these adaptations help desert plants conserve water.

Figure 7.2 ▲
These two plants live on opposite sides of the world. However, they have similar adaptations because they both live in dry habitats.

Related Organisms Organisms may have similar adaptations because they are related to each other. Large groups of organisms have the same general adaptations needed for survival. For example, all plants have cell walls and almost all plants have chlorophyll to capture energy from sunlight.

Groups of more closely related organisms also have adaptations in common. All birds have wings and use beaks to get food, no matter where they live. All fishes have gills and fins. Frogs and toads both have strong back legs for hopping. Sea turtles have shells similar to the shells of pond turtles.

Organisms that are related to each other may have similar structures, even though the structures are used differently. Look at the different front limbs in Figure 7.3. How are these structures similar? How is each used?

Figure 7.3 ▲
Humans, cats, whales, and all other mammals have similar front limbs. They are made up of the same kinds of bones put together in the same way. Only the shape and size of each bone vary.

Species

Living things that share a large number of characteristics and adaptations are identified as one kind of organism, called a **species**. A species is made up of organisms that look alike. Members of a species can mate and reproduce young that can reproduce.

All the members of a species have some adaptations that distinguish them from other species. For example, the panda has a sixth finger for stripping leaves off bamboo stems. This special finger developed from a wrist bone. It is an adaptation that is not shared by any other animal. Consequently, pandas are not the same species as bears, even though they look a lot alike.

Any two individuals in a species are never exactly the same, however. For example, you and your friends all look different from each other, but you are all human beings. Sometimes it is very difficult to tell whether two organisms belong to the same or different species

Figure 7.4 ▲
All pandas belong to the same species.

SkillBuilder *Estimating*

The Effect of Adaptations

Use small white beans and dark beans, such as lima beans, to represent mice. You'll need about 40 white beans and 40 dark beans altogether. Pretend you are an owl that preys on mice. A 10-second pickup period represents one week.

Scatter 20 dark beans and 20 white beans over a square white surface that measures 9 sq m. Pick up beans for 10 seconds. Pick up only one bean at a time and put it down before picking up another. Record the number picked up. For each bean you missed, add 2 beans of each color to the square. Repeat this procedure two more times. Be sure to record the numbers.

1. In three "weeks," how many light "mice" could the "owl" pick up from the surface? How many dark mice could the owl pick up?

2. Which color of mouse is most protected from the owl? How is color an adaptation?

3. Make a graph like the one shown below to show the trend of the decrease or increase of the mouse population over time. Use one color for white and one color for dark to show your estimations.

---

because of individual variation. For example, German shepherds and French poodles look different, but they belong to the same species.

Look at the elephants in Figure 7.5. Are they members of the same species? They have similar adaptations, but they are not exactly the same. What differences do you notice? One is an African elephant and the other is an Indian elephant. You may be surprised to know that they belong to different species.

Science and You
Helping Out Your Adaptations

You share adaptations with people all over the world. All people are endothermic and have a protective coating of skin. All people see things in three dimensions, and most people see things in color.

Sometimes your adaptations are limited. You probably don't notice how you overcome these limitations. For example, your body temperature remains constant, but you still get cold. How do you adapt? You help maintain your internal temperature by wearing warm clothing and by heating your surroundings.

How do you adapt to the limitations of your eyes? For example, if you can't see something from a great distance, you may use a telescope or binoculars to overcome this limitation. Many people wear corrective lenses to see things more clearly, both up close and far away. What other limitations do you have? How do you adapt to these limitations?

Figure 7.5 ▲
The African elephant (top) and the Indian elephant (bottom) are different species.

Check and Explain

1. What is an adaptation? Give a few examples from both humans and other organisms.

2. What adaptations do humans have that make it possible for them to ride a bicycle?

3. **Compare and Contrast** Explain how the bones in Figure 7.3 on page 141 are adapted for the survival of each organism.

4. **Infer** Explain how sight, touch, and smell are useful adaptations for a family of new kittens.

7.2 Variation and Reproduction

Objectives

▶ **Describe** how the members of a species may vary.

▶ **Explain** how sexual reproduction helps produce variation in a species.

▶ **Compare** and **contrast** the amount of trait variation possible in sexual and asexual reproduction.

▶ **Estimate** the amount of trait variation that can occur in a group.

---

ook at the kittens in Figure 7.6. How are they alike? How are they different? Even though they have similar ears and body shapes, their color patterns and sizes are not the same. Still, each kitten resembles its parents. As you know, this resemblance is the result of inheriting genes from both parents. Because each kitten looks a little different from its parents and from its brothers and sisters, this family of kittens has a variety of traits.

Variation

The differences among the kittens is an example of **variation** within a species. Variation is easy to see among humans. We are all different shapes, sizes, and colors. In what ways do you vary from your friends and the members of your family?

If you look closely, you can see that differences exist among the individuals of almost every species. Dogs, horses, apple trees, goldfish, and other species can have a great deal of variation. The variation in these species is increased intentionally by the people who breed them.

Species that reproduce in the wild also have variations. For example, individual ladybugs have different numbers of spots. Two pine trees of the same species will have different shapes. Even bacteria show differences in their ability to resist the drugs that were designed to kill them. Within a species, individual variation shows up in physical traits and in the genetic material.

Figure 7.6 ▲
Kittens in a litter often have very different color patterns.

Sexual Reproduction

Remember that when two members of the same species reproduce, each contributes genetic material to the offspring. This form of reproduction is called **sexual reproduction**. Sexual reproduction results in a new combination of genetic material that is unique in the species.

Since each new combination of genes is unique, each individual in a species varies slightly from the others. Sexual reproduction is responsible for the variation within a species.

Sexual reproduction produces new genetic combinations for two reasons. During the formation of gametes, or sex cells, the genetic material of the individual is shuffled. Recall that the gametes are the result of meiosis. During meiosis, the chromosome pairs intertwine and trade genes. In humans, the genes on the 23 pairs of chromosomes can be shuffled into at least eight million different combinations. Consequently, each gamete has a unique combination of genes.

Remember also that each parent contributes one set of genes. The two sets of genes combine when two gametes come together to form a fertilized egg, or **zygote**. The zygote contains a completely random and unique assortment of genes.

Most species reproduce sexually. However, not all living things need a partner to reproduce. A single-celled organism, for example, divides by fission to form two new individuals. The new cells get their genes from just one parent. Thus the two cells are exact copies of each other. When reproduction takes place through the copying of just one individual's genetic material, it is called **asexual reproduction**.

A large number of species that reproduce asexually can also reproduce sexually. Some have developed other ways of exchanging genetic material. The paramecium, for example, can join with another of its kind and trade pieces of DNA. This process creates variation among parameciums.

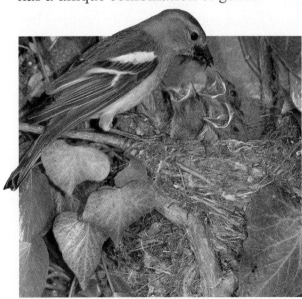

Figure 7.7 ▲
These chaffinch chicks were produced sexually. Each has a unique set of genes.

Figure 7.8 ▲
These parameciums are conjugating, or exchanging genetic material.

Genetic Diversity

Variation within a species occurs when there are different forms of the same genes. You learned that sexual reproduction creates new combinations of genes, but how are different genes created in the first place? Genes change when a mutation occurs.

Mutations happen all the time in a species. A small number of the genes changed by mutation survive and are passed on. They become part of the species' gene pool. As a result of mutation and sexual reproduction, the genes of the individuals in a species show variety.

 Science and You *Variation in Humans*

Look at the variety of features in human beings. Not only are eyes different colors, but often the color and texture of hair is not the same. Body parts, such as legs, arms, ears, and noses, are different sizes and shapes. Fingerprints are different. Each human is unique.

In other ways, however, all humans are very much alike. Many of the features that make individuals look different are really only "skin deep." Differences in skin color, for example, are very noticeable. However, these differences are simply the result of a greater or lesser amount of a protein called melanin.

Despite variation, every human being shares a huge number of the same genes and proteins with humans living all over the world.

Skills WorkOut

Classify Look through old magazines to find as many photographs of the *same* animal species as you can. Cut out the photos and decide on an order in which to arrange them on a posterboard. For example, you may choose to arrange the animals by size. Glue the pictures onto the posterboard. Describe the characteristics you used to arrange the individuals. In what other ways could you arrange the photographs? How much variation occurs in the species? Describe the average individual in the species.

Check and Explain

1. How is a single individual alike and different from the other members of its species?

2. Explain how reproduction affects variation in a species.

3. **Define Operationally** Why are so many gene combinations possible in sexual reproduction?

4. **Estimate** Measure and record your arm length from the tip of your middle finger to your elbow. Estimate the arm length of ten classmates. Find out the actual lengths and graph the results. How much do arm lengths vary?

Activity 7   *How do beans vary?*

Skills   Measure; Observe; Classify

Task 1   Prelab Prep

1. Collect the following items: 2 sheets of paper, pencil, metric ruler, 10 beans of the same variety. Use pinto beans or any kind of striped or textured bean.
2. On a sheet of paper, draw 10 squares. Number each square from 1 to 10. Place one bean in each square. Use this grid for identifying the beans.

Task 2   Data Record

1. On the other sheet of paper, prepare a data table like the one shown.
2. Record each observation and measurement in the data table.

Table 7.1   Bean Observations

Bean	Color	Length	Markings	Texture
1				
2				
3				
4				
5				
6				
7				
8				
9				
10				

Task 3   Procedure

1. Note and record the color of each bean. Look carefully for small differences among the beans. Include any variation of color in your data.

2. Measure and record the length of each bean.
3. Examine each bean for stripes, spots, or any other kind of marking. Note all your observations of each bean in the data table.

Task 4   Analysis

1. What is the range of length for this variety of bean?
2. How many color variations did you observe? What color is the most common?
3. What kind of marking and/or texture do the beans have? Which marking is the most common? Which marking is the least common?
4. Did you find any bean with a characteristic shared by no other bean? What is this unique characteristic? If you examined 10 other beans, would you expect to see another bean with this characteristic?

Task 5   Conclusion

Write a short paragraph describing the variations that appear in this variety of bean. Include the most varied trait you observed in the beans. Identify as many variations as you can.

Everyday Application

Suppose this kind of bean must be soaked in water before cooking, and each bean doubles in volume when soaked. The beans are sorted and sold by size. What would be the difference in the volume of water for one liter of the largest-sized and one liter of the smallest-sized beans? Explain your conclusions.

Extension

Use reference books to find out how other organisms of the same species are different. You can choose a species of plant, a species of mammal, or another kind of animal. Write down all the characteristics that make the members of the species both alike and different.

7.3 Natural Selection

Objectives

▶ **Describe** some of the observations that puzzled Darwin on his voyage.

▶ **State** Darwin's theory of evolution by natural selection.

▶ **Explain** how a new species may arise.

▶ **Communicate** how changes in traits are important to the survival of a species.

Imagine that you are asked to go on a voyage around the world. Of course, the journey could be dangerous and might take several years. You're excited about going, but your parents try to discourage you. This was the situation of young Charles Darwin during the autumn of 1831.

At age 22, Darwin accepted the offer. In December, he set off on the *Beagle*, a medium-sized sailing ship. The main goal of the voyage was to study and chart stretches of the South American coastline. Darwin was to be the ship's naturalist, a person who studies the world of nature.

The voyage lasted five years. During that time, Darwin saw an incredible number of different living things. The variety of patterns in nature puzzled him. He spent the years after his return working out a theory to account for his observations. This theory eventually caused a revolution in the study of biology.

Voyage of the *Beagle*

Darwin had studied the plants and animals of England before he set sail on the *Beagle*. He was also familiar with the ideas of the scientists of his time. Most scientists believed that the earth and life on it had always been the same.

During the first part of the voyage, Darwin explored the tropical forests, the plains, and the very cold places in South America. He noticed that nearly every living thing there was very different from living things in England. Even in South American climates similar to those in

Figure 7.9 ▲
This is a portrait of Darwin about 19 years after his voyage on the *Beagle*.

England, organisms were more similar to organisms in other parts of South America than they were to English organisms. Darwin wondered why the life forms in these two places were so different when the climates were similar.

Darwin also found many fossils. They were the remains of organisms that no longer existed. Why did they die out? Many of the fossils were similar to living organisms. But curiously, they were always much bigger. One fossil find was very perplexing. High up on a mountain, Darwin found fossils of organisms that had once lived in the ocean. Why were they now so far from the sea?

Galápagos Islands   Darwin's ideas were greatly influenced by the life forms on the Galápagos Islands. These 16 islands form a chain off the west coast of South America near the equator. Almost all the organisms Darwin found on these islands were not found anywhere else. Giant tortoises roamed the islands. Iguanas sunned themselves on the rocky shores and ate food from the ocean. Even more interesting to Darwin was that each island had many plants and animals that were different from those on the other islands.

Darwin collected 13 species of finches on the Galápagos Islands. Each had a different kind of beak, as you can see in Figure 7.10. Some had large, thick beaks for cracking seeds. Others had narrower beaks for eating insects. A few species had beaks suitable for eating cacti. The finches puzzled Darwin. In most places, finches had one kind of beak. The other kinds of beaks belonged to very different kinds of birds.

Theory of Evolution   After his return to England, Darwin worked over 20 years to answer the many questions raised by his observations. Darwin had seen evidence everywhere that the surface of the earth had changed and was still changing. He concluded that if organisms in this changing world did not change along with it, they could not survive. In 1859, he published his ideas in a book, *The Origin of Species*.

Darwin claimed that organisms are the products of historical change and that new species gradually developed from previous ones. He concluded that all life shares a single and complex history. These ideas make up Darwin's theory of **evolution**. In biology, evolution is the process by which species change over time.

Figure 7.10 ▲
Notice how the beaks of the Galápagos Islands finches vary. Why is a large, thick beak most suitable for cracking seeds?

Natural Selection

In addition to claiming that life forms had evolved, Darwin hypothesized on *how* they evolved. Darwin called his hypothesis **natural selection**. Natural selection is the process by which those organisms best adapted to their environment survive and pass their traits on to the next generation. Natural selection works on a **population** of organisms, not individuals. A population is a group of individuals of the same species living in a particular area.

Darwin based natural selection on four conditions he observed in nature.

Overproduction   Living things produce more young than can survive. Populations tend to stay the same size over a period of time, despite the large number of young produced.

Limited Resources   Food, water, space, and other resources are limited. Members of a population must compete for these limited resources. Darwin called this the *struggle for existence*.

Variation   Not all individuals in a population are exactly the same. Their traits vary slightly. These variations can be passed from parents to offspring.

Advantage of Some Variations   Some variations can determine which individuals will survive the struggle for existence and reproduce.

When these conditions hold true, organisms best adapted to a particular habitat live and produce more offspring like themselves. Organisms that are not well adapted have a greater chance of dying before they can reproduce. Over

generations, the number of well-adapted individuals increases. As a result, the traits and characteristics of the population as a whole change.

Darwin did not know about the genetic basis of inheritance. Today we know that natural selection changes the genetic makeup of a population. Certain genes that result in better adaptations become more common than others. Because of natural selection, a population always tends to be adapted to its habitat. When a habitat changes, individuals adapted to the new conditions survive and reproduce.

Darwin's theory of natural selection competed with other explanations of how organisms evolved. Jean Lamarck, a French biologist in the early 1800s, argued that a species changed because offspring inherited traits that their parents developed during their lives. Thus, if a giraffe's neck became longer from stretching for leaves high in trees, the giraffe's offspring would inherit the longer neck.

Many people accepted Lamarck's hypothesis. However, most scientists gradually realized that natural selection better explained evolution.

Figure 7.11 ▲
The brook trout overproduces offspring. Which ones are most likely to survive?

New Species

Just as natural selection can explain changes in a species, it can also explain how one species evolves from another. This evolutionary process is called *speciation*. Speciation begins when a portion of the population of a species becomes isolated. A population is referred to as separate when its members are not able to breed with other members of the population. Speciation can occur in several ways. Populations may be divided by a newly formed canyon or mountain range. Fish populations might be separated by the division of a lake. A pair of birds might fly to an island and start a separate population there.

Once a population is isolated, it can change in a different way from other groups. Mutations might occur in the isolated population. A gene might become more common through the process of natural selection. Over a period of time, members of the isolated population

Skills WorkOut

Classify   Explore a vacant lot. Take a leaf sample from each different kind of plant growing there. Classify each leaf by color, size, and shape. Think about the climate of the lot. What characteristics do the plants have in common that are suited to the climate?

Historical Notebook

Natural Selection in Action

The peppered moth lives around the city of Manchester, England. The moth rests on the trunks of trees. Color varies in this species, so the moths can be either light or dark.

Before 1848, only light-colored moths were seen. Then people began to notice fewer light-colored moths, and began to see dark-colored ones. By 1898, nearly all of the moths around Manchester were dark-colored.

In the 1950s, H. B. Kettlewell looked for a reason why the color of the moth population had changed. He suspected that the increased burning of coal in the 1800s had changed the moths' habitat. Soot from Manchester's factories had blackened the nearby trees. Did this make the light-colored moths more visible to predators? Kettlewell set up an experiment to test this hypothesis. He found that dark-colored moths did have an advantage when the trees were darkened with soot.

1. How did the peppered moths' habitat change in the late 1800s?

2. **Write**   How did the change in the moths' habitat affect the moths' traits? Write how this is an example of natural selection.

Figure 7.12 ▲
Australian animals have been isolated for millions of years. As a result, species like the swamp wallaby (top) and the wombat (bottom) are found nowhere else.

may look very different. Their genes may be different enough to make interbreeding impossible with the organisms that were once part of the same species. The isolated population has become a different species.

The finches on the Galápagos Islands developed into 13 separate species in this way. The population on each island was separate from the others. As each population evolved, the beaks of the finches adapted to eating the form of food most available on the island. The pouched animals of Australia are another example of organisms that evolved as separate species because of isolation.

Science and Technology *Germplasm Banks*

Just as you put money in a bank for safekeeping, there are banks for keeping safe the genetic information in seeds, or the plant's germplasm. Germplasm banks located throughout the United States make up the National Plant Germplasm System. A typical seed bank contains about a billion seeds. Almost 500,000 types of seed samples are stored throughout the United States.

The purpose of these banks is to collect, store, catalog, and distribute the germplasm of every species and variety of plant in the world. This system not only stores seeds and plant parts, but it also preserves living plants. Germplasm repositories store species of plants that lose their variation if they are stored only as seeds.

The banks are important because they ensure against losing the genetic material of wild plants. Also, they provide germplasm with traits for breeding crop plants that can resist certain kinds of pests and disease.

Check and Explain

1. What did Darwin notice that was unique about the animal and plant life on the Galápagos Islands?

2. What important hypothesis did Darwin develop by studying the beaks of finches?

3. **Reason and Conclude**   Why did Darwin's concept of natural selection cause a revolution in biology?

4. **Communicate**   Explain how changes in the traits of a species can be important to its survival.

Chapter 7 Review

Concept Summary

7.1 Diversity and Adaptation

▶ An adaptation is a characteristic that helps an organism reproduce and survive in an environment.

▶ Adaptations are similar in different species if the adaptation is necessary for survival, or if the organisms are related to one another.

▶ The variety of organisms that live in an environment is called diversity.

7.2 Variation and Reproduction

▶ The different traits in the individuals of a species is variation within the species.

▶ Since both parents contribute genetic material during sexual reproduction, the traits of the offspring are a unique combination of genes.

▶ Asexual reproduction occurs when a single organism divides to produce another organism with identical genetic material.

7.3 Natural Selection

▶ Charles Darwin observed many plant and animal species in South America that did not exist anywhere else.

▶ The fossils of ocean organisms discovered in high mountains caused Darwin to infer that the earth's environment changes over time.

▶ Darwin based his theory of evolution on the hypothesis that species change when the organisms most adapted to an environment survive and pass their genes to the next generation.

▶ Speciation occurs when a population of organisms is isolated, or when survival depends on a certain characteristic and those individuals without it die.

Chapter Vocabulary

adaptation (7.1)	species (7.1)	zygote (7.2)	natural selection (7.3)
habitat (7.1)	variation (7.2)	evolution (7.3)	population (7.3)
diversity (7.1)	sexual reproduction (7.2)	asexual reproduction (7.2)	

Check Your Vocabulary

Use the vocabulary words above to complete the following sentences correctly.

1. A group of the same species living in a particular area is a _____ .

2. The concept that new species develop from the previous ones is called _____ .

3. Variation within a species is possible because of _____ .

4. A structure that helps an organism survive in its environment is a(n) _____ .

5. A _____ is made up of organisms that look alike.

6. An environment with a large variety of organisms has _____ .

7. A fertilized egg, or _____ , results from sexual reproduction.

8. A new organism is formed from one parent cell during _____ .

9. An organism's adaptations help it survive in a particular _____ .

10. Darwin's hypothesis about how life changed through time is called _____ .

11. The differences among individuals within a species is called _____ .

Write Your Vocabulary

Write sentences using each of the vocabulary words above. Show that you know what each word means.

Chapter 7 Review

Check Your Knowledge

Answer each question in a complete sentence.

1. Why do some organisms have similar adaptations?

2. On what four conditions did Darwin base his hypothesis of natural selection?

3. Why are the traits of humans unique for each individual?

4. What happens when a mutation occurs?

5. What diverse adaptation did Darwin discover in the finches of the Galápagos Islands?

6. Name one adaptation necessary for the survival of the following organisms: bat, anteater, jackrabbit, dandelion, and turkey vulture.

7. Give two reasons why sexual reproduction produces new genetic combinations.

Determine if each statement is true or false. Write *true* if it is true. If it is false, change the underlined word(s) to make the statement true.

8. Overproduction limits the variation of genetic material in an organism.

9. A gamete is a fertilized egg that forms when two sets of genes combine.

10. Natural selection occurs when the individuals that are most adapted to an environment are able to pass on their genes.

11. Darwin located some fossils of birds in the mountains of South America.

12. Speciation occurs when a population of organisms is isolated.

13. Within a species, individual variation shows up in physical traits and in the genetic material.

Check Your Understanding

Apply the concepts you have learned to answer each question.

1. Explain how isolation can play an important role in speciation.

2. **Contrast** Explain how *variation* and *diversity* differ.

3. Why is time important in evolution?

4. Explain why such a large number of gene combinations are possible for humans.

5. **Mystery Photo** The grizzled mantis pictured on page 138 eats only live prey. What adaptation does the grizzled mantis have that protects it from its predators? How is it adapted for killing its prey?

6. **Application** Use the pictures of three different breeds of dogs to identify the variation in the different characteristics given below. Explain how these differences affect the dogs' ability to breed with each other.

Body shape	Eye color
Height	Tail
Snout	Foot size
Coat	Ears

7. **Application** Use the information below to describe the beak and feet of a bird that lives in a salt marsh.

▶ The water depth is 10 to 30 cm, depending on the tide.

▶ Small crabs live year-round in the muddy bottom. Insects burrow in the stems of grass during spring.

▶ Seeds ripen during the late autumn months. Flowers with a high amount of nectar bloom during summer.

Develop Your Skills

Use the skills you have developed in this chapter to complete each activity.

1. **Interpret Data** The graph below shows the variation of leaf widths in one species of plant.

a. What is the width of the narrowest leaf? Of the widest leaf?

b. What leaf width occurs most often?

c. Under what conditions might small leaves be helpful to the survival of the plant? When might large leaves be helpful to survival?

2. **Data Bank** Use the information on page 630 to answer the following questions.

a. In which era and period or epoch did each of the following first appear on the earth: insects, primates, reptiles, sea scorpions, and mastadons?

b. The first flowering plants appeared during the Permian period. What animals that lived during this period probably would depend on flowering plants to survive?

Make Connections

1. **Link the Concepts** Below is a concept map showing how some of the main concepts in this chapter link together. Only parts of the map are filled in. Copy the map. Using words and ideas from the chapter, complete the map.

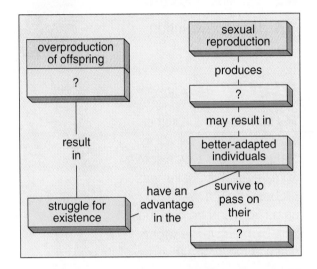

2. **Science and Social Studies** Humans are not adapted naturally to very cold weather. Write a report on the kinds of clothing made for people living in cold winter climates. Identify the industries that meet the need for winter clothing.

3. **Science and Technology** Research how seed banks get the seeds and plants that they store. Identify the locations on the National Plant Germplasm System and explain why each location is important.

Chapter 8 — History of Life

What do you see?

"I see a cricket in some yellow material. The yellow matter is amber, which comes from trees. This cricket was probably on the tree this came from and he got stuck in it. By being in the wrong place at the wrong time, he got stuck. I think the cricket has been there for a long time. The cricket has been there since the dinosaurs ruled the earth."

Isaac Villa
Byrnedale Junior High
School
Toledo, Ohio

To find out more about the photograph, look on page 172.
As you read this chapter, you will learn about living things from the past and how life on the earth has changed through time.

8.1 Geologic Time

Objectives

▶ **Name** the major eras of geologic time.

▶ **Describe** the organisms living during each era.

▶ **Describe** methods to determine the age of rocks.

▶ **Predict** how life would be different if the earth had remained one large landmass.

Skills WarmUp

Make a Graph Make a timeline that shows at least ten important events in your life. Include events such as your date of birth, when you started school, when you moved, memorable vacations, and so on. Also include some important world events that have happened during your lifetime.

Y ou are suddenly transported back in time 200 million years. Everything around you is different. You don't recognize any landmarks. If you went exploring, you would see that whole mountain ranges are missing. Even the continent you stand on is a different shape and in a different place.

None of the living things you see around you are familiar. The trees look very strange. Insects as large as birds fly by you. You don't see a single animal with fur.

History of Life on Earth

The earth and its life have a very long history. The earth is about 4,600 million years old. This is such an enormous amount of time that it is hard to comprehend. If 4,600 million years were condensed into one single year, a human lifetime would be only a tiny fraction of a second!

Life did not exist on the earth until about 3,500 million years ago. The organisms alive at that time were simple cells without nuclei. The world around them was very different than it is today. For one thing, the atmosphere was made up of gases that would be poisonous to most of today's living organisms!

Since that time, the earth has changed in many ways. You can see in Figure 8.1 how the continents shifted and moved apart. Mountain ranges formed. Sheets of ice covered parts of the earth and then retreated. All these changes have affected living things and the way they have evolved. Living things, in turn, have changed the earth. Through photosynthesis, organisms have filled the atmosphere with oxygen.

200–250 million years ago

65 million years ago

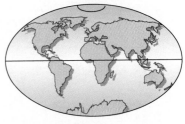

Present

Figure 8.1 ▲
At one time, the earth's continents were one large landmass (top). Notice how much the earth's land has changed since then.

Earth's Timeline

Scientists use a timeline to show the 4,600 million-year history of the earth and its life. This timeline is called a scale of **geologic time**. As you can see below, scientists divide the earth's geologic time into parts, much like a year is divided into months, weeks, and days. The largest kind of division is called an **era**. Eras are measured in millions of years. How many millions of years did the Precambrian era last?

Precambrian Era

After the earth formed, hundreds of millions of years passed before the first cells evolved, about 3,500 million years ago. After millions more years, fungi and algae evolved. Then, near the end of the era, the oceans began to fill with life. Many-celled sponges, jellyfish, and worms were among the simple organisms that began to appear.

Paleozoic Era

Many new life forms gradually appeared. Trilobites and other animals without backbones became common in the oceans. Then fishes evolved. Organisms began living on land about halfway through this era. Reptiles and insects appeared. At the end of the era, most of the animal species living in the oceans died out.

2,000 million years ago

There are four eras, but they are not equal lengths. Notice that the Precambrian era is much longer than the other three combined. One era ends and another begins at times in the earth's history when important changes were occurring. For example, few traces of animal and plant life from the Precambrian era exist. In fact, a variety of life forms did not appear until the Paleozoic era. Therefore, geologists separate the Precambrian era and the Paleozoic era at about 640 million years ago. What distinguishes the Paleozoic era from the Mesozoic era?

Mesozoic Era
Dinosaurs of all sizes were the most common form of animal for much of this era. Mammals evolved early in the era, and birds appeared about midway through. Also around the middle of the era, the earth's landmass began an important change. The one giant continent called Pangaea began to break up into separate continents.

Cenozoic Era
Mammals became very numerous and evolved into many different species. The horse and camel appeared about 37 million years ago. Large grazing animals and whales evolved. Four times in the last 2 million years of this era, huge sheets of ice spread over much of the land. During this time, the first humans appeared.

640
million years ago

245
million years ago

66
million years ago

History Preserved in Rock

How do scientists piece together the earth's history? When landforms are worn down by wind and water, pieces of rocks called sediments are created. Sediments pile up, layer by layer. They are squeezed together to form layers of rock, as shown in Figure 8.2. Rocks formed in this way are called **sedimentary rocks**. They provide clues to how the earth has changed over time.

Layers of rocks closest to the surface formed after the layers below them. Thus, the lower layers are older than the upper layers. The *relative* age of a layer of sedimentary rock can be determined by its position among other layers.

The Grand Canyon in Figure 8.2 has many layers of sedimentary rocks exposed to view. Here the scale of geologic time is laid out on the canyon walls. The layers of rock range from 200 million years old at the top to 2,000 million years old at the bottom.

Figure 8.2 ▲
How do the different rock layers of the Grand Canyon help scientists learn about the earth's history?

SkillBuilder *Making a Model*

Geologic Time Scale

The geologic time scale spans about 4,600 million years and is divided into eras. Fossils that show life forms are associated with each era. A model that shows the relative length of time in each era can help you to understand how the length of each era is different.

Collect a metric ruler, a meter stick, 4 different colored pencils, transparent tape, 1.5 m of adding-machine tape, or narrow strips of paper taped together. Copy the table below and complete the third column, using the scale of 1 cm for each 100 million years.

1. Measure out the correct amount of tape for each era. Label each era and color it a different color.

2. Use the information on pages 158–159 and the Data Bank on page 630 to draw or write in examples of life during each era.

3. Which era has the most new life forms?

4. Which era is the longest? Why is this era so much longer than the others?

5. How many times longer is the Precambrian era than the Paleozoic?

6. Does it make sense to divide the Precambrian era into two eras? If so, where would you draw the dividing line?

Geologic Time Scale		
Era	**Length of Time (millions of years)**	**Tape Length (cm)**
Precambrian	3,960	
Paleozoic	395	
Mesozoic	180	
Cenozoic	66	

Radioactive Dating

The position of a layer of rock tells scientists its relative age. However, scientists sometimes need to know more exact ages of rocks to learn about the earth's history. To determine the actual age of a rock layer in years, they use a method called radioactive dating.

In radioactive dating, the amounts of two elements in the rock are measured. One is a radioactive element, which changes into another element at a constant rate. The other is the element the first one changes into. When the amounts of the two elements are compared, a rock's age can be determined. In the oldest rocks, most of the radioactive element has changed into the other element.

Science and Technology
Clues to Continental Movement

The earth is like a giant bar magnet. A magnetic field stretches between the North and South Poles. The magnetic field is invisible, but it can affect objects on the earth. A compass needle, for example, points north in order to line up with the earth's magnetic field.

In a similar way, particles of iron in certain rocks tend to line up with the magnetic field while the rocks are being formed. When the rocks cool, the particles are frozen in one place, "pointing" to the North Pole. Later, if the rock moves, it will no longer point to the North Pole. By determining where a rock's iron particles point now, scientists can figure out where and how the rock has moved since it was formed. This method has allowed scientists to learn how the continents have moved.

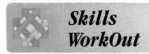

Skills WorkOut

Research The Paleozoic and Mesozoic eras are broken down further into periods. Find out the names of the periods in each era and the factors that distinguish each period. The Cenozoic era is divided into epochs. Find out the names of the epochs and the factors that distinguish each epoch. Make a chart of your findings listing the eras, periods, and epochs. Include a few highlights from each.

Check and Explain

1. List the four eras of geologic time in order.

2. Identify the era in which each of the following first appeared: humans, fishes, birds, worms, reptiles.

3. **Reason and Conclude** What were some important adaptations for animals living during the Cenozoic era?

4. **Predict** Refer to Figure 8.1 on page 157. How might life on the earth be different today if Pangaea had not split apart to form separate continents?

Make a Model Cut a sheet of paper into about eight differently shaped parts. Exchange pieces with a partner, and put them back together. Check each other's puzzles. How do you think looking for clues about the earth's past is like doing a puzzle? How do you think scientists go about putting pieces of the earth's "puzzle" together?

8.2 The Fossil Record

Objectives

▶ **Describe** different types of fossils and explain how they form.

▶ **Explain** how fossils provide evidence for evolution.

▶ **Generalize** about evolutionary relationships using an evolutionary tree.

▶ **Make inferences** about past life on the basis of the fossil record.

Think about how your life has changed since you were born. What records could you use to help explain the history of your life to a friend? After you have died, how can others learn about your life? People often leave behind such things as photographs, diaries, videotapes, letters, and other personal items. These records of people's lives can be used by others to understand how people lived and what they looked like.

In a similar way, scientists can use the records left by organisms that once lived to learn about past life on the earth. Bones, teeth, shells, and prints from leaves, plus animal footprints and outlines from body parts left in rocks are part of life's record.

Fossils

The remains and traces of organisms that lived in the past are called **fossils**. Fossils show that many of the organisms living in the past were different from those living today. Fossils also provide evidence that earlier forms of life have died out, or become **extinct**. Fossils provide a record of life called the **fossil record**. The fossil record extends back in time to the Precambrian era, though few fossils from this era actually exist.

Even though there are many fossils, most of the individual organisms that lived in the past have left no trace of their existence. The typical fossil was formed under fairly unusual conditions.

Figure 8.3 ▲
Scientists use fossils to reconstruct the skeletons of extinct animals.

Fossil Formation

Most fossils are found in rocks that formed from layers of sand, mud, or silt. They show the shape or outlines of the hard parts of the organism, such as its shell or bones.

Organisms that left these kinds of fossils were covered by sediments after they died. The soft parts of the organisms decayed. Over a long period of time, the sediment covering the organism's hard parts became a layer of rock. Water seeped through the rock and dissolved the bones or shells, leaving an impression called a **mold**.

For many fossils, one last step occurred. Minerals carried by the seeping water built up in the mold to form a **cast**. You can see a cast in Figure 8.4.

Fossils formed in many other ways, too. Sometimes the soft part of an organism was preserved when it was buried where it could not be decayed by bacteria. Leaves have been found that are millions of years old and still contain chlorophyll. Organisms have also been trapped in the sap from trees or frozen in ice. They have had their entire bodies preserved. The footprints, tracks, and burrows of organisms have been preserved in rock.

Figure 8.5 ▲
What can be learned from the fossil record?

Reading the Fossil Record

Fossils provide clues to how organisms and the earth have changed. They tell a story that scientists can piece together by making inferences.

The fossil record, for example, has been used to determine the order in which different forms of life have appeared. The oldest layers of rock in which reptile fossils occur are always above layers of rock containing fossils of fishes. Based on this observation, scientists conclude that fishes appeared on the earth before reptiles.

Fossils can also provide clues to how different life forms are related to each other. Imagine that fossils of fishes with leglike fins are found in layers above fossils of fishes. And above both layers, there are fossils of animals that have legs. These animals look like they lived in water part of the time. And above this layer are fossils of reptiles. What would you conclude from this evidence? It supports the idea that reptiles evolved from fishes.

Figure 8.4 ▲
A trilobite left behind this cast.

The Evolutionary Tree

By piecing together the clues provided by the fossil record, scientists have determined the likely ancestry of the earth's life forms. They have constructed tree-shaped diagrams that show evolutionary relationships among the different groups of organisms. A simple evolutionary tree is shown in Figure 8.6. The base of the tree represents the earliest forms of life that gave rise to all others. Each branch leads in a different evolutionary "direction."

Figure 8.6
This simplified evolutionary tree gives you an idea of how organisms are related. ▼

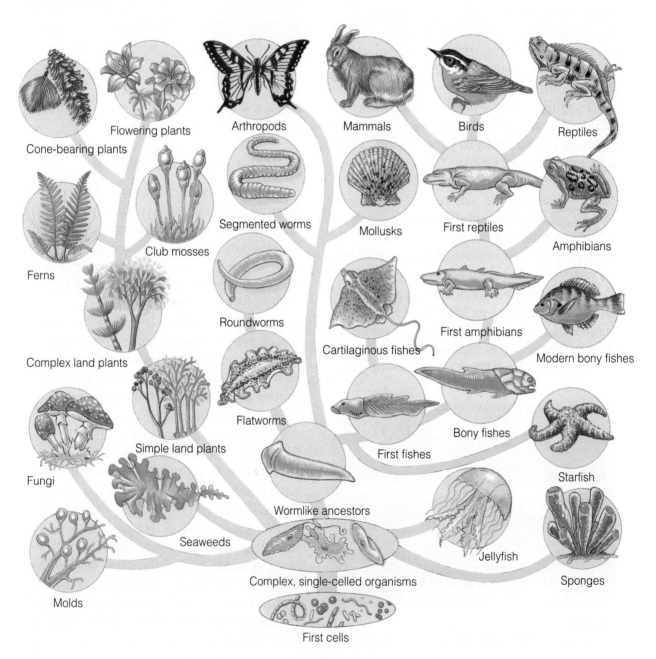

Flowering plants

Cone-bearing plants

Arthropods

Mammals

Birds

Reptiles

Ferns

Club mosses

Segmented worms

Mollusks

First reptiles

Amphibians

Complex land plants

Roundworms

Cartilaginous fishes

First amphibians

Modern bony fishes

Fungi

Simple land plants

Flatworms

First fishes

Bony fishes

Starfish

Molds

Seaweeds

Wormlike ancestors

Jellyfish

Sponges

Complex, single-celled organisms

First cells

Other Evidence for Evolution

The fossil record leaves no doubt that life forms have changed over time. In addition, there are other kinds of evidence for evolution. For example, many animals look similar during their early stages of development. Look at Figure 8.7. Species with similar embryos probably have a common ancestor.

Similarities in the DNA of different organisms also show how closely they are related. And, on a large scale, the fact that all life uses the same genetic code is evidence of the common ancestry of all living things.

Science and Technology *Finding Oil*

Big pockets of natural gas and oil lie under the earth in layers of sedimentary rock. Millions of years ago, when organisms died and were buried, their bodies were slowly changed into these "fossil fuels."

Scientists use many methods to find these hidden pockets of oil and natural gas. For example, they measure the magnetic field in areas of the earth's crust. The sedimentary rocks in which oil might be found have weaker magnetic fields than other kinds of rocks. Scientists also measure the pull of gravity in different locations. Objects weigh more when they are above large masses of dense rock than when above the light, porous rocks that may contain oil deposits. If data from these tests suggest oil is present, a hole is drilled in the earth's crust to see if oil is really there.

Fish

Rabbit

Human

Figure 8.7 ▲

Similar embryos mean evolutionary relationships. Here, you can see that the embryos of the fish, rabbit, and human are quite similar, even though they look very different as adults.

Check and Explain

1. How does a mold form?

2. What kinds of evidence do fossils provide about life's history?

3. **Reason and Conclude** Why do different branches of an evolutionary tree never intersect each other?

4. **Infer** Fossils of organism X are always found in rock layers below those with fossils of organism G. Both are always found in layers below fossils of organism A. Which of these organisms appeared on the earth first? Which evolved most recently?

Activity 8 *What is the difference between a mold and a cast?*

Skills Model; Observe; Infer; Classify

Task 1 Prelab Prep

Collect the following items: modeling clay; seashell; petroleum jelly; paper cup or plastic food container; plastic spoon; plaster of Paris; objects such as coins, keys, leaves, washers; paper plates; lab apron.

Task 2 Data Record

Copy Table 8.1 on a sheet of paper. You will be identifying objects in casts that other groups will be making. Use the table to record your observations.

Task 3 Procedure

1. On a paper plate, roll a piece of modeling clay into a flat, smooth slab. Make the piece of clay about 3 by 5 cm.
2. Coat the seashell with petroleum jelly. Press the seashell into the clay. Make sure that you have a definite imprint of the shell. Remove the seashell and observe the imprint. You have made a mold.
3. Use more clay to build a low wall around the seashell imprint.
4. Use the food container and spoon to prepare a mixture of plaster of Paris according to the directions.
5. Fill the seashell imprint to the top of the wall with plaster.
6. Wait about 20 to 30 minutes for the mold to harden. Then carefully remove the clay. You have made a cast.
7. In your group, use a leaf, key, washer, or other object to make another clay imprint. Don't let anyone see the cast your group is making. Give your cast a number. After everyone is finished, go around the room and identify the object that each group's cast represents. Write the cast number in Table 8.1 and identify it.

Table 8.1 Mystery Casts

Cast Number	Object

Task 4 Analysis

1. How are the molds and casts similar to the original objects? How are they different from the original objects?
2. What does the plaster of Paris represent?
3. Explain why an imprint would not form if the seashell were just laid on the clay.
4. Explain why an imprint would not form if the clay were dried out or frozen.
5. What are some of the clues that the cast tells you about the object? What information about the object is not revealed from a cast?
6. What clues helped you identify the objects in casts that your classmates made?

Task 5 Conclusion

Write a paragraph explaining the difference between a mold and a cast. Then discuss how casts help scientists find out more about the earth's past.

Extension

Research what fossils can be found in your area. What kind are they? What era in geologic history are they from? Find out details about your area at that time, including climate, kinds of living things, and any changes that were occurring on land, such as earthquakes and volcanoes.

8.3 Human Evolution

Objectives

▶ **Describe** the adaptations of primates.

▶ **Explain** the origin of hominids.

▶ **Describe** Neanderthals and Cro-Magnons.

▶ **Summarize** the changes that scientists hypothesize occurred in the process of human evolution.

▶ **Make a graph** showing the average brain sizes of extinct hominids.

Define Operationally How does your body enable you to climb things safely, like trees? Describe some adaptations you have that help you to climb. How would your body need to be different for you to climb higher? What if you wanted to move faster? How would your body need to be different? Compare the adaptations you have for moving on the ground and moving in trees.

Compare your body to a dog's or a cat's. In what ways is your body different? What characteristics make you human? All your human features are adaptations that evolved over many millions of years. You share some of these adaptations with animals that have a similar ancestry. Other adaptations are unique to humans. The evolutionary history of humans can be traced back from the present through species that are now extinct.

Primate Ancestry

The human species belongs in a group of mammals called the **primates**. Primates appeared more than 65 million years ago as animals adapted to living in trees. Life in trees requires several special adaptations. The hands must be able to grasp branches. The arms must have a wide range of motion to allow swinging from branch to branch. The eyes must be able to judge distance accurately for rapid movement. This means that the eyes must face forward so that their fields of vision overlap. Even though humans do not live in trees, you will recognize these traits in your own body.

After the first primates appeared, they evolved in different directions. Some continued to be tree-dwellers and evolved into the many species of lemurs, monkeys, and other similar primates alive today. Others adapted to living at least part of the time on the ground. They evolved into the many species of modern apes, which include chimpanzees, gorillas, and orangutans.

Figure 8.8 ▲
An orangutan walks on all fours when on the ground. In the trees, it swings or walks from branch to branch.

Human Origins

Between 4 and 8 million years ago, some apelike primates began to adapt to living entirely on the ground. A skeleton for standing and walking upright on two legs evolved. These primates were ancestors of modern humans. They were the first **hominids** (HAHM uh nihdz), or humanlike primates. In Figure 8.9, you can see one of the earliest known hominids. This 3.6-million-year-old skeleton was found in Africa in 1974.

Many other fossils of extinct hominids have been found. Scientists have classified them and determined their age. Some of these hominids are represented in Figure 8.10. Scientists are not sure how these and other species are related to each other. What they do know is that more than 2 million years ago, a species of *Australopithecus* developed a larger brain and began to use tools. This hominid was the first member of the genus *Homo*, which includes modern humans.

Figure 8.9 ▲
The skeleton of this female hominid was nicknamed "Lucy" by the research team that discovered her.

Historical Notebook

The Leakey Team

In 1931, anthropologist Louis Leakey began searching for hominid fossils in northern Tanzania, a country in East Africa. He found an ideal spot for his search in the canyons of the Serengeti Plain. Here the exposed rocks revealed strata dating back nearly 2 million years.

For years Leakey searched for human bone fragments. He was joined by his wife, Mary, also an anthropologist. After searching for decades, Mary made the first major discovery in 1959. She found fragments of a human skull and two large teeth! The Leakeys' first discovery turned out to be an extinct hominid whose branch had died out.

Louis Leakey died in 1972 after writing many books about the origin of humans. Mary Leakey has continued her work with her son, Richard Leakey, who is the director of the National Museum of Kenya.

1. Why was Mary Leakey's discovery important to scientists researching human evolution?

2. **Research** Find out about the research and discoveries of Richard and Mary Leakey. Write a short report about their contributions to the field of physical anthropology.

Neanderthals

The most widely known early hominids that are classified as *Homo sapiens* are the Neanderthals (nee AN dur THAWLZ). These early humans lived about 130,000 years ago. Even though they belong to the same species as modern humans, they looked much different. Neanderthals ranged in height from 1.5 m to 1.7 m. They had large bones and heavy brows.

Neanderthals were intelligent hunters who used tools and fire. They made their own clothes from animal hides. They lived in cooperative social groups and cared for the aged and sick. They practiced forms of art and music. Most importantly, they used language and could pass on knowledge and traditions from generation to generation. Neanderthals disappeared about 30,000 years ago.

Cro-Magnons

The first group of modern humans were the Cro-Magnons (KROH MAG nuhnz). They appeared about 100,000 years ago, possibly in Africa. Later they migrated to other areas. They arrived in Europe about 35,000 years ago. Some scientists think they caused the extinction of the Neanderthals.

Cro-Magnons looked very similar to modern humans. They had smaller teeth, longer faces, and straighter foreheads than Neanderthals. If you saw a Cro-Magnon walking down the street dressed in modern clothes, you would probably think he or she looked pretty normal.

Cro-Magnons used language and created music and art. Their colorful and expressive paintings have been found in more than 200 caves in Europe. They also created sculptures.

Figure 8.10
This timeline shows approximately when different hominids lived. Notice how the skull structures changed over time. ▼

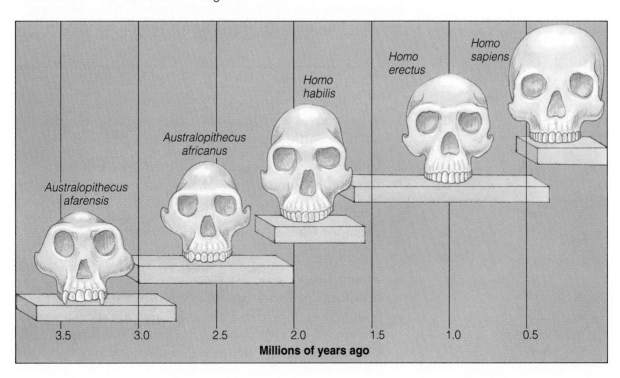

Australopithecus afarensis

Australopithecus africanus

Homo habilis

Homo erectus

Homo sapiens

3.5   3.0   2.5   2.0   1.5   1.0   0.5

Millions of years ago

Science and Society *The Piltdown Hoax*

On December 12, 1912, newspaper headlines all over the world announced the discovery of the "missing link" between apes and humans. Pieces of a skull and jaw, tools made of bones and rocks, and remains of ancient mammals had been found in a gravel pit in Piltdown, England. The skull had room for a large brain and was the same as modern humans. However, the jaw was apelike.

The find was named Piltdown Man. The Piltdown Man was exactly what many scientists were looking for at that time. For years they had searched for a primitive human halfway between modern humans and apes. For this reason, many accepted it as real.

But in 1953, Piltdown Man was exposed as a forgery. The skull was from a modern human and the jaw was from an orangutan. Both had been stained brown so they would look old. The teeth in the jaw had been filed down to look more human. The reasons for the fraud are still unknown.

The discovery of the forgery shows how science should work. Science is self-correcting. Even though many scientists were fooled for 40 years, the truth was finally revealed. Piltdown Man was not a missing link. In fact, there was no missing link to be found, because humans are not descended from apes. Rather, modern humans and modern apes share a common ancestor.

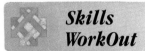

Skills WorkOut

Research Find out more about the discoveries of hominid fossils made in the 1900s. Where was each find made? Which hominid species does each fossil belong to? What is the importance of each fossil to the understanding of human origins? Write a report describing the discoveries.

Check and Explain

1. What characteristics do humans share with apes, such as chimpanzees?

2. In what ways are modern humans different from the first hominids?

3. **Uncover Assumptions** What is incorrect about cartoons that show humans and dinosaurs living together?

4. **Make a Graph** The average brain size of extinct hominids ranges from 400 cc in *Australopithecus afarensis* to 750 cc in *Homo habilis,* to 900 cc in *Homo erectus,* to 1500 cc in Neanderthals. Make a bar graph that shows this information.

Chapter 8 Review

Concept Summary

8.1 Geologic Time

▶ The earth is 4,600 million years old. The first living things appeared about 3,500 million years ago.

▶ The earth's history is divided into parts called eras. The four eras are the Precambrian, the Paleozoic, the Mesozoic, and the Cenozoic.

▶ Because of the way it forms, sedimentary rock preserves a record of how the earth has changed.

8.2 The Fossil Record

▶ Fossils are remains and traces of past life. They provide evidence that many kinds of organisms once lived on the earth but are now extinct.

▶ Fossils form when the shape or substance of all or part of an organism is somehow preserved after its death.

▶ When a fossil is formed in rock, it is often in the form of a mold and a cast.

▶ Fossils provide clues to how living things have evolved. They help scientists construct tree diagrams showing the ancestry of modern organisms.

8.3 Human Evolution

▶ Humans belong to the primates, a group of mammals that appeared over 65 million years ago.

▶ The basic primate characteristics are adaptations for living in trees.

▶ The first humanlike primates, or hominids, appeared between 4 and 8 million years ago. Hominids evolved larger brains and began using tools.

▶ Neanderthals lived just before modern humans evolved. The earliest modern humans were the Cro-Magnons.

Chapter Vocabulary

era (8.1)	fossil (8.2)	mold (8.2)	primate (8.3)
geologic time (8.1)	extinct (8.2)	cast (8.2)	hominid (8.3)
sedimentary rock (8.1)	fossil record (8.2)		

Check Your Vocabulary

Use the vocabulary words above to complete the following sentences correctly.

1. The remains of an organism can leave an impression, called a _____ , in sedimentary rock.

2. A species is _____ when all of its members have died out.

3. Scientists use the _____ to determine the ancestry of modern species.

4. A humanlike primate is called a _____ .

5. The earth's history is divided into four _____ .

6. A _____ is created when mineral-containing water seeps into a fossil mold.

7. The earth's history is shown on a scale of _____ .

8. Sediments collect in layers and may in time form _____ .

9. Many of the characteristics of a _____ are adaptations for living in trees.

10. The footprint of an extinct animal preserved in rock is an example of a _____ .

Explain the difference between the words in each pair.

11. Fossil, extinct

12. Hominid, human

13. Fossil record, evolutionary tree

Chapter 8 Review

Check Your Knowledge

Answer the following in complete sentences.

1. What is a primate? What distinguishes it from other animals?

2. What is the age of a layer of sedimentary rock compared to those above it?

3. Why did soft-bodied organisms leave few fossils?

4. In what ways were Neanderthals like modern humans? How were they different?

5. What important change occurred at the beginning of the Paleozoic era?

6. What must form first, a mold or a cast?

Choose the answer that best completes each sentence.

7. Horses evolved before (jellyfish, insects, birds, humans).

8. The earth is about (4,600, 3,500, 420, 66) million years old.

9. A primate is classified as a hominid if it (can learn, has forward-facing eyes, walks upright, has hair).

10. The oldest and longest era was the (Precambrian, Cenozoic, Mesozoic, Paleozoic).

11. When two organisms have similar (behaviors, diets, adaptations, embryos), it is evidence that they evolved from a common ancestor.

12. Scientists use (bar graphs, evolutionary trees, chemical equations, pie charts) to show how organisms have evolved and how they are related.

Check Your Understanding

Apply the concepts you have learned to answer each question.

1. **Critical Thinking** Will people living 100 years from now find fossils of the humans living now? Explain.

2. **Classify** Which of the following can be considered a fossil? Why or why not?
   a. A clamshell buried in sand
   b. An old bone
   c. An impression of a snail shell in a piece of rock
   d. A footprint in hardened mud

3. **Infer** In an area rich in fossils, you find a hillside cut away by erosion. In one layer of rock, you discover a fossilized horse jaw. Where would you look to find the fossils of dinosaurs?

4. **Mystery Photo** The photograph on page 156 shows a cricket millions of years old sealed inside a piece of hardened tree sap called amber.
   a. How do you think the cricket ended up inside the amber?
   b. Is the cricket a fossil? If so, how is it different from most fossils?

5. **Find Causes** Why do you think the mammals began to evolve rapidly about the same time that the dinosaurs became extinct?

6. **Infer** What can you infer about a species that is placed at the end of a branch on an evolutionary tree? How is it different from a species placed at the base of a branch?

7. Suppose a form of life is discovered that does not use DNA for its genetic code. How would this discovery change scientists' view of the evolution of life?

Develop Your Skills

Use the skills you have developed in this chapter to complete each activity.

1. **Interpret Data** The timeline below shows some major events in the earth's history.

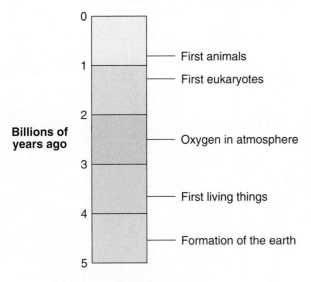

a. How many billions of years ago did the earth form? What is this number in millions?

b. Where on the timeline is the present?

c. For how long has there been oxygen in the earth's atmosphere?

d. Where on the timeline would you mark a line to show the beginning of the Cenozoic era?

2. **Calculate** For what percentage of the earth's history was there no life?

3. **Data Bank** Use the information on page 630 to answer the following questions.

a. When did the first amphibians appear?

b. The Mesozoic era is divided into how many periods?

c. Which appeared first, bats or mastodons?

Make Connections

1. **Link the Concepts** Below is a concept map showing how some of the main concepts in this chapter link together. Only part of the map is filled in. Finish the map, using words and ideas you find in the chapter.

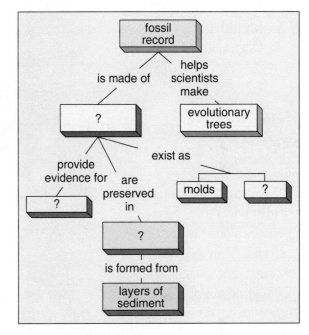

2. **Science and Social Studies** One of the most important events in the evolution of humans was the beginning of the use of language. Research the importance of language in human society. How does it make the human species different from any other? How does language shape the way humans interact with their environment?

3. **Science and Art** Find photographs of cave paintings done by Cro-Magnons and earlier humans. Study them carefully and decide what they were meant to show. Then research what scientists say they mean. Present your findings and ideas to the class.

Chapter 9 Classifying Living Things

What do you see?

66In this picture, I see a starfish and coral. They both are living animals. The picture shows one starfish and one coral. They both live in the water, but the starfish can move and coral doesn't. They both eat other animals in the water.99

Payam Tehranian
Ferry Pass Middle
*   School*
Pensacola, Florida

To find out about the photograph, look on page 188. As you read this chapter, you will learn about the variety of living things and how they are classified.

174

9.1 Classification

Objectives

▶ **Explain** why organisms are organized into groups.

▶ **Describe** how scientists name organisms.

▶ **Identify** the major classification groups.

▶ **Make a model** showing a classification system.

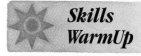
Did you know that a dog is more closely related to a wolf than either animal is to a fox? Since similarities in appearance can be misleading, people need a better way to classify, or organize into groups, the many different types of organisms on earth. In this way, patterns in nature can be more clearly understood. Long ago, people began developing classification systems for this purpose. These systems help make sense of the relationships among organisms by clearly defining what makes them similar and different.

History of Classification

As a small child, you learned to classify things by their use, shape, size, or color. As you grew older, you learned to classify things by smaller and more meaningful categories. Throughout time, people have classified living things in some way, usually based on how they affected the people's lives.

For instance, the earliest systems of classification probably grouped plants and animals by whether they were useful, harmful, or neither. People of the ancient Near East recognized five animal groups: domestic animals, wild animals, creeping animals, flying animals, and sea animals. More than 2,300 years ago, the Greek philosopher Aristotle defined two groups of animals: those that had red blood and those that did not. He classified plants as herbs, shrubs, or trees.

In the 1700s, the Swedish scientist Carolus Linnaeus classified about 12,000 organisms into groups based on similar characteristics. His basic system is still used today. The science of classifying living things using this system is called **taxonomy**.

Figure 9.1 ▲
Which two animals are more closely related: the gray wolf (top), Akita Inu dog (middle), or red fox (bottom)?

Levels of Classification

There are seven major levels of classification. Each successive level contains fewer organisms with more characteristics in common than the level above it.

Kingdom Most scientists today group all living things into five **kingdoms**. Classification by kingdom depends largely on an organism's cell structure, how it gets energy, and its movement and reproductive characteristics. A polar bear, for example, belongs to the kingdom Animalia (animals). Members of this kingdom have complex cells, consume other organisms for food, use energy, usually move about, and reproduce sexually.

Phylum The largest group in the animal kingdom is a **phylum** [FY luhm] (plural: phyla). (Plants are grouped into divisions instead of phyla.) For example, polar bears are classified in the phylum Chordata. Animals in this phylum have a flexible, skeletal rod called a *noto-chord*. Frogs, fishes, and birds are also classified in this phylum.

Figure 9.2
Classification of the Polar Bear

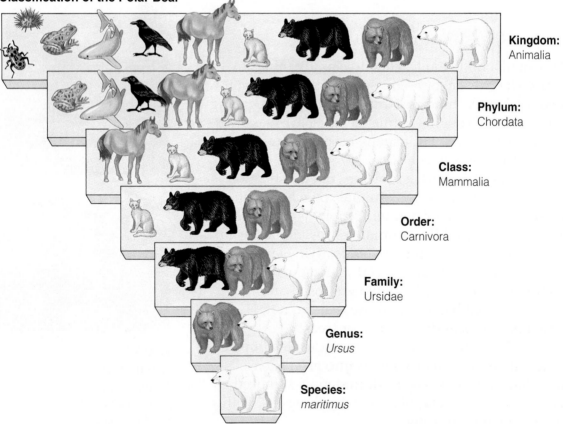

Kingdom:
Animalia

Phylum:
Chordata

Class:
Mammalia

Order:
Carnivora

Family:
Ursidae

Genus:
Ursus

Species:
maritimus

Table 9.1 Classification of Five Different Organisms

	Human	Yogurt-making Bacterium	Bread Mold	Ameba	Sunflower
Kingdom	Animalia	Monera	Fungi	Protista	Plantae
Phylum	Chordata	Eubacteriaces	Zygomycota	Sarcodina	Tracheophyta
Class	Mammalia	Schizomycetes	Phycomycetes	Lobosa	Anthophyta
Order	Primates	Eubacteriales	Mucorales	Amoebina	Asterales
Family	Hominidae	Lactobacilla	Mucoracease	Amoebidae	Compositae
Genus	*Homo*	*Lactobacillus*	*Rhizopus*	*Amoeba*	*Helianthus*
Species	*sapiens*	*bulgaris*	*stonifer*	*proteus*	*annus*

Class A phylum is divided into **classes**. Polar bears belong to the class Mammalia (mammals), endothermic animals whose females produce milk. Cats, horses, and humans are mammals. Fish and birds form separate classes in the phylum Chordata.

Order A class is divided into **orders**. Polar bears are members of the order Carnivora, animals that mainly eat meat and have well-developed tearing teeth. Cats and dogs also belong to Carnivora, while horses and humans belong to other orders in the same class.

Family An order is divided into **families**. The polar bear, like all bears, belongs to the family Ursidae. Other members of Carnivora, such as dogs and cats, form different families.

Genus Each family consists of at least one **genus** (plural: genera). The polar bear belongs to the genus *Ursus,* which includes large bears, such as the grizzly. Smaller bears, such as the American black bear, are grouped in different genera.

Species A genus contains one or more **species**. A species is made up of related organisms that are able to mate and reproduce offspring of the same type. In their natural environments, one species cannot successfully mate with another.

Figure 9.3 ▲
According to Figure 9.2, to which order does the polar bear belong?

Scientific Names

The name *pine* is used for hundreds of tree species. Yet silver pine and sugar pine are both common names for the same species. A single organism may have 50 different common names in 30 languages.

When Linnaeus invented his classification system, he realized the importance of using a unique name for each type of organism. He used Greek and Latin words to name organisms by genus and species. Those languages were understood by most scientists of his day. Today, biologists still use his system to name organisms. The system is called binomial nomenclature, a Latin phrase that means "two-name naming." For example, scientists of all countries know the polar bear by its scientific name, *Ursus maritimus,* which means "seagoing bear." *Ursus* is the genus, *maritimus* the species. Similarly, all pine trees belong to the genus *Pinus,* but *Pinus monticola* identifies only one species.

SkillBuilder *Classifying*

Classification Systems

Imagine that you are the manager of a grocery store or supermarket. You have to develop a classification system for displaying items in your store. How will you go about it?

Follow the steps below to organize your store.

1. Make a list of eight to ten different categories of items based on common characteristics.

2. Break each category down into smaller subcategories, using two or more levels based on common characteristics. Use the diagram below as an example.

3. Draw a layout of your store, showing the locations of the different items you identified in steps 1 and 2.

4. Compare your store design with the designs of three other students. Discuss why you organized your systems the way you did. Write a short report comparing the strengths and weaknesses of the different classification systems.

Science and You
Finding One Book Among Millions

When you look for a book in the library, you can see how a classification system works. Books can be classified one of two ways. You are probably familiar with the Dewey Decimal Classification System used in many school and public libraries. However, most large research libraries use a system developed by the Library of Congress in Washington, D.C.

In this system, two capital letters identify the category of a book. Numbers and other letters identify the individual book. Consider, for example, a book identified as QH309.A88 1984. The Q stands for science, the H for life on earth, and the 309 for environmental science. The code A88 identifies the book as *The Living Planet* by David Attenborough. The date 1984 distinguishes this edition from later editions that might include changes.

The Library of Congress classification system is not exactly like the system used to classify living things, but the two systems do have some similarities. For instance, they both provide many levels of classification and exactness in classifying items. Also, they both provide a way to include new items, such as newly discovered species or new categories of living things, or newly published books.

Figure 9.4 ▲
To help people find books, libraries group and arrange books using a classification system.

Check and Explain

1. What is the name of the science of classifying living organisms?

2. The chimpanzee belongs to the family Pongidae of the order Primata. Its genus is *Pan* and its species is *troglodytes*. What is its scientific name?

3. **Classify** List three characteristics of birds that identify them as a group and make them distinct from other types of animals.

4. **Make a Model** Develop a classification system for sports equipment. Make a chart to illustrate your classification system. Use at least three categories of equipment and at least three levels of classification within each category.

Skills WarmUp

Make a Chart Make a chart that shows the relationships between people in your family.

9.2 The Five Kingdoms

Objectives

▶ **Name** and **describe** the five kingdoms of living things.

▶ **Explain** the relationship between classification and evolution.

▶ **Classify** a variety of living things.

For many years, biologists recognized only two kingdoms: animal and plant. Animals included all organisms that moved about, ate food, and stopped growing at a certain size. Plants included all organisms that did not move, used photosynthesis, and grew as long as they lived.

These categories were not exact. Fungi and bacteria were classified as plants even though they do not photosynthesize. The one-celled Euglena seemed to belong to both kingdoms—or neither. It has chlorophyll for photosynthesis, like a plant, but it moves about like an animal. Today's five-kingdom taxonomy is more precise. It is based on what scientists have learned about the structure of different types of cells.

**Figure 9.5
The Five Kingdoms**

Kingdom: Fungi
- Cells with cell walls, nuclei, and organelles
- Mostly many-celled
- Absorb nutrients from other organisms
- Do not move about
- Most reproduce both sexually and with spores

Kingdom: Monerans
- Simple cells with no nuclei or organelles
- Single-celled; may live in colonies
- May eat or make food
- Reproduce by cell division

Classification and Evolution

Classification shows the evolutionary relationships among living things. The more groups two organisms share, the more closely they are related. This is possible because all organisms share a common history.

Humans and octopuses, for example, belong to the same kingdom. They had a common ancestor about 600 million years ago. Humans and polar bears belong to the same kingdom, phylum, and class. They had a common ancestor about 100 million years ago. Humans and gorillas had a common ancestor about 9 million years ago. They share the same kingdom, phylum, class, and order. Therefore you are more closely related to a gorilla than to a polar bear, and more closely related to a polar bear than to an octopus.

Kingdom: Animals
- Cells with nuclei and organelles
- Many-celled
- Can move about
- Eat food
- Most reproduce sexually

Kingdom: Plants
- Cells with cell walls, nuclei, and organelles
- Many-celled
- Do not move about
- Use photosynthesis
- Most reproduce sexually

Kingdom: Protists
- Cells with nuclei and organelles; some with cell walls
- Mostly single-celled
- May make or eat food
- Reproduce by cell division; some sexually

Skills WorkOut

Research Find out about the work of zoologist Jane Goodall. How has her work helped scientists learn about the close evolutionary relationship of humans and chimpanzees? Write a one-page report on your findings.

Science and Technology *Clues to the Past*

Scientists have studied the evolutionary paths of similar species for hundreds of years. Much of the research has been based on a method called *comparative anatomy*. In the science of comparative anatomy, relationships among different species are charted based on similarities in their physical structures or anatomies. Bone patterns and glands are two of the physical structures that are charted. The development of embryos is also charted. For example, birds, bats, turtles, and horses all have the same bone structures in their forelimbs. Similarities in anatomy lead comparative anatomists to hypothesize that these animals descended from a common ancestor millions of years ago.

A more recent technique for studying similarities among species has come about through DNA research. Using a technique called DNA sequencing, researchers examine long DNA strands. DNA strands are contained in the nucleus of a cell. The more similar the DNA strands are in two organisms, the more closely related the organisms probably are. Through DNA sequencing, biologists have discovered that humans and chimpanzees are more closely related than previously thought. In fact, humans and chimpanzees are each other's closest genetic cousins.

Today, the study of DNA molecules is changing classification schemes. As new DNA techniques are developed, scientists may make other startling discoveries about how species are related to one another.

Check and Explain

1. List the five kingdoms. Give an example of an organism from each kingdom.

2. What characteristic distinguishes monerans from all other kingdoms?

3. **Reason and Conclude** Why do organisms in the same classification group have characteristics that are similar?

4. **Classify** Make a chart in which you classify each of the following organisms: mushroom, sunflower, starfish, stegosaurus, dog, chimpanzee, human.

9.3 Identifying Organisms

Objectives

▶ **Explain** how to use a taxonomic key.

▶ **Compare** and **contrast** taxonomic keys and field guides.

▶ **Make a model** of a taxonomic key.

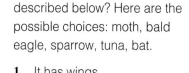
While walking through the woods one day, you find a clump of attractive mushrooms. You want to take them home to eat, but you do not know whether they are safe. How can you tell a delicious edible mushroom from a poisonous one?

Taxonomic Keys

A taxonomic key is a guide to identifying organisms on the basis of physical characteristics. Taxonomic keys show evolutionary relationships by arranging similar organisms in a series of numbered statements.

Figure 9.6 shows part of a key for the family of trees that includes pines, spruces, and other evergreens. Follow the steps below as you use the taxonomic key.

Figure 9.6   Taxonomic Key for Part of the Pine Family

1. Read parts a and b of statement 1. Choose the appropriate description. The numbers at the right, 2 and 4, tell you which statement to read next. For example, since the leaves are not in clusters, you go to statement 4.

2. Because the leaves are arranged alternately on the stem, go to statement 5.

3. Because the leaves are four-sided, go to statement 6.

4. The leaves are 6–12 mm long. You can identify the tree as a black spruce (*P. mariana*).

1a.	Leaves in clusters...................2
1b.	Leaves not in clusters..............4
2a.	Leaves in clusters of 5............White pine (*Pinus strobus*)
2b.	Leaves in clusters of 2 or 3......3
3a.	Leaves 8–15 cm long.............Norway pine (*Pinus resinosa*)
3b.	Leaves 2–4 cm long................Jack pine (*Pinus banksiana*)
4a.	Leaves alternate or scattered..5
4b.	Leaves opposite or whorled....Juniper (*Juniperus utahensis*)
5a.	Leaves four-sided...................6
5b.	Leaves flattened......................7
6a.	Leaves 6–12 mm long.............Black spruce (*Picea mariana*)
6b.	Leaves 15–25 mm long...........White spruce (*Picea glauca*)
7a.	Leaves 12–28 mm long...........Tideland spruce (*Picea stichensis*)
7b.	Leaves 18–28 mm long...........Weeping spruce (*Picea Breweriana*)

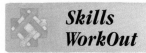
Communicate Make a list of five organisms. Create a series of four clues for identifying only one organism among the five. Have each successive clue eliminate one organism as a possible answer. Then see if a classmate can use the clues to identify the correct organism from the list.

Field Guides

A field guide is another tool for identifying organisms. It is designed to be used in the field, such as on a nature hike or a trip to an aquarium or natural history museum. A field guide does not give as much scientific information as a taxonomic key. Instead, it has pictures and descriptions that help you identify what you see. Unlike taxonomic keys, field guides are not based on classification. Although guides may group organisms by order and family, they sometimes make groups on the basis of color, size, behavior, or location.

Field guides are especially popular for identifying birds, wildflowers, and other animals and plants you might encounter in nature. They usually give information on habitat, range, migration patterns, seasonal changes in appearance, and other helpful facts. Field guides are also useful for identifying nonliving natural objects, such as fossil rocks and minerals.

Career Corner *Scientific Photographer*

Who Takes the Photographs for This Book?

You will probably never be near an erupting volcano or a hibernating bear. You may never see cells dividing or observe heart-transplant surgery. However, you probably are familiar with all these events through the work of scientific photographers.

Scientific photographers take pictures of everything from animals to microscopic surgery. Their work may take them to tropical rain forests, the ocean floor, or inside a laboratory. Some specialize in photographs for magazines, scientific journals, field guides, textbooks, or other books. Others make films or videotapes for research, education, or entertainment.

Scientific photographers often use special techniques and equipment. To photograph animals from a distance, they use a telephoto lens. To record cell processes, they use a special camera mounted on a microscope. To record events that happen very quickly, such as a frog capturing a fly, they use slow-motion photography. For taking pictures underwater, they use a watertight camera built to stand pressure.

Most scientific photographers specialize in a particular field, such as medicine or wildlife. They may take college courses in their field. They develop their photographic skills in college, other special courses, or on-the-job training.

Science and You *Birding*

Do you enjoy watching the birds at a backyard feeder or in a park? Do you like the outdoors and learning about nature? Then you might enjoy birding, the sport that is also a science. Birding, or birdwatching, involves observing and identifying birds. Most birders keep a log of the date and location of each species they see. They identify birds by such characteristics as size, color, shape, song or other call, distinctive body parts, and feeding and nesting behavior.

To begin birding, you need only a field guide, a pair of binoculars, and a notebook. Take a walk through your neighborhood or a local park and try to identify the different birds you see. Many areas have bird walks that are guided by experts who can help you spot and recognize a variety of birds.

Figure 9.7 ▲
Birdwatchers may use a field guide (above) to help identify the birds they see and hear.

Check and Explain

1. Explain the difference between a taxonomic key and a field guide.

2. Use the key on page 183 to identify an evergreen tree with two-leaf clusters that are 3 cm long.

3. **Classify** Lizards and snakes belong to the same order in the class Reptilia (reptiles). How would a taxonomic key distinguish between them?

4. **Make a Model** Make a list of ten animals. Create a taxonomic key that identifies all of them.

Activity 9   *How do you use a taxonomic key?*

Skills   Observe; Classify

Task 1   Prelab Prep

1. Collect the following items: 12 or more screws and bolts, all differing in size, head type, threading, and other characteristics (see Table 9.2).
2. Divide the objects into two groups. Make sure that all items in a group share at least one defining characteristic.
3. Divide each group into two smaller subgroups. Again, make sure that all items in each subgroup share at least one characteristic.
4. Continue to separate the items into smaller and smaller groups until you end up with single items ("species").

Task 2   Data Record

1. Assign each item a name. Use real names or creative names.
2. List the characteristics you used to classify the items in each group.

Task 3   Procedure

1. Use your data to create a taxonomic key for identifying bolts and screws. You can use the one for identifying trees, on page 183, as a model.
2. Have another group use your key to identify one of your items.

Task 4   Analysis

Was the other group able to identify an item using your key? If not, discuss with your group whether the problem may have been due to inexact classification. Rethink your classification system and prepare another key.

Task 5   Conclusion

Write a short paragraph explaining the way you created your key and what the activity taught you about creating and using taxonomic keys.

Table 9.2
Characteristics of Screws and Bolts

Screw	
Bolt	
Wood screw	
Machine screw	
Automotive screw	
Flat-head screw	
Round-head screw	
Pan-head screw	
Slotted head	
Phillips head	
Round bolt	
Square-head bolt	
Hex-head bolt	
Eye bolt	

Everyday Application

Suppose you needed a supply of screws for a home project. Explain how a classification system would help you find them in the hardware store.

Extension

Develop a taxonomic key for something you use every day. The taxonomic key could be for identifying items of clothing, types of TV shows, or movies you have seen.

Chapter 9 Review

Concept Summary

9.1 Classification
▶ Taxonomy is the science of classifying living things based on similar characteristics.
▶ The modern system of taxonomy has seven major levels of classification: kingdom, phylum, class, order, family, genus, and species.
▶ The basis of modern classification was developed by Linnaeus. In this system, each organism is given a two-part name—its genus and species.

9.2 The Five Kingdoms
▶ The five-kingdom system of classification consists of monerans, protists, fungi, plants, and animals.
▶ Scientific classification outlines evolutionary relationships among living things.

9.3 Identifying Organisms
▶ Living things can be identified by taxonomic keys and field guides.
▶ Taxonomic keys identify organisms by physical characteristics. The keys show evolutionary relationships.
▶ Field guides identify organisms by pictures and descriptions of an organism's location, color, size, or behavior.

Chapter Vocabulary

taxonomy (9.1)	order (9.1)	species (9.1)	fungus (9.2)
kingdom (9.1)	family (9.1)	moneran (9.2)	plant (9.2)
phylum (9.1)	genus (9.1)	protist (9.2)	animal (9.2)
class (9.1)			

Check Your Vocabulary

Use the vocabulary words above to complete the following sentences correctly.

1. A shark is an _____, because it does not have cell walls, moves about, eats food, and reproduces sexually.

2. The science of classifying living things is called _____.

3. A _____ makes food by photosynthesis and has a cell wall.

4. An organism that absorbs food from other organisms, does not move, and reproduces sexually or by spores is a _____.

5. Most scientists today group all living things into five _____.

6. Plants are grouped into divisions instead of _____.

7. A class is divided into _____.

8. A _____ is made up of organisms that are able to mate and reproduce offspring of the same type.

9. Polar bears belong to the _____ of mammals.

10. A bacterium is a member of the _____ kingdom.

11. Each family consists of at least one _____.

12. An ameba belongs to the _____ kingdom.

13. All bears belong to the same _____, Ursidae.

Write Your Vocabulary

Write sentences using each vocabulary word above. Show that you know what each word means.

Chapter 9 Review

Check Your Knowledge

Choose the answer that best completes each sentence.

1. Linnaeus developed a (one-, two-, three-, four-) name system for naming organisms.

2. Bread mold belongs to the (animal, plant, fungi, moneran) kingdom.

3. The science of naming organisms and putting them in groups is called (biology, ecology, taxonomy, filing).

4. A slime mold belongs to the (fungi, moneran, protist, plant) kingdom.

5. A taxonomic key is a way of identifying organisms based on (habitat, behavior, seasons, physical characteristics).

6. Dogs belong to the (genus, order, family, species) Carnivora.

Determine whether each statement is true or false. Write *true* if it is true. If it is false, change the underlined term(s) to make the statement true.

7. Humans and <u>octopuses</u> had a common ancestor about <u>100 million</u> years ago.

8. The largest group in scientific classification is the <u>species</u>.

9. In the 1700s, Linnaeus classified about 12,000 organisms into groups based on <u>similar</u> characteristics.

10. A field guide usually identifies organisms using <u>classification</u>.

11. The scientific name for an organism includes its <u>class</u> and species.

12. Humans, <u>ameba</u>, and polar bears are examples of animals.

13. Taxonomy is a science that <u>names</u> organisms and puts them into groups.

Check Your Understanding

Apply the concepts you have learned to answer each question.

1. How are protists different from monerans?

2. When might you use a field guide? When would a taxonomic key be more useful?

3. **Sequence** Order the following groups from most general to least general: class, genus, family, kingdom, phylum, species, order.

4. **Apply** Suppose an organism had three common names in different parts of the United States. How might these names lead to confusion?

5. **Mystery Photo** The photograph on page 174 shows a starfish crawling on a soft coral tree. The coral is a colony of small animals with stinging tentacles. What characteristics do these animals share?

6. Which of the following three organisms are most closely related: *Picea rubra, Morus rubra, Picea mariana?*

7. Use the key on page 183 to identify the following trees. Give the common and scientific names.

   a. Tree with opposite leaves growing on a stem

   b. Tree with 2-leaf clusters that are about 13 cm long

   c. Tree with 2-leaf clusters that are 3 cm long

   d. Tree with 5-leaf clusters

   e. Tree with flattened leaves (about 12 mm long) growing alternately on a stem

Develop Your Skills

Use skills you have developed in this chapter to complete each activity.

1. **Interpret Data** The chart below shows a system of classification.

   a. What problems can you see with this system?

   b. What important invention made scientists begin to understand that this system was not accurate?

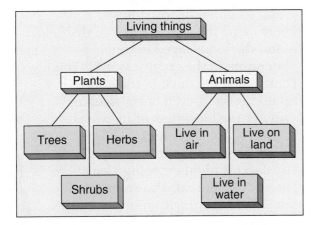

2. **Data Bank** Use the chart on page 628 to answer the following questions:

   a. At what level is the skunk related to the polar bear?

   b. According to the tree, how does the dog differ from the wolf?

3. **Design an Experiment** There are many different species of grasses. Using grass seeds or grasses, design an experiment to prove that two types of grass are different species. Describe the question, materials, procedure, control and variable, observations, and conclusion.

4. **Research** Choose five common organisms and use reference books to classify them from kingdom to species. Write their scientific names.

Make Connections

1. **Link the Concepts** Draw a concept map showing how some of the main concepts in this chapter link together. Use words and ideas from the chapter to draw your map.

2. **Science and Language Arts** Using what you have learned about field guides, develop a field guide to something nonliving. You may want to use automobiles or the utensils used in the school cafeteria.

3. **Science and You** Make a list of common plants and animals found in your area. Use a reference book to find the scientific name of each. Write the scientific names next to the common names. Include pictures or drawings of your organisms.

4. **Science and Language Arts** Many libraries use the Dewey Decimal System to group books by similarities. Visit your school or local library. Choose a science topic (such as whooping cranes, evolution, genetics). List five books related to your topic. Include the book's title, author, publisher, year of publication, and Dewey decimal number. Write a brief description about the information in each book.

5. **Science and Technology** Use your library to find out more about DNA sequencing. Draw a series of steps to explain how scientists examine the DNA strands. Describe the different uses of DNA sequencing.

6. **Science and Social Studies** Draw a timeline that shows the events that led to the modern classification system. You will need to research this topic in your library. Include advances in technology on your time line.

Science and Literature Connection

"In the Night, Still Dark"

The following poem comes from the book In the Night, Still Dark *by Richard Lewis*

Darkness of the sun,
darkness of the
night, nothing but
night.
In this darkest night, in
this darkest sea,
After the coral was born,
there came the mud-
digging grub, and its child, the earth
worm.
There came the pointed star-fish, and the
rock-grasping barnacle,
and its child, the oyster,
and its child, the mussel.
There came the moss which lives in
the sea,
And the ferns which grow on the land.
In this the darkest night
There came the fish, and all the creatures
of the sea.
There came the lurking shark, and the
darting eel, moving quickly through the
high weeds.
There came the stinging ray, and the
hiding octopus, waiting shyly in the
deep waters.
There came all the creatures who swim,
rise and dive,
swallowing, swallowing,
as they go.

In this the darkest night
The darkest night just
breaking into dawn,
There came all the small,
weak, and flying
things.
There came the furred
caterpillar,
and its child, the moth.
There came the scurrying ant,
and its child, the dragonfly.
There came the grasshopper of the field,
and the long-legged heron,
standing in the quietness of its shadow.
There came the duck of the pond,
and the swift-eyed crow, sleeping
under the blackness of its wings.
In this the darkest night,
The darkest night falling away,
The darkest night creeping away,
There came the rat who runs, here
and there, and with him the hairless
red dog.
And out of the slime, roots began
to grow.
Leaves began to branch.
And a great calmness,
And a great stillness
came about.
And in this time men and women
began to be born.
Here on the ocean's edge,
Here in the damp forest,
Here in the cold mountains,
People spread over the land.
People were here,
And so it was:
DAY

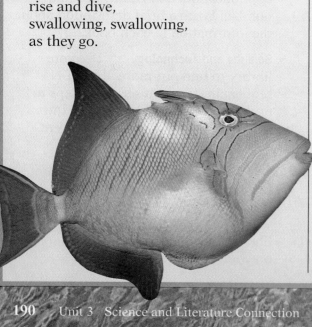

"The Weasel"

The following poem appears in the book Consider the Lemming *by Jeanne Steig.*

The weasel is clever, the weasel is spunky,
The weasel when peeved smells decidedly funky.
He's long in the torso and short in the legs.
He's a merciless hunter—they say he sucks eggs.

In summer the weasel, like ferret and stoat,
Goes out in a nondescript frumpy brown coat.
But if, as may happen, his winter vacation
Is spent in a more or less frigid location,

An astounding transmogrification occurs:
The weasel puts on the most luscious of furs.
He turns into an ermine! How does he achieve it?
A fact is a fact, you can take it or leave it.

Skills in Science

Reading Skills in Science

1. **Evaluate Sources** The poem "In the Night, Still Dark" infers that plants such as mosses and ferns existed on the earth before there was light. Is this possible? Explain your answer.

2. **Infer** What does the author mean when she writes "the weasel when peeved smells decidedly funky"?

Writing Skills in Science

1. **Communicate** Write a poem that describes a particular organism in its environment.

2. **Predict** Suppose you were able to interview a human that was among those described in "In the Night, Still Dark." With a partner, write the interview complete with the person's responses. Share your interview with the class, having one student act as the interviewer and the other as the first human.

Activities

Evaluate Sources Determine the order in which the five kingdoms appeared on the earth as detailed in "In the Night, Still Dark." Use your text and other sources to assess the poem's scientific validity.

Communicate Research the similarities and differences between two of the following animals: ferret, stoat, weasel, ermine. Communicate your findings to the class in the form of a chart or diagram.

Where to Read More

In the Beginning; Creation Stories from Around the World by Virginia Hamilton. Harcourt Brace Jovanovich, 1988. Different creation myths explore how diverse cultures envision the origins of life.

Darwin and the Voyage of the Beagle by Felicia Law. Deutch, 1985. This fictional account of the voyage to the Galápagos Islands is based on Darwin's diary.

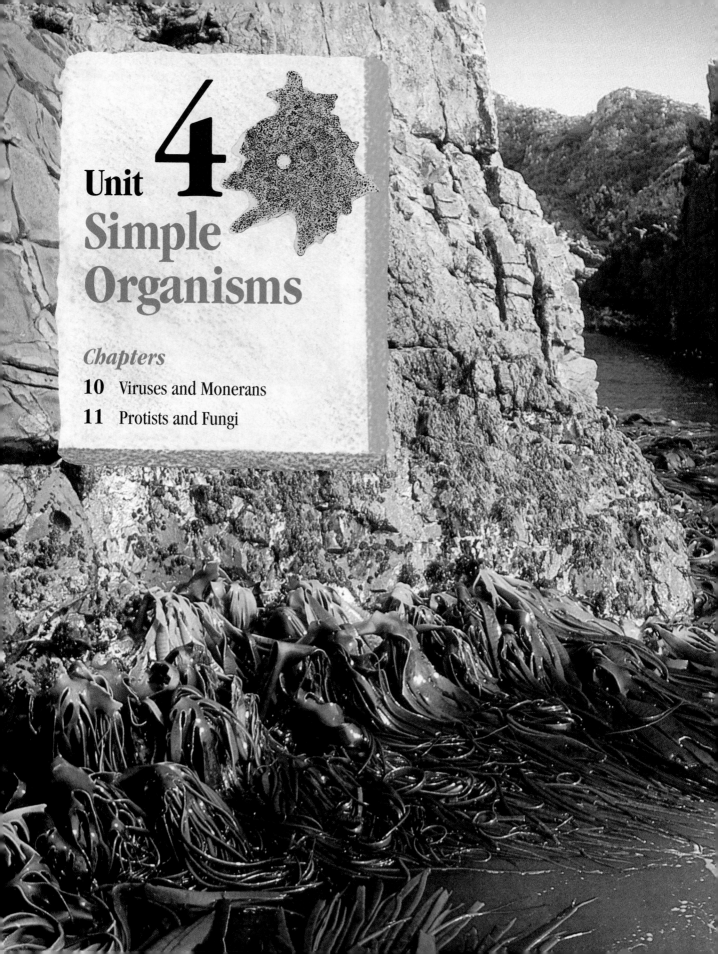

Unit 4
Simple Organisms

Data Bank

Use the information on pages 624 to 631 to answer the following questions about topics explored in this unit.

Interpreting Data

What is the approximate size of most bacteria? Most viruses?

Comparing

Which is larger, a protein or a virus?

Reading a Diagram

A virus can be seen through what kind of microscope?

Classifying

Name all the living things listed on the diagram. Then name all the nonliving things listed. On which list did you place a virus?

The photograph to the left is of a kelp bed in New Zealand. What kind of water do you think the kelp is living in, salt water or fresh water?

Viruses and Monerans

What do you see?

66 I see in this picture what appear to be many microscopic organisms. The organisms look like small bacteria or viruses of some sort. These organisms are small enough to fit one thousand of them on the point of a needle. **99**

Jay Rhine
Intermediate School West
Toms River, New Jersey

To find out about the photograph, look on page 208. As you read this chapter, you will learn about viruses, bacteria, and other monerans.

10.1 Viruses

Objectives

▶ **Describe** the characteristics of viruses.

▶ **Explain** why viruses do not fit easily into any classification system.

▶ **Explain** how viruses reproduce.

▶ **Calculate** a mathematical problem that shows an understanding of the relative size of a virus.

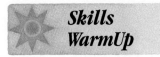

Skills WarmUp

Classify Make a list of all the diseases you know about. Then classify them into groups. Write on your list why you classified the diseases the way you did.

You're sneezing and coughing. Your nose is runny. You may even have a fever. You feel just plain awful. What's the problem? You have the common cold. What's the cause? Your body cells have been invaded by particles so small that they can't even be seen under a light microscope. The particles are **viruses**. A virus is a piece of hereditary material with a coat of protein.

Characteristics of Viruses

Viruses are not cells. They do not have any cell structures. There is no cytoplasm, cell membrane, or nucleus in a virus. Viruses can't move, feed, or grow outside the cell of another organism. They can't carry out any life processes. They appear to be nonliving when outside a living thing. However, they can replicate, or reproduce themselves, inside a living cell. The ability to reproduce, and the genetic code used in the process, are the only similarities that viruses share with cells.

Look at Figure 10.1. It shows three different kinds of viruses. Notice how their shapes vary. Viruses have many other kinds of shapes, too. Each virus is only a strand of RNA or DNA with a protein coat called a capsid. The capsid makes up most of the virus and gives the virus its shape.

Viruses are so small that they were not seen until the 1930s. At this time, the invention of the electron microscope enabled scientists to see viruses. To give you an idea of their size, about 100,000 average-sized viruses could be lined up end-to-end on the period at the end of this sentence.

Capsid — Nucleic acid

Tail

Tail fibers

Bacteria virus

Flu virus

Polio virus

Figure 10.1 ▲
Although viruses come in many shapes, all viruses have capsids with RNA or DNA.

Classifying Viruses

Because viruses do not fit into the ideas of the cell theory, scientists have a hard time classifying them. They do not fit into any of the five kingdoms. Scientists can't even agree on whether viruses are living or nonliving.

Viruses are classified according to the **host** that the virus invades. A host is the living thing another organism lives in. Some viruses use bacteria as hosts. Other viruses infect plants, and still others live inside animals.

Viral Replication

You know that organisms reproduce by passing on their genetic material. Viruses do the same thing, except they do not have cell parts to carry out reproduction. Instead, viruses use the reproductive machinery of the cells they invade. The virus uses the cell like a factory, causing the cell to make new viruses. Figure 10.2 explains the reproduction of bacterial viruses, or bacteriophages (bak TEER ee uh FAYJ uhs).

Figure 10.2
Viral Replication

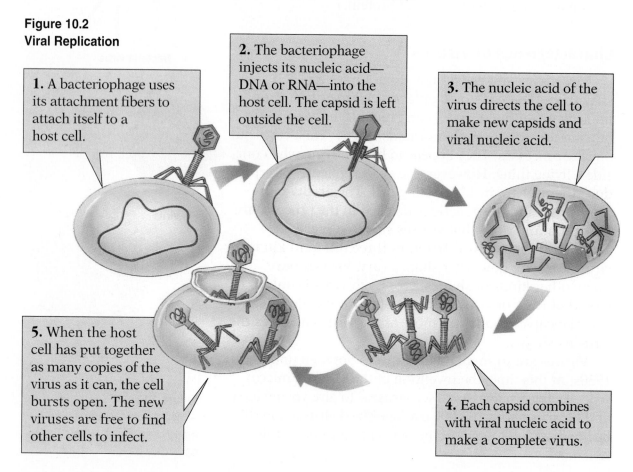

1. A bacteriophage uses its attachment fibers to attach itself to a host cell.

2. The bacteriophage injects its nucleic acid—DNA or RNA—into the host cell. The capsid is left outside the cell.

3. The nucleic acid of the virus directs the cell to make new capsids and viral nucleic acid.

5. When the host cell has put together as many copies of the virus as it can, the cell bursts open. The new viruses are free to find other cells to infect.

4. Each capsid combines with viral nucleic acid to make a complete virus.

Viruses and Disease

When a virus invades an organism's cells, it usually means disease or illness for the host organism. Some viral infections, such as those that cause cold sores in humans, are relatively harmless. Others, such as AIDS, are deadly.

Most viruses can only infect a specific kind of organism. The plant virus that causes disease in tobacco plants, for example, can't harm a human, or even an orange tree. The AIDS virus, called HIV (human immunodeficiency virus), only infects humans.

Humans, unfortunately, are hosts to many different kinds of viruses. Table 10.1 lists some human diseases that are caused by viruses. Most human viruses can invade only certain kinds of cells or tissues. For example, the virus that causes hepatitis infects only liver cells. The tissues affected by other human viruses are shown in the table.

Table 10.1
Viral Diseases in Humans

Disease	Tissue Infected
Smallpox	Skin
Hepatitis	Liver
Polio	Nerves
Rabies	Nerves
Common colds	Respiratory tract
Influenza	Respiratory tract
AIDS	Immune system

Career Corner Virologist

Who Finds Out Which Viruses Cause Disease?

The word was in from San Diego. Schools were closed, and many people were forced to stay home from work. As everyone at the Centers for Disease Control in Atlanta, Georgia, had been expecting, a new virus was spreading. It had reached San Diego and was causing a flu epidemic. The virus had been identified in Asia and probably arrived on a naval ship.

Virologists have a major role in trying to keep epidemics like this one under control. In this case, virologists helped prepare a vaccine, which was sent to health centers around the country. Flu shots were given to those most likely to become very ill from the disease.

Virologists often grow viruses in human tissue cultures. They observe what the virus does to find out if it causes disease, and if so, how. Many virologists use an electron microscope to help them see the viruses they study.

Virologists sometimes provide information to the general public about how a viral disease is transmitted. They are also at the center of the search for a cure for AIDS.

Virologists also study the viruses that cause diseases in

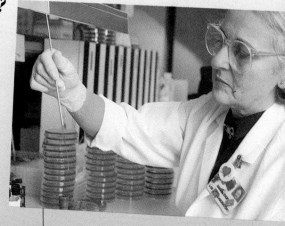

agricultural animals and plants. They help prevent epidemics among sheep and cattle as well as in many crops.

If you would like to become a virologist, you will need a college degree in biology with courses in microbiology.

Common Cold More than 100 different viruses cause the common cold. Your body can build up cell defenses, called antibodies, against a particular cold virus. But the antibodies you build up after being exposed to one cold virus are useless against a different cold virus.

Cold viruses travel on dust and water droplets in the air. When a person with a cold sneezes or coughs, cold viruses are sprayed into the air. If you breathe in the viruses or pick them up on your hands from your surroundings, you can catch a cold.

Hepatitis The hepatitis virus causes a disease of the liver. Hepatitis makes people feel very tired. Hepatitis is spread to people by contaminated food or drinking water. When food is prepared by a person with hepatitis, the hepatitis virus can be transmitted, or passed, to others who eat the food.

Herpes Several kinds of herpes viruses cause human diseases. A fever blister or cold sore on your lips is caused by herpes virus 1. The blisters heal within a week, but the new viruses formed during the infection remain inactive within the body for a long time. Later, a fever, emotional stress, or overexposure to the sun can trigger another outbreak. Herpes virus 2 causes sores in the area of the sex organs. This herpes virus, too, can remain inactive and then become active again. Herpes virus 3 causes chicken pox and shingles.

AIDS HIV causes AIDS—acquired immune deficiency syndrome. As HIV attacks the cells of the body's immune system, the body loses its ability to defend itself against all diseases. The virus enters the body in blood or other body fluids. Scientists have not been able to prepare a vaccine against HIV because it changes constantly.

Figure 10.3
With the development of electron microscopes, it became possible to view viruses such as these.

AIDS virus ▶

▲ Cold virus

◀ Herpes virus

▲ Hepatitis virus

198

Science and Technology
Curing the Common Cold

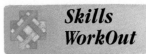
Medical researchers have been searching for the cure for the common cold for a long time. They are experimenting with a drug called WIN 51,711. Because the researchers know about the structure of a virus and the way viruses reproduce themselves, they think WIN 51,711 may be able to be used to cure the common cold. WIN 51,711 keeps cold viruses from shedding their protein coats. If the capsid of a virus can't be left outside the host cell, the medical researchers hypothesize that the virus will not be able to inject its nucleic acid into the cell.

The researchers are not exactly sure how or why WIN 51,711 works. They know that the drug attaches itself to certain points on the virus's capsid. They hypothesize that the drug keeps the capsid from falling away from the virus. But their studies and experiments are not complete.

WIN 51,711 has not been tested on humans yet. It has only been tested on animals and in test-tube cell cultures. Will WIN 51,711 work in humans? Researchers will not know until it is tested on humans. Often, a drug works on animals or in test-tube cultures but does not work inside the human body. WIN 51,711 could also have unforeseen side effects. But who knows? Someday WIN 51,711 may be available by prescription from your doctor, and the common cold will not affect people anymore.

Infer Think about the time of year that you most often catch colds. Is it during the winter months or summer months? Most people catch colds more often during the winter than they do in the summer. State at least two inferences that could explain this.

Check and Explain

1. List the characteristics of a virus.

2. In what ways does a virus differ from an organism? In what ways are they alike?

3. **Find Causes** Why does the reproduction of a virus in the cells of an organism cause disease or illness for the organism?

4. **Calculate** If a very large virus were enlarged 10,000 times, it would be about the size of a grain of salt. How tall would you be if you were enlarged 10,000 times?

10.2 Monerans

Objectives

▶ **Describe** the characteristics of monerans.

▶ **Classify** bacteria according to shape.

▶ **Distinguish** between harmful and helpful bacteria.

▶ **Make a graph** showing how a moneran population can increase over time.

Take a survey of the living things in your classroom. How many did you count? Compare your count to the counts of three classmates. Are your numbers in the millions? If not, they should be! All around you, on your skin, in your body, and in the food you eat, are millions of organisms so small you can't see them without a microscope. These microscopic organisms are classified as **monerans**. Monerans are single-celled microscopic organisms. Unlike other cells, they do not have a nucleus surrounded by a membrane. Instead they have a nuclear area that contains a circular molecule of DNA.

Monerans live nearly everywhere—in the air, in soil, in water, in certain foods, inside other organisms. More monerans are living at this moment than any other group of organisms. With so many of them in so many different places, monerans affect your life in a variety of ways.

Characteristics of Monerans

Look at the moneran in Figure 10.4. Notice that the cell is very simple, with few structures. Find the nuclear area with its molecule of DNA. Look at the outside borders of the moneran. It, like all monerans, has both a cell membrane and a cell wall. This moneran also has many whiplike structures called **flagella** (fluh JEHL uh). Monerans that have flagella can move in liquids.

Although monerans are single cells, some monerans live together in groups of two or four. Some form long chains of several hundred or more. Still others form grapelike bunches.

Capsule

Ribosome

Cell wall

DNA

Flagella

Cytoplasm

Cell membrane

Figure 10.4 ▲
This moneran has a cell membrane and a cell wall but no nucleus or other internal structures.

Kinds of Monerans

Scientists classify monerans into two main groups: bacteria and blue-green bacteria. Blue-green bacteria are different from bacteria because they have the green pigment chlorophyll just like plant cells. Blue-green bacteria also have a blue pigment. The two pigments give blue-green bacteria their color.

Because blue-green bacteria have chlorophyll, they can get energy through photosynthesis. Unlike plant cells, however, the chlorophyll in blue-green bacteria is not in chloroplasts. In fact, scientists hypothesize that the first chloroplasts were really blue-green bacteria that began to live inside another bacterium.

Bacteria are more common than blue-green bacteria. Most bacteria get energy from food in their surroundings. Some bacteria, however, can get energy through photosynthesis. But these bacteria either don't have chlorophyll or use a simpler kind of chlorophyll than do blue-green bacteria.

One way scientists classify bacteria is by their shape. There are three common shapes. Round or egg-shaped bacteria are called **cocci** (KAHK sy). Rod-shaped bacteria are called **bacilli** (buh SIHL EYE). Spiral-shaped bacteria are called **spirilla** (spy RIHL uh). Read about these three kinds of bacteria below.

Bacteria are also classified by whether or not they need oxygen to live, grow, and reproduce. Bacteria that require oxygen are called **aerobes** (AIR ohbs). Bacteria classified as **anaerobes** (AN ur OHBS) do not need oxygen. Anaerobic bacteria get energy from food through the process of fermentation.

Cocci
Some cocci form pairs called diplococci. *Di-* means two. Others form long chains. These are called streptococci. Others form clusters called staphylococci. ▼

Bacilli ▲
The rod-shaped bacilli can grow in pairs or chains. They do not form clusters. Pairs of bacilli are called diplobacilli.

Spirilla
Spirilla only live as single cells. They are shaped like spirals or corkscrews. ▼

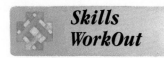
Calculate A colony of 100 bacteria begin to reproduce every 20 minutes. How many bacteria will there be after 2 hours?

Bacterial Reproduction

Bacteria reproduce asexually by a process called **binary fission**. During binary fission, one bacterial cell divides into two identical bacterial cells.

Conditions have to be right for a bacterial cell to divide. For most bacteria, this means being in a warm, moist place with a good food source. Under ideal conditions, bacterial cells can reproduce rapidly. Some bacteria can reproduce every 20 minutes or less.

Before binary fission begins, a bacterial cell usually has to grow to twice its normal size. Look at Figure 10.5. As the bacterial cell grows, the bacterium makes enough cell material, including new DNA, for each new cell. Then the cell membrane and cell wall begin to pinch inward until a cross-wall forms. Two new cells are formed, each with a set of identical hereditary material. As this process continues, large numbers of bacteria can be produced. A group of bacteria that started with one bacterium is called a colony.

Some bacteria can live through very unfavorable conditions. If the temperature is too hot or the environment is too dry, they form a thick wall around themselves. A bacterium with a thick protective wall is called an **endospore**. Some endospores can withstand boiling and freezing. When environmental conditions are favorable again, the endospore breaks open, and the bacterium becomes active again.

Figure 10.5 Binary Fission ▼

Cell membrane

1. Bacterial cell grows twice its size.

2. DNA replicates.

3. Cell membrane grows; DNA molecules pull apart.

4. Cell wall pinches off.

5. Two identical cells form.

Helpful Bacteria

Even though harmful bacteria often get all the attention, helpful bacteria far outnumber harmful bacteria. Bacteria play an important role in the lives of all living things, including you.

Bacteria and Plants Plants need nitrogen to grow. Even though the atmosphere is about 70 percent nitrogen, plants can't use it directly from the air. Some bacteria, called nitrogen-fixing bacteria, can change nitrogen gas to a form that plants can use. These bacteria grow on the roots of beans, peas, peanuts, and other plants. Others live in the soil. Animals, in turn, get usable nitrogen when they eat plants.

Bacteria and Animals Some bacteria live in the intestines and stomachs of animals. They help the animals digest food. Plant-eating animals, such as cows, sheep, and camels, feed on grasses. Bacteria help these animals digest the plant material, releasing nutrients in plants that the animals need to live.

Figure 10.7 ▲
Factory-produced cheeses are made in large molds, then cut up and packaged.

Bacteria and Food Bacteria are used widely by humans in food making, especially in producing dairy products. Milk is changed to cheese, yogurt, and sour cream through the action of bacteria. Bacteria are also involved in making soy sauce, tea, and cocoa. Many of the flavors in your food are produced by bacteria. Cheddar, Swiss, Parmesan, and other cheeses would all taste about the same without bacteria. The sour taste of vinegar and sauerkraut is also caused by bacteria.

Bacteria and Soil Soil is made up of very small rock particles and decaying plant and animal material called humus (HYOO muhs). Humus holds the large amounts of nutrients that plants need to grow. Bacteria are among the most important makers of humus. They are **decomposers**, organisms that feed on dead plants and animals for energy. As decomposers feed, they break down dead organisms into simpler substances. These substances are released into the environment. Decomposers recycle minerals into the ecosystem and help to keep soil fertile.

Figure 10.6 ▲
Bacteria in the stomachs of cows digest plant matter and release nutrients.

Consider This

Should Food Be Irradiated?

The word *irradiation* sounds dangerous to many people. To irradiate means to expose to radiation. When people are exposed to radiation, it can cause cancer and birth defects. Irradiating food, however, is a very effective way of preserving it.

Consider Some Issues

Spoiled food is an expensive and dangerous problem. Those who support food irradiation say that it is a perfectly safe way to prevent food spoilage and food poisoning.

When food is irradiated, the food itself doesn't become radioactive. The radiation kills molds, bacteria, worms, and other organisms that can cause spoilage or disease.

Japan, Mexico, and Canada are currently using the food irradiation process. The United States also approved food irradiation in the 1980s. Many people in the United States, however, are worried that food irradiation may be harmful. Irradiation can create new substances in food that give it a bad taste or smell. The substances seem to be harmless, but their effects are not fully known. Another problem is that food irradiation creates dangerous radioactive waste products.

Think About It Most people feel safe eating canned, frozen, and microwaved food. Is irradiated food something people should also accept? How can scientists make sure that food irradiation is safe?

Write About It Write a paper stating your position for or against food irradiation. Include all your reasons.

Harmful Bacteria

Bacteria cause many kinds of diseases in plants and animals. In humans, tuberculosis and pneumonia are the result of bacterial infection. Bacteria also cause common problems, such as acne and tooth decay.

Once inside a living thing, bacteria can reproduce rapidly. The inside of the human body is the ideal temperature for bacterial growth. As the bacteria multiply, they produce waste products that are poisons to the living thing. The poisons cause the symptoms of the disease. In humans, the body tries to fight back by raising its body temperature. That's when you have a fever.

You get food poisoning when you eat food in which bacteria have grown. The poisons produced by salmonella food poisoning cause headache, chills, nausea, diarrhea, and stomach cramps. The symptoms are usually gone after two or three days. Salmonella bacteria

Figure 10.8 ▲
What effects from the bacterial blight do you see on the soybean plant?

most commonly infect eggs, ground meat, chicken, and sausage. Another kind of food poisoning, called botulism, can be fatal. Fortunately, botulism is not common. The bacteria that cause botulism are harmful only when they are trapped in improperly canned or jarred food.

Skills WorkOut

Research Choose one of your favorite foods. Find out the different ways it can be safely preserved.

Science and Technology *Foul Food*

Food poisoning and food spoilage are caused by the growth of bacteria in foods that are not packaged or stored properly. Using scientific knowledge about the needs of bacteria, food manufacturers can package or treat foods so that they last longer. The methods they use slow or stop bacterial growth.

Table 10.2   Methods of Preventing Food Spoilage

Method	Description
Canning	Foods are cooked at high temperatures. Then they are stored in airtight containers.
Curing	Foods are dried or cooked. Salt, vinegar, sugar, or chemical preservatives are added. These substances slow or stop bacterial growth.
Cold Storage	Many foods need to be stored at temperatures between −1°C and 10°C.
Drying	Removing most of the water from foods slows or stops bacterial growth.
Freezing	Foods are stored at temperatures below −18°C to help slow or stop bacterial growth.
Irradiation	Fruits and meats are bombarded with ultraviolet or gamma rays.

Check and Explain

1. What are the characteristics of monerans?

2. How are monerans classified?

3. **Compare and Contrast** Explain the main ways that bacteria are helpful and the ways they are harmful.

4. **Graph** One bacterium divides to form two; two divide to make four. Make a graph that shows how this pattern continues as the bacteria divide. How many bacteria will there be after five generations?

Activity 10 *How effective are common antiseptics?*

Skills Measure; Observe; Infer; Control Variables

Task 1 Prelab Prep

1. Collect the following items: grease pencil, 1 package instant chicken broth, a 1-liter beaker or 4-cup glass measuring cup, graduated cylinder, 5 small jars, 4 different everyday products claiming to have antiseptic properties (such as mouthwash, rubbing alcohol, hydrogen peroxide, cleaning products). **CAUTION! Some of these products may be dangerous, especially when mixed together; read the labels and observe all warnings and cautions**.
2. Using the grease pencil, label the jars from 1 to 5.

Task 2 Data Record

1. On a separate sheet of paper, draw the data table shown.
2. Record all your observations in the data table.

Table 10.3 Product Tests

Jar	Product Name	Condition on Day 2	Condition on Day 3
1			
2			
3			
4			
5			

Task 3 Procedure

1. Following the directions on the package, make up 3 cups of chicken broth (about 750 mL) in either the glass measuring cup or the beaker. Use very warm water from the faucet. Make sure the broth dissolves completely. Stir if necessary.

2. Using the graduated cylinder, measure 100 mL of chicken broth into each jar.
3. To each of jars 1 through 4, add 2 dropperfuls of a different "antiseptic" product. Make sure you write the name of each product in the data table before you add it to the jar.
4. Do not add anything to jar 5.
5. Place all the jars together in an open place where they will be out of direct sunlight.
6. On the second and third days, record your observations in the data table.

Task 4 Analysis

1. Identify the control variable in this activity.
2. **Infer** How can you tell if bacteria are growing in a jar of chicken broth?
3. In which jars were bacteria growing on the second day? On the third day?
4. **Infer** Which of the products prevented the growth of bacteria?
5. Read the labels from your antiseptic products. What do the labels claim these antiseptic products do?

Task 5 Conclusion

Based on your analysis of your observations, explain which of the products is the most effective antiseptic and why.

Everyday Application

What are each of the products you tested usually used for? Why would it be important to keep bacteria from growing out of control in each case?

Extension

Choose one of the antiseptics you used in this activity. Develop an experiment to test how much of the antiseptic you need to add to 100 mL of chicken broth in order to keep the bacteria from growing.

Chapter 10 Review

Concept Summary

10.1 Viruses

▶ Viruses are microscopic, noncellular, and unable to carry out basic life processes except inside the cells of another organism.

▶ Viruses are difficult to classify because they are not made of cells and appear to be nonliving when outside of a living thing.

▶ Viruses replicate by using the reproductive machinery of the cells they invade.

▶ Viral infection usually causes disease in the host. In humans, viruses can cause colds, hepatitis, herpes, and AIDS.

10.2 Monerans

▶ Monerans are single-celled microscopic organisms. They have both a cell membrane and a cell wall but do not have a nucleus.

▶ Monerans are classified as blue-green bacteria or bacteria. Bacteria are classified according to shape as cocci, bacilli, or spirilla.

▶ Bacteria can reproduce rapidly under good conditions by binary fission.

▶ Most bacteria play a positive role, such as aiding animals in digestion, decomposing dead organisms, and helping plants get nitrogen.

▶ Some bacteria are harmful and cause diseases in plants and animals. In humans, bacteria can cause tuberculosis, pneumonia, and food poisoning.

Chapter Vocabulary

virus (10.1)	flagella (10.2)	spirilla (10.2)	binary fission (10.2)
host (10.1)	cocci (10.2)	aerobe (10.2)	endospore (10.2)
moneran (10.2)	bacilli (10.2)	anaerobe (10.2)	decomposer (10.2)

Check Your Vocabulary

Use the vocabulary words above to complete the following sentences.

1. Bacteria reproduce asexually by means of a process called ____ .

2. The living thing in which another organism lives is called a ____ .

3. Organisms that feed on dead plants and animals are ____ .

4. Round or egg-shaped bacteria are called ____ .

5. A piece of hereditary material with a coat of protein is a ____ .

6. Some monerans have a whiplike structures called ____ that allows them to move in liquids.

7. Rod-shaped bacteria are classified as ____ .

8. A bacterium that requires oxygen is called an ____ .

9. A bacterium with a thick protective wall is an ____ .

10. Bacteria and blue-green bacteria are two kinds of ____ .

11. Spiral-shaped bacteria are called ____ .

12. Bacteria that do not require oxygen are classified as ____ .

Write Your Vocabulary

Write complete sentences using the vocabulary words. Show that you know what each word means.

Chapter 10 Review

Check Your Knowledge

Answer the following in complete sentences.

1. What are three different ways to classify bacteria?

2. Why are viruses difficult to classify?

3. How do viruses reproduce?

4. What are some characteristics of monerans?

5. What are some ways bacteria are helpful?

6. What are some human diseases caused by viral infection?

7. How do the two main groups of monerans differ?

Choose the answer that best completes the sentence.

8. Some monerans are able to move in liquid by using (capsids, flagella, spirilla, endospores).

9. AIDS is caused by a (bacterium, moneran, virus, flagellum.)

10. Viruses cannot move, feed, or grow outside the cells of a (decomposer, cow, human, host).

11. Bacteria are classified according to (size, need for oxygen, harmfulness, shape) as cocci, bacilli, or spirilla.

12. Bacteria reproduce (sexually, with the machinery of a host cell, by binary fission, using endospores).

13. A bacterium may become an endospore (for protection, to reproduce, to infect, to decompose).

14. Bacteria are classified as aerobic or anaerobic depending on whether or not they (have capsids, are round, are harmful, need oxygen).

Check Your Understanding

Apply the concepts you have learned to answer each question.

1. **Compare and Contrast** What do viruses and monerans have in common? How are they different?

2. **Reason and Conclude** Scientists disagree whether viruses are living, nonliving, or something in between. Based on what you know about viruses, how would you classify them? Give reasons to support your conclusion.

3. **Reason and Conclude** Since bacteria and viruses can cause so much disease, do you think it would be a good idea to destroy all of them? Why or why not?

4. Why are foods preserved? What methods can be used?

5. **Infer** What would happen if the population of bacteria acting as decomposers were significantly reduced?

6. When you have a bacterial infection, you often develop a fever. Why do you think that raising your body temperature is helpful in fighting the bacteria?

7. **Mystery Photo** The photograph on page 194 shows bacteria (yellow) on the head of a household pin. Based on their shape, what type of bacteria are they?

Develop Your Skills

1. **Make a Model** Make a model showing a bacteriophage infecting a bacterium. Label the parts of the virus and the bacterium. Describe in five steps how the bacterium is infected.

2. **Data Bank** Look on page 625 to answer the following questions.

   a. How much bigger is a bacterium than a virus?

   b. How much bigger than a bacterium is a grain of salt?

3. **Interpret Data** *Escherichia coli* is a bacteria that lives in the human large intestine. It digests some foods your body can't and even produces vitamins for you. *Dipplococcus pneumoniae* is a bacteria that causes pneumonia. Use the graph below to answer the following questions. What appears to have happened on Day 3? What happened on Day 5? What happened to the population of both types of bacteria after Day 5? Why?

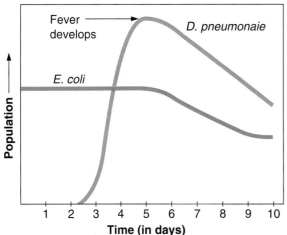

Number of Bacteria in Human Host

Make Connections

1. **Link the Concepts** Below is a concept map showing how some of the main concepts in this chapter link together. Only part of the map is filled in. Copy the map and complete it using words and ideas from the chapter.

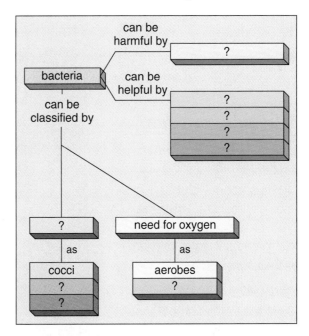

2. **Science and Art** Most types of bacteria are not harmful and do not cause disease. Design an advertisement to inform people about helpful bacteria. Draw pictures or find photographs from old magazines. Think up slogans. Include reasons why the bacteria are helpful.

3. **Science and Society** Read about one of the diseases listed in Table 10.1 on page 197. Find out as much of the following as possible: how the disease affects the body, where and when the disease was most widespread, how it affected society, how society responded to it, and if and how it was brought under control. Get into groups of three and report your findings to one another.

Chapter **11** Protists and Fungi

Chapter Sections

What do you see?

66In this picture I see a mushroom. It looks like one big mushroom with little ones all around it. I think the grooves are so these mushrooms can get water, oxygen, and air.99

Kim Rice
Honea Path Middle School
Honea Path, South Carolina

To find out more about the photograph, look on page 230. As you read this chapter, you will learn about fungi and protists.

11.1 Diversity of Protists

Objectives

▶ **Describe** how protists differ from monerans.

▶ **Compare** and **contrast** protozoa and algae.

▶ **Explain** the role of plankton in food chains.

▶ **Make inferences** about how protozoa obtain their nutrition.

You watch a group of submarine-shaped creatures whizz by through the murky water. The long hairs covering their bodies beat rapidly. Suddenly an even larger beast appears, its scary mouth gaping open. Is it chasing the others? Then you notice a huge jellylike blob oozing toward you.

Are you on an alien planet? No, you're still on the earth, at the bottom of a pond. But you've been shrunk down to the size of the tiniest speck. The creatures you've been observing are single-celled, animal-like organisms called **protozoa** (PROH tuh ZOH uh). Protozoa (singular: protozoan) belong to kingdom Protista.

Kingdom Protista

Members of kingdom Protista are called **protists** (PROH tihsts). Protozoa like the ones living in the pond are one major group of protists. The other major group of protists is made up of plantlike organisms, both single-celled and many-celled, called **algae** (AL jee). Seaweeds are common kinds of algae (singular: alga).

Why do scientists classify these two different groups of organisms in the same kingdom? All protists have one thing in common. They are **eukaryotes** (yoo KAIR ee OHTS), meaning their cells are complex, like the cells of plants and animals. They have nuclei, mitochondria, and other organelles. Having complex cells is what separates the protists from the monera.

However, protists aren't as complex as plants or animals. The protozoa are only single-celled. The algae are either single-celled or do not have all of the many specialized parts that plants have. Kingdom Protista, therefore, includes all eukaryotes that are not plants, animals, or fungi.

Figure 11.1 ▲
Algae are plantlike protists often found growing in masses on the surface of ponds. How do algae differ from plants?

Protozoa

Animal-like protists, the protozoa, live wherever there is water. Besides ponds, you can find them in soil, in the ocean, and inside other organisms. They have no chloroplasts, so they must take in food from their surroundings.

Most protozoa are microscopic. Even so, they are much larger than bacteria. If an average protozoan were the size of a soccer field, then a bacterium would be the size of a soccer ball.

Even though it is made up of only one cell, a protozoan can do almost everything a many-celled animal can do. It moves and senses changes in its environment. It eats and reproduces.

A protozoan has a cell membrane, but no cell wall. The absence of a cell wall is another way in which protozoa differ from monerans and most algae.

Most protozoa reproduce asexually. In a process called fission, the protozoan divides into two similar daughter cells. Some protozoa exchange genetic material before undergoing fission. This is a simple form of sexual reproduction.

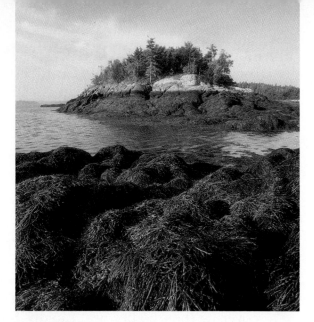

Figure 11.3 ▲
Many-celled algae grow on rocks at the ocean's edge.

Algae

Protists with chloroplasts are classified as algae. Algae undergo photosynthesis, and most have rigid cell walls. It is because they share these characteristics with plants that they are considered plantlike.

Unlike protozoa, some algae are many-celled organisms. These algae are known as seaweeds and can grow larger than many land plants. But their simple organization and lack of transport vessels are characteristics of the protists.

Algae reproduce in a variety of ways. Some groups of algae reproduce asexually by fission. Other groups have developed forms of sexual reproduction. In some many-celled algae, special sex cells are used to exchange genetic material.

Single-celled algae living in the ocean are called plankton. They form the first level of the food chain. Chloroplasts within these organisms harness the sun's radiant energy and convert it into glucose. Animals that feed upon these protists absorb their stored energy.

Figure 11.2 ▲
Protozoa called foraminifera make hard shells. The shell at the right is magnified 105 times.

Figure 11.4 ▲

Edible algae are dried on a beach in Japan (left). Sushi is a popular dish in many Japanese restaurants (right).

Science and Society *Algae as Food*

When was the last time you ate algae? It was probably very recently, because many foods contain extracts of algae. Carrageen, for example, is a substance obtained from an alga called Irish moss. Carrageen is added to such foods as ice cream and puddings to make them thicker. It is also found in many toothpastes.

Algin is another substance made from algae that you may have eaten. Extracted from kelps, algin is added to ice cream to prevent its ingredients from separating. Like carrageen, algin also adds body to foods.

Many people in the world eat algae from the sea, both fresh and dried. In Japan, raw seafood and rice are wrapped in sheets of dried algae to make the delicacy called sushi. Sushi is also popular in the United States. Japanese people also use algae in soups, teas, biscuits, and as a flavoring.

Check and Explain

1. How are protists different from monerans?

2. What are plankton? What role do they have in the food chains of the ocean?

3. **Compare and Contrast** Why are algae and protozoa grouped together in the same kingdom? What characteristics separate protozoa and algae?

4. **Infer** What do protozoa eat? Name a possible food and explain why protozoa are likely to eat it.

11.2 Protozoa

Objectives

▶ **Name** the different structures protozoa use to move.

▶ **Identify** and **describe** protozoa that cause disease in humans.

▶ **Make inferences** about the habitats of protozoa based on the ways they move.

▶ **Organize data** about the four major groups of protozoa.

One characteristic that many protozoa share with animals is the ability to move. Organisms that get their energy through photosynthesis may stay in one place, but those that must take in food often have to search for their meals.

Animals have developed a variety of structures that help them move, such as wings, legs, and fins. In a similar way, protozoa have evolved different ways of moving, each using a different kind of structure. Protozoa that move in similar ways tend to have many other similarities. Just as you find it easy to classify vehicles as cars, boats, or planes, scientists have grouped the protozoa according to how they move.

Sarcodines

One group of protozoa, the sarcodines (SAR kuh deens), move using footlike projections of cell matter called **pseudopodia** (soo duh POH dee uh). A typical sarcodine extends a pseudopod, and cytoplasm begins to flow into it. The entire cell oozes into the pseudopod, and at the same time a new pseudopod forms. The cell is always changing shape.

Most sarcodines are free-living, meaning they don't live inside other organisms. A few, however, are parasites. One sarcodine causes an illness in humans called amebic dysentery (uh MEE bihk DIHS uhn TAIR ee).

Look at Figure 11.5. It shows a common sarcodine, the ameba (uh MEE buh). Sarcodines such as the ameba use their pseudopods for capturing food. The ameba engulfs the food and stores it within a food vacuole.

Cell membrane
Pseudopods
Food vacuole
Nucleus

Figure 11.5 ▲
The bloblike ameba oozes around in search of food. What structures does it use to move?

Ciliates

The ciliates are another group of mostly free-living protozoa. Ciliates move using tiny, hairlike structures called **cilia** (SIHL ee uh). The cilia work like little oars, moving back and forth in the water to move the organism along.

With cilia covering much of their bodies, many ciliates are able to swim very fast, for a protozoan. Ciliates can move forward and backward, and they can turn quickly.

A common ciliate is the paramecium, shown in Figure 11.6. Its tapered body is enclosed by a hard covering. On one side of the body is a channel lined with cilia called the oral groove. Food particles are swept down this oral groove into the paramecium's mouth.

Food passing through the paramecium's mouth enters a food vacuole. As this vacuole circulates through the cytoplasm, its contents are digested and distributed around the cell.

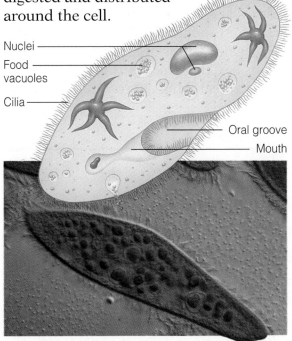

Nuclei
Food vacuoles
Cilia
Oral groove
Mouth

Figure 11.6 ▲
How does a paramecium move?

Figure 11.7 ▲
Victims of African sleeping sickness have this parasitic flagellate in their blood.

Flagellates

A third group of protozoa, the flagellates (FLA juh LAYTS), use a whiplike organelle called a flagellum to move. Lashing of the flagella creates a current of water that propels the flagellate. Look at the flagellate in Figure 11.7. Can you see the flagella? Some flagellates have one flagellum, others have many.

You may remember that monerans, too, have structures called flagella. Moneran flagella, however, are very different from the flagella of flagellates. They are made of different parts and materials and are moved in a different way. Why do you think these two different structures have been given the same name?

Although most flagellates are free-living, some members of this group live inside other organisms. A termite's gut, for example, contains a population of flagellates. These flagellates help the termite by digesting wood.

Some of the flagellates that live inside other organisms are parasites that can injure or kill their host. For example, African sleeping sickness is a deadly human disease caused by a flagellate. It is transmitted by the bite of the tsetse fly.

Sporozoa

Unlike the other groups of protozoa, sporozoa (SPOH roh ZOH uh) have no special organelles used for movement. They are all parasites, living inside the bodies of cattle, birds, humans, and other animals. All sporozoa produce special reproductive cells called **spores**, from which new sporozoa can grow.

One well-known sporozoan causes malaria. A mosquito bite transfers the organism into a person's body. There, it reproduces and infects red blood cells. Mosquitos that feed on infected blood pick up the sporozoan. Spores are produced in the insect's gut. They migrate to the mosquito's salivary glands, where they can be transferred into someone else.

Figure 11.8 ▲
An *Anopholes* mosquito infects a person with the sporozoan that causes malaria.

Science and Society *Malaria*

In places such as Central Africa, Brazil, India, and the Far East, malaria is a very common disease. In fact, over 150 million people are stricken with malaria each year. Malaria doesn't usually cause death, but a person infected with it often has symptoms of the disease for a long time. Headaches, high fever, and violent shivering are the main symptoms.

In the 1960s, drugs and the use of insecticides helped prevent the disease from spreading. Today, however, the disease is spreading again. This is because the mosquitos that infect organisms have become resistant to the insecticides. Scientists are researching alternative vaccines to this serious disease.

Check and Explain

1. What is a pseudopod?

2. Describe two human diseases caused by protozoa.

3. **Infer** Based on what you know about how different protozoa move, which group would you say is most common in soil?

4. **Organize Data** Make four columns on a piece of paper and write the name of a group of protozoa at the top of each. Below each name, write down all that you have learned about that group.

11.3 Algae

Objectives

▶ **Identify** and **describe** six groups of algae.

▶ **Explain** the causes and dangers of red tide.

▶ **Describe** human uses of some algae.

▶ **Classify** algae based on their characteristics.

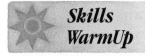
Skills WarmUp

Classify In order to grow, algae need sunlight and fresh water or salt water at different temperatures. List the places in your neighborhood that you think can support algae growth.

The algae, whether single-celled or many-celled, all use chlorophyll to capture the sun's energy to make glucose. Algal cells also have other light-absorbing substances, or pigments. These extra pigments help transfer the sun's energy to chlorophyll.

Because the extra pigments can hide the green color of chlorophyll, many kinds of algae are not green. Instead they appear brown, red, or yellow. The pigments contained in algae form the basis for their classification. Of the six major groups of algae formed in this way, three have mostly single-celled members, and three contain mostly many-celled forms.

Dinoflagellates

One major group of algae is made up of the single-celled dinoflagellates. Most dinoflagellates live in the ocean. Their cells are encased in rigid plates of cellulose. Two flagella extend from a groove in the plates. As these flagella lash about, they make the dinoflagellate spin. Dinoflagellates often contain large amounts of an extra red pigment.

When the population of certain types of dinoflagellates grows rapidly, they color the water red. This condition, known as red tide, is dangerous because these protists also contain a poison. Animals that eat the dinoflagellates keep the poison in their bodies. When people eat these poison-containing animals, such as clams, they can get sick and even die.

Some dinoflagellates can change stored chemical energy into light. If you've walked on a beach at night, you may have seen glowing dinoflagellates. They make the waves sparkle as they crash on the sand.

Figure 11.9 ▲
Dinoflagellates have different shapes, but all have two flagella.

Diatoms

Single-celled, gold-colored algae make up another group called diatoms (DY uh TAHMS). The gold color comes from large amounts of yellow, orange, and brown pigments. Diatoms are important producers in both freshwater and saltwater environments. In the ocean, they make up part of the plankton.

The diatom cell is covered by a shell made from a glass-like material. The shells come in two halves that fit together like a pillbox. The shells have many beautiful and delicate shapes as you can see in Figure 11.10. Each species has its own shape and markings.

When a diatom dies, the shell sinks to the sea bottom. Over millions of years, diatom shells have formed thick deposits on the ocean floor. When geologic processes raise these deposits above sea level, they can be mined. They are used for products that need a fine grit, such as cleansers and polishes.

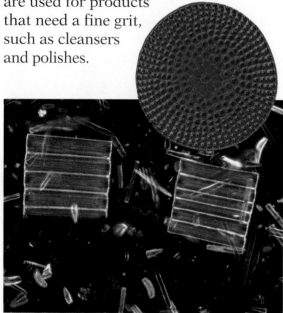

Figure 11.10 ▲
The extra-fine details of diatom shells were once used to test a microscope's focusing ability.

Flagellum · Chloroplasts · Nucleus · Cell membrane · Eyespot

Figure 11.11 ▲
Euglenas have characteristics of both algae and protozoa. In what ways are they animal-like?

Euglenas

Ponds and similar environments are home to single-celled, grass-green protists called euglenas (yoo GLEE nuhs). Look at Figure 11.11. Most euglenas have chloroplasts and undergo photosynthesis. Unlike other types of algae, however, euglenas are able to live without sunlight because they can eat.

In dark conditions, euglenas dine on monerans and other protists. They are also active swimmers, using flagella to propel themselves. These animal-like characteristics show that the boundary between algae and protozoa is blurry.

Euglenas have tapered bodies encased in tough but flexible coverings. At the base of the single flagellum is an eyespot. Of course, the eyespot isn't actually an eye. Light striking the eyespot directs the action of the flagellum, causing the protist to swim toward light. Why is an eyespot a valuable adaptation for a euglena?

Green Algae

Both single-celled and many-celled algae are included in a large group called the green algae. Green algae live in freshwater habitats and the ocean. They are abundant in soil, and some live inside other organisms. Green algae are bright green because they contain large amounts of chlorophyll.

Green algae have a great variety of forms. The simplest green algae are single-celled. Other types of green algae form colonies, groups of cells that live together but do not show much specialization. Some of these colonial algae exist as long filaments. Another kind of colonial green algae has its cells arranged in a hollow ball.

Other types of many-celled green algae have structures adapted for certain functions. They are more complex than colonial green algae. For example, a green algae called sea lettuce has its cells arranged in thin, leaflike sheets.

Many-celled green algae are similar in many ways to plants. In fact, the cells of all green algae are more plantlike than those of any other group of algae.

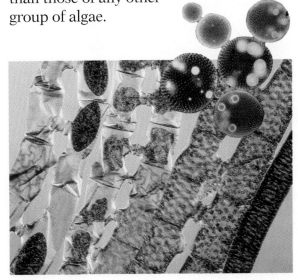

Figure 11.12 ▲
Volvox (top) and *Spirogyra* (bottom) are colonial green algae.

Brown Algae

Many of the seaweeds that carpet rocky shores belong to the brown algae. Brown algae are all many-celled, and nearly all live in the ocean. Like the many-celled green algae, their cells are grouped to form specialized structures. The cell walls of brown algae contain a jellylike material called algin. Algin's rubberiness helps protect brown algae from battering by waves.

Many kinds of brown algae look very plantlike because their specialized structures resemble those of plants. Many brown algae have a rootlike structure called a *holdfast* that anchors the algae to a stable surface. They also have stalks and leaflike blades.

Some brown algae also have air bladders, structures plants don't have. Air bladders enable brown algae to keep their bodies near the ocean's surface. Why does being at the surface benefit an alga?

The kelps are the largest brown algae. Their giant blades form an underwater environment much like a forest. Its canopy protects many different types of organisms.

Figure 11.13 ▲
Many kinds of brown algae are harvested for food and fertilizer.

Red Algae

Many of the brown algae's characteristics are shared by the group called red algae. All red algae are many-celled, and most live in saltwater habitats. They are large enough to be called seaweeds, and they have specialized structures such as holdfasts and stalks.

Red algae get their name from a reddish pigment that other kinds of algae do not have. Unlike other pigments, it can harness the energy of the dim light that penetrates below the ocean's surface. The amount of this pigment in a red alga depends on the depth at which it grows. Those growing near the surface do not need very much of it, so they are green. Those growing at medium depths are red. Red algae growing deep below the surface contain so much of this pigment that they appear almost black.

The bodies of red algae are divided into thin filaments. Often these filaments are branched or interwoven, creating

Figure 11.14 ▲
Some red algae, called coralline algae, have hard calcium deposits in their cell walls.

Career Corner   *Marine Life Technician*

Who Studies Ocean Organisms?

As you collect your last specimen, your diving buddy communicates that it is time to surface. Slowly you rise among the kelp, tracing the path made by your rising bubbles. Surfacing, you carefully place your specimens in a collection pail and head off to the laboratory.

Inside the laboratory, you catalog your collection and begin a series of tests and experiments as directed by a scientist. These observations and experiments will help scientists learn more about the life that inhabits the oceans.

Marine life technicians can be found helping scientists in many different ways. Some technicians work on research ships where they collect and catalog marine specimens. Others use scuba diving to observe organisms.

Most marine technicians, however, work in the laboratory. There, they assist scientists in studying the biology of sea-dwelling organisms. Some technicians may care for the organisms used in experiments.

To become a marine life technician, you should have a science background and enjoy working in a laboratory. A two-year college degree that includes courses in general science and laboratory techniques is recommended. Even with a college background, however, most of the laboratory skills you will need to know will be learned on the job.

lacy designs. Some red algae have hard calcium deposits in their cell walls. They are called coralline algae. Red algae are most common in warm tropical seas, where many different species live.

Red algae are often harvested by humans for use as food. Some contain substances used as food thickeners. One red alga is harvested for making agar. Agar is a jelly-like material used for growing bacteria in the laboratory.

Science and You *Polishing Up on Diatoms*

Have you ever rubbed a liquid or paste polish between your fingers? If so, you may have discovered that the polish contained very small particles of grit. When rubbed over a rough surface, these particles smooth out pits and bumps.

Many polishes, including some brands of toothpaste, contain grit made of ancient deposits of diatom shells. As you may recall, these deposits were formed on the ocean floor as the shells of dead diatoms settled to the bottom. These deposits are called diatomaceous (DY uh tuh MAY shus) earth.

Diatomaceous earth is made up of silica, the same substance that makes up the common mineral quartz. So why aren't polishes made from ground-up quartz? If you look at diatomaceous earth under a microscope, you can see the answer. The individual diatom shells are still there. The shells have many sharp edges. These edges are what make diatomaceous earth good for polishing.

Figure 11.15 ▲
The remains of diatom shells are preserved in diatomaceous earth.

Check and Explain

1. Which two groups of algae contain only many-celled species?

2. Describe one way in which humans use algae.

3. **Reason and Conclude** In some older classification systems, euglenas were placed in the animal kingdom. Explain why this classification made sense.

4. **Classify** Divide the six groups of algae you have studied into two large groups. What will you call the groups? On which characteristics do you base your classification?

Find Causes   Add a small
amount of active dry yeast to
two containers of warm water.
Add sugar to one of the containers. Mix well and wait about ten
minutes. What do you see?
Explain your observations.

11.4 Fungi

Objectives

▶ **Explain** why fungi are different from members of the other four
kingdoms.

▶ **Describe** the basic characteristics of each major fungus group.

▶ **Describe** the lichens and slime molds.

▶ **Hypothesize** about what fungi need to grow best.

Have you ever uncovered a slice of bread with a
dark, furry coating? If so, then you observed a
bread mold. A bread mold is a common example
of a **fungus**, a spore-producing organism with complex
cells and no chlorophyll. The plural of fungus is fungi
(FUHN gee), which is also the name of the kingdom in
which these organisms belong.

The fungi can be found nearly everywhere. Like
monerans, they cause disease, spoil food, and damage
crops. But also like monerans, fungi are important in
the earth's ecology and help humans in many ways.

Characteristics of Fungi

How are fungi different from organisms in the other
four kingdoms? Fungi, first of all, are eukaryotes, which
separates them from the monera. Unlike plants and algae,
fungi lack chlorophyll and can't photosynthesize. Unlike
animals and protozoa, fungi cannot ingest food either.
Instead, fungi *absorb* nutrients from their environment.

Most fungi feed upon dead organisms or other nonliving organic matter. They digest this food outside their
cells by releasing digestive juices. These chemicals
break down the organic matter into simpler substances
that fungi can use as nutrients. Organisms that obtain
their nutrition in this way are called decomposers.
Although most fungi are many-celled, some fungi, such
as yeast, exist as single cells.

The bodies of the many-celled fungi are formed
from branching, threadlike filaments called **hyphae**
(HY fee). Figure 11.17 shows what hyphae look like. In
most fungi, the hyphae are divided into single cells.

Figure 11.16 ▲
These mushrooms are the
reproductive structures of a
fungus. How do fungi differ
from other kinds of organisms?

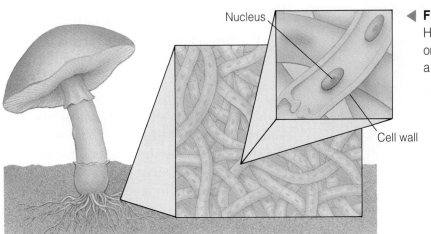

Nucleus

Cell wall

Having a body made of hyphae helps a fungus obtain its nutrients. Hyphae can grow rapidly, reaching wherever there might be food to digest and absorb. And because hyphae are only one cell thick, all cells can be in contact with the food source.

Hyphae are also good building blocks. In complex fungi, the hyphae form a broad underground mat called a mycelium (my SEE lee uhm). Hyphae can also grow in closely packed bunches to form fruiting bodies. The fruiting bodies of some groups of fungi are commonly called mushrooms. Mushrooms and other fruiting bodies function to produce and release the spores that fungi use to reproduce.

Diversity of Fungi

Mycologists (my KAHL uh jihsts), the scientists who study fungi, recognize over 100,000 species of fungi. Among these many fungi, there are three different ways of producing spores through sexual reproduction. Each way of producing spores involves a different spore-producing structure. Mycologists use these different structures to classify fungi into three groups: threadlike, sac, and club.

Some fungi, however, do not reproduce sexually at all. Or at least they are not known to have sexual reproduction. So they are placed in a fourth major group, the imperfect fungi. Occasionally, a member of this fourth group is found to have a sexual stage in its life cycle and is moved to another group.

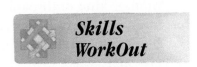

Skills WorkOut

Predict Write a paragraph describing what would happen if suddenly all the fungi and bacteria on the earth died out.

Spore cases

Spores

Hyphae

Figure 11.18 ▲

The tiny dark spots you see on bread mold are the spore cases of a threadlike fungus.

Threadlike Fungi

One group of fungi produces spores in round spore cases at the tips of hyphae. Members of this group are called threadlike fungi. Perhaps the best known threadlike fungus is the black bread mold, *Rhizopus stolonifer*.

When a *Rhizopus* spore germinates, it gives rise to a loose mat of hyphae. Some of the hyphae anchor the mold to the substance on which it grows and release digestive chemicals. These root-like hyphae are called rhizoids.

Other types of hyphae grow upward and bear the cases in which spores are produced. You can see these spore cases in Figure 11.18. The spores released from the cases float around in the air, and a few find good places to grow.

Another kind of threadlike fungus has more control over where its spores go. This fungus lives on animal dung. It aims its spore cases toward bright light, where grass is likely to be growing. Then it shoots its spores like little cannonballs! The spores stick to the grass, and when cows eat it, they disperse the spores.

Sac Fungi

The largest group of fungi consists of the sac fungi. Sac fungi include diverse forms, such as the single-celled yeast, plant parasites, blue-green molds, mildews, and the edible mushrooms called morels and truffles. When reproducing sexually, all these fungi produce spores in saclike structures.

Yeasts have a huge impact on human society. They obtain the energy they need through a process called fermentation. During fermentation, sugar is broken down and its stored energy released. Carbon dioxide gas and alcohol are produced as wastes. Yeasts growing in bread dough produce bubbles of carbon dioxide gas, which cause the dough to rise.

In addition to reproducing sexually, yeasts use a form of asexual reproduction called **budding**. When a yeast cell buds, part of the cell wall swells and is eventually pinched off from the parent as a separate yeast cell.

Other sac fungi are harmful or annoying. Dutch elm disease is caused by a sac fungus. Humans are infected by a sac fungus when they get athlete's foot.

Figure 11.19 ▲

Morels are a kind of sac fungus. They are highly prized for cooking.

Spores

Gills

Cap

Stalk

Hyphae

◀ **Figure 11.20**
The fruiting body of a club fungus begins as a small, round mass of hyphae. The mature fruiting body can release billions of spores from the many clublike structures lining its gills.

Club Fungi

The mushrooms that spring up in lawns and top some kinds of pizza belong to the club fungi. This group also includes the rusts and smuts, both of which cause plant diseases. What these fungi have in common is a spore-producing structure shaped like a club.

In most of the common mushrooms, these club-shaped structures are found lining the gills on the underside of the mushroom's cap. When the spores are ready, they drop from the gills and are scattered by the wind.

However, a mushroom is only a small part of a larger, hidden mass. Beneath the soil's surface, a club fungus exists as a mycelium that can spread through a large area of soil.

The fruiting bodies of some types of club fungi are edible. Other types of club fungi, however, contain poisons that can cause serious sickness and death.

Imperfect Fungi

Fungi that have no known sexual reproductive cycle are classified as imperfect fungi. This group includes the fungi that produce the antibiotic penicillin and those species that give certain cheeses their distinct flavors.

Lichens

Have you noticed colorful, crustlike blotches on rocks or trees like the ones in Figure 11.21? They are organisms called lichens (LY kuhns). A lichen is made up of a fungus *and* an alga. Living together, these organisms from different kingdoms help each other survive.

The alga produces glucose for both itself and the fungus. The hyphae of the fungus anchor the lichen and keep in moisture. The hyphae are also able to absorb minerals and other necessary nutrients from the air and the surface on which the lichen grows. A lichen is able to grow in habitats where neither the fungus nor the alga could live alone.

Figure 11.21 ▲
What two kinds of organisms make up a lichen?

Slime Molds

Figure 11.22 ▲
Many slime molds are very colorful. Where do you think you could find one?

Funguslike organisms called slime molds present a problem in classification. As organisms without chlorophyll, they are like fungi. However, they are also very much like protists because they can move. In addition, the cells that germinate from some slime-mold spores have flagella. Many scientists place the slime molds with the protists, but they are studied by mycologists.

One kind of slime mold is a large mass of cytoplasm with many nuclei. It engulfs food particles and grows by extending pseudopodia through the soil. When conditions become too dry for growth, it reproduces sexually.

Another kind of slime mold exists most of the time as separate cells. For one stage of their life cycle, these cells come together in one mass and resemble a giant, many-celled ameba. This mass of protoplasm can move and even crawl over objects in its way. When it stops migrating, it produces asexual fruiting bodies.

SkillBuilder *Classifying*

A Key to Fungi

You know that scientists often use a taxonomic key. Recall that a taxonomic key is a series of statements that describe an organism's physical characteristics. Keys help scientists classify organisms.

Look at the simple key shown. This key can be used to place a fungus into one of the four major fungi groups. Study the key, then answer the questions.

1. What are the four main fungi groups in this key?

2. Based on information in the key, what are some characteristics that distinguish the four groups of fungi?

3. Why didn't you have to go to another step in the key after Step 1b?

4. Why did you have to go to another step in the key after Step 2b, but not Step 2a?

Key to Fungi
1a. Has sexual stage…GO TO 2 1b. Has no sexual stage…IMPERFECT FUNGI
2a. Spores produced in cases at tips of upright hyphae…THREADLIKE FUNGI 2b. Spores produced in another kind of structure…GO TO 3
3a. Sexual spores formed in a saclike structure…SAC FUNGI 3b. Sexual spores formed on club-shaped structures…CLUB FUNGI

Using this key as a guide, make your own key that can be used to place protozoa into one of the four groups discussed earlier. However, instead of placing the names of each group of protozoa on your key, leave a blank space. Then have a partner go through your key and fill in the name of each protozoa. Check your partner's answer. Is the key correct?

Science and Society *Penicillin*

Fungi, like most organisms, have several defenses against harmful bacteria. Perhaps their best known defense is an adaptation found in a group of imperfect fungi. These fungi produce toxins, called antibiotics, that target and kill bacterial cells. The fungi that produce these poisons belong to the genus *Penicillium*. The poisons they produce are called penicillin.

Penicillin's antibacterial action was first discovered in 1928 by British scientist Alexander Fleming. Fleming was growing cultures of bacteria when one was accidentally contaminated with a *Penicillium* mold. Fleming observed that bacteria would not grow near the mold. He hypothesized that the *Penicillium* produced a substance that killed bacteria.

Ten years later, Howard Florey purified the antibacterial substance. Since this poison did not affect human cells, he proposed that it be used as a drug to fight bacterial infection. Soon, penicillin began to be used to treat bacterial diseases and infections. The drug has saved many lives and has revolutionized the practice of medicine.

Since the discovery of penicillin, many other antibiotics have been developed. Penicillin, however, remains the best treatment for many kinds of bacterial infections. Today, penicillin is obtained from special cultures of *Penicillium*. These molds are maintained in large vats of nutrient broth. The penicillin extracted from these vats is purified, then shipped to drug suppliers.

Figure 11.23 ▲
The fungus *Penicillium* is the source of one of the most important drugs ever developed.

Check and Explain

1. Why are the fungi placed in a kingdom of their own?

2. To which group of fungi do most mushrooms belong?

3. **Predict** Two slices of bread are placed on a table. One is covered. On which slice will mold first start growing? Explain.

4. **Hypothesize** What do fungi need to grow best? Form hypotheses about the ideal temperature, amount of light, level of moisture, and type of food for a bread mold. Then design experiments to test these hypotheses.

Activity 11 How does temperature affect yeast growth?

Skills Observe; Infer; Interpret Data

Task 1 Prelab Prep

1. Collect the following items: wax marker, packet of yeast, sugar, 3 large test tubes, three 250-mL beakers, 3 medium balloons, ice, clock, spoon.
2. Use the wax marker to label the test tubes 1, 2, and 3.

Task 2 Data Record

1. On a separate sheet of paper, draw Table 11.1.
2. Record all your observations about the balloon size, the appearance of the yeast mixture, and any other observations in the table.

Task 3 Procedure

1. Divide the contents of the yeast packet into approximately three equal parts. Place one part in each of the three test tubes.
2. Use a spoon to add about 5 mL of sugar to each test tube.
3. Carefully fill each tube halfway with warm water.
4. Place a balloon over the mouth of each tube. (Make sure that all the air has been squeezed out of the balloon.)
5. Place tube 1 in a beaker filled with ice water.

Place tube 2 in a beaker filled with room-temperature water. Place tube 3 in a beaker filled with warm water.

6. Observe each tube, then record your observations in the table. Repeat at the end of 5, 30, and 60 minutes.

Task 4 Analysis

1. Identify the variable in this activity.
2. How did you know when the yeast was growing?
3. In which beaker did the largest change occur?
4. What caused the observed changes? What gas did the yeast produce?
5. Why was sugar added to the test tubes? What would have happened without sugar?
6. Why did you place balloons on the test tubes?

Task 5 Conclusion

Write a short paragraph explaining what happens when yeast is placed in a warm sugar-water solution.

Everyday Application

How could you increase the rate at which baking dough rises?

Extension

Design an experiment that could be used to discover the best temperature for yeast growth.

Table 11.1	Yeast Observations	Observations			
Test Tube Number	**Temperature of Bath**	At Beginning	After 5 Minutes	After 30 Minutes	After 60 Minutes

Chapter 11 Review

Concept Sumary

11.1 Diversity of Protists

▶ Protists have complex cells.
▶ The two main groups of protists are protozoa and algae.
▶ Protozoa are single-celled. Algae can be single-celled or many-celled.
▶ Single-celled algae make up plankton, which is the first level of the food chain in lakes and oceans.

11.2 Protozoa

▶ Sarcodines use pseudopodia to move, ciliates use cilia, and flagellates use flagella.
▶ Sporozoans have no special structures for movement.
▶ Sporozoans are parasites and can cause diseases such as malaria.

11.3 Algae

▶ The groups of algae include the single-celled dinoflagellates and diatoms, the single- and many-celled green algae, and the many-celled brown algae and red algae.
▶ Red tide is caused by dinoflagellates that grow rapidly and contain poison.
▶ Humans use algae for food and to make food additives and fertilizer.

11.4 Fungi

▶ Fungi are eukaryotes that absorb food.
▶ Threadlike fungi produce round spore cases at the tips of hyphae.
▶ Sac fungi include diverse forms such as yeast, truffles, and mildews.
▶ Club fungi include many mushrooms, rusts and smuts. They have a spore-producing structure shaped like a club.
▶ Lichens are made up of a fungus and an alga living together.

Chapter Vocabulary

protozoan (11.1)	eukaryote (11.1)	spore (11.2)	hyphae (11.4)
protist (11.1)	pseudopodia (11.2)	fungus (11.4)	budding (11.4)
alga (11.1)	cilia (11.2)		

Check Your Vocabulary

Use the vocabulary words above to complete the following sentences correctly.

1. Sarcodines use ____ to move.

2. Members of the kingdom Protista are ____ .

3. A yeast cell reproduces asexually by ____ .

4. Ciliates use ____ to move.

5. Organisms with complex cells are called ____ .

6. A spore-producing organism with complex cells and no chlorophyll is a ____ .

7. Single-celled animal-like organisms belonging to the kingdom Protista are ____ .

8. Plantlike organisms of the kingdom Protista are ____ .

9. Sporozoans produce reproductive cells called ____ .

10. Many-celled fungi bodies are formed by filaments called ____ .

Write Your Vocabulary

Write sentences using each vocabulary word. Show that you know what each word means.

Chapter 11 Review

Check Your Knowledge

Answer the following in complete sentences.

1. Are red algae many-celled or single-celled? Where do they usually live?

2. Describe two examples of green algae. Are they many-celled or single-celled?

3. How are slime molds usually classified? What are the reasons for this classification?

4. What are protozoa? Where do they live?

5. How are sporozoans different from other protozoa?

6. Describe diatoms. Are they single-celled or many-celled? Where do they fit in the food chain?

Determine whether each statement is true or false. Write *true* if it is true. If it is false, change the underlined word to make the statement true.

7. The flagellates move using a whiplike organelle called a cilia.

8. The sarcodines move using footlike projections of cell matter called pseudopodia.

9. Fungi have three different ways of producing spores through asexual reproduction.

10. A lichen is made up of a fungus and alga.

11. Protists that have chloroplasts are classified as algae.

12. The two major groups of protists are the protozoa and the algae.

13. The kingdom Protista includes all organisms that are not plants, animals, or fungi.

14. The ameba is one of the best-known ciliates.

Check Your Understanding

Apply the concepts you have learned to answer each question.

1. Some algae are used in food. Which of the five types of algae have you eaten? Which would you never want to eat?

2. **Extension** If you had an aquarium, would you consider algae a welcome or unwanted addition? Why?

3. Which of the protozoa is the least animal-like? Why?

4. **Mystery Photo** The photograph on page 210 shows the underside of mushrooms. The grooves covering the underside are called gills. This is where mushrooms produce spores. A single mushroom can produce billions of spores.

   a. Infer why the gills are on the underside of the mushroom, pointing toward the ground.

   b. The mushroom is only part of the fungus. What part is it?

   c. These mushrooms are not morels or truffles. What type of fungi are they?

5. Describe two major differences between algae and protozoa.

6. **Infer** Fungi are decomposers. What is a decomposer? What are some of the advantages of being a decomposer?

7. How does a paramecium use cilia? Describe two uses.

8. **Application** Every year you notice a ring of mushrooms growing in the school lawn. Each year the ring gets larger. What can you infer about the location of the mushrooms' mycelium and its growth?

Develop Your Skills

Use the skills you have developed in this chapter to complete each activity.

1. **Interpret Data** The table below shows the number of species included in each group of fungi.

   a. How many species of fungi are there in all the groups combined?

   b. Which group of fungi has the fewest species? The most species?

Type	Number of Species
Threadlike fungi	600
Club fungi	25,000
Imperfect fungi	25,000
Lichens	25,000
Sac fungi	30,000

2. **Communicate** Using what you have learned in this chapter, create a poster that shows different kinds of protists. In addition to the examples shown in the chapter, use the descriptions of each group to infer what other protists may look like.

3. **Data Bank** Use the information on page 625 to answer the following questions.

   a. Which is larger, a typical plant cell or a euglena?

   b. Is a euglena visible to the unaided eye?

4. **Classify** Refer to Figure 11.11 on page 218. Which of the euglena's structures are animal like? Which are plantlike? Are there any structures that fit both categories?

Make Connections

1. **Link the Concepts** Draw a concept map showing how the concepts below link together. Add terms to connect, or link, the concepts.

   algae   single-celled
   protists   flagellates
   ciliates   sarcodines
   euglena   protozoa
   brown algae   sporozoa
   many-celled

2. **Science and Language Arts** Write a paragraph describing how fungi can be beneficial to humans. Write another paragraph describing how they can be harmful to humans. Before writing, you may want to create a list of harmful and beneficial interactions between fungi and humans.

3. **Science and You** Fungi and algae can be used as food, or to make food additives. Research ways fungi and algae are used as food. Then describe a breakfast, lunch, and dinner, each including at least one fungus or alga.

4. **Science and Research** You have learned about the phenomenon known as red tide. Red tide is caused by a population explosion, or algal bloom, of dinoflagellates. Find out where red tide occurs most often in the world. Also research the most common environmental conditions under which red tide occurs. Include what methods, if any, are currently being used to fight red tide.

Science and Literature Connection

This year [for their mother's birthday, Sue and Alan Hancock] wanted something special—something different, something no one else's mother had. They searched the usual shops, and were not satisfied. Indeed, it was not until the very day before the birthday that they walked past the greengrocer on the corner near their school and saw the very thing.

Outside the shop were two shallow wooden boxes from which bubbled a profusion of gleaming white mushrooms: crisp fresh delicious-looking mushrooms. And alongside the boxes was a notice: GROW YOUR OWN MUSHROOMS! A NEW CROP EVERY DAY!

They looked at each other. Their mother had grown just about everything in her time, but never mushrooms. They went into the shop. They bought a small plastic bag labelled MUSHROOM SPORE, another bag of earthy stuff in which you were supposed to plant it, and an instruction leaflet.

"The Great Mushroom Mistake"

The following excerpt is from the short story "The Great Mushroom Mistake" by Penelope Lively.

Mrs. Hancock was thrilled. She couldn't wait to get going. The instruction leaflet said that the mushrooms like to grow indoors in a darkish place. A cellar would do nicely, it said, or the cupboard under the stairs. The Hancocks had no cellar and the cupboard under the stairs was full of the sort of thing that takes refuge in cupboards under the stairs: old shoes and suitcases and a broken tennis racket and a chair with only three legs. Mrs Hancock decided that the only place was the cupboard in the spare room, which was used by guests only and no guest was threatening for some while. The children helped her to spread the earthy stuff out in boxes and scatter the spore. Then, apparently, all they had to do was wait.

During the night, Alan woke once and thought he heard a faint creaking sound, like a tree straining in the wind. And when, in the morning, they opened the door of the spare room cupboard there in the boxes was a fine growth of mushrooms—fat adult mushrooms and baby mushrooms pushing up under and around them. Mrs Hancock was delighted; the children preened themselves on the success of their present; everyone had fried mushrooms for breakfast.

The next day they found the cupboard door half open and mushrooms tumbling out onto the floor. "Gracious!" said Mrs Hancock. "It'll be mushroom soup for lunch today." The instruction leaflet said DO NOT SOW MORE SPORE TILL CROPPING CEASES, so they decided to wait and see what happened. . . .

That night, the creaking was more definite. Both children heard it; a sound something between rustling and a splitting—the sound of growth. And in the morning there were mushrooms all over the spare room floor, a clump on the stairs and several clusters under the table in the hall. The Hancocks gazed at them in astonishment. "They *are* doing well," said Mrs Hancock, with a slight trace of anxiety in her voice. . . .

Over the next few days, the mushroom invasion continued. They found mushrooms in the bathroom and beside the cooker and in the toy chest. When they got up in the mornings they had to walk downstairs on a carpet of small mushrooms which squeaked faintly underfoot, like colonies of mice. It was when Mrs Hancock had to vacuum mushrooms from the sitting room carpet that they realized the situation had got quite out of control.

Skills in Science

Reading Skills in Science

1. **Classify** Classify this selection as fiction or nonfiction. Support your classification with information contained in the selection.

2. **Evaluate Sources** The selection paints a rather unique portrait of the life processes of a mushroom. Identify at least three descriptions that are scientifically accurate.

Writing Skills in Science

1. **Find the Main Idea** Write an article for a local newspaper that describes the great mushroom invasion of the Hancock home.

2. **Infer** Describe what happened in the guest room cupboard that first night while the Hancocks slept. Include information you learned in this unit about mushrooms.

Activities

Communicate Certain types of mushrooms can cause illness or even death if eaten. Visit a library to learn more about poisonous mushrooms. Make a chart to show the symptoms and effects of eating two types of poisonous mushrooms.

Collect Data Sometimes mushrooms grow in a circle in the wild. Use reference tools to explain how this occurs. What folklore has arisen about these rings of mushrooms?

Where to Read More

Uninvited Guests and Other Stories by Penelope Lively. New York: E.P. Dutton, 1985. Contains "The Great Mushroom Mistake" and other stories.

The Mushroom Hunter's Field Guide by A.H. Smith and N.S. Weber. University of Michigan Press, 1980. This field guide will help mushroom hunters classify specimens.

Unit 5
Plant Life

Data Bank

Use the information on page 624 to 631 to answer the following questions about topics explored in this unit.

Calculating

How much taller is the California redwood than the cedar?

Reading a Graph

How many metric tons of root crops are produced worldwide?

Making a Graph

Make a bar graph that shows the essential nutrients in plants. Your graph should show the form available for each element listed and the percent of dry weight.

Comparing

What is the tallest tree shown? What is the shortest tree shown?

The photograph to the left is of wildflowers and a yucca tree in the Mojave Desert in California. What time of year do you think this photograph was taken?

Chapter **12** A World of Plants

What do you see?

❝ I see a cactus. It is very big and has repeating sections. The purple things are prickly thorns. The cactus uses these thorns for protection from animals and people. **❞**

Chavon Webb
Carl Albert Junior High School
Oklahoma City, Oklahoma

To find out more about the photograph, look on page 250. As you read this chapter, you will learn more about the origins of plants and their life processes.

12.1 Plant Origins

Objectives

▶ **Describe** the origins of modern plants.

▶ **Compare** and **contrast** vascular and nonvascular plants.

▶ **Infer** the uses of plant adaptations.

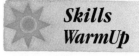
Define Operationally   Make a list of plants and plant products you use every day. What do the plants on your list have in common? How many different ways do plants affect your life?

How many different plants do you know? Probably quite a few. Grasses and garden flowers, such as tulips, roses, and orchids, are plants. Pine, elm, and maple trees are plants. Mosses and ferns are also plants. Every day you probably eat parts of such common food plants as corn, rice, wheat, or potatoes.

People all over the world have long depended on plants for food, clothing, housing, medicines, and many other needs. Look at Figure 12.1. Plants from faraway places produce items that are part of your everyday life. The banana you ate for breakfast comes from a plant native to Malaysia. Bananas have been cultivated in Southeast Asia for more than 1,000 years. Vanilla, chocolate, and coffee come from plants grown in South America and Africa. Many spices, such as cinnamon and nutmeg, come from Asia and Africa. An early form of paper was made from papyrus reeds in ancient Egypt.

Characteristics of Plants

When you see a plant, you can probably tell that it is a plant. However, some organisms, such as algae, look like plants, but aren't. You need to know about the chemicals and cells inside a plant to see why it is classified as a plant. Plants have the following characteristics:

▶ All plants are many-celled.
▶ All plants are made of tissues and organs.
▶ All plants have cell walls.
▶ Almost all plant cells contain chlorophyll.

Plants, unlike most animals, continue to grow throughout their entire lives. Plants differ from many-celled algae because they have adaptations for living on land. These adaptations include a waxy coating to keep the cells moist and reproductive organs enclosed in protective tissue.

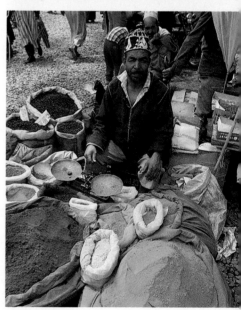

Figure 12.1 ▲
The bananas you eat are grown on plantations like this one in Costa Rica (top). Many different spices are available at this African market (bottom).

Plant Evolution and Classification

Plants evolved from many-celled green algae. Cells of green algae are very similar to plant cells. Both green algae and plant cells have the same pigments used in photosynthesis. Both have cell walls made of cellulose and store carbohydrates in the form of starch. Evidence from fossils shows that the first plants appeared about 400 million years ago.

The first plants were small and lived close to the water's edge. They had to stay very close to water because they had no system for transporting water throughout the plant. One cell would simply transfer materials to its neighbor, much like a sponge soaks up water. Plants that absorb water in this way are called **nonvascular** (NAHN VAS kyuh lur) **plants**. Nonvascular plants lack specialized tissues to transport water. Bryophytes (BRY oh FYTS), such as mosses, are living representatives of these early plants.

To grow successfully on land, plants evolved tissues with tubelike structures that can transport water. Plants with these vascular tissues are called **vascular** (VAS kyuh lur) **plants**. Over millions of years, this adaptation allowed vascular plants to colonize the land. Eventually vascular plants evolved other adaptations that let them live in a wide variety of land environments. The two most important adaptations to evolve in the vascular plants were the seed and the flower. Today, plants without vascular tissue, without seeds, and without flowers still exist along with flowering plants.

Bryophytes

Mosses are the most common bryophytes. These non-vascular plants have a variety of shapes and are generally less than 2 cm tall. More than 20,000 species are known to exist. Liverworts, shown at right, are also bryophytes. There are about 8,000 species of liverworts.

Nonvascular plants

Ferns ▲

Like club mosses and horse-tails, ferns are an ancient group of vascular plants. More than 12,000 species of ferns are now living. Most ferns live in the tropics and other moist forest areas.

Angiosperms ▲

The first flowering plants, called **angiosperms** (AN jee oh SPURMZ), appeared about 120 million years ago. All angiosperms produce seeds enclosed in a fruit or pod. More than 235,000 species are known.

Gymnosperms ▲

The first plants to evolve seeds were the **gymnosperms** (JIHM noh SPURMZ). All gymnosperms produce naked seeds not enclosed in a fruit. Seeds and other adaptations allowed gymnosperms to live in dry places. More than 7,000 species exist today.

Vascular plants

Club Mosses ▲

These vascular plants are one of the oldest groups. About 1,000 species exist today. Large treelike club mosses, now extinct, lived millions of years ago.

Horsetails ▲

These vascular plants are considered "living fossils." They have changed very little over millions of years. Only about 15 species survive.

Adaptations of Flowering Plants

Flowering plants grow in practically all land habitats—from seashores to mountain tops, from the tropics to the arctic, and from marshy areas to deserts. To survive such diverse conditions, these plants have developed special adaptations. Unlike animals, plants can't move from one place to another when conditions for growth become unfavorable. Most plants are firmly anchored to the ground and must adapt to changes in the environment.

Many desert plants, like this creosote bush, have adapted to dry conditions in a variety of ways. The plants use water efficiently. They grow slowly, so they need little water. The small waxy leaves of the creosote bush are adapted to slow water loss from the hot desert sun. The creosote bush also has a large, shallow root system to absorb water over a large area. ▼

▲ Many plants in the tropical rain forest grow in the sunny treetops, high above the ground. Their roots cling to the tree. Some have leaves that form a cup shape to store water.

Plants growing in the shade of the rain forest trees look different from plants growing in treetops. They have large leaves to absorb as much light as possible. ▼

▲ Cacti, like this saguaro (suh WAR oh), have a thick, green stem that can store water and capture energy from sunlight. A waxy coating on the stem keeps the plant from drying out. Spines protect the plant from animals and shade the stem.

Although these African euphorbias ▲ (yoo **FOR** bee uhz) look very similar to American cacti, they are unrelated. What environmental conditions are the euphorbias adapted for?

Alpine plants, like this cushion plant, are small and grow close to the ground. Plants in high mountain areas face short growing seasons with high winds and low temperatures. ▼

Historical Notebook

Plant Classification

Identifying and classifying plants has been important to people throughout history. One early classification system was developed by Greek scientist Theophrastus about 300 B.C. He classified plants into four groups: herbs, undershrubs, shrubs, and trees. Illustrated books for identifying plants were published in China in the eleventh century. These had both medical and scientific importance, because plants were widely used for medicine in China. During the Middle Ages in Europe, plants were also classified by medicinal use. Herbalists named plants after the human organ or disease they were used to treat.

The plant classification system used today is based on observations of reproductive structures of flowers and other plants. This system was developed in 1735 by Swedish botanist Carl von Linné, also known as Carolus Linnaeus. He used two words, a genus name followed by a species

name, to name each plant. A drawing from his notebook is shown here. Since Latin was the most important scientific language in Linnaeus' time, scientific names are still in Latin or a Latinlike form. For example, the scientific name for red oak is *Quercus rubra*. *Quercus* is the genus of all oaks. The species name, *rubra,* is Latin for "red."

Dryas octopetala

1. Explain how plant classification changed through history.

2. Obtain a field guide to plants from the library. Look up the scientific name for three plants common in your area.

Figure 12.2 ▲

These plants are being grown hydroponically. What are some advantages and disadvantages to this method?

Science and Technology *Hydroponics*

Hydroponics (HY droh PAHN ihks), shown in Figure 12.2, is a method of raising plants without soil. Instead, the plants are grown in water enriched with plant growth nutrients, such as nitrogen, phosphorus, and potassium. These and other plant nutrients are usually present in the soil and are essential for plant growth. Hydroponics has several advantages over traditional soil methods. More plants can be grown in a limited amount of space. Food crops mature more rapidly and produce greater yields. Some food crops that grow well hydroponically are tomatoes, lettuce, kale, spinach, and cucumbers.

The word *hydroponics* comes from two Greek words meaning "water working." The word was coined in 1936 by W. F. Gericke at the University of California. Dr. Gericke grew tomato vines more than 7 m tall in basins of water and nutrients. His experiments caused a sensation. Some people thought hydroponics could make traditional farming methods obsolete.

While hydroponic gardening didn't replace soil methods of growing plants, it has become useful in urban areas and other places with limited space. Hydroponics probably will be used to grow crops in future space stations and space colonies. Using hydroponics, every factor affecting plant growth can be regulated. As a result, the plants grow faster, taste better, and look more attractive.

Check and Explain

1. Distinguish between nonvascular and vascular plants.

2. List several ways in which cacti have become adapted to living in a dry environment.

3. **Find Causes** Environmental conditions caused different types of plants to evolve from one common ancestor. Describe three environmental conditions and the type of plant that adapted to each condition.

4. **Infer** Some vascular plants such as trees can grow to be more than 100 m tall. Discuss the advantages to being tall.

12.2 Chemistry in Plants

Objectives

▶ **Describe** the two stages of photosynthesis.

▶ **Give examples** of chemical activities of plants.

▶ **Communicate** how energy is stored and used in a plant.

Skills WarmUp

Hypothesize Plants need light for photosynthesis. Hypothesize what would happen to plants grown in the dark. Consider how darkness would affect the amount of food they produced, their growth, their color, and their overall health. What experiment would be needed to test your hypothesis?

You can think of a plant as a chemical factory. Part of this chemical factory makes the sugar glucose. To make glucose, the plant uses energy from sunlight and raw materials from air and water. This process is called *photosynthesis*. Look at the plant in Figure 12.3. Which part takes in energy from the sun?

Some glucose made by the plant is stored for later use. The rest is transported throughout the plant. The glucose is used for energy to help the plant convert soil nutrients to body tissues and grow larger. The energy is also used to make other plant products, such as plant oils.

A plant's chemical factory also produces hormones. Hormones are complex chemicals that regulate growth and development. Plant hormones direct plant growth. As a result, stems grow toward light and roots toward water. Hormones also stimulate the growth of new leaves and flowers.

Figure 12.3
A plant is a natural chemical factory. ▼

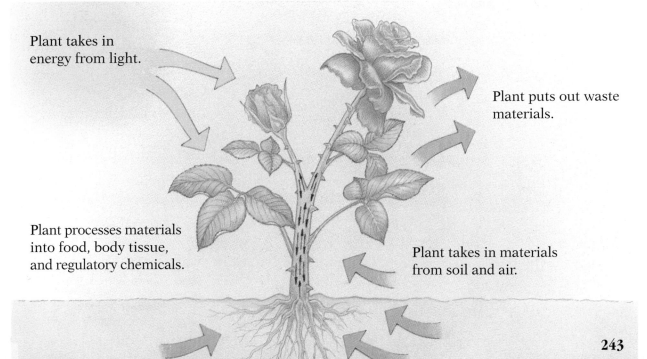

Plant takes in energy from light.

Plant puts out waste materials.

Plant processes materials into food, body tissue, and regulatory chemicals.

Plant takes in materials from soil and air.

Photosynthesis

The green parts of a plant make glucose for the whole plant, using light as an energy source. Light is absorbed by the green pigment chlorophyll. Chlorophyll is located inside the organelles called chloroplasts. The plant obtains the raw materials from the environment. Water is taken up from the soil. Carbon dioxide from the air enters openings on the plant surface, called **stomates** (STOH mayts). Carbon dioxide dissolves and travels into the cells that manufacture glucose. Glucose is used for plant growth or is stored. Oxygen is produced along with glucose. The oxygen that is not needed by the plant is released into the air through the stomates. The overall process of photosynthesis is shown in the following chemical reaction:

$$6CO_2 + 12H_2O \xrightarrow{\text{Light}} C_6H_{12}O_6 + 6H_2O + 6O_2$$

Carbon Dioxide and Water — Light → Glucose, Water, and Oxygen

This process actually takes place in two stages, shown in Figure 12.4.

First Stage A molecule of chlorophyll absorbs light and becomes energized. The energized chlorophyll is capable of transferring its energy in two ways. Some energy is used to split the water molecule (H_2O) into hydrogen and oxygen. The rest of the energy is used to make ATP, a molecule used by cells of all organisms to store energy.

When water is split into hydrogen and oxygen, the hydrogen stays in the chloroplasts to continue more chemical reactions. The oxygen passes out of the leaf through the stomates.

Second Stage Carbon dioxide is combined with the hydrogen and ATP made in the first stage. Unlike the first stage, the chemical reactions of the second stage do not require light. These chemical reactions, called the **Calvin cycle**, produce glucose and other simple sugars. The plant uses these sugars for metabolism, growth, and other life processes. Some sugars are used for energy. Other sugars may combine chemically to form complex starches, or they may undergo chemical reactions to form oils or proteins.

Figure 12.4
Two Stages of Photosynthesis

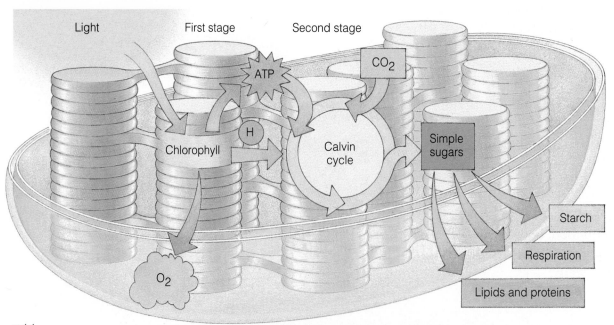

Respiration

During photosynthesis, plant cells convert light energy into chemical energy stored in glucose. To release this energy, plant cells, like animal cells, use the reverse process known as respiration. In respiration, oxygen combines with glucose, releasing energy in the form of ATP. Respiration takes place in the cell's cytoplasm. The chemical reaction is:

$$C_6H_{12}O_6 + 6O_2 \text{ — Enzymes} \rightarrow 6CO_2 + 6H_2O + ATP$$

Glucose and Oxygen — Enzymes → Carbon Dioxide, Water, and Energy

Plants use less oxygen during respiration than they produce during photosynthesis. The excess oxygen is released into the air, and used by animals for respiration. This oxygen is the plant's contribution to the global oxygen–carbon dioxide cycle. Notice in Figure 12.5 that animal respiration, in turn, produces waste carbon dioxide that is used by plants for photosynthesis.

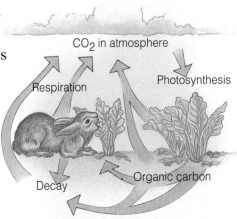

Figure 12.5 ▲
Plants play an important role in the global, oxygen–carbon dioxide cycle.

SkillBuilder *Interpreting Data*

Factors Affecting Photosynthesis

Light intensity and temperature affect the rate of photosynthesis in plants. The graph shows the relationship between the rate of photosynthesis, light intensity, and temperature for two plants. Use the graph to help you answer the questions.

1. What happens to the rate of photosynthesis as light intensity increases?

2. At which temperature, 20°C or 30°C, is the rate of photosynthesis higher? How can you tell by looking at the graph?

3. Based on the graph, describe the trend you see in the relationship between temperature, light, and the rate of photosynthesis.

4. Trace the graph on a sheet of paper. If the temperature is 25°C, predict the rate of photosynthesis by plotting a third line on your drawn graph.

5. Describe the conditions present when the rate of photosynthesis is almost the same for the two plants. Based on this observation, which factor affects photosynthesis more, temperature or light intensity? Explain your conclusions.

Figure 12.6a ▲
The sugar maple has bright green leaves during the long days of summer.

Figure 12.6b ▲
As the days get shorter, the green pigment in the leaves starts to break down. Red and yellow pigment begins to show through. What will happen to the leaves by the end of autumn?

Chemical Interactions of Plants

In addition to manufacturing glucose within their cells, plants have many other chemical activities. Some of these chemical activities allow plants to react to conditions in the environment. A plant in a window grows toward the light. If a potted plant is laid on its side, the stem responds to gravity and gradually grows upward while the roots grow downward.

During autumn, as the days grow shorter, the green coloring in the leaves of many trees fades and other colors become visible. You can see how leaves change color in Figure 12.6. As longer days return with the coming of spring, chemical activities stimulate the plant to develop new growth. All these responses, and many more, are controlled by hormones produced by the plant.

Plants also produce chemicals that affect other plants and animals. Some desert plants produce chemical substances in their roots that "poison" the ground around them. The poisons prevent other seeds from sprouting. This keeps other plants from growing nearby and using scarce water. When attacked by insects, many plants begin to produce small amounts of toxic chemicals. These chemicals serve to repel the insects.

Science and Society *Too Few Food Plants?*

As you know, food plants you enjoy daily come from all over the world. In fact, about 150 different species of plants are cultivated for food by people worldwide. Of these, the 12 plants listed in Table 12.1 are especially important staple foods. These 12 plants stand between human survival and starvation.

The three most important food plants are known as cereal grains: wheat, corn, and rice. These grains are among the oldest cultivated plants, going back more than 10,000 years. Each cereal grain was cultivated and developed by cultures from different regions of the world. Wheat was cultivated in Africa, Europe, and the Middle East. Corn was cultivated in North, South, and Central America. Rice was cultivated in Asia. All cereal grains are seeds and contain a high amount of starch and small amounts of oil and protein. They are low in water, are easily transported, and can be stored for long periods without spoiling.

Table 12.1 Twelve Essential Plants

Plant	Origin	Food Value
Wheat	Middle East, Africa	Starch, protein, oil
Corn	Central America, South America	Starch
Rice	Asia	Starch
Potato, Yam	South America	Starch
Cassava	South America	Starch
Sugar cane	Asia	Sugar
Sugar beet	Europe	Sugar
Soybeans	Asia	Protein, starch
Beans	South, North, and Central America	Protein, starch
Coconut	World tropics	Oil, protein
Bananas	Southeast Asia	Starch, sugar, protein, oil

Food plants known as root crops, such as potatoes and yams, are also from different regions of the world. The potato was cultivated for many thousands of years by Native Americans in the Andes mountain areas of South America. Some of the many varieties of potatoes they developed are shown in Figure 12.7. Potatoes were brought to Europe in 1570. They became widespread because the potato plants were easy to grow. They grew even in areas with poor soil where other food plants failed.

Figure 12.7 ▲
Many unusual varieties of potatoes are still available in this Andean market.

Check and Explain

1. What chemical activities take place in plants, beside making glucose?

2. Where does photosynthesis take place in a plant? When does photosynthesis take place?

3. **Generalize** Sometimes it is said that plants use carbon dioxide to produce oxygen, while animals use oxygen to produce carbon dioxide. In what way is this statement misleading?

4. **Communicate** In your own words, explain how a leaf makes and uses glucose.

Activity 12 Do plants breathe?

Skills Observe; Predict

Task 1 Prelab Prep

1. Collect the following items: 3 labels, a pencil, 3 small jars with lids, cabbage-juice indicator, sprig of *Elodea* or other water plant, aluminum foil, a straw.
2. Fill each jar full of the cabbage-juice indicator. **CAUTION! This liquid will stain clothing and skin.**
3. Make the following three labels: *Control, Elodea, Breath.*

Task 2 Data Record

1. On a sheet of paper, draw the data table shown.
2. Record all your observations about the color of the cabbage-juice indicator in the data table.

Task 3 Procedure

1. Place the *Elodea* into one of the jars filled with cabbage-juice indicator. Put the lid on the jar. Record your observations.
2. Attach the *Elodea* label to the jar. Cover the outside of the jar with aluminum foil.
3. Put the lid on the second jar filled with cabbage-juice indicator. Record your observations in the data table.
4. Attach the *Control* label to the jar. Cover the outside with aluminum foil.
5. Use the straw to blow for 2 minutes into the cabbage-juice indicator in the third jar.
6. Put the lid on the jar and record your observations.

7. Attach the *Breath* label to the jar. Cover the outside of the third jar with aluminum foil.
8. Set the three jars where they will not be disturbed.
9. After 24 hours, remove the aluminum foil and record your observations. Replace the aluminum foil.
10. After 48 hours, remove the aluminum foil and record your observations.
11. Remove the *Elodea* sprig and pour the cabbage-juice indicator down the sink. Be sure to rinse the jars.

Task 4 Analysis

1. What chemical in your breath made the cabbage-juice indicator change color?
2. Why did you prepare a jar with only cabbage-juice indicator?
3. How did the indicator react when the *Elodea* leaf was placed in the jar? What happened 24 hours later? What happened 48 hours later? Explain your observations.
4. Explain why the jars were covered with aluminum foil.

Task 5 Conclusion

Write a paragraph summarizing what you observed in this activity. Do plants breathe? Explain.

Everyday Application

Explain how a plant would be affected if you exposed it to constant light using a "grow lamp."

Table 12.2 Cabbage-Juice Observations

Jar	Prediction	Immediate	24 Hours	48 Hours
Control				
Elodea				
Breath				

Chapter 12 Review

Concept Summary

12.1 Plant Origins

▷ Plants evolved from many-celled green algae about 400 million years ago. However, plants differ from algae because they have adaptations for living on land.

▷ Vascular plants have systems for transporting water through the plant, whereas nonvascular plants lack these structures.

▷ Gymnosperms are vascular plants that produce seeds, and angiosperms are vascular, flowering plants with seeds enclosed in a fruit.

▷ Flowering plants have developed many special adaptations for surviving in many different environments.

12.2 Chemistry in Plants

▷ Photosynthesis is the process by which a plant makes simple sugars from water and carbon dioxide, using energy from the sun. Oxygen is produced as a result.

▷ Photosynthesis occurs in a plant's chloroplasts.

▷ Photosynthesis has two stages. The first stage requires light to split water into hydrogen and oxygen, making ATP. In the second stage, the Calvin cycle produces glucose and other simple sugars.

▷ The plant uses the simple sugars for metabolism, growth, and all its life processes.

▷ Plants, like animals, breathe by taking in oxygen to break down glucose.

▷ Chemical activities occur in plants that enable them to react to environmental conditions.

Chapter Vocabulary

nonvascular plant (12.1) gymnosperm (12.1) stomate (12.2) Calvin cycle (12.2)

vascular plant (12.1) angiosperm (12.1)

Check Your Vocabulary

Use the vocabulary words above to complete the following sentences.

1. Plants with tubelike structures for transporting water are called _____ .

2. Plants with no specialized system for conducting water are _____ .

3. Carbon dioxide enters a plant through _____ located on the plant's leaves.

4. The conversion of carbon dioxide, hydrogen, and ATP into glucose occurs during the _____ of photosynthesis.

5. Flowering plants are _____ .

6. Plants that produce seeds not enclosed in a fruit are _____ .

Find Word Relationships

Pair each numbered word(s) with a vocabulary word. Explain in complete sentences how the words are related. You may use the vocabulary words more than once.

1. Gas exchange
2. Tubelike vessels
3. Bryophyte
4. Simple sugars
5. Rose
6. Mosses
7. Spongelike
8. Flowers
9. Chemical reactions
10. Fruit

Write Your Vocabulary

Write sentences using each vocabulary word above. Show that you know what each word means.

Chapter 12 Review

Check Your Knowledge

Answer the following in complete sentences.

1. Why are most nonvascular plants small and live near water?

2. What is the function of stomates?

3. Describe three ways in which plants respond to their environment.

4. Name six major groups into which plants are classified.

5. What does a plant produce as the result of photosynthesis?

6. In what plant structure does photosynthesis occur?

7. What characteristics do all plants have in common?

Choose the answer that best completes each sentence.

8. Plants evolved from (green algae, sponges, fungi, club mosses).

9. Plants that grow slowly and have fleshy leaves probably live in the (rain forest, high mountains, desert, marsh).

10. A product of the Calvin cycle is (carbon dioxide, hormones, chlorophyll, simple sugars).

11. During respiration, energy is released in the form of (ATP, hormones, enzymes, glucose).

12. Plants are important to animal life because they release (water, oxygen, carbon dioxide, nitrogen) into the atmosphere.

13. Photosynthesis has (one, two, three, six) stages.

14. The first stage of photosynthesis requires (oxygen, starches, enzymes, light).

Check Your Understanding

Apply the concepts you have learned to answer each question.

1. In a table, compare and contrast respiration and photosynthesis.

2. The word *photo* comes from the Greek word meaning "light," and *synthesis* comes from the Greek word meaning "to make." Using this information, write a definition for photosynthesis. How does this definition relate to what occurs during photosynthesis?

3. Most mosses are small plants. A fern can grow as tall as a small tree. Which one is vascular? Nonvascular? Why is the plant's size a clue to the answers?

4. **Mystery Photo** The photograph on page 236 shows a close-up view of a barrel cactus. What is the function of the spines shown in the photograph? List other successful plant adaptations to the desert environment.

5. When would you expect a plant to take in more carbon dioxide, at night or during the day? Why?

6. **Infer** The water plant *Elodea* was put in a fishbowl with a goldfish. One day later bubbles appeared underneath the plant's leaves.

   a. What gas is in the bubbles? Explain.

   b. Predict what might happen to the goldfish if you removed the *Elodea* from the fishbowl.

7. A friend of yours used to live in the tropics of Hawaii where she had a lush fern garden. She moved to the desert area of Nevada. She wanted to grow another fern garden in her new backyard. Is this a good idea? What will probably happen to her garden?

Develop Your Skills

Use the skills you have developed in this chapter to complete each activity.

1. **Interpret Data** The graph below shows the relationship between the rate of photosynthesis and the amount of carbon dioxide in the air.

a. Describe what happens to the rate of photosynthesis as the amount of carbon dioxide increases.

b. What happens to the rate of photosynthesis at a carbon dioxide level of 0.09 percent?

c. Infer why photosynthesis levels off at higher levels of carbon dioxide.

d. What happens when there is no carbon dioxide present?

2. **Observe** Look at several plants that grow near your home or school. Record how each plant reacts to conditions in the environment.

3. **Data Bank** Use the information on page 624 to answer the following questions.

a. What elements make up the largest percentage of dry weight in plants?

b. Hydrogen is available to plants in what form?

Make Connections

1. **Link the Concepts** Below is a concept map showing how some of the main concepts in this chapter link together. Only parts of the map are filled in. Copy the map. Using words and ideas from the chapter, complete the map.

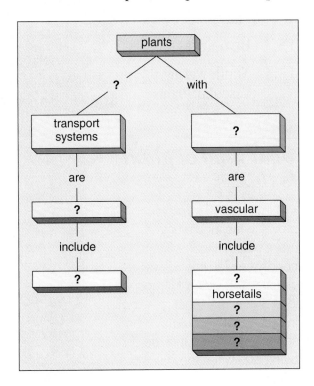

2. **Science and Math** Collect pictures of different types of plants found around the world. The entire collection is your set. Create subsets from this main set. How many different subsets did you create? What did you use as the basis for forming your subsets?

3. **Science and Technology** Research how scientists are planning to use hydroponics in space stations of the future. Find out what kinds of plants will be grown and how their needs will be met. List the problems plants may have living in space.

Chapter 13 Nonflowering Plants

What kind of plant is this?

❝ I think this is a plant that grows in the jungle or in a moist place. It looks like it needs a moist, humid, wet climate. The yellow clumps look like animals that grow on the plant. They could also be seeds that grow out of the plant, and when they fall they will create a new plant. ❞

Rodrigo Figueroa
Antioch Junior High School
Antioch, California

To find out more about the photograph, look on page 268. As you read this chapter, you will learn about different nonflowering plants and how they grow and reproduce.

13.1 Characteristics of Nonflowering Plants

Objectives

▶ **Give examples** of common nonflowering plants.

▶ **Explain** how nonflowering plants adapted to living on land.

▶ **Compare** plant and animal life cycles.

▶ **Infer** reasons why vascular plants are larger than nonvascular plants.

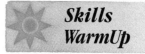

Skills WarmUp

Classification How many nonflowering plants can you find? Collect leaves and other parts of plants you think are nonflowering. Also collect photographs from magazines. Arrange your collection into groups. When you finish this chapter, evaluate your method of classifying.

Imagine a forest without any broad-leaf trees or other flowering plants. What kind of plants would grow in such a forest? To find out, look at Figure 13.1. A forest of nonflowering plants would include mosses, ferns, horsetails, and cone-bearing trees. When dinosaurs walked the earth, the ancestors of these plants grew in vast forests and swamps.

Origins and Adaptations

Four hundred million years ago, nonflowering land plants began to evolve from water-living green algae. Eventually, nonflowering plants completely colonized and changed the land environment. To colonize the land, nonflowering plants had to solve many problems that plants living in water don't have. A land plant must adapt to both soil and air. The air space above the soil has sunlight but no water and no support. The soil has water and minerals but no sunlight. To live on land, nonflowering plants evolved more specialized tissues and organs that satisfied some of their needs in air and some in soil.

In three separate stages of evolution, nonflowering plants solved each of the major problems of living on land. Bryophytes developed a waxy covering to keep their cells from drying out in the air. Club mosses, horsetails, and ferns evolved vascular tissue to transport water from the roots to above-ground stems. With vascular tissue they could grow upward into the air and downward into the soil. Finally the gymnosperms evolved a way to reproduce that didn't depend on water.

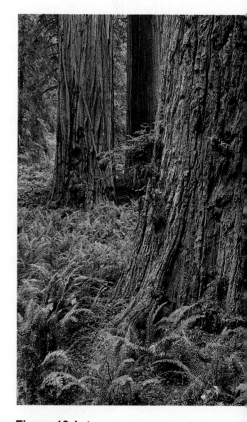

Figure 13.1 ▲
What kinds of nonflowering plants can you see in this photograph?

Life Cycles

Like the algae they evolved from, nonflowering plants have a life cycle made up of two different stages. Look carefully at Figure 13.2. Notice that plants alternate between a sexual stage and a nonsexual stage. In the sexual stage, a plant called the **gametophyte** (guh MEET uh FYT) produces egg and sperm cells. The sperm and egg combine to form a fertilized egg cell, which grows into an embryo. The embryo grows into a **sporophyte** (SPOH roh FYT), the plant that makes up the nonsexual stage. The sporophyte produces **spores**. A spore is a nonsexual reproductive cell with a protective coat. A spore develops into a gametophyte. The gametophyte reproduces sexually, and the cycle continues. Some plants have separate male and female gametophytes. In other plants, one gametophyte produces both eggs and sperm.

This two-stage life cycle evolved in a water environment, where the gametophyte and sporophyte could be separate organisms. The least complex plants have kept this arrangement. They have to make do with rainwater to transport the eggs and sperm. This limits where they can live.

Other plants adapted more completely to land by modifying their sexual stage. It became shorter, and the gametophytes became smaller. These two changes allowed the sporophyte to evolve ways of protecting the gametophyte and helping the eggs and sperm to come together without water.

In the most complex nonflowering plants, the gymnosperms, the sexual stage takes place almost completely within the sporophyte. This adaptation was made possible in part by the evolution of the seed, shown at right. A seed is made up of an embryo, a stored energy supply, and a protective seed coat.

Figure 13.2 ▼
Life Cycle of a Nonflowering Plant

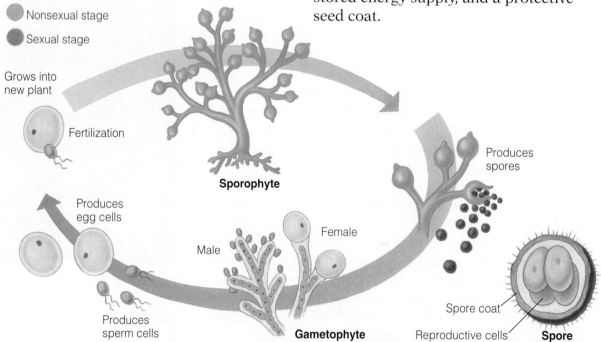

Nonsexual stage
Sexual stage

Grows into new plant
Fertilization
Produces egg cells
Produces sperm cells
Male
Female
Sporophyte
Gametophyte
Produces spores
Spore coat
Reproductive cells
Spore

Seed
Young plant
Stored food
Seed coat

Science and You *Using Nonflowering Plants*

As you go through your day, you may encounter many things made from nonflowering plants. First of all, this page is paper that probably contains wood pulp from cone-bearing trees, such as pine and fir. Your pencil, your chair, your desk, and even your classroom may be constructed of wood or wood products from these same nonflowering trees. In fact, most paper products and many wood products come from cone-bearing trees. In addition, cleaning products containing pine oil may help keep your classroom clean.

If you look inside a potted plant or flower arrangement, you may find sphagnum (SFAG nuhm) moss, another nonflowering plant. Florists use sphagnum moss as a packing material because it is highly absorbent. In landscaped areas and gardens, sphagnum moss in the form of peat may be mixed in with the soil.

Are you reading this page with the help of a light bulb? Its light may come from electricity produced by the burning of coal. The coal formed from ancient nonflowering plants that grew during the Carboniferous period, about 350 million years ago. These plants were buried when they died and changed into coal by heat and pressure deep underground.

If you have ever tasted food containing pine nuts, you know that some nonflowering plants are good to eat. Pine nuts are high in protein and carbohydrates, but lower in fat than other nuts. Another nonflowering plant that people eat is the young curled frond of a fern, called a fiddlehead.

Figure 13.3 ▲
Ponderosa pines (top) are a major source of wood and paper products. Ancient plants like the seed fern (bottom) contributed to the earth's supply of coal.

Check and Explain

1. Name four common nonflowering plants. Describe how they differ from one another.

2. Describe three adaptations gymnosperms have for living on land.

3. **Compare and Contrast** How are the life cycles of nonflowering plants different from those of animals? How are they similar?

4. **Infer** Why can ferns and gymnosperms grow much larger than bryophytes?

Skills WarmUp

Research Look up the word *bryophyte* in the dictionary. Discover the root words from which it was formed.

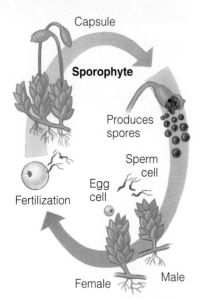

Capsule

Sporophyte

Produces spores

Sperm cell

Egg cell

Fertilization

Female **Male**

Gametophyte

Figure 13.4 ▲

The life cycle of a moss is shown in the diagram. What are the structures at the tips of the moss plants in the photograph?

13.2 Bryophytes

Objectives

▶ **Describe** where bryophytes grow and explain why they grow there.

▶ **Compare** and **contrast** the characteristics of mosses and liverworts.

▶ **Infer** how environmental conditions affect bryophyte reproduction.

Imagine you are walking through a cool, moist forest. On the ground you see a fuzzy patch of deep green. What could it be? You bend down to examine it closely and notice that the fuzzy patch is made of many small plants like the one in the photograph in Figure 13.4. You have encountered a member of the group of plants known as *bryophytes*. Bryophytes are nonvascular plants that grow only in moist environments.

Mosses

Study the plant in Figure 13.4. The tiny green leaflike structures arranged in a spiral on a short stalk are characteristic of a bryophyte called a **moss**. A moss attaches to the ground by small **rhizoids** (RY zoydz). These are rootlike structures found in bryophytes.

Rhizoids are not true roots because they do not have vascular tissue to carry water. Water travels through a moss by osmosis, and glucose travels between cells by diffusion. These processes are slow and support only a small plant.

Look at the moss life cycle shown in Figure 13.4. In the first stage, spores develop into separate male and female gametophytes. The male gametophyte grows sperm-producing sex organs, and the female gametophyte grows egg-producing sex organs. The sperm cells use water from rain or dew to swim to the egg cell and fertilize it. The fertilized egg remains in the female sex organ and develops into a sporophyte. The sporophyte, still attached to the female gametophyte, grows a stalk with a capsule on the end. In the capsule, cell divisions produce spores that will be released to continue the cycle.

Liverworts

In wet areas of a forest or bog, you may find bryophytes like the **liverwort** shown in Figure 13.5. The bodies of most liverworts have the flat, leaflike structures that you see here. Other liverworts have bodies divided into rounded sections, or lobes. Liverworts got their unusual name because the shape of the lobed liverwort looks somewhat like a mammal's liver. Both kinds of liverworts have rhizoids.

The life cycle of liverworts is similar to that of mosses. The leaflike structures belong to the gametophyte, which is the most noticeable stage. The smaller sporophyte produces capsules that contain special spring-loaded cells. These cells launch the spores and help them disperse.

Close relatives of the liverworts are the hornworts. The gametophytes of both plants look very much alike. However, their sporophytes look very different. Hornworts get their name from their sporophytes, which are hornlike.

Figure 13.5 ▲
Notice the difference between the male and female gametophytes on this liverwort.

Who Studies How Plants Grow and Reproduce?

Imagine cutting a trail through thick jungle vegetation in Brazil. Every so often, you find an unfamiliar plant that you carefully dig up and place in a special container. You hope one of these plants contains a substance that will kill cancer cells. You are a botanist at work.

A botanist may study any aspect of the plant kingdom. Many botanists work in laboratories, studying plant life processes and reproduction. Others may focus on developing new varieties of food crops or controlling plant diseases.

Some botanists work outside much of the time. They may explore an area to see if rare plants live there, for example. If rare plants are discovered, it may mean that the land cannot be developed.

Many research positions in botany require a doctorate degree. However, for many careers related to botany, you need only a bachelor's degree or some college-level training in botany. These careers include forester, forest ranger, landscaper, florist, environmental educator, botanical illustrator, and nursery manager.

A bachelor's degree in botany may also qualify you for an entry-

level job as a technician or lab assistant. This kind of job may involve helping scientists perform research projects for private companies, universities, or government agencies.

Figure 13.6 ▲

In Ireland, a man stacks peat to dry it. The peat will eventually be used for fuel.

Science and Society *Peat Resources*

Peat has been used for thousands of years as a fuel. It forms from the compacted bodies of dead sphagnum moss plants. As the moss grows in a bog, each new generation grows on top of the others. The weight of the new plants compacts the layers beneath. The compacted moss decays slowly, forming peat. Large peat deposits occur in Europe, North America, and Asia.

Dried peat burns readily. In many places in the world, peat fires heat homes and cook meals. In Ireland and Scotland, some people still cut peat in blocks using hand tools. They dry it and store it in piles near their homes.

Large amounts of peat fuel electrical power generating plants in Europe and Asia. In the United States and Canada, mined peat is sold for landscaping and gardening. The peat is mixed into the soil to increase its ability to hold moisture and nutrients. Various techniques are used to harvest the large quantities of peat needed. For example, a steel drum with spikes is dragged across a bog, churning up the peat. After the peat dries, vacuum machines collect the top layer.

Sphagnum moss itself has other important uses. Highly absorbent, it is used for wound dressings and baby diapers by people from many different cultures. It contains sphagnol, a compound with antibacterial properties. Traditional healers in China and North America use the moss to prepare medicinal teas and salves.

Check and Explain

1. If you were chosen to lead an expedition looking for unusual mosses and liverworts, where would you go? Describe two environments you would choose.

2. Explain why you selected each environment in the first question.

3. **Compare and Contrast** What characteristics do mosses and liverworts have in common? How are they different?

4. **Infer** How might a long drought affect the reproduction of mosses?

13.3 Nonflowering Vascular Plants

Objectives

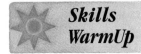

▶ **Describe** ferns, horsetails, club mosses, and gymnosperms.

▶ **Explain** the importance of pollen as a plant adaptation.

▶ **Compare** and **contrast** the life cycles of ferns and pine trees.

▶ **Make a model** of an ancient landscape dominated by nonflowering vascular plants.

Skills WarmUp

Make a Graph   There are about 1,000 species of club mosses, 15 species of horsetails, and 12,000 species of ferns living today. Display this information on a circle graph.

Imagine walking the length of a football field. Now imagine a plant that grows taller than that distance! Such a plant is a nonflowering vascular plant known as a redwood tree. Redwood trees are among the tallest of all living things, reaching heights of over 100 m.

Why can a redwood tree grow so tall? As plants evolved on land, they developed tubelike vascular tissues to carry water and nutrients. The bundles of vascular tissue gave the plants support, allowing them to grow taller. The tubelike vascular tissue could also transport water from the soil to the rest of the plant. Because of this adaptation, vascular plants could grow almost anywhere on land.

Look at Figure 13.7. By about 300 million years ago, tall vascular plants that looked like giant feather dusters, asparagus stalks, and tree-sized ferns covered the earth. Descended from those fantastic forest plants are today's horsetails, ferns, and club mosses, as well as the giant redwood.

Ferns

Nonflowering vascular plants called ferns were important members of the ancient forests. Ferns still grow today in forests around the world. Most grow in warm, tropical regions, but some species are found in regions where seasonal changes occur. A few species of tropical ferns are tree-sized like those living millions of years ago, but most of the 12,000 or so species of ferns alive today are smaller.

Unlike mosses, ferns have true roots, stems, and distinctive leaves. These organs all contain vascular tissue. The leaves of ferns are sometimes called fronds. Each is

Figure 13.7 ▲
With the evolution of vascular tissue, nonflowering plants could form forests.

Figure 13.8 ▼
Life Cycle of a Fern

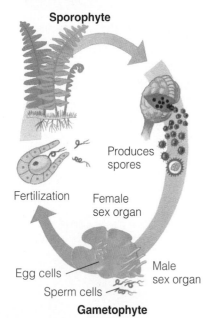

Sporophyte

Produces spores

Fertilization

Female sex organ

Egg cells

Sperm cells

Male sex organ

Gametophyte

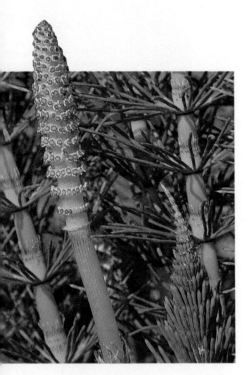

Figure 13.9 ▲
What do you think is the pointed structure at the end of this horsetail plant?

divided into leaflets. They have a waxy coating to protect them from drying out. The stems of most ferns are underground stems called *rhizomes* (RY zohmz). Roots grow from the underside of the rhizome and leaves grow from the topside. Tree ferns have tall, upright stems.

The life cycle of a fern is shown in Figure 13.8. The plant that you know as a fern is the sporophyte part of the life cycle. On the underside of its mature fronds grow spore cases called *sori* (SOH ree) that look like small brown spots. Inside the sori, special cell divisions occur, producing spores. The sori have springlike structures that can fling the spores several meters when they are mature. Once released in this way, spores travel greater distances by wind and water.

If a spore lands in moist, shaded soil, it develops into a small, heart-shaped gametophyte with both male and female sex organs. Sperm cells produced by the male organ swim to the female sex organ containing the egg cell. Fertilization occurs, and the zygote develops into an embryo. The embryo, protected and nourished by the gametophyte, develops into the familiar leafy sporophyte.

How is the fern life cycle different from the life cycle of a moss? In a moss, the gametophyte is the largest and longest-lived generation. In a fern, it is the sporophyte that grows larger and lives longer.

Horsetails

The plants that look like giant bottle brushes in Figure 13.7 are the ancestors of the horsetails. Some grew up to 15 m tall. Modern horsetails, shown in Figure 13.9, are much smaller. They are common in many damp places, but there are only 15 species.

Horsetails have jointed stems. A circle, or whorl, of narrow leaves grows from each joint, making the plant look something like the bushy tail of a horse. Horsetails were once called scouring rushes, because people used them to scrub cooking pots. The cell walls of the stem contain hard grains of silica, making the plant abrasive.

The life cycle of a horsetail is similar to that of a fern. The sporophyte is much larger and longer-lived than the gametophyte. Spores produced by the sporophyte grow into tiny free-living gametophytes that produce both egg and sperm cells. The fertilized eggs grow into new sporophytes.

Club Mosses

The plants shown in Figure 13.10 can be found growing on forest floors in temperate regions. They are members of another group of nonflowering vascular plants called club mosses. The club-shaped structures at the tips of their stems are spore cases.

Although these plants have the word *moss* in their name, they are not mosses. Unlike true mosses, club mosses have vascular tissue. Their life cycles are similar to those of the horsetails and ferns. The plants you see in Figure 13.10 are sporophytes.

Most species of club mosses grow in tropical areas on the branches and trunks of trees. Hundreds of millions of years ago, relatives of modern club mosses grew as large as trees. The treelike club mosses all became extinct, however, when the earth's climate changed. The club mosses alive today are descendants of a group of smaller club mosses that survived.

Figure 13.10 ▲
The most common club mosses in North America are these *Lycopodium.*

SkillBuilder *Estimating*

Fern Spore Cases

Ferns store spores in spore cases, or sori, located under the frond leaflets. Each sori contains thousands of tiny spores. To increase the chances of new fern growth, a fern plant has many sori.

1. Obtain a fern frond.

2. Observe the underside of the frond. Look for the sori.

3. Copy the table below on a sheet of paper.

4. Based on your observation, estimate the total number of sori on the frond. Record your estimate.

5. Count the total number of sori on ten leaflets. Record in your table. Calculate the average number of sori for each leaflet. Record.

6. To calculate the estimated number of sori on the entire frond, count the total number of leaflets on the frond. Record. Multiply the total number of fronds by the average number of sori for each leaflet.

Write a paragraph comparing your estimation to the calculated estimation for sori found on the frond. Give reasons why your observed estimate was different from the calculated estimate.

Estimation from Observation	Number of Sori on Ten Leaflets	Average Number of Sori for Each Leaflet	Total Number of Leaflets	Calculated Estimation

Gymnosperms

Nonflowering vascular plants that produce seeds are called gymnosperms. Cone-bearing trees, such as pine and redwood, are the most common gymnosperms alive today. Because of their seeds and other adaptations, these plants live and reproduce in places where ferns, horsetails, and club mosses cannot.

A seed is an adaptation for protecting and nourishing a plant embryo. Along with an embryo, a seed contains an energy supply. It is surrounded by a protective coat. The embryo inside a seed may remain dormant for a long period of time. Then, when the conditions are right, it can begin growing. Seeds can travel over a distance to establish new plants in new places.

Gymnosperms have another important adaptation to living on land. Recall that ferns, horsetails, and club mosses need standing water so that sperm cells can swim to the egg cells. Gymnosperms evolved a way to get around the need for water. Their sperm cells don't need to swim. Instead, they develop inside protective cases that can be carried by moving air. These dustlike particles are known as **pollen**. Pollen made it possible for gymnosperms to survive and reproduce away from damp environments. As a result, gymnosperms grow in deserts and on dry, windy mountaintops.

There are four main groups of gymnosperms alive today. One member of each group is shown below. Study the photographs carefully. What do all the plants have in common?

▲ The most common living gymnosperms, the **conifers**, have needle-shaped leaves and seeds produced in cones. What conifers can you name?

Cycads (SY kadz) are relics of the ancient forests. This cycad is native to the state of Florida. ▼

◄ This plant belongs to a group called gnetophytes (NEE toh FYTS). It has long straplike leaves and bears clusters of small cones on short stalks.

The ginkgo, also called the maidenhair tree, has fan-shaped leaves and fleshy cones. Unlike other gymnosperms, the leaves of a ginkgo fall from the tree in autumn. ▼

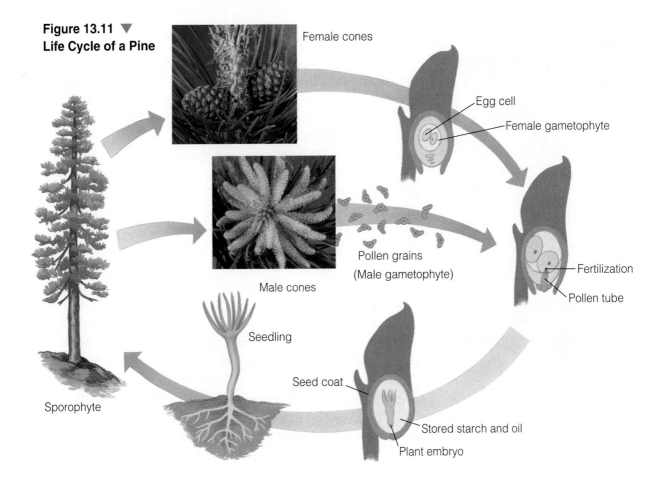

Figure 13.11 ▼
Life Cycle of a Pine

Female cones

Egg cell

Female gametophyte

Pollen grains
(Male gametophyte)

Fertilization

Pollen tube

Male cones

Seedling

Seed coat

Sporophyte

Stored starch and oil

Plant embryo

Pine Tree Life Cycle

The life cycles of gymnosperms differ greatly from the life cycles of ferns, horsetails, and club mosses. The pine tree provides a good example of how the gymnosperm life cycle works.

The pine tree is the sporophyte generation. It has two types of cones. The large woody cones produce spores that develop into female gametophytes. Smaller, nonwoody cones produce spores that develop into male gametophytes. Unlike the gametophytes of ferns, horsetails, and club mosses, these gametophytes are not free-living.

Look at Figure 13.11. The female gametophyte remains in the cone. It grows into a many-celled mass in which several egg cells begin to develop. The male

gametophyte is packaged into a tiny pollen grain. These are released and carried by the wind.

When the wind-borne pollen reaches a cone where the female gametophyte is developing, **pollination** occurs. The male gametophyte grows a pollen tube through which sperm can reach the egg cell. Fertilization occurs as the sperm and egg fuse. Notice in Figure 13.11 that the fertilized egg develops into an embryo. The embryo is packaged into a seed, along with a food supply. When the seed sprouts and grows into a young sporophyte, the cycle is complete.

In this life cycle, the gametophyte generation is very small. For this reason, reproduction in gymnosperms *appears* to involve only one generation producing male and female sex cells.

Figure 13.12 ▲
These fossils of cones (top) and ginkgo leaves (bottom) are the kinds of evidence scientists use to piece together the history of gymnosperms on the earth.

Gymnosperms and Geologic Time

Fossils like those in Figure 13.12 tell the history of gymnosperms. The first gymnosperms appeared about 350 million years ago. At that time, the earth's land masses were joined together in a supercontinent called Pangaea. The climate was warm and wet. Club mosses, horsetails, and ferns dominated the landscape.

About 250 million years ago, geologic processes began to change the landscape. Mountains formed, and many shallow seas drained. Conditions on land became much drier. Gymnosperms, particularly conifers, were well adapted for the dry conditions. Gymnosperms did not require standing water to reproduce. The conifers had needlelike leaves with thick waxy coatings and sunken pores to conserve water.

When dinosaurs roamed the earth, about 200 million years ago, gymnosperms were the most common plant life. The dinosaurs lived among forests of conifers and cycads the size of small palm trees. Large fernlike plants that reproduced with seeds were also common. When the climate cooled dramatically about 70 million years ago, dinosaurs became extinct, but conifers continued to thrive. Other gymnosperms were less successful under the new conditions, and many species died out. The newly evolved flowering plants took over much of the landscape. Today gymnosperms grow mostly in dry areas with poor soil.

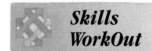

Science and Technology *Making Paper*

Think of all the paper you handle in one day. Most of this paper is made of wood fibers from conifer trees. The method used to make all this paper was developed in China about 2,000 years ago. First, wood is crushed and mixed with water to form a pulp. The pulp is poured onto a flat screen, which is shaken to intermesh the wood fibers. The water is suctioned off, leaving a thin sheet of fresh paper.

Although the basic method is similar, papermaking today takes place on a huge scale. One metric ton of paper needs wood from more than 17 mature trees. The trees are cut down and trucked to a paper mill. There the bark is removed. The trees are ground with water or treated with heat and chemicals to form pulp.

Figure 13.13 ▲
Most papermaking takes place on a huge scale, as you can see in this photograph of a paper mill.

Figure 13.14 ▲
Some paper is still made by hand. This photograph, taken in Japan, shows a man making paper in the traditional way.

Pulp is pumped through pipes to a papermaking machine. The pulp is sprayed onto a wide, moving belt with a screen. Water drains through the screen, leaving a damp mat of wood fibers. This is the newly made paper. The paper is lifted from the end of the moving belt and dried over a series of steam-heated rollers, like the one in Figure 13.13.

If paper is recycled, the papermaking process is much simpler. Waste paper is mixed with water in a machine resembling a giant kitchen blender. The action of the blades forms a pulp that is just like the pulp made from trees.

Check and Explain

1. Name and describe four groups of nonflowering vascular plants.

2. What is pollen? Why is pollen a useful adaptation to gymnosperms?

3. **Compare and Contrast** How do the life cycles of pines and ferns differ? How are they alike?

4. **Make a Model** Depict a forest landscape that may have existed when dinosaurs lived.

Activity 13 *Which plant absorbs the most water?*

Skills Measure; Observe; Collect Data; Infer

Task 1 Prelab Prep

Collect the following items: 4 small cups or petri dishes, water, 2 samples of other nonflowering plants beside mosses, moss sample, hand lens, graduated cylinder, paper towels.

Task 2 Data Record

1. Place one sample of each plant in a cup or petri dish.
2. On a separate sheet of paper, draw the table shown to the right. Make the space for the drawing larger than it is shown. Write the names of the plant samples you chose in the table.
3. Record all your observations in the table.

Task 3 Procedure

1. Using the hand lens, observe the three nonflowering plant samples.
2. Draw each sample in your data table.
3. Measure 5 mL of water in the graduated cylinder. Add the water to one of the samples. Record this amount in your table. Repeat for each of the other two plant samples.
4. Wait 5 minutes. As you wait, wipe up any spills, and observe the samples.
5. Without disturbing the plant sample, pour off the remaining water from one of the samples into the empty cup. Measure the amount of water in the graduated cylinder. Record the amount. Dispose of the sample water. Dry the cup with the paper towel.
6. Repeat step 5 for each of the other two plant samples.

Task 4 Analysis

1. Which plant absorbed the largest amount of water?
2. What is it about the structure of this plant that makes it absorbent?

Table 13.1   Water Absorbed

Plant	Drawing	Water Added	Water Left	Water Absorbed

3. Why do you think it is important for this nonflowering plant to be able to absorb water?
4. List the variables in this activity.
5. Why was it important to dry the cup and graduated cylinder after each water sample measurement?

Task 5 Conclusion

Write a short paragraph comparing the absorption of the nonflowering plants in this activity. If the plants didn't absorb the same amount of water, explain why.

Everyday Application

Dead moss plants are often placed in the pots of indoor plants or around the base of potted trees. Explain why mosses are used for this purpose.

Extension

Try planting your own simple terrarium with various nonflowering plants. Before you make the terrarium, be sure to make a list of the necessary conditions for successful plant growth. Keep a record of any changes that occur.

Chapter 13 *Review*

Concept Summary

13.1 Characteristics of Nonflowering Plants

▶ Bryophytes, mosses, and ferns are examples of nonflowering plants.

▶ Nonflowering plants evolved specialized tissues and organs that enabled them to live on land.

▶ The plant life cycle has a sexual gametophyte stage and nonsexual sporophyte stage.

13.2 Bryophytes

▶ Bryophytes grow only in moist environments. The gametophyte is the largest and longest-lived part of their life cycle.

▶ Mosses have small leaflike structures arranged in a spiral on a short stalk. They have rhizoids.

▶ Liverworts have flat leaflike or lobed structures that make up the main part of their bodies. Hornworts are close relatives of liverworts.

13.3 Nonflowering Vascular Plants

▶ Ferns are nonflowering vascular plants with true roots, stems, and leaves. The sporophyte is the largest and longest-lived part of their life cycle.

▶ Horsetails have jointed stems and leaves arranged in whorls.

▶ Club mosses have club-shaped spore cases at the tips of their stems.

▶ Gymnosperms are nonflowering vascular plants that produce seeds.

▶ Pollen makes it possible for gymnosperms to survive and reproduce away from damp environments.

Chapter Vocabulary

gametophyte (13.1)   moss (13.2)   liverwort (13.2)   conifer (13.3)
sporophyte (13.1)   rhizoid (13.2)   pollen (13.3)   pollination (13.3)
spore (13.1)

Check Your Vocabulary

Use the vocabulary words above to complete the following sentences correctly.

1. The _____ stage in the plant life cycle reproduces sexually.

2. Nonsexual reproductive cells with a protective covering are called _____ .

3. _____ have needle-shaped leaves and seeds produced in cones.

4. Bryophytes have rootlike structures called _____ .

5. Gymnosperms' sperm cells are packaged inside grains of _____ .

6. The _____ stage of a plant reproduces nonsexually with spores.

7. When pollen reaches the female gametophyte, _____ occurs.

8. A bryophyte with green leaflike structures arranged in a spiral on a short stalk is called a _____ .

9. The body of a _____ is divided into rounded sections, or lobes.

Explain the difference between the words in each pair.

10. Spore, seed

11. Rhizoid, root

12. Pollen, sperm

Write Your Vocabulary

Write sentences using each vocabulary word above. Show that you know what each word means.

Chapter 13 Review

Check Your Knowledge

Answer the following in complete sentences.

1. Why don't the cells of bryophytes dry out in the air?

2. How do club mosses, horsetails, and ferns transport water from the roots to the above-ground parts of the plant?

3. Where can you find club mosses growing?

4. What was the climate like when the first gymnosperms appeared on the earth? What was the name for the earth's land masses at that time?

5. How are ferns different from mosses? Name three differences.

6. What are the most common living gymnosperms?

7. The plant you know as a fern is just part of its life cycle. What is the other part of the life cycle called?

Determine whether each statement is true or false. Write *true* if it is true. If it is false, change the underlined word to make the statement true.

8. In the first stage of the moss life cycle, <u>spores</u> develop into separate male and female gametophytes.

9. A plant that lives on land must adapt to two separate substances: soil and <u>rain</u>.

10. As plants evolved on land, they developed tubelike vascular tissues to carry water and <u>soil</u>.

11. The club-shaped structures at the tips of the stems on club mosses are <u>spore cases</u>.

12. About 200 million years ago, when dinosaurs roamed the earth, <u>giant ferns</u> had become the most common plant life.

Check Your Understanding

Apply the concepts you have learned to answer each question.

1. How is the life cycle of a fern different from the life cycle of a moss?

2. **Compare and Contrast** All land plants have a way to disperse their offspring, which means to scatter them over a large area. In what stage of its life cycle can a fern disperse offspring? In what stage does this occur in a gymnosperm? How do nonflowering plants compare in their methods of dispersal?

3. Are club mosses really mosses? Explain why or why not.

4. **Mystery Photo** The photograph on page 252 is a close-up view of a fern. The yellow clumps are sori on the underside of the leaf. They contain spores. These spores are an important part of the fern's reproductive cycle. What happens if a spore lands in moist, shaded soil?

5. Gymnosperm sperm cells do not have flagella for swimming. How do they travel instead? What advantage do they have over sperm cells that must swim?

6. Describe how pollination occurs in the life cycle of a pine tree.

7. **Extension** Which process is simpler: making paper from trees or from recycled paper? Why?

8. **Compare and Contrast** How do non-flowering plants differ from many-celled algae? How are they similar?

9. Why can a redwood tree grow as tall as 100 m high? Describe the adaptation that allows plants to grow far above the soil.

Develop Your Skills

Use the skills you have developed in this chapter to complete each activity.

1. **Interpret Data** Bracken fern spreads quickly in cleared areas as its rhizomes grow outward and make new plants. The map below shows where bracken fern grew in a certain field at the beginning of 1989. It also shows the edge of bracken fern growth at the beginning of each following year.

 a. How many places in the field did bracken fern grow at the beginning of 1990?

 b. During which year did the fern grow the slowest?

 c. Predict how many years it will take for bracken fern to cover the field.

2. **Data Bank** Use the information on page 627 to answer the following questions.

 a. What do the seven tallest trees in the United States all have in common?

 b. What species of conifer grows closest in height to the California redwood?

3. **Compare and Contrast** How are seeds and spores different? How is each a part of the plant life cycle?

Make Connections

1. **Link the Concepts** Below is a concept map showing how some of the main concepts in this chapter link together. Only part of the map is filled in. Finish the map, using words and ideas you find in the chapter.

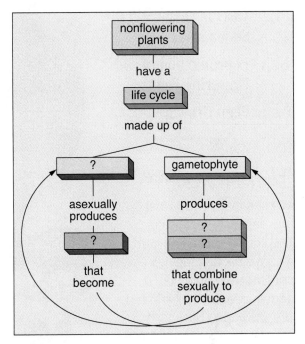

2. **Science and Art** Using information in this chapter, as well as your own research, create a poster showing what the swampy forests on the earth looked like 300 million years ago.

3. **Science and Language Arts** Liverworts can have lobes shaped like a mammal's liver. Hornworts have long, hornlike spore capsules. Investigate other plants that are named after a familiar object or part of the body.

4. **Science and You** Pollen makes gymnosperm reproduction possible. It also makes many people sneeze. Research pollen allergies. How does pollen affect allergic people?

Chapter **14** Flowering Plants

What do you see?

66 I see many seeds that are many different colors. The corn kernel came from a corn stalk and the helicopter seed came from a certain tree. Each, if planted, will grow up to be what it came from. It is kind of like a chain. First a seed must be planted and then a tree or a plant or whatever grows. Later the plant will make new seeds to be planted. **99**

Erica Severns
Whittier Middle School
Sioux Falls, South Dakota

To find out more about the photograph, look on page 292. As you read this chapter, you will learn about flowering plants.

14.1 Characteristics of Flowering Plants

Objectives

▶ **Explain** what all flowers have in common.

▶ **Discuss** adaptations of flowering plants.

▶ **Compare** gymnosperms and angiosperms.

▶ **Organize data** about monocots and dicots.

Imagine you are walking through a beautiful flower garden. What do you see? You can usually see a variety of shapes, sizes, and colors. You may wonder how there can be so many different kinds of flowers. For example, you might find a colorful, complex orchid, or a simple, white daisy. Perhaps you'll see a bee, or a butterfly landing on a flower. You might also notice hummingbirds hovering nearby. Although the flowers look very different, they all have one thing in common. Do you know what it is?

Origins and Adaptations

Fossils show that flowering plants, called angiosperms, first evolved about 130 million years ago. Scientists infer that angiosperms evolved from a gymnosperm ancestor—both have vascular tissue and both produce pollen. But unlike gymnosperms, angiosperms produce seeds within a flower.

Flowers contain the sex organs for an angiosperm. The male sex organs make pollen and the female sex organs make egg cells. Some flowers, such as tulips, contain both male and female sex organs within one flower. Other flowers, such as the squash blossoms shown in Figure 14.1, may contain either male or female sex organs.

Flowers have many adaptations for reproduction. Plants with colorful and complex flowers usually depend on insects, bats, or hummingbirds to carry pollen from one flower to another. Shape, scent, and color are flower adaptations that help plants

Figure 14.1 ▲
Squash plants have separate male and female flowers. The flower in the top photograph has male sex organs. The flower in the bottom photograph has female sex organs.

Figure 14.2 ▲
The world's largest flower, *Rafflesia*, grows in the forests of Malaysia. The rare flower is more than 1 m in diameter and smells like rotting meat.

attract specific pollen carriers. A specific pollen carrier is more likely to take the pollen to another plant of the same species, increasing the chances of successful reproduction. Plants that depend on wind to carry their pollen do not have this advantage.

Most angiosperms produce flowers grouped together in clusters. These flower clusters vary greatly in size, shape, and the number of flowers they contain. Other angiosperms, such as the daffodil, have only one single flower. Can you think of other angiosperms that have one flower?

More than 275,000 species of angiosperms are found in the world today—from the equator to the poles, and from the oceans to the mountains. They come in different forms: trees, shrubs, vines, herbs, and succulents, such as cacti. Angiosperms range in size from tiny floating plants only 10 mm long to enormous flowering trees over 100 m tall. The plant shown in Figure 14.2 has the world's largest known single flower.

SkillBuilder *Collecting Data*

Sowing Information About Seeds

There are probably as many seed variations as there are different types of flowers. Obtain a bag of assorted seeds. Examine the seeds very closely. Divide your seeds into groups, according to color, size, shape, or whatever characteristic you choose.

Copy the table shown on a separate sheet of paper. Record the characteristic you observed, the different variations you observed for this characteristic, and the number of groups you obtained.

After you finish, collect your seeds into one group. Divide your seeds again according to a different characteristic. Record your data in the table. Continue regrouping and sorting your seeds for several new characteristics. Study your table, then answer the following questions.

1. Describe the characteristics you observed.

2. Which seed grouping did you think was the best? Why?

3. Which characteristic had the least number of groups? The largest number of groups?

4. What seed characteristic would you use to place all seeds in the same group?

5. Explain how seeds are similar. Explain how they vary.

Observed Seed Characteristics		
Characteristics	**Different Types**	**Number of Groups**

Angiosperm Classification

Angiosperms are classified into two groups based on the number of seed cotyledons (KAHT uh LEED uhns). Cotyledons are leaflike parts of the plant embryo inside the seed.

Monocots Look at the characteristics of a **monocot** (MAHN oh KAHT) in Figure 14.3.

- ▶ *Mono-* means "one." A monocot seed has only one cotyledon.
- ▶ Monocot leaves are narrow with a parallel vein pattern.
- ▶ Inside a monocot stem, the bundles of vascular tissue are scattered.
- ▶ Monocots have fibrous roots.
- ▶ The parts of a monocot flower are found in multiples of three.

Some monocots are grasses and food plants, such as corn, and garden flowers, such as tulips. Palms are the only monocot trees.

One cotyledon

Flower parts in threes

Parallel veins

Vascular bundles scattered

Fibrous roots

Figure 14.3 ▲
This plant, *Lilium regale*, has the characteristics of a typical monocot.

Dicots Figure 14.4 shows the characteristics of a **dicot** (DY kaht).

- ▶ *Di-* means "two." A dicot seed has two cotyledons.
- ▶ Dicot leaves have a branching pattern of veins.
- ▶ The bundles of vascular tissue inside a dicot stem are arranged in a ring.
- ▶ Dicots have a large, thick taproot.
- ▶ The parts of a dicot flower are found in multiples of four or five.

Dicots are thought to have evolved before monocots. About five times more dicot species than monocot species exist today. Common dicots include all broadleafed trees, such as oak, maple, cottonwood, and fruit trees. Food plants such as tomatoes, potatoes, peas, squash, lettuce, and broccoli are dicots. Dicot flowers include sunflowers, roses, and violets.

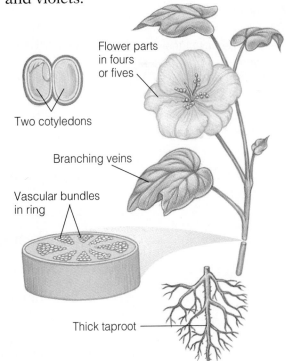

Flower parts in fours or fives

Two cotyledons

Branching veins

Vascular bundles in ring

Thick taproot

Figure 14.4 ▲
This plant, *Fremontia californica*, has the characteristics of a typical dicot.

Figure 14.5 ▲

Tribal legends say that the medicinal properties of the cinchona tree were discovered during an epidemic. Everyone who drank water from a shallow lake with these trees growing at the water's edge got well.

Science and Society *Plant Medicines*

Did you know that aspirin and many other medicines originally came from flowering plants? For centuries, many cultures around the world used tea made from the bark of willow trees as a pain remedy. In 1827, the active ingredient of willow bark was identified. In 1899, a synthetic form of the active ingredient was made and given the name aspirin. Aspirin is still widely used to relieve pain and reduce fever.

For thousands of years, people all over the world suffered and died from a disease called malaria. Malaria is caused by a parasite and produces very high fevers. Long before the cause of malaria was understood, native peoples in South America knew an effective cure. They treated malaria and other fevers with bark from a tree they called the *quina* or *querango*. The flowers and leaves of this life-saving tree from the Andes Mountains are shown in Figure 14.5.

During the 1600s, Spanish expeditions gathered the bark, collected the flowers and seeds, and took the plant to Europe. There the bark became famous for curing many prominent people, including the Countess of Chinchón, a Spanish noblewoman. In honor of her cure, Linneaus named the plant cinchona (sihn KOH nuh).

Until the early 1800s, powdered cinchona bark was the only cure for malaria. Plantations of cinchona trees supplied the worldwide demand. About 1820, the active ingredient in the bark, called quinine (KWY nyn), was discovered. Soon after, drug manufacturers began to make synthetic quinine. Today doctors use synthetic quinine to treat malaria patients all over the world.

Check and Explain

1. What do all flowers have in common?

2. What adaptations do flowering plants have to ensure pollination?

3. **Compare and Contrast** How are angiosperms similar to gymnosperms? How are they different?

4. **Organize Data** Make a table comparing the characteristics of monocots and dicots.

14.2 Vascular Plant Systems

Objectives

▶ **Describe** a root system and **explain** how it works.

▶ **Explain** how each part of a shoot system works.

▶ **Compare** and **contrast** three types of roots.

▶ **Make a model** of water transport in plants.

Skills WarmUp

Hypothesize Write a hypothesis for what would happen to a plant if you removed its roots. Design an experiment to test your hypothesis.

Think about how your body systems work. For example, your circulatory system transports food, oxygen, water, minerals, and other materials throughout your body. Your circulatory system is made up of many different cells, tissues, and organs. All parts of the system work together. Your circulatory system also interacts and works with other systems of your body.

Vascular plants also have systems. The shoot system is the aboveground part of the plant. Below the ground is the root system. Each system is made of cells, tissues, and organs working together.

Water, Sugar, and Mineral Transport

Vascular tissue forms a plant's pipeline, connecting the root system and the shoot system. Follow the pipeline through the plant in Figure 14.6. One part of the vascular tissue is a set of linked cells called the **xylem** (ZY luhm). The xylem forms a pipeline for water and minerals. From the root system, water and minerals travel upward through the xylem to the shoot system. Some water is used in photosynthesis, but most of it evaporates through stomates in the leaves. The loss of water through the stomates of leaves is called **transpiration**.

A leaf is a shoot system organ. Leaves capture light and make glucose by photosynthesis. Glucose made in the leaves must travel to other parts of the plant. A second set of linked cells in the vascular tissue, called the **phloem** (FLOH ehm), transports glucose and other sugars. In the root system, the sugars provide energy for root growth. The shoot system receives sugars for growth and flower production. The plant storage organs store glucose in the form of starch for later use.

Phloem
Xylem

Figure 14.6 ▲
Inside every vascular plant there are xylem and phloem tissues. Water and minerals move through the xylem. Sugars, dissolved in water, move through the phloem.

Root System

The root system of a plant is usually about the same size as its shoot system. For example, a maize plant 2 m tall often has roots that are 2 m long and extend 1 m on all sides.

Root Functions   The root system has several functions.

▶ Roots support and anchor the plant.

▶ Roots absorb water and minerals from the soil.

▶ Roots store glucose in the form of starch.

Figure 14.7 Root System

The root cap protects the end of the growing root. Root cap cells make a slime that coats the root, enabling it to pass more easily through the soil.

Water and minerals absorbed by root hairs enter xylem cells inside the root by osmosis.

The epidermis is an outer protective layer. It covers the entire plant like a skin.

Cambium cells divide, producing either new xylem cells or new phloem cells.

Root Structure   Study the root in Figure 14.7. At the tip of the growing root is a dome-shaped root cap. Tiny structures called root hairs project near the tip. Root hairs increase the area of root exposed to the soil. The greater the exposed surface area, the easier it is for the root to absorb needed water and minerals. The root hairs extend from the **epidermis** (EHP uh DUR mihs). The epidermis is an outer layer of protective cells. Beneath the epidermis is a starch storage layer. In the center are the xylem and phloem. Between the xylem and phloem is the **cambium** (KAM bee uhm). The cambium is growth tissue that makes new xylem and phloem cells.

Roots and Soil Formation   In rocky environments, plant roots make soil by breaking apart solid rock. The root cap secretes slime-containing acids that dissolve rock. The force of the root growth wedges the rock apart. As fallen leaves and other plant parts decay and mix with the rock fragments, soil forms.

Food storage layer

Epidermis

Cambium

Phloem

Xylem

Root Types

The roots of a plant are adapted to the plant's environment. For example, some desert plants have roots more than 18 m long to reach water deep underground.

Although plant roots vary in size and structure, there are three general types: fibrous roots, taproots, and aboveground roots. Monocots produce a fibrous root system. Gymnosperms and dicots usually produce a taproot system. Aboveground roots are specialized roots that grow from stems or leaves. Some plants, such as corn, normally produce aboveground roots. Other plants, such as orchids, develop aboveground roots in response to their environment. Some plants develop aboveground roots in response to injuries.

Fibrous Roots

The plant shown here has fibrous roots. Fibrous roots branch out in all directions. Fibrous roots absorb water efficiently from near the ground surface. They also hold soil together, preventing erosion. ▼

Taproots ▲

This plant has a taproot. A taproot is a thick main root that grows straight into the ground. Smaller roots grow out from the sides. A taproot securely anchors a plant in the soil and may store starch. Vegetables such as carrots and beets are taproots. They contain starch stored by the plants.

Aboveground Roots

Many rain forest plants, such as the epiphyte shown below, grow high in trees. They have aboveground roots that cling to the tree and absorb water and nutrients. Other aboveground roots start on the plant stem and grow down into the soil. They support large trees. ▼

Shoot System

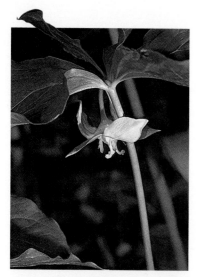

The shoot system includes stems, leaves, and flowers. Some stems are flexible and slender. These are called herbaceous (hur BAY shuhs) stems. Other stems, such as those of trees, are large and woody.

Stem Functions   Stems have several functions.

▸ Stems support the plant.

▸ Stems hold the leaves up toward the light.

▸ Inside a stem, water and minerals move through the xylem and sugars move through the phloem.

▸ Stems of some plants also store water or starch. Green stems make glucose through photosynthesis.

Woody Stems

A woody stem is hard, strong, and rigid. Most plants with woody stems are dicot trees and shrubs that live for many years. Look at the growth rings on this cut tree. Each year's growth has dark and light bands of xylem cells. During wet weather, large xylem cells are produced. In the dry summer, the xylem cells are small and close together. Which cells would appear as a dark band?

▼

Stem Adaptations ▲

Plant stems have many unusual adaptations. Cacti, shown in the photograph, have green succulent stems that store water. The stored water is used to make glucose for the plant. Some plant stems can climb. For example, the stem of the bean plant grows in a spiral to climb up a tree or post.

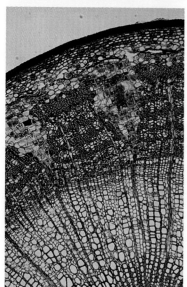

Herbaceous Stems ▲

A herbaceous stem is green, soft, and flexible. Smaller flowering plants, such as wildflowers, grasses, and most vegetables, have herbaceous stems. The top photograph shows the outside of a herbaceous dicot stem. The bottom photograph shows the inside of a dicot stem magnified 100x. Plants with herbaceous stems usually live only one or two years.

Leaf Functions Each leaf is a specialized organ with three main functions.

▶ Leaves capture light from the sun.

▶ Leaves make glucose through photosynthesis.

▶ Leaves exchange gases with the environment.

Leaf Structure Look carefully at Figure 14.8. Notice that a leaf is made of layers. The surface layers are the waxy cuticle and the epidermis. Inside is the moist mesophyll (MEHZ oh FIHL) layer, where photosynthesis occurs. Gases are exchanged with the environment through stomates in the plant's surface.

Leaf Adaptations The shapes and sizes of leaves vary, depending on their environment. Plants in shady forests have large leaves to capture light. Plants in dry environments have small, thick, wax-coated leaves to prevent drying.

**Figure 14.8
Leaf Structure** ▼

Beneath the waxy cuticle, the epidermis covers the upper and lower surfaces of a leaf.

Mesophyll is moist, spongy tissue inside the leaf. It contains cells that photosynthesize and a system of veins.

Stomates are openings in the lower epidermis.

Guard cells open and close the stomates, letting carbon dioxide in and oxygen out.

A vein has xylem, phloem, and supporting tissue. Water and minerals enter a leaf through the xylem. Glucose made in the leaf exits through the phloem.

Science and You *Plant Edibles*

Think about the vegetables you ate during the past week. Chances are you tasted the roots, stems, or leaves of many different flowering plants. Maybe you even ate them raw.

In a salad, you might eat leaves from a lettuce plant, sliced radish roots, and diced celery stems. If you eat a potato, you swallow an underground part of the potato plant stem. Onion and garlic, used to flavor many foods, are the stems and the leaves from two different lily plants. You can even have roots for dessert! Carrot cake is made from the sweet, orange roots of the carrot plant. Tapioca comes from the root of the cassava plant, and spicy gingerbread is flavored with ginger root.

The plant part eaten as a vegetable is usually the plant's storage organ. Lettuce and cabbage plants save sugars in their thick leaves. Celery, rhubarb, and asparagus plants store sugars and starches in their stems. Carrot, beet, and jicama plants use their roots for storage. The stored sugars and starches give many fresh vegetables a sweet taste.

Other roots, stems, and leaves serve as spices. Bark from the stem of a tropical tree is the source of cinnamon. Mint comes from the leaves of the peppermint or the spearmint plant. Leaves from bay laurel trees, rosemary, sage, and oregano shrubs are used to flavor soups. Roots, such as ginger, produce "hot," aromatic spices.

Figure 14.9 ▲
The brightly colored edible leaves are from a plant called red chard. You probably recognize the edible turnip and red potato. What are some leaves, stems, and roots that you eat?

Check and Explain

1. Describe the main functions of a plant's root system. Explain how each function is carried out.

2. What are the parts of a plant's shoot system? Explain how each part functions.

3. **Compare and Contrast** Describe three types of roots. How are the roots different from one another? How are they similar?

4. **Make a Model** Trace the path of water as it moves through a plant. Using references, first draw the plant, then use arrows to show how the water moves. Be sure to label important plant parts.

14.3 Reproduction of Flowering Plants

Objectives

▶ **Identify** the parts of a flower and **describe** their functions.

▶ **Explain** what a fruit is and how it develops.

▶ **Discuss** vegetative propagation.

▶ **Infer** how to make seeds germinate.

Have you ever watched a honeybee or a bumblebee after it has landed on a flower, such as a daisy? If you have, you probably know that the bee was searching for nectar to eat. But did you know that the daisy also benefits from the bee's visit?

If you could closely watch a bee on a daisy, you might notice a yellow dust on the bee's body. The yellow dust is an important part of the daisy's life cycle. The yellow dust is pollen from the daisy's male sex organs. The pollen is carried by wind or animals to the female part of another daisy. The pollen fertilizes the egg cells, producing a young daisy embryo that is packaged into a seed. From the seed, a new daisy plant grows.

Flower Structure

Look carefully at the flower parts in Figure 14.10. Flowers have four sets of specialized structures growing from a short stem. At the flower's base are the **sepals** (SEE puhls). Sepals are often green. They enclose and protect the flower as it develops. Just above the sepals are petals. Petals are often brightly colored.

The **stamen** (STAY muhn) is the male reproductive part of a flower. It has two parts, a long filament and a saclike **anther** (AN thur). The anther produces the pollen grains. The **pistil** is the female reproductive part of the flower. Forming the base of the pistil is a swollen ovary. From the ovary a slender stalk, called the style, arises and supports the **stigma**. The stigma is the part of the pistil that collects pollen. Its sticky or feathery quality enables it to capture pollen.

Figure 14.10 Flower Structure

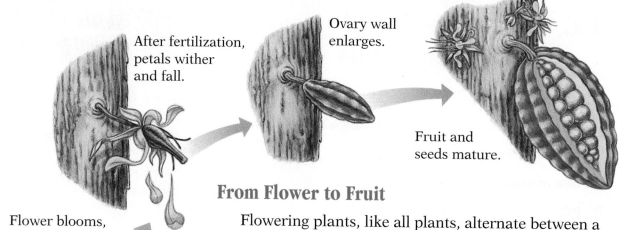

After fertilization, petals wither and fall.

Ovary wall enlarges.

Fruit and seeds mature.

Flower blooms, attracting pollinators.

Figure 14.11 ▲

The cacao flower develops into a podlike fruit with large seeds called cocoa beans. Aztec and Maya people cultivated this plant in ancient Mexico.

From Flower to Fruit

Flowering plants, like all plants, alternate between a gametophyte and a sporophyte generation. You usually see the sporophyte. The tiny male and female gametophytes are produced inside the flower. The male gametophyte is the pollen grain. The female gametophyte grows inside the ovary and produces the egg cells.

Look at how the cacao flower develops into a fruit in Figure 14.11. A flower produces fruits and seeds only after pollination. Pollination is the transfer of the pollen from the anther to the stigma. Following pollination, a pollen tube begins to grow toward the egg cells in the ovary. Sperm cells travel down the pollen tube, and fertilization occurs. Fertilized eggs grow into plant embryos. Structures develop around each plant embryo, forming seeds.

As the seeds form inside the ovary, the ovary wall enlarges to become a fruit. All fruits develop from flowers and contain seeds. Fruits also protect and help disperse seeds. Like cherries and apples, squashes and tomatoes are fruits. Not all fruits are juicy and edible. Some fruits are winged seed covers, or dry pods. The dry, podlike fruit of the cacao tree contains cocoa beans. Cocoa beans are the source of chocolate.

Figure 14.12

Kiwi, lemons, and papaya are fleshy fruits. The pea pod is a dry fruit. ▼

New Plants from Seeds

Just as flowers and fruits differ in shape, color, and size, so do seeds. Compare the seeds in Figure 14.12. The seeds look different, but they all share common features. All seeds have a seed coat, a plant embryo, and stored energy for the young plant. The stored energy is in the form of sugars, starches, and oils.

When a seed forms, the plant embryo usually stops growing, becoming dormant. A dormant seed can withstand freezing temperatures, or drought. Some seeds remain dormant for a few days, some for a few months, and others for many years.

If a seed lands in a suitable environment, it sprouts, or germinates. Seeds need water, oxygen, and a suitable temperature to germinate. Look at the germination process shown in Figure 14.13. Germination begins when water enters the seed coat and the seed swells. The embryo grows, using the sugars, starches, and oils stored in the cotyledons. The root tip emerges first and anchors the seed to the ground. Root hairs begin to absorb water. Then the shoot, with its tiny leaves, sprouts from the soil. The tiny leaves turn green and begin to manufacture sugars. The stored energy in the cotyledons is used, and they may shrivel and fall off.

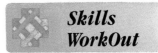

Skills WorkOut

Classify Make a list of plants that produce seeds. Classify the seed-producing plants according to whether each plant seed is also a human food product.

**Figure 14.13
Seed Germination** ▼

▲ Shoots grow upward and break the ground surface.

▲ Roots grow downward. Root hairs absorb water and minerals.

▲ True leaves begin to grow. Cotyledons contain stored energy for plant growth.

▲ True leaves open. Plant begins photosynthesis.

Reproduction Without Seeds

Skilled gardeners do not need seeds to grow many similar plants in a short time. Instead they use the method shown in Figure 14.14. They cut pieces of stems or leaves from plants and place them in a moist environment. Within a few weeks, roots develop, and the cuttings grow into mature plants. This is called **vegetative propagation** (prahp uh GAY shuhn). New plants produced this way are genetically identical to the parent plant. Vegetative propagation is possible with a root, a stem, or a leaf of the parent plant.

Some plants reproduce this way naturally. For example, strawberry plants produce runners. At the end of a runner, a new plant develops. Some grasses do this also. A small patch of grass spreads in this way until it covers hundreds of square meters. The spider plant, a common houseplant with straplike leaves, produces many small spiderlike plants with their own roots.

Figure 14.14 ▲
Under controlled conditions, vegetative propagation can be used to grow many hundreds of similar plants.

Career Corner *Horticulturist*

Who Raises Plants for Landscaping?

The beautiful flowers in a floral arrangement or a botanical garden are cultivated by a horticulturist (HOR tih KUHL chur UHST).

Horticulture comes from two Latin words: *hortus*, which means "garden," and *colere*, which means "to cultivate." Horticulture combines both the art and science of gardening.

The work performed by horticulturists is very diverse. It includes fruit growing, vegetable production, flower use and growing, and landscape gardening. Horticulturists may work in orchards, commercial gardens, nurseries, greenhouses, or research facilities. Horticultural scientists experiment to determine the conditions necessary for good plant growth. They also develop ways to control plant diseases and produce new varieties of plants.

Horticulturists have a strong interest in flowers and plants. Most people in this field earn a four-year degree in biology, botany, or agricultural studies. Some two-year colleges offer a degree in architectural landscaping, which is a branch of horticulture. You can also choose to be a horticultural technician and learn about plants through on-the-job training.

If you like gardening, you can prepare to work in horticulture by taking classes in botany and by joining groups interested in gardening, such as the 4H Clubs of America.

Science and You *Pollen Allergy*

If your eyes water and you sneeze during certain times of the year, you may be allergic to pollen. Pollen allergy is sometimes called hay fever. People named it hay fever when they noticed that the pollen allergy symptoms occurred when hay grasses were common.

People suffer most from pollen allergy during the spring, summer, and fall seasons. In the early spring, flowering trees, such as oak, elm, maple, and walnut, release windborne pollen. In the summer, the small flowers of grasses shed their pollen. In the fall, ragweeds release large clouds of pollen.

Pollen allergy is a reaction of your body's immune system to pollen grains, like the ragweed pollen pictured in Figure 14.15. The tiny, dustlike pollen grains enter your nose and nasal passages as you breathe. Proteins in the pollen irritate cells in the membranes lining your nasal passages. The irritated membranes usually swell and secrete fluids.

If you have pollen allergies, you know that they are accompanied by a number of annoying symptoms. A runny nose and irritated throat are the most common symptoms of pollen allergy. Many people also get itchy, watery eyes. Sneezing and coughing, other symptoms of pollen allergy, are the responses of the body to irritations in the air passages. When particles are in the air passages, a sneeze or a cough often clears them away. But when allergy is the cause of the irritation, repeated coughing and sneezing do not help.

Figure 14.15 ▲
Ragweed pollen (bottom) has been magnified 325×. It comes from the flowers of the ragweed plant (top).

Check and Explain

1. Name the parts of a flower, and describe the function of each part.

2. What is a fruit? Describe the flower parts from which a fruit develops.

3. **If . . . Then Arguments** You notice a tiny sprout in the dirt next to your favorite plant. If this is vegetative propagation, what will happen? What will happen if it isn't?

4. **Infer** Your friend has some unusual seeds. What advice can you give on getting the seeds to grow?

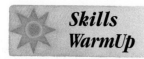
14.4 Plant Growth

Objectives

▶ **Explain** how plant growth and animal growth differ.

▶ **Describe** two plant hormones and their effects on plant growth.

▶ **Explain** why some plants bloom in summer and other plants bloom in autumn.

▶ **Hypothesize** about how to prove if a plant is an annual, a biennial, or a perennial.

Think about how you grow. As your height increases, your arms and legs get longer. As you get taller, the distance between your arms and the ground increases. If you have lived in the same neighborhood for a long time, you have probably noticed that the trees have also grown taller. However, as trees grow, you may have observed that their branches always remain the same distance off the ground. This observation tells you something about how trees grow. How is it different from the way animals and humans grow?

How Plants Grow

Plants, unlike humans, continue to grow larger as long as they live. In plants, growth occurs at special growth tissue sites. The plant's root and shoot grow longer from their tips, where growth tissues are found. Growth tissue cells are small and divide constantly, making new cells. Notice the growing tips in Figure 14.16. Growth occurs in two stages. First, more cells are made. Second, those cells increase in length. This process in plants is called primary growth.

In addition to increasing in length, a tree trunk or plant stem grows wider, or thicker. This process is called secondary growth. Examine the cross section of a woody stem in Figure 14.16 to see how secondary growth occurs. The cambium, a layer of growth tissue in the stem, continues to divide. It makes a layer of new xylem cells toward the center of the stem and a layer of new phloem cells toward the outside of the stem.

Primary growth

Secondary growth

Figure 14.16 ▲
In primary growth, the tips of roots and shoots grow longer. In secondary growth, the stem, trunk, or branches widen.

The Role of Plant Hormones

Hormones play a part in regulating a plant's growth. One example is gibberellin (jihb ur EHL ihn). Hundreds of years ago, Japanese rice farmers observed that some of their rice seedlings grew abnormally tall. This was the first clue to the effects of gibberellin. Gibberellin can make dwarf plants grow tall, flowers produce seedless fruits, and plants flower prematurely. Young leaves, roots, and plant embryos make gibberellin.

Figure 14.17 shows gibberellin's effect on stem length. The hormone also plays a role in seed germination and the growth of new leaves, branches, fruits, and flowers. These effects make gibberellin useful in agriculture. For example, it is used on seedless grapes to make the fruit grow larger.

Plants in a window usually bend toward the light. You may wonder how the plant is attracted to the light. Turning in response to an environmental stimulus, such as light or gravity, is called **tropism** (TROH PIHZ uhm). When a plant turns toward light, it is called phototropism. Tropisms are controlled by a plant hormone called auxin (AWK sihn). The growing tips of plants produce auxin. The amount of auxin in the cells controls the amount of cell elongation.

The way auxin controls phototropism is shown in Figure 14.18. Experiments show that auxin is sensitive to light. As a result, auxin concentrations are always higher on the shaded side of a stem. Auxin causes the stem cells on the shaded side to grow longer, making the stem bend toward the light.

Figure 14.17 ▲
Notice the difference in the size of the plants. Why do you think the plants on the right are larger?

◀ **Figure 14.18**
Light affects the amount of auxin available (left). Why is the plant in the photograph bending toward the window?

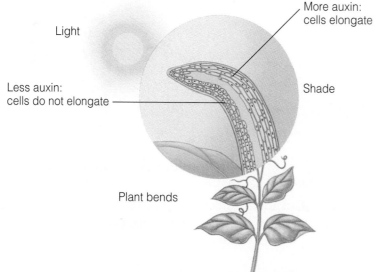

Light

Less auxin: cells do not elongate

More auxin: cells elongate

Shade

Plant bends

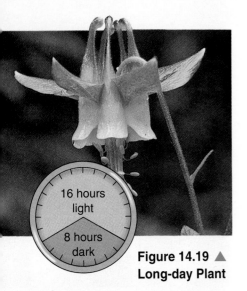

Figure 14.19 ▲
Long-day Plant

16 hours light / 8 hours dark

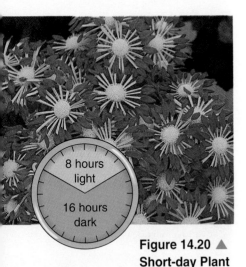

Figure 14.20 ▲
Short-day Plant

8 hours light / 16 hours dark

Seasonal Responses

Why do some plants always flower in summer and not at any other time of year? Plants have a light-sensitive chemical that helps them measure the length of periods of darkness and light. Examine the relationship between day length and flowering in Figures 14.19 and 14.20. Summer-blooming plants, such as columbines, are long-day plants. They need long days and short nights to trigger flowering. Autumn-blooming plants, such as chrysanthemums, are short-day plants. They flower when there are short days and long nights. Broad-leaf trees also respond to seasonal changes in day length. As days become shorter in autumn, the green chlorophyll in leaves is destroyed and other colors, such as reds and yellows, can then show through.

The life span of a flowering plant is measured in one-year growing seasons. Compare the life spans of the plants in Figure 14.21. Some plants, called annuals, complete their entire life cycle within one growing season. After setting seed, the plant dies. Plants that live for two growing seasons are called biennials.

During the first growing season, the plant germinates and develops roots, stems, and leaves. It stores energy in underground organs. During the second growing season, the plant flowers, produces seeds, then dies. Other plants, called perennials (pur EHN ee uhls), live for many growing seasons. They develop thick, woody stems and reproduce over and over again.

Grows, sets seed — Dies after one year

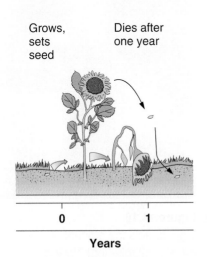

Years

Figure 14.21a ▲
Annual Growth Pattern

Grows, stores food — Flowers, sets seed — Dies after two years

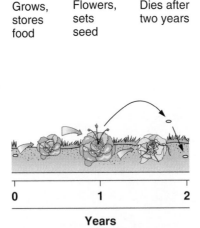

Years

Figure 14.21b ▲
Biennial Growth Pattern

Grows, sets seed — Grows, sets seed — Lives many years

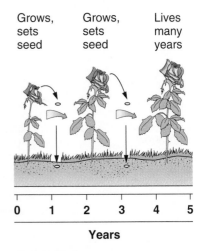

Years

Figure 14.21c ▲
Perennial Growth Pattern

Science and Technology *Future Superplants*

Potatoes that resist disease; tomatoes that last for weeks without spoiling; strawberry blossoms that survive a freeze—these are just some of the potential uses for biotechnology in agriculture. Biotechnology combines genetic engineering and tissue culture. Genetic engineering takes a chosen trait from the DNA of a plant or a bacterium and splices it into host plant cells. The new cells multiply in a nutrient-rich tissue culture. These cells grow to form new plants.

For thousands of years, plant breeders all over the world introduced genes into crops through selective breeding. This process is very effective, but also very slow. Also, plant breeders can't always find the characteristics they want. Through biotechnology, scientists can insert desired traits into plants, and it takes only months to develop a desired plant strain. For example, biotechnology produced genetically altered tomatoes that do not spoil quickly. Genes from bacteria inserted into tomatoes interrupt the release of the chemical pectin. Because the release of pectin was stopped, a tomato that would spoil in one week can now last for several weeks.

In another study, tomatoes received a spliced gene from a bacterium resistant to a disease-causing virus. The plants were protected against the virus that destroys many tomato crops. Genetically altered strawberries may also be in the future. A gene from "ice minus" bacteria inserted into strawberry blossoms results in "frost-free" plants.

Figure 14.22 ▲

The genetic material of plants can be manipulated in the laboratory using genetic engineering techniques.

Check and Explain

1. How is plant growth different from animal growth?

2. Name two plant hormones. Describe where each one is produced and its effects on plant growth.

3. **Compare and Contrast** What do plants that bloom in the summer have in common? How do they differ from plants that bloom in the autumn?

4. **Hypothesize** Write hypotheses you could use to prove that an unfamiliar plant was an annual, a biennial, and a perennial.

Activity 14 *What are the parts of a flower?*

Skills Observe; Classify

Task 1   Prelab Prep
Collect the following items: A gladiolus, tulip, or lily flower; paper towel; black paper; scalpel. A hand lens is optional. If you can't get a flower, use the photograph for your observation.

Task 2   Data Record
1. On a separate sheet of paper, draw the data table shown.
2. Record your observations about the color and number of flower parts in the table.

Table 14.1   Flower Parts

Flower Part	Number	Color
Sepals		
Petals		
Anther		
Pollen grains		
Filament		
Pistil		

Task 3   Procedure
1. Place your flower on a paper towel. Closely examine your flower.
2. Locate the outer parts, the sepals. Record the color and number of sepals in your table.
3. Inside the sepals are the petals. Examine the petals and record your observations.
4. Gently remove the sepals and the petals. Find the stalklike stamens. Remove one stamen. Observe the anther and the filament. Record your observations.
5. Tap the anther against the black paper to release pollen grains. Record the color and an estimate of the number of grains.
6. Remove the stamens. The remaining structure is the pistil. In the table, record your observations about the pistil.
7. With a scalpel, cut the pistil in half from top to bottom. **CAUTION! Be careful when using sharp instruments.** Look at the structures inside the ovary. Record your observations in the table.

Task 4   Analysis
1. What are the differences between the sepals and the petals?
2. Compare the number of stamens, petals, and sepals.
3. What did you see in the pistil?
4. List the parts of a flower.

Task 5   Conclusion
Is your flower a monocot or a dicot? Write a short paragraph explaining how you know.

Everyday Application
Flowers can be pollinated by hand. Explain the steps you would use to pollinate a flower yourself.

Extension
Collect and observe pollen grains under a microscope. What is the shape of the pollen grains?

Chapter 14 Review

Concept Summary

14.1 Characteristics of Flowering Plants
▶ All angiosperms have flowers containing reproductive organs.
▶ Shape, color, and scent are flower adaptations to attract pollen-carriers.
▶ Angiosperms are classified as monocots and dicots.

14.2 Vascular Plant Systems
▶ Vascular plants have a shoot system and root system connected by xylem and phloem tissues.
▶ Root systems absorb materials from soil, store glucose, and anchor plants.
▶ Stems and leaves are parts of the shoot system. Stems support the plant and transport materials. Leaves make glucose through photosynthesis.

14.3 Reproduction of Flowering Plants
▶ Flowers have petals, sepals, and reproductive organs. The male reproductive organ is the stamen. The female organ is the pistil.
▶ After pollination, the flower forms seeds inside a fruit. The fruit protects and disperses the seeds.
▶ Vegetative propagation is growing new plants from pieces of the parent plant.

14.4 Plant Growth
▶ Plants have primary and secondary growth.
▶ The plant hormones auxin and gibberellin affect plant growth.
▶ Angiosperms differ in their seasonal responses and in their life spans.

Chapter Vocabulary

monocot (14.1)	phloem (14.2)	stamen (14.3)	stigma (14.3)
dicot (14.1)	epidermis (14.2)	anther (14.3)	vegetative propagation (14.3)
transpiration (14.2)	cambium (14.2)	pistil (14.3)	tropism (14.4)
xylem (14.2)	sepals (14.3)		

Check Your Vocabulary

Use the vocabulary words above to complete the following sentences.

1. The outer layer of protective cells on a root is the ____ .

2. A seed with one cotyledon is a ____ .

3. Vascular tissue cells that transport glucose are called the ____ .

4. The male part of a flower is the ____ .

5. The structures growing from the stem that protect the developing flower are the ____ .

6. Plant growth in response to an environmental stimulus is called ____ .

7. A seed with two cotyledons is a ____ .

8. The plant pipeline that transports water and minerals is the ____ .

9. The growth tissue for making new xylem and phloem cells is the ____ .

10. The female reproductive part of the flower is the ____ .

11. Growing new plants from pieces of stems, leaves, or roots from a parent plant is called ____ .

12. The male part of the flower that produces pollen grains is the ____ .

13. The female part of the flower that collects pollen is the ____ .

Chapter 14 Review

Check Your Knowledge

Answer the following in complete sentences.

1. Describe three features of a monocot.

2. List the functions of leaves.

3. What is the angiosperm's male gametophyte?

4. List the requirements for seed germination.

5. What is secondary plant growth?

6. What is a long-day plant? A short-day plant?

7. How is the life span of flowering plants measured?

8. What is the purpose of fruits for plants?

9. Define pollination.

10. How can angiosperms reproduce without seeds?

Choose the answer that best completes each sentence.

11. Dicots have (parallel veined leaves, flower parts in multiples of ten, a thick taproot, four cotyledons).

12. The phloem transports (minerals, water, starch, sugars) throughout the plant.

13. The cambium makes new (root hairs, xylem and phloem cells, epidermis cells, shoot and root cells).

14. Stems that are flexible and slender are called (filament, woody, herbaceous, taproot) stems.

15. In leaves, photosynthesis occurs in the (mesophyll, cuticle, stomates, xylem).

16. The stamen is composed of the (pistil and stigma, anther and stigma, filament and anther, filament and pistil).

Check Your Understanding

Apply the concepts you have learned to answer each question.

1. Describe how fertilization occurs in flowering plants. Start from the formation of the pollen grain.

2. Explain three possible ways that a cherry could help disperse the seed contained inside the fruit.

3. Why would a gardener choose to grow plants using vegetative propagation?

4. **Infer** Some flowers have stamens that extend far beyond their petals. Would this be an advantage or a disadvantage for such a plant? Why or why not?

5. What nutritional value do taproots have to humans?

6. **Mystery Photo** The picture on page 270 shows seeds from a variety of angiosperms, including pumpkins, corn, sunflowers, walnuts, beans, and maples.

   a. Why do the seeds look so different? What do they all have in common?

   b. From what you see in the photograph, classify the seeds as monocots or dicots.

7. **Critical Thinking** You observe two plants that have similar leaves. What conclusions can you make about these plants? Explain how you came to each conclusion.

8. **Application** Poinsettias are often seen during the winter holiday season. Poinsettias are short-day plants. Explain how you could manipulate a poinsettia plant into blooming during the summer.

Develop Your Skills

Use the skills you have developed in this chapter to complete each activity.

1. **Interpret Data** The drawing below shows a plant as it changes with time.

   a. Is this plant an example of a mono-cot or a dicot? Describe at least two characteristics shown in the drawing that support your decision.

   b. What type of root system does this plant have? How can you tell?

   c. Which plant process is shown in the drawing?

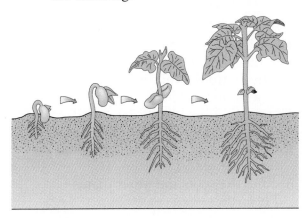

2. **Design an Experiment** New jade plants can be grown by vegetative propagation. Design an experiment to test what pieces of a jade plant will develop new plants. Remember to change only one variable at a time.

3. **Data Bank** Use the information on page 625 to answer the following questions.

   a. Which crops are most abundant in the world?

   b. **Research** Find out examples of oil-bearing and sugar-bearing crops. What countries grow these crops?

Make Connections

1. **Link the Concepts** Draw a concept map showing how some of the main concepts in this chapter link together. Use words and ideas from the chapter to draw your map.

2. **Science and Math** Calculate and record the number of possible petals for a monocot and a dicot. Estimate the maximum petal number for each group.

3. **Science and Social Studies** Before manufactured goods were available, people depended on common local plants for a variety of uses. A single species of plant could be a source of food, fiber, medicine, and building material. In the library, do research on local native plants, their uses, and the people who used them in the past or use them today.

4. **Science and You** Count the number of angiosperm varieties that you encounter on your way to school. Describe what features you used to determine whether a plant is an angiosperm.

5. **Science and Social Studies** Many of the common plants that you have probably seen in gardens came here from other countries. For example, tulips originated in western and central Asia. How did these plants travel so far? During the 19th and early 20th centuries, thousands of plant collectors travelled far distances in search of unkown plants. Many of these people were faced with obstacles during their travels. Research to find out more about the discoveries of these early plant collectors. Write a report of your findings. Include examples of the types of plants that were discovered.

Science and Literature Connection

The sacred blue corn-seed I am planting,
In one night it will grow and flourish,
In one night the corn increases,
In the garden of the House God.

The sacred white corn-seed
    I am planting,
In one day it will grow and ripen,
In one day the corn increases,
In its beauty it increases.

With this it grows, with this it grows,
The dark cloud, with this it grows.
The dew thereof, with this it grows,
The blue corn, with this it grows.

With this it grows, with this it grows,
The dark mist, with this it grows.
The dew thereof, with this it grows,
The white corn, with this it grows.

This it eats, this it eats,
The dark cloud,
Its dew
The blue corn eats,
This it eats.

This it eats, this it eats,
The dark mist,
Its dew
The white corn eats,
This it eats.

The great corn-plant is with the bean,
Its rootlets now are with the bean,
Its leaf-tips now are with the bean,
Its dewdrops now are with the bean,
Its tassel now is with the bean,

"Songs in the Garden of the House God"

The following Navajo poem is from
In the Trail of the Wind,
a book of Native-American poems
and ritual orations
edited by John Bierhorst.

Its pollen now is with the bean,
And now its silk is with the bean,
And now its grain is with the bean.

Truly in the East
The white bean
And the great corn-plant
Are tied with the white lightning.
Listen! It approaches!
The voice of the bluebird is heard.

Truly in the East
The white bean
And the great squash
Are tied with the rainbow.
Listen! It approaches!
The voice of the bluebird is heard.

From the top of the great corn-plant the
    water gurgles, I hear it;
Around the roots the water foams,
    I hear it;
Around the roots of the plants it foams,
    I hear it;
From their tops the water foams,
    I hear it.

The corn grows up. The waters of the
    dark clouds drop, drop.
The rain descends. The waters from the
    corn leaves drop, drop.
The rain descends. The waters from the
    plants drop, drop.
The corn grows up. The waters of the dark
    mists drop, drop.

Since the ancient days, I have planted,
Since the time of the emergence,
    I have planted,
The great corn-plant, I have planted,

Its roots, I have planted,
The tips of its leaves, I have planted,
Its dew, I have planted,
Its tassel, I have planted,
Its pollen, I have planted,
Its silk, I have planted,
Its seed, I have planted.

Since the ancient days, I have planted,
Since the time of the emergence,
    I have planted,
The great squash-vine, I have planted,
Its seed, I have planted
Its silk, I have planted,
Its pollen, I have planted,
Its tassel, I have planted,
        Its dew, I have planted
        The tips of its leaves, I have planted,
                Its roots, I have planted.

            Shall I cull this fruit
            Of the great corn-plant?
        Shall you break it? Shall I break it?

Shall I break it? Shall you break it?
    Shall I? Shall you?

Shall I cull this fruit
Of the great squash-vine?
Shall you pick it up? Shall I pick it up?
Shall I pick it up? Shall you pick it up?
    Shall I? Shall you?

Skills in Science

Reading Skills in Science

1. **Infer** What does the phrase "since the time of the emergence" refer to?

2. **Find Context Clues** Which parts of the poem describe the connection between plants and the water cycle?

Writing Skills in Science

1. **Compare and Contrast** Imagine that a drought occurs during one growing season. Write a poem that describes how this lack of rain affects the corn-plant.

2. **Predict** The poem identifies various parts of a corn-plant and states that they are "with the bean." Think about products of a corn-plant. Write a paragraph that describes other items that are "with the bean."

Activities

Collect Data Use reference texts to identify nonfood products made from corn. Share your findings with the class in the form of a collage that shows these products.

Communicate Make a flow chart to show how a corn-plant reproduces sexually.

Where to Read More

In the Trail of the Wind edited by John Bierhorst. New York: Farrar, Straus and Giroux, 1971. Contains Native-American poems and ritual orations including "Songs in the Garden of the House God."

The Lore and Legend of Flowers by Robert L. Crowell. New York: Crowell, 1982. This beautifully illustrated text describes the origins of ten flowering plants and the impact of each on history.

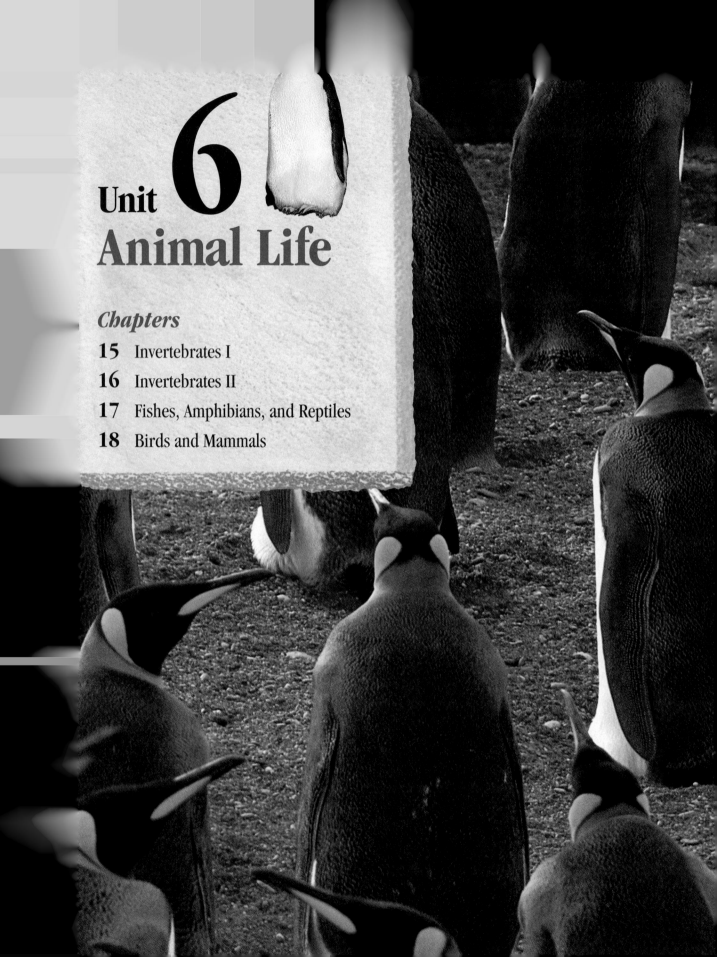

Unit 6

Animal Life

Chapters

Data Bank

Use the information on pages 624 to 631 to answer the following questions about topics explored in this unit.

Calculating

How much longer is a king cobra than a rattlesnake?

Reading a Table

During which period in the earth's history did reptiles begin to take over the land?

Classifying

Is the polar bear included in the same genus as the grizzly bear? Name the genus that each bear on the tree belongs to.

Making a Graph

Make a graph that shows the average life spans of the mammals listed in the table. Which mammal lives the longest? The shortest?

The photograph to the left is of king penguins on the South Georgia Island near Antarctica. Why do you think the penguins live in groups?

Chapter **15** Invertebrates I

What do you see?

66In this photo there are tiny organisms called coral. Corals are invertebrates and belong to the phylum Coelenterata. Coelenterates have hollow body cavities. Have you ever wondered why corals have walls around themselves? They build the walls by using lime, a mineral found in the water. Coral can grow quite large; in some cases they form reefs.99

Sherri Coates
Washington Middle School
Newport News, Virginia

To find out more about the photograph, look on page 318. As you read this chapter, you will learn about sponges, corals, jellyfish, earthworms, and other similar invertebrates.

298

15.1 The Animal Kingdom

Objectives

▶ **Describe** the main characteristics of animals.

▶ **Explain** the major differences in the body plans of animals.

▶ **Distinguish** between vertebrates and invertebrates.

▶ **Make inferences** about the relationship between an animal's body plan and the way it moves.

▶ **Make a graph** comparing the number of vertebrate and invertebrate species.

Skills WarmUp

Model Draw a circle. How many ways can you fold the paper through the center of the circle to make two similar halves? Now draw a simple human figure facing forward. How many ways can you fold the paper through the center of this shape to form two similar halves? What does this tell you about the difference between the circle shape and the human shape?

Look at Figure 15.1. Does it show any animals? Which organisms do you think are animals? Why? Even though the organisms shown in the photograph do not look like the animals you are familiar with, many of them are animals. The animal kingdom includes an amazing variety of living things, from microscopic worms to giant clams to elephants to you.

Characteristics of Animals

All animals share characteristics that separate them from plants, fungi, monerans, and protists. Animals are many-celled, which makes them different from monerans and protozoa. They lack chlorophyll in their cells, so they can't make glucose through photosynthesis like plants and algae.

Animals obtain their food by *ingesting* it. They take in food from their environment and then digest it. Because they eat their food, animals differ from fungi, which digest their food outside their bodies and then absorb the nutrients.

What other characteristic do animals share? If you answered that they have the ability to move, you are right. The animals you have seen crawl, swim, jump, fly, walk, and run. But what about the animals in Figure 15.1? Do they move? Actually, many of the animals pictured stay in one place as adults. However, they were able to move at an earlier stage in their lives. For an animal, why may movement be important?

Figure 15.1 ▲
To which kingdom do these tidepool organisms belong?

Radial symmetry

Bilateral symmetry

No symmetry

Figure 15.2 ▲

Animal bodies have either radial symmetry, bilateral symmetry, or no symmetry.

Classification of Animals

The first animals evolved from single-celled protists hundreds of millions of years ago. Since then, the animals have evolved a variety of different body plans, or kinds of overall body structures. These different body plans are the basis for animal classification.

Four levels of organization exist among animals: cells, tissues, organs, and organ systems. One major way that animal bodies differ is in their level of organization. The simplest kind of animal body has many cells but no true tissues. Animals called sponges have this kind of structure. Another group called the cnidarians (ny DAIR ee uhns) includes animals whose bodies are made up of tissues but have no organs. Several groups of animals have bodies in which tissues work together as organs. These include the flatworms and roundworms. In the earthworms, organs work together as organ systems.

Animals can also be classified by their shape. Look at Figure 15.2. Animals with *radial symmetry* have bodies organized around a center, like a wheel. They have a top and bottom, but no front, back, or head. Animals with *bilateral symmetry* have bodies with two similar halves. They have a head end that faces in the direction the animal moves. The head contains the animal's sense organs. A sponge's body can't be divided into parts. It has no symmetry.

Many of the animals with bilateral symmetry, such as dogs and birds, have an extra degree of complexity. These animals have a backbone. Animals with back-

Figure 15.3 ▶

Four basic body types have evolved in the animal kingdom. What characteristics separate the four types?

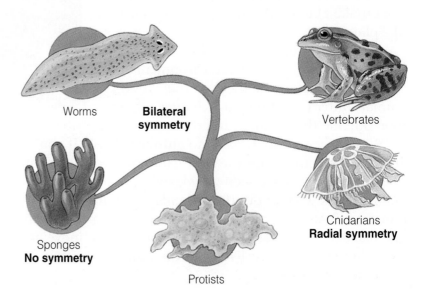

Worms

Bilateral symmetry

Vertebrates

Sponges
No symmetry

Cnidarians
Radial symmetry

Protists

bones are called **vertebrates** (VUR tuh brihts). You are a vertebrate. All the other animals without backbones are called **invertebrates**.

Based on these and other differences in the bodies of animals, scientists have divided the animal kingdom into 28 large groups called phyla.

 ## Science and Technology
Deep-Sea Exploration

The ocean is rich in animal life, but most of these organisms live at or near the surface, within reach of sunlight. Algae living there are the first link in the ocean's many food chains. The deep ocean bottom, in contrast, has very little life. No sunlight reaches into these depths, so no algae exist as a food supply.

Until the 1970s, no firsthand exploration had been made of the deep sea. Then scientists built special research submarines designed to withstand the great pressures of the deep sea. The best known of these vessels is *Alvin*, owned by the Woods Hole Oceanographic Institute. Using *Alvin*, scientists found hot springs around which live many kinds of strange new invertebrates, including sea anemones, crabs, and giant tube worms.

At first, the scientists did not know how these organisms obtained food. Then they found that the water around the hot springs is filled with special bacteria. These bacteria use hydrogen sulfide from the hot spring water as an energy source. The other organisms of the community feed upon the bacteria by filtering them from the water.

Check and Explain

1. What characteristics separate the animals from the plants, algae, protozoa, monerans, and fungi?

2. What is the difference between radial symmetry and bilateral symmetry?

3. **Infer** What kind of symmetry would you expect most animals that hunt for food to have? Explain.

4. **Make a Graph** Invertebrates make up 95 percent of all known animal species. Make a circle graph that shows this and identifies the other 5 percent.

Generalize What can a
many-celled animal such as a
sponge do that a single-celled
protist cannot? Make a list of
the comparisons.

15.2 Sponges

Objectives

▶ **Describe** the main characteristics of sponges.

▶ **Identify** the functions of a sponge's three cell types.

▶ **Explain** how sponges reproduce.

▶ **Make a model** that shows how a sponge gets its food.

Examine the sponge in your kitchen or bathroom closely and you'll see it has little holes, or pores, everywhere. These pores are what make a sponge able to hold water.

Most likely your sponge was made by humans. But some sponges are natural. They are the soft skeletons of animals harvested from the ocean. These living animals are called sponges, too.

Characteristics of Sponges

Living sponges are full of pores, like your kitchen sponge. These pores are what give sponges their scientific name, Porifera (poh RIHF uhr uh).

A sponge uses its pores to get food. The sponge remains in one place, often attached to a rock. It makes water from its environment come through its pores and into the middle of its saclike body. There the sponge removes algae, tiny animals and protozoa, and bits of organic material. The water leaves the sponge through one larger hole. This way of getting food is called *filter feeding*.

Because of these characteristics, a sponge seems very plantlike. You could watch one for a whole day and not see it move. A sponge is the simplest of animals. Its cells do different jobs, but they do not form true tissues.

Look at Figure 15.4. It shows the structure of a sponge's body and its three kinds of cells. The collar cells in the inside layer use their flagella to move the water through the sponge. They also catch the food. The amebalike cells in the jelly layer carry food and waste to and from the other cells.

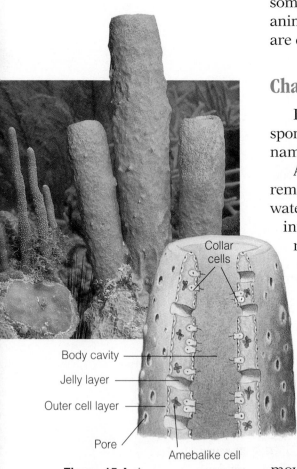

Collar
cells

Body cavity

Jelly layer

Outer cell layer

Pore

Amebalike cell

Figure 15.4 ▲
What is the function of each
kind of cell in a sponge?

Some sponges, like the one in the diagram, are just one large sac. Others are made up of many very small sacs joined together as one organism. Most sponges have neither radial nor bilateral symmetry and no definite body shape. They are asymmetrical.

Sponges have skeletons that give support to their cells. These skeletons are made of different materials. Some are stiff and made of a glasslike substance or lime. Others are made of a flexible material.

Reproduction of Sponges

Sponges reproduce sexually and asexually. To make new sponges asexually, a sponge may bud or pinch off small sponges that will grow into new sponges. Or, if a piece of a sponge breaks off accidentally, the piece can grow to form another whole sponge.

Look at Figure 15.5. To reproduce sexually, sponges produce both eggs and sperm. Most release their sperm into the water but keep their eggs inside their bodies. When sperm cells from another sponge are drawn into a sponge's body, they are not eaten but are used to fertilize that sponge's eggs. The fertilized eggs stay inside the sponge until they have grown into tiny **larvae** (LAR vee), organisms in an early stage of development that look different from their parents.

The larvae leave the sponge through the large openings and float around. Then they drift to the bottom, attach themselves, and grow into new sponges.

Figure 15.5
In what stage of its life cycle is a sponge able to move?
▼

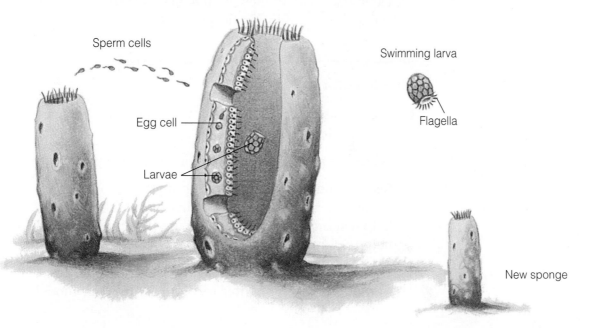

Sperm cells

Egg cell

Larvae

Swimming larva

Flagella

New sponge

Figure 15.6 ▶

After live sponges are collected, they are often hung up on boats for a few days (right). They are then cleaned, dried, and trimmed (bottom).

Science and You *Household Sponges*

Since ancient times, people have used sponges for bathing and cleaning because sponges can hold so much water. What do you use a sponge for? Today, most people use artificial sponges made in factories.

Some people, however, still prefer natural sponges. They say that natural sponges hold more water, last longer, and are easier to clean than artificial ones. Artists and some other workers use natural sponges, too. Have you ever seen or used a natural sponge?

Natural sponges used for cleaning have skeletons made of a tough, flexible material called spongin. The living cells are removed before the sponge is sold.

Some natural sponges come from the Mediterranean Sea. Others come from the Caribbean or the Gulf of Mexico. People in boats gather them with hooks or harpoons. Divers collect sponges that live in deeper waters.

Check and Explain

1. What jobs do the cells lining the inside of a sponge's body perform?

2. What happens to the sperm that a sponge produces?

3. **Reason and Conclude** Some sponges live on the shells of crabs. How could living on a crab's shell help a sponge? How could having the sponge there help the crab?

4. **Make a Model** What familiar objects could you use to model a sponge's filter feeding? Draw your model.

15.3 Cnidarians

Objectives

▶ **Describe** the characteristics of cnidarians.

▶ **Explain** how cnidarians reproduce.

▶ **Compare** and **contrast** the two body forms of cnidarians.

▶ **Make inferences** about the survival value of cnidarian adaptations.

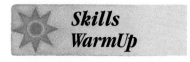

Skills WarmUp

Interpret Data Choose ten small islands from a map of the South Pacific. Look up the names of these islands in an encyclopedia. How many of the islands are made of coral? What does this tell you about the importance of coral in this ocean?

You're walking along the beach with a friend. Suddenly the two of you come to a large blob of—you're not quite sure what. You start to poke it with your foot. Your friend says, "Hey, don't do that! It's a jellyfish. It might sting you."

Your friend may be right. But the blob on the beach looks nothing like the jellyfish it once was, swimming gracefully in its ocean habitat. A jellyfish is a **cnidarian**, an organism armed with stinging cells.

Characteristics of Cnidarians

Cnidarians are common in most ocean habitats, and a few live in freshwater habitats. A habitat is the area or place where an organism lives. Some cnidarians live attached to a surface and look like flowers or tiny trees. Others, like the jellyfish, swim freely in the ocean. Yet in spite of this diversity, all cnidarians have features in common.

Cnidarians have two main body forms, the *polyp* (PAHL ihp) and the *medusa* (muh DOO suh). You can see these two body forms in Figure 15.7. Medusas swim freely, and polyps usually live attached to a surface. Some cnidarians exist only as polyps. Some are medusas for most of their lives after being polyps for only a short time. In other cnidarians the two forms are equally important in the life cycle.

Both cnidarian body forms have radial symmetry. They look the same from all sides. This type of body plan helps cnidarians detect food or enemies from any direction.

Cnidarians have several features that make them different from sponges. First, cnidarians have a mouth that leads to a digestive cavity. The mouth is the cavity's only opening. Cnidarians also have tissues. The cells

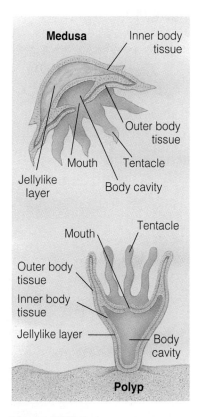

Figure 15.7 ▲
How is a cnidarian polyp similar to a medusa?

covering the outside of a cnidarian make up one kind of tissue. The cells lining the inside are a different kind. Both contain simple muscles and nerves. The two layers are separated by jellylike material.

Cnidarians' most striking adaptation is their tentacles, which are lined with stinging cells. Stinging cells help cnidarians defend themselves and catch food. When prey is stunned or killed by the stinging cells, the tentacles carry the food to the mouth.

Reproduction of Cnidarians

Cnidarians can reproduce both sexually and asexually. When it occurs, asexual reproduction is carried out by polyps. A small piece of the animal breaks off and grows into a new polyp. This process is called budding.

To reproduce sexually, cnidarians release eggs and sperm into the water. Each fertilized egg forms a larva. The larva grows into a new polyp or medusa.

Look at the life cycle of the jellyfish in Figure 15.8. Notice that a medusa and a polyp are part of the cycle. Many cnidarians have a life cycle that has both a medusa stage and a polyp stage. In these cnidarians, it is the medusa that reproduces sexually. In cnidarians without a medusa stage, the polyp reproduces sexually.

Figure 15.8

Jellyfish have a life cycle that includes a medusa stage and a polyp stage. Each polyp produces many young medusas.

▼

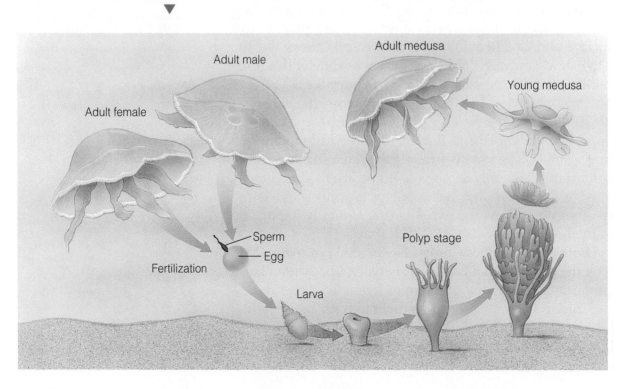

Diversity of Cnidarians

Cnidarians are divided into three main groups. Each has a different kind of life cycle. Within each group there are many shapes and sizes, and differences in habitat. Even though all the cnidarians you see on this page live in the ocean, your nearest cnidarian may be only as far away as the closest pond, river, or stream. Those are places where the *Hydra* lives. It is one of the few freshwater cnidarians.

◄ Hydrozoans
This sea fan belongs to a second group called the hydrozoans (HY droh ZOH uhnz). A single fan contains many polyps. Most hydrozoans have both polyp and medusa stages.

Jellyfish ▲
Jellyfish make up the third cnidarian group. They spend most of their lives as medusas.

Staghorn Coral
This staghorn coral has a shape very different from that of the reef coral. Yet it, too, is made of tiny polyps and a hard skeleton. Corals like the staghorn live on coral reefs but do not themselves help to form the reef. ▼

Sea Anemones
One group of cnidarians includes the sea anemones (uh NEHM uh NEES). Their scientific name means "flower animals." They are polyps all their lives. Some fish can live safely inside the tentacles of sea anemones. The anemones protect the fish. The fish, in turn, lure other fish that the anemone might eat. ▼

Reef-building Corals ▲
Tropical reefs are formed by tiny cnidarians called corals. Corals are in the same group as sea anemones. Reef corals spend their whole lives as tiny polyps living together in colonies. They make hard skeletons of calcium.

Fringing reef

Barrier reef

Atoll

Figure 15.9 ▲

There are three kinds of coral reefs. A fringing reef is closer to shore than a barrier reef. An atoll is a reef atop a sunken volcanic island.

Coral Reefs

Coral reefs are found in warm ocean waters around the world. They provide homes for a greater variety of living things than any other place in the ocean. Reefs can be very large. The Great Barrier Reef off the coast of Australia is over 2 000 km long. Many tropical islands were once coral reefs that have been left dry by changing sea levels.

It is hard to believe that these large and important structures are built by tiny cnidarians. The surface of all living reefs is coated with coral polyps, each with its own hard skeleton. Below the surface are layers and layers of skeletons left by coral polyps that are now dead. The reef grows as new live corals replace ones that die on the surface.

One reason corals can produce huge reefs is that they have help from algae. Algae live inside the polyps and make part of the polyps' food. The algae also give the coral its color. Coral must therefore live in shallow water so that their algae can get enough sunlight.

In many places where there are coral reefs, scientists are worried that the coral polyps are dying off. They are not being replaced by new living corals. Scientists are not sure why this is happening, but some blame pollutants in the ocean water.

Science and You *Stinging Jellyfish*

Each cnidarian stinging cell contains a tiny harpoon at the end of a coiled, hollow thread. When something touches the cell, the long thread uncoils suddenly, and the harpoon shoots into whatever touched the cell. While jagged barbs hold the harpoon in place, a poison passes through the hollow thread. Any animal that touches a cnidarian is hit by thousands of these tiny poisoned harpoons.

The stinging cells of most cnidarians are too weak to break through human skin. Some hydrozoans and jellyfish have stinging cells that can harm people, however. The Portuguese man-of-war, a hydrozoan, and the sea nettle, a jellyfish, are examples of cnidarians harmful to humans.

If you encounter a jellyfish on the beach, it's best to avoid it. If you get tentacles from a Portuguese man-of-war on you, try to put vinegar on the tentacles as soon

Consider This

Should Protection of Coral Reefs Come First?

The kind of climate reef corals need to grow is also the kind of climate humans like to live in. On Key Largo, an island off the coast of Florida, developers want to build a new community called Port Bougainville. Environmentalists, however, say that building the community would endanger nearby coral reefs.

Consider Some Issues Scientists believe that human activity is damaging coral reefs worldwide. People damage reefs by polluting the ocean water with sewage, by anchoring boats on the reefs, and by letting logging and digging on land wash dirt into the sea.

Coral reefs are home to an amazing array of living things, and they protect shores from erosion by waves. For these reasons and others, some people argue that reefs should be protected by limiting what humans can do in the areas around them.

Others point out that protecting the reefs has costs, too. Resorts such as Port Bougainville provide jobs and places for people to live. Other activities that damage reefs, such as tourism, logging, and fishing, are also important to the economy.

Think About It How can the needs of people be balanced against the need to protect the reefs?

Debate It Have a class debate in which opposing teams discuss the pros and cons of the Port Bougainville Project.

as possible. The vinegar will keep more stinging cells from firing. A paste made of baking soda and water will do the same for the sea nettle. Meat tenderizer can also stop jellyfish stings because it chemically changes the poison.

Check and Explain

1. What features do cnidarians have that sponges do not?

2. In which cnidarian body form does asexual reproduction occur?

3. **Compare and Contrast** How are the structures of polyps and medusas alike and different?

4. **Infer** How do you think each of the following help a jellyfish survive: being transparent, having stinging cells, having radial symmetry, being able to swim?

15.4 Worms

Objectives

▶ **Explain** how worms differ from cnidarians.

▶ **Identify** and **describe** the three major worm phyla.

▶ **Explain** the importance of a segmented worm's coelom.

▶ **List** worms that live as parasites in humans.

▶ **Estimate** the size of a worm population based on a sample.

When it rains all night, what might you find on the streets and sidewalks in the morning? Worms! Have you ever wondered why they leave their homes in the soil? The rain floods their underground burrows. They escape drowning by crawling to the surface.

Earthworms are just one of the many kinds of worms in the animal kingdom. Other kinds of worms are too small to see. Some build hard shells and live in the ocean. In fact, worms live almost everywhere and have a large impact on human life.

Characteristics of Worms

Worms differ in two important ways from cnidarians. First, they have bilateral symmetry and a definite head. Nerves and sense organs are concentrated in the head. Second, instead of just two layers of tissue, they have three. And the middle layer of tissue, called the mesoderm (MEHS oh DURM), forms organs that serve particular functions.

With this added complexity, worms can live in a greater variety of habitats than cnidarians. Like cnidarian medusas, some worms swim. Like polyps, some worms attach themselves to one place. But worms also burrow in mud, crawl on surfaces, and live in other organisms. And some, like the earthworm, can live in soil.

Scientists place worms in several main groups, or phyla. A worm's body structure determines which phyla it belongs to. The three most common worm phyla are flatworms, roundworms, and segmented worms. Which group do you think earthworms belong to?

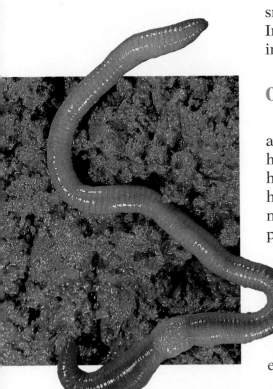

Figure 15.10 ▲
What do you notice about the body of this earthworm?

Flatworms

Worms with a flattened shape are called **flatworms.** Flatworms have the simplest body organization of any worm. They have organs and three layers of tissue. But like cnidarians, their digestive cavity has only one opening.

Flatworms are either free-living or parasitic. A common flatworm that lives in fresh water, the planarian, is a good example of the free-living type of flatworm. Most kinds of planaria are only a few centimeters long. They eat tiny animals in the water and are harmless to humans.

Look at Figure 15.12. It shows the structure of a planarian. The eyespots on the top of the head do not transmit images. Instead, they sense light. The nerve cells in the head form a simple brain. Food enters through the mouth, and undigested food leaves through the same opening.

A single planarian is both male and female. When two planaria exchange genetic material, each fertilizes the other. Planaria reproduce asexually by dividing their bodies in two. Each half then grows back the missing part. If you cut a planarian into several pieces, each piece will regenerate into a new worm.

There are two groups of parasitic flatworms: flukes and tapeworms. Flukes mainly live in the body tissues of animals. Some live in human tissues and cause sickness. Most tapeworms live in the intestines of different vertebrates, including humans. The tapeworm drops pieces of its body, full of fertilized eggs, into its host's waste. If another animal eats the tapeworm pieces, worms will grow in that animal's body. Tapeworms have no digestive cavity because they absorb the digested food of their host.

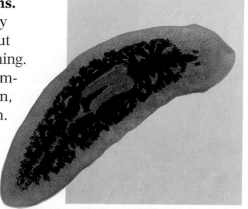

Figure 15.11 ▲
A planarian is about 2.5 cm long. What is the function of the eyespots?

Figure 15.12
Planaria have a simple body structure. ▼

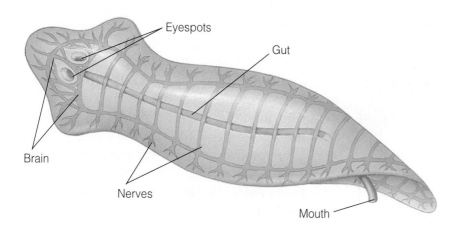

Eyespots

Gut

Brain

Nerves

Mouth

Roundworms

Go outside and pick up a handful of moist garden soil. What are you holding? In addition to the soil, you may have in your hand about one million tiny worms. These worms have round bodies and belong to the **roundworm** group, also called nematodes (NEHM uh TOHDS).

Besides their round shape, roundworms have something no flatworm has: a one-way digestive tube with two openings. Look at Figure 15.13. Food enters a roundworm through the mouth located at the head. As it passes through the digestive tube, it is digested and then absorbed. Undigested food leaves the tube through the anus. In roundworms, different parts of the gut can have different functions because food moves in only one direction.

Roundworms reproduce sexually. Unlike many flatworms, the sexes are separate. In many species, females are larger than the males and can produce over 100,000 eggs in a day.

Many roundworm species attack the roots of plants. Some of their favorite plants are crops grown by humans. On the other hand, some roundworms benefit crops by killing insect pests.

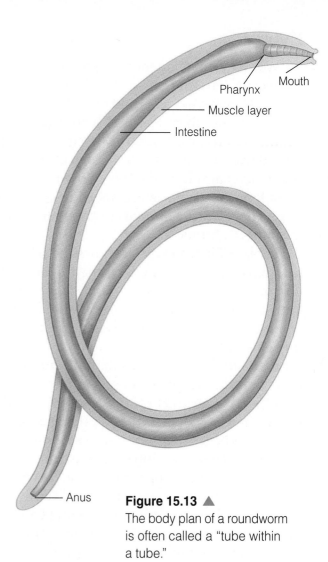

Figure 15.13 ▲
The body plan of a roundworm is often called a "tube within a tube."

Figure 15.14 ▲
In this photo you can see a *Trichinella* inside muscle tissue.

About 50 kinds of roundworms are parasites in humans. Hookworms enter a human host by boring through the skin of the feet. Using the bloodstream, they move to the lungs. They are coughed up and then swallowed. In the intestines, they attach themselves and feed on digested food. When they have grown into adult worms, they reproduce and send eggs out with the host's waste to start the cycle over. Another roundworm parasite is *Trichinella*, which causes trichinosis. It can enter your body if you eat under-cooked meat.

Segmented Worms

Earthworms are common examples of a third worm group, the **segmented worms**. Segmented worms have bodies divided into small units or segments. A segmented body is like a beaded necklace. Just as you could thread together a large red bead, five blue beads, and eight yellow beads, a segmented worm's body is built of similar and different segments.

The segmented worms are unlike flatworms and roundworms because they have a fluid-filled space, or cavity, inside the middle tissue layer. This cavity is called a **coelom** (SEE luhm). Look at Figure 15.15 to see where the coelom is in a segmented worm's body.

A coelom provides the space needed for complex organs. The segmented worms were the first group of animals to evolve organ systems, groups of specialized organs working together.

The common earthworm is a good example of how organ systems are arranged in a segmented worm's body. Look at the earthworm in Figure 15.16. Notice the crop and gizzard. These organs help the worm digest the soil it eats. They grind up the soil and remove organic matter from it. Notice also that the earthworm has five hearts and a brain. The brain is connected to a nerve

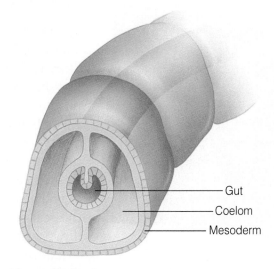

Figure 15.15 ▲
What is the function of the coelom?

cord that runs all the way down the worm's body.

Earthworms can move in a variety of ways. Stiff bristles on the outside of the body act as anchoring points. They hold a part of the worm in place while another part pushes forward through the soil.

In these ways and others, an earthworm is well adapted to life in the soil. Its lifestyle is made possible by its segmented organization and its organ systems.

Figure 15.16
Which organs are part of an earthworm's digestive system?

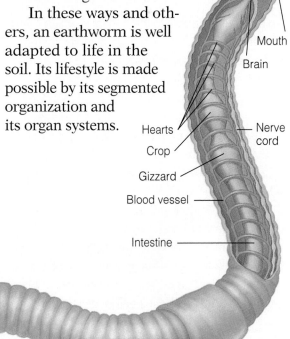

Earthworms and Soil

Earthworms help enrich and improve the soil. They eat organic matter in the soil that plants can't use directly. They digest this matter and take nutrients from it. What is left over are simpler substances, such as nitrates, that plants can use. Earthworms eliminate this waste from their bodies, adding it to the soil. Pellets of earthworm waste, called castings, are so full of plant nutrients that people use them as garden fertilizer.

Earthworms also improve the soil by burrowing in it. Their tunnels allow air and water to reach deep into the soil. They move organic matter from the surface down into deeper soil levels.

Many hundreds of earthworms can live under the surface of a square meter of ground. Each earthworm eats and discards its own weight in soil every day. Because it is full of living things like earthworms, soil is constantly changing.

Figure 15.17 ▲
In what ways do earthworms affect the soil they live in?

SkillBuilder *Making a Model*

Design an Invertebrate

An animal is adapted to the habitat in which it lives. The characteristics of particular animals, therefore, depend on the characteristics of their habitats.

Choose a habitat. It can be a familiar one, such as a forest, a desert, or a coral reef. Or it can be a strange one, such as the deep sea, the atmosphere, or even another planet. Make notes about the features of this habitat. Is it hot or cold? Wet or dry? How much sunlight does it receive? What is there to eat? What plants grow there? Are there predators to watch out for? Are there any other dangers such as waves or high winds?

Now design an invertebrate to fit the habitat you chose. Think about the features that your animal will need to do well in this habitat. As you design your invertebrate, think about these questions:

1. Will your invertebrate have radial or bilateral symmetry, or will it have no symmetry?

2. How big will it be?

3. What adaptations will it have?

4. Where will it fit in the animal kingdom? What living animals are its closest relatives?

5. What will it eat? How will it get its food?

6. What sense organs will it have?

7. How will it move?

8. How will it reproduce?

9. How will it defend itself?

Write a short report describing your animal and explaining how it is adapted to its environment. Include pictures of your animal, showing what it looks like and what internal organs it has. Present your invertebrate design to the class.

Science and Society *Worms as Parasites*

Several kinds of worms live as parasites in human beings. They include tapeworms, a kind of flatworm, and roundworms, such as hookworm and *Trichinella*. Some of these worms spend part of their lives in the bodies of other animals. *Trichinella* worms live in pigs, for example, and can be present in the pork eaten by people.

Parasitic worms take nutrients from a person's body. As a result, people with worms do not have enough nutrients for their own needs. Such people often feel weak and tired. They have lowered resistance to infections from microorganisms. They usually have digestive problems. *Trichinella* worms live in muscle tissue and cause muscle pains.

There are things you can do to prevent parasitic worms from entering your body. For example, if you wear shoes outside, hookworms can't bore into your feet. If you are careful to keep human and animal waste from food, you can't get tapeworms. If you eat only well-cooked meat, you can't get trichinosis.

Few people in the United States today suffer from parasitic worms. These worms still weaken people in other parts of the world, however. They are a special problem in tropical countries where, for example, most people can't afford sanitary ways to dispose of human waste. Medicine can get rid of the worms, but people quickly become reinfected.

Figure 15.18 ▲
This tapeworm was removed from the intestine of a cat.

Check and Explain

1. How do flatworms differ from cnidarians?

2. Name the three main groups of worms. For each, describe how it differs from the others.

3. **Predict** Suppose you removed all the earthworms from an acre of soil. What would happen to the soil? Why?

4. **Estimate** You dig up a small area of moist soil 10 cm wide, 10 cm long, and 10 cm deep and find five earthworms. Assuming that this number is average, how many earthworms would there be in a square plot of land 100 m on a side and 1 m deep?

Activity 15   How do earthworms change soil?

Skills   Measure; Observe; Infer; Interpret Data

Task 1   Prelab Prep

1. Collect the following items: earthworms, 200 mL each of three kinds of soil with different colors and textures, a 1 L jar, 250 mL of humus (partly decayed leaves and other plant matter), 125 mL of apple peelings, dark construction paper, a rubber band.
2. To collect the earthworms, carefully dig them up yourself or buy them from a bait shop.

Task 2   Data Record

1. On a sheet of paper, draw the data table shown.
2. Record all your observations about the earthworms in the data table.

Task 3   Procedure

1. Put a layer of each kind of soil in the jar.
2. Wet the soil. Be sure that the soil is damp throughout.

Table 15.1   Earthworm Observations

Date	Time	Observations

3. Spread the humus over the soil.
4. Place the worms in the jar.
5. Add the apple peelings.
6. Wrap the paper around the jar and fix it in place with the rubber band. Put the jar in a cool place.
7. Remove the paper and observe the jar once every day for a week. Each time, record your observations and then return the jar to its place. **CAUTION!: Keep the soil moist at all times. Add water when needed, but do not make the soil soggy.**

Task 4   Analysis

1. **Observe**   How soon do tunnels appear in the soil?
2. What happens to the apple peelings and humus?
3. What happens to the layers of soil? Do they stay as separate layers, or are they mixed?
4. What appears on the surface of the soil?
5. **Infer**   In which soil layer do the earthworms spend the most time? Do they like this layer because of the soil type or because of its position? How could you find out?

Task 5   Conclusion

Write a short paragraph explaining how earthworms live in the soil and how they change the soil.

Everyday Application

If you were planting a garden, why might you want earthworms in it? How could you encourage earthworms to live there?

Extension

Based on what you have learned in the activity, develop a hypothesis about how well plants grow in soil that contains earthworms as compared to soil that does not contain earthworms. Write down your procedure and test your hypothesis. Make a chart of your comparisons.

Chapter 15 Review

Concept Summary

15.1 The Animal Kingdom
▶ Animals have cells, tissues, organs, and organ systems.
▶ All animals are many-celled, ingest their food, and move during some part of their life cycle.
▶ Animals can have radial symmetry, bilateral symmetry, or no symmetry.
▶ Animals with backbones are vertebrates; animals without backbones are invertebrates.

15.2 Sponges
▶ Sponges are filter feeders that have no definite body shape and no symmetry.
▶ Sponges have cells to move water through their bodies, to catch food, and to carry food and waste to and from other cells.
▶ Sponges reproduce both sexually and asexually.

15.3 Cnidarians
▶ Cnidarians have radial symmetry in both of their two forms: polyp and medusa.
▶ Cnidarians have two layers of tissue and stinging cells.
▶ Cnidarians reproduce both sexually and asexually.
▶ Cnidarians have tentacles that help them get food. Tentacles also help cnidarians defend themselves.

15.4 Worms
▶ Worms have bilateral symmetry, a head with sense organs, and three layers of tissue.
▶ The three major worm phyla are flatworms, roundworms, and segmented worms.
▶ Segmented worms have a coelom that provides space for complex organs.

Chapter Vocabulary

vertebrate (15.1)	larva (15.2)	flatworm (15.4)	segmented worm (15.4)
invertebrate (15.1)	cnidarian (15.3)	roundworm (15.4)	coelom (15.4)

Check Your Vocabulary

Use the vocabulary words above to complete the following sentences correctly.

1. An organism armed with stinging cells is called a ____ .

2. An earthworm is a ____ ; its body is divided into small segments.

3. Animals without backbones are classified as ____ .

4. A worm with a round shape and a one-way digestive tube with two openings is a ____ .

5. Organisms in an early stage of development that look different from their parents are called ____ .

6. Only segmented worms have a ____ , or cavity with space for organ systems.

7. Animals with backbones are classified as ____ .

8. A worm with a flat shape, such as a planaria, is a ____ .

Write Your Vocabulary

Write a sentence for each vocabulary word above. Show that you know what each word means.

Chapter 15 Review

Check Your Knowledge

Answer the following in complete sentences.

1. What are the two main body forms of cnidarians?

2. How do earthworms affect soil?

3. How do animals obtain food?

4. Name four ways animals move.

5. Name a roundworm that is a human parasite. How does the parasite enter a human body?

6. What type of animal is responsible for producing coral reefs?

7. Do roundworms reproduce sexually or asexually? Do they have two separate sexes?

Determine whether each statement is true or false. Write *true* if it is true. If it is false, change the underlined word to make the statement true.

8. <u>Flatworms</u> have the simplest body organization of any kind of worm.

9. Worms are classified into <u>two</u> phyla.

10. Reef corals make hard skeletons of <u>phosphate</u>.

11. Roundworms have a <u>two-way</u> digestive tube with two openings.

12. <u>Planaria</u> reproduce asexually by dividing their bodies in two. They can also reproduce sexually.

13. All worms have <u>bilateral</u> symmetry and a definite head.

14. Each cnidarian stinging <u>organ</u> has a tiny harpoon at the end of a coiled, hollow thread.

Check Your Understanding

Apply the concepts you have learned to answer each question.

1. How do cnidarians use their tentacles lined with stinging cells?

2. How is the body organization of segmented worms different from the body organization of flatworms and roundworms?

3. How does a sponge take in food? What is its method of eating called?

4. **Extension** Classify each of the following animals as a vertebrate or invertebrate.

   a. Sponge

   b. Snake

   c. Flatworm

   d. Jellyfish

   e. Human

   f. Fish

5. **Mystery Photo** The photo on page 298 shows coral polyps. Their limestone home is in the background. Each polyp is a different coral animal, though they often live in colonies like this one. Do the coral polyps have radial or bilateral symmetry? Are the coral polyps vertebrates or invertebrates?

6. **Infer** Animal X has radial symmetry. It often lives in ocean habitats. You might find it attached to a surface, or moving freely. It has tissues, a mouth, and a digestive cavity. It can reproduce sexually or asexually. What is the phyla of animal X? What is another important distinguishing feature of the phyla?

Develop Your Skills

Use the skills you have developed in this chapter to complete each activity.

1. **Interpret Data** The bar graph shows the number of earthworms per cubic meter in different samples of soil.

   a. Which sample contains the most earthworms? How many are there?

   b. What can you infer about soil sample E?

2. **Compare and Contrast** How is the body of a sponge similar to and different from the body of a cnidarian?

3. **Classify** Which of the following animals have bilateral symmetry? Which have radial symmetry? Which have neither?

   a. Earthworm   c. Sponge
   b. Sea star   d. Hydrozoan

4. **Data Bank** Use the information on page 629 to answer the following questions.

   a. How many species of roundworms exist? How many species of sponges ?

   b. **Infer** Why do so many more species of roundworms exist than any other invertebrate shown on the graph?

Make Connections

1. **Link the Concepts** Below is a concept map showing how some of the main concepts in this chapter link together. Only part of the map is filled in. Finish the map, using words and ideas from the chapter.

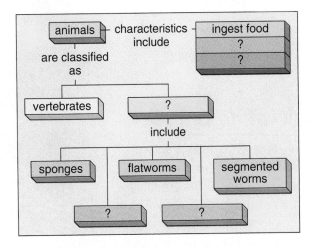

2. **Science and Art** Using what you've learned in this chapter and any additional sources from the library, design a poster of a coral reef. Include coral of different sizes and colors. What determines the different colors of coral?

3. **Science and Technology** *Alvin* is a special research submarine. What other types of vessels are used for sea exploration and research? Use the library to find out about the technology scientists use to explore the sea.

4. **Science and Society** Natural sponges are a living resource. If one type of sponge is collected too frequently, the population could be depleted. What can be done to prevent the loss of sponge diversity due to human use? Hint: you may want to review sponge reproduction.

Chapter 16   Invertebrates II

What do you see?

“I see a parade of colors flashing. It seems like a kind of wing—more like a butterfly's or dragonfly's wing. The colors are green, yellow, red, blue, and blue-green with black spots all over. It seems like some sort of wing because you can see the scales a little bit. You can almost see the shape of the wing, too.”

Erik Gomez
Clifton Middle School
Houston, Texas

To find out more about the photograph, look on page 342. As you read this chapter, you will learn about many different kinds of invertebrates.

16.1 Mollusks

Objectives

▶ **Describe** the characteristics of mollusks.

▶ **Compare** mollusks to other invertebrates.

▶ **Describe** the features of each class of mollusks.

▶ **Make inferences** about geologic history based on mollusk fossils.

How fast do you move when you're getting ready for school in the morning? Do you move at a "snail's pace"? When your teacher asks you a question in class, do you just "clam up"? These expressions describe human behavior, but they also tell you something about snails and clams. Snails and clams are invertebrates called **mollusks** (MAHL uhsks). All mollusks have soft bodies, and many are covered by hard shells.

Characteristics of Mollusks

Mollusks live mostly in the ocean, but some can be found in freshwater habitats. A number of mollusks have also adapted to life on land. Snails and slugs are common in damp places in your backyard.

There are more than 100,000 species of mollusks. They range in size from tiny snails only a few millimeters across to the 20-m-long giant squid.

No matter what their shape or size, all mollusks have the same basic body plan. Like the bodies of segmented worms, mollusks' bodies contain organs organized into systems. However, their bodies are not built of segments like the segmented worms. Instead, mollusks have all their organs in one area called a visceral (VIS ur uhl) mass. The visceral mass is made up of the digestive, excretory, circulatory, respiratory, and reproductive organs.

Another characteristic of the mollusk body plan is a muscular foot. The foot is used by most mollusks for movement. In addition, a mollusk's soft body parts are covered by a skinlike tissue called a mantle. In many mollusks, the mantle produces a hard, protective shell.

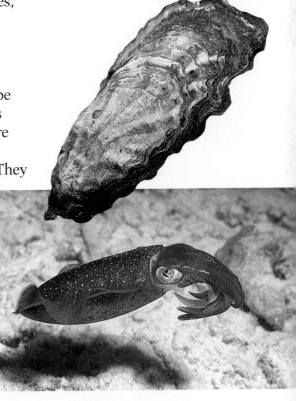

Figure 16.1 ▲
This oyster (top) and squid (bottom) may look very different, but they are both mollusks.

Evolution of Mollusks

The oldest known mollusk fossil is a clamlike organism that lived about 570 million years ago. After this time, mollusks evolved a variety of body forms. Many were common in the ancient oceans. Then about 225 million years ago, most mollusk species became extinct. The survivors are the ancestors of the kinds of mollusks alive today.

Mollusks have larvae similar to the larvae of segmented worms, or annelids. For this reason, some scientists think mollusks evolved from segmented worms. However, because of mollusks' lack of segmentation, other scientists hypothesize that mollusks evolved from ancient worms more similar to flatworms.

Diversity of Mollusks

You can tell that snails are very different from clams and that both differ from an octopus. Would you classify these three mollusks in different groups? That is what scientists do. Each of these kinds of mollusks is a member of a different group, or class.

Gastropods   Mollusks that glide along on a foot underneath their bodies are called **gastropods** (GAS troh PAHDZ). Snails, limpets, slugs, and the sluglike nudibranchs are all gastropods. Most gastropods have one coiled shell. The shells of limpets, however, are flattened cones. Slugs and nudibranchs have no shell at all.

If you watch a snail moving on the ground, you might think it is scooting on its stomach. Actually, a gastropod's muscular foot spreads out under its body and is separate from the stomach. Locate the snail's foot in Figure 16.2. A rippling motion of the foot muscle moves the snail along.

Many gastropods eat plants and algae. Some eat other invertebrates. As an adaptation for getting their food, gastropods have a tonguelike organ covered with rows of teeth. It is called a radula (RAJ oo luh). A gastropod moves its radula back and forth to scrape off and scoop up food. Gastropods that live in water have respiratory organs called gills. As water flows over the gills, oxygen is extracted. Gastropods living on land have evolved a cavity inside their bodies that serves as a lung.

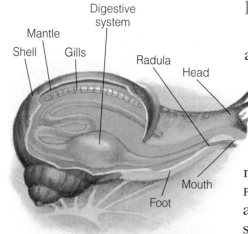

Mantle
Shell
Gills
Digestive system
Radula
Head
Mouth
Foot

Figure 16.2 ▲
Snails are typical gastropods. Does this one live in water or on land?

Bivalves Mollusks with two shells hinged together make up a second class called the **bivalves** (BY valvz). Clams, oysters, mussels, and scallops are all bivalves. Like gastropods, bivalves have a muscular foot. But the foot is shaped and used differently than a gastropod foot. It is normally hidden inside the two shells. Some bivalves move by hooking the foot in sand, and then pulling themselves along.

Bivalves have no head, and most move very little. Some remain attached to one place. Movement isn't important because they are filter feeders. Look at Figure 16.3 and find the gills of the clam. Cilia move water across the gills. Tiny food particles, such as plankton, are trapped by mucus on the gills. Cilia push the food into the animal's mouth.

The gills in bivalves have a large surface area and a rich supply of blood. Oxygen from the water passing over the gills diffuses into the blood. Carbon dioxide, a waste product of animals, diffuses from the blood into the water.

In some kinds of bivalves, water flows over the gills when the shells are open. In clams, the water enters through a muscular tube called a siphon. After it flows over the gills, it leaves through another siphon.

Figure 16.4 ▲
The tentacles of a cephalopod are attached at the animal's head.

Cephalopods The octopus and squid are the major members of a third class of mollusks called **cephalopods** (SEF uh loh PAHDZ). In these mollusks, the foot is divided into tentacles. The tentacles are located at the head, away from the rest of the body. Look at the octopus in Figure 16.4. How many tentacles does it have?

Cephalopods are the only mollusks to have a closed circulatory system. In a closed system, the blood stays in blood vessels.

Modern cephalopods all evolved from now-extinct mollusks with external shells. In the octopus, the shell has disappeared during the process of evolutionary change. Squids have only small internal shells. Only cephalopods called nautiluses (NAWT uh luhs uhz) still have the external shells of their ancestors. Cephalopods live in the oceans and most move about freely. Unlike the filter-feeding bivalves, they are active predators. Their tentacles are covered with suction cups for grasping prey. The octopus lives mostly on the ocean floor, crawling around in search of prey. Squid swim in the open water.

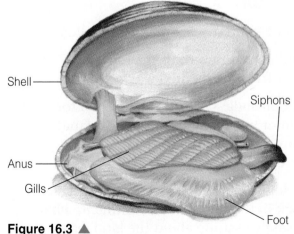

Shell

Siphons

Anus

Gills

Foot

Figure 16.3 ▲
The clam is a typical bivalve.

Science and Society *People and Mollusks*

Throughout the world, mollusks are known mainly as food. The oyster, a kind of bivalve, is a great delicacy to some people. Many popular dishes are made of mollusks, such as abalone, Oysters Rockefeller, clam chowder, calamari, and escargots (EHS kar GOH). Calamari is squid, and escargots are land snails. Many mollusks from all three classes are edible. In some parts of the world, people eat mollusks every day. What kinds of mollusks have you eaten?

Mollusks are also the producers of pearls. When a grain of sand gets into an oyster shell and lodges between the shell and mantle, the oyster gradually coats the particle with thousands of layers of the substance known as mother-of-pearl. In time a pearl forms. Mother-of-pearl is the same material that makes up the inside of the oyster shell. In Japan and other parts of the world, small particles are purposely placed inside oysters to make "cultured" pearls.

Bivalve and gastropod shells are used for jewelry, buttons, and other types of ornaments. Early civilizations made cooking utensils out of mollusk shells and also used them as money.

The internal shell from a type of squid called a cuttlefish is familiar to bird owners. It is the cuttlebone hung in bird cages to provide the birds with calcium. In all these ways, mollusks have been important to people throughout history.

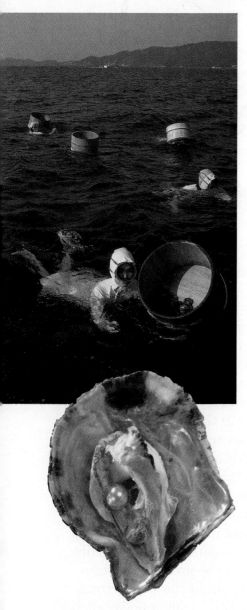

Figure 16.5 ▲

In Japan, divers collect oysters. Each oyster may contain one or more pearls.

Check and Explain

1. What are some similarities among all mollusks?

2. How are mollusks different from cnidarians? How do they differ from segmented worms?

3. **Reason and Conclude** Give an explanation for why bivalves cannot live on land. In your explanation, consider how they differ from gastropods, some of which do live on land.

4. **Infer** If geologists found clamshell fossils in sedimentary rock in the middle of a continent, what could they safely assume about the land where the fossil was found?

16.2 Arthropods

Objectives

▶ **Describe** the characteristics of arthropods.

▶ **Identify** the major kinds of arthropods.

▶ **Explain** how arthropods are classified.

▶ **Communicate** why spiders are important organisms.

No matter where you go on the earth, you can find invertebrates with jointed appendages called **arthropods** (AR throh PAHDZ). With more than a million different species, arthropods make up the largest phylum of animals. They include spiders, butterflies, bees, crabs, lobsters, shrimps, and millipedes.

Arthropods live in water, on land, and even in the air. Some, such as mites, are so tiny you can barely see them. Others, such as the Japanese spider crab, grow to more than 4 m across!

Characteristics of Arthropods

Arthropods are the only invertebrates with jointed appendages. Appendages are parts that extend from the body. Jointed appendages, as you have probably guessed, have joints, just as your arm has an elbow joint. Arthropods use their appendages for movement, defense, feeding, sensing, and even reproduction. A single arthropod may have a great variety of appendages, each adapted for a particular use.

Arthropods share one important characteristic with segmented worms. They both have segmented bodies. However, most arthropods have fewer repeated segments. Instead, their bodies are divided into dissimilar regions: the head, **thorax**, and **abdomen**. Look at Figure 16.6. In most arthropods, the thorax holds legs used for movement. The abdomen contains many of the animal's organs. The head has appendages that are used for sensing and feeding.

Arthropods have another important characteristic. Their bodies are covered by an outer support structure called an **exoskeleton**. An exoskeleton is much like a

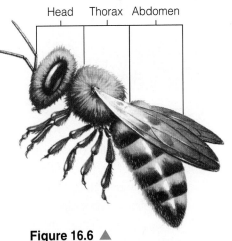

Head   Thorax   Abdomen

Figure 16.6 ▲
The three body regions characteristic of arthropods are easy to see in this honeybee.

Figure 16.7 ▲
The compound eyes of a Mediterranean fruit fly are shown above enlarged 21 times. In the photograph on the right, a cicada has just finished molting. Can you tell which object is the old exoskeleton and which is the cicada?

Skills WorkOut

Communicate Choose an arthropod to report about. Find information about the organism and a picture of it. Trace or photocopy the picture. Neatly print the information on an index card. Display your picture and information on a bulletin board.

suit of armor worn by a medieval knight. It is waterproof and helps prevent the loss of body fluids. Most of it is hard for protection, yet around the joints it is flexible.

The exoskeleton, however, does not grow with the animal. It must be shed and a new, larger exoskeleton made. The process of growing a new exoskeleton and shedding the old one is called molting. Arthropods may molt many times during their lives.

Arthropods have sense organs for sight, smell, taste, and touch. Many have eyes with multiple lenses, called compound eyes. Look at the compound eyes of the insect in Figure 16.7. Vision with compound eyes is not very sharp, but compound eyes are very sensitive to light and movement.

Evolution of Arthropods

Arthropods have been on the earth a long time. Some arthropod fossils are more than 500 million years old. Arthropods called trilobites (TRY loh BYTS) were very common in the oceans for hundreds of millions of years. They became extinct about 280 million years ago.

Arthropods most likely evolved from segmented worms. In the process of evolution, groups of repeated segments were fused, or joined, to create the head, thorax, and abdomen of arthropods. Arthropods' jointed appendages probably evolved from shorter, unjointed appendages present in ancient segmented worms. With their hard exoskeleton and walking legs, arthropods were among the first animals to live successfully on land.

Diversity of Arthropods

A wide variety of animals are included in the arthropod phylum, from mites to millipedes, ladybugs to lobsters. These very different animals are organized into different classes.

Arachnids Spiders, ticks, scorpions, and mites are all **arachnids** (uh RAK nihdz). Arachnids generally have two main body regions. The head and thorax are fused, forming a cephalothorax (SEF uh loh THOR AKS). An abdomen is the other body region. In ticks and mites, the cephalothorax and abdomen are also fused together. Arachnids have four pairs of legs attached to the cephalothorax. Near the mouth is another pair of appendages called chelicerae (kuh LIHS ur EE).

In spiders, the chelicerae are like fangs and have poison glands. They are used to attack prey, which is mainly insects. Spiders also produce a liquid form of silk in glands and spin the silk into thread with spinnerets. When the liquid silk is exposed to air, it becomes solid and strong. Spiders make different kinds of silk for

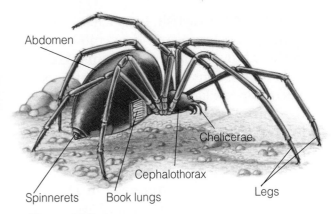

Abdomen
Chelicerae
Cephalothorax
Legs
Spinnerets
Book lungs

Figure 16.8 ▲
How many legs does a spider have?

catching prey, making sacs for eggs, and anchoring webs. Not all spiders spin webs, but they all produce silk.

Spiders have thin slits in their exoskeletons that allow air into their bodies. In some spiders, the oxygen in the air diffuses directly into cells. In other spiders, the oxygen in the air diffuses into the spider's blood through book lungs. Find the book lungs in Figure 16.8. Book lungs are made up of sheets of tissue like the pages of a book. This gives them a large surface area for gas exchange. Some spiders use both for gas exchange.

Figure 16.9 ▲
What differences do you notice in the bodies of these spiders?

Crustaceans Crayfish, barnacles, crabs, shrimps, lobsters, water fleas, pill bugs, and sow bugs are all **crustaceans** (kruhs TAY shunz). Crustaceans have many specialized appendages. At the head are jaw-like appendages called mandibles (MAN duh buhlz), used for chewing and crushing food. Also attached to the head are two pairs of appendages used for balance and sensing called **antennas** (an TEHN uhz). Other arthropod classes have antennas, but crustaceans are the only ones that have two pairs. Unlike spiders, which have simple eyes, most crustaceans have compound eyes.

Look at the crayfish shown in Figure 16.10. It is a typical crustacean. The crayfish uses the large claws on its thorax to grab food and to protect itself. Behind the claws are legs used for walking. Like all crustaceans, the crayfish also has appendages on its abdomen. The crayfish uses these for swimming.

Figure 16.11 ▲
A ghost crab's claws are good weapons.

You may have seen crayfish, lobsters, crabs, or shrimps, but tiny crustaceans called copepods (KOH puh PAHDS) greatly outnumber all the other crustaceans on the earth. Copepods make up part of the plankton. They are an important part of ocean food chains.

Most crustaceans move around freely, but some crustaceans, called barnacles, remain attached to one place. Many barnacles produce hard, volcano-shaped shelters. Inside one of these shelters is a crustacean with jointed appendages. Most of these appendages are used to paddle food into the barnacle's mouth when it is under water.

Figure 16.10 ▲
How many different kinds of appendages can you see on this crayfish? What is the function of each kind?

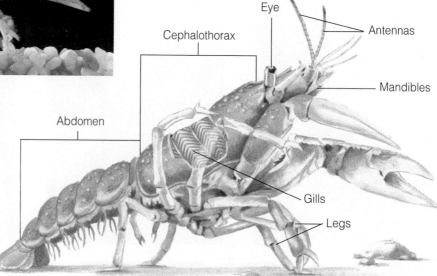

Cephalothorax

Eye

Antennas

Mandibles

Abdomen

Gills

Legs

Centipedes and Millipedes One variation on the basic arthropod body plan is a long, wormlike body with many walking appendages. Two classes of arthropods, the centipedes (SEHN tuh PEEDZ) and millipedes (MIHL ih PEEDZ), share this type of body structure. They resemble segmented worms because of their many repeated segments. Their jointed legs, however, identify them as arthropods.

Although the word *centipede* means "100 legs" in Latin, most centipedes have about 30 legs. Each body segment has one pair of legs. Centipedes are predators. They eat insects, snails, slugs, and worms. Their adaptations for hunting include poison claws, antennas, mandibles, and the ability to move very quickly.

Millipedes, in contrast, are slow-moving and eat mainly plants and decaying organic matter. A millipede has more segments than the typical centipede. And each segment has two pairs of legs. As a millipede walks, the many legs move in a wavelike motion.

Figure 16.12 ▲
Look at these arthropods' legs. Which is the millipede?

SkillBuilder *Collecting Data*

Arthropod Search

Look for arthropods in your yard or in pictures in magazines. Start searching for them in both places after you copy the table below. When you encounter an organism you think is an arthropod, observe it for the characteristics in the table. Record your observations. Determine whether the organism is an arthropod. Give the organism a name, and write it down next to the number. If you are observing live organisms, release them after you complete your data collecting. Once you have observed 12 different organisms, answer the following questions.

1. How many arthropods did you observe?

2. Which characteristic of arthropods was easiest to observe? Explain why.

3. If you observed 100 different organisms, how many do you think would belong to the arthropod phylum? Explain your reasoning.

4. How might your results change if you conducted your search six months from this date?

Write a short paragraph comparing the characteristics of arthropods to other animal phyla.

	Jointed Appendages?	Segmented Body?	Exoskeleton?	Is it an Arthropod?
1.				
2.				
3.				
4.				

Figure 16.13 ▲
Without spiders, the world might be overrun with insects.

Science and Society *Friendly Spiders*

If you saw a spider right now, what would you do? Despite popular belief, spiders are not out to get you. In fact, most spiders will bite only when frightened. Some spider bites may cause a reaction, but most do not harm people.

Spiders are generally shy creatures who spend most of their time hunting and killing insects. In fact, spiders are insects' worst enemies. Spiders kill more insects than all the birds in the world do. Spiders also kill more insects than commercial pesticides do.

Some farmers in China know how useful spiders are for killing insects that harm their rice crops. Before these farmers flood their rice fields, they set out stacks of rice straw. Spiders crawl inside the stacks, which are then moved to save the spiders. The farmers can move the stacks to places where insects are damaging the rice crop. The spiders come out and eat the insects.

Research is now being done on the kind of poisons spiders make to capture and kill insects. These substances may be useful in the development of natural insecticides. Some pharmaceutical companies are even studying spider poisons as a source of drugs to treat heart and nervous system disorders.

Check and Explain

1. Describe at least three characteristics shared by all arthropods.

2. For each of the following arthropods, name the class in which it belongs: lobster, spider, barnacle, tick, shrimp, scorpion.

3. **Compare and Contrast** How are arthropods similar to mollusks? How are they different? Do arthropods have more in common with mollusks or with segmented worms? Explain.

4. **Communicate** Suppose you share a garden with someone who is afraid of spiders. You want to encourage spiders to live in the garden to help reduce the number of harmful insects. How would you convince your partner that this is a good idea?

16.3 Insects

Objectives

▶ **Describe** the characteristics of insects.

▶ **Distinguish** between incomplete and complete metamorphosis.

▶ **Explain** how social insects differ from other insects.

▶ **Make a model** of the body structure of an insect.

Have you ever been on a picnic and had uninvited guests show up? Maybe there were ants crawling on the cheese, or flies landing on the potato salad. Or possibly mosquitoes bit you and bees buzzed around. Insects seem to be everywhere!

These six-legged invertebrates are arthropods. They belong to a single class, but there are more species in this class than in all the other arthropod classes put together. In fact, in their number of species, insects outnumber all other forms of life combined!

The Success of Insects

Insects appeared about 400 million years ago. By the beginning of the Cenozoic era, they had evolved an amazing variety of shapes, sizes, and behaviors. The great number of insect species is a sign that insects have been very successful as a life form. They have been able to adapt to many different habitats, from high mountains to dry deserts to rivers and wetlands to your backyard. They have been able to survive when other organisms could not. Insects owe their success to a body plan that has many advantages over others.

One important characteristic of the insect body is its flexibility. In the process of evolution, insect body parts have been modified for different ways of living. Changes in mouthparts, for example, have resulted in the adaptation of different species for eating different food. Figure 16.14 shows some of the different mouthparts insects have evolved.

Another major insect advantage is the ability to fly. Flight helps insects find food, escape predators, locate mates, and reach new places to live.

Grasshopper

Moth

Housefly

Figure 16.14 ▲
Compare the mouthparts of these insects. What kind of food does each one eat?

Skills WorkOut

Observe Get a piece of string about 50 cm long and a hand lens. Go outside and lay the string in a circle on a lawn, in a field, or under a tree. Sit quietly for three minutes and look for insects in the circle. What are they doing? Write your observations.

Figure 16.15 ▲
What parts of the grasshopper can you find in the photograph above?

Body Structure of Insects

Insects, like all arthropods, have exoskeletons, segmented bodies, and jointed appendages. They differ from other arthropods in having three pairs of legs. In addition, they are the only arthropods with wings. All insect bodies are divided into the three basic arthropod body regions: head, thorax, and abdomen.

The grasshopper shown in Figure 16.15 is a good example of an insect. Notice where its body is divided into the three regions. Now look at the head. The grasshopper has a pair of compound eyes and three simple eyes. Its antennas are for touch and smell. The grasshopper's mouthparts are adapted for chewing.

The grasshopper's thorax is divided into three segments. It has a pair of legs attached to each segment. The first two pairs are for walking. The hind pair are powerful legs used for jumping. Notice that the grasshopper has two pairs of wings, attached to the second and third segments of the thorax. Many other insects have two pairs of wings, but some have only one pair, and others are wingless.

A grasshopper's abdomen has ten segments. Notice the tympanum (TIHM puh nuhm), which is like an eardrum; it senses sound. Other insects have tympanums on their thorax or legs.

Like other insects, a grasshopper has tiny slits in its thorax and abdomen. Air enters these slits and flows through a series of tubes called tracheae (TRAY kee EE). Oxygen diffuses from tiny tubes into the body cells.

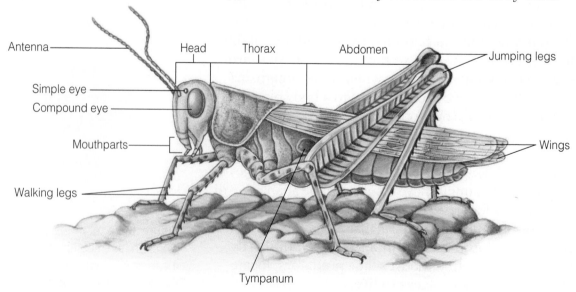

Antenna — Head Thorax Abdomen Jumping legs

Simple eye
Compound eye

Mouthparts

Wings

Walking legs

Tympanum

Insect Development

All insects reproduce sexually. In most species the eggs are fertilized inside the female's body by a male's sperm. Many insects lay eggs on a food source so the young can begin to eat right after they hatch.

Most insects don't look exactly like their parents when they hatch from their eggs. As they grow, they undergo a process called **metamorphosis** (MEHT uh MOR fuh sihs). During metamorphosis, a young organism changes its appearance to become an adult.

Incomplete Metamorphosis Some insects, such as grasshoppers and lice, go through an incomplete metamorphosis. This is a series of molts in which the insect changes from an egg to a **nymph** (NIHMF) to an adult. A nymph looks like a little adult, but it has no wings and is not yet able to reproduce.

Complete Metamorphosis Look at Figure 16.17. Most insects go through complete metamorphosis, which involves a more complete change of appearance. Bees, wasps, flies, beetles, butterflies, and moths are among the insects that go through complete metamorphosis. They change from eggs to larvae to pupae to adults.

In the larva stage, the insect usually looks something like a worm. You have probably seen caterpillars, which are the larvae of butterflies or moths. During the **pupa** (PYOO puh) stage, the insect does not eat or move around. In many species the pupa is surrounded by a cocoon. During this stage, amazing changes are taking place. Most of the larva's cells are destroyed and others divide rapidly. When metamorphosis is complete, an adult insect emerges.

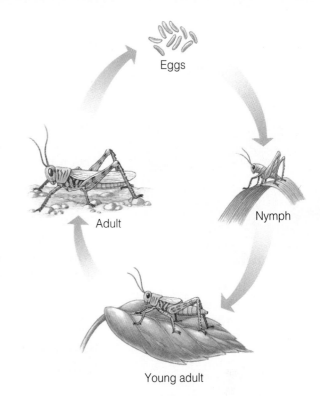

Figure 16.16 ▲ Incomplete Metamorphosis

Eggs

Adult

Nymph

Young adult

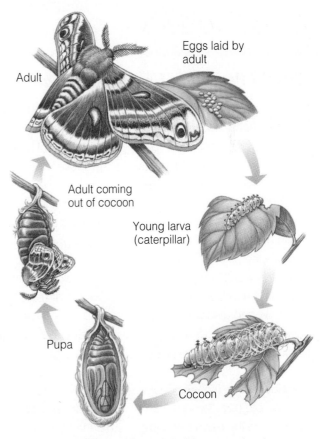

Figure 16.17 ▲ Complete Metamorphosis

Adult

Eggs laid by adult

Adult coming out of cocoon

Young larva (caterpillar)

Pupa

Cocoon

Social Insects

Most insects live on their own, but some species live together in colonies. They are called social insects. Social insects include termites, most ants, and some wasps and bees. A colony of social insects is in many ways like a single organism. The members of the colony have specialized functions, much like different cells. They also have systems of communication that allow them to work together smoothly.

In an ant colony, or nest, most of the ants are wingless female workers. They build the nest, gather food from outside, care for the young, and defend the nest against invaders. They communicate with each other through touch and chemicals. The worker ants do not reproduce. That job is reserved for the queen ant. She lays eggs all during her long life. The eggs are fertilized by stored sperm the queen receives after a single mating with a winged male ant.

Figure 16.18 ▲
How are these ants cooperating? Could a single ant do the job alone?

Consider This

Should Pesticide Use Be Reduced?

Crops are prime targets for hungry insects. Most farmers rely heavily on pesticides to control insect pests, which lets them produce more and better-looking crops.

Some pesticides cause health problems for the people who use them. They may remain in small amounts on the food you eat. They may kill birds, fish, and many invertebrates when they drain into rivers and lakes. Some pesticides enter the food chain.

Consider Some Issues People who want to reduce pesticide use believe the harm pesticides cause outweighs the benefits.

They point out that pesticides kill beneficial insects that may help control harmful ones. They propose switching to other methods of controlling pests, including the use of organisms that attack the pests.

Supporters of pesticide use believe the alternative methods won't work as well as pesticides. They claim that reducing the use of pesticides will also reduce the amount of food that can be grown, leading to hardship for farmers.

Think About It Does the harm done by pesticides justify limiting their use? Can the problems

caused by reducing the use of pesticides be overcome? What is the best policy over the long term?

Debate It Find out more about all sides of the pesticide issue. Choose a position. Debate the issue with other students in your class.

Science and Technology *A Robot Honeybee*

All insects communicate in some way with others of their kind. Ants, for example, give off a chemical that marks a trail to a food source. They also touch each other's antennas. Fireflies communicate with flashes of light.

One of the most studied methods of insect communication is the "waggle dance" of the honeybee. The dance is used by a worker bee to communicate information about the location of a food source to other members of the hive. A bee performing the dance wiggles its abdomen, vibrates its wings, and runs around in a figure-eight pattern.

To study how information is communicated in this dance, a group of scientists in Denmark and Germany have developed a robot honeybee that can imitate the dance. Its movements are controlled by a computer. The scientists had the robot perform dances based on what they already knew about how a bee's movements communicated directions.

The scientists found that the robot could communicate enough information for some bees to find the location of a food source. But it could not do as well as a real bee. This result suggested that there is more to honeybee communication than the scientists had thought. One discovery was that the kind of sound produced by the vibration of the bee's wings seems to be important. The sound has to be just right for the correct message to be communicated.

Figure 16.19 ▲

Even though the robot honeybee looks nothing like a bee, real bees can still get information from it.

Check and Explain

1. How does oxygen reach an insect's body cells?

2. What is a social insect? Give an example, and explain why social behavior helps the group survive.

3. **Compare and Contrast** What is the difference between a larva and a nymph? How is each different from an adult insect?

4. **Make a Model** Choose an insect, other than a grasshopper, with which you are familiar. You may want to observe one for a while. Write a paragraph describing its body structure. Draw a picture and label its body parts.

Activity 16 *What are the stages in fruit fly reproduction?*

Skills Observe; Collect Data; Infer

Task 1 Prelab Prep
Collect the following items: wide-mouth jar, half of a ripe banana, nylon stocking, rubber band, small spoon, microscope slide, coverslip, microscope, hand lens.

Task 2 Data Record
1. On a sheet of paper, draw the data table shown below. Write the date you begin this activity in the first box.
2. Mark the date in each box as you record your observations.
3. Record all your observations about the changes you observe in the jar. Describe what you see with words and pictures.

Table 16.1 Fruit Fly Observations

Date	Observations

Task 3 Procedure
1. Peel the banana and put it in the jar. Leave the jar open.
2. Check the jar every day. When you see a few small flies in the jar, put the stocking over the mouth of the jar. Fasten it with a rubber band.
3. Carefully observe the flies over the next three days. Notice their features. Do not remove the stocking from the jar.
4. After three days, remove the stocking from the jar. Let all the flies go outside. Put the stocking back on the jar and fasten it.

5. For the first day or two, spoon out a tiny bit of the banana and smear it on a slide. Look at it under a microscope. Record your observations. Wash the slide.
6. Continue checking the jar every day. Use a hand lens or microscope if you want. Record your observations.
7. When you see flies in the jar again, let them go outside.
8. Clean out the jar and wash it well.

Task 4 Analysis
1. What changes did you observe in the jar?
2. What did you expect to see under the microscope in step 5? What did you see? Explain.
3. What would have happened if you had not cleaned out the jar in step 8 above?
4. Is a fruit fly's metamorphosis complete or incomplete? Explain. Which stages did you observe?
5. About how long is the life cycle of a fruit fly? Explain.

Task 5 Conclusion
Write a paragraph describing the stages of metamorphosis in a fruit fly. Explain how you know, whether you did or did not observe all the stages in this activity.

Everyday Application
Some supermarkets sell slightly overripe fruits and vegetables at bargain prices. How should this produce be packaged for sale? Why?

Extension
Many people a long time ago believed in "spontaneous generation." They thought living things could come from decaying food. How could you use what you learned in this activity to refute spontaneous generation?

16.4 Echinoderms

Objectives

▶ **Describe** the characteristics of echinoderms.

▶ **Identify** the five classes of echinoderms.

▶ **Describe** the adaptations of starfish.

▶ **Infer** the evolutionary history of echinoderms.

Skills WarmUp

Research Look in a dictionary or encyclopedia to find out the meaning of the Greek roots that make up the word *echinoderm*. Why do you think this phylum was given this name?

What kind of stars are never seen in the sky but often found in the sea? What kind of dollars are you more likely to find on a beach than in a bank? What kind of cucumber is an animal, not a plant? If you can't guess the answers to these riddles now, you will be able to soon. They are all about invertebrates with radial symmetry called **echinoderms** (ee KY noh DURMZ).

Characteristics of Echinoderms

Echinoderms live in the ocean. Like humans, they have hard endoskeletons, which are support structures inside their bodies. Many echinoderms also have hard spines or bumps extending from the endoskeleton.

Like cnidarians, adult echinoderms have radial symmetry. They develop, however, from larvae with bilateral symmetry. In the center of an echinoderm's rounded body, or disk, is a mouth. In most echinoderms, the mouth faces downward. Some echinoderms have arms radiating out from the disk, and some don't.

Echinoderms are the only animals with tube feet, thin-walled hollow tubes or tentacles used for movement and feeding. Most echinoderms have many tube feet, each as thin as spaghetti and a few centimeters long. The tube feet are part of a system of water canals that run throughout an echinoderm's body.

Even though echinoderms have radial symmetry like the cnidarians, they are not related to cnidarians. In fact, these simple-looking organisms are more closely related to vertebrates than to the other invertebrates. Echinoderm larvae begin their development much like vertebrate embryos.

Figure 16.20 ▲
Sand dollars are pancake-shaped echinoderms that bury themselves in sand.

Diversity of Echinoderms

The 6,000 or so species of echinoderms are organized into five classes. Starfish make up the largest class. The other four classes are the brittle stars, the sea urchins, the sea cucumbers, and the sea lilies.

◀ Brittle stars look something like starfish, but they have long, whiplike arms. If you tried to pick up a brittle star, its arms would break off. What do you think is the purpose of this adaptation? Brittle stars eat dead or decaying matter.

Sea lilies look like ▶ flowers, with their cup-shaped bodies attached to the ocean floor by stalks. Their branched arms are used to catch food. Sea lilies were very common hundreds of millions of years ago. The few sea lilies that exist today look very much like sea lily fossils 500 million years old.

▲ Sea urchins have no arms. Their bodies are covered with spines. The spines are for protection and locomotion. Sea urchins have five sharp teeth for scraping and chewing. They eat mostly many-celled algae. In Japan, people eat the reproductive organs of sea urchins. Sand dollars are also included in this class of echinoderms.

Sea cucumbers do not ▶ look very much like other echinoderms. They have long, flexible bodies with a reduced endoskeleton and no arms. Using their tube feet, they burrow into the sand on the bottom of the sea. They move more freely than other echinoderms. Some people eat dried sea cucumbers.

Starfish

If you've seen an echinoderm, it was probably a starfish. They are often found clinging to rocks at the ocean's edge. Starfish have five or more arms. Look at Figure 16.21. Notice that the arms are not just appendages. They contain internal organs. The undersides of the arms are covered with tube feet.

Starfish have adapted to eating filter-feeding bivalves, such as mussels and clams. Although the hard shells of these mollusks keep most predators away, starfish have no problem with them. The starfish wraps its strong arms around the bivalve, holding on tightly with the suction cups on its tube feet. Slowly the starfish pulls open its prey's shell just a little. Then it turns its stomach inside out and pushes it into the shell. Digestive enzymes kill the mollusk, and the starfish has a meal.

Like all echinoderms, starfish have a system of water canals attached to the tube feet. Water pressure inside the canals helps keep the tube feet rigid. An opening on top of the body strains the water as it flows into the canal system.

Starfish and other echinoderms can regrow, or regenerate, lost body parts. One starfish arm including just part of the central disk can regenerate into an entire new animal.

Skills WorkOut

Infer   Starfish eat the mollusks harvested as shellfish. At one time, when shellfish farmers found starfish, they cut up the starfish and threw them back into the sea. But the starfish population just got larger and did even more damage. Why do you think this happened?

Figure 16.21 ▲
The red patterns on this African red starfish (above) are parts of its endoskeleton. The endoskeleton is not shown in the drawing to the left so that you can see the system of water canals inside the starfish's body.

Ring canal

Radial canal

Stomach

Body cavity

Arms

Tube feet

When Europeans began to settle in California in the 1700s, huge "forests" of kelp grew in a band just offshore. Kelp are many-celled algae that grow as big as trees. Air bladders keep their leaflike blades at the surface. Living in the band of kelp were many thousands of sea otters, marine mammals with thick fur.

In the 1800s the sea otters were hunted for their fur. By the early 1900s, they were nearly extinct. People noticed that while the population of otters was falling, the kelp forests were also disappearing.

The connection between the decline of both the sea otter and the kelp was the sea urchin. Sea urchins eat kelp. Normally, the population of sea urchins was kept in balance by their major predator—the sea otter. But as the sea otter began to disappear, the urchins greatly increased their numbers. They munched away on the kelp, and eventually there was little kelp left.

Then in 1911, an international treaty ended the otter fur trade. In 1938, a few sea otters were found off the California coast and immediately protected. In 1973, the Marine Mammal Protection Act was passed. These actions have helped the sea otter make a comeback.

Not surprisingly, the return of the sea otter has helped the kelp forests grow back. This is restoring the diversity of the marine ecosystem. There are fewer sea urchins, but more fishes, crabs, shrimps, and mollusks.

Figure 16.22 ▲
A sea otter floats in kelp off the California coast.

Check and Explain

1. What makes echinoderms different from other invertebrates?

2. List and describe the five classes of echinoderms.

3. **Reason and Conclude** Most predators, such as octopuses, spiders, and tigers, are fast-moving and have good eyesight. Explain why starfish, which are also predators, can be slow-moving and blind.

4. **Infer** Modern species of one class of echinoderms are often called living fossils. Can you guess which class? Explain the reason for your answer.

Chapter 16 *Review*

Concept Summary

16.1 Mollusks

▶ Mollusks have soft, nonsegmented bodies with a mantle and a muscular foot. They have complex organ systems.

▶ The three classes of mollusks are the gastropods, the bivalves, and the cephalopods.

16.2 Arthropods

▶ Arthropods have jointed appendages and bodies divided into a head, thorax, and abdomen.

▶ Arthropods' bodies are enclosed in an exoskeleton.

▶ The major classes of arthropods are the arachnids, the crustaceans, the centipedes and millipedes, and the insects.

16.3 Insects

▶ Insects are six-legged arthropods. Many have wings.

▶ Insects go through either incomplete or complete metamorphosis to become adults.

▶ Termites and some ants, bees, and wasps are social insects.

16.4 Echinoderms

▶ Echinoderms live in the oceans. They have hard endoskeletons, radial symmetry, and tube feet.

▶ The five classes of echinoderms are the brittle stars, the sea urchins, the sea cucumbers, the sea lilies, and the starfish.

Chapter Vocabulary

mollusk (16.1)	arthropod (16.2)	arachnid (16.2)	nymph (16.3)
gastropod (16.1)	thorax (16.2)	crustacean (16.2)	pupa (16.3)
bivalve (16.1)	abdomen (16.2)	antenna (16.2)	echinoderm (16.4)
cephalopod (16.1)	exoskeleton (16.2)	metamorphosis (16.3)	

Check Your Vocabulary

Use the vocabulary words above to complete the following sentences correctly.

1. Arthropods have an outer support structure called an _____ .

2. _____ make up a phylum of soft-bodied animals with a muscular foot.

3. An insect with incomplete metamorphosis begins life as a _____ .

4. _____ are sensory organs on the heads of arthropods.

5. Crabs and lobsters belong to the arthropod class called the _____ .

6. The body region between the head and abdomen of an arthropod is called the _____ .

7. Insects undergo _____ to become adults.

8. A _____ has a one coiled shell.

9. The body region of an insect farthest from the head is the _____ .

10. _____ make up a phylum of invertebrates with jointed legs.

11. _____ are mollusks with two hinged shells.

12. During the _____ stage, an insect undergoes most of the changes of complete metamorphosis.

13. Invertebrates with endoskeletons and radial symmetry are called _____ .

14. Squid belong to a mollusk class called the _____ .

Chapter 16 Review

Check Your Knowledge

Answer the following in complete sentences.

1. What is the difference between a spider and an insect?

2. What different functions can the appendages of arthropods serve? Name at least three functions and describe the kind of appendage used in each case.

3. Give two reasons why insects have been successful as a life form.

4. What echinoderm characteristic is shared by no other kind of animal? How is this characteristic useful?

5. An octopus's tentacles are similar to what part of a snail?

6. How do millipedes and centipedes differ from segmented worms?

Choose the answer that best completes each sentence.

7. A tissue called the (visceral mass, radula, foot, mantle) produces a shell in many mollusks.

8. Starfish are (cnidarians, echinoderms, arthropods, fish).

9. During the (pupa, egg, larva, nymph) stage, an insect is often wrapped in a cocoon.

10. Arthropods with many legs and repeated segments are (insects, spiders, millipedes, annelids).

11. An insect's wings are attached to the (head, thorax, abdomen, cephalothorax).

12. Cephalopods are the most (common, colorful, fast-moving, dangerous) of the mollusks.

Check Your Understanding

Apply the concepts you have learned to answer each question.

1. **Compare and Contrast** How do echinoderms and arthropods differ?

2. **Application** A red tide is a population explosion of dinoflagellates, one-celled algae that contain a poison. During a red tide, bivalves in the area are not safe to eat, but most gastropods are safe. Explain.

3. Why do you think starfish are not used by humans for food?

4. **Mystery Photo** The photograph on page 320 shows the surface of a moth's wing. What kinds of parts and materials do you think make up this wing? What would happen if you touched it with your finger?

5. **Extension** You discover a spider that has evolved adaptations for life in the ocean. What might some of these adaptations be? How is the spider different from other spiders? What spider characteristics does it still have?

6. Why is a gastropod's shell not considered an exoskeleton?

7. What do barnacles have in common with sponges, bivalves, and sea anemones?

8. **Application** What kind of echinoderm– sea urchins or sea cucumbers–are you most likely to find living where the ocean has a muddy bottom? Explain your answer.

9. Why have no echinoderms adapted to living on land?

10. Why is it impossible for insects to be as large as humans?

Develop Your Skills

Use the skills you have developed in this chapter to complete each activity.

1. **Interpret Data** The graph below shows the results of an experiment in a farm field.

   a. Describe what happens to the insect population and to the spider population.

   b. What seems to be the cause of these changes?

   c. Why does the insect population rise rapidly after falling for a time?

   d. What is likely to happen to the population levels as more time passes?

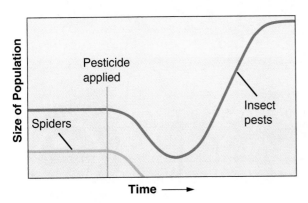

2. **Infer** Many squid that live in the ocean can produce their own light. How do you think this adaptation helps them survive? Explain.

3. **Data Bank** Use the information on page 627 to answer the following questions.

   a. Which arthropods have the fewest number of species?

   b. What percentage of the total number of arthropod species are arachnids?

   c. In number of species, insects outnumber all non-insect arthropods by how many times?

Make Connections

1. **Link the Concepts** Below is a concept map showing how some of the main concepts in this chapter link together. Only part of the map is filled in. Finish the map, using words and ideas you find in the chapter.

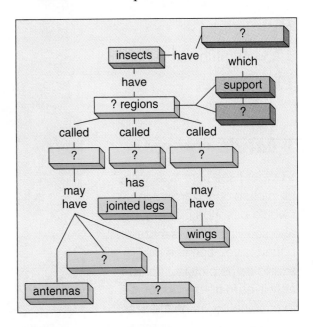

2. **Science and Society** To control insect pests, some farmers and gardeners bring in organisms that prey upon the pests. Find out what organisms are used for this purpose, and which kinds of pests each will eat. Write a report on this form of biological pest control.

3. **Science and You** Do research on the life cycle of fleas to find out why they are so hard to get rid of. Based on what you learn, explain how you would try to control fleas in your home and on your pets.

4. **Science and Art** Start a butterfly collection, using photographs instead of real butterflies. Draw your own pictures of each butterfly. Make hypotheses about the purposes of their colors and patterns.

Chapter 17

Fishes, Amphibians, and Reptiles

What do you see?

66 What I see here is a close-up picture of a lizard's eyeball. I would describe it as colorful and scaly. I think it is a lizard because you can see the scales in the picture. It probably lives in trees in a tropical forest. The colors on the lizard would suggest a forest-type environment. 99

Jason Bonte
Sara Scott Junior High
Terre Haute, Indiana

To find out more about the photograph, look on page 364. As you read this chapter, you will learn about fishes, amphibians, reptiles, and some of their common characteristics.

17.1 Common Traits of Vertebrates

Skills WarmUp

Objectives

▶ **Describe** the characteristics vertebrates have in common.

▶ **Distinguish** between endothermic and ectothermic animals.

▶ **Discuss** the evolutionary development of vertebrates.

▶ **Classify** invertebrates and vertebrates by constructing a diagram.

Compare and Contrast
Make a list of five important differences between an insect and a frog. Compare your list with a classmate's list. How does your list differ from your classmate's? How are the two lists the same?

U p and down the middle of your back are bones that make up your vertebrae (VUR tuh BREE). The bones in your vertebrae are joined together with cartilage to form a flexible but supportive column called the backbone.

Humans aren't the only organisms with backbones. You share a backbone with fishes, amphibians, reptiles, birds, and other mammals. Recall that these animals with backbones are called vertebrates.

Characteristics of Vertebrates

All vertebrates belong to a single phylum. The name of the phylum is Chordata. Animals in this phylum are called chordates (KOR dayts). Among the chordates are several types of animals that do not have backbones.

All chordates share several traits. One chordate trait is the presence of gills or gill slits at some stage of development. Chordates also have a flexible skeletal rod called a notochord (NOHT uh KORD). The notochord protects a chordate's hollow nerve cord.

In vertebrates, the notochord is present only in the embryo stage. As a vertebrate develops, its notochord is replaced by a backbone that surrounds and protects the spinal cord. The backbone is the central part of an internal support structure called an **endoskeleton**. A vertebrate's endoskeleton is very different from the exoskeleton of an arthropod.

Even though vertebrates share many traits, they have important differences, too. Birds and mammals are **endotherms** (EHN doh THURMS), animals with constant

Nerve cord

Gill slits

Notochord

Figure 17.1 ▲
The lancelet is a chordate but not a vertebrate. What does it have in common with vertebrates?

internal body temperatures. Their body cells produce enough heat to keep their bodies warm despite the changing temperature outside their bodies. Endotherms are commonly described as warm-blooded.

Fishes, amphibians, and reptiles, in contrast, can't keep their body temperatures constant. Their body temperatures depend on the temperature of their environment. Animals with bodies that receive heat from the outside are called **ectotherms** (EHK toh THURMS). Ectotherms are sometimes described as cold-blooded. All the animals you will read about in this chapter are ectotherms.

Figure 17.2
This evolutionary tree shows that fishes living hundreds of millions of years ago are the ancestors of all the kinds of vertebrates alive today. ▼

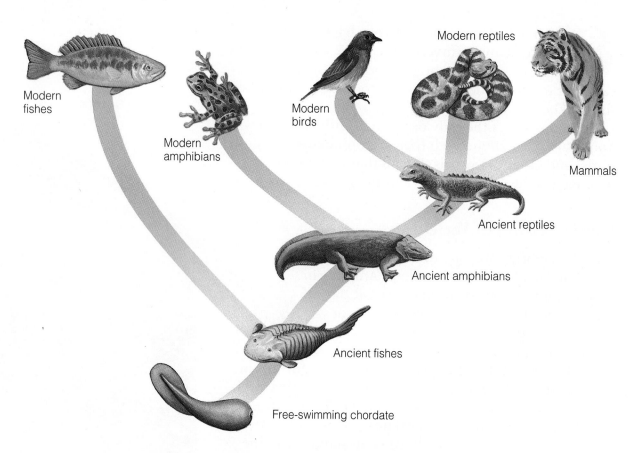

Modern fishes

Modern amphibians

Modern birds

Modern reptiles

Mammals

Ancient reptiles

Ancient amphibians

Ancient fishes

Free-swimming chordate

Origin of Vertebrates

The first vertebrates appeared on the earth about 500 million years ago. They were water-dwelling, fish-like animals. Over time they evolved into many different kinds of fish. For many millions of years, fish were one of the most successful life forms on the earth.

Eventually, some fishes developed adaptations that permitted them to move from the water onto the land.

One of these adaptations was strong, lobelike fins that could be used like limbs to crawl across land. Once out of the water, another adaptation—lungs—helped these animals survive on land. Lungs allowed the organisms to exchange gases with the atmosphere. These early land-dwelling vertebrates were the first amphibians.

Look at Figure 17.2. Notice that the amphibians evolved into reptiles, and the reptiles gave rise to mammals and birds. Each of these vertebrates is classified as a separate class. There are seven classes of vertebrates because the fishes are divided into three classes.

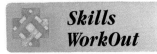

Skills WorkOut

Classify Find out the class names for the seven groups of vertebrates. Then make a poster that lists the group's name, such as mammals, next to the class name. Use old magazines to find photos of each class of vertebrates. Tape or glue your photos next to the class of vertebrate to which it belongs. Show your poster to your class.

Science and You *Fever Biology*

The temperature of your home is controlled by a mechanical device called a thermostat. You may be surprised to discover that your body also contains a type of thermostat. Unlike your home's thermostat, your body's "thermostat" is made up of living cells. The cells are located in the part of your brain called the hypothalamus (HY poh THAL uh muhs).

Like that of all endotherms, your body temperature stays about the same all the time. Most often, your "thermostat" is set at about 37°C (98.6°F). Sometimes, when you are sick, a fever may cause your body temperature to rise above 37°C. You run a fever when chemicals act on the hypothalamus to "turn up" your thermostat. Doctors and scientists are not sure what function a fever has. Some have suggested that a fever may speed up the metabolism of your body. This would allow the body to produce germ-fighting particles at a faster rate.

Check and Explain

1. What are vertebrae?

2. Which classes of vertebrates are ectothermic?

3. **Predict** If the outdoor temperature increases by 20°C, what will happen to a reptile's body temperature?

4. **Classify** Construct a diagram that shows how the following animal groups are classified: chordates, invertebrates, vertebrates, fishes, amphibians, reptiles, birds, and mammals.

Communicate Make a list of nonfishes that have fish names, such as *crayfish*. Then explain why each is not a fish.

17.2 Fishes

Objectives

▶ **Describe** the main characteristics and adaptations of fishes.

▶ **Distinguish** between the three classes of fishes.

▶ **Compare** and **contrast** the feeding methods of jawless fishes and cartilaginous fishes.

▶ **Collect data** relating to the classification of fishes.

If you have been inside a pet store, you have probably seen aquariums containing many kinds of fishes. Fishes come in many shapes, sizes, and colors. Although different kinds of fishes have different features, all fishes are adapted to life in the water. They have fins used for swimming. Most have streamlined bodies that allow them to move through the water with little resistance. What other adaptations for life in water do fishes have?

Characteristics of Fishes

Like all vertebrates, fishes have a backbone that develops from a notochord during the embryo stage. Fishes also have **gills**. Gills are organs that remove dissolved oxygen from water. The gills are located on either side of a fish's head. As a fish swims, water passes over its gills. Oxygen in the water diffuses into cells at the surface of the gills. At the same time, carbon dioxide diffuses out of blood vessels and into the passing water. Recall that all chordates have gills or gill slits at some stage of their development. Unlike most other vertebrates, fishes keep their gills throughout their lifetimes.

The 31,000 different species of fishes are grouped into three classes. Fishes in all three classes share the following characteristics:

▶ All fishes are ectotherms.

▶ Most fishes have streamlined bodies and use fins for locomotion.

▶ Most fishes have a very good sense of smell.

▶ All fishes have highly developed nervous systems.

Figure 17.3 ▲
Fishes live in rivers, streams, lakes, and the ocean. These are blue striped grunts swimming off the coast of Florida.

Jawless Fishes

The first fishes to appear on the earth were covered by thick, bony plates. Like the fishes of today, they had backbones and were considered vertebrates. However, these early fishes lacked jaws. Scientists infer that like their invertebrate ancestors, they probably were filter feeders.

A few species of fishes without jaws still exist today. They are the lampreys and the hagfish. These jawless fishes do not have the bony plates of the first fishes, but they are placed in the same class.

Lampreys and hagfish seem to have changed little since they first evolved. Unlike their more ancient relatives, however, lampreys and hagfish are not filter feeders. They are parasites. Look at the mouth of the fish shown in the upper left photograph in Figure 17.4. You can see that the mouth is a type of sucker. Lampreys and hagfish use these suckers to attach to their hosts. Once attached, these fishes rip into their host's flesh using rasp-like tongues. They then feed upon the blood and body fluids of the host.

Cartilaginous Fishes

Gently move the outer part of your ear back and forth with your fingers. Your ear holds its shape but is flexible because of a type of tissue called **cartilage** (KART uhl ihj). Cartilage is a firm but flexible connective tissue that makes up some parts of your skeleton.

Members of the second class of fishes have skeletons made up entirely of cartilage. They are called cartilaginous (KART uhl AJ uh nuhs) fishes. This group of fishes includes sharks, rays, and skates.

Unlike the jawless fishes, cartilaginous fishes have jaws. The jaws evolved from the skeletal rods that supported the gills of jawless fishes.

Most cartilaginous sharks are carnivores. Their sharp senses and sharp teeth make them well adapted for life as predators. Some of the largest sharks, however, are filter feeders. The whale shark strains water to remove the plankton it contains.

Cartilaginous fishes are more dense than ocean water, so they must keep swimming to stay above the sea floor. Swimming is also what makes a current of water pass over the gills, supplying the fish with oxygen.

Figure 17.4 ▲
The lamprey (upper left) is a jawless fish. The great white shark (lower left) and winter skate (above) are examples of cartilaginous fishes.

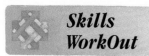
Bony Fishes

The greatest number of fish species belong to the bony fishes. The bony fishes first appeared around the same time as the cartilaginous fishes, more than 350 million years ago. As their name implies, bony fishes have skeletons made of bone. Other adaptations, too, help them live in many kinds of water habitats.

Buoyancy Control Bony fishes have an organ called a swim bladder. This organ helps them conserve energy as they swim through the water. The swim bladder is similar to a balloon.

Fishes use their swim bladders to adjust their depth in the water. Inflating the swim bladder with just the right amount of air keeps the fish from sinking to the bottom of the ocean or floating to the surface. The swim bladder, therefore, allows the fish to maintain a *buoyancy* that is just right in water.

Consider This

Should Sharks Be Protected?

Would you swim in shark-infested waters? Probably not. Sharks are often described as terrifying creatures that kill for no apparent reason. However, this reputation is not completely deserved. Although people are killed and injured by sharks, most sharks do not attack humans. In fact, it is human attacks on sharks that have scientists concerned.

Each year about 100 million sharks are killed. As a result, the population of these predators is declining. The decline of the shark population may be causing a shift in ocean food webs. This shift could be unhealthy for many kinds of ocean life.

Consider Some Issues Unlike whales, dolphins, and seals, sharks are not protected by special laws. Some people believe that sharks should be protected because they are just as important as these other animals.

Others disagree, for a variety of reasons. Some of these people fish for sharks as part of their livelihood. Others claim that sharks do more harm than good, or simply aren't worth the fuss.

Think About It Should sharks be protected? Can you think of a compromise that might make everyone happy?

Write About It Write a newspaper editorial stating your position on the protection of sharks.

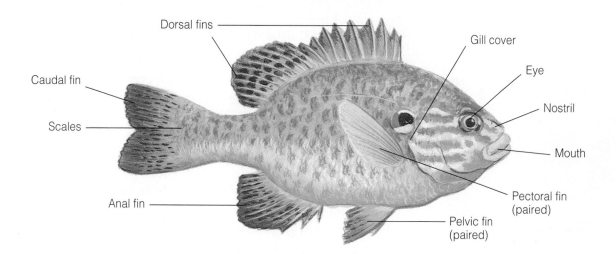

Dorsal fins

Gill cover

Eye

Caudal fin

Nostril

Scales

Mouth

Anal fin

Pectoral fin (paired)

Pelvic fin (paired)

Buoyancy is the force of fluid pushing an object up. Buoyancy acts against the weight of an object. It makes an object seem like it weighs less in a fluid. If the weight of an object under water is greater than the buoyant force, the object will sink. If the weight is less than the buoyant force, the object will rise to the surface and float. If you have been swimming, you may know what it is like to float. If the weight is equal to the buoyant force, the underwater object will stay at any level. This is what happens to a fish.

Scales and Fins The outside of a bony fish is covered with a layer of smooth scales. Notice how the scales of the fish shown in Figure 17.5 overlap each other. The scales also are covered with a thin layer of mucus. The mucus and overlapping of the scales are adaptations that help the fish move through the water with little resistance. Also notice the different kinds of fins on the bony fish. The fins are adapted for swimming and guiding the fish.

Gills and Lungs Unlike the cartilaginous fishes, bony fishes do not have to swim to move water over their gills. They can pump water through the mouth and into the gill chamber. The water is pumped by movements of a special flap of tissue in the gill chamber.

Most bony fishes depend only upon gills for their gas exchange. However, some bony fishes have both gills and lungs. The lung developed from part of the swim bladder. One of these fishes, called the African lungfish, uses its lungs to help meet its oxygen needs. When it needs to take in more oxygen, the lungfish swims to the surface of the water and "gulps" fresh air.

Figure 17.5 ▲
Bony fishes have paired and unpaired fins. A fish uses its paired pectoral and pelvic fins to steer, brake, back up, and move up and down. The caudal fin propels the fish.

Figure 17.6 ▲
The African lungfish is a bony fish that lives in shallow waters and gets most of its oxygen from the air.

Science and Society   *A Fishy Diet*

What are your ten favorite foods? If you eat such foods as hamburgers, steaks, ice cream, french fries, and eggs, you may be placing yourself at risk for heart disease. Heart disease is a condition associated with diets high in cholesterol. What causes a diet to be high in cholesterol? Cholesterol is naturally found in animal products. It is especially common in red meats, dairy products, and eggs. Diets that include these foods are high-cholesterol diets.

One group of people with diets especially high in cholesterol are Native Americans living in the Arctic. They call themselves Inuits (IHN oo wihts). The name given to them by Europeans—Eskimo—comes from a Native American term meaning "eater of raw meat." As this name suggests, Inuits eat much uncooked meat. Their diet includes very fatty meat taken from marine mammals, such as seals, walruses, and whales. The Inuits also eat sea birds and caribou.

With a diet high in fatty meats, Inuits should suffer from heart disease. However, a recent study performed on these people showed that Inuits actually have very healthy hearts. How can these findings be explained?

One explanation is that the Inuit diet also includes a large amount of fishes. Many fishes contain oil that seems to reverse the effects of cholesterol. A diet rich in fishes containing this oil may actually prevent the formation of deposits in the arteries, the cause of heart disease. The fishy diet of the Inuits seems to make them resistant to heart disease.

Figure 17.7 ▲
An Inuit man fishes through a hole in the ice. Fish is an important food in the diets of Inuits.

Check and Explain

1. List five characteristics of fishes that make them adapted to life in water.

2. Explain why a cartilaginous fish must swim constantly. What adaptations make it unnecessary for a bony fish to swim all the time?

3. **Compare and Contrast** How do jawless and cartilaginous fishes differ in their methods of feeding?

4. **Collect Data** In three columns, list the characteristics used to classify the three classes of fishes.

17.3 Amphibians

Objectives

▶ **Describe** the origin of amphibians.

▶ **Describe** the characteristics and adaptations of amphibians.

▶ **Explain** the process of metamorphosis in frogs.

▶ **Hypothesize** if an amphibian is mostly a land-dweller or water-dweller.

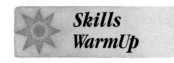
Have you ever touched a frog? If so, you may have observed that the frog felt slippery and cool. Frogs have a slick, slimy skin through which respiratory gases are exchanged. They are also ectotherms, which explains why they are cool to the touch.

Frogs are amphibians (am FIHB ee uhns). Other amphibians are toads and salamanders. Most amphibians spend part of their lives in water and part on land. A few, such as the mud puppy, spend their entire lives in water. Others, such as the brightly colored tree frogs that live in tropical rain forests, spend their entire lives as land-dwelling vertebrates.

Movement onto Land

Imagine seeing a fish crawl across the highway. In some places, such as parts of Florida, this sight is not uncommon. When ponds dry up or food sources become scarce, fishes called walking catfish drag themselves across the ground. They "walk" to new water holes.

Millions of years ago, this kind of ability to move over land for short periods of time led to the evolution of amphibians. Amphibians evolved from a group of lobe-finned fishes that are now extinct. The lobed fins of these fishes were strong and bony. As they evolved, the fins became stronger and more supportive. They made possible both swimming and a kind of crawling on land. Fossil records suggest that these fins evolved into the two pairs of legs that allow modern amphibians to live both on land and in water.

Figure 17.8 ▲
Study this frog's body. In what kind of habitat do you think it lives?

Figure 17.9

The bony fins of lobe-finned ▶ fishes evolved into the four limbs of the amphibians.

Early amphibian

Lobe-finned fishes

Characteristics of Amphibians

Look at Figure 17.9. As amphibians evolved, these four-legged vertebrates continued to adapt to a land environment. The gills and simple lungs that developed in their fishlike ancestors evolved into lungs better able to exchange gases with the atmosphere. Amphibians also began to use their skin for respiration. No longer covered by bony scales, the skin could be an extra site for gas exchange. In fact, some amphibians today lack lungs and gills and use the moist surface of their skin and mouth to meet all their respiratory needs.

Although most amphibians are adapted to life on land, they remain dependent upon water. Except for some species, such as desert toads, amphibians require moist environments. Most live in or near bodies of water, or spend much of their time in moist burrows.

Amphibians also depend on water for reproduction. Their eggs lack a protective, waterproof shell. Since the eggs can easily dry out, most amphibians must return to the water to reproduce. In most species, the female lays eggs in a pond, swamp, or stream, and they are fertilized externally by the male. A few species have evolved interesting ways of adapting to living where water is scarce. Some desert toads, for example, produce a moist foam in which they lay their eggs.

The eggs of many amphibians develop into a fishlike larva stage called a tadpole. In amphibian species where the adult remains a water-dweller, the changes from the tadpole stage to the adult stage are minor. In amphibians such as frogs and toads, the tadpole changes completely as it becomes an adult.

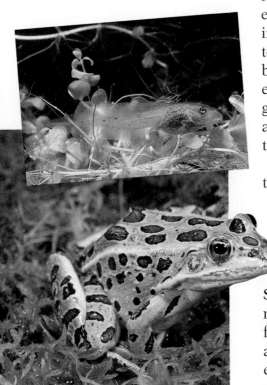

Figure 17.10 ▲
Many amphibians, such as the leopard frog (bottom), begin life as a tadpole (top).

Frogs and Toads

Amphibians are divided into several groups. One group includes frogs and toads, the two kinds of amphibians that do not have tails as adults. Most frogs spend their lives in and around water.

When frogs reproduce, the female lays hundreds of jellylike eggs. As the eggs pass out of her body, the male fertilizes them. Within several weeks, the eggs hatch into tadpoles. Tadpoles are a water-dwelling stage in amphibian development. Like fishes, tadpoles have gills, fins, tails, and a streamlined body form.

As a tadpole develops, it undergoes great changes in appearance. These changes during development make up a process called *metamorphosis*. The stages of frog metamorphosis are shown in Figure 17.12. When metamorphosis is complete, the adult frog emerges from the water as a land-dwelling vertebrate. Most toads have a similar metamorphosis. Not all frogs and toads have a tadpole stage, however. In some species, a tiny frog or toad emerges directly from the egg.

Figure 17.11 ▲
Toads spend most of their lives on land. Here, toads bury themselves in mud to keep cool.

Figure 17.12
Stages of Frog Metamorphosis

The tadpole develops front legs. The tail begins to disappear. Lungs form. The tadpole becomes an air-breathing frog.

When the young frog becomes sexually mature, it reaches the adult stage.

The tadpole develops two small limb buds. The buds grow into hind legs.

During spawning, eggs released by the female are fertilized externally by the male.

Several days after fertilization, a tadpole emerges from the egg. It has many fishlike characteristics, including gills.

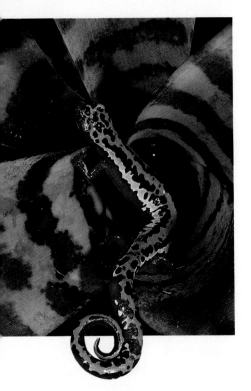

Figure 17.13 ▲
This salamander lives in a tropical rain forest.

Salamanders and Newts

Amphibians with tails make up another group that includes the salamanders and newts. Like frogs, salamanders and newts have a smooth, moist skin. Some live in relatively dry habitats similar to where toads live. Others prefer very moist places, and a few even live in water their entire lives.

Science and Society *Vanishing Amphibians*

How long does it take for an organism to become extinct? It may be faster than you think. As many as 100 species may become extinct each day.

The gastric brooding frog once lived in the rain forests of Australia. The female swallowed her eggs after they were fertilized and kept them inside her stomach until they developed into fully formed young. Until 1980, this frog appeared to be a hearty species. Then, within several months, it vanished.

Today many amphibians are faced with extinction. Biologists blame much of the threat on the destruction of habitats. The cutting down of rain forests, for example, is a major cause of amphibian extinction.

Amphibians are also especially vulnerable to chemical pollution. In Puerto Rico, three species of miniature frogs have vanished. Salamanders that once lived in the mountains of Colorado have also disappeared. Scientists think these species were victims of acid rain. Acid rain may affect amphibians more than other groups of organisms because amphibians' skin absorbs poisons as easily as it absorbs oxygen.

Check and Explain

1. From what structure of early fishes did the legs of amphibians most likely evolve?

2. List several characteristics of amphibians. For each, explain whether it is an adaptation to land or to water.

3. **Compare and Contrast** Write about how an adult frog is like a tadpole and how it is different.

4. **Hypothesize** Design a test to determine if an unknown amphibian lives mostly on land or mostly in water.

17.4 Reptiles

Objectives

▶ **Discuss** the evolutionary history of reptiles.

▶ **Describe** the characteristics and adaptations of reptiles.

▶ **Identify** the different groups of reptiles.

▶ **Make inferences** about the relationship between the body size of reptiles and the climates they live in.

Look at the lizard in Figure 17.14. Have you seen this animal before? You've probably never found one in your backyard, but you may have seen one on your television screen. Lizards similar to this marine iguana are commonly used in science fiction movies to represent prehistoric dinosaurs.

Lizards actually are related to the extinct dinosaurs. Both are vertebrates with scaly skin adapted to life on land. But unlike dinosaurs, lizards are living today all over the earth. Together with snakes, turtles, tortoises, alligators, and crocodiles, they make up the reptiles.

History of Reptiles

Scientists can learn many things about extinct animals by studying their fossil remains. For example, scientists can infer the kind of food an animal ate by the shape of its teeth. The length and thickness of leg bones are clues about the body size of an animal. Even footprints can provide clues about an animal's movement and behavior. Using such evidence, scientists have assembled a history of reptiles. This history began when reptiles' amphibianlike ancestors developed adaptations for living their entire lives on land.

These adaptations included a body covering that reduced water loss and eggs that could be laid on land. About 300 million years ago, these adaptations appeared in a group of ancestral reptiles. These early reptiles evolved in many different directions. One path of their evolution resulted in the dinosaurs. But even before the dinosaurs evolved, the ancestors of modern turtles, lizards, and snakes had appeared.

Figure 17.14 ▲
The marine iguana is a harmless vegetarian.

Figure 17.15 ▲
Dinosaurs and modern reptiles share a common ancestor.

Characteristics of Reptiles

Because of the way snakes move, many people expect them to be slimy and slippery. However, if you touch a snake, you discover that the animal is not slimy at all. Unlike amphibians, whose outer skin *is* slimy, snakes and other reptiles have a dry, waterproof body covering made up of scales. This covering helps these land-dwellers conserve water. Scales also prevent the exchange of oxygen and carbon dioxide across the skin. Reptiles must therefore rely on their lungs to meet their respiratory needs.

Unlike amphibians, reptiles produce eggs that are covered by a tough, leathery shell. The shell prevents moisture from escaping, but it also keeps sperm from entering. For this reason, fertilization takes place inside the body of the female, before the eggshell develops.

Reptiles have circulatory systems more highly developed than those of amphibians. Like those of amphibians, their hearts are three-chambered. But a partial wall inside the main chamber lessens the mixing of low-oxygen blood and high-oxygen blood. The result is a heart that works nearly as well as the four-chambered hearts of birds and mammals.

Even though reptiles are ectotherms, most are very good at regulating their internal temperatures. They bask in the sun when the air is too cool and seek shade when it is too hot. Through these behavioral adaptations, many reptiles keep their body temperatures about as warm as yours throughout much of the day.

Skills WorkOut

Research Use the resources of a school or public library to make a list of local amphibians and reptiles and their habitats.

Lizards and Snakes

They may look very different, but lizards and snakes are closely related. All snakes and most lizards are carnivores. Both have a type of jaw hinge not found in other reptiles. It allows lizards and snakes to swallow their prey whole by increasing the size of their mouths.

The main difference between lizards and snakes is that snakes don't have legs. Snakes have developed ways of moving about without appendages. But some snakes still have hipbones and remnants of hind legs. These are signs that they evolved from reptiles that did have legs.

Snakes have very poor hearing and most have poor eyesight. They do, however, have keen senses of smell and taste. Snakes use their tongues to find prey and to gather other information about the environment. A snake sticks out its tongue to sample the air or the ground. The tip of the tongue picks up chemicals. The snake then places its tongue into an organ in the roof of its mouth. This sense organ detects the odors in the air or on the ground.

Turtles and Tortoises

Members of another group of reptiles all have shells. They are the turtles and tortoises (TOR tuh suhs). These reptiles have hardly changed since they appeared hundreds of millions of years ago. Their shells have proved to be important adaptations. When in danger, most turtles and tortoises can pull their heads, legs, and tails into their shells.

The shells of turtles and tortoises form from bony plates connected to their ribs and vertebrae. The shell is covered by a layer of skin. The skin is responsible for the markings and color patterns on the shell.

Turtles and tortoises differ in the structures of their shells. Most turtles have flat, streamlined shells. Tortoises have dome-shaped shells. Turtles and tortoises also live in different environments. Tortoises are land animals. Most turtles live in ponds, lakes, rivers, or the ocean. Turtles that spend most of their lives in water must return to land to lay their eggs.

◄ **Figure 17.16**
What main characteristic distinguishes snakes from lizards? Why is the shell an important adaptation for the turtle?

Alligators and Crocodiles

Among the reptiles, the closest living relatives of the dinosaurs are the alligators and crocodiles. They are lizardlike in shape and can grow as long as a small boat. Their backs have large, deep scales.

Alligators and crocodiles are very similar in appearance. However, they can be distinguished by the shapes of their heads. Crocodiles have a narrow head with a triangle-shaped snout. Alligators have a broad head with a rounded snout.

Both alligators and crocodiles live in tropical areas and spend most of their time in the water. Alligators live mostly in North America and Asia. Crocodiles inhabit areas of tropical America, Africa, Asia, and Australia.

Unlike most other reptiles, alligators care for their young. The female guards her eggs, and after they hatch, both male and female protect the babies.

Figure 17.17 ▲
Both alligators (top) and crocodiles (bottom) live in the Everglades region of Florida.

Career Corner Pet Store Owner

Who Takes Care of All Those Pet Store Animals?

Imagine caring for 125 birds, 30 hamsters, 22 mice, 4 snakes, 25 dogs, 12 cats, and more than 1,000 tropical fish! For a pet store owner or manager, this is a typical everyday responsibility.

If you like animals, you might like working in a pet store. Pet store workers must make sure that every animal remains healthy. This means feeding the animals daily and keeping their cages and tanks clean. A pet store worker must also watch for sick or injured animals. The sooner an unhealthy animal is treated, the better its chances for recovery.

In order to tell customers how to care for their pets, pet store workers must also learn about each kind of animal. They need to be able to give advice about feeding, living quarters, treatment of diseases, and breeding. They should know what kinds of fish can live in the same tank together. A pet store worker must also be familiar with the supplies and equipment stocked by the store.

Much of this information can be learned on the job. You can also learn about the care of animals by reading books. Classes in biology at any level are very helpful.

With experience, you could take on the responsibility of managing a pet store. This includes buying and selling products, paying employees, and making sure the animals are cared for. After a while, you could be on your way to owning your own pet store!

Science and You *Know Your Fangs!*

Most snakes are quite harmless to humans. But several snakes are poisonous. Their poison, called venom, can be deadly. You should know what snakes in your area are poisonous, or venomous, and what kind of habitats they live in.

If you are bitten by a snake, the first thing to do is find out if the snake is venomous. You can often tell whether a bite was made by a venomous snake by observing the shape of the wound. Non-venomous snakes have tiny teeth set in both the upper and lower jaws. When a non-venomous snake bites, it leaves an almost circular mark formed from the impressions of a complete set of teeth.

Most venomous snakes leave a different kind of bite mark. It is made of two small skin punctures. The punctures are from a set of two long, sharp, hollow fangs. As the snake bites, a poison produced by a special gland flows through the hollow fangs into the wounds.

If you have any reason to believe that you were bitten by a venomous snake, you must get medical attention as soon as possible. If more than one kind of venomous snake lives in the area, the doctor will want to know what kind of snake it was. Here is a situation in which your scientific skill of observation may even save your life. You should be able to describe the snake in enough detail for it to be identified. Some snakes have venom that affects the blood cells. The venom of other snakes targets the nerve cells. The doctor must know the species of snake in order to use the correct method of treatment.

Figure 17.18 ▲
This eastern diamondback rattlesnake is being "milked" to make an anti-venom serum. You can see the venom dripping out of its fangs.

Check and Explain

1. Why is it inaccurate to say that reptiles evolved from dinosaurs?

2. Identify the characteristics of reptiles that make them suited to life on land.

3. **Classify** Explain the similarities and differences among the three groups of reptiles.

4. **Infer** The largest reptiles all live in areas where it is warm year-round. Based on what you know about reptiles, suggest a reason why this is so.

Activity 17 What changes occur during metamorphosis?

Skills Measure; Observe; Infer

Task 1 Prelab Prep
Collect the following item: a metric ruler.

Task 2 Data Record
On a separate sheet of paper, copy Table 17.1. Make four rows, one for each drawing below.

Task 3 Procedure
1. Look at the drawings of the tadpoles and frogs shown on this page. In your data table, measure and record the animal's length and width for each stage of metamorphosis shown.
2. Identify the drawing in which the frog's hind legs first appear. Measure and record the length of a hind leg in the drawing. Repeat this step for the other drawings.
3. Identify the drawing in which the frog's front legs first appear. Then measure and record the length of a front leg. Repeat this step for each of the remaining drawings.
4. In drawings 1, 2, and 3, measure and record the length of the animal's tail section. Make your measurement from where the hind legs begin to the tip of the tail.

Task 4 Analysis
1. Make a line graph that illustrates the relationship between the length of the animal and its age. Make a similar graph for tail length.
2. Why is the tail so much longer in drawing number one?
3. In which stage might the lungs first appear?

What information did you use to make this inference?
4. How does the development of the hind legs differ from the development of the front legs?
5. Tell what environment each organism lives in.

Task 5 Conclusion
Write a short paragraph explaining the changes that occur as a tadpole undergoes metamorphosis and develops into an adult frog. Include how these changes enable the frog to adapt to land.

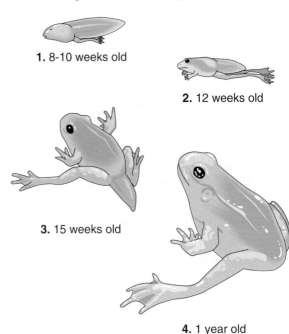

1. 8-10 weeks old

2. 12 weeks old

3. 15 weeks old

4. 1 year old

Extension
Compare and contrast the metamorphosis of frogs with the evolution of land-dwelling amphibians from fish ancestors.

Table 17.1 Frog and Tadpole Measurements

Drawing Number	Age	Body Length	Body Width	Tail Length	Hind Leg Length	Front Leg Length

Chapter 17 Review

Concept Summary

17.1 Common Traits of Vertebrates

▶ All vertebrates belong to the phylum Chordata and have endoskeletons.

▶ Some vertebrates are endotherms and others are ectotherms.

▶ The first vertebrates were fishlike animals. Amphibians evolved into reptiles, and reptiles gave rise to mammals and birds.

17.2 Fishes

▶ Most fishes have streamlined bodies, fins, a good sense of smell, and complex nervous systems. They are

▶ ectotherms.
Fishes are divided into three classes:

▶ jawless, cartilaginous, and bony. The greatest number of fish species belongs to the bony fishes. All bony fishes have scales and swim bladders. Swim bladders help them conserve energy in the water.

17.3 Amphibians

▶ Amphibians were the first vertebrates to live on land.

▶ Most amphibians are dependent upon water.

▶ Many amphibians begin life as water-dwelling tadpoles and become land-dwelling vertebrates through metamorphosis.

17.4 Reptiles

▶ Reptiles are adapted to living their entire lives on land.

▶ Reptiles have dry, waterproof, scaly bodies. They produce eggs with a leathery coating.

▶ The main difference between snakes and lizards is that snakes do not have legs.

▶ The shells of the turtle and tortoise are important adaptations for protection.

Chapter Vocabulary

endoskeleton (17.1)   ectotherm (17.1)   gill (17.2)   cartilage (17.2)
endotherm (17.1)

Check Your Vocabulary

Use the vocabulary words above to complete the following sentences correctly.

1. Animals with constant internal body temperatures are called _____ .

2. Some parts of your skeleton are made of _____ , a firm, flexible connective tissue.

3. The central part of the _____ is the backbone.

4. Animals with bodies that receive heat from the outside are called _____ .

5. Organs that remove dissolved oxygen from water are called _____ .

Explain the difference between the words in each pair.

6. Endoskeleton, exoskeleton

7. Gill, lung

8. Ectotherm, amphibian

9. Endotherm, endoskeleton

10. Cartilage, vertebrae

11. Vertebrate, chordate

Write Your Vocabulary

Write sentences using each vocabulary word above. Show that you know what each word means.

Chapter 17 Review

Check Your Knowledge

Answer the following in complete sentences.

1. What are animals with backbones called? Give some examples.

2. How can you tell the difference between a crocodile and an alligator?

3. How are lizards like dinosaurs? How are they different?

4. Describe two characteristics of bony fishes. When did they first appear on the earth?

5. When did the first vertebrates appear on the earth? Where did the first vertebrates live, and what did they look like?

6. How is a tadpole different from a frog? Name two differences. How is a tadpole like a fish? Name two similarities.

7. Which amphibians have tails? Describe one characteristic of this group.

8. What kind of shell covers reptile eggs? What is one advantage of this type of egg covering?

9. Why do reptiles bask in the sun when the air is cool and seek shade when it is hot?

Choose the answer that best completes each sentence.

10. All fishes have a very good sense of (sight, hearing, balance, smell).

11. A newt is a type of (reptile, amphibian, mammal, plant).

12. Most cartilaginous fishes swim constantly to (stay warm, find food, move water across their gills, stay awake).

13. There is a total of (seven, five, four, six) classes of vertebrates.

Check Your Understanding

Apply the concepts you have learned to answer each question.

1. Describe one difference and one similarity between snakes and lizards.

2. How does a snake use its tongue? Describe the process and two uses.

3. What is a common nickname for ectotherms? Why do you think they are called this?

4. **Mystery Photo** The photograph on page 344 shows the eye and part of the head of a chameleon. Chameleons are able to change colors, primarily to camouflage themselves. When you look at the photograph, how do you know that the subject is a reptile? Is the chameleon slimy? Why or why not?

5. **Extension** If you read a story about an alligator attacking a human in an African river, would you believe it? Why or why not?

6. What are some of the fossil clues scientists have used to learn about the history of reptiles? Give two examples. What inferences are made from these clues?

7. **Compare and Contrast** What characteristics do tortoises and turtles have in common? How do they differ?

8. Which fishes are included in the cartilaginous group?

9. **Infer** Some salamanders have no lungs and use only their skin for gas exchange. How large do you think these lungless salamanders are, compared to other amphibians? Why?

Develop Your Skills

Use the skills you have developed in this chapter to complete each activity.

1. **Interpret Data** The graph below shows the body temperature of a lizard over a 24-hour period.

   a. How cold does the lizard's body get? How warm?

   b. What happened in the lizard's environment at the time labeled A? What happened at B.

   c. What do you think the lizard was doing between time A and time B?

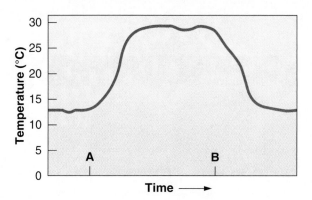

2. **Hypothesize** When frogs reproduce, the female lays hundreds of jellylike eggs. Why do you think a single frog lays hundred of eggs?

3. **Data Bank** Use the information on page 631 to answer the following questions.

   a. What is the longest reptile? How long is it?

   b. Which is longer, the rattlesnake or the giant tortoise?

4. **Communicate** Make a poster that shows examples from each of the seven classes of vertebrates. You should include one of each of the fish classes.

Make Connections

1. **Link the Concepts** Below is a concept map showing how some of the main concepts in this chapter link together. Only part of the map is filled in. Finish the map, using words and ideas you find in the chapter.

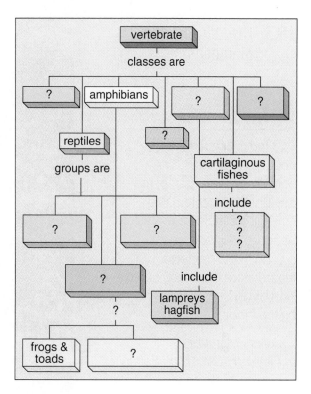

2. **Science and PE** How does a reptile move? How about an amphibian, or a fish? Practice moving as if you were a reptile, then an amphibian, then a fish. Use the information from the chapter, as well as your imagination.

3. **Science and Society** Crocodiles and alligators are often portrayed as villains in popular culture. Find examples of alligators and crocodiles in movies, comic strips, television, or books. Investigate how the alligator or crocodile is portrayed. Write a report on your findings. Include at least two examples.

Chapter 18 Birds and Mammals

What do you see?

66 It looks like a male peacock's feathers. The purple spots are part of the design to attract females. I think it's a male peacock, because they are more colorful while the female feathers are plain. You can kind of tell they're feathers by the fringed edges. 99

Julie Motomura
Fleming Junior High School
Lomita, California

To find out more about the photograph, look on page 386. As you read this chapter, you will learn about birds and different types of mammals.

18.1 Birds

Objectives

▶ **Describe** the main characteristics of birds.

▶ **Explain** how birds are adapted for flight.

▶ **Interpret** how the shape of a bird's wings helps a bird fly.

▶ **Compare** and **contrast** bird reproduction and reptile reproduction.

▶ **Make inferences** about a bird's diet and lifestyle by observing its beak, wings, and feet.

Skills WarmUp

Infer   You have seen birds in many places. You have probably watched them fly, look for food, and interact with each other. Based on what you have observed, describe birds as living organisms.

Have you ever dreamed you could fly? Imagine that you could soar over hills and valleys and flap across town to drop in on a friend. Write down what it would be like.

For most birds, flight isn't just a dream but an everyday event. As fliers, birds can easily escape enemies and cover large areas in their search for food. They can move over great distances to find good places to live. For these reasons, birds have been able to make many kinds of habitats home. As you will find out, most of what makes birds unique has to do with flying.

Characteristics of Birds

Like reptiles, fishes, and amphibians, birds are vertebrates. But birds are different from these other vertebrates in an important way. They are endotherms, organisms that have a constant internal body temperature. Reptiles and amphibians obtain heat from their external environment. When it is cold out, they are sluggish. Birds, however, can be active no matter what the temperature of their environment. The cells of their bodies stay warm and can work normally all the time.

All birds share certain other characteristics, too. You can probably guess what most of them are. Birds are the only group of animals to have feathers. They have beaks instead of teeth. Although not all birds can fly, all birds have wings. And, like reptiles, birds lay eggs with shells. How do you think each of these characteristics relates to a bird's ability to fly?

Figure 18.1 ▲
How are birds' bodies designed for flight?

Skills WorkOut

Research Find out more about *Archaeopteryx*. What dinosaurs lived during the same period? How was it similar to a dinosaur? How did it probably catch its prey? How well did it fly? Find out why scientists debate whether or not *Archaeopteryx* was truly a bird.

Origin of Birds

One day in 1861, a man in Europe split apart two layers of rock in a quarry. Inside he found the fossil imprint of an amazing organism. Like a reptile, it had scales, jaws with teeth, and claws on its front limbs. But also visible in the stone was the unmistakable imprint of feathers. The 150-million-year-old fossil was an ancient bird! Scientists called it *Archaeopteryx* (AR kee OP tur ihks).

The fossil of *Archaeopteryx* was convincing evidence that birds evolved from a reptile ancestor. Since then, other evidence has been collected to back up this conclusion. But scientists still don't know the exact evolutionary relationship between reptiles and birds. They know that feathers evolved from reptile scales, but they don't know why. There had to be some in-between animal that couldn't fly but that could take advantage of having feathers. Perhaps the first birds were fast runners who used their feathered wings to catch insects.

Historical Notebook

Exposing the Silent Truth

In the 1950s, an ecologist named Rachel Carson began to notice a spooky quietness around her home. She wondered why she heard so few bird songs. Puzzled, she began to do research to explain the "spring without voices."

In 1962, she published *Silent Spring*, a book that offered a reason for the decrease in the numbers of birds. She argued that when farmers used pesticides such as DDT, they destroyed more than just crop-threatening insects.

Other scientists agreed that DDT was harming organisms throughout the entire food web, including birds. One problem was that DDT killed the insects that many birds relied upon for food. But this chemical also caused the eggshells of many birds to become too thin. When the eggs were incubated, the shells broke.

Silent Spring had a tremendous impact. In 1972 Congress passed laws prohibiting use of DDT in

the United States. But many dangers to birds still exist. DDT is used in countries where many birds migrate in winter. Other pesticides affect the food web, too. Birds are also threatened by the destruction of their habitats.

1. What did Carson argue in *Silent Spring*?

2. **Research** Find out what is being done in your area to protect birds.

Diversity of Birds

There are almost 9,000 species of birds. They are often grouped into four main types: birds of prey, perching birds, water birds, and flightless birds. Even within a group, birds have an amazing variety of shapes and sizes. Each bird is adapted to eating a certain kind of food and living in a certain kind of habitat. A bird's lifestyle is reflected in its beak, wings, and feet.

Birds of Prey ▲

Birds of prey eat mammals, fish, and other birds. They have sharp, hooked beaks good for tearing flesh, and claws made for grasping. Birds of prey include eagles, hawks, owls, falcons, and vultures. This osprey lives near the ocean and eats fish.

Water Birds

Water birds have a variety of beaks, wings, and feet. Many have webbed feet for swimming. Other water birds, like this flamingo, have long legs for wading. Some have long wings they can use to fly great distances. ▼

Flightless Birds ▲

Flightless birds have lost the ability to fly. They have lifestyles that make flight unnecessary. Many flightless birds, such as this rhea, have become fast runners.

Seed Eaters

Other perching birds are seed eaters. Seed-eating birds like this cardinal have thick, strong beaks for cracking open seeds. ▼

◄ **Perching Birds**

Many of the perching birds are insect eaters. They have long, pointed beaks that work like tweezers. The beaks of woodpeckers are used as drills for boring into wood to find insects. Swifts have wings that let them fly fast and turn quickly in pursuit of flying insects.

Adaptations for Flight

Like airplanes, birds must be streamlined to fly. Their bones must be lightweight. In addition, they must use large amounts of energy, just as an airplane uses fuel. A bird's body releases the energy stored in food quickly and efficiently. Its cells do this work at a much faster rate than the cells of reptiles and amphibians. In the process, they create more heat. The extra heat produced by cells rapidly burning fuel is what makes birds endotherms. Adaptations for low weight and high activity are present in all parts of a bird's body.

Vision
As fliers, birds must rely on their sense of sight to avoid flying into things and to see food from far away. Most birds have large eyes and very sharp vision.

Bones
The skeletons of most vertebrates living on land are heavy. If birds had heavy bones, they couldn't fly. To save as much weight as possible, bird bones are hollow. Inside they have thin cross-supports for added strength.

Muscles
Moving wings fast and hard enough to overcome gravity takes great muscular effort. Birds have powerful flight muscles attached to a large breastbone.

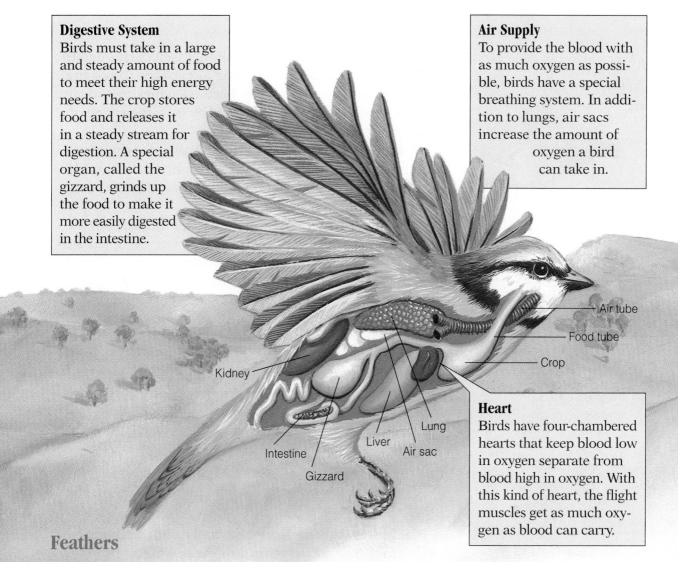

Digestive System
Birds must take in a large and steady amount of food to meet their high energy needs. The crop stores food and releases it in a steady stream for digestion. A special organ, called the gizzard, grinds up the food to make it more easily digested in the intestine.

Air Supply
To provide the blood with as much oxygen as possible, birds have a special breathing system. In addition to lungs, air sacs increase the amount of oxygen a bird can take in.

Air tube

Food tube

Crop

Kidney

Intestine

Liver

Gizzard

Lung

Air sac

Heart
Birds have four-chambered hearts that keep blood low in oxygen separate from blood high in oxygen. With this kind of heart, the flight muscles get as much oxygen as blood can carry.

Feathers

Feathers are perhaps a bird's most important adaptation. Without feathers birds could not fly no matter how light their bodies. In Figure 18.2 you can see a feather called a contour feather. A contour feather is both strong and light. These feathers together make up most of a bird's wings and tail, the most important structures in flying. Shorter contour feathers cover a bird's body, making it streamlined. Contour feathers have many rows of interlocking barbs. These barbs are what make a feather strong and firm.

Under the contour feathers and next to a bird's body are down feathers, also shown in Figure 18.2. The fluffiness of down feathers traps a layer of air next to the body. This layer of air prevents heat loss. Birds could not be endotherms without the insulation provided by down feathers.

Figure 18.2
How does the structure of each kind of feather match its function? ▼

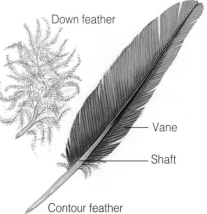

Down feather

Vane

Shaft

Contour feather

Figure 18.3 ▲

The wings of birds and airplanes both make use of the same physical principle to provide lift.

Physics of Flight

Birds use their wings to push themselves through the air. But if birds relied on flapping alone, they would tire quickly. Flying is made easier because wings provide lift, even without being flapped. The key is in the shape of the wing.

You may have noticed that an airplane's wings are not flat. The upper surface is rounded. Look at Figure 18.3 to see the shape of an airplane wing. Notice how it is similar to the shape of a bird's wing.

When a wing with this shape moves through air, the air has a longer way to go around the curved upper surface than it does across the flat bottom surface. The air above the wing must move faster to cover this longer distance in the same amount of time. This difference in air speed above and below the wing creates a difference in air pressure. The pressure under the wing is higher. So there is more force pushing up, under the wing, than there is force pushing down, on top of the wing. The result is lift. The larger the wing, the greater the lift. Birds with large wings can soar and glide for a very long time. Once they are airborne, they can cover great distances without flapping.

Migration

In places where winters are cold, many animals face a shortage of food for part of the year. Plants stop growing. Insects and other invertebrates die or bury themselves. Some animals deal with the shortage of food by becoming inactive, or hibernating. Birds, however, can go somewhere else to find food.

Taking advantage of their ability to fly, many birds **migrate**, or move to a different place during part of every year. Some birds in the northern hemisphere, for example, fly south to warmer places for the winter months.

When migrating, many birds travel along certain flying routes. Many of these routes follow coastlines, sea currents, wind currents, or land contours.

Some migrating birds travel distances that are hard to imagine. The short-tailed shearwater flies up to 32 000 km every year, circling the Pacific Ocean. The arctic tern enjoys the endless days of arctic summers, then flies all the way to Antarctica in time for summer!

Skills WorkOut

Make Models Experiment with making different types of paper airplanes. Which design will glide the longest distance? In what ways is a paper airplane like a bird? In what ways is it different?

Reproduction of Birds

Birds reproduce much like their distant relatives, the reptiles. The male passes sperm to the female, and the eggs are fertilized inside her body. Shells form around the eggs. Then the female moves the eggs outside her body for the embryos to develop.

Unlike reptiles, however, birds have eggs that must stay warm while the embryos develop. Birds must therefore **incubate** their eggs, or use their body heat to keep the eggs warm. The need to incubate their eggs causes birds to have reproductive behavior different from that of reptiles.

Incubation can't be interrupted for long. How does one bird incubate its eggs and find food at the same time? In some species of birds, the male and female take turns sitting on the eggs. In other species, one of the parents sits on the eggs and the other finds food for both of them. Either kind of cooperation requires an attachment, called a pair-bond, between male and female. Not all birds have pair-bonds.

Figure 18.4 ▲
Many birds build nests in trees to protect the eggs from predators.

To help keep the eggs warm and protected, birds build nests. In contrast, most reptiles bury their eggs in soil. The nests of many kinds of birds are very complex structures. Look at the nest in Figure 18.4. How long do you think it took to build? In many species, nestmaking is shared by males and females. This is another reason for pair-bonding.

How do you think bird eggs and reptile eggs differ? Bird eggs have a hard shell compared to the leathery shell of reptile eggs. The hard shell keeps the embryo from being crushed during incubation.

Look at the bird egg in Figure 18.5. Along with the embryo, a bird egg contains yolk and albumen. The albumen is the "white" of the egg. Both yolk and albumen provide food for the embryo.

At the end of the incubation period, the chick breaks open the shell. The chicks of some species are fully developed when they hatch. They are ready to move and find food. In other species, the chicks are blind, helpless, and almost featherless. They must be fed and taken care of by one or both parents before they are ready to be on their own.

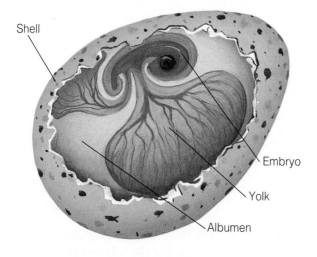

Shell

Embryo

Yolk

Albumen

Figure 18.5 ▲
A bird egg supports a growing embryo.

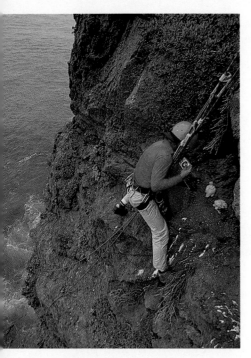

Figure 18.6 ▲

A peregrine chick is returned to its nest after being hatched in the laboratory.

Science and Society *Back from the Brink?*

The peregrine falcon was once common throughout North America. But by 1970, only two nesting pairs were counted in California. In 1978, no nesting pairs could be found in the eastern United States. The main reason for the decline was the presence of DDT in the food chain. Peregrines ate other birds with DDT in their bodies. As a result, peregrines produced eggs with shells so thin they broke when incubated.

Now peregrine falcons are on the increase. Banning DDT in the United States has helped. But peregrines still pick up DDT because they eat birds that winter in countries where DDT is still used. So for peregrines to reproduce, scientists have had to help them.

Scientists help the birds by taking peregrine eggs from the nest just after they are laid. The eggs are then incubated in a laboratory so they will hatch even if the shells are thin. Then comes the task of returning the birds to the wild. One method is to place peregrine chicks into the nests of the more common prairie falcon, who raise the foster peregrine chicks as their own.

Another successful method is bringing the chicks back to the same nest they came from. This can be done if "dummy" eggs are left in place of the real eggs. The parents continue to incubate and will accept the chicks when they are returned to the nest.

As a result of these methods, peregrines are making a comeback. But they are far from being out of danger. Many peregrine embryos die in the egg, poisoned by other chemicals present in the environment.

Check and Explain

1. Describe three adaptations that help a bird fly.

2. Why do the wings of both birds and airplanes provide lift when passing through air?

3. **Compare and Contrast** How is reproduction in birds and reptiles the same? What are the differences?

4. **Infer** A certain bird wades in marshes hunting fish. It travels long distances between the places it feeds. Describe what this bird might look like, including its wings, beak, legs, and feet.

Activity 18 *How do contour and down feathers compare?*

Skills Observe; Infer; Hypothesize

Task 1 Prelab Prep
Collect the following items: a contour feather, a down feather, unlined paper, a microscope.

Task 2 Data Record
Record your observations of feathers on the unlined paper. Write a note about each characteristic. Make drawings to illustrate what you see.

Task 3 Procedure
1. Examine a contour feather. In one hand, hold the base of the central shaft where it was attached to the bird. Gently bend the tip of the feather with your other hand. Now, hold the shaft with one hand and wave the feather through the air. How strong is the feather? Record your observations on your paper.
2. Look at the shape of the feather. How long is it? Is it curved or straight? Is one side wider than the other side? Record your observations.
3. Examine the structure of the feather. Is the feather solid or does it come apart? Hold the tip of the feather with one hand and run the fingers of the other hand down toward the base. What happens? Now that you have "unzipped" the feather, can you "zip" it back together? What different parts does a feather seem to be made of? Make a close-up drawing of the feather's structure on your paper.
4. Now examine a down feather. Do you see a difference in the shape, size, and structure of the down feather compared with the contour feather? Record your observations.
5. Examine a contour feather under the low-power setting of the microscope. Note the individual barbs that are attached to one another. Draw what you see.
6. Examine a down feather under the low-power setting of the microscope. Are the individual barbs attached or separate from one another? Draw what you see.

Task 4 Analysis
1. How do the barbs of a contour feather seem to be attached to one another? How does this method of attachment make the feather strong?
2. **Infer** Suggest a reason why the barbs of a down feather do not fit together like the barbs that attach themselves together in the contour feather.
3. How is the structure of a contour feather related to its function? How is the structure of a down feather related to its function?
4. **Hypothesize** Based on your observations of its size and shape, hypothesize where on the bird the contour feather came from. Explain the reasons for your guess.

Task 5 Conclusion
Complete your examination of bird feathers by summarizing what you have learned in a short paragraph. Be sure to compare and contrast contour feathers and down feathers.

Everyday Application

What kind of clothes are best for keeping warm? How could you dress to copy the way a bird insulates itself with down feathers?

Extension

Find out about other feathers on a bird's body and how they contribute to a bird's flying abilities. Research the following kinds of feathers, all of which are used by pigeons when they fly: coverts, outer flight feathers, inner flight feathers, tail feathers. Make a table listing these feathers and their functions. Include contour feathers.

If you can, observe a bird for a short time. Watch the bird as it preens. What is it doing to its feathers? Why is preening necessary?

Compare and Contrast
Think of one mammal you know
well, like a dog or cat. Then think
of one kind of reptile. Write all
that you know about each animal.
Then compare one with the other.

18.2 Mammals

Objectives

▶ **Describe** the characteristics of mammals.

▶ **Explain** how mammals differ from other animal groups.

▶ **Compare** and **contrast** mammals and birds.

▶ **Infer** what kinds of teeth various mammals have.

L ook closely at the surface of your forearm. What do
you see? The little hairs poking out of your skin are
a characteristic shared by none of the animals you
have studied so far. Only one group of animals has hair.
They—and you—are the mammals.

Like birds, mammals are vertebrates and endotherms.
They also have four-chambered hearts. What sets the
mammals apart are their hair and their mammary glands.
Mammary glands, active only in female mammals, produce milk to feed offspring. The milk is a balanced diet of
fats, sugars, protein, minerals, and vitamins.

Origin of Mammals

Mammals evolved from ancient reptiles, just as the
birds did. The early mammals and the early birds were
both endotherms, adapted for a more active life than
their reptile ancestors. Otherwise, the first mammals
were very different from the first birds. While birds
evolved feathers as a body covering, mammals developed
hair. Birds evolved wings from their front limbs.
The limbs of mammals, in contrast, became more
efficient at moving on land or in trees.

The earliest mammals lived during the age of
dinosaurs. Fossils show that they were probably
no bigger than rats and similar to rats in appearance. They were very likely active at night, hiding
from meat-eating dinosaurs by day. When the
dinosaurs died out, however, mammals began to
evolve rapidly. In taking the place of the dinosaurs,
they developed a variety of shapes, sizes, and lifestyles.
After a while mammals came to live in nearly every
habitat on the earth.

Figure 18.7 ▲
The first mammals were small
and probably ate insects.

Characteristics of Mammals

The ability to maintain a constant internal temperature is a major reason why mammals have been so successful. In addition, mammals have several other characteristics different from those of birds, the other group of endotherms.

Hair and Skin   All mammals have hair at some time in their lives. For many mammals, hair insulates the body, preventing heat loss. For others, however, hair is not important. Adult dolphins, for example, have no hair at all. They rely instead on a layer of fat under the skin to keep in body heat.

Skin is also an important insulator for land mammals that live in cold environments, such as polar bears. In addition to their heavy coats, polar bears have a thick layer of skin that keeps their bodies from losing heat. For mammals living in warm environments, the ability to sweat is an important adaptation. Sweat evaporates from their bodies, keeping them cool.

Many mammals run on land using all four limbs. This cheetah can reach speeds of almost 90 km per hour. ▼

Teeth   Mammals have three different kinds of teeth: incisors, canines, and molars. Incisors are chisel-shaped teeth that are used for cutting and gnawing. Canines are long, pointed teeth that can stab prey and tear flesh. Molars are broad, flat teeth that are good for grinding food. The kinds of teeth a mammal has depends on the food it eats. Some mammals with a varied diet have all three kinds of teeth and can handle any kind of food.

Movement   Mammals are active animals. They move to find food and escape enemies. All mammals, except dolphins and whales, have two pairs of limbs they use to move. The structure of these limbs, however, varies considerably. Depending on the species, they can be adapted for running, swimming, climbing, or flying. Some mammals, such as rabbits, move by hopping.

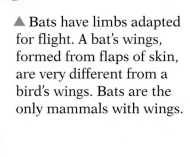

▲ Bats have limbs adapted for flight. A bat's wings, formed from flaps of skin, are very different from a bird's wings. Bats are the only mammals with wings.

◀ Dolphins are among the mammals with limbs adapted for swimming. They have adapted so completely to life in the ocean that they can't move at all on land.

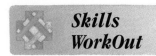
Body Systems

Like birds, mammals have organ systems adapted for an active life. The four-chambered heart transports oxygen to body cells more efficiently than the simpler hearts of reptiles, amphibians, and fishes.

A mammal's lungs are made up of millions of tiny sacs. These sacs greatly increase the surface area of lung tissue in contact with air. As a result, the lungs can transfer more oxygen into the blood. Another adaptation for breathing is a muscle in the chest called the diaphragm (DY uh FRAM). The diaphragm expands and contracts the chest cavity, causing the lungs to draw in air.

Mammals also have complex nervous systems. Their brains are large, especially the part called the **cerebrum** (SUR uh bruhm). The cerebrum is where the higher brain functions occur. With their large cerebrums, mammals are able to perform complex behaviors such as learning. Some mammals also have well-developed senses.

Consider This

Should Products Be Tested on Animals?

For many years, scientists and doctors have used animals to help them develop new products and inventions. They test drugs and cosmetics on animals to see if these substances have harmful side effects. They inject disease-causing microorganisms into rats to help find ways of controlling infections in humans. They try out new kinds of surgery on monkeys.

To develop many of the drugs and inventions that save human lives today, many animals were killed or made to endure pain. Each year, between 17 and 22 million animals are used for testing or experimentation.

Consider Some Issues
Opponents of animal research say that too many animals are killed or injured. They believe people do not have the right to harm animals, regardless of the benefit to humans.

Scientists, however, claim that animal research is necessary for testing medicines and discovering cures that help sick people and save lives. They say that animals in labs are treated as humanely as possible.

Think About It Is it right to kill animals for human benefit? Or, on the other hand, is it right to put limits on what can be done to save human lives?

Write About It Write a paper stating your position on animal experimentation.

Science and Society
Saving Endangered Mammals

In the last few hundred years, humans have drastically changed the face of the earth. In the process, people have killed off many species. At least 36 species of mammals have become extinct in the last 400 years.

But today there are at least three times as many mammal species threatened with extinction. They are called endangered species. Endangered mammals include the African elephant and the blue whale. Many endangered mammals have simply been hunted so heavily there are few left. Others are in danger because their habitats have been destroyed.

Many people around the world are trying to prevent endangered species, especially mammals, from becoming extinct. This work is going on in many different areas.

Scientific research is often an important part of saving a species. Scientists try to find out, for example, what the species needs to increase in number. Another part of saving a species involves protecting the places it lives. Parks, wildlife refuges, and reserves are set aside as places where the animal can live and reproduce.

To protect species that are hunted for certain products, laws are made to ban the hunting of the animal or the buying and selling of any of its parts. It is against the law, for example, to buy or sell elephant tusks.

Some endangered species would probably not survive on their own in nature, even with protection. The only way to prevent these species from becoming extinct is to breed them in captivity.

Figure 18.8 ▲
The black-footed ferret (top), snow leopard (middle), and Florida manatee (bottom) are all endangered mammals.

Check and Explain

1. How do mammals with little or no hair stay warm?

2. Name and describe two characteristics unique to mammals.

3. **Compare and Contrast** Explain how mammals and birds are similar and different.

4. **Infer** Write down the kinds of teeth you think each of the following mammals has and why: giraffe, beaver, horse, human, elephant, mouse, lion, goat, and dog.

Skills WarmUp

Classify Write the names of all the mammals you can think of. Then classify them into different groups based on common features or behaviors. Choose any classification system you wish.

18.3 Diversity of Mammals

Objectives

▶ **Distinguish** between egg-laying, pouched, and placental mammals.

▶ **Infer** why most egg-laying and pouched mammals live in one part of the world.

▶ **Classify** the major orders of placental mammals and give examples of each.

If you've been to a zoo, then you've seen many of the different kinds of mammals that live on the earth. Elephants, giraffes, lions, zebras, monkeys, and anteaters make up a very diverse bunch. But common zoo animals don't cover all the major mammal groups. Most zoos don't have bats or shrews, few have koalas or duck-billed platypuses, and hardly any have whales. And don't forget more common mammals like dogs, mice, rabbits, goats, and cows!

Life scientists begin to make sense of this diversity by separating two kinds of mammals from all the rest. These two groups, the egg-laying mammals and the pouched mammals, reproduce very differently from most other mammals.

Egg-Laying Mammals

As you probably know, most mammals give birth to live young. Living in Australia and New Guinea, however, are mammals that lay eggs. They are the duck-billed platypus and two species of spiny anteater. These egg-laying mammals are called **monotremes** (MAHN oh TREEMZ).

Monotremes have the two unique mammal characteristics: hair and mammary glands. Their eggs are soft-shelled and hatch after ten days. When the young emerge, they are fed milk. The milk comes from glands on the mother's belly. Since the glands have no special opening, the milk seeps out and the baby sucks it off of the mother's fur. Spiny anteaters nurse their young for up to six months.

Figure 18.9 ▲
This monotreme is a short-nosed spiny anteater from Australia.

Pouched Mammals

The other group of mammals with unusual reproduction is called **marsupials** (mar SOO pee uhlz). Marsupials are mammals with pouches in which the young complete their development. You have probably heard of two marsupials, the koala and the kangaroo. They both live in Australia. Another marsupial, the opossum, is common throughout North America. About 80 species of marsupials live in South America, including the rat opossum.

Marsupial eggs are fertilized inside the female's body and begin their development there. The embryos grow inside an organ called the uterus (YOOT ur uhs). They are nourished by a limited food supply that was part of the egg. When that food supply is used up, the young are born while still embryos. The tiny, blind babies then crawl into the mother's pouch. Each finds a nipple, where milk comes out of a mammary gland, and begins to suckle. The babies stay in the pouch for one to two months, until their development is complete.

Placental Mammals

Most mammals neither lay eggs nor have pouches. Their young complete their development inside the uterus. There, an embryo receives nutrients and oxygen from the mother's body through an organ called the **placenta** (pluh SEHN tuh). The placenta also takes away waste products and carbon dioxide from the embryo. Thus the placenta provides for all the embryo's needs during the entire time it is developing. Mammals with placentas are called **placental mammals**.

The length of time an embryo develops inside its mother varies, depending on the kind of placental mammal. Mice have a short, 21-day period of development. Humans are born after 9 months of growth inside the uterus. Elephants take 22 months before they are born.

After they give birth, placental mammals spend more time caring for their young than do other animals. Cnidarians, for example, release many eggs and sperm into the ocean. Placental mammals care for their young until they can be on their own. However, the degree of parental care varies. An elephant invests more time and energy into raising each offspring than a rabbit does.

Figure 18.10 ▲
What is the function of this western gray kangaroo's pouch?

Diversity of Placental Mammals

Scientists classify placental mammals into nearly 20 large groups called orders. The mammals in each order share certain important characteristics and adaptations. Here are some of the orders of placental mammals.

Carnivora ▲

As you might guess from the name, these mammals are carnivores, or meat eaters. They have teeth adapted for tearing flesh, clawed toes, and a well-developed brain. This group includes not only dogs, cats, wolves, and bears, but also seals, otters, and walruses.

Insectivora

Moles and shrews belong to this group of insect-eating mammals. Most have long skulls, narrow snouts, five-clawed feet, and are smaller than 46 cm. Their bodies, habits, and diet are similar to those of the first ancient mammals. ▼

Rodentia ▲

Rodents make up the largest order of mammals. They have chisel-like front teeth adapted for gnawing. Rodents include squirrels, beavers, rats, mice, porcupines, and gophers.

Proboscidea

This order is named for the long, muscular trunks of its members, the elephants. Elephants have extra-long teeth called tusks. ▼

Cetacea ▲

Whales and dolphins belong to this group of mammals that live in the ocean. They have evolved fishlike bodies with fins and paddle-like front limbs.

Primates ▲

Mammals placed in this order have thumbs adapted for grasping objects. Their eyes face forward and they eat both plants and animals. Monkeys and apes are members of this group. What other common mammal belongs to the primates?

Chiroptera ▲

Bats, the mammals adapted for flight, make up this order. Their wings are flaps of skin stretched between their bodies and their long fingers. Bats are active mainly at night.

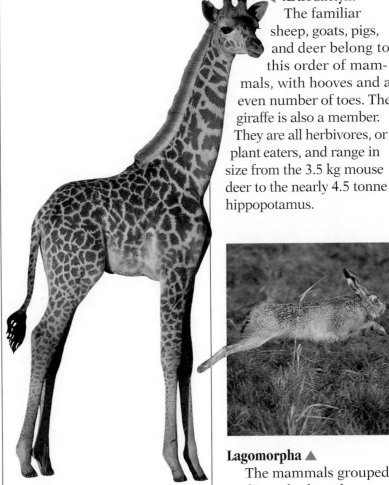

◄ Artiodactyla

The familiar sheep, goats, pigs, and deer belong to this order of mammals, with hooves and an even number of toes. The giraffe is also a member. They are all herbivores, or plant eaters, and range in size from the 3.5 kg mouse deer to the nearly 4.5 tonne hippopotamus.

Lagomorpha ▲

The mammals grouped in this order have long rear limbs adapted for jumping. They include rabbits and hares.

Perissodactyla ▶

Like sheep and goats, the mammals in this group have hooves and are plant eaters. But instead of having an even number of toes on each foot, they have an odd number. This order includes horses, zebras, and rhinoceroses. They have large, flat teeth used for grinding their food.

Figure 18.11 ▲

Humans and dogs are both mammals, but what makes you different?

Science and You *Humans as Mammals*

You are a mammal. You therefore share many characteristics with dogs, cats, rabbits, goats, even whales and moles. Your hair is one obvious sign of your membership in the mammal group. You don't call it fur, but it is present all over your body. You wear clothes and live in shelters to stay warm, but your internal body temperature is constant.

If you think about it, many mammals can do things better than humans can. For example, cheetahs can run much faster. Dolphins can swim much faster. Whales can hold their breath much longer. Dogs have a better sense of smell. Cats can see better in the dark. Monkeys are better tree climbers. Tigers have longer teeth.

What can humans claim to be the best at? As a species, humans are not specialized. Instead, humans are fairly good at many things. Not many mammals can run fairly fast *and* swim *and* climb trees *and* jump. Not many other mammals can eat and survive on so many different kinds of food. Few mammals can live in every environment from the arctic to the tropics.

Humans also rely on two important characteristics: a hand that can grasp and a brain that can think and reason. Monkeys and apes, too, have grasping hands and well-developed brains. That is why humans, apes, and monkeys are all primates. But humans alone have put brain and hand together to make many things. Humans have built cities and invented computers. Humans use written language. The ability to create makes you a very different kind of mammal indeed.

Check and Explain

1. Name two species of pouched mammals.

2. How are placental mammals different from egg-laying and pouched mammals?

3. **Infer** Find Australia and New Guinea on a map. Why do you think most egg-laying and pouched mammals live only in this part of the world?

4. **Classify** For each of the following mammals, name the order to which it belongs, and give one characteristic: mouse, tiger, giraffe, elephant, dolphin.

Chapter 18 Review

Concept Summary

18.1 Birds
▶ Birds are endothermic vertebrates. They all have beaks, feathers, wings, and lay eggs with shells.
▶ Birds must incubate their eggs to keep them warm. They build nests to protect the eggs.
▶ Birds have special adaptations for flight, including special vision, bones, muscles, and body systems.
▶ Bird wings are shaped to create lift in flying.
▶ Many birds migrate to different places during part of every year. Many birds travel along certain routes.

18.2 Mammals
▶ Mammals are active endotherms with hair, mammary glands, and specialized teeth.

▶ Mammals move in different ways because the structure of their limbs varies. However, most mammals use two pairs of limbs to move.
▶ Mammals have a four-chambered heart, a diaphragm, and a complex nervous system.

18.3 Diversity of Mammals
▶ Two types of mammals, egg-laying and pouched mammals, reproduce differently than most other mammals.
▶ Most mammals are placental mammals. Scientists classify placental mammals into nearly 20 different orders.
▶ Placental mammals have a placenta that allows the embryo to be nourished while it is developing. The mother's blood supply provides the nourishment.

Chapter Vocabulary

migrate (18.1)   cerebrum (18.2)   marsupial (18.3)   placental mammal (18.3)

incubate (18.1)   monotreme (18.3)   placenta (18.3)

Check Your Vocabulary

Use the vocabulary words above to complete the following sentences correctly.

1. Egg-laying mammals, such as spiny anteaters or the duck-billed platypus, are called _____ .
2. An embryo receives nutrients and oxygen from the mother's body through an organ called the _____ .
3. Many birds _____ , or move to a different place during part of every year.
4. Mammals with pouches in which the young complete their development are called _____ .
5. Mammals with placentas are called _____ .

6. The largest part of a mammal's brain is called the _____ .
7. Birds _____ their eggs, using their bodies to keep the eggs warm.

Explain the difference between the words in each pair.

8. Placenta, uterus
9. Monotreme, marsupial
10. Migrate, fly

Write Your Vocabulary

Write sentences using each vocabulary word above. Show that you know what each word means.

Chapter 18 Review

Check Your Knowledge

Answer the following in complete sentences.

1. Describe two methods by which birds are able to incubate their eggs and find food at the same time.

2. List three characteristics that have helped mammals adapt to a variety of environments.

3. Describe the three ways in which mammals reproduce.

4. Describe the difference between bird eggs and reptile eggs. What is the reason for this difference?

5. Name the three different types of teeth that mammals have. What are the uses of each type of tooth?

6. List two examples of marsupials. Where do they live?

7. Name three mammal orders and give an example of an animal from each.

8. What are the four main types of birds? Do all the birds of one general type look the same?

Choose the answer that best completes each sentence.

9. The fossil of (*Archimedes, Chioptera, Archaeopteryx, Artiodactyla*) was convincing evidence that birds evolved from a reptile ancestor.

10. The extra heat produced by cells rapidly burning fuel for energy is what makes birds (endotherms, exotherms, exotic, extroverted).

11. The embryo in a bird egg gets food from the (placenta, albumen, eggshell, feathers).

Check Your Understanding

Apply the concepts you have learned to answer each question.

1. Do all mammals have hair? Describe the main function of hair.

2. When did the earliest mammals live? What did they look like?

3. **Mystery Photo** The photograph on page 366 shows the feathers of a male Asian pheasant, a relative of the peacock. The male uses the feathers for courtship displays. You may notice in the photograph that the spots of the feathers look like eyes. This may also confuse predators. Sometimes a male and female bird work together to incubate their eggs, and form an attachment. What is this relationship called? What is another function of that type of relationship?

4. Explain why birds must eat large and steady quantities of food.

5. **Application** How do flightless birds survive without flying? Give an example.

6. How does a bird get an adequate air supply?

7. What happens at the end of the incubation period? Are newborn chicks fully developed?

8. **Extension** Both bats and birds can fly. What are two differences between bats and birds?

9. **Infer** There are a few species of birds that are flightless. They include the kiwi, emu, penguin, and ostrich. Describe why being flightless is not a disadvantage to these birds. How do you think the birds adapt to being flightless?

Develop Your Skills

Use the skills you have developed in this chapter to complete each activity.

1. **Interpret Data** The figure below shows the tracks of a hopping bird and a walking bird.

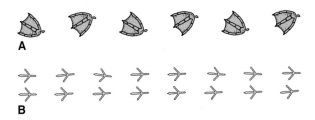

A

B

a. One bird is larger than the other. Guess which is larger, and then infer the relationship between size and type of movement.

b. How can you tell that the hopping tracks are from hopping rather than walking?

c. Were the hopping tracks made by a bird of prey, a perching bird, or a water bird? How about the walking tracks?

2. **Data Bank** Use the information on page 630 to answer the following questions.

a. When did the first flying animals appear? What were they?

b. How long ago did the first humans evolve?

c. How long ago did the first birds evolve? What were the dominant animals at that time?

3. **Communicate** Make a poster to show the characteristics of mammals. Choose one mammal, then illustrate and label the major characteristics.

Make Connections

1. **Link the Concepts** Draw a concept map showing how the concepts below link together. Add terms to connect, or link, the concepts.

birds	fly
endotherms	energy
adaptations	feathers
hollow bones	heat loss
wings	air sacs
	sharp vision

2. **Science and Social Studies** Most states have a state bird. Research the state bird for your state. Where does it live? Why do you think it is the bird chosen to represent your state?

3. **Science and Society** Humans have domesticated many other mammals as pets and to use their labor. Choose a pet or a work animal and find out when it was first domesticated and by whom.

4. **Science and You** Of the millions of species of birds and mammals in the world, you have probably seen only a few. Find out about an animal you have never seen. Write a report on how it is adapted to its habitat, and draw a picture of it.

5. **Science and Writing** Many stories have been written about humans and their relationships with animals. For example, in *Julie of the Wolves*, by Jean Craighead George, Julie is saved and protected by a pack of wolves. Write your own adventure story in which a person has a special relationship with an animal or group of animals. You can either be the main character in the story or narrate the story. Present the story to your class.

Science and Literature Connection

Yosaku marched up and down the neat rows of radishes and cabbages and beans. He was proud as a warrior inspecting his soldiers. . . .

Between two cabbage stalks stretched a spider-web, and in the center sat a handsome spider. Its body, dark as polished teak, was striped with gray that shone like silver in the sunlight.

"Greetings," said Yosaku politely. "You honor me by visiting my garden." He stepped back, so as not to disturb his guest. His heel struck something much too soft for a cabbage, far too thick for a bean.

"Sssssss!" A huge and ugly snake slipped over his sandal.

"*Ara!*" exclaimed Yosaku, waving his hoe.

The snake's tongue darted in and out of its mouth, its bright, cold eye fixed upon the spider. The spider froze, as if tied in its own ropes.

"Off with your head!" Yosaku shouted at the snake.

But as he brought down his hoe, the handle caught and ripped the full sleeve of his *kimono*. Yosaku missed, and the snake slithered away. The spider ran down from its web and disappeared among the cabbages.

Yosaku looked at his torn sleeve. The *kimono* was beyond mending and he had no other, for Yosaku was poor. "Just so!" he said, but sadly now, and went home to his bowl of rice and bed-mat.

That night Yosaku slept soundly until the Hour of the Ox, when a tiny voice, calling from the courtyard, awakened him.

"Mr. Yosaku!"

"Eh?" mumbled Yosaku. Perhaps his

"The Cloud Spinner"

The following Japanese folktale is adapted from the story "The Spider Weaver" *in* Japanese Children's Favorite Stories

ears were playing tricks.

"Honorable Mr. Yosaku!" Yosaku tied his old *kimono* tight and padded to the door. There stood a young girl. Her robe was of rich black silk stitched with rows of silver thread. Yosaku blinked. Perhaps his eyes tricked him, too.

The girl bowed low. "You are in need of new *kimono*?"

Yosaku stared down on the girl's dark glossy head. She reminded him of something, but he was too sleepy to remember what. "So I am," he answered.

She looked up at him and smiled shyly. "If you will allow, I would be pleased to weave new cloth for *kimono*."

Yosaku, astounded by such a grand offering, slid the door wide. "You are welcome in my house."

He offered tea to the girl, but she refused and went directly to the weaving room. . . . Yosaku went back to sleep on his mat again, and soon was snoring to the rhythm of the loom. When he awoke in the morning, there were seven new *kimono*, neatly laid out next to his mat.

Yosaku rubbed his eyes. "How can this be?" He ran to the weaving room. "Already you made new *kimono* for every day of the week!"

"Do not question, Honorable Yosaku." The girl looked modestly down at her hands. "And please do not come into this room while I work."

Yosaku bobbed his head. "It shall be as you wish," he agreed. . . .

Yosaku asked nothing, not even the girl's name, but his curiosity was growing even greater than the stack of *kimono* in his cupboard. So, at the week's end, he tip-toed to the window of the weaving room. Slowly, softly he slid back the ricepaper screen. In the center of the room sat his visitor at the newly strung loom. Only it was not the young girl. It was a giant spider!

"Aaaah!" Yosaku clapped his hand over his mouth. . . .

She was swallowing great mouthfuls of cotton and spinning it out as finished thread.

No wonder the girl was not hungry!

Yosaku watched as all eight of the spider's legs, working together, wove the thread into cloth. . . .

Yosaku crept away from the window. He had come close to spoiling the spider-girl's secret. But he had an idea of his own.

Skills in Science

Reading Skills in Science

1. **Evaluate Sources** This folktale contains scientific accuracies as well as inaccuracies. Identify three of each.

2. **Predict** During the course of the tale, the reader is given clues regarding the identity of the girl. Reread the selection and identify these clues.

Writing Skills in Science

1. **Predict** Write an ending to the tale describing Yosaku's idea and what happens when he carries it out.

2. **Accurate Observations** At one point Yosaku interferes in the natural relationship between two organisms. Identify Yosaku's action. What might have occurred had he not interfered?

Activities

Classify List the physical traits of the spider in this tale. Use your list and reference tools to identify a particular species to which the spider might belong.

Communicate In a library, research types of spider webs and the reasons for the differences in structure. Use string or yarn to create a model of one type of web.

Where to Read More

Someone Saw a Spider by Shirley Climo. New York: Crowell, 1985. Contains the complete text of "The Cloud Spinner" and other spider facts and folktales.

Shelf Pets: How to Take Care of Small Wild Animals by Edward Ricciuti. New York: Harper and Row, 1971. Details how to care for wild animals that are appropriate to keep as pets.

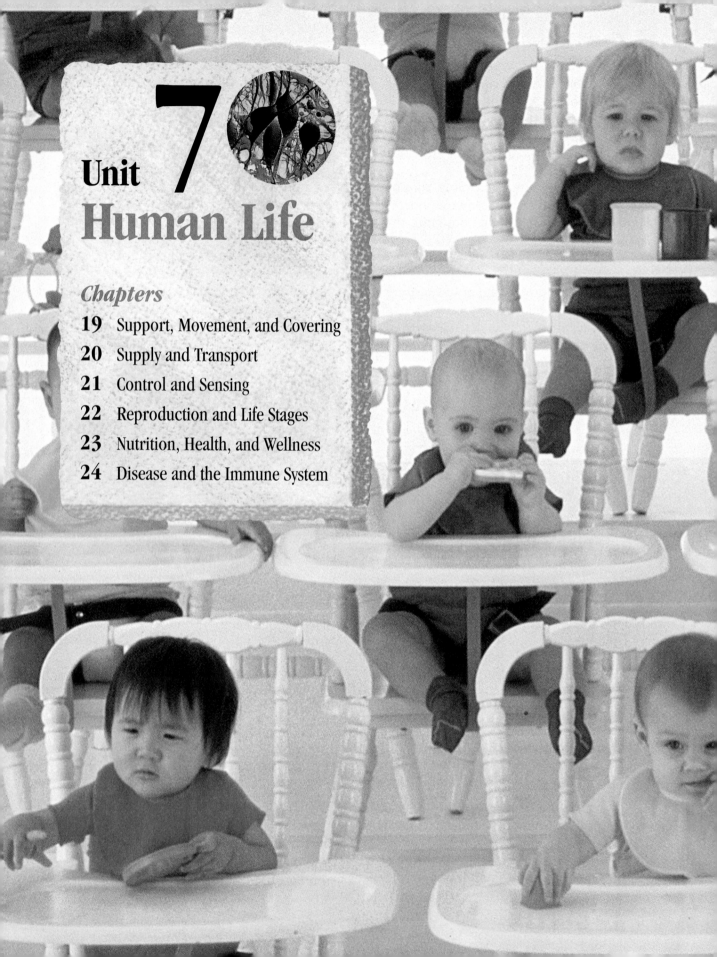

Unit 7

Human Life

Data Bank

Use the information on pages 624 to 631 to answer the following questions about topics explored in this unit.

Classifying

How many bones are in the human torso? List some of the major bones that you think are part of the torso.

Interpreting Data

What are some of the risk factors for skin cancer? What warning signals are associated with detecting skin cancer?

Reading a Table

How many red blood cells are contained in the amount of blood shown on the table? How many white blood cells are contained in the same amount of blood?

Approximately how old do you think the infants are in the photograph to the left? Do you think they can feed themselves at this stage?

Chapter **19**

Support, Movement, and Covering

What do you see?

❝I see a knee joint. I use it to run and to walk. Without it I couldn't do a lot of things like sports and stuff. On the knee joint is the patella, or kneecap.**❞**

Kai Bates
Hilsman Middle School
Athens, Georgia

To find out about the photograph, look on page 412. As you read this chapter, you will learn about systems that support and protect your body and allow for movement.

19.1 Skeletal System

Objectives

▶ **Name** and **classify** some bones in the skeleton.

▶ **Describe** the structure of a typical long bone.

▶ **Write** in your own words the functions of the bones and the skeleton.

▶ **Identify** and **compare** the different types of joints and the movements they allow.

▶ **Make analogies** between parts of the skeletal system and everyday things.

Can you imagine yourself without any bones? Just as the girders and beams are a building's framework, the human skeleton is the body's framework. Your bones—about 206 of them—make up this framework. The girders and beams of a building also support and give shape to a building. Your skeletal system also supports and gives shape to your body.

Unlike many organisms, such as insects, your skeleton is inside your body. An internal skeletal system is an **endoskeleton** (EHN doh SKEHL uh tuhn). All vertebrates have an endoskeleton. Insects and some other animals, such as lobsters and crabs, have exoskeletons (EHKS oh SKEHL uh tuhn). An exoskeleton is on the outside of the body.

When describing the skeleton, you can say that it is made up of two parts. One part called the axial (AK see uhl) skeleton is made of the bones of your skull, ribs, and the small bones, or **vertebrae** (VUR tuh BREE), in your backbone. Look at Figure 19.1. Notice all the vertebrae of the backbone. As an infant, your backbone had 33 separate bones. As you got older, nine bones grew together, or fused, to form larger bones. The other 24 vertebrae have remained as separate bones.

 The other part of the skeleton is called the appendicular (AP uhn DIHK yuh luhr) skeleton. It includes all the bones attached to the axial skeleton. These bones make up the appendages: your arms and legs. Your collarbones, hipbones, and shoulder bones are also part of the appendicular skeleton.

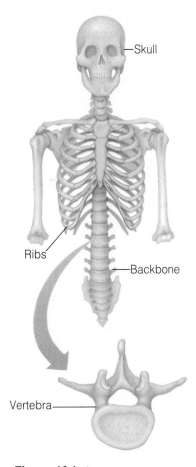

Skull

Ribs

Backbone

Vertebra

Figure 19.1 ▲
The bones of the axial skeleton are shown. The backbone is part of the axial skeleton.

Bones

The figure below shows some of the bones in the human skeleton. Notice that the bones have different shapes. There are four main types of bones: flat, long, short, and irregular. The shape of a bone is related to its function. Many of these bones have the same name, shape, and function as the bones of other vertebrates.

Flat Bones

The ribs, breastbone, and shoulder bones are flat bones. They protect and support body organs. ▶ For example, your ribs protect your lungs.

Long Bones

The arms and legs are long bones. These bones are strong, hollow, and light. They support weight and are used for ▶ movement. Your leg bones, for example, act like the pillars of a building. They support you when you stand.

Short Bones

There are short bones in the feet. These bones support weight and allow for ▶ many small movements.

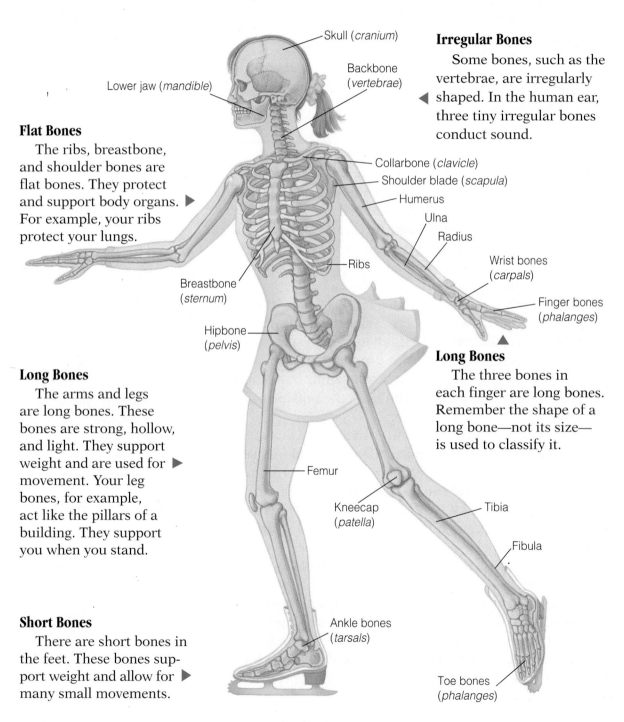

Skull (*cranium*)
Backbone (*vertebrae*)
Lower jaw (*mandible*)
Collarbone (*clavicle*)
Shoulder blade (*scapula*)
Humerus
Ulna
Radius
Wrist bones (*carpals*)
Ribs
Finger bones (*phalanges*)
Breastbone (*sternum*)
Hipbone (*pelvis*)
Femur
Kneecap (*patella*)
Tibia
Fibula
Ankle bones (*tarsals*)
Toe bones (*phalanges*)

Irregular Bones

Some bones, such as the vertebrae, are irregularly ◀ shaped. In the human ear, three tiny irregular bones conduct sound.

Long Bones

The three bones in each finger are long bones. Remember the shape of a long bone—not its size—is used to classify it.

Structure of Bones   All bones are made of living bone cells surrounded by nonliving materials. These nonliving materials are protein and minerals, such as calcium and phosphorus. Protein gives bones their flexibility. The minerals calcium and phosphorus give bones their strength and hardness.

The structure of a long bone, such as the femur, is a good bone to take a close look at. Look at Figure 19.3. Notice that the bone has a long shaft and two large knoblike ends.

Think of the shaft as a cardboard tube. The shaft is made up of mostly compact bone surrounding a hollow cavity or space. Compact bone is dense and looks smooth. It helps bones withstand bangs and bumps. The cavity of the shaft contains yellow marrow. Yellow marrow is a soft tissue that contains fat.

Although the compact bone in the shaft looks solid, under a microscope you would see tiny passageways called the Haversian (huh VUR zhuhn) canals. These canals run throughout the shaft. They contain nerves and blood vessels. The blood vessels carry food and oxygen to the living bone cells and carry away wastes.

The shaft of a long bone is covered with a tough, white membrane called the periosteum (pehr ee AHS tee uhm). It is made up of connective tissue and bone-forming cells. Blood vessels in the periosteum carry oxygen and food. Nerve fibers are also present in the periosteum.

The knoblike ends of the long bone contain spongy bone. Spongy bone is softer and lighter in weight than compact bone. As you might infer from its name, spongy bone also has a lot of open spaces and holes in it. Spongy bone contains red marrow, which is where blood cells are made.

Figure 19.2 ▲

The small dark ovals are bone cells. Each cell is surrounded by larger circles of nonliving materials. What two minerals make up most of bone?

Figure 19.3

The femur is the longest bone in the human body.

▼

Periosteum

Compact bone

Central Haversian canal for nerves and blood vessels

Spongy bone

Artery

Shaft

Hollow cavity containing yellow marrow

Spongy bone

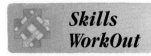
Calculate and Observe

Count as many bones and joints as you can in each hand. Then look at Figure 19.4 (right). Count the number of bones and joints in the adult hand. Compare your findings.

Functions of Bones   What are the functions of the bones that make up the skeletal system? With the muscle and skin systems, the skeletal system gives the body shape and support. In addition to providing shape and support, bones also have other important functions.

▶ Many bones protect your body organs. For example, the vertebrae protect the spinal cord, and the ribs protect your lungs.

▶ Many bones work with certain muscles to move the body and its parts. As a result, you can run, walk, grasp, and breathe.

▶ Most blood cells are made in the red marrow of certain bones.

▶ Bones store fat and minerals. Fat is stored in yellow marrow. Minerals, such as calcium and phosphorus, are stored in the bone itself. When the minerals are needed by the body, they are released into the blood and carried to all parts of the body.

Cartilage

Besides bone, the skeletal system has a tissue called **cartilage** (KART uhl ihj). This strong, flexible tissue gives shape to some parts of your body. For example, your ears and the tip of your nose are made of cartilage. If you bend your ears with your fingers, you can see how flexible and strong cartilage is. Cartilage also covers the ends of some bones or makes up disks between vertebrae. Cartilage keeps bones from grinding against each other. Between the vertebrae, cartilage disks act as shock absorbers. If you have ever injured your knee or suffered the pain of a "slipped disk" in your spine, you can appreciate the function of cartilage.

Bones usually develop from cartilage. Before birth, the skeleton is made mostly of cartilage. The cartilage has a covering that contains bone-forming cells. After birth, these cells begin to absorb calcium that is dissolved in the blood. The bone-forming cells change the dissolved calcium into calcium compounds that cannot dissolve in the blood. These calcium compounds are deposited in the cartilage, causing it to harden and become bone. The process of bone formation is called ossification (AHS uh fih KAY shuhn). Your bones lengthen

◀ **Figure 19.4**
The X-rays show the hands of a baby (left) and an adult (right). Notice that in the baby's wrist, the cartilage has not been replaced completely by bone.

until all cartilage is ossified. Ossification begins after birth and continues for about 20 years. It stops when you are between 18 and 25 years old.

Dairy products, such as milk and cheese, are rich in calcium and phosphorus. You have probably heard someone say, "Drink your milk; it's good for you." Why do you think someone would say this?

Skeletal Connections

Almost every bone in the human body forms a **joint** with at least one other bone. A joint is where two or more parts meet. The 206 bones of your body need to be held together in some way. At some joints, the bones are fused together, such as the flat bones that form the skull. In other joints, however, several bones meet but are not fused together. These joints, such as the joints at your knees and your elbows, allow you to move. The bones in these joints are connected by **ligaments**. Ligaments are connective tissues that can stretch. Bones and ligaments make up most of the skeletal system.

For the human body to move, muscles and bones need to work together. So, the muscles need to be connected to bones. Muscles are connected to bones by connective tissues called **tendons**.

Figure 19.5 ▲
Notice that three leg bones and the kneecap are at the knee joint. The bursa is a fluid-filled sac that helps cushion bones, preventing the ends of the bones from wearing down. What three leg bones meet at the knee joint?

Joints

There are many joints in the skeletal system. The large number of joints enables the human body to move in many different and graceful ways. Without all these joints, you would move like a robot.

At some joints, there is no movement. These are immovable joints. In adults, the joints between the flat bones of the skull are immovable joints. In a newborn baby, the joints in the skull are movable.

As the child grows, the skull bones fuse.

Some joints allow a little movement. The joints between your vertebrae are slightly-movable joints. Slightly-movable joints allow some bending and twisting movements in all directions. Most immovable and slightly-movable joints are in the axial skeleton.

Most joints are freely-movable joints. These joints allow large movements, and most of them are in the appendicular skeleton.

Ball-and-Socket Joints

A ball-and-socket joint allows movement in all directions. The antenna on a portable radio is attached to the radio with a ball-and-socket joint. You can move the antenna any way you want. A ball-and-socket joint connects your shoulder and your upper arm. These joints permit you to swing your arms in a circle.

▼

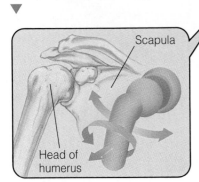

Scapula

Head of humerus

◄ Pivotal Joints

Nod your head. Then turn your head from side to side. The skull is joined to the first vertebra of your backbone by a pivotal joint. Pivotal joints allow two kinds of movement—side-to-side and up-and-down.

First vertebra of backbone

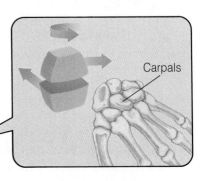

Carpals

▲

Gliding Joints

Your wrist has many gliding joints. If you move your wrist in as many ways as you can, you will notice there is some movement in all directions. In gliding joints, the bones slide along each other. The vertebrae in your backbone are also connected by gliding joints.

Hinge Joints

Bend your arm at the ▶ elbow. There is a hinge joint there—just like the hinge on a door. A hinge joint allows bones to move backward and forward in only one direction.

Humerus

Radius

Ulna

Science and Technology
Fiber Optics! Television! Surgery!

Imagine a surgeon performing knee surgery through a tiny incision, or cut, in your knee. With advances in medicine and fiber optics technology, many joint operations are performed just this way. It is called arthroscopic (AR throh SKAHP ihk) surgery.

Arthroscopic surgery is usually performed on knee, shoulder, elbow, and hip joints. Many athletes have arthroscopic surgery to help prolong their sports careers. The technique uses a straight, tubelike instrument called an arthroscope. It contains lenses and bundles of optical fibers. The lenses magnify, and the optical fibers transmit light.

During arthroscopic surgery, the arthroscope is put into a small incision. The surgeon can look through the arthroscope and see what the problem is. An image is also transmitted to a television monitor. Through a second incision, the surgeon can correct the problem by using special small instruments. The image on the monitor helps surgeons see what they are doing.

Because the incisions are so small, there is little tissue damage and little discomfort. Therefore, people heal quickly, and often can be released from the hospital on the same day as their surgery.

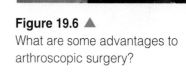

Figure 19.6 ▲
What are some advantages to arthroscopic surgery?

Check and Explain

1. Look at the skeleton on page 394. What are the scientific names for the breastbone, hipbone, wrist bones, and upper arm bone? Classify each bone.

2. Describe how each freely-movable joint moves.

3. **Infer** How is the shaft of a long bone related to the function of the bone?

4. **Make Analogies** Match the everyday object to the part of the skeleton that shows the best analogy. Explain your choices.

   a. Skull   Door hinge
   b. Any bone   Elastic band
   c. Ligament   A broken and glued together cup
   d. Knee joint   A storage warehouse

Activity 19   *What gives a bone its hardness and flexibility?*

Skills   Observe; Predict; Interpret Data; Infer

Task 1   Prelab Prep

1. Collect the following items: 1 chicken bone, 1 small beef bone, 2 cups, a hand lens, vinegar, a metric ruler, and a balance.
2. In Task 3, you will need to gather a variety of art materials to make a model. You may wish to gather toothpicks, glue, drawing paper, pens, pencils, or clay.

Task 2   Data Record

1. Discuss with several other classmates the different observations that you can make about each bone, such as color, size, shape and so on.
2. Identify a way to organize the observations. You may want to use a table, a list, a chart, or some other way.
3. Make as many observations as you can about each bone. Record your observations in the table or chart.

Task 3   Illustrate by Modeling

1. Make a model of each bone you observed. You may draw pictures, use clay, papier-mâché, sticks, toothpicks, or any other material suitable for making models. Be sure to label the parts of each bone model.
2. Study the bones carefully and decide whether each bone is a long, flat, irregular, or short bone. *Hint:* The beef bone may be part of a larger bone.
3. Can you name the bones? If so, record their names.

Task 4   Procedure

1. Place the chicken bone into one cup. Place the beef bone into the other cup.
2. Pour enough vinegar into each cup to cover the bone.

3. Set the two cups in a place where they will not be disturbed for two days.
4. **Predict**   Acids interact with calcium compounds. Predict what you think will happen to each bone.
5. After two days, remove the bones from the vinegar. Be sure to rinse each bone thoroughly with water.
6. Examine each bone carefully. Make as many observations as you can about each one after it was in the vinegar. Record all your observations in your table or chart.

Task 5   Analysis

1. a. Is vinegar an acid? If so, how do you know?
   b. **Name**   If vinegar is an acid, use reference books to identify the acid of vinegar.
2. What happened to each bone when it was left in the vinegar for two days?
3. **Infer**   What substance was removed from the bones? How do you know?
4. **Infer**   What substance remains in the bones? How do you know?

Task 6   Conclusion

1. Write a short paragraph explaining how the chemical makeup of a bone is related to its strength and flexibility. Be sure to describe how the bones changed.
2. **Infer**   You have worked with the bones of two vertebrates, a chicken and a cow. What can you infer about the chemical makeup of the bones of other vertebrates, including human bones?

Everyday Application

Your teeth are covered with enamel. Acids can erode enamel; however, enamel is resistant to vinegar. The acid content of a cola drink is much greater than the acid content of vinegar. What do you think might happen to your teeth if you drink a lot of cola drinks?

19.2 The Muscular System

Objectives

▶ **State** the main function of the muscular system.

▶ **Compare** the three types of muscles.

▶ **Describe** how muscles work in pairs.

▶ **Identify** three lever systems in the body.

▶ **Classify** the type of muscle in different parts of the body.

Skills WarmUp

Apply Definitions Write a definition for *work*. Use a dictionary to find out the meaning of the word *work*. How many definitions are given? Which definition do you think is used in science? Write this definition in your own words. After you read about the muscular system, revise your definition of *work*.

Muscles are tissues that can shorten, or contract. All muscles do work this way. They pull. When a muscle pulls or contracts, it is doing work. Keep in mind that in science "work" means that a force causes something to move over some distance.

The human muscular system is the force behind the skeletal system. Without the action of muscles, bones could not move at their joints. You couldn't walk, run, or pick up things. Without muscles, you couldn't breathe. Your heart wouldn't beat. You couldn't even swallow food without muscles.

Muscle Structure

Look at Figure 19.7. It shows the scale and structure of muscle. Muscles are made up of hundreds to thousands of long, thin cells, or muscle fibers. Groups of muscle fibers are wrapped by a thin covering of connective tissue. Many bundles of muscle fibers make up a muscle. Because each muscle is an organ, there are also blood vessels and nerve fibers within each muscle.

Figure 19.7
Each muscle fiber (cell) is made of smaller fibers. These fibers are made of two kinds of protein filaments. These filaments slide past one another, causing muscles to contract. What are the names of these two filaments?
▼

Actin filament

Myosin filament

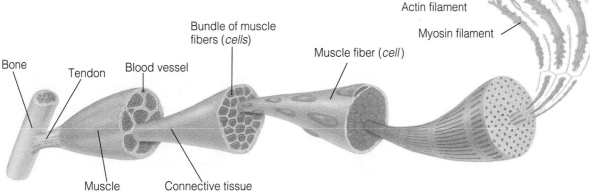

Bundle of muscle fibers (*cells*)

Muscle fiber (*cell*)

Bone

Tendon

Blood vessel

Muscle

Connective tissue

Types of Muscles

Trapezius! Biceps! Pectoralis! Do these words sound Greek to you? Many of the more than 600 muscles that make up the muscular system get their names from Greek or Latin words or word roots. Look at Figure 19.8. It shows some of the major muscles of the body. The white tissues that you see are tendons.

Some muscles can be moved when you want them to move. These are the voluntary muscles. Other muscles are not under your voluntary control. They are controlled automatically by your brain. These are the involuntary muscles. For example, the involuntary muscles in your stomach help you digest food, but you cannot "tell" them to make your stomach work harder to grind and digest food.

**Figure 19.8
The Human Muscular System**

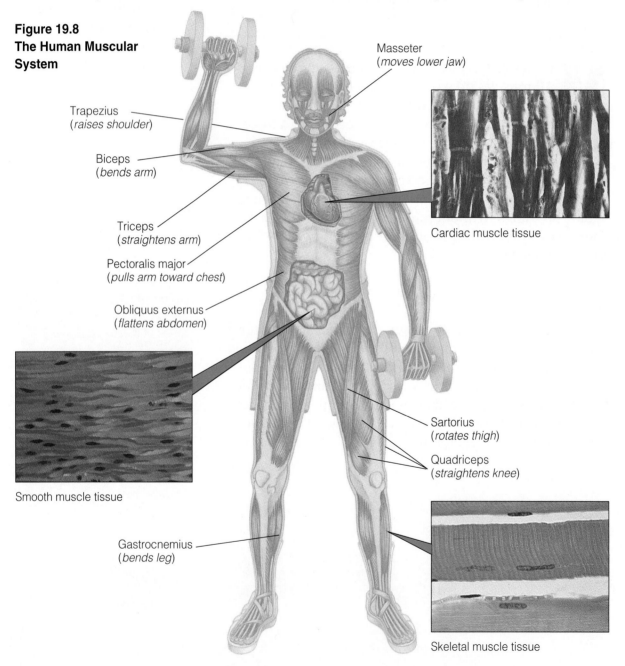

Masseter
(*moves lower jaw*)

Cardiac muscle tissue

Trapezius
(*raises shoulder*)

Biceps
(*bends arm*)

Triceps
(*straightens arm*)

Pectoralis major
(*pulls arm toward chest*)

Obliquus externus
(*flattens abdomen*)

Smooth muscle tissue

Sartorius
(*rotates thigh*)

Quadriceps
(*straightens knee*)

Gastrocnemius
(*bends leg*)

Skeletal muscle tissue

Skeletal Muscle You can make **skeletal muscle** move any time you want. Skeletal muscle makes movement at joints possible. It is attached to the bones by tough, elastic tendons. Look at the skeletal muscle in Figure 19.8. Its cells look striped, or striated. Skeletal muscle is sometimes called striated muscle.

Smooth Muscle Involuntary muscle is called **smooth muscle**. Look at Figure 19.8. Notice that smooth muscle doesn't have any stripes in it. Smooth muscle is in the walls of most internal organs, such as the walls of your stomach and blood vessels. You can't voluntarily control these muscles. Smooth muscles keep your internal organs working all the time, even when you are asleep.

Cardiac Muscle Did you know that your heart is a muscle? The heart is made up of **cardiac** (KAR dee AK) **muscle**. This type of muscle is only in the heart. Look at Figure 19.8. Cardiac muscle is unusual because its cells seem to branch and weave together. Also, it looks like striated muscle and acts like smooth muscle. You have no direct control over cardiac muscle in your heart. However, some people claim to be able to voluntarily slow down or speed up their heartbeat. Your heartbeat is the contraction of the heart. These contractions pump blood through the heart and to the rest of your body. Your brain will speed up or slow down your heartbeat automatically whenever your body needs a larger or smaller supply of blood.

Career Corner *Exercise Specialist*

Who Sets Up Exercise Programs?

You visit a health club, and the exercise specialist asks, Do you want to tone or develop your muscles? The exercise specialist will probably measure your height and weight, and run some tests. From the information gathered, the exercise specialist will develop an exercise program just for you.

Exercise specialists perform many different tasks in their jobs. They also may work in different industries. Corporations, health clubs, and hospitals often hire exercise specialists. They may teach exercise classes or give lectures about exercise and health.

In a hospital, exercise specialists may develop special exercise programs for patients who have had heart attacks or who are overweight. These specialists will monitor a person's heart rate, blood pressure, and so on. Therefore, they must be able to use some medical instruments.

A good understanding of the parts of the body and how they work is important to exercise specialists. To become an exercise specialist, you need a

four-year college degree. However, many community colleges and organizations, such as the YM/YWCA, offer certificates in exercise. You may want to write to your local college to find out more about this career.

Classify

1. Blink your eyes five times.
2. Try *not* to blink for as long as you can. Time yourself and record the time.
3. Repeat step 2 four times.
4. Calculate your average time. Compare your time to the time of four classmates.

Do you think your eye-blinking muscles are controlled by voluntary or involuntary muscles? Explain.

Muscle Action

A muscle cannot contract unless it receives an electrical message from a nerve. These electrical messages are sent to nerves by the brain and spinal cord. The electrical message signals the muscle fibers to contract.

To move the body, most muscles work in pairs. When one muscle contracts, it pulls on a bone to which it is attached. At the same time, another muscle relaxes. Remember that muscles always pull; they cannot push bones apart. The contraction of one muscle can bend your leg, but another muscle is needed to straighten your leg.

To see how this works, lift one of your legs a few centimeters off the floor. Place one hand firmly on the front of your leg just above the knee. Place your other hand on the back of your leg just above the knee. Now, straighten your leg. The muscle in the front of your leg contracts. This muscle is an **extensor**. A muscle that straightens a joint is an extensor. The back muscle contracts as the knee is bent. This muscle is a **flexor**. A muscle that bends a joint is a flexor.

Figure 19.9   Lever Systems

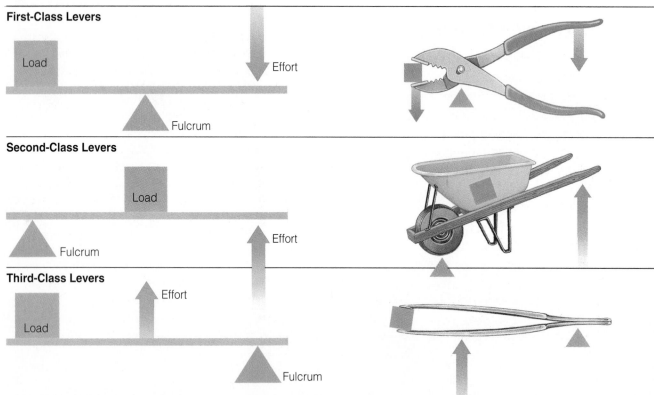

First-Class Levers

Load   Effort   Fulcrum

Second-Class Levers

Load   Fulcrum   Effort

Third-Class Levers

Effort   Load   Fulcrum

Lever Systems in the Human Body

In the human body, most bones and muscles work together as a lever system. In a lever system, the lever is a rigid bar that moves on a fixed point called the fulcrum. A force is applied to another place, causing movement. In your body, your joints are the fulcrums. In a lever system, a force, or effort, is used to move the load. In your body, muscle contraction is the force. Force is applied where muscles are attached to the bones. The muscles pull. The load includes the bones and the tissues that are moved and anything that you are lifting or moving.

A lever reduces the amount of force needed to move something. Usually, the applied force is less than the force needed to move the object directly.

There are three kinds of levers: first-class levers, second-class levers, and third-class levers. The positions of the fulcrum, effort, and load determine how a lever works. The positions also classify a lever. Look at Figure 19.9. It shows the different kinds of levers, some everyday tools that are levers, and lever systems in the human body.

Gastrocnemius
(*extensor*)

Biceps
(*flexor*)

Triceps
(*extensor*)

First-Class Lever: Load-Fulcrum-Effort
When you lift your head or nod your head, you use a first-class lever system. The muscles in the back of your neck are the effort. The joint at the top of your backbone and the base of your skull is the fulcrum. The bones in your face are the weight that is lifted.

Second-Class Lever: Fulcrum-Load-Effort
Standing on tiptoe activates a second-class lever in your body. The joints in the balls of your feet are the fulcrum. The muscles in your calves pull up on the heel bones of your foot. The load is the weight of your body.

Third-Class Lever: Load-Effort-Fulcrum
Whenever you use your arm to drink something, you operate a third-class lever. The biceps in your arm provide the effort. The fulcrum is the hinge joint at your elbow. The load is your hand, your forearm, the container, and the liquid.

Relate Concepts

1. Write your name 15 times on a sheet of paper. Record how long it takes.
2. Open and clench your writing hand as many times as you can in 45 seconds.
3. Repeat steps 1 and 2 three times.
4. Rest for 2 minutes. Then write your name 15 times.

How did your hand feel? How did your writing change? Define *muscle fatigue*.

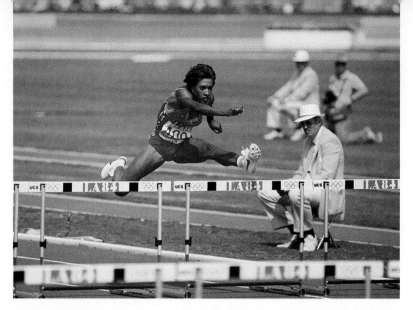

Figure 19.10 ▲
During training, the hurdler may stretch muscles more than she would during everyday activities. This stretching may cause small tears that usually cause soreness.

Science and You *Those Aching Muscles*

Are your muscles sore after exercise? Are they sore the next day? This soreness is caused by two different things. Some muscle fibers contract very quickly and give short bursts of energy. When these muscle fibers are working, they produce a waste product called lactic acid. Usually lactic acid is removed from the muscles by the blood. However, when lactic acid builds up and is not removed from your muscles quickly, you feel pain. Lactic acid usually builds up during heavy exercise. If you are still sore the next day, the exercise has caused microscopic tears and bruises in the muscle.

Check and Explain

1. What is the main function of the muscular system?

2. Compare the structure and function of the three types of muscle tissue: skeletal, smooth, and cardiac.

3. **Apply Definitions** Use the words *flexor* and *extensor* to explain how muscles work in pairs.

4. **Classify** Which of the three types of muscles would you find in your heart, small intestine, blood vessels, and toes?

19.3 The Skin

Objectives

▶ **Describe** the structure of the skin.

▶ **State** the functions of the skin.

▶ **Make analogies** between parts of the skin, their functions, and common objects.

▶ **Demonstrate** the cooling effect of evaporation.

O nce the girders and beams of a building are in place, the outside walls are added to the framework. The inside walls are also constructed. Some of the inside walls help support the building. The outside walls protect the people who live or work in the building. Just like the walls of a building, your skin is the outer covering of your body. Your skin also helps to support and protect your body.

The Largest Organ

Skin is the body's largest organ. Not only does it cover the outside of your body, but it also covers many organs inside your body. You may not think of skin as an organ, but it is. The skin is made up of four tissues: muscle tissue, connective tissue, nerve tissue, and epithelial (ehp ih THEE lee uhl) tissue. Epithelial tissue consists of cells that cover all body surfaces.

Look at the skin cells in Figure 19.11. They make up the top layer of your skin. Notice that the cells are flattened and fit closely together like the pieces of a jigsaw puzzle. Because the cells fit so closely together, they form a protective barrier. Your skin keeps out harmful bacteria and keeps in moisture. Skin cells also contain a protein called keratin (KER uh tihn) that makes the skin waterproof.

Hair and nails are part of the skin system. Both hair and nails are made up of dead cells and keratin. If you have ever wondered why you can cut your hair and nails without pain, it is because they are made up of dead cells. Just like the keratin in animal horns, claws, and birds' beaks, keratin in your nails makes them hard.

Figure 19.11 ▲
Human skin cells form a watertight and bacteria-proof covering.

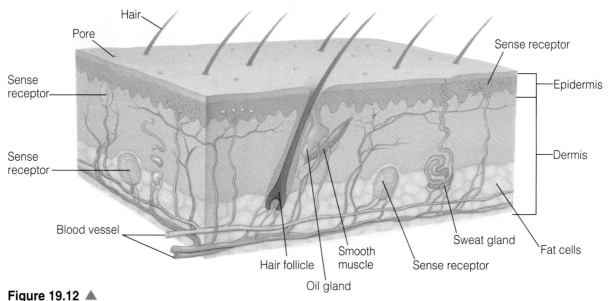

Figure 19.12 ▲
The human skin has two main layers—the epidermis and dermis—
with many different structures in the dermis.

Structure of the Skin

The skin is layered. It has two main layers. The upper layer is called the **epidermis**. The lower layer is called the **dermis**. Figure 19.12 shows a model of the skin. Notice that the dermis is much thicker than the epidermis.

Epidermis   Under a microscope, you would see that the epidermis has five layers. The upper layer of the epidermis is made up of dead skin cells. Rub your hands together and you will have rubbed off thousands of dead skin cells. The dead cells of the epidermis flake off or are rubbed off all the time. Therefore, they must be replaced.

The dead cells are replaced by cells in the deepest layer of the epidermis. Here a steady supply of skin cells is made. These cells move upward toward the top layer of the dermis. As these cells move through each layer, they receive less oxygen and nutrients from the blood. Eventually they die. These dead cells form the skin that you can see.

Dermis   The dermis is beneath the epidermis. A thin membrane separates the dermis from the epidermis. The dermis is thicker than the epidermis: it is the living layer of skin. The dermis is made up of protein fibers and cells that form a strong network. This layer gives your skin its strength and elasticity. If you pinch the skin on the back of your hand, you will notice that it springs back just like an elastic band.

Within the dermis, there are many blood vessels, glands, and tubelike hair follicles (FAHL ih kuhlz). There are hundreds of thousands of hair follicles in the dermis. Each one grows a hair.

Oil and Sweat Glands   There are oil glands and sweat glands in the dermis. The oil glands open into hair follicles. Oil passes into a hair follicle and then to the skin surface. The oil keeps both hair and skin from drying out. Your scalp and face have more oil glands than any other part of your body.

Your skin helps remove wastes from

your body through the sweat glands. Sweat glands are coiled tubes that lead to a pore, or opening, on the skin's surface. Water, salt, and some body wastes are released through the pore. You know this liquid as perspiration, or sweat.

Sweating also helps control your body's temperature. During heavy exercise, on hot days, or when you have a fever, you sweat. As the sweat evaporates from your skin, your skin gets cooler. Blood flowing through the skin also cools. Heat is lost from the body. In this way, the skin acts like a built-in air-conditioning system. When you are cold, the blood vessels narrow. There is less blood flowing near the skin's surface, less heat is lost from the body, and you are kept warm.

Sense Receptors   Think about all the sensations that your skin can feel. The skin is a sense organ. The dermis contains several kinds of nerve endings called sense receptors. There are special sense receptors for cold, hot, pain, pressure, and touch. Each receptor responds to a change, or stimulus, in the environment.

You do not have the same number of each kind of sense receptor. For example, there are more pain receptors than any other kind. Also, some parts of your body have more of one kind of receptor than other parts. For example, you have more touch receptors in your fingertips, the palms of your hands, on the tip of your tongue, and on your lips than any other parts of your body.

SkillBuilder   *Evaluating Sources*

Acne Medication Advertisements

There are many different kinds of acne medications for sale. Most of the information that you get about these medications is from newspaper or magazine ads, and radio and television commercials. The advertisement is usually put together by someone working for the company. Before you buy a product, you should evaluate its advertisement claims.

1. Find a newspaper or magazine advertisement for an acne medication.

2. Write the name of the product.

3. Read the advertisement carefully. Then make a list of questions you would like to have answered before you decide whether or not to believe what the ad claims.

4. Analyze your questions.

   a. If a question asks for more information, write *MI* next to the question.

   b. If the question asks about the source of the information, write an *S* next to the question.

   c. If the question asks about evidence or proof of the claims in the ad, write a *P* next to the question.

5. What reasons might you have for questioning the claims in the ad?

6. What questions could you ask to help decide whether the claims in the ad are truthful?

7. What could you do to decide if the product works the way the ad claims it does?

8. What would you tell someone to think about when a person reads or hears an ad?

9. Would you buy and use the product in your ad? Explain your answer.

Skin and Hair Color

Skin, hair, and eye color are visible differences among people. These inherited traits are caused by a pigment, or coloring, called melanin (MEHL uh nihn). Melanin is produced by a layer of cells in the epidermis. The amount of melanin that you have in your skin determines the color of your skin. There is a wide range of skin colors. People with a lot of melanin have black or dark-brown skin. People with melanin and another substance called carotene have reddish or yellow skin. People with little melanin have light-tan or brown skin. Some people have no melanin. Their skin is white or pinkish. Their hair is also white.

Table 19.1

Skin Care Hints
Wash your face regularly—2 or 3 times per day—with soap and water.
After washing, use a lotion or cream on your skin.
Avoid using oily cosmetics. Remove all makeup before going to bed.
Eat a healthful diet. Avoid sweets.
Exercise regularly.
Sleep 7 to 8 hours per day.

Science and You *Zits and Zats!*

Everybody gets a pimple, but some people, especially teenagers, suffer from acne. Acne is a skin disorder caused by oil, clogged pores, and bacteria. Acne is most common in people with oily skin. The increased amount of oil produced by the oil glands clogs the skin's pores. Bacteria grow in the oil. These bacteria cause changes in the oil that irritate the surrounding skin. The result is usually a pimple. Sometimes a blackhead forms when air causes a chemical change. Table 19.1 gives some helpful hints for controlling acne. However, people who have severe acne should see a dermatologist, or skin doctor. Medical treatment can help prevent acne scars.

Check and Explain

1. What are the two main layers of the skin?

2. List the functions of the skin.

3. **Make Analogies** Name the part of the skin that shows the best analogy to the function of these common objects: an air conditioner, a lube job on a car, a thermometer, and paint.

4. **Demonstrate** Use a cotton ball and water or rubbing alcohol to show the cooling effect of evaporation on the skin. **Caution! Rubbing alcohol is poisonous.** Write a paragraph explaining how evaporation cools your skin.

Concept Summary

19.1 Skeletal System

▶ Bones, cartilage, tendons, and ligaments all make up the human skeletal system.

▶ Bones are classified by their shape as flat, long, short, or irregular.

▶ The human skeleton has immovable, slightly-movable, and freely-movable joints. Four types of freely-movable joints are hinge, ball-and-socket, pivotal, and gliding.

▶ The functions of the skeletal system are support, protection, storage, and blood cell formation.

19.2 Muscular System

▶ The muscular system allows voluntary movement of the skeletal system and involuntary movement of organs.

▶ Skeletal, smooth, and cardiac muscles are made of bundles of muscle cells.

▶ Muscles do work only by contracting. Muscles work in pairs consisting of an extensor and a flexor.

▶ Skeletal muscles work together with bones as lever systems.

19.3 The Skin

▶ The skin is the body's largest organ. Its functions include protection, cooling, waste removal, lubrication, support, and sensory reception.

▶ The two main layers of the skin are the epidermis and the dermis. Sweat glands, hair follicles, oil glands, and sense receptors are all found in the dermis.

▶ Melanin is the pigment that gives skin, hair, and eyes their color.

Chapter Vocabulary

endoskeleton (19.1)	ligament (19.1)	smooth muscle (19.2)	flexor (19.2)
vertebra (19.1)	tendon (19.1)	cardiac muscle (19.2)	epidermis (19.3)
cartilage (19.1)	skeletal muscle (19.2)	extensor (19.2)	dermis (19.3)
joint (19.1)			

Check Your Vocabulary

Use the vocabulary words above to complete the following sentences correctly.

1. Most of the the skeleton of the newborn baby is made of ____ .

2. A chicken, a cow, and a human have an internal bone framework called an ____ .

3. Muscles are connected to bones by ____ .

4. The backbone is made of ____ .

5. Only the heart muscle is made of ____ .

6. Hinge, ball-and-socket, pivotal, and gliding are types of movable ____ .

7. The layer of skin you can see is the ____ .

8. The ____ connect bones at the joint.

9. You move your body by contracting ____ .

10. A muscle that straightens a joint is called a ____ , while a muscle that bends a joint is called a ____ .

11. Sweat glands, oil glands, and hair follicles are all found in the ____ .

12. You can't control the ____ in the walls of your internal organs.

Write Your Vocabulary

Write sentences using each of this chapter's vocabulary words. Show that you know what each word means. Check with a partner to see if your sentences are correct.

Chapter 19 Review

Check Your Knowledge

Answer the following in complete sentences.

1. Give an example of a flexor and an extensor muscle.

2. What are some characteristics of skeletal muscles?

3. What substances are produced in the dermis?

4. Give an example of a ball-and-socket, a hinge, a pivotal, and a gliding joint.

5. What type of muscle is the heart?

6. What are the functions of the skeletal system?

7. How are bones classified? What are the four classifications?

8. What are the two main layers of the skin?

Determine whether each statement is true or false. Write *true* if it is true. If it is false, change the underlined term(s) to make the statement true.

9. Skeletal muscles do work by <u>contracting</u>.

10. Many of your muscles and bones work together as a lever system in which a <u>joint</u> serves as the fulcrum.

11. Sweat glands, oil glands, and sense receptors are located in the <u>epidermis</u>.

12. Bones, cartilage, tendons, and ligaments are parts of the human <u>muscular</u> system.

13. The functions of the skin include cooling and <u>sensory reception</u>.

14. The pigment that gives skin, hair, and eyes their color is <u>melanin</u>.

15. Both <u>skeletal</u> and <u>smooth</u> muscles are involuntary muscles.

Check Your Understanding

Apply the concepts you have learned to answer each question.

1. **Classify** Which of the following organisms have exoskeletons? Which have endoskeletons?

   a. Human   d. Lobster
   b. Cow   e. Chicken
   c. Grasshopper   f. Beetle

2. a. Which types of joints are named for the kind of movement they allow?

   b. Which type of joint is named for the way the bones meet at the joint?

3. **Compare and Contrast** What are three common characteristics of the three muscle types?

4. **Compare and Contrast** Identify two differences each between the following pairs of muscle types: cardiac and skeletal; skeletal and smooth; smooth and cardiac.

5. **Generalize** Apply what you know about evaporation and the body's cooling system. Identify one reason you're cold when you get out of the shower. Identify one way to cool yourself when you're hot.

6. List three flexor muscles in your body. Next to each one, describe the movement it causes. List the extensor muscle that makes a pair with each flexor listed and describe the movement each one causes.

7. **Infer** More than half of your 206 bones are in your feet and hands. Why do you think there are so many bones in human feet and hands? How is this fact important to you every day?

8. **Mystery Photo** The photograph on page 392 is a color-enhanced X-ray of a human knee joint. Make a drawing of the bones as you see them in the X-ray. Label the bones.

Develop Your Skills

Use the skills you have developed in this chapter to complete each activity.

1. **Interpret Data** The diagram shows a map of sense receptors in a patch of skin.

Key ● = Cold receptor ■ = Hot receptor
◇ = Pressure receptor ▲ = Pain receptor

a. Which type are there the most of? Which type are there the least of?

b. What part of the body might this map be showing? Why?

2. **Data Bank** Use the information on page 626 to answer the following questions.

a. How many bones are in the head? How many are in the hands?

b. **Calculate** Determine the percentage of bones in each area listed. Make a circle graph of this data.

3. **Accurate Observations** Observe how you can move the following joints: hip, elbow, thumb knuckle. What type of joint do you think each is? Why?

Make Connections

1. **Link the Concepts** Below is a concept map showing how some of the main concepts in this chapter link together. Only parts of the map are filled in. Copy the map and complete it using words and ideas from the chapter.

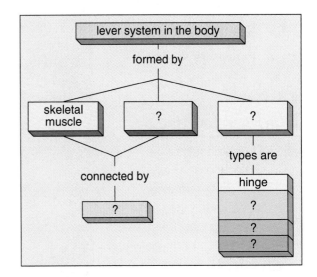

2. **Science and Art** Draw or make a model for each of these tissue cells.

a. Skin cell
b. Smooth muscle cell
c. Bone cell

3. **Science and You** Have you ever fractured a bone? Three kinds of fractures are greenstick, simple, and compound. Use reference books to find out about each kind of fracture. Illustrate each type of fracture in some way, such as a drawing or a clay model. Write a description of each type of fracture.

4. **Science and Math** Measure as many long bones in your arms, legs, and fingers as you can. Organize your data in a table. Which long bone is the longest bone in your body? How many times longer is it than the shortest long bone that you measured?

Chapter **20**   Supply and Transport

Chapter Sections

What do you see?

❝I see large donuts flowing in some type of liquid. I think that they are red blood cells. I predict that they are the size of this period → . I think that they carry oxygen to the body.**❞**

Aneeshia Russum
Leeds Middle School
Philadelphia, Pennsylvania

To find out more about the photograph, look on page 440. As you read this chapter, you will learn about the different systems in your body that help supply and transport nutrients essential to your health.

414

20.1 Digestive System

Objectives

▶ **Trace** the passage of food through the digestive system.

▶ **Name** and **describe** the organs used in digestion.

▶ **Communicate** how mechanical digestion helps chemical digestion occur.

Why do you need food? You need food because the cells of your body require a constant supply of energy and materials to build new cells and repair old ones. Food provides the materials and the energy. But your body can't use food the way it exists when you eat it. Food must be broken down into simpler parts that your body can use. This process is called **digestion.**

Digestion

The substances in food that your body needs in order to live and grow are called **nutrients.** Carbohydrates, proteins, and fats are three important kinds of nutrients in food. When your body digests food, the nutrients in it are broken down so that they dissolve in water. The dissolved nutrients are absorbed into your blood and carried to your body's cells.

Digestion occurs in a series of organs called the digestive tract. As food moves through these organs, it undergoes both chemical and physical changes.

The physical changes are a result of **mechanical digestion.** During mechanical digestion, food is broken into smaller pieces. Look at Figure 20.1. Mechanical digestion begins in your mouth as your teeth cut, grind, and mash food.

The chemical changes are a result of **chemical digestion.** Chemical changes occur when the nutrients in food are broken down into simpler molecules that dissolve in water.

Food is changed chemically by substances called acids, bases, and enzymes. Different glands throughout the digestive system produce these substances. Enzymes are molecules that speed up chemical reactions.

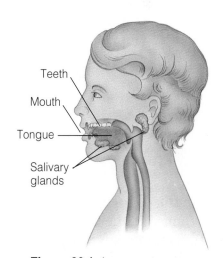

Teeth

Mouth

Tongue

Salivary glands

Figure 20.1 ▲
Both mechanical and chemical digestion begin in the mouth.

Process of Digestion

When you eat, food travels for about 8 m through your digestive tract. This journey can last a day or more. Each organ in the digestive tract performs different functions of mechanical and chemical digestion. As you read, follow the path of digestion in Figure 20.2.

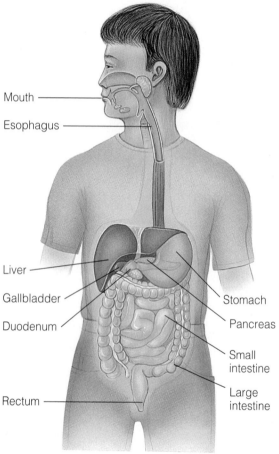

Figure 20.2 ▲
The food you eat makes a long journey through your digestive system.

Mouth   Digestion begins in your mouth. When you chew a bite of food, it is broken into smaller pieces and mixed with saliva.

Saliva contains water, mucus, and an enzyme. The enzyme changes starch, a complex molecule in food, into simpler molecules of sugar. The water and mucus in saliva make the food softer and easier to swallow. Your tongue moves the food around in your mouth as it is chewed. When you swallow, the food moves into your esophagus.

Esophagus   Food travels from your mouth to your stomach by a muscular tube called the esophagus (ih SAHF uh guhs). Look at Figure 20.2 and locate the esophagus. It is about 25 cm long. Food is pushed down the esophagus by the contraction and relaxation of the muscles in the esophagus. This type of muscle action is called *peristalsis* (PEHR uh STAHL sihs).

A ring of muscles at the bottom of the esophagus guards the entrance to your stomach. The muscles relax to allow food to pass into your stomach. Then they contract again to prevent food from coming back into your esophagus.

Stomach   Rhythmic contractions of powerful muscles in your stomach wall mash food into a pulp and mix it with gastric juice. The gastric juice, which is made in the stomach wall, contains the enzyme pepsin, hydrochloric acid, and mucus. The thick layer of mucus protects the membranes that line the stomach from the acidic gastric juice.

The hydrochloric acid in gastric juice begins breaking down proteins and destroys microorganisms in the food. The enzymes help break down protein and fat.

The food becomes a thick, soupy mixture in your stomach. Little by little this mixture squirts out through another ring of muscles into your small intestine. After a meal, it takes about 2 to 6 hours for your stomach to empty.

Small Intestine The next stop in the digestive tract is a narrow, folded tube where food is further digested and absorbed. This is your small intestine, which is about 2.5 cm wide and 7 m long. Your small intestine is four or five times as long as you are tall! Find the small intestine in Figure 20.2.

The first 25 cm of the small intestine are called the *duodenum* (DOO oh DEE nuhm). As the thick, soupy mixture moves from the stomach to the duodenum, more digestive juices are added. These digestive juices are produced in the liver, the pancreas (PAN kree uhs), and the small intestine itself. The digestive juice produced by the small intestine contains enzymes and substances that neutralize the acidic food mixture.

While digestive juices are working, the thick, soupy food mixture is pushed through the small intestine by peristalsis. During this part of the journey, amino acids from proteins, simple sugars from carbohydrates, and broken-down fats are gradually absorbed into the blood. This absorption occurs through the small intestine's lining.

Liver

Your liver has many functions, including aiding in digestion. In Figure 20.3, you can see a close-up view of the liver. Find the liver in the digestive system in Figure 20.2. Where is it located?

The liver produces bile, a mixture of substances. Although bile doesn't contain digestive enzymes, it does contain bile salts. Bile salts aid in the digestion of fats. They are important because fats are completely undigested when they reach the small intestine.

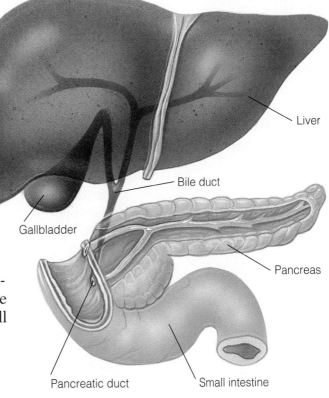

Figure 20.3 ▲
The liver, pancreas, and small intestine produce chemicals used in digestion. What is the function of the gallbladder?

Bile made by the liver is stored in the gallbladder. Find the gallbladder in Figure 20.3. The gallbladder moves bile into the small intestine through a duct. In the small intestine, the bile breaks down fat globules into smaller droplets of fat.

Pancreas

Figure 20.3 also shows the pancreas. The pancreas aids digestion by supplying pancreatic juices to the small intestine. Pancreatic juices are delivered to the small intestine with the bile from the gallbladder. Both enter the small intestine through the same duct. The many enzymes in pancreatic juices help to break down carbohydrates, fats, and proteins.

Skills WorkOut

Observe In a medium-sized bowl of water, drip about ten drops of vegetable, peanut, or canola oil. Observe what happens for a few minutes. Then drip five or six drops of liquid dishwashing detergent into the middle of the bowl. What happens? Explain why this is similar to how bile breaks up fats in the small intestine.

Figure 20.4

Millions of villi line the small intestine. The structure of villi is shown at left. The photograph shows villi magnified 300x. ▼

Absorption

Most nutrients are absorbed from food in your small intestine. For this reason, the small intestine has a huge surface area. In fact, if the total lining of the small intestine were spread out flat, it would cover a baseball diamond!

You may think the inside of the small intestine is smooth, but it isn't. The small intestine has ridges. These ridges are lined with tiny fingerlike projections called **villi** (VIHL eye). You can see the villi in Figure 20.4. The villi and ridges are the structures that increase the surface area of the small intestine. Most nutrients would not be absorbed without this large surface area.

The lining of the small intestine is connected to a vast network of blood vessels. Simple molecules of broken-down nutrients pass through the lining of the small intestine into these blood vessels. The blood vessels carry these nutrient molecules throughout the body.

The watery leftovers that can't be digested move from the small intestine through another ring of muscles to the large intestine. The large intestine is about 1.5 m long and about 6 cm wide. The walls of the large intestine absorb the leftover water.

As the excess water is gradually absorbed, the contents of the large intestine become semisolid. This material, called feces (FEE seez), is still more than half water. Feces also contain food that can't be digested, such as apple skins and cucumber seeds. These fibrous foods are important, however, because they help to keep food moving through your digestive tract. Other parts of the feces include dead bacteria and bits of the lining of the digestive tract that rubbed off as food passed through.

Villi

Blood vessels

Intestinal wall muscle

The feces move into the rectum at the lower end of the large intestine, where they collect. At the end of the rectum is a small opening called the anus. Muscle action excretes the feces through the anus and out of the body.

Problems of the Digestive System

If you are like most people, you have experienced digestive disorders. Stomachaches, nausea, diarrhea, and other similar disorders are very common. Your digestive system has to deal with a steady stream of substances from outside your body. Every day there is a chance that these substances will contain microorganisms or chemicals that upset the normal functions of your stomach or intestines.

Table 20.1 lists some of the common disorders of the digestive system. Many of these disorders are related to a person's diet or lifestyle. Ulcers and indigestion, for example, are most common in people with high levels of stress. You probably know from experience, too, that your emotions affect your digestion. In general, the best way to prevent digestive disorders is to eat a balanced diet of the right amounts of food and to drink plenty of water.

Table 20.1   Digestive Disorders

Disorder	Description	Cause	Treatment
Appendicitis	Swollen and infected appendix	Trapped food and bacteria	Surgery
Constipation	Feces too hard	Too much water absorbed in large intestine	Medication
Diarrhea	Feces too watery	Not enough water absorbed in large intestine	Medication
Gallstones	Pain in abdomen	Hard "stones" formed in gallbladder	Medication or surgery
Heartburn	Pain below heart	Stomach contents backed up into esophagus	Change of diet; medication
Indigestion	Pain in abdomen, nausea, cramps	Food not fully digested	Change of eating habits or diet
Ulcer	Open sore in stomach or duodenum	Tissue eroded by excess stomach acid	Change of diet; reduction of stress; medication

Science and Society *Eating Disorders*

Have you ever gone on a diet to lose weight? For some people, losing weight can get out of control. When this happens, they are in danger of being affected by eating disorders called anorexia nervosa (an uh REHKS ee uh nur VOH suh) and bulimia (buh LEEM ee uh). The two disorders mostly affect women in their teens and twenties. Both disorders are often related to a person's self-image.

People with anorexia nervosa are convinced they are overweight no matter how thin they are. They eat little or no food and often exercise too much. Lack of food can cause them to become nervous and act "edgy" all the time. Anorexia nervosa can severely damage a person's health. In some cases, it can lead to death.

People with bulimia actually eat large amounts of food. However, they purge their bodies of the food to avoid gaining weight. To purge, bulimics may force themselves to vomit after eating. They may take laxatives to move food through the digestive tract before it can be absorbed. Bulimia can damage the stomach and esophagus, the liver, the gallbladder, the pancreas, and even the teeth. Bulimia can also cause kidney failure or heart failure, which can lead to death.

The treatment for these eating disorders usually requires hospitalization. Patients learn about nutrition and get psychological counseling. These treatments are not really cures for the disorders, though. Instead, they are treatments for the symptoms. People who have had anorexia nervosa or bulimia may always fight the urge to lose a few more pounds or to purge after eating.

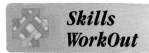

Skills WorkOut

Collect Data Have you noticed how foods affect your digestive system? For example, how does your stomach feel after you've eaten too much food? Over a three-day period, list all the foods you eat along with approximate amounts. Then write how you feel, if anything, after you've eaten the foods. Describe how different foods and the amounts you consume affect your digestive system.

Check and Explain

1. What are the organs of the digestive system? What does each organ do in the process of digestion?

2. Explain how digested nutrients enter the blood.

3. **Reason and Conclude** What would happen if a person had half of his or her small intestine surgically removed? Would this person survive? Explain.

4. **Communicate** How does mechanical digestion help chemical digestion occur? Explain.

20.2 Circulatory System

Objectives

▶ **Describe** the structure and function of the heart.

▶ **Trace** the path of blood through the circulatory system.

▶ **Identify** functions of the lymphatic system.

▶ **Explain** how blood types interact with each other.

▶ **Hypothesize** about the interaction of blood pressure and blood vessels.

Think about how you move through the school building each day. You walk through the halls between your locker and the classrooms. You carry books and papers into and out of class. You are joined by many other students who move as you do through the school building.

Blood cells circulate through the body in the same way that you and your classmates circulate through the school building. However, blood can't move on its own. Blood is pumped through blood vessels in your body by the heart. Together the heart, blood, and blood vessels make up the circulatory system.

The Heart

Clench your fist. Your heart is about the same size and very similar in shape. Your heart is a strong muscle that expands and contracts in rhythmic beats as it pumps blood through the blood vessels. Your heartbeat changes in response to your body's need for blood. What happens to your heart when you exercise? What happens to it when you relax?

The inside of the heart is shown in Figure 20.5. Notice that each side of the heart has an atrium at the top and a ventricle at the bottom. Both atria receive blood coming into the heart, and both ventricles pump blood out of the heart. A small tissue, called a valve, opens and closes to let blood flow into the atrium and then from the atrium to the ventricle. The action of the valves keeps the blood flowing in one direction. Your heartbeat is the rhythmic sound of the opening and closing valves.

Right atrium

Left atrium

Valve

Valve

Right ventricle

Left ventricle

Figure 20.5 ▲
The Human Heart

Blood Vessels

Blood is carried through your body by more than 95 000 km of blood vessels. Look at Figure 20.6. Blood leaving the heart is forced into **arteries**, which transport it to all your organs and muscles. Arteries are tubes with thick, strong, elastic walls. They can withstand the pressure of the blood that is forced into them when the ventricles contract. Blood leaving the heart is forced through smaller and smaller arteries to all parts of your body.

The smallest blood vessels are called **capillaries**, which are finer than a human hair. Some capillaries are so small that only a single line of blood cells can move through them. Some capillaries carry blood from the heart to your muscles and organs, and other capillaries carry blood back toward the heart.

Capillaries that carry blood back toward the heart join larger blood vessels called **veins**. The heart does not push blood through veins. Valves in the veins force the blood through. Because veins are close to the surface, you can see them in your hands and feet where the skin is thin.

Heart Rate

Put two fingers on the side of your neck directly under your jaw. The rhythmic surge under your fingers is your heart pushing blood through the neck artery. Each time the ventricle forces blood into the main artery, the pressure causes every artery in your body to expand and contract. Every surge you feel is a heartbeat.

The number of times your heart beats in one minute is your heart rate, or your pulse. A normal heart rate at rest is between 65 and 75 beats per minute. Your heart rate changes throughout the day, depending on your

Figure 20.6 ▲
Arteries, veins, and capillaries are all blood vessels. What is the function of each blood vessel?

activity. For example, it increases when you exercise. It even changes when you stand up.

Blood Pressure

The next time you pump up a bicycle tire, hold onto the hose. Notice that with each surge of air, the hose stiffens and then relaxes. The same thing happens to your arteries when your heart pumps blood through them. The surge of blood puts pressure on the artery wall. This pressure is called your blood pressure. Blood pressure can indicate the condition of the arteries.

Blood-pressure readings are stated with two numbers. For example, normal blood pressure is 120 over 80. The first number is the amount of pressure on the artery wall when the heart contracts and forces more blood into the artery. The smaller number is the amount of pressure on the blood moving through the artery between surges.

Many people have their blood pressure checked regularly. High blood pressure can lead to strokes or heart attacks.

Circulation

The main function of the heart is to circulate blood, which transports food, oxygen, and waste products. The heart's two pumps work together in perfect rhythm to circulate your blood through your lungs and your body.

Systemic Circulation Look at Figure 20.7. Blood is forced from the heart by contraction of the left ventricle. The blood enters the aorta, which is the largest artery in the body. The aorta distributes the blood to smaller arteries and then to the capillaries.

As the cells throughout your body remove oxygen from the blood, they release carbon dioxide. Capillaries and veins carry the oxygen-poor blood back to the heart. The inferior vena cava is the final collection point for blood from the veins. Blood flows from the vena cava into the right atrium.

Circulation of blood from the heart to the body and back again is called systemic circulation. It moves blood throughout the entire body system.

Pulmonary Circulation The function of pulmonary circulation is to oxygenate the blood. This is done by passing it through the lungs.

The oxygen-poor blood entering the right atrium is pumped into the right ventricle. The right ventricle then forces this blood into the pulmonary artery connected to the lungs. In your lungs, oxygen diffuses into the blood. In addition, carbon dioxide is given up so it can be exhaled. When blood leaves the lungs, it is once again rich in oxygen. Blood enters the left atrium and repeats the cycle. The entire cycle of blood, including both pulmonary and systemic circulation, occurs in less than one minute.

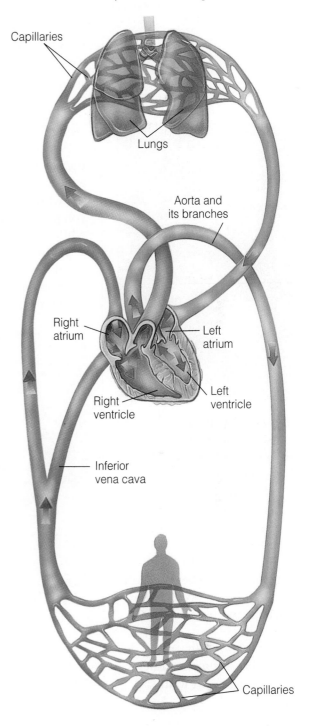

Oxygen diffuses into, and carbon dioxide diffuses out of, capillaries in the lungs.

Capillaries

Lungs

Aorta and its branches

Right atrium

Left atrium

Right ventricle

Left ventricle

Inferior vena cava

Capillaries

Oxygen diffuses out of, and carbon dioxide diffuses into, capillaries in the body.

Figure 20.7 ▲
The Human Circulatory System

Blood

What are you giving away when you donate half a liter of your blood? Actually you are sharing many elements that are vital to life. Blood is a complex substance made up of different kinds of cells, particles of protein, and dissolved salts and nutrients.

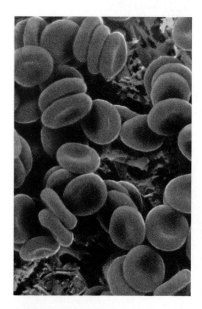

Red Blood Cells ▲

Oxygen is carried in your blood by red blood cells. These cells are specialized for this function. Unlike other cells in your body, they have no mitochondria or nuclei.

How do red blood cells carry oxygen? They contain hemoglobin, a protein that attracts and holds oxygen molecules.

Red blood cells are made in the bone marrow. Each lives only a few months.

White Blood Cells

A whole army of cells in the blood protect your body against disease. These are the white blood cells. When you get sick, the number of white blood cells increases.

White cells begin their development in the bone marrow and mature in the lymph organs and nodes.

▼

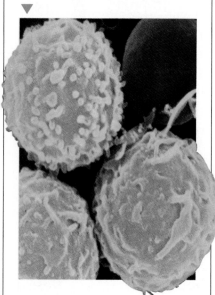

Plasma ▶

When red blood cells, white blood cells, and platelets are removed from blood, what's left is a watery yellow fluid called plasma. Plasma contains important salts that help your muscles function. It also carries dissolved nutrients.

Platelets ▲

Colorless bits of cells, called platelets, cause your blood to clot. When a blood vessel is injured, proteins in the plasma form long sticky threads called fibrin. The fibrin traps platelets, which then collect, form a clot, and plug the hole.

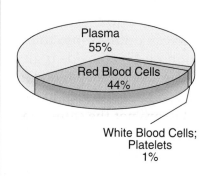

Plasma
55%

Red Blood Cells
44%

White Blood Cells;
Platelets
1%

Lymphatic System

Do you ever notice small, sore lumps in your neck when you are sick? These little lumps are swollen lymph nodes that are helping you get well. Lymph nodes are part of a network of lymph vessels that extend throughout your body. The main function of this network, called the lymphatic system, is to return to the bloodstream small amounts of fluid and proteins that seep out of the capillaries. Figure 20.8 shows the network of lymphatic vessels in the body.

The clear yellow fluid that flows through the lymphatic vessels is called lymph. Lymph travels through your body to a location near your shoulders. Here it drains into the circulatory system. During its journey, lymph is filtered through the lymph nodes, where bacteria and viruses can be trapped. These nodes are filled with white blood cells, called lymphocytes. Lymphocytes fight infections. When bacteria and viruses are present, the lymphocytes multiply rapidly and the lymph nodes are tender and swollen. Lymphocytes are also manufactured in the spleen, which is part of the lymphatic system. In addition to fighting infection, the lymphatic system helps keep the right level of fluid and proteins in your blood.

Blood Types

Everyone has blood made up of the same physical components. There are, however, differences among people in the chemical makeup of their blood. Your red blood cells belong to a group that identifies an important molecule, called an antigen, on its surface. Individuals with the A antigen on the surface of their red cells have type A blood. Those with the B antigen have type B blood. If the red cell surface has both A and B antigens, then the blood is type AB. If the red cell surface has neither the A nor the B antigen, the blood is type O.

Blood typing is important if you give or receive blood. The plasma of your blood can produce special proteins, called antibodies, that will bind to the antigens on red cells that are not the same type. For example, type A blood plasma makes an antibody that binds to type B blood cells. This antibody is referred to as an anti-B antibody. If type B blood is mixed with type A blood, the anti-B antibodies

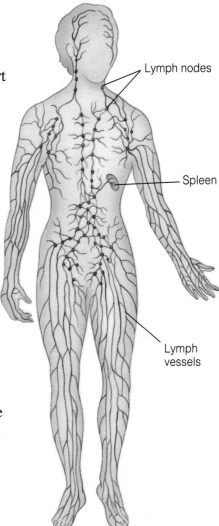

Figure 20.8 ▲
The lymphatic system includes lymph nodes, lymphatic vessels, and the spleen. How does the lymphatic system help fight infections?

Table 20.2   Blood Types, Donors, and Recipients

Blood Type	Cell Surface Antigen	Can Donate Blood To	Can Receive Blood From
A	A	A, AB	A, O
B	B	B, AB	B, O
AB	A, B	AB	A, B, AB, O
O	None	A, B, AB, O	O

cause the type A cells to clump and form a clot. Clots are dangerous because they prevent the flow of blood through the blood vessels. They can cause death.

The same thing happens with the other blood types. Type B blood contains anti-A antibodies that bind to type A blood. Type AB blood cells have both A and B antigens, so AB blood contains neither anti-A nor anti-B antibodies. People with type AB blood can receive all

SkillBuilder *Interpreting Data*

Antibody Formation

Before blood transfusions are done, the donor blood is cross-matched with the blood of the person receiving it. The purpose of cross-matching the two blood types is to ensure that the blood transfusion will work. If blood clotting occurs, then a new donor must be found.

Copy the table shown on a piece of paper. Use Table 20.2 and the information on blood types to complete the table. For each blood type, place an X in the antigen row if antibodies form. Study the table and answer the following questions:

Antigen	Blood Types			
	A	B	AB	O
A				
B				

1. Type AB blood has antibodies against which antigens?

2. Type O blood has antibodies against which antigens?

3. Donated blood is safe only if it is given to a person whose blood does not contain anti-

bodies against it. Which blood type(s) can be donated to a person with AB blood?

4. Which blood can be donated to a person with type A blood? Type B blood?

5. Although type AB blood is rare, donor blood does not have to be type AB. Why do you think this is so? Explain.

6. Type O blood is the most common. However, the number of compatible blood types is limited. Why do you think this is so? Explain.

types of blood, but they can donate blood only to other people who are type AB. Type O blood cells have neither A nor B antigens, so O blood contains both anti-A and anti-B antibodies. People with type O blood can donate to anyone, but they can receive only type O blood.

Use the information in Table 20.2 to determine blood type, donors, and recipients. Remember, two blood types can't be combined if one contains antibodies that conflict with the surface antigen(s) of the other.

Cardiovascular Disease

Do you know someone who has had a heart attack or a stroke? If you do, you know that heart attacks and strokes are very serious. Disease of the heart and blood vessels is called cardiovascular disease. It is the most common cause of death in the United States.

Cardiovascular disease starts in the blood vessels. Normally the blood flows freely through the arteries. However, with time, fatty deposits of cholesterol can build up on the walls of the arteries. The opening inside the artery is narrowed by these deposits. This condition is called atherosclerosis (ATH ur oh skluh ROH suhs). It becomes serious when a large number of the major arteries are narrowed.

As the arteries become narrower, the amount of blood flow is reduced, and the heart and blood vessels are affected. The heart has to work harder to force blood through the arteries, so the blood pressure increases. Increased pressure inside the arteries causes them to lose their elasticity and bulge. If the bulge is great, the artery wall becomes thinner and can rupture.

Blood clots are likely to form at the fatty deposits. These clots can break loose and completely close a blood vessel anywhere in the body: the lung, the brain, or the heart muscle itself. When a clot lodges in the heart muscle, a person has a heart attack. When a brain artery ruptures or is clogged by a clot, a stroke occurs.

Just about everyone, even children, has some amount of fatty deposits in their blood vessels. As you age, these deposits increase in size and amount if you don't take care of yourself. Controlling your weight, not smoking, eating a diet low in animal fats, exercising regularly, and controlling your blood pressure are all important in preventing cardiovascular disease.

Skills WorkOut

Make a Graph Record the heart rate of everyone in your class. What is the highest heart rate? What is the lowest heart rate? Graph the results. What is the average range for most students?

Figure 20.9 ▲
The yellow shapes are fat deposits. How does the buildup of fat deposits affect the arteries?

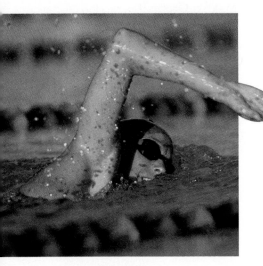

Figure 20.10 ▲

How can regular exercise help lower the risk of heart disease?

Science and You *Have a Healthy Heart*

What is your risk of ever having a heart attack? If very few people in your family have had heart attacks, you might be at low risk. However, if your family has a long history of high blood pressure and cardiovascular disease, you could be in a higher risk group. You can't change what you inherited from your family, but you can control some factors that contribute to cardiovascular disease.

Medical studies show a link between heart disease and a high-fat diet. Limiting the amount of such foods as butter, eggs, red meat, and cheese reduces the amount of fat in your diet. You can make decisions about what you eat.

Exercise is another important factor in lowering your risk of heart disease. Swimming, biking, running, hiking, and brisk walking are all good for your cardiovascular system. They are aerobic exercises in which you must breathe deeply. However, it's important that you do them consistently for at least 20 minutes at a time. To get the best results, you can decide to do aerobic exercises three times a week.

Weight control and not smoking are also important in lowering your risk of heart disease. You can control the amount of food you eat, how much you exercise, and whether or not you smoke. No one knows exactly what your risk of cardiovascular disease is. However, good health habits beginning now will more than likely lower your risk.

Check and Explain

1. How is blood moved through the arteries? Through the veins?

2. Explain how the lymphatic system fights infection. Describe one other function of the lymphatic system.

3. **Find Causes** The left ventricle of the heart is the largest chamber. How is this important to systemic circulation?

4. **Hypothesize** Explain how blood pressure and the health of your blood vessels are related. Why is it important to periodically have your blood pressure checked?

20.3 Respiratory System

Objectives

▶ **Explain** the function of the ribs in inhaling and exhaling.

▶ **Describe** the flow of air through the respiratory system.

▶ **Predict** how the respiratory system is affected by cigarette smoking.

Whether you are playing football, cheering in the stands, or playing in a band, you need energy. The food you eat is a source of energy. In order for your body to release energy from the food you eat, you need oxygen. Your cells use oxygen to "burn" the molecules that your digestive system supplies.

Breathing and Air Pressure

The air around you is about one-fifth oxygen. You get the oxygen you need by breathing in air. Organs that help with breathing make up the respiratory system.

Put your hands on either side of your ribs. Take a deep breath and hold it a few seconds. What happens? When you inhale, your ribs move up and out as air moves into your lungs. When you exhale, your ribs move down and in as gases move out of your lungs.

Look at Figure 20.11. Your ribs move up and out when you inhale because the muscles between your ribs are contracting. Below your ribs and lungs is a large, flat muscle called the diaphragm (DY uh FRAM). When you inhale, your diaphragm contracts and moves down. The contracting diaphragm works with the contracting muscles between your ribs to increase the space in your lungs. When the space inside your lungs increases, the air pressure inside your lungs decreases. Because the air pressure outside your lungs is greater than inside your lungs, air moves into your lungs.

When you exhale, the contracted rib muscles and diaphragm relax. Your ribs move down and in, the diaphragm moves up, and the space in your lungs decreases. The air pressure inside your lungs is greater than the air pressure outside. In order to equalize the air pressure, air moves out of your lungs.

Air in

Inhaling

Diaphragm contracts

Ribs

Air out

Lung

Exhaling

Diaphragm relaxes

Figure 20.11 ▲
The diaphragm contracts when you inhale. What happens to the diaphragm when you exhale?

Path of Air

Each time you take a breath, air travels through the organs of your respiratory system. Figure 20.12 traces the path of air, which begins in the nose.

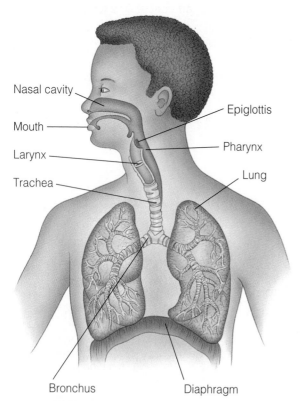

Nasal cavity

Mouth

Larynx

Trachea

Epiglottis

Pharynx

Lung

Bronchus

Diaphragm

Figure 20.12 ▲
The Human Respiratory System

Nose The main entrance and exit to your respiratory system is your nose. The nose is connected to the winding passages that warm and filter the air as it passes through the respiratory system.

When you breathe in, hairs in your nasal passages filter dust, pollen, and other small particles from the air. These particles also stick to the mucous membranes that line your nasal passages. If they build up, sneezing forces them out.

Tiny blood vessels in the nasal passages warm the air as it passes through.

The air also collects moisture in the nasal passages.

Sometimes breathing through your nose can be difficult, such as when you have a cold. So you breathe through your mouth. When you run or exercise, you need to take in air at a faster rate. Your air supply is increased by breathing through your mouth and nose.

Pharynx Another name for the throat is the pharynx (FAIR ihnks). The pharynx is like a funnel that leads from your nose and mouth to your windpipe. Locate the pharynx in Figure 20.12. The pharynx is lined with cilia. Cilia are tiny hairlike parts that help filter air on its way to your lungs.

Trachea Air travels from your pharynx to a tube called the trachea (TRAY kee uh). Another name for the trachea is the windpipe. This ringed tube is about 10 cm long and 1.5 cm wide.

The trachea is a tough, flexible passageway that air can move through all the time. When you move your head and neck, the trachea twists and stretches. Notice the epiglottis in Figure 20.12. The epiglottis closes off the trachea when you swallow. This keeps food from entering your lungs. The epiglottis opens when you breathe or talk.

At the top of the trachea is the larynx (LAR ihnks), or voice box. Air passing over the vocal cords in the larynx produces sounds. You form these sounds into speech with your mouth.

Like the pharynx, the trachea is lined with cilia. The cilia continue to clean air as it passes by. The bottom of the trachea branches into two narrow tubes called **bronchi** (BRAHN kee). Each bronchus leads into one lung. Locate the bronchi in Figure 20.12.

Lungs

The oxygen you inhale with air is exchanged for waste gases from the body in the lungs. Inside your lungs, the bronchi branch into thousands of tiny bronchioles (BRAHN kee OHLS). Each bronchiole ends in a cluster of tiny air sacs called **alveoli** (al VEE uh LY).

The bronchioles and alveoli look like the branches of a tree. The biggest branches are the bronchi. Bronchi are covered by cilia and a thin film of mucus. Dust and pollen are trapped by the mucus before they can reach the alveoli.

There are about 300 million alveoli in each lung. Although each lung is only about the size of a football, the large number of alveoli greatly increases the surface area of the lungs. If the total surface of the lungs were spread out flat, it would cover a tennis court! This large surface area is important for the quick exchange of oxygen and waste gases.

Exchange of Gases

As oxygen moves into the bloodstream, carbon dioxide moves into the alveoli. The gases exchange places by diffusion. Look at Figure 20.13. Notice that the capillaries surround the alveoli. The alveoli are coated with a moist film. Oxygen dissolves in this film and diffuses into the capillaries. The red blood cells in the capillaries release the carbon dioxide and replace it with oxygen. The carbon dioxide diffuses out of the capillaries and into the moist film on the alveoli. The carbon dioxide is then exhaled from the lungs.

Every cell of your body needs oxygen for respiration to take place. After the blood receives oxygen from your lungs and releases carbon dioxide to the lungs, the blood flows back to the heart. The heart pumps this oxygen-rich blood into all your cells. Carbon dioxide diffuses from the cells into the blood.

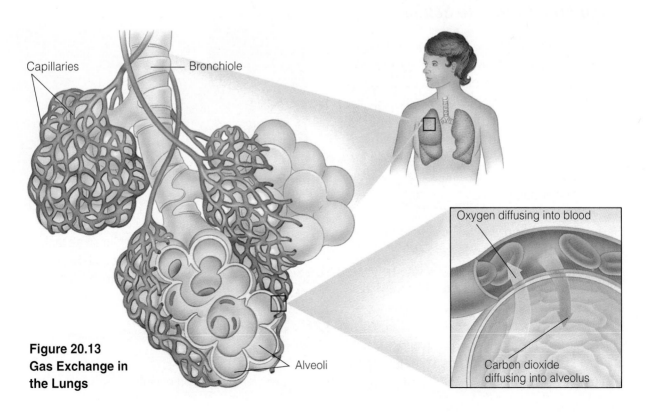

Capillaries

Bronchiole

Oxygen diffusing into blood

Carbon dioxide diffusing into alveolus

**Figure 20.13
Gas Exchange in
the Lungs**

Alveoli

Respiratory Disorders

The function of the hairs, cilia, and mucous membranes in the respiratory system is to filter out substances that might be harmful to your lungs. Sometimes harmful substances get past these filters and cause respiratory problems. The most common respiratory problem is the common cold, caused by any one of 100 viruses.

Asthma is a respiratory problem that occurs when muscles in the bronchi and bronchioles contract. When this happens, the size of the airways into the lungs is reduced. This narrowed airway makes breathing difficult and causes wheezing. Asthma can be brought on in a number of ways, including allergies and extreme cold.

Bronchitis is an inflammation of the mucous membranes that line the bronchi. Bronchitis causes coughing and high fevers. Pneumonia is a respiratory disorder that infects the lungs. It is usually caused by bacteria. Symptoms include chest pains and coughing.

Historical Notebook

From Free Diving to Scuba

Finding methods of underwater exploration has interested people for many centuries. As early as 4500 B.C., divers in the Mediterranean Sea held their breath and dived for pearls and sponges. By 100 A.D., divers in Greece and Italy were using hollow reeds as snorkels. The diver could search the sea floor underwater for a long time by breathing through a snorkel, which has one end above water.

The first apparatus used for breathing underwater was the diving bell. In 1690 Edmund Halley built the first diving bell that held more than one person. Halley's wooden bell had glass portholes. Oxygen was supplied by two barrels.

The first safe underwater breathing device was the *aqualung*, which was invented by Jacques-Yves Cousteau, a naval officer, and Emile Gagnan, an engineer. The aqualung, which is an air tank and regulator, is part of the scuba equipment used today.

Scuba, which stands for self-contained underwater breathing apparatus, has an air tank, goggles, snorkel, fins, and a weight belt. Scuba equipment enables a diver to explore the ocean depths for long periods of time.

1. Name two kinds of apparatus used for breathing underwater.

2. Explain how a snorkel works.

Science and Society *Indoor Air Pollution*

In the late 1970s, many people found ways to make their homes and businesses more energy-efficient. However, they did not know that they were contributing to air pollution. For example, many people put better insulation and tighter seals around windows and doors to save energy. Unfortunately, these devices also lessen the flow of natural air into and out of a building.

Studies by the Environmental Protection Agency (EPA) show that indoor air often contains more pollutants than outdoor air. Examples of pollutants include aerosol sprays, cleaning products, paint products, and air fresheners. Concentrations of these pollutants can be as much as 100 times higher inside the building than in the open air.

Some indoor pollutants cause itchy eyes, nausea, and headaches. Other pollutants are linked to diseases that may take years to develop, such as cancer. Thirty of the indoor air pollutants identified by the EPA are known to cause cancer. These substances include asbestos and a radioactive gas called radon. Radon seeps into buildings from underground. There are ways to check for radon and asbestos in buildings. In many communities, asbestos is being removed from schools.

To combat indoor air pollution, you can be more careful about using household products that contain harmful chemicals. A lot of people are using natural products instead. Many office workers are getting better ventilation in their offices by using desktop air purifiers. Smoking is no longer allowed in many buildings.

Figure 20.14 ▲
Asbestos is a material that has been used for insulation and fireproofing in many older buildings. It has been linked to lung cancer. Here, workers begin removing asbestos.

Check and Explain

1. Describe how air moves through the respiratory system.

2. What happens to the diaphragm when you breathe in and out? What do you think happens to the diaphragm when you have the hiccups?

3. **Compare** Write how the process of photosynthesis in plants compares to the exchange of gases in animals.

4. **Predict** What respiratory problems might a person who smokes be more likely to develop than a non-smoker? How do you think smoking can make some respiratory problems worse?

Activity 20 *How does lung capacity vary?*

Skills Measure; Collect Data; Interpret Data

Task 1 Prelab Prep
1. Collect the following items: a large, clear plastic drinking jug, a large cake pan, a half-meter length of plastic tubing, a grease pencil, a 500-mL beaker, liquid soap.
2. Find a large sink or tub.

Task 2 Data Record
1. On a sheet of paper, draw the table shown. Write your name at the top. Also write the names of people whose lung capacity you plan to measure.
2. After you measure the lung capacity of each person listed, record the volume in the table.

Table 20.3 Measuring Lung Capacity

Name	Lung Capacity

Task 3 Procedure
1. Fill the jug to the top with water.
2. Put the cake pan in the sink. Completely fill the pan with water.
3. Hold your hand tightly over the opening of the jug.
4. Turn the jug upside down over the sink. Put the upside-down jug in the cake pan so the opening is underwater. Remove your hand.
5. Slip one end of the tubing into the jug. Hold on to the jug so it doesn't fall over. Pinch the other end of the tubing.
6. Take a deep breath. Release the pinch at the end of the tubing. Exhale all the air in your lungs into the tubing. Quickly pinch the tubing shut again.
7. Use a grease pencil to mark the water level on the side of the jug.
8. Put your hand over the opening of the jug and remove it from the pan.
9. Pour out the water in the jug. Refill the jug with water up to the line you marked.
10. Use the beaker to measure the amount of water in the jug. Record this volume amount as your lung capacity.
11. Repeat steps 1 to 10 to determine the lung capacity of each person. Be sure to wash the tubing with soap and water between each use.

Task 4 Analysis
1. What is your lung capacity?
2. How does your capacity compare to the lung capacities of your classmates?
3. Find the average lung capacity of your group.
4. Create a chart that shows the lung capacity of each person in your group.

Task 5 Conclusion
What factors affect a person's lung capacity? For example, how might the lung capacity of a person who exercises a lot be different from someone who doesn't exercise very often? Explain why lung capacity varies among people.

Extension
Explain how measuring lung capacity could be used in the diagnosis and treatment of some respiratory illnesses. Find out actual methods used to measure lung capacity.

20.4 Excretory System

Objectives

▶ **Describe** how the skin rids the body of wastes.

▶ **Describe** how the kidneys remove wastes from the body.

▶ **Define operationally** the path of urea from the liver through its excretion from the body.

Infer Set up this simple activity. You'll need a piece of filter paper that is cone-shaped, a funnel, a measuring cup, a clear cup, water, and sand. Put sand and about 200 mL of water into the measuring cup. Put the filter paper into the funnel. Pour the sand-water mixture into the empty cup through the filter. What happens? How do you think this is like your kidneys?

You know that the lungs remove carbon dioxide from your body. Your cells produce other wastes as well. For example, when your tissues contain too much salt and water, they become wastes. If wastes are not removed, or excreted, they build up to dangerous levels in your body.

Your liver and skin are excretory organs. They play an important part in removing certain wastes from your body. However, the main organs of excretion are the kidneys.

Liver

You learned about some of the functions of the liver when you read about the digestive system. During metabolism, wastes with nitrogen are released. These wastes are toxic to the body. Your liver combines the wastes with carbon dioxide to form urea. Urea is a nitrogen compound that is poisonous in large amounts and must be removed from your body. Urea enters the bloodstream through the capillaries in the liver. The circulatory system carries urea to your kidneys, where it is separated from the blood and flushed from your body in urine. Urine is made up of urea, water, and excess salts.

Skin

You know that your skin has several layers. Within your skin layers are sweat glands and hair follicles. Wastes and excess water are removed from your blood by the sweat glands. The waste and water form sweat, which is released onto the skin surface through pores in your skin.

Did you ever notice that if sweat from your face gets into your mouth, it tastes salty? Along with excess water, salt is removed from your blood in the form of sweat.

Figure 20.15 ▲
The green objects shown are bacteria in a pore of skin. Why is the skin an excretory organ?

Kidneys

Reach back and touch your lower back, just above your waist. You have found approximately where your two kidneys are located. They are about 10 cm long and shaped like large beans.

Each time your heart beats, about 20 percent of your blood enters the kidneys through the renal artery. As you can see in Figure 20.16, the artery branches off into a network of capillaries. Some parts of blood, such as blood cells and proteins, are too large to enter the capillaries. They remain in the bloodstream. Other substances, such as water, some salts, and nutrients, enter the capillaries. They are filtered by tiny structures called **nephrons** (NEHF rahnz). You can see a diagram of a nephron in Figure 20.16. The substances pass through the collecting tubes in the nephron. They are then absorbed back into the bloodstream and leave through a vein. Why is it necessary for water, nutrients, and some salts to reenter your bloodstream?

The liquid that remains in the collecting tube of the nephron is urine. Notice the ureter in Figure 20.16. Here urine flows from the core of the kidney into the urinary bladder. The bladder is a muscular sac of tissue. The bladder will store about 1 L of urine. When the bladder is full, its strong muscular walls squeeze urine

Figure 20.16 ▲
In the body, urine is excreted from the kidneys to the ureter to the urinary bladder. Through what tube does urine leave the body? What is the function of the nephron?

Kidney — Vein — Renal artery — Ureter — Urinary bladder — Urethra

Capillaries — Renal artery — Vein — Ureter

Vein — Renal artery — Collecting tubule — Capillaries

Kidney   **Nephron**

out through the urethra. The urethra is a tube that leads from the bladder to the outside of the body. Look at Figure 20.16 and trace the flow of urine to the outside of the body.

Excretory Disorders

Sometimes microorganisms get into the organs of the excretory system. Microorganisms may enter the body through the urethra, other body organs, or the blood. When microorganisms get into the urinary tract, they cause infections. Some infections can be treated by drinking a lot of water, resting, changing your diet, or taking antibiotics. Other infections are more serious.

When the nephrons of the kidneys become infected, a disease called *nephritis* may result. Repeated infections can damage the kidneys to the point that they can't remove wastes anymore. A person with severe kidney damage may have to be connected to an artificial kidney. If the kidneys no longer function, a transplanted kidney may be necessary. Fortunately, one kidney can do the work of two.

Another kidney disorder occurs when salts in the urine form crystals, or kidney stones. They are usually the result of frequent bacterial infections. If the kidney stones are too large to pass in the urine, they can lodge in the ureter and keep urine from leaving the kidney. Kidney stones can be very painful. They are often treated with a technique called *ultrasound*. The ultrasound vibrations break up the kidney stones the same way that a certain sound pitch can shatter glass. Once broken up into small crystals, the kidney stones can easily pass through the ureter.

Skills WorkOut

Make Analogies Refer back to the activity you did in the *Skills WarmUp* on page 435. What part of the human body best represents the filter paper? What body part best represents the water to be filtered? What body part best represents the clear water that passes out of the filter?

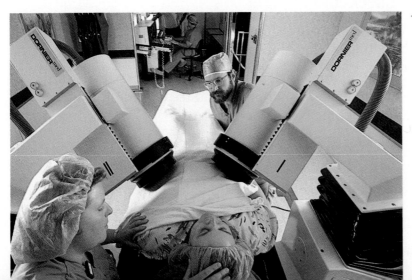

◀ **Figure 20.17**
Today, ultrasound is often used to break apart most large kidney stones so they can be passed out of the body.

437

Science and Technology
Dialysis—The Amazing Machine

Sometimes a person's kidneys fail to function at all. However, a person whose kidneys fail is still able to lead a normal life, thanks to the kidney dialysis machine. A kidney dialysis machine takes over the functions of the kidneys and removes all waste products from the blood.

During dialysis, a person's blood flows into special tubing. The tubing is made of a material that allows only certain substances to diffuse through its walls. Inside the dialysis machine, the tubing is surrounded by a special fluid. Wastes and other unneeded substances in blood diffuse from the tubing into the fluid. Certain substances from the fluid diffuse into the blood. The blood then flows back into the person. The dialysis process takes six to eight hours. A person might need dialysis two or three times a week.

In some cases, temporary kidney failure is caused by sudden trauma or illness. The patient may have dialysis done in the hospital until the kidneys heal and no longer need the dialysis.

When kidney failure is permanent, dialysis may be done in a hospital or elsewhere. A new type of dialysis machine was developed in recent years. This machine is cheaper, less traumatic, and requires less time. Most importantly, kidney dialysis patients are able to perform the procedure themselves. They hook up to the machine at bedtime and let the machine work through the night. This amazing machine allows people to go on with their daily lives.

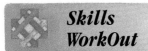

Skills WorkOut

Classify Make a list of body organs you have read about in this chapter. Find ways to group the organs based on how they are alike and different. Think about their locations, functions, and so on. Which organs fit in more than one group? Why?

Check and Explain

1. What substances does the kidney remove from the body? What substances does it keep?

2. Explain why death would occur if a person's kidneys no longer functioned, and treatment on a dialysis machine was not possible.

3. **Infer** Why is water important for the excretory system to function properly?

4. **Define Operationally** Explain the process by which the waste from the liver is excreted from the body.

Chapter 20 Review

Concept Summary

20.1 Digestive System

▶ Digestion is the process of breaking down food into particles small enough to cross cell membranes.

▶ Mechanical digestion involves mashing and grinding food. Chemical digestion occurs when food is broken down into simpler molecules with the aid of enzymes, acids, and bases.

▶ The main parts of the human digestive tract are the mouth, esophagus, stomach, small intestine, large intestine, and rectum.

20.2 Circulatory System

▶ The heart serves as a muscular pump that moves blood through the vessels of the circulatory system.

▶ The left side of the heart pumps blood to the organs of the body. The right side of the heart pumps blood to the lungs.

▶ Blood has liquid and solid parts. Blood transports oxygen, carbon dioxide, nutrients, and wastes. Blood also helps the body fight disease and repair damaged blood vessels.

▶ The lymph system returns fluid to the capillaries and aids in nutrient absorption and body defense.

20.3 Respiratory System

▶ The diaphragm and rib muscles work together during breathing to change the air pressure in the lungs. Air moves into and out of the lungs through the nose or mouth, pharynx, trachea, and bronchial tree.

▶ Gas exchange occurs in the alveoli and body cells by diffusion.

20.4 Excretory System

▶ In humans, the lungs, liver, skin, and urinary system all aid in excretion.

▶ The kidneys remove wastes carried by the blood and restore nutrients.

Chapter Vocabulary

digestion (20.1)
nutrient (20.1)
mechanical digestion (20.1)
chemical digestion (20.1)
villi (20.1)
artery (20.2)
capillary (20.2)
vein (20.2)
bronchi (20.3)
alveoli (20.3)
nephron (20.4)

Check Your Vocabulary

Use the vocabulary words above to complete the following sentences correctly.

1. Blood leaving the heart travels through _____ to all organs and muscles.

2. In the kidneys, a _____ is a system of tubes acting as a filter.

3. Gas exchange occurs in the tiny air sacs of the lungs called _____ .

4. Carbohydrates, proteins, and fats are three important _____ in food.

5. Your teeth cutting, grinding, and mashing food are examples of _____ .

6. The smallest kind of blood vessel is a _____ .

7. Tiny fingerlike projections, or _____ , line the walls of the small intestine.

8. Blood leaves the organs and travels through _____ back to the heart.

9. The breakdown of food into simpler parts that your body can use is called _____ .

10. Air enters a lung after having passed through the _____ .

11. Acids, bases, and enzymes change food during _____ .

Chapter 20 Review

Check Your Knowledge

Answer the following in complete sentences.

1. Name the two ways food may change during digestion.

2. Suppose your blood pressure was 120 over 80. What do the two numbers mean?

3. Name three things you can do to help prevent cardiovascular disease.

4. Why are alveoli covered with a moist film and surrounded by capillaries?

5. Describe three digestive disorders and list their treatments.

6. Where does blood flow after it leaves the right side of your heart?

7. Name three organs that remove wastes from the body.

8. What are the four blood types?

Choose the answer that best completes each sentence.

9. Blood is oxygenated during (digestion, pulmonary circulation, systemic circulation, excretion).

10. Gallstones, heartburn, and ulcers are all disorders of the (digestive, circulatory, respiratory, excretory) system.

11. The lungs, pharynx, and trachea are all parts of the (digestive, circulatory, respiratory, excretory) system.

12. Excess salts, water, and nitrogen wastes form (sweat, urine, nephrons, urea).

13. Nutrients are carried in the blood by (red blood cells, white blood cells, platelets, plasma).

14. Most nutrients are absorbed in the (gallbladder, small intestine, stomach, liver).

Check Your Understanding

Apply the concepts you have learned to answer each question.

1. How is each of the following important in food processing?

   a. Muscle action

   b. Villi

   c. Enzymes

2. Match the body part on the left with its function on the right.

   a. Ureter   Digests proteins

   b. Platelet   Clots blood

   c. Lung   Traps viruses and bacteria

   d. Stomach   Exchanges gases

   e. Lymph node   Carries urine to bladder

3. **Sequence** Where in the human body is carbon dioxide produced? Describe the path it follows until it leaves the body.

4. **Mystery Photo** The photograph on page 414 shows red blood cells. What is the function of these cells? What are the other parts of blood and their functions?

5. Which is richer in oxygen—inhaled air or exhaled air? Which is richer in carbon dioxide?

6. Can you feel a pulse in your veins? Why or why not?

7. **Sequence** Order the basic steps for food digestion and absorption below.

   a. Water is absorbed.

   b. Food is liquified.

   c. Nutrients pass into bloodstream.

   d. Food is broken into smaller pieces.

   e. Wastes are removed from the body.

   f. Food is digested into nutrient forms that cells can use.

Develop Your Skills

Use the skills you have developed in this chapter to complete each question.

1. **Interpret Data** Use the table below to answer the following questions.

   a. During normal weather, what causes the major loss of water to the body?

   b. How does water excretion change during heavy exercise? Why?

   c. On a normal day, the average person takes in about 2.2 L of water. What will happen to you if you do not increase this amount during hot weather?

Table 20.4   Daily Loss of Water in Humans (in mL)

	Normal Weather	Hot Weather	Extended Heavy Exercise
Lungs	350	250	650
Urine	1400	1200	500
Sweat	450	1750	5350
Feces	200	200	200
Total	2400	3400	6700

2. **Data Bank** Use the information on page 627 to answer the following questions.

   a. Which activity uses the least amount of oxygen per hour? The most oxygen?

   b. Which activity probably needs the least amount of energy? The most energy?

   c. **Infer** Explain the relationship between oxygen use and energy need.

3. **Make a Table** Design a table that lists in order the organs of the digestive system. List the functions of each organ. Identify the types of nutrients digested or absorbed at each stage.

Make Connections

1. **Link the Concepts** Below is a concept map showing how some of the main concepts in this chapter link together. Only part of the map is filled in. Copy the map. Using words and ideas from the chapter, finish the map.

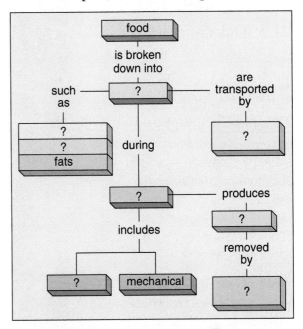

2. **Science and Language Arts** Write a series of metaphors and similes for various human body organs. For example: "The heart is like a geyser that explodes every few seconds."

3. **Science and You** Hold one arm up in the air and let the other arm hang down at your side for two minutes. Compare the color of each hand and how much your veins stand out. What do you think causes the difference?

4. **Science and Technology** Astronauts in space must be able to eat, breathe, and remove wastes from their bodies. Research how scientists meet the oxygen and food needs of astronauts as well as reduce or remove carbon dioxide and food waste buildup.

Chapter 21   Control and Sensing

What do you see?

66This picture seems to have a bunch of nuclei with a stringy substance going to and from each one. I think the surroundings of the picture give it away, because I think they are magnified nerve cells.99

Mike Eaton
Northeast Middle School
Kansas City, Missouri

To find out more about the photograph, look on page 464. As you read this chapter, you will learn about how you control your body and how your senses work.

21.1 Nervous System

Objectives

▶ **Name** the parts of the nervous system and **describe** their functions.

▶ **Explain** how neurons carry impulses throughout the body.

▶ **Describe** the parts of the brain and their functions.

▶ **Make a model** of a reflex.

Skills WarmUp

Infer   Have a partner hold a ruler vertically above the floor. Position your thumb and forefinger around the bottom of the ruler, but don't touch it. Your partner will then drop the ruler at any time. Catch the ruler as soon as you see it falling. Try this a few times. Did you catch it each time? Why did you react to the falling ruler?

H as this ever happened to you? The muffin you heated in the oven smells so good, you can't wait to try it. But as soon as you pick it up, you drop it. Your fingers can't hold the muffin. It's too hot! Even before you knew it was hot, your fingers received the message to let go. What might have happened had you held on to the muffin? What made your fingers let go of the muffin?

Functions of the Nervous System

The reason you'll let go of anything hot, such as the muffin fresh out of the oven, is because of your nervous system. Your nervous system is a communication and control system made up of the brain, spinal cord, and billions of nerves. The nervous system receives information from your environment and from inside your body. The system interprets this information and causes the body to respond to it.

Your nervous system lets you know if something is hot or cold, sweet or bitter, rough or smooth. It controls your movements. It protects you from harm by letting you feel pain. The nervous system even lets you solve problems and learn music. In addition, the nervous system controls reactions that involve emotion. It lets you be happy or sad, angry, or calm.

You wouldn't be wrong if you thought that the nervous system is the most important system in your body. You couldn't even raise an eyebrow without the nervous system. But remember, all human body systems work together to keep you alive.

Figure 21.1 ▲
Reacting to the taste of a bitter lemon is possible because of your nervous system.

Calculate Try the ruler activity again with a partner. This time, have your partner hold the ruler with the zero end closest to the floor. Catch the ruler five times. Record in centimeters the distance the ruler falls past zero before you catch it. Then calculate your average reaction time. How does it compare with your classmates' averages?

Parts of the Nervous System

In the study of the human body, the nervous system is divided into two parts. Look at Figure 21.2. The central nervous system, or CNS, is made up of the brain and spinal cord. The peripheral (puh RIHF uhr uhl) nervous system, or PNS, connects the central nervous system to the rest of the body. It is made of the spinal nerves and the many nerves that branch from the brain and spinal nerves.

Think about the two words that describe the nervous system. *Central* means the main part or most important part of something. *Peripheral* means lying on the outside or away from the central part. By looking at these definitions, you can tell how the two parts of the nervous system were named.

Brain

The brain is the main control center of your body. It directs and coordinates all body processes, thoughts, behaviors, and emotions. It is often compared to a computer. Yet no computer has as much memory or as many connections.

Spinal Nerves

Thirty-one pairs of spinal nerves branch out into both sides of the body from between the vertebrae. Spinal nerves carry messages to and from other nerves. Each nerve contains thousands of nerve fibers.

Spinal Cord

Extending from the base of your brain down your back is a bundle of nerve fibers called the spinal cord. If you want a first-hand idea of where your spinal cord is, try this. Feel the vertebrae in the back of your neck and down your spine. The vertebrae cover and protect the spinal cord.

Nerves

Many nerves branch to all parts of your body. Some go to body organs, such as your heart and lungs. The actions of these nerves are controlled automatically by the brain. Some nerves connect the spinal cord to muscles. These nerves cause muscles to contract.

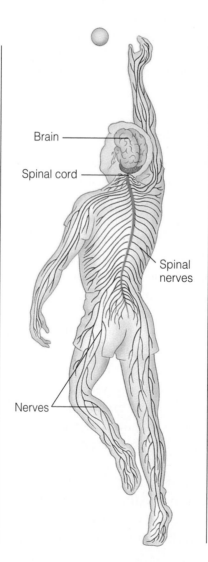

Brain

Spinal cord

Spinal nerves

Nerves

Figure 21.2 ▶
The Human Nervous System

Neurons

Your brain, spinal cord, and nerves are made of nerve cells, or **neurons** (NOO rahns). Each neuron receives and sends electrical and chemical messages.

Look at Figure 21.3. It shows the parts of a neuron. The cell body is like a telephone switchboard that receives and relays incoming messages. Notice that the cell body has a nucleus just like all cells.

The cell body receives electrical messages from branched cell parts called dendrites. Notice that the many short dendrites are close to neighboring neurons. The cell body relays the messages to the long axon. The axon carries nerve impulses away from the cell body. The axon ends in branches, too. These branches of the axon transmit nerve impulses to the dendrites of another neuron.

Nerve Impulses

A neuron uses both electrical and chemical energy to send a nerve impulse. Look again at Figure 21.3 to follow the process. An electrical impulse travels from the dendrites to the cell body. From the cell body, the electrical impulse travels down the axon. But the end of the axon doesn't touch the next neuron. There is a small space between one neuron and the next one. This space between neurons is called a **synapse** (SIHN aps). The electrical impulse stops at the gap. That's when the axon releases a chemical into the synapse.

Chemical energy is used to carry the nerve impulse to the dendrite of the next neuron. The chemicals travel across the synapse. They join with molecules in the dendrites of the next neuron. The chemical energy causes an electrical impulse in the dendrites of this neuron.

Figure 21.3 ▲
Follow the path of an impulse from one neuron to the next. The photo at left shows a neuron magnified 100 times.

Movement — Cerebrum — Touch

Reasoning —

Hearing

Speech —

Vision

Taste —

Balance

Smell —

Cerebellum

Medulla —

Breathing and heart rates

**Figure 21.4
The Human Brain**

The Brain

The brain is made up of more than 10 billion neurons, forming a spongy nerve tissue. The nerve tissue is surrounded by membranes that nourish and protect the brain. The main job of the brain is to receive and interpret messages from outside and inside your body. You can see the three main parts of the brain in Figure 21.4. They are the cerebrum, the cerebellum, and the medulla.

Cerebrum The largest part of your brain is the cerebrum (SUR uh bruhm). The folds in the cerebrum greatly increase the surface area of this part of the brain. More surface area means more neurons.

The cerebrum controls many functions, including all conscious body movement, such as running in a race. The cerebrum also interprets nerve impulses that come from your sense organs—the eyes, ears, nose, tongue, and skin. The cerebrum enables you to see this page.

The cerebrum is divided into two halves. The left half of the cerebrum

controls your ability to speak, use mathematics, and think logically. The right half is the center for musical ability, the creation of art, and the expression of emotions. Nerve paths between the two halves allow them to communicate.

Cerebellum The second largest part of the brain is the cerebellum (SUR uh BEHL uhm). When the cerebrum directs your body to move, the cerebellum makes the motion smooth. It adjusts the impulses of the motor neurons so the motion they cause is not robotlike or jerky. A violinist moves the bow across the strings of the violin when the cerebrum sends impulses to the musician's hands and arms. The cerebellum fine-tunes that motion so the violinist creates a soothing sound.

Medulla The brain stem is a bundle of nerves connecting the cerebrum to the spinal cord. The medulla (mih DUHL uh) is the lowest part of the brain stem. Nerve impulses from the medulla control many automatic body processes, such as heartbeat, breathing, and blood pressure.

The Spinal Cord

The spinal cord connects the brain to the peripheral nervous system. It acts as a highway for the passage of nerve impulses both to and from the brain. Nerve impulses pass through the spinal cord when your brain tells your body to move, such as when you reach for a glass of water. As you grasp the glass, nerve impulses pass through the spinal cord in the other direction to tell the brain that the glass feels cold.

The spinal cord connects with nerves all over your body through spinal nerves. These nerves are made of two kinds of nerve fibers. Some of the fibers lead from the spinal cord to the muscles and cause the muscles to contract. They are made up of neurons called **motor neurons**. Other nerve fibers carry sense information to the spinal cord, which then sends it on to the brain. These fibers are made up of **sensory neurons**. Impulses are carried between sensory and motor neurons by association neurons.

Spinal cord

Vertebrae

Spinal nerve

Figure 21.5 ▲
The nerves in the spinal cord are protected by vertebrae.

Career Corner *Speech Pathologist*

What Does a Speech Pathologist Do?

A ten-year-old boy is struggling to conquer stuttering. A hearing-impaired teenager is learning to speak. A six-year-old girl is working to overcome a lisp. An adult who has suffered a stroke is slowly regaining his speech. The person helping each of these people with problems in speaking is called a speech pathologist. The work of speech pathologists is as varied as the speech disorders they treat.

When treating patients, the pathologist uses various methods. The methods used depend on many factors, including age, type of speech disorder, and case history. A pathologist may use video and audio recording machines. This way, patients can see their lips move on the television screen and hear their speech errors on the tape recorder. The patients learn to speak correctly by watching and listening to the pathologist pronounce the sounds and words correctly. The pathologist will eventually have patients do tongue exercises and drills to help them improve their speech.

If you would like to help people with speech problems, many universities offer training in speech therapy. You need a master's degree in the field to work as a speech pathologist.

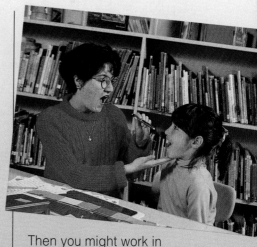

Then you might work in schools, hospitals, or university speech clinics. Speech pathologists with doctorate degrees may teach in colleges or universities. They may also engage in research.

Reflex Actions

Remember the hot muffin? It was too hot to hold, so you immediately dropped it without having to think about dropping it. Dropping the muffin was a reflex action.

A reflex action is a simple response to a stimulus. Sneezing is a reflex. It is automatic. Blinking is also a reflex. It can be automatic or it can be controlled. Reflex actions are controlled by the spinal cord.

Look at the diagram of the reflex in Figure 21.6. The incoming message is switched in the spinal cord directly to outgoing motor neurons. The nerve impulse then travels quickly to the hand or to another part of the body in danger. It causes the body part to move away from the source of the stimulus. The message from the sensory neurons is also sent to the brain. But by the time the message of pain is registered in the brain, the body has already responded.

Figure 21.6

Some quick movements happen as a result of short impulse pathways. ▼

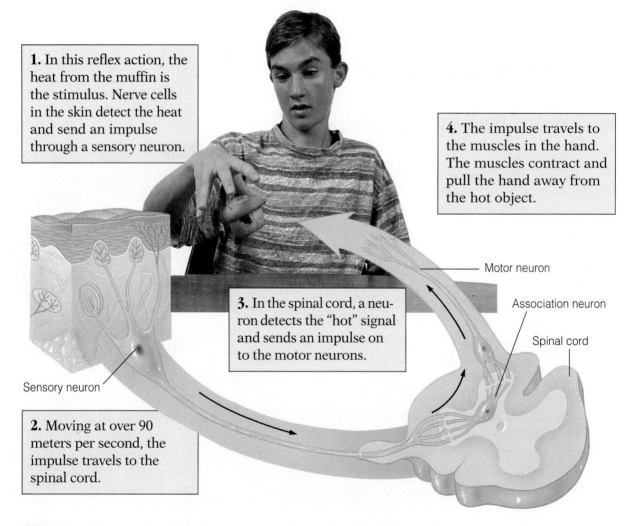

1. In this reflex action, the heat from the muffin is the stimulus. Nerve cells in the skin detect the heat and send an impulse through a sensory neuron.

4. The impulse travels to the muscles in the hand. The muscles contract and pull the hand away from the hot object.

3. In the spinal cord, a neuron detects the "hot" signal and sends an impulse on to the motor neurons.

Motor neuron

Association neuron

Spinal cord

Sensory neuron

2. Moving at over 90 meters per second, the impulse travels to the spinal cord.

Science and Technology *PETs and CATs*

Did you know that it is possible to take a picture of the brain? Pictures of the brain are achieved through a process called computerized tomography, or CT. At one time, X-rays were the only method for obtaining information about the inside of a human body. This method often gave insufficient results because X-rays are most sensitive to bony structures. CT imaging is different. It is like taking a slice out of a loaf of bread without cutting the bread. However, a person is much more complex than bread.

There are two main types of computerized tomography: computerized axial tomography, or CAT, and positron-emission tomography, or PET. A CAT machine is shaped like a human-sized doughnut. When a patient is placed inside the tube, the tube shoots an X-ray beam into the skull. The different tissues in the brain collect the radiation in different ways. The computer takes this information and translates it into a detailed picture of the scanned brain slice. Often many different slices of the brain are imaged. CAT is used to scan for tumors, brain damage from accidents, and cancer.

PET patients ingest a small dose of a radioactive substance. The PET scanner picks up the radiation sent out from the brain. A computer creates pictures of the brain's activity in blues and yellows. PET scans have been used for research on people affected by mental illness, Alzheimer's disease, and epilepsy.

Figure 21.7 ▲
CAT scans are used to detect problems in the brain, such as tumors.

Check and Explain

1. List the parts of the nervous system and describe the function of each.

2. Which part of the brain did you use in answering the first question?

3. **Infer** Drugs called anesthetics are used during surgery. An anesthetic stops the transmission of nerve impulses at the synapses. How does this help a patient being operated on?

4. **Make a Model** Create a model that shows how a nerve impulse travels through a neuron and across a synapse.

21.2 The Senses

Objectives

▶ **Describe** the function of sensory receptors.

▶ **Identify** the different stimuli the senses can detect.

▶ **Outline** the processes of seeing, hearing, smelling, tasting, and touching.

▶ **Make inferences** about possible causes of deafness.

How would your life be different without your sense of sight? How would you communicate with people if you couldn't hear? Would you enjoy eating if you couldn't taste your food? Your senses work together with your brain to keep you informed about your environment. They provide pleasure, keep you from danger, and help you interact with others.

Sensory Receptors

You know that you use your eyes to see, your ears to hear, your nose to smell, your tongue to taste, and your skin to feel. Each of these sensory organs is sensitive to certain parts of the world around you. Each is able to detect a certain kind of stimulus. Your eyes see, for example, by picking up the stimulus provided by rays of light.

How are your sensory organs able to perform their functions? They contain special nerve cells called sensory receptors. The function of a sensory receptor is to take in a stimulus and convert it into nerve impulses. These impulses can then be transmitted to the brain. Here they become the experience of sight, sound, taste, touch, or smell.

The sensory receptors in your eyes detect light rays. The receptors pick up different colors and brightnesses and create nerve impulses to match. The sensory receptors in your tongue and nose sense different chemicals. In your ears, sensory receptors respond to sound waves. One kind of receptor in your skin detects pressure and another senses heat.

Figure 21.8 ▲
How do your senses help you experience a roller coaster ride?

**Figure 21.9a
The Human Eye** ▼

Optic nerve

Iris

Lens

Pupil

Cornea

Aqueous
humor

Retina

Choroid

Sclera

Figure 21.9b ▲
The photograph above
shows a cross section of
the human eye.

Light and Seeing

Light doesn't just let you see, it *is* what you see. Light rays enter your eyes. Your eyes and your brain work together to form and interpret images of the objects that you see.

Structure of the Eye Look at Figure 21.9a. Your eye is made up of three layers. The tough, white, outer covering of most of the eye is called the sclera (SKLUR uh). The middle layer is the choroid (KOR oyd) layer. Lining the back and sides of the inner eye is the **retina** (REHT ih nuh).

In the front of the eye, the choroid layer has an opening called the **pupil**. Surrounding the pupil is a round, colored disk called the **iris**. The iris controls how much light enters the eye by changing the size of the pupil. Behind the pupil is a piece of clear tissue called the lens. The lens is attached to muscles that can change its shape.

The retina is a layer of nerve tissue made up of receptors called rods and cones that detect light and color.

Light and Image Light bounces off objects in the world. Some of it enters your eye. The lens then focuses, or gathers together, the rays of light. By changing its shape, the lens changes how the light rays bend when they pass through it. In this way, the lens focuses the rays of light so that they form a clear image when they strike the retina. This image is an upside-down likeness of the object the light rays are bouncing off of.

The rods and cones in the retina detect the image. They convert it, piece by piece, into nerve impulses sent to the brain along the optic nerve. The brain uses the impulses to remake the image. In the process, it turns the image right-side up. It also combines the two slightly different images from each eye to make a three-dimensional image.

Sound and Hearing

Extend your ruler over the edge of your desk. Lightly flick the end of the ruler. What do you hear? Notice that as the ruler vibrates, it makes a sound.

Sound Waves   All sound comes from vibration. When an object vibrates, it causes the molecules in the air around it to push together and stretch apart. This movement of air molecules is a sound wave. Sound waves move outward from the source of the vibration. They can travel through solids, liquids, and gases.

The ear picks up sound waves and converts them into nerve impulses. With the help of the brain, you experience sound waves as sound.

Hearing   Look at Figure 21.10. As you can see, most of your ear is hidden inside your head. The external ear is only a funnel that helps collect sound waves. Sound waves pass through the ear canal and strike a thin, round, tightly stretched membrane called the **eardrum.** When sound waves strike the eardrum, it vibrates.

A chain of three tiny bones is attached to the inner surface of the eardrum. The eardrum's vibrations are transmitted to these three bones. The bones pass the vibrations on to the **cochlea** (KAHK lee uh). It is a fluid-filled structure that makes up the inner ear.

The vibrations move through the fluid in the cochlea. The cochlea contains nerve endings that detect the vibrations and convert them into nerve impulses. The nerve impulses are carried to the brain by the auditory nerve.

Balance   The semicircular canals you can see in Figure 21.10 are not involved with hearing. They enable you to keep your balance. The canals are filled with fluid and motion receptors. When you move or rotate your head, the fluid in the canals shifts, affecting the receptors. The receptors send nerve impulses to the brain, which detects the way you moved and coordinates muscle movements that keep you balanced.

Figure 21.10 ▲
The curved tubes in the photograph are the semicircular canals.

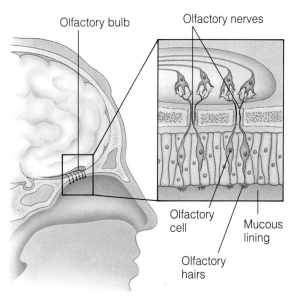

Figure 21.11 ▲
Smell receptors in the nose

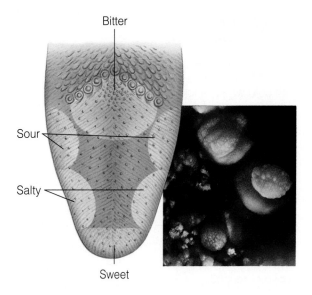

Figure 21.12 ▲
Taste buds in the tongue (left); photograph of clusters of taste buds (right)

Smell

Think about what happens to you when a meal is being cooked near you. What are the odors, and how does your brain detect them? All odors are chemicals carried in the air.

The food you'll eat at a meal gives off different chemicals as it is cooked. These chemicals are molecules in the gaseous state. When you breathe, you take in some of these molecules. The molecules dissolve in the mucus that lines the tissues inside your nose. They stimulate sensory receptors located in this tissue. The receptors change odor stimuli into nerve impulses. Look at Figure 21.11. These nerve impulses are carried by the olfactory nerves to the brain.

It is not clearly understood how you can tell one odor from another. It may be that different odor receptors respond to different kinds of chemicals. At least 7, and perhaps as many as 50, basic odors can be distinguished. Most smells are different combinations of several of these basic odors.

Taste

The aroma of a food you like makes you want to taste it. Like smell, taste is the result of chemicals being detected by sensory receptors. The sensory receptors on your tongue, however, respond to molecules in the liquid state or molecules dissolved in liquid.

Look at Figure 21.12. Your tongue's sensory receptors are called taste buds. Taste buds give you four different kinds of taste sensations: salty, sweet, bitter, and sour.

Your taste buds are all very similar, but some are more sensitive to each of the four taste sensations. This may explain how areas of the tongue specialize in sensing either saltiness, sweetness, sourness, or bitterness. Find where these areas are located in Figure 21.12.

Have you noticed that when you have a cold it is harder to taste food? That is because most "tastes" are actually combinations of tastes and smells. When your nose is blocked, it can't detect the odors of food very well.

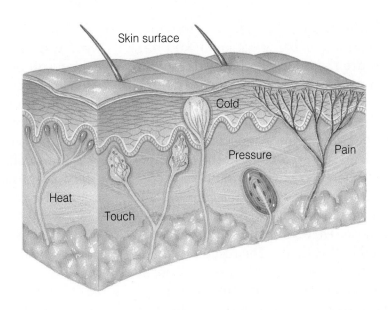

Skills WorkOut

Observe Fill one jar or bowl with cold water, another with warm water, and a third with water just hot enough to touch. Label each jar. Place one forefinger in the hot water and the other forefinger in the cold water for one minute. Then put both fingers in the warm water jar. Describe what happens. What does this tell you about your sense of touch?

Figure 21.13 ▶
There are different kinds of receptors in the skin. Touch receptors are located near the surface of the skin. Pain receptors are located deep within the skin.

Touch

What are the different sensations you can feel with your skin? You can detect cold and heat. You can tell the difference between the touch of a feather and the touch of someone's hand. You can feel pricking pain and aching pain. Each of these sensations is detected by a certain kind of sensory receptor in the skin.

You can see in Figure 21.13 that these receptors occur at different levels in the skin. They are also distributed unevenly. You have many more pain receptors than cold receptors, for example. Touch and pressure receptors are concentrated on the hands and fingertips. Where else do you have large numbers of touch receptors?

Even though the skin contains many kinds of receptors, they fall into three main groups. Touch receptors and pressure receptors both detect movement or pressure. Cold and heat receptors both respond to temperature changes. Pain receptors detect many kinds of stimuli but are placed in a group of their own.

Skin surface
Cold
Pain
Pressure
Heat
Touch

Pain is an especially important sense for survival. Imagine, for example, if you couldn't feel the burning sensation of a hot muffin. Pain is felt in different ways. For example, if you've cut yourself, you know that the result is an intense, quick pain. If you've burned yourself, the painful feeling usually develops slowly and is long lasting. Have you ever had an aching pain? What does it feel like?

Tasting Without Smelling?

Prepare small, peeled cubes of an apple, potato, carrot, turnip, and onion—all the same size. Place the pieces on a plate. Blindfold a partner, so she can't see what kind of cube you choose. Tell your partner to hold her nose while you place a cube on her tongue with a spoon.

Copy the table at right. After your partner chews the cube, ask which food she has eaten. Make a check mark on the chart under that food. Draw a star under what the cube really is. If your partner guesses correctly, the check and the star will be in the same box. After your partner tastes each food, switch roles. This time you will taste while your partner records.

Trial	Apple	Potato	Carrot	Turnip	Onion
1					
2					
3					
4					
1					
2					
3					
4					

1. Why was it difficult to determine which food you were eating?

2. Which foods were the hardest to distinguish? Why?

3. What clues did you use to determine what you were eating?

4. When have you not been able to taste food? Write why it is important to be able to smell food.

Science and You *Too Close or Too Far?*

How many people do you know who wear glasses or contact lenses? What are some reasons people wear glasses?

People's eyes are not always able to function normally. Glasses or contact lenses correct many people's vision problems. Two of the most common vision problems are nearsightedness and farsightedness.

When you view a distant object, your lens flattens to project the image of the object farthest from the lens. For a person with normal vision, the image falls on the retina. If the eyeball is too long, the image forms in front of the retina, as you can see in Figure 21.14. Nearsighted people can't see distant things clearly. Nearsightedness can be corrected by wearing lenses that are thinner in the middle than at the edges. These lenses bring the image back on the retina, where it should be, and into focus.

Nearsighted vision

Farsighted vision

Concave lens

Convex lens

Nearsighted, corrected

Farsighted, corrected

Figure 21.14 ▲
A concave lens (left) corrects nearsighted vision. A convex lens (right) corrects farsighted vision.

When you view a close object, your lens thickens to project the image of the object closer to the lens. If the eyeball is too short, the image forms behind the retina. People are farsighted if they can't see near things clearly. A farsighted person wears lenses that are thicker in the middle than at the edges. These lenses bend the light so the image is focused somewhat sooner, making it fall on the retina.

Focusing on close objects often becomes more difficult as you grow older. The reason is that the lenses in your eyes harden and lose their ability to change shape. The lenses cannot become thick enough to see close objects.

Check and Explain

1. What is the function of a sensory receptor?

2. Explain how you can see the words on this page.

3. **Compare and Contrast** How is the eye like a camera? In what ways is it different from a camera?

4. **Infer** At which places could the transmission of sound from object to brain be blocked, causing deafness?

Activity 21 *Are two eyes better than one?*

Skills Observe; Infer; Interpret Data

Task 1 Prelab Prep
1. Collect the following items: a cup and several pennies.
2. Put the cup on a table.

Task 2 Data Record
1. On a sheet of paper, draw the data table shown. Write the number of each trial.
2. Use the table to record your observations about where the penny falls.

Table 21.1 Guiding the Pennies

One Eye Closed	
Trial	Result
1	
2	
3	
4	
5	

Both Eyes Open	
Trial	Result
1	
2	
3	
4	
5	

Task 3 Procedure
1. Sit at least a meter away from the cup. Cover one of your eyes while a friend holds a penny at arm's length above the cup. The penny should be held slightly in front of the cup.
2. Watch only the cup and the penny. Tell your friend where to move his or her hand so the penny appears to be directly above the cup.
3. Remind your friend to move the penny exactly as you say—no more, no less. When you think the penny will fall into the cup, say, "Drop." Check how close you came. Record your results.
4. Repeat steps 1–3 four more times with the same eye closed.
5. Repeat steps 1–3 five times with both eyes open.

Task 4 Analysis
1. Identify the variable in this activity.
2. With one eye closed, why were you not able to judge the right position from which your friend should drop the penny?
3. How much did your accuracy improve with two eyes open instead of one?
4. Why weren't you told to cover the other eye for some of the drops?

Task 5 Conclusion
Write a short paragraph explaining how two eyes help you judge distances and depth.

Everyday Application

Suppose the eye doctor orders you to wear a patch over one eye for three weeks. What are some activities you should avoid? What are a few clues that might help you to judge depth?

Extension

Most mammals have eyes set at the sides of their heads. The primates, however, have eyes that face forward, and as a result they have stereoscopic vision, or the ability to perceive depth. Develop a hypothesis to explain why primates have depth perception and other mammals do not.

21.3 Endocrine System

Objectives

▶ **Describe** the major endocrine glands and their functions.

▶ **Explain** how hormone levels in the body are regulated.

▶ **Identify** several disorders of the endocrine system.

▶ **Predict** the effects of extra growth hormone on a normal person.

When can you run the fastest—racing in a 100-meter dash, or trying to escape an attacking dog? Most likely, the fear of the dog would boost your speed more than the desire to win a race. Why can you run faster when you are afraid?

The answer is that a substance called adrenaline (uh DREHN uh luhn) gives you a boost when you are frightened. Adrenaline causes many quick changes in your body. These changes make you faster and stronger for a short period of time. At what other times do you feel a boost from adrenaline?

Adrenaline is produced by a body system called the endocrine (EHN doh krihn) system. The endocrine system works closely with the nervous system. Like the nervous system, it functions to control many body processes. But the endocrine system uses chemicals, not nerve impulses, to perform its function.

Endocrine Glands

A gland is an organ that produces a chemical needed somewhere in the body. You have already learned about the glands that have ducts. They distribute their chemical directly to another organ. Another kind of gland, an **endocrine gland**, does not have a duct. An endocrine gland releases the chemicals it makes directly into the bloodstream.

Endocrine glands are the major organs of the endocrine system. The chemicals made by endocrine glands are called **hormones** (HOR mohnz). Hormones cause changes in other organs and regulate many body activities. There are 7 major endocrine glands in the human body, and more than 50 different hormones.

Pituitary Gland   Look at Figure 21.15. At the base of the cerebrum is a pea-sized gland called the pituitary (pih TOO uh TAIR ee) gland. Despite its small size, some people call it the "master gland" because it releases hormones that control several other glands. The pituitary has two lobes, each of which produces and stores a different set of hormones.

Among the many hormones produced by the pituitary is human growth hormone, or HGH. HGH controls how fast your muscles, bones, and organs grow. It determines the height you will reach when you are an adult.

The pituitary also stores hormones made by a part of the brain called the hypothalamus (HY poh THAL uh muhs). These hormones regulate blood pressure, water absorption in the kidneys, and the contraction of some smooth muscles in the body. The hypothalamus and the pituitary are closely connected and serve as a link between the nervous system and the endocrine system.

Thyroid Gland   One gland that the pituitary controls is the thyroid (THY royd). Find this gland in Figure 21.15. The thyroid gland produces the hormone thyroxine (thy RAHKS een), which regulates your body's metabolism. Remember that metabolism is all the chemical reactions that provide energy for the body and allow it to grow. The thyroid is located at the base of the neck beneath the larynx. It lies on the trachea. It also produces calcitonin (KAL sih TOH nihn), a hormone that controls the levels of calcium and phosphorus in the body.

Pancreas   You have already learned about the pancreas as a digestive gland. Locate the pancreas in Figure 21.15. A part of the pancreas is an endocrine gland as well. The pancreas releases a

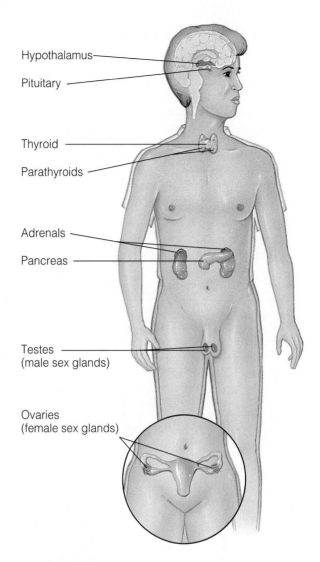

Figure 21.15 ▲
The endocrine systems of males and females are somewhat different. What endocrine glands are found only in females?

hormone called insulin (IHN seh lihn). This hormone helps transport sugar from the blood into the body cells, where it can be used for energy. This lowers the level of sugar in the blood.

The pancreas also produces glucagon (GLOO kuh GAHN). Its function is the opposite of insulin. Glucagon raises the blood sugar level. It does this by causing the liver to release the glucose stored there, making it available to the cells.

Table 21.2   Endocrine Glands

Gland	Hormone	Function
Pituitary	Growth hormone	Regulates growth of bones
	Thyroid-stimulating hormone	Stimulates thyriod to secrete hormones
	Gonadotropic hormone	Affects development of sex organs
Thyroid	Thyroxine	Increases metabolism
	Calcitonin	Controls level of calcium and phosphorus in the blood
Parathyroids	Parathyroid hormone	Regulates amount of calcium in bone
Adrenals	Adrenaline	Stimulates organs to respond to emergencies
Pancreas	Glucagon	Stimulates release of glucose from liver
	Insulin	Stimulates storage of glucose in liver
Ovaries	Estrogen	Produces female secondary sex characteristics
	Progesterone	Promotes growth of uterine lining
Testes	Testosterone	Produces male secondary sex characteristics

Feedback Control of Hormone Levels

Too much or too little of a hormone can cause serious health problems. Hormone levels are tightly controlled by a feedback system that automatically turns an endocrine gland on or off. You can compare feedback to a thermostat in a building. When the temperature inside the building drops below a set temperature, a signal turns the furnace on. What happens when the building temperature reaches the set temperature? The thermostat then signals the furnace to turn off.

The feedback mechanism in your body works like this. When a hormone is needed, a chemical signal tells the right gland to make more of it. When there is enough hormone to do the job, it causes a certain effect in the body. This effect acts as a signal for the gland to stop producing that hormone.

Look at Figure 21.16, which shows how the feedback mechanism controls blood sugar levels. When blood glucose levels fall below normal, the pancreas responds by releasing glucagon into the bloodstream. Glucagon acts on the liver to increase the rate at which the stored glucose is

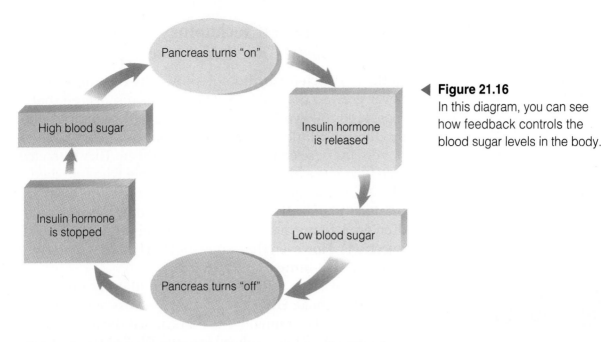

◀ **Figure 21.16**
In this diagram, you can see how feedback controls the blood sugar levels in the body.

changed to sugar. As the level of sugar rises in the blood, insulin is released by the pancreas. Insulin increases the transport of glucose from the blood into cells, causing the level of sugar in the blood to fall again. The level of sugar in the blood, therefore, is balanced by the two hormones.

Disorders of the Endocrine System

The endocrine system is in a state of delicate balance. Sometimes one of the endocrine glands fails to work properly, and the balance of the system is upset. The result is one of the endocrine disorders listed in Table 21.3.

Table 21.3   Endocrine Disorders

Disorder	Description	Cause
Diabetes	Inability of cells to properly use glucose	Too little insulin
Dwarfism	Below-normal growth	Too little human growth hormone
Gigantism	Above-normal growth	Too much human growth hormone
Goiter	Enlargement of thyroid and neck	Too little iodine in the diet
Hyperactivity	Weight loss and high level of nervousness	Too much thyroxine

Science and Technology
Synthetic Growth Hormone

In the past, scientists did not know why certain people never grew to normal size. Then it was discovered that most kinds of dwarfism occurred when the pituitary gland produced too little human growth hormone (HGH). With this discovery, scientists could treat dwarfism. They extracted HGH from the pituitary glands of people who had died. This HGH was injected into the bodies of children whose pituitary glands did not produce enough HGH. The children grew to normal height if they received regular HGH injections. However, the supply of HGH collected in this way was very limited.

Then in 1979, scientists succeeded in programming bacteria to make HGH through the process of genetic engineering. The human gene that carried the instructions for making HGH was spliced into the DNA of the bacteria. Large numbers of bacteria containing the HGH gene were cloned. The HGH produced by the bacteria was collected and purified. HGH produced in this way was approved for use in 1985. It is used in treating children whose growth is far below normal.

The synthetic hormone has helped many children grow to a normal height. Taking the hormone is not without some risk, however. Regulating the dose given to each child is very difficult. Also, the hormone can stimulate the leg bones to grow so fast that they slip out of the hip socket. Most people, however, think that using HGH is worth the risk.

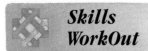

Skills WorkOut

Research Find out more about the disease diabetes. How is diabetes currently being treated? What advances have been made in the search for a cure? Write a one-page report on your findings.

Check and Explain

1. List the major endocrine glands, the hormones they produce, and the function of each hormone.

2. What does it mean for hormone levels to be controlled by feedback?

3. **Infer** Knowing that lack of iodine in the diet causes a disorder affecting the thyroid gland, what can you infer about the hormone thyroxine?

4. **Predict** A normal adult takes a dose of human growth hormone. What might happen? Why? What might happen if a normal teenager took HGH?

Chapter 21 Review

Concept Summary

21.1 Nervous System

▶ The nervous system is the communication and control system of your body. It includes the brain, spinal cord, and nerves.

▶ Nerve impulses travel through neurons using electrical and chemical energy.

▶ The brain consists of the cerebrum, cerebellum, and medulla. The spinal cord connects the brain to the rest of the body.

21.2 The Senses

▶ Sensory receptors in your body allow you to convert stimulus to sense.

▶ The senses allow you to smell, taste, touch, see, and hear.

▶ Your senses work with your brain to keep you informed about your environment.

21.3 Endocrine System

▶ Endocrine glands release chemicals needed by the body directly into the bloodstream.

▶ The major endocrine glands are the pituitary, thyroid, parathyroid, adrenal, pancreas, ovaries (in females) and testes (in males).

▶ Hormone levels in the body are regulated by endocrine glands. Hormones cause changes in other organs and regulate many body activities.

▶ Diabetes, dwarfism, gigantism, goiter, and hyperactivity are disorders of the endocrine system.

Chapter Vocabulary

neuron (21.1)	sensory neuron (21.1)	iris (21.2)	endocrine gland (21.3)
synapse (21.1)	retina (21.2)	eardrum (21.2)	hormone (21.3)
motor neuron (21.1)	pupil (21.2)	cochlea (21.2)	

Check Your Vocabulary

Use the vocabulary terms above to complete the following sentences correctly.

1. The three tiny bones of the ear transfer sound vibrations to the _____ .

2. Hormones are released directly into the bloodstream by _____ .

3. A nerve cell, or _____ , receives and sends electrical messages.

4. Nerve tissue in the _____ is made of light and color receptors.

5. Light entering the eye is controlled by the _____ , a round, colored disk.

6. Thyroxine is a _____ that regulates your body's metabolism.

7. Nerve fibers that lead from the spinal cord to the muscles are called _____ .

8. Nerve fibers carrying sense information to the spinal cord are called _____ .

9. In the front of the eye, the choroid layer has an opening called the _____ .

10. Chemicals are released into the small space, or _____ , that exists between one neuron and the next.

11. Sound waves strike the _____ , causing it to vibrate.

Write Your Vocabulary

Write sentences using each vocabulary word above. Show that you know what each word means.

Check Your Knowledge

Answer the following in complete sentences.

1. What is the function of the nervous system?

2. Name the two main parts of the nervous system.

3. Name three endocrine glands and their role in the endocrine system.

4. Describe what sensory receptors do. Give an example.

5. What is a reflex action? Where are reflex actions controlled?

6. Describe two disorders of the endocrine system, and their causes.

7. List the parts of the brain.

Determine whether each statement is true or false. Write *true* if it is true. If it is false, change the underlined word to make the statement true.

8. The largest part of the brain is the <u>cerebrum</u>.

9. Hormones are produced by the <u>nervous</u> system.

10. Taste is the result of <u>motion</u> being detected by sensory receptors.

11. The ear picks up <u>sound waves</u> and converts them into nerve impulses.

12. Human growth hormone is produced by the <u>thyroid</u> gland.

13. Hormone levels are tightly controlled by a feedback system that automatically turns a(n) <u>endocrine</u> gland on or off.

14. The brain is called the main <u>control center</u> of the body because it directs and coordinates all body processes, thoughts, behaviors, and emotions.

Check Your Understanding

Apply the concepts you have learned to answer each question.

1. **Critical Thinking** Describe the path of the reflex that occurs when a person steps on a sharp object.

2. Why can having a cold affect your sense of taste?

3. **Critical Thinking** Compare the endocrine system and the nervous system. How are they similar? How are they different?

4. **Mystery Photo** The photo on page 442 shows human nerve cells, or neurons. The photograph is a false-color electromicrograph: a photograph taken through an electron microscope.

   a. What are neurons and what do they do?

   b. What is the space between neurons, and how do impulses cross the gap?

5. **Application** Describe three things you could not experience without your senses. Identify the sense necessary to fulfill that experience.

6. **Extension** Reflex actions that involve heat receptors are faster than any other kind of reflex action. Why do you think this is important for your body?

7. What endocrine gland(s) could help you win a swimming race? Describe how the gland(s) can help you in this situation.

8. **Infer** After riding on a roller coaster that takes you on a series of loops, and comes to a stop, you still feel like you are spinning. What sense is related to this sensation? Why?

9. When you are in bright light, your pupils become small. When you move into dim light, they become large. What part of the eye controls this change?

Develop Your Skills

Use the skills you have developed in this chapter to complete each activity.

1. **Interpret Data** Sound is measured in hertz (Hz). Humans cannot hear sounds that measure much more than 10,000 Hz. The graph below shows the hearing ranges for various organisms. Study the graph, then answer the following questions.

   a. Which organisms have similar hearing ranges?

   b. Which organism is most sensitive to sounds? Explain why you think this organism has a wide hearing range.

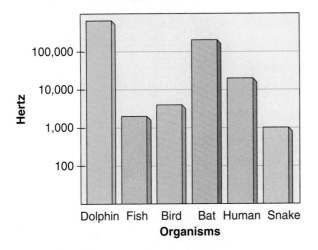

2. **Data Bank** Use the information on page 626 to answer the following questions.

   a. How long do brain cells live?

   b. **Infer** Why does a brain cell live so much longer than a skin cell?

3. **Define Operationally** Decide whether each of the following is a reflex action or a voluntary action:

   a. Coughing after eating spicy food.

   b. Climbing a tree.

   c. Blinking when a bug flies in your eye.

Make Connections

1. **Link the Concepts** Below is a concept map showing how some of the main concepts in this chapter link together. Only part of the map is filled in. Copy and finish the map, using words and ideas from the chapter.

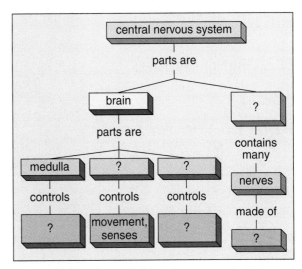

2. **Science and Art** Look through art reference books and find examples of optical illusions. For example, drawings and paintings by M.C. Escher are famous for their optical effects. After studying some optical illusions in drawings and paintings, see if you can draw some of your own. Test them out on a partner. See if your partner can "figure out" your illusion. Why do you think you see optical illusions?

3. **Science and You** Think of some things you do every day, like brushing your teeth or eating your lunch. Which of your senses do you use to do these activities? Imagine what it would be like to do the same activities if you had lost one of your senses, such as vision. What other senses might you use instead?

Chapter 22 Reproduction and Life Stages

What do you see?

❞I see the fetus of a human baby. It is in the mother's uterus. It has been developing for about 3¾ months. The fetus has all its toes and fingers. Its body is catching up to its head in size. This image was created by ultrasound.❞

Tim Kelley
Memorial Junior High
Minot, North Dakota

To find out more about the photograph, look on page 484. As you read this chapter, you will learn about growth and reproduction in humans.

466

22.1 Human Reproductive Systems

Objectives

▶ **Name** and **describe** the male and female reproductive organs and their functions.

▶ **Explain** the process of menstruation.

▶ **Communicate** how hormones are part of the reproductive systems in males and females.

D o you ever look at your old school pictures and wonder who that little kid was? You have been growing and changing since you were born. You'll change and grow up in different ways over the next few years, too. Sometime between ages 10 and 15, girls and boys usually experience a growth spurt. They not only get taller, but their bodies also begin to change in other ways. In girls, the mammary glands in their breasts develop and their hips widen. Boys begin to develop facial hair. Their voices deepen, and their shoulders broaden.

These changes in females and males are caused by the hormones produced in the reproductive system. They signal the beginning of sexual maturity, which is the ability to reproduce. The time when the human body becomes sexually mature and capable of reproducing is called puberty. Puberty usually occurs between ages 9 to 14 for females, and 11 to 16 for males. However, it can occur earlier or later, too.

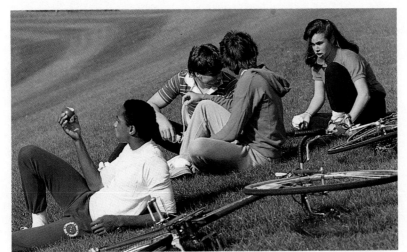

Figure 22.1
◀ Females and males both experience many physical and emotional changes during puberty.

The Male Reproductive System

The changes in the body of a male are triggered by the hormone testosterone (tehs TAHS tur OHN). Testosterone is produced in the male sex glands, the **testes** (TEHS teez). Look at Figure 22.2 and find the testes. Notice that they are inside the **scrotum** (SKROHT uhm), a protective sac.

Because the scrotum is outside the male's body, the testes can maintain a cooler temperature than the rest of the body. This is important for the production of sperm cells. Sperm cells are male sex cells. Sperm can only survive at a temperature that is a few degrees cooler than the body. Production of sperm begins at puberty. During the rest of a male's lifetime, the testes will make hundreds of billions of sperm.

Notice in Figure 22.2 that the testes connect to two sperm ducts. Sperm are stored in these ducts after they are produced in the testes. The two sperm ducts connect to the urethra. As sperm move from the sperm ducts to the urethra, they are mixed with fluids. These nutrient-rich fluids are produced by glands. The fluids protect the sperm, and provide sperm with energy. With this energy, sperm can swim as well as survive outside the male's body. The mixture of sperm cells and fluids is called **semen** (SEE muhn).

As you can see in Figure 22.2, the urethra extends through the **penis**. The penis is the external male organ through which both semen and urine flow out of the body. However, they do not mix. Only one fluid at a time enters the urethra. The penis also releases semen into the female's body during sexual intercourse.

Figure 22.2

The male reproductive system; a close-up view of a testis is shown. ▼

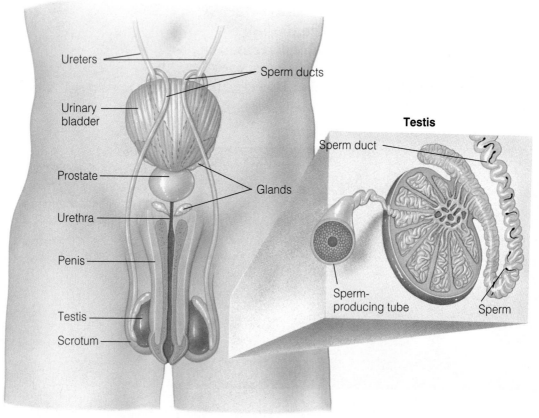

The Female Reproductive System

The changes in the body of a female are triggered by the hormone estrogen (EHS truh juhn). Estrogen is produced in the female sex glands, the **ovaries** (OH vuh reez). Find the ovaries in Figure 22.3.

The ovaries contain egg cells. When a female is born, her ovaries already hold all the eggs she will ever have. At birth, these eggs are tiny. During the years that a female can have children, one egg will mature each month. A mature egg is the largest cell in the human body.

Look at Figure 22.3. When an egg matures in one of the two ovaries, it is released into an **oviduct** (OH vih DUHKT). The oviducts are close to the ovaries, but they aren't actually connected to them. In an oviduct, **fertilization** occurs. Fertilization is the process in which an egg cell and sperm cell unite to form one cell, called a zygote.

The egg is swept through the oviduct by cilia into the **uterus** (YOOT uhr uhs). The uterus is a hollow organ with muscular walls. A zygote will embed itself into the lining of the uterus. There the zygote begins to divide and grow. Eventually, the egg will develop into a baby. If the egg is not fertilized, it dies and passes out of the female's body.

Notice that the lower end of the uterus opens to a canal called the cervix (SUR vihks). The cervix is connected to the **vagina** (vuh JY nuh), a passageway leading to the outside of the female's body. The vagina receives the male penis during sexual intercourse. The penis releases semen into the vagina. A female has a separate opening for releasing urine.

The vagina is also called the birth canal. When a baby is born, it passes from the uterus, through the cervix, and out of the body through the vagina.

Figure 22.3

The female reproductive system; a front and side view is shown. ▼

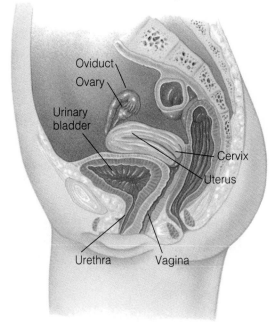

The Female Reproductive Cycle

The female reproductive cycle is actually two cycles and two hormones working together. Both cycles, the menstrual (MEHN struhl) cycle and the ovulatory (AHV yoo luh TOR ee) cycle, occur each month within 14 days of each other. During the ovulatory cycle, which is controlled by the hormone estrogen, an egg matures and is released. The menstrual cycle, which is controlled by the hormone progesterone, prepares the uterus for the fertilized egg. Look at Figure 22.4 as you read about the interaction of the menstrual and ovulatory cycles.

Together, both cycles take about 28 days to complete, although it may vary from month to month. A female's first menstrual cycle usually begins between the ages of 11 and 14.

Figure 22.4

In the female reproductive system, the menstrual cycle occurs each month. On what day does ovulation begin? ▼

Menstrual Cycle   During the menstrual cycle, progesterone causes the lining of the uterus to thicken. The blood vessels and fluids that develop there will nourish the fertilized egg. If the egg is not fertilized, the lining breaks down and **menstruation** (MEHN STRAY shun)

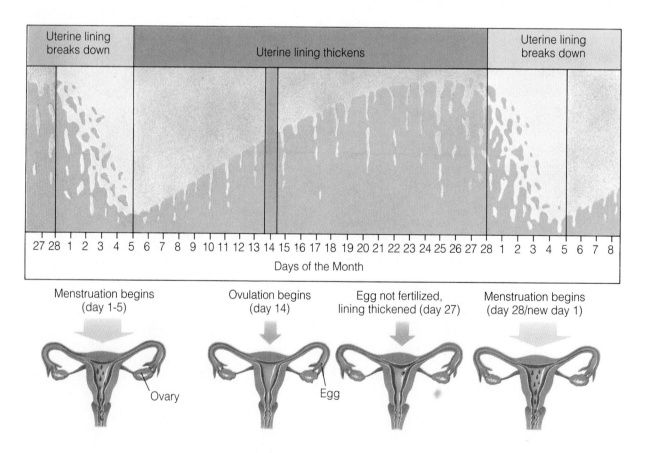

Uterine lining breaks down | Uterine lining thickens | Uterine lining breaks down

27 28 1 2 3 4 5 6 7 8 9 10 11 12 13 14 15 16 17 18 19 20 21 22 23 24 25 26 27 28 1 2 3 4 5 6 7 8

Days of the Month

Menstruation begins (day 1-5)

Ovulation begins (day 14)

Egg not fertilized, lining thickened (day 27)

Menstruation begins (day 28/new day 1)

Ovary

Egg

begins. During the menstrual period, which lasts for three to seven days, the blood and tissue of the uterine lining and the unfertilized egg flow from the uterus. The flow leaves the body through the vagina.

These bodily changes that occur during the menstrual cycle sometimes cause abdominal cramps. In the week before menstruation, some women also experience premenstrual syndrome, or PMS. PMS can bring on a number of symptoms, including headaches, weight gain, tension, or depression. Although many women are not affected by PMS, it can be a serious problem for some.

Ovulatory Cycle   About 14 days after the onset of menstruation, a drop in the estrogen level triggers the release of a mature egg from the ovary. This marks the beginning of the ovulatory cycle. If the egg is fertilized, it attaches itself to the lining of the uterus and pregnancy begins. If the egg is not fertilized, menstruation occurs about 14 days after ovulation.

SkillBuilder   *Making a Model*

Charting the Menstrual Cycle

You will be modeling a female's 28-day menstrual cycle. Choose any 2-month period. Use a large sheet of paper and colored pencils to make a timeline showing all the dates of these 2 months. Be sure to label the days and the dates on your timeline.

Assume that the menstrual period lasts 5 days, that an egg is released from the ovary on the 14th day of the month, and that the egg is not fertilized. Refer to Figure 22.4 on page 470. Use the illustration to label what is happening each day of the month. Be sure to mark the following events on the timeline:

▶ Day when the uterine lining breaks down.

▶ Days when the uterine lining builds up.

▶ Day when the menstrual cycle begins.

▶ Day when ovulation begins.

After labeling the dates, make drawings of the uterine lining that show what is happening to it during the cycle. Draw the oviducts, the ovaries, and the movement of the egg. Then label all of these parts. Compare your drawing to Figure 22.4.

1. When could fertilization occur in this cycle?

2. When will ovulation begin again?

3. When will the first menstrual period begin? The second? Mark the start of the second period on your timeline.

4. Why does the uterine lining thicken? Why does it break down?

Sometimes a female's menstrual cycle is affected by factors such as stress and strenuous exercise. In a paragraph, infer how these factors might affect the cycle.

Science and Society *STDs*

A serious problem in many countries today is the spread of diseases by sexual contact. A sexually transmitted disease, or STD, is caused by either a virus or a bacterium. For example, chlamydia (kluh MID ee uh) and gonorrhea (GAHN uh REE uh) are two STDs caused by bacteria. Both of these diseases can cause painful urination or a cloudy discharge from the sex organs. However, there are often no symptoms, especially in the early stages. Complications, such as severe infections, may eventually occur if an infected person does not seek treatment. If caught in time, chlamydia and gonorrhea can be cured with antibiotics.

Syphilis (SIHF uh luhs) is also a bacterial disease that causes serious problems if it is not treated. Symptoms include sores on the mouth and sex organs, rashes, and a fever. Although these symptoms disappear, the bacteria remain in the blood. Years later the bacteria can cause blindness, paralysis, mental disorders, or heart failure.

Genital herpes (HUR peez) is a viral disease that causes painful, contagious blisters on the sex organs. Although the blisters go away after a few weeks, the virus continues to live in the body. The blisters may reappear again and again for years. Although the symptoms of genital herpes can be treated, there is no cure.

AIDS is usually transmitted through sexual contact. However, people can also get AIDS from contaminated blood and intravenous drug use. AIDS is caused by HIV, which attacks and weakens the cells of the immune system. A person with AIDS becomes less resistant to infections and diseases. Many people have died as a result of AIDS. So far, there is no cure.

Skills WorkOut

Collect Data Find out how many new cases of each of the following STDs were reported in the United States in the last three years: gonorrhea, AIDS, chlamydia, syphilis, genital herpes. Make a chart of your findings. Which disease occurred most often? Which disease occurred least often? Is any disease declining in numbers? Is any disease increasing in numbers? Write a report on your findings.

Check and Explain

1. Describe the two main functions of the testes and two functions of the ovaries.

2. What is menstruation? What causes it to occur?

3. **Compare and Contrast** In what ways are eggs and sperm different? In what ways are they alike?

4. **Communicate** Explain how hormones are involved in a male's and female's reproductive developments.

22.2 Fertilization, Pregnancy, and Birth

Objectives

▶ **Describe** the process of fertilization.

▶ **Describe** the development of the fertilized egg, embryo, and fetus.

▶ **Summarize** the stages of labor.

▶ **Infer** the importance of understanding the birth process.

Observe Look for a photograph of a newborn baby in a book or magazine, or think of a newborn you may have actually seen recently. Write down everything you observe about the baby. What makes a newborn baby so special?

Is there a newborn baby in your family or a friend's family? If so, you may know that pregnancy and birth are special times for both women and men. Pregnancy is the period of time between fertilization and birth. Pregnancy lasts for about nine months in humans. It is a time of dramatic changes in a woman's body.

Fertilization

During sexual intercourse, the male's penis enters the vagina of the female. The penis releases semen, which is filled with millions of sperm. The sperm swim rapidly from the vagina, through the cervix and uterus, and on into both oviducts.

Depending on the female's menstrual cycle, an egg may be present in one of the oviducts. If it is, the egg sends out a chemical that attracts and guides the sperm to the egg. Often many sperm will surround the egg and stick to it. Although many sperm may attach to the jellylike coating of the egg, only one sperm can penetrate through the egg's cell membrane beneath this jelly coating. The nuclear material of this single sperm then enters the cytoplasm of the egg cell and fertilizes it.

Immediately following fertilization, the egg releases chemicals that form a protective membrane around the fertilized egg, or zygote. The membrane prevents other sperm from entering.

The zygote now contains 46 chromosomes: 23 from the egg and 23 from the sperm. The zygote will begin to develop into a human being.

Figure 22.5 ▲
This photograph shows sperm on an egg. The sperm and egg have been magnified 3,400 times.

Development Before Birth

The zygote, smaller than a grain of salt, will undergo dramatic changes and growth. Over the next nine months, the zygote will develop into a human baby that is made of billions of cells. As the zygote travels down the oviduct, cell division begins. One cell becomes two, two cells become four, and so on, until it forms a small ball. It continues to divide and change, reaching the uterus about six days after fertilization. The zygote attaches to the inner wall of the uterus. In Figure 22.6b, notice that the developing individual, called an embryo, does not yet look much like a human.

Within the uterus, a placenta forms. The placenta is an organ that brings nutrients to the embryo and takes away wastes. Connecting the embryo to the placenta is the umbilical cord, a soft rope of blood vessels. The umbilical cord allows the embryo to float freely within its fluid-filled sac. Although materials can pass back and forth between mother and embryo, their blood does not mix. The blood is kept apart by a thin layer of cells.

After nearly eight weeks, the embryo begins to look like a human. Fingers, toes, and eyelids have developed. All of the major internal organs have formed. From eight weeks until birth, the developing baby is called a **fetus**. You can see the fetus at ten weeks in Figure 22.6c.

From the third to sixth month of pregnancy, the fetus grows rapidly. The mother begins to feel its kicks and somersaults as it moves around. At this time, the fetus has a little hair on its head, and its fingernails have grown. It begins a regular pattern of sleeping and waking.

Most of the fetus's growth takes place during the last three months of pregnancy. A layer of fat develops under the skin, and the bones harden. Near the end of the ninth month, the fetus is about 45 cm long and weighs 3 to 3.5 kg.

Figure 22.6
From Zygote to Newborn

a. In this phase of mitosis, the zygote has divided eight times.

b. At 5 weeks, the 1 cm long embryo has a head, buds where arms and legs will form, and a beating heart.

c. At 10 weeks, the fetus has a human shape and is about 5 cm long. Its mass is about 25 g.

The Birth Process

After about nine months of development and growth inside the uterus, the fetus is large, strong, and developed enough so life is possible outside the mother's body. Near the end of the pregnancy, the fetus is positioned for birth, usually upside down in the mother's body. The head points toward the cervix. The birth process begins when muscles of the uterus start to contract and relax at regular intervals. The muscular contractions, called **labor**, push the baby out of the uterus and through the vagina, or birth canal.

There are three stages of labor. The first stage lasts from about 2 to 24 hours. At the beginning, contractions are about 15 to 20 minutes apart. By the end of the first stage, the contractions have gotten much stronger and are only 1 or 2 minutes apart. The cervix widens from its normal 1 cm opening to about 10 cm. Contractions push the baby's head against the cervix. Crowning, or the appearance of the baby's head in the cervix, marks the beginning of the second stage of labor.

The baby is born during the second stage of labor, which usually lasts from two minutes to one hour. The mother uses the muscles in her abdomen to push the baby toward the birth canal. Strong contractions, along with this pushing, squeeze the baby out of the mother's body.

After birth, the baby is still connected to its mother by the umbilical cord. The cord is then clamped and cut. This does not hurt the baby or the mother. Within a few days, the rest of the cord falls off and the navel, or belly button, marks the spot where the cord was attached.

In the third stage of labor, contractions push fluid, blood, the rest of the umbilical cord, and the placenta out of the mother's body. This stage lasts about 15 or 20 minutes.

▲ **d.** At 16 weeks, the fetus begins moving around inside the uterus. Notice the umbilical cord.

▲ **e.** At 22 weeks, the fetus is nearly 35 cm long and weighs about 600 g. Its body is covered with fine hair.

▲ **f.** A baby soon after birth. Compare the newborn's development to the photographs of the embryo and fetus.

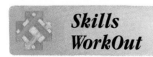
Problems of Reproduction

Human reproduction is a complex process made of many steps. Problems can occur at each step. For example, there may be problems fertilizing the egg due to a blocked oviduct or too few sperm in the semen.

Other problems can occur later in a pregnancy. Occasionally an embryo begins to develop inside an oviduct instead of in the uterus. This condition is called an ectopic, or tubal, pregnancy. It requires immediate surgery. In other cases, a pregnancy may end suddenly. This is called a miscarriage. The causes of miscarriages are sometimes unknown.

Sometimes a baby is born prematurely—before it is fully developed. Premature babies are very small. Often their organ systems are not fully developed. These babies may suffer from lung problems, brain damage, and blindness. They may not survive without intensive hospital care.

Historical Notebook

The Apgar Score

"Birth is the most hazardous time of life," wrote Dr. Virginia Apgar. When Dr. Apgar began studying childbirth, she learned that newborns were typically wrapped in blankets and examined later. Because serious problems went unnoticed in these first few moments after birth, many babies died. So Dr. Apgar devised a quick way of checking a newborn's health before it was given a thorough exam by a pediatrician. This quick check is called the Apgar Score. Dr. Apgar, who became one of the first female graduates of the Columbia University Medical School, introduced the Apgar Score in 1952.

Using the Apgar Score, a baby's health can be quickly rated at one and five minutes after birth. For example, a healthy baby breathes easily, shows good muscle tone and reflexes, and has a normal heart rate and rosy-colored skin. Each of these newborn characteristics—respiratory

effort, muscle tone, reflexes, heart rate, and skin color—is given a score of 0 to 2, with a total score of 10 showing excellent health.

1. Why is it important to test newborns right away?

2. **Research** Find out what other kinds of medical advances have been made in recent years to test a newborn's health.

Science and Technology
Health Before Birth

Did you know that some children have baby pictures taken before they are even born? These "pictures" are actually ultrasound scans. The scans are often used to make an image of a fetus in the mother's uterus. Scans are done by moving a special device over the mother's abdomen. The device sends out sound waves that echo off the fetus. The sound waves are changed to electrical impulses and are shown on a video monitor as a picture of the fetus.

Ultrasound scans are used to check the fetus's organs for defects and to diagnose ectopic pregnancies. Sometimes these defects can be surgically corrected while the fetus is still in the uterus, or, in other cases, shortly after the baby is born. Ultrasound scans are taken at any time during pregnancy; they do not hurt the fetus or the mother.

Another useful tool for identifying problems before birth is amniocentesis (AM nee OH sehn TEE sihs). As the fetus develops, it sheds cells into the amniotic fluid, the fluid that surrounds and cushions the fetus. A doctor uses a hollow needle to withdraw a small amount of amniotic fluid. Fetal cells in the fluid are checked to determine if the baby has certain diseases or genetic disorders. The cells and fluid also indicate the age and sex of a fetus. When a baby is expected to be premature, amniocentesis may be used to find out if the baby's lungs are fully developed. In most cases the best time for this kind of test is around the sixteenth week of pregnancy.

Figure 22.7 ▲
Using ultrasound, a doctor checks a pregnant woman. They are looking at an outline of her baby on the video monitor.

Check and Explain

1. In a paragraph, summarize the steps of fertilization of a human egg.

2. Describe the development of an individual from fertilized egg to birth.

3. **Evaluate** What are the possible advantages and disadvantages of testing a fetus or embryo with ultrasound or amniocentesis? Explain.

4. **Infer** How might prior knowledge of the birth process be useful to a woman in labor or a father attending the birth?

22.3 Human Life Stages

Objectives

▶ **Identify** the main life stages in humans.

▶ **Describe** the characteristics of each life stage.

▶ **Predict** the impact of the aging population in the United States.

L ook around you the next time you are in a crowd. All the people you see began life in the same way— as a single cell that divided and developed into a baby. As you know, those first nine months of development involved amazing changes. After birth, a new period of growth and change began. Everyone you see is still in the process of change. Change occurs throughout a person's lifetime.

Infancy

When you were born, you could cry, suck, grasp objects, hear, and follow light with your eyes. You probably spent about 16 hours a day sleeping. And you depended on other people to feed, diaper, clothe, shelter, and protect you. These first 12 months of life are called infancy.

Infancy is a time of rapid growth. The lower body, legs, and arms grow fastest. An infant's mass also increases greatly. Infants begin to react to stimuli, such as light and noise, just a few weeks after birth. They begin to respond to familiar voices. As their muscles grow stronger, they shows signs of controlling body movements. Infants can usually lift their heads after about 3 or 4 months and soon they can grasp objects. Within the first 7 or 8 months, the infant usually learns to crawl, sit up, and roll over. Baby teeth develop.

By the age of 8 months, infants can often speak simple words. By 12 months, infants can usually understand simple commands, and many can take their first steps. From 1 to 3 years of age, infants enter the toddler stage. During this stage, most toddlers learn to walk. They are very curious about their environment, touching and grabbing at objects, and putting things in their mouths. It is a very active time of life.

Figure 22.8 ▲
All infants are dependent on the care provided by an adult.

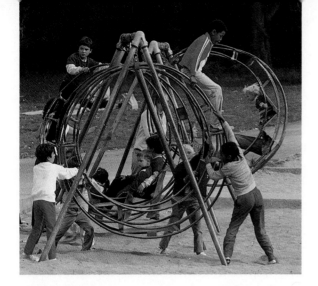

Figure 22.9 ▲
Why is play an important part of childhood?

Childhood

After infancy, physical growth slows down, and mental and emotional growth take the lead. This period of growth, from infancy to about age 11 or 12, is called childhood. During childhood, most body systems mature, and the brain reaches its full size.

By age 2, a child has a vocabulary of a few hundred words and can speak in two-word phrases. By age 3, most children speak in sentences. Later, children learn to draw, read, and write. They begin feeding and dressing themselves.

Children also learn that they are part of a community and that their actions can affect others. They learn to cooperate and to make friends. They learn many skills through play, which is an important part of their lives.

Adolescence

You are in a stage of life called adolescence. Adolescence occurs from about age 11 to 20. It is a period of transition from childhood to adulthood.

Many cultures celebrate the transition to adulthood with special ceremonies. For example, some Native-American girls are initiated into their tribe in a ceremony. Each teenage girl shares a blanket with an older woman who promises to protect her for life.

During adolescence, the body grows to its full height, and the reproductive organs develop. As you know, the time when a person's body becomes capable of reproducing is called puberty. At this time, males and females go through many changes, both physically and emotionally. The hormones that trigger puberty also affect the emotions and may cause sudden mood swings.

Just as with other life stages, puberty does not occur at the same age for everyone. Those who mature first may feel uncomfortable with their looks. Those who mature later often worry that they are not developing as quickly as everyone else. The changes brought on by adolescence can be very confusing. Keep in mind, however, that all the changes are a natural part of growing up.

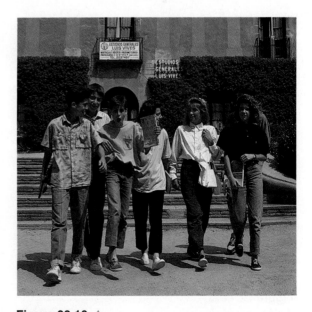

Figure 22.10 ▲
During adolescence, young people spend a great deal of time socializing.

Adulthood

Once the body has grown to its full height and has sexually matured, a person enters adulthood. At this time of emotional and physical maturity, usually starting between age 18 and 21, all body systems are fully developed. Bones and muscles are large and strong, coordination is good, and the anxieties of adolescence are generally over.

During adulthood, there is no additional growth, only replacement of damaged cells. Although the body starts a gradual decline after age 30, exercise and a healthy diet can help slow the decline.

The reproductive systems of men and women age differently. Men continue to produce sperm throughout most of their adult lives. But usually sometime after age 40, women experience menopause, a time when the menstrual cycle stops. After menopause, no more eggs are released from the ovaries, and a woman can no longer reproduce.

Old Age

As people grow older, their body systems may change. It may become more difficult for people to fight off disease and heal from physical injuries. Many older people have problems with their eyesight and hearing.

In the past, a normal life span was only about 40 years. Today people live longer and healthier lives thanks to better nutrition, exercise, and advances in medicine. In addition, staying interested in activities and other people is a key to staying healthy. Some older people continue their careers. Others retire and devote time to special interests, such as swimming, gardening, reading, or travelling. Many enjoy spending time with their grandchildren.

Figure 22.11 ▲
Adulthood is often a time of many new responsibilities, such as rearing families and establishing careers.

Figure 22.12 ▲
Even in later years, many people continue to work. In Poland, a man creates beautiful violins.

Science and Society *Our Aging Population*

As medical advances help people live longer, the number of people in the United States who are over 65 is rapidly increasing. In addition, there are many more very old people, those over 85. How will our society respond to a population that includes more old people than ever before?

The very old often have physical problems. As a result, they generally have more health care needs than younger adults. In previous generations, these needs were often met by adult children. But today many adult children work full time, live far away from their parents, or have little money to spare.

Another problem facing the elderly is the financial burden of rising health care costs. Most working people contribute to social security insurance, and many have company retirement funds. However, the cost of living is rising faster than the increase in social security, and many retirement benefits are inadequate. As a result, elderly people are finding it harder to pay their medical bills and maintain healthy lifestyles.

To respond to the financial burdens and needs of the elderly, many communities now provide day-care services. These services are especially useful for adult children who work and care for their parents. In addition, some employers today assist employees making arrangements for care of their aging parents. And many older people are taking action. Large organizations of senior citizens offer special services at reduced costs.

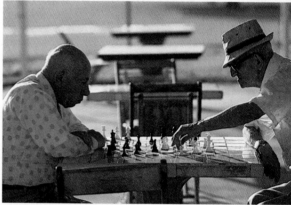

Figure 22.13 ▲
In the United States, many elderly people live in nursing homes. As the aging population increases, more and more communities are faced with a shortage of nursing homes.

Check and Explain

1. What are the main life stages?

2. Explain why adolescence is sometimes a difficult stage.

3. **Classify** Make a table showing some of the events that occur in infancy and childhood. For example, include when a baby begins to talk and walk.

4. **Predict** How might a growing population of older people affect your community? How could the community help them? Explain.

Activity 22   Is age related to learning development?

Skills Communicate; Collect Data; Observe

Task 1   Prelab Prep

1. Collect the following items: blank labels, ball of clay, 2 identical clear containers, a taller and thinner clear container, 8 pennies, measuring cup.
2. Arrange individual meetings with at least one child between age 2 and 7 and one child between age 7 and 11.
3. Before each meeting, label the identical containers *A* and *B*. Label the other container *C*. Fill A and B with exactly the same amount of water, about halfway full.

Task 2   Data Record

On separate sheets of paper, draw the data table shown. Make one for each child you will be meeting with. Circle the children's responses in your data tables.

Table 22.1   A Child's Responses

Child's Name and Age			
Which has more clay?	Ball	Sausage	Same
Which has more water?	A	B	Same
	A	C	Same
Which has more pennies?	Short row	Long row	Same

Task 3   Procedure

1. Meet with one child. Record the child's name and age.
2. Show the child a ball of clay. Then roll the ball of clay into a sausage shape.
3. Ask the child whether the ball or the sausage contains more clay, or if they are the same. Record the response.

4. Show the child containers A and B. Ask which contains more water, or if they are the same. Record the response.
5. Pour all of the water from container B into container C. Ask whether A or C contains more water, or if they are the same. Record the response.
6. Show the child a row of eight pennies. Then spread out the pennies a little to make a longer row. Ask the child which row has more pennies, or if they are the same. Record the response.
7. Repeat steps 1 through 6 with another child.

Task 4   Analysis

1. Compare the responses and ages of the children. What differences do you notice? What trends do you notice?
2. Compare your results to those of your classmates. How are they the same? How are they different?

Task 5   Conclusion

You know that the amount of matter stays the same in an object regardless of changes in its shape or position. Based on this activity, write a paragraph describing when children seem to develop an understanding of this concept. Does the activity show that age is related to learning? Explain.

Everyday Application

Why is it important to know a child's developmental stages when trying to teach difficult concepts, such as matter and energy, to a child?

Extension

Jean Piaget was a French scientist who developed a theory that identified different stages of learning development. Write a report about Piaget and his theory.

Chapter 22 Review

Concept Summary

22.1 Human Reproductive Systems

▶ Male sex organs include the testes and penis. The testes produce sperm.

▶ Female sex organs include the ovaries, uterus, and vagina. The ovaries release mature egg cells.

▶ In sexually mature females, ovulation and menstruation take place in a cycle that is usually about 28 days long.

▶ The major sex hormones are testosterone in males and estrogen and progesterone in females.

22.2 Fertilization, Pregnancy, and Birth

▶ Fertilization occurs when a sperm penetrates the egg and combines its genetic material with that of the egg.

▶ Over a nine-month period, called pregnancy, the fertilized egg grows into an embryo and then a fetus. It is nourished by the placenta, which is attached to the uterus by the umbilical cord.

▶ A baby is born during the process of labor.

22.3 Human Life Stages

▶ Infancy is a time of rapid growth during the first 12 months of life.

▶ During childhood, body systems mature and the brain reaches its full size.

▶ The life stage between childhood and adulthood is adolescence. It includes puberty, the time when a person reaches sexual maturity.

▶ After a long period of maturity, called adulthood, a person reaches old age.

Chapter Vocabulary

testes (22.1)	penis (22.1)	fertilization (22.1)	menstruation (22.1)
scrotum (22.1)	ovaries (22.1)	uterus (22.1)	fetus (22.2)
semen (22.1)	oviduct (22.1)	vagina (22.1)	labor (22.2)

Check Your Vocabulary

Use the vocabulary words above to complete the following sentences correctly.

1. An unfertilized egg and the uterine lining leave the body during _____ .

2. Estrogen is produced in the _____ .

3. The mixture of sperm cells and fluid is called _____ .

4. Testosterone is produced in the _____ .

5. After the third month of pregnancy, the growing embryo becomes a _____ .

6. Fertilization occurs in an _____ .

7. The testes are enclosed in the _____ .

8. A baby is born during the second stage of _____ .

9. Sperm cells are delivered into the vagina through the _____ .

10. When a sperm cell penetrates the lining of the egg, a process called _____ occurs.

11. Another name for the _____ is the birth canal.

12. The development of the embryo and fetus takes place inside an organ called the _____ .

Write Your Vocabulary

Write sentences using each of the vocabulary words above. Show that you know what each word means.

Chapter 22 Review

Check Your Knowledge

Answer the following in complete sentences.

1. What is the purpose of the uterus in reproduction?

2. Which is the shortest human life stage? Which is the longest?

3. What is puberty? During which life stage does it occur?

4. Why are the testes held in the scrotum away from the rest of a male's body?

5. What occurs during menstruation? Why is it called a cycle?

6. What is labor? What occurs during the birth process?

7. What hormones are produced in the female reproductive system? What hormones are produced in the male reproductive system?

Choose the answer that best completes each sentence.

8. Menstruation occurs (after, before, just before, during) ovulation.

9. A male does not have (testes, hormones, a urethra, ovaries) in his body.

10. A child usually learns to talk in complete sentences by age (6 months, 1 year, 3 years, 5 years).

11. Between the uterus and the vagina is the (urethra, placenta, zygote, cervix).

12. A common symptom of premenstrual syndrome is (weight loss, tension, a runny nose, drowsiness).

13. In the uterus, the embryo is connected to the placenta by the (fetus, umbilical cord, zygote, oviduct).

Check Your Understanding

Apply the concepts you have learned to answer each question.

1. **Compare and Contrast** What are the differences and similarities between sperm production and egg production?

2. **Extension** Describe how your body will have changed by the time you reach adulthood.

3. **Infer** Of all the animals, humans take the longest to reach maturity. How do you think humans' long period of childhood relates to the other characteristics that make the human species unique?

4. **Mystery Photo** The photograph on page 466 shows a human fetus in the uterus of its mother. The image was created through a process called ultrasound. How old do you think the fetus is? On what did you base your answer?

5. The placenta does the work of three different body systems for the developing fetus. What are these three body systems? Which important body system is functioning on its own in the fetus?

6. **Application** Why do you not remember anything about the time you spent in your mother's uterus or your whole first year or two of life?

7. **Application** A person with type A blood cannot receive a transfusion of type B blood. The combination causes the blood to clot. However, a woman with type A blood can safely have a baby with type B blood. Explain.

Develop Your Skills

Use the skills you have developed in this chapter to complete each activity.

1. **Interpret Data** The graph below shows the mass of a developing baby at different stages of pregnancy.

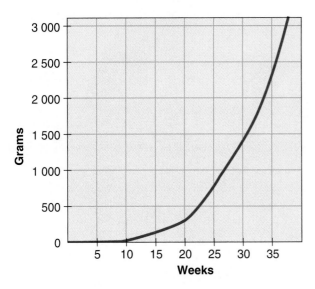

a. How many weeks old is the fetus when it reaches 1 000 g?

b. When does the baby increase its mass most rapidly?

2. **Make a Graph** Refer to pages 474 and 475 to make a graph showing the length of a developing baby at different stages of pregnancy. Add the following statistics to the graph: 14 weeks—18 cm; 26 weeks—38 cm; 32 weeks—41 cm. Use the same scale of weeks as in the graph above. How does the increase in length compare to the increase in mass?

3. **Data Bank** Use the information on page 625 to answer the following questions.

a. What animal has a longer life span than humans?

b. Which animal lives longer, a lion or an elephant?

Make Connections

1. **Link the Concepts** Below is a concept map showing how some of the main concepts in this chapter link together. Expand the map by adding the following concepts: embryo, placenta, vagina, fetus, and labor.

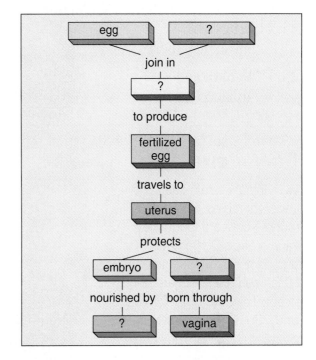

2. **Science and Society** Birth is a special event that can be difficult. Many different methods of making childbirth easier for the mother and better for the baby have been developed. Research different methods of childbirth and choose one to report on.

3. **Science and Social Studies** Find out how life expectancies differ in countries around the world. In which countries do people tend to live the longest? What are the causes of short life expectancies?

Chapter **23** Nutrition, Health, and Wellness

Chapter Sections

What do you see?

66 In this picture, I see fruits and vegetables. Some are round, some are long. They vary in color. Some have bumps and some are smooth. I think some of them are good to eat. They are good for your body. Some have protein and vitamins C and B. They give the body energy to run, play, and participate in sports and other school activities. 99

Paula Lee
Pace Middle School
Milton, Florida

To find out more about the photograph, look on page 508. As you read this chapter, you will learn about human nutrition and health.

23.1 Nutrients

Objectives

▶ **Explain** the body's need for protein, carbohydrates, and fats.

▶ **Describe** the importance of fiber.

▶ **Describe** the characteristics of a balanced diet.

▶ **State** the dangers of improper nutrition.

▶ **Make a model** of a menu that provides a balanced diet.

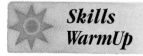
What did you eat for dinner last night? For breakfast this morning? What are your favorite snacks? The foods you eat affect your health and physical fitness in many ways.

Food provides energy for you and your body's cells. It also supplies raw materials that cells need for growth and repair. The substances in food that your body needs are called nutrients. Many nutrients are necessary for good health. Foods vary in the kinds and amounts of nutrients they contain. That's why paying attention to what you eat is necessary for good health. A balanced diet is one that includes all the nutrients your body needs.

Most nutrients can be classified as organic nutrients. Organic nutrients are essential compounds found in living things. They include carbohydrates, fats and oils, proteins, vitamins, and fiber.

Carbohydrates

Your body gets most of its energy from organic nutrients called **carbohydrates**. They are made of carbon, hydrogen, and oxygen. Starch is a carbohydrate made of large molecules. Corn, potatoes, and rice are good sources of starch. So are foods made from wheat, such as bread.

When starches are broken down into smaller molecules, they form sugars. Table sugar, or sucrose, is only one of many sugars. During digestion, sucrose splits into two smaller molecules of a simple sugar called glucose. In the cells, glucose combines with oxygen during the process of respiration. During respiration, the stored energy of glucose is released.

Figure 23.1 ▲
The grain of the rice plant is high in starch. In some cases, the grain is ground into a flour, but usually it is husked, boiled, and eaten in its original state.

Fats and Oils

What makes foods greasy? Greasy foods contain either fats or oils. At room temperature, fats are solid, while oils are liquid. In general, animals produce fats and plants produce oils. Together, fats and oils are called **lipids**. Lipids are made up of carbon, hydrogen, and oxygen.

In your body, deposits of fat serve as a source of stored energy. Gram for gram, fats supply more than twice as much energy as carbohydrates. Fat deposits stored under the surface of your skin also help insulate your body.

Eating too much fat can be harmful. High-fat food, such as french fries, hot dogs, and chocolate bars, are high in Calories and tend to make you gain weight. Moreover, fats seem to increase the amount of **cholesterol** (kuh LEHS tuh ROHL) in the blood. Cholesterol is a fatty sustance found in all animal tissues. High cholesterol levels can cause solid deposits to clog the arteries, resulting in heart disease. To cut down on the amount of fat in your diet, substitute low-fat foods like fruits and vegetables or cereal grains.

Proteins

Your cells need nutrients called **proteins** for growth and repair. Your body uses the proteins you eat to build its own proteins. These are used to make new cell material and substances important in all life processes. Within your body are thousands of different proteins, each doing a different job.

Proteins are large, complex molecules made up of smaller units called *amino acids*. Twenty different amino acids, combined in different ways, make up all the different proteins in your body. Just as the 26 letters of the alphabet form an endless number of words, amino acids join together to create many kinds of proteins.

Proteins in food are classified as complete or incomplete. Complete proteins contain all the amino acids your body needs to make its own proteins. Incomplete proteins are missing one or more of the essential amino acids. Cheese, eggs, meat, fish, and milk are good sources of complete proteins. Grains, nuts, and dried peas and beans contain incomplete proteins. Grains and beans eaten together, however, combine to provide you with complete protein.

**Figure 23.2
Nutrients and Food**

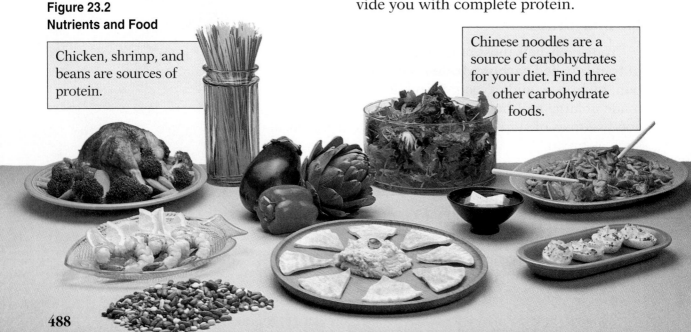

Chicken, shrimp, and beans are sources of protein.

Chinese noodles are a source of carbohydrates for your diet. Find three other carbohydrate foods.

Vitamins

Your body also needs organic nutrients called vitamins. Vitamins help regulate the chemical reactions that convert food into energy and living tissue. Vitamins are needed only in small amounts. If you don't have enough of any one vitamin in your diet, however, disease will result.

Because your body can't produce most of the 13 vitamins it needs, they must be supplied daily. Look at Table 23.1 to see which foods contain the vitamins you need. Find some of these foods in Figure 23.2.

Fiber

Plant cell walls contain indigestible substances called *fiber*. Fresh fruits and vegetables, dried beans and peas, and whole grain cereals are all good sources of fiber. Fiber helps move food through your intestines more quickly. This may help to prevent cancer from occurring in the walls of the intestines. Because most high-fiber foods are low in Calories, substituting these foods for high-Calorie foods can help you lose weight.

Table 23.1   Vitamins

Vitamin	Sources	What It Does
A	Milk, eggs, green and yellow vegetables, liver	Promotes healthy bones, teeth, eyes, skin
B-complex	Whole-grain breads and cereals, most vegetables, eggs, milk products, meat	Helps body cells use energy and oxygen; needed for healthy skin, nerves, blood, and heart
C	Citrus fruits, tomatoes, potatoes, strawberries, cabbage	Promotes healthy bones, teeth, healing of wounds
D	Fortified milk, eggs, tuna, salmon, liver	Promotes healthy bones and teeth
E	Grains, fish, meat, lettuce, vegetable oils, margarine	Protects cell membranes
K	Green leafy vegetables, tomatoes, pork	Essential for blood clotting

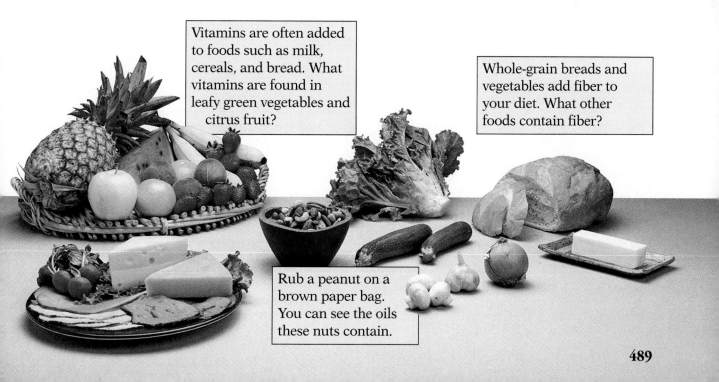

Vitamins are often added to foods such as milk, cereals, and bread. What vitamins are found in leafy green vegetables and citrus fruit?

Whole-grain breads and vegetables add fiber to your diet. What other foods contain fiber?

Rub a peanut on a brown paper bag. You can see the oils these nuts contain.

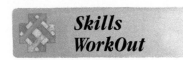
Inorganic Nutrients

Your body needs certain substances, such as water and minerals, that are not manufactured by living things. These substances are called inorganic nutrients.

Water You could live without food for up to a month, but only about a week without water. Your body can't function properly without water. It needs to take in about 2 liters of water a day.

Most of the chemical reactions in your body take place in water solutions. Water carries dissolved nutrients to the cells and carries away soluble wastes. Water makes up most of the saliva that helps you swallow food.

Minerals A supply of minerals is necessary for building many important substances in your body. Your bones, for example, are made in part from the minerals phosphorus and calcium. Like vitamins, minerals are needed only in small amounts for your body to function properly. But some minerals are required in greater amounts than others. They include calcium, phosphorus, potassium, sodium, and magnesium. Table 23.2 lists sources and functions of minerals.

Table 23.2   Minerals

Mineral	Sources	What It Does
Calcium	Milk, cheese, eggs, leafy vegetables	Promotes strong bones and teeth; necessary for blood clotting
Phosphorus	Protein-rich foods, grains	Promotes strong bones and teeth; used in energy-rich molecules like ATP
Magnesium	Milk, cheese, cereals, vegetables, nuts	Aids nerve and muscle contractions
Potassium	Most foods, especially fruits and vegetables	Helps regulate water balance inside and outside body cells
Sodium	Table salt, most foods	Helps regulate water balance inside and outside body cells
Iron	Liver, red meat, grains, eggs, leafy vegetables, dried beans	Enables blood to carry oxygen
Iodine	Iodized salt	Controls normal functioning of thyroid gland
Zinc	Meat, fish, eggs, milk, oysters	Helps heal wounds; aids growth and reproduction

A Healthy Diet

Your body needs varying amounts of more than 40 different nutrients. If you choose your diet by taste or convenience alone, you risk getting too little of some nutrients and too much of others. To have a healthy diet, follow the guidelines below.

▶ Eat a variety of foods. Most foods are rich in just a few nutrients. The best way to make sure your body gets all the many nutrients it needs is to eat many different kinds of foods. Table 23.3 shows one way in which foods are divided into groups according to the nutrients they contain. Eating foods from all these groups ensures a varied diet.

▶ Reduce your intake of fat and cholesterol. The diets of many Americans include too much fat and cholesterol. Eggs and red meat contain a large amount of cholesterol. Red meat, butter, ice cream, and all fried foods are high in fat. The bulk of the lipids in your diet should be from unsaturated oils, such as olive oil.

▶ Eat plenty of fruits, vegetables, grains, and dried beans. Most foods that come from plants are naturally low in fat and contain no cholesterol. In addition, most contain large amounts of fiber. For these reasons plant foods are good replacements for foods high in fat. If you greatly reduce the amount of meat, milk, and cheese in your diet, dried beans and peas and foods made from them can provide you with needed proteins.

▶ Use sugar and salt in moderation. Sugar and salt help many foods taste better. But both are unhealthy in large amounts. Many snack foods and packaged and processed foods contain much more salt or sugar than you may realize.

Skills WorkOut

Classify Write down all the foods you ate yesterday. Then place each food into one of the food groups in Table 23.3. You may need to divide some dishes into the foods they are made from. If you ate spaghetti and meatballs, for example, the spaghetti goes into the grain group, the meatballs into the meat group, and the sauce into the vegetable group.

Table 23.3 Food Groups and Their Nutrients

Fruits	Vegetables	Breads, Cereals, Rice, Pasta	Meat, Poultry, Fish, Eggs, Dry Beans, and Nuts	Milk, Cheese, and Yogurt
Vitamins A and C, minerals, carbohydrates	Vitamins A and C, minerals, carbohydrates, fiber	Carbohydrates, B vitamins, iron, fiber	Protein, iron and other minerals, B vitamins	Protein, B vitamins, vitamin D

Science and Society *Staple Foods*

Think about the food you eat. You probably eat a variety of foods. However, you and your family may eat one kind of food more often than others. A food that makes up the bulk of a diet is called a staple. What might be your family's staple food?

About half the world's people eat rice as their staple food. Southeast Asians were probably the first to use rice. Today, thousands of kinds of rice are grown in warm, wet regions around the world.

In many countries of Latin America and Africa, corn is the staple food. It was first used about 10,000 years ago by Native Americans living in what is now Mexico. Many varieties are now grown in temperate and tropical regions.

Rice and corn are versatile foods: that is, they can be prepared many ways. Greeks wrap rice in grape leaves, for example, while the Chinese fry it with pork. Some Latin Americans eat a mixture of beans and rice called *gallo pinto* for breakfast. Corn can be eaten fresh or made into cornmeal. Tortillas and tamales are popular Mexican foods made from cornmeal.

Grains, such as rice and corn, are staple foods in developing countries because they are easy to grow and cost less than other foods. Depending too much on these single foods, however, has a serious disadvantage. While grains are good sources of starch, vitamins, and fiber, they supply only small amounts of incomplete protein. People who have no other source of protein in their diet will suffer from malnutrition.

Figure 23.3 ▲

Rice (top) is grown in areas where there is enough water to flood the fields, or paddies, in which it is planted. Corn products can be found in open-air markets (bottom) of Mexico, where it is a staple crop.

Check and Explain

1. Name the three main organic nutrients and explain why your body needs them.

2. Why should you eat foods that contain fiber?

3. **Predict** How might your body be affected by a diet made up mainly of junk food?

4. **Make a Model** Make up a menu for an entire day that provides a balanced diet.

Activity 23 *What information is found on food labels?*

Skills Observe; Infer; Interpret Data

Task 1 Prelab Prep
1. Collect the following items: 2 sheets of paper, pencil or pen.
2. Read the information on the labels shown on this page.

Task 2 Data Record
On a separate piece of paper, copy Table 23.4 and use it to compare the nutrients in the milk and chicken noodle soup.

Task 3 Procedure
1. Enter the data from the labels into your table. Note: Always use a capital *C* when referring to food Calories.
2. Calculate the number of Calories in one serving of milk that come from protein by multiplying the number of grams of protein listed by 4.
3. Calculate the number of Calories in the milk that come from carbohydrates by multiplying the number of grams of carbohydrate by 4.
4. Calculate the number of Calories that come from fat by multiplying the number of grams of fat by 9. Enter these figures for milk in your table.
5. Do the same set of calculations for one serving of chicken noodle soup. Enter these figures in your table.

Table 23.4 Comparing Nutrients

Nutrients in 1 Serving	Milk	Soup
Total Calories		
Grams of protein		
Calories that come from protein		
Grams of carbohydrate		
Calories that come from carbohydrates		
Grams of fat		
Calories that come from fat		

Task 4 Analysis
1. Compare the fats and carbohydrates provided by one serving of each food.
2. Which food is the best source of carbohydrate? Of protein?
3. Which food contains the least amount of fat?

Task 5 Conclusion
Write a short paragraph describing the information available on a food label.

Everyday Application

How can reading food labels help you to control the amount of fats and carbohydrates in your diet? Read the labels of all the packaged foods you ate in one day and add up how much fat and carbohydrate you consumed.

Look at the labels again and add up how much sodium, or salt, you consumed. Compare this figure to the daily recommended allowance of 1 100 to 3 300 mg of salt. Did you consume too much salt? Why is a low-salt diet important to your health?

Chicken Noodle Soup
Serving Size..........250g
Calories..................131
Protein.....................6.5g
Carbohydrate..............9g
Fat.............................7.4g

Milk
Serving Size 250g
Calories 200
Protein 13g
Carbohydrate...........20g
Fat 7g

23.2 Exercise and Rest

Objectives

▶ **Explain** the role of exercise in maintaining a healthy body.

▶ **State** how stress affects the body.

▶ **Interpret** the role of rest and relaxation in maintaining health.

▶ **Estimate** the stress level of events and situations.

Every day, you make personal choices about eating, exercise, and rest. You may also face choices about whether to smoke, drink alcoholic beverages, or use drugs. The decisions you make will determine your lifestyle. How does your lifestyle affect your health and well-being?

Exercise

Regular exercise is part of a healthy lifestyle. Exercise does more than strengthen muscles. It improves your flexibility and builds endurance. Actually, endurance is the most important result of exercise. Building endurance strengthens your body's most important muscle—your heart muscle.

The best way to improve your endurance is to do aerobic (air OH bihk) exercise. Aerobic exercise is vigorous activity that increases your muscles' need for oxygen. Oxygen is used in the chemical reactions that provide muscles with energy. Because of the increased demand for oxygen, your lungs work harder, and more oxygen is delivered to the blood. Your heart also works harder to pump more blood to the muscles. The object is not to make the heart beat as fast as it can but to make it beat somewhat faster than when the body is at rest. Aerobic exercise benefits your heart and lungs because the hard work improves their strength. As a result, they work more efficiently when your body is at rest.

Aerobic exercises include bicycling, dancing, jogging, rowing, skating, and swimming. Even ordinary activities like walking or mowing the lawn can become aerobic when you do them at a fast pace. Exercise also helps you maintain a healthy body weight.

Figure 23.4 ▲
Exercise that strengthens muscles is not limited to any age group.

As you probably know, food is rated in Calories. A Calorie is a measure of the energy in food. A food Calorie (spelled with a capital *C*) is actually a kilocalorie (1000 Calories). The number of Calories in a serving of food tells how much heat energy is available in the food for the body to use. Foods high in Calories provide a lot of energy. Foods low in Calories provide less energy.

Like wood, food can be "burned." The heat given off by burning food can change the temperature of water. Scientists define a calorie as the amount of heat needed to raise the temperature of one gram of water 1°C. Of course, food energy in your body is not used to heat water. It is used to keep your body temperature close to 37°C. What else does food energy help you do?

Your body weight depends on the balance between Calories taken in and Calories used. Burning Calories as you exercise can help you lose weight. Which activities in Table 23.5 use the most Calories?

Table 23.5   Burning Calories

Exercise	Burned per Hour
Dancing (moderate)	210
Recreational swimming	220
Softball	230
Tennis	336
Bowling	336
Basketball	348
Football	414
Soccer	480

Based on body weight of 56.8 kg

SkillBuilder *Interpreting Data*

Measuring Calories Used

Different activities use different amounts of Calories. For example, shoveling snow uses more than twice as many Calories as raking leaves. Using the data in the tables on this page, calculate the number of Calories you use in an average 24-hour period. Create your own table on a separate sheet of paper. It should include space for the estimated number of hours you spend doing each activity and space for the total Calories used for that activity.

Study your completed table, then answer the following questions.

1. What activity used the greatest number of Calories?

2. What activity used the least number of Calories?

3. Write the total number of Calories used by ten of your classmates. Then write a short statement comparing your Calorie use with their Calorie use.

Activity	Calories Burned per Hour
Sleeping	60
Reading, watching television	60
Playing a computer game	100
Playing a musical instrument	120
Doing household chores	190
Mowing grass	200
Walking	240
Bicycling	250

Using your results, write a paper discussing whether or not you get enough exercise. To support your position, give examples of the activities you do and the Calories used.

Stress and Your Body

Do you sometimes feel tense? Pressured? Depressed? Everyone has these feelings at times. If you feel this way very often, however, you are probably experiencing a lot of stress. Stress is an unbalancing of your emotions or mental state. Learning to handle stress is necessary for a healthy lifestyle.

Stress is a normal part of everyday life. It is usually caused by unhappy events, but stress can also stem from happy events, such as getting a job. Stress can also build up gradually, without being caused by any single event. For example, you may feel a need to always excel in school or sports.

Your body's built-in stress response equips you to handle dangerous situations. Your heart beats faster, your blood pressure increases, and your nervous system goes on the alert. When triggered too often, however, this response can cause chronic headaches, depression, loss of sleep, and other health problems.

What can you do about stress? Reducing stress might be as simple as getting up 15 minutes earlier than you usually do in the morning, or writing down school assignments so you don't forget them. One of the best ways to relieve stress is to exercise. Sometimes stress is brought on by holding in your feelings. If you are troubled, don't bottle up your feelings. Find someone you can talk to—a family member, counselor, teacher, or friend.

Figure 23.5 ▲
The strenuous activity of competitive sports releases tension and keeps your body in good condition. How might art classes relieve stress?

Relaxation and sleep also help reduce stress. Any activity that differs from your normal routine can be relaxing. Plan to spend a little time each day doing something you enjoy. Growing teenagers need more sleep than adults. The amount of sleep needed varies from person to person, but your body probably does best on at least eight hours of sleep a night.

Science and Technology *Toning Up*

For many people, using an exercise machine is the most convenient way of staying fit. For one thing, exercise machines can be used at home. People who own machines can exercise at any time, in any kind of weather.

One reason people use exercise machines is to strengthen the heart and lungs through aerobic exercise. Another goal is to tone specific muscle groups.

There are many types of exercise machines that help people design their own fitness programs. For example, many stationary bicycles, called ergometers, calculate your work output as you pedal. This makes it possible to carefully monitor your exercise program. Small trampolines, or rebound exercisers, are great for your heart, lungs, and leg muscles. Some runners use treadmills for exercising indoors during bad weather. Treadmills are revolving belts that can be powered either manually or by a motor. Weight machines help a person concentrate on toning specific muscle groups. There are also exercise machines that imitate the movements used in rowing, cross-country skiing, or climbing stairs.

Figure 23.6 ▲
How does a stair-stepping machine help you keep fit?

Check and Explain

1. Why should a person exercise regularly?

2. List several ways stress affects the body.

3. **Reason and Conclude**   Does regular exercise increase or decrease the number of hours of sleep you need? Why?

4. **Estimate**   Make a list of situations that cause stress. Then give each item a number from 1 to 10 according to how much stress you think it causes. Compare your list with those of your classmates.

Communicate Think about the following questions, then write a short paragraph that communicates your feelings about drugs. Do you know anyone who uses drugs? What happens to someone who gets "hooked" on drugs? What happens to a drug abuser's family?

23.3 Drugs and Substance Abuse

Objectives

▶ **Describe** the major kinds of drugs.

▶ **Describe** the effects of drug abuse.

▶ **Classify** commonly abused drugs.

▶ **Analyze** the reasons why people abuse drugs.

What do you know about drugs? Are all drugs harmful? Write your own definition of a *drug*. Then make a list of all substances that you think are drugs. Did you classify alcohol, nicotine, or caffeine as drugs?

Any substance that changes the way your body or mind works is a drug. Medicines are drugs used to relieve pain and cure diseases. Generally, drugs are helpful when used for their intended purposes. But any drug can be harmful when not used properly. Any harmful or nonmedical use of a drug is called *substance abuse*.

Types of Drugs

Drugs you can buy at the supermarket are over-the-counter, or nonprescription, drugs. Aspirin, cold remedies, and insulin are just a few of the hundreds of over-the-counter drugs available. While they are fairly safe, you still need to use these drugs carefully. Always read the label and use the drug exactly as recommended.

Other drugs can be purchased only with a doctor's prescription. You may have taken a prescription drug such as penicillin or tetracycline. These drugs fight bacterial infections like strep throat. Other prescription drugs are used to treat such illnesses as heart disease and cancer. Because they are more powerful than over-the-counter drugs, prescription drugs should always be taken under a doctor's supervision. Misuse of prescription drugs can be very dangerous. For example, some athletes use drugs called steroids to develop bigger muscles. This practice may lead to serious health problems and even death.

Figure 23.7
Finding the right medication in this pile of pills could be a problem. What steps can you take to guard against taking the wrong drug? ▼

You may be surprised to learn that caffeine, alcohol, and nicotine (NIHK uh TEEN) are also classified as drugs. Nicotine is found in tobacco. As you know, only adults can legally buy and use products containing alcohol and nicotine.

The possession, use, or sale of certain drugs is forbidden by federal law. These drugs, such as cocaine, crack, and marijuana, have the potential to greatly harm the user.

Dangers of Drug Abuse

Improper use of drugs can damage your health, threaten your safety, interfere with your performance at school or work, and hurt your personal relationships. Abusers may spend thousands of dollars a year on drugs. Anyone convicted of drug charges faces strict penalties and a criminal record.

Long-term abuse of certain drugs causes physical dependence, or **addiction**. An addict's body gets so used to the drug that a painful condition called withdrawal results if the drug is withheld. The body also develops a drug tolerance. This means that users need to take more and more of a drug to get the same effects.

Whereas some drugs cause a physical dependence, regular use of any drug can lead to psychological dependence. This means that using the drug is a habit because the mind craves it. A drug that your mind craves can be as hard to stop using as a drug your body is addicted to.

There is a limit to how much of a drug a person can take safely at one time. When this limit is exceeded, an overdose results. An overdose may lead to death. Mixing drugs increases the risk of an overdose. For example, using alcohol and sleeping pills together greatly increases the danger of a sleeping pill overdose.

Commonly Abused Drugs

Five types of drugs are commonly abused: stimulants, depressants, marijuana, narcotics, and hallucinogens. Some of these drugs cause physical dependence and all can cause psychological dependence. While many commonly abused drugs are illegal, quite a few can be obtained with a doctor's prescription, and some can even be purchased over-the-counter.

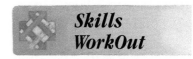

Skills WorkOut

Research Find out the penalties for drug-related crimes in your state. You can interview a police officer, judge, or district attorney. Or you can find the information in a library.

Stimulants Does sipping a cola pep you up? Cola contains a **stimulant**, a substance that stimulates the nervous system. Stimulants also raise blood pressure and make the heart beat faster. The stimulant in cola is caffeine. Caffeine is also found in coffee and tea. Tobacco contains nicotine, a mild stimulant. Amphetamines (am FEHT uh MEENZ) are a group of stimulants often referred to as "speed." They are very powerful stimulants.

Amphetamines are popular mood-enhancing drugs. Small doses create a feeling of limitless energy and a sense of pleasure called euphoria. Amphetamines also curb the appetite and reduce the desire for sleep. Doctors prescribe small doses of these drugs to treat depression and for supervised weight-loss programs.

Cocaine is also a stimulant. On the street, a form of cocaine is often sold as "crack." Long-term abusers of crack and cocaine may become tense and suspicious. They may suffer from depression and other kinds of temporary mental illness. Heavy use causes permanent brain damage, and sometimes death.

Depressants Another group of drugs relaxes the central nervous system, causing the heart rate to slow and blood pressure to fall. These drugs are **depressants**. The most commonly used depressant is alcohol. Others include barbiturates (bar BIHCH ur ihts) and tranquilizers. Some drug abusers routinely take depressants to relax and sleep. They then take stimulants to get going again. This creates a dangerous cycle.

Barbiturates are highly addictive to both the body and the mind. They change how people view things. They also slow down normal responses. Users may become confused about how many pills they have taken and die of an accidental overdose. Sudden withdrawal causes painful cramps, nausea, convulsions, and sometimes death.

Tranquilizers are widely used prescription drugs that calm people down without making them sleepy. Doctors use these drugs to treat such illnesses as depression and anxiety. Abuse of some tranquilizers can result in addiction. Mixing tranquilizers and alcohol is especially dangerous and can cause death.

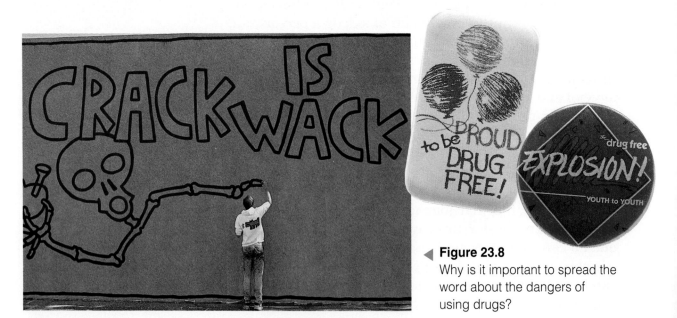

◀ **Figure 23.8**
Why is it important to spread the word about the dangers of using drugs?

Marijuana A popular illegal drug is marijuana. It is prepared by shredding the dried leaves and flowers of the hemp plant and then smoked in cigarettes or in pipes. Smokers experience a disoriented state. Moods can vary from excitement to depression.

Marijuana contains a compound called THC, which acts on the brain and nervous system. THC reduces a person's ability to concentrate and react. There is evidence that prolonged use of marijuana damages brain cells. Marijuana's effect on the lungs is similar to that of tobacco smoke.

Figure 23.9 ▲
The leaves, flowers, and resin from the hemp plant are used to produce marijuana.

Narcotics Heroin, morphine, and codeine are powerful drugs made from the opium poppy. These drugs are called **narcotics**. The word *narcotic* means "to numb." Morphine and codeine are used legally as painkillers.

When injected into a vein, heroin produces a warm, pleasurable sensation followed by a dreamy high. Heroin is physically and psychologically addictive. Heroin addicts risk getting hepatitis or AIDS if they share needles.

Hallucinogens The drug LSD causes hallucinations, or dreamlike "trips," in which a person sees, hears, smells, or feels things that do not exist. LSD and other drugs that cause hallucinations are called **hallucinogens** (huh LOO sih nuh juhnz). Another hallucinogen is mescaline, a drug obtained from peyote cactus.

After taking LSD, a person feels the effects of the drug for 10 to 12 hours. In the unreal world of a "good trip," colors seem more brilliant and patterns unfold. Senses merge into one another: music may appear as a color, or colors may even seem to have a taste. Sometimes it seems as if flying or floating is possible. Some people under the influence of LSD have fallen to their deaths thinking they could fly.

LSD trips are unpredictable. One trip may be good, the next frightening. During a "bad trip," people may appear to be horrible monsters. These visions can repeat themselves in flashbacks. Flashbacks may occur without warning—days, even months— after an individual stops using LSD.

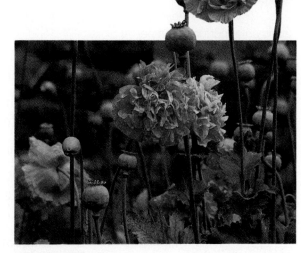

Figure 23.10 ▲
Narcotics are extracted from the seed pods of the opium poppy.

Figure 23.11 ▲

Helping others is a rewarding and productive way to spend time. Activities like these give teens an opportunity to meet new people and learn new things.

Science and You *Critical Choices*

One of the most important decisions you will ever make is whether or not to use drugs. It's a fact that most people who abuse drugs begin using them in their early teens or early twenties. For many teens, the pressure to use drugs comes mainly from their friends or peers.

Think about how peer pressure affects you. For example, what would you do if you went to a party where some of your classmates were smoking marijuana or drinking alcohol? Imagine that you were offered one of these substances. What is the best way to react to this kind of situation?

There are effective ways to resist the pressure to "join in." First, decide how you feel about the situation and then stick to your opinion. You can politely say "No thanks." You can walk away. You can seek out someone who feels the same way you do and supports your feelings.

There are many alternatives to using drugs. Below is a list of some healthy alternatives. What activities can you add?

▶ Exercise, outdoor hobbies, sports

▶ Talking to friends, family members, teachers

▶ Volunteer work

▶ Reading books, writing stories and poems, drawing, painting, playing an instrument

▶ Joining a club or an organization

Check and Explain

1. Name the major types of drugs and describe how each affects the body.

2. What may happen to someone who abuses drugs?

3. **Classify** Make a list of commonly abused drugs. Then classify each drug as illegal, legal with a prescription, or legal over-the-counter.

4. **Communicate** Write a letter to a friend, real or imaginary, whose use of drugs is having a bad effect on his or her life. Explain the dangers that person faces and suggest ways of dealing with the problem.

23.4 Alcohol and Tobacco

Objectives

▶ **Describe** the effects of alcohol on the body.

▶ **Explain** alcohol abuse.

▶ **Name** the chemicals present in tobacco smoke.

▶ **Describe** the long-term effects of tobacco on the body.

▶ **Collect data** about the alcohol content of beverages.

Why do you think alcohol and tobacco are sometimes called *social drugs*? It is because people often use them in social gatherings. People tend to forget these substances are drugs because they see others using them so often. However, just because alcohol and tobacco are legal drugs does not mean they are safe to use.

Alcohol Abuse

Any person who drinks to the point of drunkenness is abusing alcohol. People who abuse alcohol may not be alcoholics, however. Alcoholics are addicts—they have lost control over their drinking. Alcohol addiction is called alcoholism. At first, many alcoholics are unaware of their drinking problem. They may even boast that they can handle their drinking better than their friends. Actually, a high tolerance for alcohol is one of the early symptoms of alcoholism. Many alcoholics cannot get through the day without alcohol. Often they do not remember what happened during a drinking bout. They often dismiss their abuse of alcohol as "social drinking."

Alcoholism strikes men and women of all ages and in all walks of life, including teenagers. It is often hard to identify alcoholics because they learn to hide their drinking problem. Like other kinds of addiction, however, alcoholism disrupts a person's life.

The abuse of alcohol can have very serious results for both the drinker and society. Among teenagers, alcohol-related accidents are the leading cause of death. Look at Table 23.6. In what other ways do alcohol and alcoholism affect people's lives?

**Table 23.6
Alcohol's Costs to Society**

In the United States alone . . .
▶ Drunk drivers are responsible for about half of the 46,000 automobile accidents that occur every year.
▶ Someone is killed by a drunk driver every 21 minutes.
▶ Alcohol is connected to as many as 2,800 drowning deaths each year.
▶ Alcoholism costs at least $100 billion a year in treatment, property damage, lowered worker productivity, and other losses.

Effects of Alcohol

The blood absorbs alcohol directly from the stomach and intestines without digestion. Once in the bloodstream, alcohol moves quickly throughout the body. The first reactions take place in the brain.

Remember that alcohol is a depressant. It dulls the senses and weakens the brain's control centers. A drinker may become confused and lose control of speech, movements, and actions. Heavy drinking over time permanently damages brain cells.

The heart and liver are also affected by alcohol abuse. Heavy drinking increases blood pressure and eventually weakens the heart muscle. The liver breaks down alcohol and removes it from the body. Excessive drinking overworks the liver and can damage it, possibly leading to a condition in which the liver is severely scarred. Figure 23.12 summarizes the major effects of alcohol on the human body.

Brain
▶ Damages brain cells
▶ Dulls the senses
▶ Slows thinking
▶ Impairs coordination

Heart
▶ Weakens heart muscle
▶ Raises blood pressure

Liver
▶ Damages liver cells

Figure 23.12 ▲
How does alcohol affect the liver?

Effects of Tobacco

Nicotine is a poisonous compound found in tobacco leaves. It acts as a mild stimulant on the heart and other organs. Because nicotine is very addictive, heavy smokers find it hard to quit.

Cigarette smoke contains more than 3,000 substances. Some, such as carbon monoxide, are poisons. Others, such as tars, have chemicals that cause cancer.

In the brain, nicotine stimulates cravings for more nicotine. It can also affect a person's moods. Nicotine dulls the sense of taste and irritates membranes in the nose and throat.

In the lungs, nicotine damages the air sacs and increases mucous secretions in the bronchial tubes. When this happens, normal breathing is affected. Nicotine also increases the heart rate. Figure 23.13 summarizes the major effects of nicotine on the human body.

Brain
▶ Makes you want more nicotine
▶ Alters moods

Mouth and Throat
▶ Dulls taste buds
▶ Irritates membranes

Lungs
▶ Damages air sacs
▶ Narrows air passages

Heart
▶ Increases heart rate
▶ Raises blood pressure
▶ Reduces oxygen in the blood

Figure 23.13 ▲
How does nicotine affect the lungs?

Diseases and Tobacco

Studies show conclusively that smoking is the leading cause of preventable death in the United States. Smoking has been linked to a number of serious diseases. For example, smokers are much more likely to get heart disease than nonsmokers. The buildup of tars in the lungs causes a respiratory disease called emphysema (EHM fuh SEE muh). Smokers are ten times more likely to die from lung cancer than nonsmokers.

Recent studies show that nonsmokers who inhale tobacco smoke are also more likely to get heart disease or lung cancer. Moreover, children of smokers have more respiratory infections than do children of nonsmokers.

For people who already smoke, there is some good news. All of these risks can be dramatically reduced by quitting smoking. Two years after quitting, for example, a person's risk of heart attack returns to normal. After ten years, the risk of lung cancer is nearly normal.

Skills WorkOut

Collect Data Use the library to find out the kinds and amounts of gases, tars, and other substances in cigarette smoke. Make a table that lists 20 of these substances. Next to each, briefly explain why they are harmful.

Consider This

Should Tobacco Advertising Be Allowed?

The health hazards of smoking have been firmly established. In the United States, federal law requires that all cigarette packages carry a statement that smoking is harmful to your health. The law also forbids cigarette advertising on radio and television. However, tobacco companies can still advertise their products on billboards and in newspapers and magazines.

Consider Some Issues
Some people believe that cigarette ads should not be allowed anywhere. They claim that such ads persuade many people to start smoking. They feel that tobacco ads project a sophisticated image that attracts teenagers. They claim that some advertising is aimed at groups that may not be aware of the problems caused by using tobacco and are easily swayed by the ads.

The tobacco companies argue that tobacco products are legal in this country, so they have a right to advertise. Tobacco companies claim that their ads are designed for adult audiences. They say ads can't make people buy cigarettes and that adults are free to choose whether or not they want to smoke.

Think About It Do tobacco companies have a right to advertise a product known to be unhealthy for people to use? How influential are cigarette ads? Do these ads affect your own attitude about smoking?

Write About It Write a paper stating your position for or against cigarette advertising. Use the ads from magazines and newspapers to support your position.

Compare your position with those of your classmates. Form two teams to debate whether or not tobacco advertising should be allowed.

Science and Society
Fetal Alcohol Syndrome

When pregnant women drink, the alcohol passes through the placenta to the baby. It affects the baby's fast-growing tissues by killing cells or slowing their growth. The brain is affected most by alcohol.

Babies born to women who drink heavily during pregnancy may have a condition known as *fetal alcohol syndrome*. This condition is actually a mixture of physical, mental, and behavioral defects. It is one of the leading known cause of mental retardation in the United States.

Babies with fetal alcohol syndrome are smaller than normal at birth. Many of these babies show some degree of permanent mental retardation. The brain damage also affects their behavior. As children, they have poor coordination and short attention spans. Many are jittery and impulsive. They often are unable to consider the consequences of their actions. As a result, even those who have normal intelligence often have difficulty succeeding at school or living on their own.

Scientists are not sure how much alcohol is harmful to an unborn baby. Studies suggest, however, that even moderate drinking may retard fetal growth. Babies of teens who drink heavily are doubly at risk since these babies are likely to be born too small or too soon.

Figure 23.14 ▲
Babies of alcoholic mothers start life at risk. How can fetal alcohol syndrome be prevented?

Check and Explain

1. What is the substance in tobacco smoke that causes addiction?

2. What are the long-term effects on the body of using alcohol and tobacco?

3. **Uncover Assumptions**   Who is most likely to be an alcoholic—a business executive who coaches little league, a single mother on welfare, or an unemployed carpenter? What assumptions did you make in reaching this conclusion? Can these assumptions cause you to make the wrong conclusions about people?

4. **Collect Data**   Find information about the alcohol content of different kinds of alcoholic beverages. Create a circle graph or chart that displays this information.

Concept Summary

23.1 Nutrients

▶ Your body needs nutrients for energy, and for growth, replacement, and repair of cell parts.

▶ Carbohydrates and lipids provide energy; proteins provide materials for growth and repair.

▶ Vitamins, fiber, and minerals help the body to function normally.

▶ Water is needed for transport of nutrients and wastes. Most of the chemical reactions in your body take place in water solutions.

23.2 Exercise and Rest

▶ Regular exercise can help keep you healthy. Aerobic exercise improves endurance.

▶ Stress is a normal part of life, but sometimes stress can overwhelm your built-in stress response or trigger it too often.

▶ Relaxation, sleep, and exercise help reduce stress.

23.3 Drugs and Substance Abuse

▶ Any substance that changes the way your body or mind works is a drug.

▶ Alcohol, nicotine, and caffeine are drugs.

▶ Substance abuse is the harmful or non-medical use of drugs.

▶ Drug abuse can lead to physical and psychological dependence.

▶ Abused drugs include stimulants, depressants, marijuana, narcotics, and hallucinogens.

23.4 Alcohol and Tobacco

▶ Alcohol and nicotine are addictive drugs.

▶ Alcohol depresses the central nervous system. It affects the brain, as well as the heart and liver.

▶ People who become alcoholics have lost control over their drinking.

▶ Tobacco smoke contains nicotine, carbon monoxide, tars, and other substances that can harm the body.

Chapter Vocabulary

carbohydrate (23.1)	protein (23.1)	stimulant (23.3)	narcotic (23.3)
lipid (23.1)	addiction (23.3)	depressant (23.3)	hallucinogen (23.3)
cholesterol (23.1)			

Check Your Vocabulary

Use the vocabulary words above to complete the following sentences correctly.

1. Physical and psychological dependence on a drug is called ____ .

2. Fats and oils are nutrients called ____ .

3. Morphine and codeine, both ____ , numb feelings.

4. Drugs that cause dreamlike "trips" are called ____ .

5. Starch is a ____ made of carbon, hydrogen, and oxygen.

6. Caffeine is the ____ in coffee.

7. Alcohol is a ____ because it relaxes the central nervous system.

8. A fatty substance found in all animal tissues is called ____ .

9. Cells need ____ for growth and repair.

Write Your Vocabulary

Write sentences using each vocabulary word above. Show that you know what each word means.

Chapter 23 Review

Check Your Knowledge

Answer the following in complete sentences.

1. Name three diseases linked to smoking.

2. How do stimulants affect the human body? Name three products that contain a stimulant.

3. Name at least two benefits of aerobic exercise.

4. Name two foods that are good sources of fiber. How is fiber beneficial?

5. What are two dangers associated with narcotics abuse?

6. Name four things you can do to ensure that you have a healthy diet.

7. Why is it dangerous for a person to drive after she or he has been drinking?

8. What does the number of Calories in a serving of food tell you?

Determine whether each statement is true or false. Write *true* if it is true. If it is false, change the underlined word to make the statement true.

9. Soybeans, cheese, meats, and fish are sources of <u>incomplete</u> proteins.

10. About <u>25</u> percent of your body is water.

11. Cross-country skiing uses <u>fewer</u> Calories than baseball.

12. THC <u>improves</u> judgment, coordination, and concentration.

13. An <u>overdose</u> is when a person takes more of a drug at one time than is safe.

14. Walking at a fast pace can be an <u>aerobic</u> exercise.

15. Foods that come from plants are naturally <u>high</u> in fat.

16. Water and minerals are <u>organic</u> nutrients.

Check Your Understanding

Apply the concepts you have learned to answer each question.

1. In planning your diet, what three factors do you think are most important? Explain.

2. Describe three methods for reducing stress.

3. Explain what is meant by dependence, tolerance, and withdrawal.

4. Assume that the three foods listed in the right column are available in equal amounts. Which food would you eat to best satisfy each of the needs in the left column?

   a. Most energy   Potato
   b. Protein   Butter
   c. Vitamin C   Fish

5. **Mystery Photo** The photograph on page 486 shows a variety of winter squash. Squash are rich in potassium and vitamins A and C. What other foods are rich in vitamins A and C?

6. Explain what happens to your body during aerobic exercise.

7. **Critical Thinking** A teenager began smoking to be sociable. After a time, smoking became a habit. Explain this change in terms of the effect of smoking on the body.

8. **Critical Thinking** Compare the effects of stimulants and depressants.

9. **Application** Suggest ways you could help a friend decide not to start smoking, and an adult to quit smoking.

10. **Application** Before athletic events, many runners and other athletes eat large amounts of foods high in carbohydrates. Why do athletes eat these foods?

Develop Your Skills

Use the skills you have developed in this chapter to complete each activity.

1. **Interpret Data** The chart below shows how the percentage of vitamin C in peas changes as peas are processed for eating.

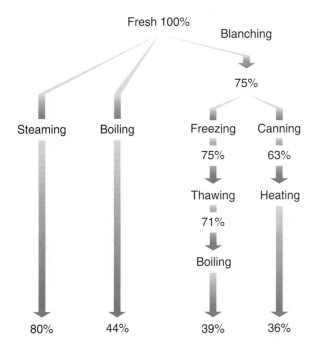

a. How should you prepare peas so that you get the most vitamin C per serving?

b. Order the methods of preparing peas from 1 to 5, with 1 being most nutritious and 5 being least nutritious. Be sure to include *not* cooking the peas as a method.

2. **Data Bank** Use the information on page 628 to answer the following questions.

a. What does BAC mean?

b. What happens to a person in this weight range after four drinks?

c. What are some activities that might be unsafe after two drinks? After five drinks?

Make Connections

1. **Link the Concepts** Below is a concept map showing how some of the main concepts in this chapter link together. Only part of the map is filled in. Finish the map, using words and ideas from the chapter.

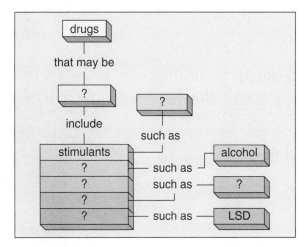

2. **Science and Art** Design an advertisement for a billboard or magazine that teaches people about the dangers of smoking, or drug or alcohol abuse.

3. **Science and PE** Drugs, smoking, and alcohol have an effect on physical abilities. Find out how each of these would affect your ability to perform in a chosen sport or activity. You may also research the use of steroids by athletes to improve muscle strength. What effect do steroids have on the body?

4. **Science and Technology** Cigarette smoking is addictive and difficult to quit. Many people who want to quit simply cannot give up smoking. Research current methods to quit smoking, such as nicotine gum, patches, acupuncture, hypnotism, and other programs. Report on the effectiveness of each program.

Chapter 24

Disease and the Immune System

Chapter Sections

What do you see?

*"*I think that this is inside the human body. The white things are probably white blood cells. The white blood cells are attaching themselves to a harmful disease. This is important because without white blood cells, diseases would infect the body and it could not function normally.*"*

Ben Wilkins
Kiser Middle School
Dayton, Ohio

To find out more about the photograph, look on page 530. As you read this chapter, you will learn about diseases, what causes them, and how your body functions to prevent them.

510

24.1 Infectious Disease

Objectives

▶ **Distinguish** between infectious diseases and noninfectious diseases.

▶ **Identify** three kinds of organisms that can cause disease in humans.

▶ **Describe** ways that disease-causing agents can be spread from person to person.

▶ **Make a graph** of the projected numbers of AIDS cases worldwide.

The feeling is all too familiar. You wake up with a tightness in your chest or a sore throat. Maybe your nose is runny and your head and muscles ache. You feel awful. You know you're getting sick.

Everyone gets sick. People catch colds and other illnesses, such as the flu, that usually go away in a few days. Unfortunately, some people also come down with illnesses that are more serious, such as cancer. When a person's body no longer functions properly, he or she may have a disorder or a disease. Learning about the causes of disease can help you to prevent them and get over them faster.

Causes of Disease

What causes a person's body not to work the way it's supposed to? You know that microorganisms, such as bacteria and viruses, can invade the body and cause disease. A disease that can be transmitted among people by harmful organisms is called an **infectious disease**. The organisms that cause infectious diseases are called **pathogens**.

Another kind of disease occurs when something goes wrong with the body itself. A body part may wear out or stop working the way it is supposed to. This kind of illness is called a noninfectious disease, or a body disorder. Some body disorders are inherited. Others are the result of old age or an unhealthy lifestyle. Whatever their cause, body disorders differ from infectious diseases because they can't be spread from person to person.

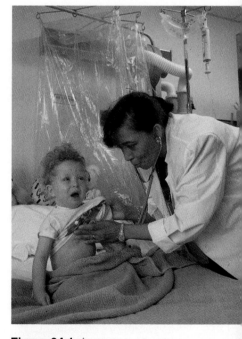

Figure 24.1 ▲
Sometimes when you're sick, a doctor may find the cause and help your body defend itself.

Figure 24.2 ▲
Newly-assembled viruses burst from a cell, ready to infect others.

Table 24.1
Some Infectious Diseases

Disease	Pathogenic Organism
AIDS	Virus
Common cold	Viruses
Gonorrhea	Bacteria
Herpes	Viruses
Influenza	Viruses
Malaria	Protozoan
Pneumonia	Viruses or bacteria
Polio	Virus
Rabies	Virus
Ringworm	Fungus
Strep throat	Bacteria
Trichinosis	Roundworm
Tuberculosis	Bacteria

Kinds of Infectious Disease

For most of human history, people had no idea that living things too small to be seen were responsible for their illnesses. As scientists discovered the pathogens that caused diseases, they found that each one infected the body in a different way. Today the treatment and prevention of an infectious disease depend on knowing what kind of organism is the pathogen at work.

Viral Diseases   As you have learned, viruses harm the body because they use the body's cells to reproduce. Cells infected by the virus are destroyed in order to make new viruses, which infect other cells. Nearly everyone has had a viral disease called the common cold. Other kinds of viral diseases are influenza, chicken pox, hepatitis, herpes, and AIDS.

Bacterial Diseases   Bacteria, as you know, are in the air, on your skin, and in the food you eat. Fortunately, most bacteria are not harmful. Those bacteria that are harmful are usually destroyed or reduced in number by the natural defenses of a healthy body.

When they cause disease, bacteria harm the body's cells in two ways. In most bacterial diseases, the pathogenic bacteria produce toxins, or poisons, that harm cells. Food poisoning, for example, is caused by toxins from bacteria growing in spoiled food. Other pathogenic bacteria harm cells directly by growing around them and preventing the normal flow of substances in and out of the cells.

Other Infectious Diseases   Some infectious diseases are caused by other kinds of organisms. Certain kinds of fungi, for example, cause disease by infecting the body and producing enzymes that digest body cells. Ringworm and athlete's foot are examples of fungal diseases.

Some protozoa are pathogens. Malaria is caused by a protozoan that lives inside liver and blood cells. A kind of ameba causes a serious form of diarrhea called amebic dysentery.

A number of worms also cause disease. Parasitic tapeworms infest the digestive system and rob the host of food. Flatworms called flukes infest the liver. Trichinosis is caused by a roundworm called *Trichina*, which lives in the skeletal and intestinal muscles.

Spread of Infectious Disease

In order for a pathogen to cause disease, it must enter the body and reproduce. Most of the time, your body's natural defenses keep pathogens from entering your body or from reproducing. Some pathogens, however, can easily overwhelm your body's defenses. Since dangerous pathogens can be almost anywhere, you should be aware of how they are transmitted to you.

People with an infectious disease may have the pathogen in their saliva, mucus, or excrement. If they get these substances on their hands, the pathogen can be transferred to anything or anyone they touch. A kiss or handshake, therefore, can spread some infectious diseases. In addition, sneezes and coughs may spray droplets of contaminated saliva into the air, which other people may breathe. ▼

Infectious diseases that are spread by the close contact of sexual intercourse are called sexually transmitted diseases. These diseases include chlamydia, herpes, gonorrhea, AIDS, and syphilis.

▲ Food and drinking water can also carry pathogens. The pathogens in food may originally come from an infected person who handled the food. Sometimes people are infected by food that has been contaminated by bacteria such as *Salmonella*. *Salmonella* bacteria live in such farm animals as chickens. Diseases, such as cholera, are commonly spread by water contaminated with sewage.

Some diseases are spread mainly by the bites of insects and other animals. A certain mosquito carries the protozoan that causes malaria. Lyme disease is carried by ticks, and mammals infected with rabies can spread the disease by biting people. ▼

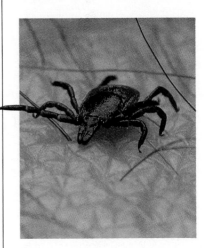

Blood from a person with a viral disease will probably contain the pathogenic virus. For this reason, needles that have been previously used can spread diseases, such as hepatitis and AIDS. ▼

Figure 24.3 ▲
The AIDS quilt is a memorial to the people who have died from the disease. It is now much larger than a football field.

AIDS

The majority of people are healthy most of the time because their bodies have natural defenses against disease. These defenses include a complex set of cells and tissues called the **immune system**. The immune system attacks invading pathogens and prevents them from growing inside the body.

Most pathogens cause disease by overwhelming the immune system on their way to infecting some other part of the body. But one pathogen, the human immunodeficiency virus, or HIV, attacks the immune system itself. HIV is the cause of the disease called AIDS, or acquired immune deficiency syndrome. Because it harms the immune system, AIDS leaves the body open to infection by many pathogens. People with AIDS suffer from infections that their bodies would normally fight off. When people with AIDS die, other infections, not HIV, kill them.

Consider This

Who Should Be Tested for HIV?

Over a million people in the United States alone are infected with HIV. Many do not even know that they are carrying the virus.

Many public-health officials would like to know who has HIV. However, getting the answer raises difficult issues about public health and an individual's right to privacy.

In order to determine who carries the AIDS virus, tests would be required of nearly everyone. Should people be tested against their will? Should an HIV test be required for jobs, medical insurance, or a marriage license?

Consider Some Issues
People who favor widespread testing for HIV believe that the AIDS threat is serious enough to justify testing. They say that accurate data are needed on how many people are carrying the virus now. The HIV test, in their view, will provide the information needed to slow the spread of the virus.

Those opposed to testing believe it threatens peoples' basic rights. They are concerned that people who are found to carry HIV may be forced to leave their jobs. Their health insurance may be canceled. They could be shunned

by others. Opponents to testing believe that no one should be forced to take an HIV test against his or her will. They feel that the test results should be given only to the patient and his or her doctor.

Think About It Who should be tested for HIV? Who should know the test results? Is HIV testing a good way to slow the spread of the virus?

Debate It Have a class debate in which you and your classmates role-play people with opposite points of view on the issue of testing for HIV.

HIV has infected millions of people all over the world, and it continues to spread. So far, there is no cure for AIDS. Researchers predict that by the year 2000, two million people will have died of AIDS. Look at Table 24.2. It shows cumulative AIDS cases in adults. How many AIDS cases are expected in North America by 1995?

Every person can take steps to keep from coming in contact with HIV. The virus can be transmitted through body fluids, such as blood, semen, vaginal fluid, and breast milk. Therefore, you can't get HIV from hugging, shaking hands, or touching toilet seats or shower stalls. You can't get HIV from a cough or sneeze. HIV is transmitted in four ways—through sexual contact, intravenous drug use, contaminated blood, and breast milk. If people abstain from sex and do not inject drugs, they greatly reduce their chances of getting AIDS.

Table 24.2
AIDS Cases in Thousands

Region	1992 Estimate	1995 Projection
N. America	257	534
W. Europe	99	279
Australia/ Oceania	4	11
Latin America	173	417
Africa	1,367	3,277
Caribbean	43	121
E. Europe	2	9
NE Asia	3	14
SE Asia	65	240

Science and You *Lyme Disease*

Have you walked through tall grass or brush lately? Did you check yourself for ticks afterward? In many parts of the United States, it is a good idea to do all you can to avoid being bitten by a tick. The deer tick can infect you with the bacteria that cause Lyme disease.

Lyme disease usually begins with headaches, back-aches, fever, and chills. If the disease is not treated, the heart and nervous system can be permanently damaged. More and more cases of Lyme disease are being reported, and many doctors consider it an epidemic.

If you find a tick attached to you, remove it immediately. Grasp it with tweezers where it meets the skin and pull straight up. Quick removal of the tick may prevent transfer of the bacteria that cause the disease.

Figure 24.4 ▲
This rash on the back of the knee is one sign of Lyme disease infection.

Check and Explain

1. Name three kinds of organisms that can be pathogens.

2. Describe three different ways you could get a disease from a friend.

3. **Find Causes** How do bacteria harm the body's cells?

4. **Make a Graph** Use the data in Table 24.2 to make a bar graph showing the projected number of AIDS cases in the world in 1995.

Skills WarmUp

Infer Name four things you could do to keep a cut from becoming infected. Explain how each precaution is effective.

24.2 The Body's Natural Defenses

Objectives

▶ **Describe** how body secretions prevent infection.

▶ **Describe** what happens during the inflammation process.

▶ **Explain** how the body can become immune to a particular pathogen.

▶ **Hypothesize** about why organ transplants may be rejected.

U sually when you cut your finger, it's no big deal. As long as the cut isn't too deep, soap and water, a bandage, and time are all that are needed to make your finger as good as new.

You probably aren't aware of all the work your body does to prevent infection the minute your skin is cut. Many lines of defense come into play. They work together to make sure bacteria that enter the cut do not grow inside your body.

The way your body fights infection in a cut is just one example of how it protects itself in an environment full of pathogens. Your body's natural defenses constantly prevent bacteria, viruses, and other pathogens from giving you diseases.

Skin

Every organism has a barrier between itself and its environment. Your barrier is your skin. Skin is thick and tough. Like bricks in a wall, the cells that make up skin are packed tightly together. Skin prevents pathogens from entering the body, where they would find ideal growing conditions.

Your skin is not only a physical barrier, it is a chemical one, too. Glands in the skin produce perspiration, or sweat. Perspiration contains enzymes that can destroy the cell walls of many kinds of bacteria.

Your skin gets a lot of wear and tear. The outer layer is constantly being rubbed, scraped, and washed away. New skin cells are always being created in the inner layer to replace them. The rapid cell division in your skin also helps it repair itself quickly when skin is damaged.

Figure 24.5 ▲
In addition to cooling the body, perspiration helps the skin be a better barrier against infection.

Body Secretions

Skin does not cover your body completely. Openings such as your mouth, nose, and eyes can be doorways for pathogens. To guard against infection, the tissues in these openings produce substances that kill pathogens or discourage their growth.

Saliva In your mouth, saliva contains strong enzymes that can destroy some kinds of bacteria.

Stomach Juices Many pathogens that reach your stomach are killed by the acids used to digest foods.

Mucus The tissues lining your nose, sinuses, throat, and windpipe produce mucus. Mucus is sticky enough to trap many of the pathogens you inhale. In the lungs and windpipe, cilia help push the mucus upward toward the mouth. There it is swallowed and carried to the stomach, where any pathogens it contains are killed by stomach acid. Pathogen-containing mucus in your nose may be removed when you blow your nose.

Tears Glands in your eyes constantly produce tears that wash away pathogens. In addition, tears contain enzymes that destroy some bacterial substances. Each time you blink, your eyelids bathe your eyes with tears and keep them free of pathogens.

Inflammation

Have you observed what your body does when you cut or scrape yourself? You bleed, of course, but the area around the wound also gets red and puffy.

When the skin is broken, bacteria can enter the body and reproduce. To prevent infection, the body begins to set up a line of defense. The injured cells in the wound produce a substance called histamine (HIHS tuh MEEN). The histamine widens blood vessels and increases blood flow to the area. At the same time, the injured tissues leak fluid. The result is a swelling and reddening called inflammation.

Inflammation of the injured area raises its temperature, which helps slow the growth of bacteria. The extra flow of blood also brings with it white blood cells. These cells seek out bacteria, which are engulfed and digested. You can see white blood cells in action in Figure 24.6.

Inflammation is a response that fights any kind of bacteria. It is a general line of defense. Your body cells have other general lines of defense, too. For example, when cells are attacked by viruses, they produce a substance called interferon. Interferon helps other cells resist further infection by the virus.

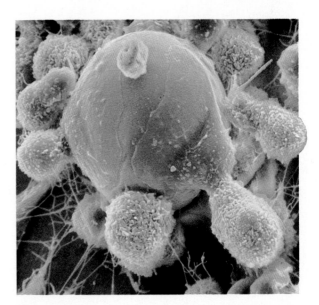

Figure 24.6 ▲
White blood cells gang up to destroy a foreign substance in the body. What do you think is the function of the bumps on the surface of the white blood cells?

The Immune System

In addition to your body's general lines of defense, a complex defensive system protects your body against specific pathogens. This defensive system is called the immune system.

The immune system is made up of several types of cells that circulate through the body. They are always on the lookout for anything that does not belong in the body. These cells are able to destroy an invading pathogen and "remember" it in case it enters the body again.

Recognition of Pathogens Imagine that you are reaching into a jar of jellybeans high on a shelf. All the jellybeans feel the same, but then you feel something you know is different. It's a piece of candy wrapped in cellophane. In a similar way,

Figure 24.7 ▲
Every pathogen has a different kind of surface. The "shapes" on its surface are determined by the chemicals that make it up. Antibodies are made to fit the surface shapes like a lock and key.

the cells of your immune system can tell the difference between your body cells and anything that is different. Cells called lymphocytes "feel" the surface of whatever they contact in the body. When lymphocytes contact a pathogen, they recognize it as a foreign substance because its surface is different.

Destruction of Pathogens When the immune system recognizes a pathogen, certain lymphocytes begin producing **antibodies** for the pathogen. An antibody is a specially shaped molecule that matches a certain part of the surface of a particular pathogen. Look at Figure 24.7. Notice how the antibodies fit onto the surface of the pathogen.

Millions of antibodies are produced. They circulate through the blood and lymph, sticking to the pathogen wherever the two come together. Once a pathogen has an antibody sticking to it, it can't infect a body cell.

Pathogens are also "tagged." Cells called phagocytes seek out tagged pathogens and eat them. Tagged pathogens may be destroyed in other ways, too. For example, certain proteins may break open the pathogen's cell membrane.

Immunity Once the immune system destroys most of the pathogens that cause a disease, you get well. Some of the lymphocytes that produced the antibodies to the pathogen stay in the blood, however. They are called *memory cells* because they remember how to produce the antibodies. If the same pathogen enters your body again, the memory cells produce antibodies right away. The antibodies destroy the pathogen before it can cause disease. You are therefore *immune* to that disease. You can become immune to a variety of diseases caused by both viruses and bacteria.

Science and Technology *The Rh Factor*

Although antibodies generally work to fight disease in the body, they can also cause problems. This is the case when a pregnant mother produces antibodies for a certain substance in the blood of her fetus. This substance is the Rh factor.

Some people, called Rh-positive, have the Rh factor on their red blood cells. Other people do not have the Rh factor and are called Rh-negative. An Rh-negative woman can become pregnant with an Rh-positive baby if the baby inherits the Rh gene from the father.

When the mother is exposed to small amounts of the fetus's blood, she develops antibodies to the Rh factor. For the first baby, this is usually no problem. But the mother's immune system "remembers" how to produce anti-Rh antibodies. If she has a second Rh-positive baby, she produces the antibodies again. The antibodies can cross the placenta in the final weeks of pregnancy and cause the baby's blood to clump. If this happens, the baby's life is in danger.

The Rh factor was a serious problem for some women during the 1950s. The blood of their newborns had to be replaced with donor blood that did not contain antibodies. Some babies died.

Fortunately, the problem of the Rh factor is easily avoided today. The mother is given an injection of anti-Rh antibodies immediately after an Rh-positive baby is delivered. The Rh-positive blood cells in the mother's blood are destroyed before her immune system can produce antibodies for them. Any Rh-positive babies she has after that will be safe.

Skills WorkOut

Communicate   Tell what would destroy bacteria that are on or in the following places: skin, eye, nose, stomach, lung, bloodstream.

Check and Explain

1. Name four body substances that fight infection.

2. Describe how the body prevents infection in a cut.

3. **Infer**   What is one danger a person faces if he or she has a severe burn on a large area of the body?

4. **Hypothesize**   When an organ is transplanted from one person to another, the body of the person receiving the organ produces antibodies against it. Explain why the immune system reacts this way.

Activity 24 *Do people blink their eyes at different rates?*

Skills Observe; Calculate; Infer

Task 1 Prelab Prep

1. Collect the following items: a stopwatch or clock with a second hand, a sheet of paper and a pencil for every other student, and a sheet of paper for each group.
2. Name one person in the class to serve as timekeeper.

Task 2 Data Record

1. Copy Table 24.3 onto a sheet of paper.
2. Use the table to record the observations of each person.

Task 3 Procedure

1. Watch your partner's eyes for three minutes. Count the number of times the person blinks. Note: Try not to think about blinking when you are being watched.
2. Write down the number of times your partner blinks. Calculate the number of blinks per minute for your partner.
3. Repeat steps 1 and 2 for each person in your group.

Task 4 Analysis

1. What is the difference between the smallest and the largest number of blinks per minute for your group?
2. How many more times per minute did the fastest blinker blink compared to the slowest blinker? Is this a big difference or a small difference?
3. Calculate the average number of blinks per minute for your group. How does your blinking rate compare to the group average?
4. What variables could explain the differences between people?

Task 5 Conclusion

Based on your data analysis, write a paragraph explaining how the rate of blinking differs among individuals and among groups of people. Infer how the blinking rate is important in protecting your eyes.

Everyday Application

What could cause your blinking rate to increase? Explain how an increased rate could protect your eyes. What would happen if you blinked less than most people? Predict what would happen if you didn't blink at all.

Extension

Graph the results for the entire class by showing the number of people at each blinking rate. How does your group's blinking-rate average compare with the other group averages? Where is your blinking rate on the graph?

Table 24.3 Blinking

Name	Length of Time Observed	Number of Blinks	Blinks per Minute	Other Observations

24.3 Body Disorders

Objectives

▶ **Identify** three different kinds of body disorders.

▶ **Explain** what cancer is and how it harms the body.

▶ **Infer** the causes of different kinds of cancer.

▶ **Classify** body disorders and their causes.

Classify   Write down the names of ten diseases. Put a check mark by the diseases that are *not caused by bacteria or viruses*. Then discuss what might cause these diseases.

Do you have older relatives with health problems? They may have arthritis, heart disease, diabetes, Alzheimer's disease, or cancer. Many people suffer from one or more of these diseases as they get older. How are these diseases different from infectious diseases such as pneumonia, influenza, and the common cold?

Body disorders, as you have learned, are not caused by pathogens. They are diseases that result from a breakdown or defect in some part of the body. Many body disorders commonly occur as the body ages. Others, however, can happen at any age. Sometimes, too, a person is born with a body disorder.

Causes of Body Disorders

There are many types of body disorders, each with a different cause. One kind of body disorder occurs when the immune system turns against the body. In diseases such as lupus and rheumatoid arthritis, the immune system attacks the body's own cells. These are called autoimmune diseases because the body treats its own cells as foreign invaders. Scientists do not fully understand what causes the immune system to malfunction in this way.

Some body disorders are caused by poor nutrition. Disease can occur if the body doesn't get enough protein, certain minerals, or vitamins. Scurvy, for example, occurs when people don't have enough vitamin C in their diets. When children have nutritional diseases for a long time, their brains and other body parts may be permanently damaged.

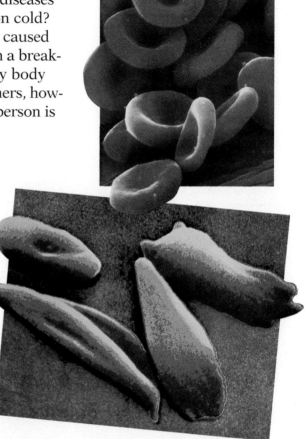

Figure 24.8 ▲
A body disorder called sickle-cell anemia causes normal red blood cells (top) to become sickle-shaped (bottom).

The most common body disorders today are caused mainly by the way people live in modern industrial societies. Cardiovascular disease, which affects the heart and blood vessels, can result from unhealthy diets, lack of exercise, and too much stress. Cancer is often caused by cigarette smoking and exposure to harmful chemicals and radiation.

Some body disorders are the result of a genetic defect. In sickle-cell anemia, for example, the body can't produce normal hemoglobin, because the wrong instructions are carried in the DNA. Genetic diseases, such as sickle-cell anemia, are hereditary because the defective gene is passed on from parent to child. Other genetic diseases, such as Down's syndrome, are not passed from generation to generation.

Cancer

Most of your body cells have the ability to divide to make new cells. Usually cell division is kept under strict control. Sometimes, however, a cell loses control and starts to divide at a rapid rate. All the cells produced also lack any control over their rate of division. A mass of cells, called a tumor, develops and continues to grow. The tumor robs the surrounding healthy cells of nutrients and oxygen. Healthy cells are crowded out and destroyed. This is what happens in the body disorder called **cancer**.

Although cancer is a body disorder, you can compare the behavior of a cancer cell to that of a pathogen. A cancer cell causes disease in the body as it grows and reproduces. The main difference between a cancer cell and a pathogen is that the cancer cell is the body's own. It's not an outside invader.

Figure 24.9

A cancer tumor in the brain shows as an orange spot in this CAT scan (left). In the cancer called leukemia, white blood cells become cancerous (right).

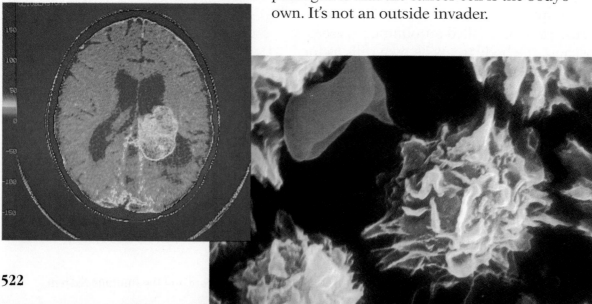

Causes of Cancer Many cancers are caused by unhealthy substances in the environment. Different substances that cause cancer are called **carcinogens**. Carcinogens include many kinds of chemicals, pollutants in the air, cigarette smoke, exposure to radiation, and substances in some foods.

Each kind of carcinogen is linked to one or more particular kinds of cancer. For example, cigarette smoke is linked to lung and throat cancer. Certain foods are associated with colon cancer. Excessive radiation can cause a cancer of the white blood cells called leukemia. Even though most cancers are probably caused by something from outside the body, heredity sometimes plays a role, too. Scientists think that certain genetic factors may increase the chances of breast, colon, and stomach cancer developing in some people.

Figure 24.10 ▲
A scientist works to develop better anticancer drugs.

Development of Cancer How does a carcinogen cause a cell to become cancerous? This is one major question cancer researchers are trying to answer. They think the carcinogen somehow changes the DNA that controls cell division.

Once a cell becomes cancerous, the immune system acts to stop its growth. Recall that the immune system recognizes anything that is not one of the body's normal cells. Since a cancer cell differs from other body cells, the immune system treats it like an invading bacterium or virus and tries to destroy it.

The immune system is not always successful in destroying cancer cells. If it is not, the tumor grows. One reason cancer is so deadly is that cells from the tumor spread the cancer to other parts of the body through the lymph system.

Treatment of Cancer Many cancers are treated by removing the tumor through surgery. However, doctors may try other ways of destroying the tumor. They can use radiation or chemicals that kill cancer cells. The use of chemicals for cancer treatment is called chemotherapy.

In some cases, the cancer patient recovers completely. However, if the cancer is discovered after it has spread to other parts of the body, the patient's chance of recovery is greatly reduced. Scientists are developing new and more effective ways of treating cancer. Cancer, however, is still a major killer.

Figure 24.11 ▲
Radiation therapy is commonly used to destroy some types of tumors.

Allergies

You probably know some people who have to stay away from dogs and cats or who get hay fever in the spring. These people have an allergy. Allergies are caused by the immune system responding to harmless substances as if they were harmful pathogens. These substances are called allergens. They can be almost anything, from pollen, to the chemicals in insect bites.

A substance becomes an allergen when a person's body produces antibodies against it. Whenever the person comes in contact with the allergen, the antibodies cause an allergic reaction. The body releases histamine, which causes the symptoms of the allergic response.

Science and Society *Electronic Pollution*

Scientists have known for a long time that air pollution is harmful to the lungs and may have a role in causing cancer. Now evidence suggests that there is another kind of pollution that may be a health hazard. It is a form of weak radiation produced by electrical appliances, power lines, radio transmitters, and video display terminals.

Studies show that in areas where people live near high-voltage power lines, there are more cases of leukemia than in the general population. Studies also indicate that some people who work at video display terminals for long periods of time report other kinds of health problems, such as eyestrain and headache. Scientists are doing more research to determine how people's health may be affected by electronic pollution.

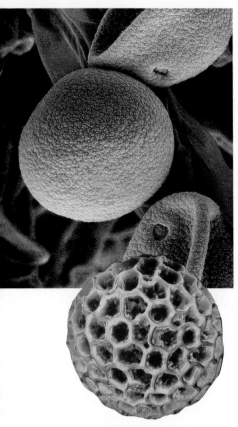

Figure 24.12 ▲
Grains of pollen, shown here magnified hundreds of times, cause an allergic reaction in some people.

Check and Explain

1. Name three different kinds of body disorders, and explain how each one occurs.

2. Why is cancer a body disorder? When is it fatal?

3. **Infer** If a person develops lung cancer, what might be the cause?

4. **Classify** Make a chart of the following body disorders and their causes: cancer, heart disease, scurvy, sickle-cell anemia, Down's syndrome, arthritis.

24.4 Medicines That Fight Disease

Objectives

▶ **Describe** how a vaccine works.

▶ **Compare** active and passive immunity.

▶ **Distinguish** between antibiotics and antibodies.

▶ **Infer** the purpose of a booster shot.

Skills WarmUp

Find Causes Write down all the infectious diseases you have had in your life. Compare your list with that of others in your class. Discuss possible reasons why everyone has not had the same diseases.

When your grandparents were your age, many children came down with infectious diseases such as measles, whooping cough, and mumps. These diseases were so common that they were called childhood diseases. Although they were not considered to be life-threatening, they were still serious illnesses, which could have side effects.

You have heard of some of these diseases. Most people don't get them anymore. Many diseases that once threatened people's lives are now easily prevented or cured. Medicines developed during the last 100 years now protect people from many infectious diseases.

Vaccines

Remember that you become immune to some types of infectious diseases once you have had them. You can't catch the disease again. Your body produced antibodies to fight off the pathogen. If the pathogen appears again later, your immune system is ready to prevent another infection.

A medicine called a **vaccine** makes it possible to become immune to a disease without having the disease. A vaccine contains dead or weakened pathogens, which can't cause disease in the body. However, the white blood cells still treat the pathogens as harmful invaders and make antibodies against them. So, when the body comes into contact with the live pathogen, infection cannot occur.

A vaccine put into the body is called a vaccination. Vaccinations are usually given to young children. You probably received vaccinations for measles, mumps, polio, diphtheria, and whooping cough.

Figure 24.13 ▲
A child in the African nation of Chad receives a measles vaccination.

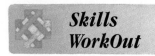
Research   Write a one-page report comparing the techniques used by Louis Pasteur and Jonas Salk to isolate pathogens. Find out why Jonas Salk developed a live vaccine for polio.

Active Immunity   A vaccine is a medicine that *prevents* disease. It can't cure a disease once infection has begun. The vaccine does not act on the pathogen itself. It "fools" the immune system into action, making it produce antibodies. When the body produces its own antibodies for a particular pathogen, **active immunity** occurs. Both vaccines and pathogens cause active immunity.

Passive Immunity   In addition to vaccination, another way to prevent certain diseases is to inject a person with antibodies that were produced by a donor. The person who receives the antibodies gains **passive immunity** against the disease. Passive immunity is only temporary. Since the lymphocytes of the person receiving the vaccine did not make the antibodies, they can't make more antibodies at a later time. Injections of antibodies are given to people who need protection from a disease for a short time.

Viruses and Vaccines   Vaccines are available for both viral and bacterial diseases. In the case of viral diseases, vaccines are especially important. Viral diseases can't be easily cured with medicines once the infection starts, so it is better to prevent them. One way a medicine can treat a viral infection is to interfere with the virus's reproduction. Development of drugs that will accomplish this task is a slow process. However, scientists recently developed some antiviral drugs. Two of these drugs are medicines that help prevent the flu. Scientists do not yet know why the drugs are effective.

Figure 24.14
Many countries have a goal of ▶ vaccinating all their children against common childhood diseases. This poster is from Burma.

Antibiotics

Although viral diseases are difficult to treat once the body's cells are infected, many bacterial diseases can be cured. The drugs that make it possible to stop bacterial infections are called **antibiotics**. Unlike vaccines, antibiotics act directly on the pathogen. They kill the bacterial cells or prevent them from reproducing.

Antibiotics have saved many lives by stopping infections that the immune system could not handle. Penicillin was the first antibiotic used commercially. It is still widely used today for such illnesses as strep throat and certain types of pneumonia. Many other antibiotics are now available. Some are created in the laboratory. Others are produced in nature by other living things.

Some people are allergic to certain antibodies. If you ever have a bad reaction to an antibiotic, it is important to remember which one. Any doctor treating you in the future will need to know.

Historical Notebook

Traditional Medicine

Hospitals, X-rays, blood tests, and miracle drugs have been around for only a short time. Not too long ago, people cured illness and disease differently than we do today. They obtained medications from flowers, grasses, seeds, roots, and animals. They also thought of illness much differently. They believed it was caused by some sort of imbalance. This kind of medicine, often called traditional medicine, is still practiced today by many people around the world.

The Chinese developed very complex and effective ways of healing beginning thousands of years ago. The goal in Chinese medicine is to restore the body's balance of vital energy, called *Qi* (CHEE). Imbalances in *Qi* are corrected with methods such as acupuncture, shown at right.

Native Americans also have a long history of traditional healing practices. In addition to herbs, they use chanting and rituals to help create the conditions

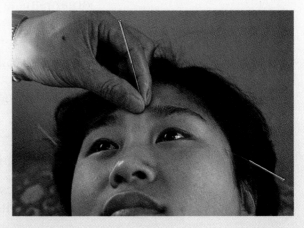

under which the sick can become well. Today traditional medicine is being studied by modern doctors. They have seen that traditional healing can sometimes work when modern medicine can't.

1. How does traditional medicine differ from modern medicine?

2. **Research** Do research on Chinese medicine or acupuncture, and write a report.

Figure 24.15 ▲

The skin of the African clawed frog produces a new and powerful antibiotic.

Nature has always been an important source of medicines for human beings. A bread mold contains the antibiotic penicillin. The bark of willow trees provided people with an aspirinlike substance. Many other living things are also sources of medicines.

Scientists think that far more useful drugs are still to be discovered in such organisms as tropical trees, corals, and frogs. These organisms may produce substances that can fight cancer, stop viral infections, and boost the immune system. Excited by these possibilities, some scientists are conducting studies in rain forests and ocean environments.

Organisms living in the ocean may be one of the largest untapped sources of new medicines. Researchers discovered a substance in an alga, for example, that greatly increases the ability of the immune system to fight infection. This substance could help **AIDS** patients live much longer. Promising substances were also discovered in certain sponges and tunicates.

Another important source of new medicines may be organisms living in tropical rain forests. Many of these organisms are still unknown to humans. Unfortunately, rain forests are being destroyed at an alarming rate.

Almost any organism might contain a useful drug. An African frog, for example, produces a chemical in its skin that kills bacteria, fungi, and protozoa. This chemical is an entirely new kind of antibiotic.

Check and Explain

1. How does a vaccine make you immune to a disease without itself causing the disease?

2. What is the difference between active and passive immunity?

3. **Compare and Contrast** What is an antibiotic? How does it differ from an antibody?

4. **Infer** Some kinds of vaccines are given more than once. The second vaccination is called a booster shot. What do you think is the effect of a booster shot on the immune system?

Chapter 24 Review

Concept Summary

24.1 Infectious Disease

▶ Infectious diseases are caused by organisms called pathogens.

▶ Pathogens may be bacteria, viruses, fungi, protozoa, or worms.

▶ Pathogens may be spread through water and food and by contact with infected animals or people.

▶ AIDS is an infectious disease caused by a virus that attacks the immune system.

24.2 The Body's Natural Defenses

▶ Skin and body secretions help protect the body against pathogens.

▶ Inflammation is a general line of defense that protects against infection when the skin is damaged.

▶ The body's immune system can recognize and destroy specific pathogens. It can remember a pathogen and prevent it from infecting the body a second time.

24.3 Body Disorders

▶ Body disorders result from a breakdown or defect in some part of the body.

▶ Cancer is an often deadly body disorder with many causes.

▶ Allergies occur when the immune system treats a harmless substance, such as pollen, as a harmful pathogen.

24.4 Medicines That Fight Disease

▶ A vaccine makes a person immune to a certain disease even though he or she has not had the disease.

▶ Antibiotics are drugs that kill bacteria or prevent them from reproducing inside the body.

Chapter Vocabulary

infectious disease (24.1)	antibody (24.2)	vaccine (24.4)	passive immunity (24.4)
pathogen (24.1)	cancer (24.3)	active immunity (24.4)	antibiotic (24.4)
immune system (24.1)	carcinogen (24.3)		

Check Your Vocabulary

Write the word or term from the list above that best matches each of the phrases below.

1. Molecules produced by lymphocytes that attach to the surface of pathogens.

2. A body disorder in which body cells divide uncontrollably, destroying healthy cells.

3. A disease caused by harmful organisms.

4. The body system that attacks invading pathogens.

5. A medicine that prevents disease by making the body produce antibodies.

6. When the body produces antibodies for a particular pathogen.

7. The name for organisms that cause infectious diseases.

8. Drugs that stop bacterial infections.

9. Substances that cause cancer.

10. A temporary immunity to a disease.

Explain the difference between the words in each pair.

11. Active immunity, passive immunity

12. Antibody, antibiotic

13. Pathogen, carcinogen

14. Infectious disease, body disorder

Write Your Vocabulary

Write a sentence using each vocabulary word above. Show that you know what each word means.

Chapter 24 Review

Check Your Knowledge

Answer the following in complete sentences.

1. List two types of body secretions that guard against infection and describe how they do their job.

2. What kind of infectious diseases can be treated with antibiotics?

3. What are memory cells? How do they help your immune system?

4. What causes sickle-cell anemia?

5. List three carcinogens.

6. What is a vaccination?

7. What is an allergen? Give two examples of allergens.

Choose the answer that best completes each sentence.

8. A disease caused by bacteria is (influenza, malaria, strep throat, polio).

9. The human immuno-deficiency virus, or HIV, causes the disease (AIDS, herpes, gonorrhea, tuberculosis).

10. During the inflammation response, (an antibody, histamine, saliva, mucus) is released and causes swelling.

11. Chemotherapy is used to treat (cancer, the common cold, diabetes, pneumonia).

12. Some body disorders, such as scurvy, are a result of (bacterial infection, allergens, stress, poor nutrition).

13. Penicillin is one example of an (antibiotic, infection, immunity, allergen).

14. If you cannot catch a disease again because your body has antibodies for the pathogen, you have developed (chemotherapy, an antibiotic, an immunity, a vaccine) to the disease.

Check Your Understanding

Apply the concepts you have learned to answer each question.

1. Explain why you continue to get colds and the flu, even though your body produces antibodies against the pathogens that cause these diseases.

2. **Compare and Contrast** How are infectious diseases and body disorders alike? How are they different?

3. Discuss how your skin prevents pathogens from entering your body.

4. **Application** You visit a friend with chicken pox, knowing you're safe from getting the disease because you have already had it. Is it possible, however, that you could spread the chicken pox virus to your brother or sister who has not had it? Explain your answer.

5. List two vaccinations that you received as a child.

6. **Mystery Photo** The photograph on page 510 shows magnified lymphocytes, or white blood cells, attacking a cancerous growth. Imagine the photograph is part of a movie. Describe the chemical and physical methods the immune system would use to destroy the cancer cell.

7. When would a doctor prescribe an antibiotic to a patient? When would a doctor give a vaccination?

8. **Extension** Make a list of the various types of infectious diseases you have had. Next to each illness, write the type of pathogen that probably caused the disease. You may want to use reference books to locate the cause of some illnesses.

Develop Your Skills

Use the skills you have developed in this chapter to complete each activity.

1. **Interpret Data** The graph below shows the occurrence of polio and measles since 1950. The dot on each line indicates when a vaccination for that disease was introduced.

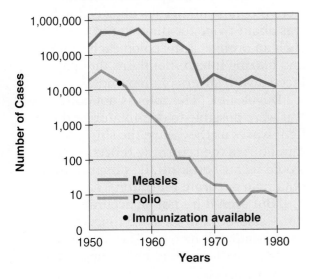

a. Which disease was, and still is, the most common?

b. Which disease has been most effectively controlled by its vaccine?

c. How does this graph visually display the effectiveness of vaccines?

2. **Data Bank** Use the information on page 629 to answer the following questions.

a. What types of cancer are linked to smoking?

b. Describe a lifestyle that would reduce your chances of getting cancer.

Make Connections

1. **Link the Concepts** Construct a concept map to show how the following concepts from this chapter link together: pathogens, active immunity, immune system, vaccines, infectious disease, antibodies, viruses, bacteria.

2. **Science and History** Research how infectious diseases have had an effect on human history. Choose a particular time in history when there was an epidemic, or uncontrolled spread of a disease. Find out the numbers of people killed during the epidemic and the results. Write a short report.

3. **Science and You** In which areas of the United States is Lyme disease most common? Find out the answer with the help of a doctor, public-health official, or librarian. Then draw a poster-sized map showing where the most and fewest cases have been reported.

4. **Science and Society** Research the occurrence of cancer in different countries. Make a graph showing the number of cases per 100,000 people. What do you think causes the differences in the cancer rate?

5. **Science and You** What things in your home may help to cause cancer? Research the kinds of chemicals, building materials, and sources of radiation that are suspected as carcinogens. Then survey your household to find if you have any of those items. If so, what can be done to make your home safer?

6. **Science and Technology** Find out what progress scientists are making in the search for a cure for AIDS. What are the most effective drugs being used? What kind of treatments do scientists have the most hope for?

Science and Literature Connection

D uval looked about with exultation. "Conceive it," he said. "Inside a human body; inside an artery. Owens! Put out the interior lights, man! " . . .

The interior lights went off, but a form of ghostly light streamed in from outside, the spotty reflection of the ship's miniaturized light beams fore and aft.

Owen's had brought the Proteus into virtual motionlessness with reference to the arterial blood stream, allowing it to sweep along with the heart-driven flow. . . .

Grant turned to the window. Almost at once he was lost in amazement at the wonder of it all.

The distant wall seemed half a mile away and glowed a brilliant amber in fits and sparks, for it was mostly hidden by the vast melange of objects that floated by near the ship.

Fantastic Voyage

The following excerpt is from the novel Fantastic Voyage *by Isaac Asimov.*

It was a vast, exotic aquarium they faced, one in which not fish but far stranger objects filled the vision. Large rubber tires, the centers depressed but not pierced through, were the most numerous objects. Each was about twice the diameter of the ship, each an orange-straw color, each sparkling and blazing intermittently, as though faceted with slivers of diamonds.

Duval said, "The color is not quite true. If it were possible to deminiaturize the light waves as they leave the ship and miniaturize the returning reflection, we would be far better off. It is important to obtain an accurate reflection." . . .

"But even if it's not an accurate reflection," said Cora in an awed tone, "surely it has a beauty all its own. They're like soft, squashed balloons that have trapped a million stars apiece."

"Actually, they're red blood corpuscles," said Michaels to Grant. "Red in mass, but straw-colored individually. Those you see are fresh from the heart, carrying their load of oxygen to the head and, particularly, the brain."

Grant continued to stare about in wonder. In addition to the corpuscles, there were smaller objects; flattened plate-like affairs were rather common, for instance. (Platelets, thought Grant, as the shapes of the objects brought up brightening memories of physiology courses in college.)

[Michaels cried out,] "See that!"

Grant looked off in the direction of the pointing finger. He saw small, rodlike objects, pushing fragments and detritus and, above all, red corpuscles, red corpuscles, red corpuscles. Then he made out the object at which Michaels was pointing.

It was huge, milky, and pulsating. It was granular and inside its milkiness there were black twinkles, flashing bits of black so intense as to glow with a blinding non-light of its own.

Within the mass was a darker area, dim through the surrounding milkiness, and maintaining a steady, unwinking shape. The outlines of the whole could not be clearly made out, but a milky bay suddenly extended in toward the artery wall and the mass seemed to flow into it. It faded out now, obscured by the closer objects, lost in the swirl.

"What . . . was that?" asked Grant.

"A white blood cell, of course. There aren't many of those; at least, not compared to the red blood corpuscles. There

are about six hundred fifty reds for every white. The whites are much bigger, though, and they can move independently. Some of them can even work their way out of the blood vessels altogether. They're frightening objects, seen on this scale of size. That's about as close as I want to be to one."

Skills in Science

Reading Skills in Science

1. **Infer** What is the *Proteus*? Where is it?

2. **Evaluate Sources** Although this story is fictional, some information it presents is scientifically accurate. Identify at least three statements that correctly describe the circulatory system.

Writing Skills in Science

1. **Predict** Imagine you are a member of the *Proteus's* crew. Write a letter to a classmate describing your journey through the human circulatory system.

2. **If . . . Then Arguments** Suppose it were possible to miniaturize a vessel to transport a crew through the passageways of the circulatory system. Write a paragraph that describes how this might affect treatment of various diseases of this body system.

Activities

Communicate Use reference tools and information from this story to make a chart that shows the components of blood, their functions, and their physical characteristics.

Compare and Contrast Research a disease that affects the blood or circulatory system. Describe how the crew's view of the blood vessel would differ if the *Proteus* were in a person who had this disease.

Where to Read More

Fantastic Voyage by Isaac Asimov. Boston: Houghton Mifflin Company, 1966. The crew of a miniaturized submarine ventures through a man's body to try to save his life.

The Body Victorious by Kjell Lindqvist and Stig Nordfeldt. New York: Delacorte, 1987. Astonishing photographs taken with an electron microscope detail the inner workings of the human body.

Unit 8
Ecology

Chapters

Data Bank

Use the information on pages 624 to 631 to answer the following questions about topics explored in this unit.

Estimating

By approximately how many British Thermal Units did the United States increase its oil usage between 1940 and 1980?

Comparing

Which continent is more densely populated, Asia or Europe?

Predicting

What type of fuel do you think will be used the most in the United States in the year 2050?

Interpreting Data

What two types of forests would you most likely find at similar altitudes?

The photograph to the left is of a coral reef in the Caribbean. What kind of interactions do you see between the different living things in this picture?

Chapter 25

Organisms and Their Environment

What helps this animal live here?

66 This is some kind of water bird in some kind of marsh. It is easy for it to blend in and hide from predators. This bird has a beak that is used for spearing fish. 99

Kevin Brown
Southwest Junior High
*   School*
Little Rock, Arkansas

To find out more about the photograph, look on page 558. As you read this chapter, you will learn how organisms interact with each other and their environment.

25.1 Ecosystems and Communities

Objectives

▶ **Describe** an ecosystem.

▶ **Identify** the abiotic and biotic parts of an ecosystem.

▶ **Distinguish** between habitats and niches.

▶ **Infer** how adaptations help determine an organism's niche.

Think of how many nonliving things you need or use to get through a day. You need air for breathing. You need water to brush your teeth and to take a shower or bath. What other nonliving things in your environment are a necessary part of your day?

You interact with nonliving things in your environment each day. You also interact with many living things. This is true of all organisms. The study of the interactions of organisms and their environments is called ecology (ee KAWL uh jee).

Scientists who study these interactions are called ecologists. They may study organisms living on a small leaf or organisms living in a huge volcanic crater.

The Biosphere

Imagine a jigsaw puzzle with more than a thousand pieces to put together. At first it may seem like an impossible task. Gradually you get all the pieces to fit together, and you have a complete picture! All the different living things and nonliving things on the earth are like pieces of a huge puzzle. Like a puzzle, they fit together, or interact to form one working system.

All organisms live at or near the earth's surface in a life-supporting zone called the *biosphere*. The biosphere includes the earth's waters, its surrounding air, and a portion of the earth's land surface. Within the biosphere are many different environments that organisms inhabit.

Figure 25.1 ▲
What are the parts of the earth's biosphere?

Ecosystems

Look at the wetland environment below. Within this environment, many kinds of interactions take place. An area in which living things interact with one another and with their environment is called an **ecosystem**. Ecosystems may be large, such as a wetland, the ocean, or a desert. They may also be small, such as a puddle or a piece of a rotting log.

The living parts of an ecosystem are called **biotic factors**. Animals are examples of biotic factors. The nonliving parts of an ecosystem are called **abiotic factors**.

Ecosystems do not happen overnight. They evolve gradually. The older an ecosystem is, the more organisms it usually contains.

Figure 25.2
A Wetland Ecosystem

Communities

How many different organisms do you recognize in the wetland ecosystem below? When two or more groups of different organisms live together and interact with each other in the same area, they form a **community**. The plants and animals shown are just a few of the types of organisms that live in a wetland ecosystem. All the organisms in a wetland are a community.

The biotic relationships in an ecosystem hold a community together. These relationships are always changing. For example, in a wetland ecosystem that has seasonal changes, there are more plants during the summer. More insects enter the community because many depend on plants for food and shelter. With more insects, the number of frogs also increases because there is a large supply of food.

Abiotic factors also contribute to changes in communities. For example, fewer plants will grow in the winter because there is less sunlight and the climate is cold. Some organisms that depend on plants will leave the community to seek food and shelter elsewhere.

Organisms interact closely with one another in the wetland. Cattails serve as landing pads for dragonflies. When danger is near, herons point their long bills and necks upward to blend in with tall marsh plants.

Reeds are common plants in wetlands. Some reeds grow up to three meters tall.

Populations

All the organisms of the same species living in a certain place make up a **population**. Notice that in the wetland community, there are many different populations. All the raccoons make up one population. Among the plants, cattails make up another population. Your school and the area around it may include populations of people, ants, grass, plants, and even spiders. The size of each population may change depending on conditions, such as available food, space, and water.

In a community, the different populations interact with one another in many ways. Some populations eat food that is produced by other populations. Some get their homes from others, and some get protection from others. Populations may also compete for food and shelter.

Wetlands support plants and animals that are adapted to living in a watery environment. Water is an abiotic factor in the wetlands. Other abiotic factors include soil, air, and sunlight.

Habitats and Niches

In a wetland ecosystem, each species lives in a certain area. The area or place where an organism lives in an ecosystem is called a *habitat*. You can think of a habitat as an organism's "address." In a wetland, the habitat of the cattails is the edge of the water. Here cattails grow well because they get plenty of water and a lot of direct sunlight.

Each organism in a wetland has a different job, or role. The specific role an organism has in its habitat is called its **niche** (nihch). A niche includes all the activities and behaviors that satisfy an organism's need for food, water, living space, and reproduction.

Each population in a habitat has a different niche. For example, herons and deer share the same wetland habitat and have similar abiotic needs. They do not, however, have the same niche. Herons live near water and eat fish. Herons make their nests high in trees. Deer have no nesting sites. They roam the wetlands in search of food, eating only plants and plant parts.

Wetlands attract a diverse group of ducks and other wildfowl. Ducks have webbed feet for swimming, and long, limber necks for finding food in the water and the water's muddy bottom.

Wetland plants take up and use nutrients in soil. Many can absorb pollutants from the soil.

Niches and Adaptations

Figure 25.3
The heron's long neck, long legs, and sharp beak for catching food are adaptations for life in its wetland niche.

All organisms have characteristics that help them survive in ecosystems. Characteristics that help organisms get food and water, protect themselves, and build homes are adaptations.

Adaptations help determine an organism's niche. For example, a heron waits in water until fish come within reach. As fish dart through the water, the heron cranes its neck, spears a fish, and tosses it around. The heron will then eat the fish whole. The heron's long legs and neck and sharp beak enable it to catch fish. These adaptations help the heron live and reproduce successfully in its niche in the wetlands.

Populations with similar adaptations occupy similar niches. They eat foods that are alike. They construct homes and seek protection in much the same way. If more than one population has the same niche, they will compete for food and shelter.

SkillBuilder *Estimating*

Sampling a Population

Scientists sometimes need to know the size of a population. However, a population is often much too large to count each organism. The size of a whole population can be estimated by counting a small part, or sample, of the population.

1. Estimate the number of ants you think are in the population shown. Record your estimate. *Note: Do not count the ants.*

2. Choose any square in the grid. Count and record the number of ants in the square.

3. Now estimate the total number of ants in the grid by multiplying the number of ants you counted by the number of squares in the grid. Record your answer.

4. Repeat steps 2 and 3 two more times. Record your answers.

5. Add the three sample estimates, then divide the total by three. This is the average. Record the average.

6. Count all the ants in the grid. Record the total.

How do you think sampling can help scientists estimate an entire population's size?

Science and Society *Balance in Ecosystems*

In any ecosystem, organisms need a balanced environment. A balanced ecosystem is one in which all living and nonliving things are interacting successfully. If any part of the ecosystem is disturbed, other parts will also be disturbed. People sometimes cause these disturbances. In some wetland ecosystems, people have affected the balanced environment.

At one time, people did not consider wetland areas to be important ecosystems. In many countries, wetlands were drained for farmland. Some wetlands were filled in so that houses could be built. Other wetland ecosystems were destroyed by pollution.

How does the destruction of wetlands cause imbalance in ecosystems? If a wetland area is destroyed, so are important plants and the habitats of many kinds of animals. You may think that the destruction of a wetland ecosystem stops there. However, wetlands protect other ecosystems, such as bays, by absorbing pollutants from industries and other sources. Wetlands also help prevent flooding in coastal areas.

Today, many people recognize the value of wetland ecosystems. Around the world, important steps have been taken to protect and preserve wetlands. In Tunisia, Africa, a wetland nature center has been built. In El Salvador, the habitat of white-winged tree ducks has been preserved because people protested the destruction of a wetland area.

Figure 25.4 ▲
This wetland ecosystem in Botswana, Africa, was saved from possible destruction. Why is it important to preserve wetland ecosystems?

Check and Explain

1. What is an ecosystem? Give an example of an ecosystem.

2. Explain the difference between an organism's habitat and its niche.

3. **Classify** Make a list of abiotic and biotic factors inside and outside your classroom. Be sure to include factors, such as insects, that may not be clearly visible.

4. **Infer** Describe a turtle's niche in a wetland ecosystem. Then describe how some of the turtle's physical features have helped it adapt to the wetland.

25.2 Food and Energy

Objectives

▶ **Identify** the producers and consumers in an ecosystem.

▶ **Distinguish** between a food chain and a food web.

▶ **Interpret** an energy pyramid.

▶ **Make a model** of a food chain.

What would the earth be like without energy from the sun? It would be a very cold and dark place. No organisms could live on the earth without energy from the sun.

All organisms get energy from some type of food, and the sun provides the energy needed for food crops to grow. Food provides you with energy for all your activities, including walking, eating, and even reading.

Food Chains

Food energy is passed from one organism to another through a sequence of events called a **food chain**. Plants are the only organisms that can capture the sun's energy, which they use to fuel their growth by the process of photosynthesis. Because they can fuel their own growth, plants are called **producers**. On a prairie, grasses are the main producers. In a forest, trees are the main producers. Algae carry on photosynthesis, so they are also producers.

Many organisms can't make their own food. They eat plants, animals, or other organisms. Organisms that eat other living things are called **consumers**. A food chain may include more than one consumer. For example, in a food chain in which a rabbit eats grass and an owl eats the rabbit, both the rabbit and the owl are consumers.

Some food chains have consumers that feed only on the bodies of dead organisms. These consumers are called scavengers. After a scavenger has fed on a dead organism, millions of tiny organisms called decomposers take over. Decomposers, such as bacteria and molds, break down the tissues of dead organisms.

Figure 25.5 ▲

A vulture is a bird that is an example of a scavenger.

A Food Chain Example

A food chain always begins with the sun, which provides energy for the producers. Producers are the next link in the chain. Look at the food chain below. It shows the following sequence: sun → plant → grasshopper → harvest mouse → marsh hawk.

Consumer

In this food chain, a marsh hawk swoops down to feed on the mouse. Animals that feed only on other animals are called carnivores (KAHR nih vorz). Carnivores have special adaptations, such as sharp teeth, for eating flesh. ▶

Consumer

In one link of the food chain, a harvest mouse eats the grasshopper. The mouse also feeds on the plants. Consumers that eat both plants and animals are called omnivores (AHM nih vorz). ▼

Decomposers

The last link in a food chain are the decomposers. After the marsh hawk has died, decomposers feed on the hawk and break down its tissues. In the process, decomposers release wastes into the soil. These wastes are then used by other organisms. ▼

Consumer

The plants are eaten by a grasshopper. Animals that eat only plants are called herbivores (HUR bih vorz). ▶ Herbivores have adaptations that enable them to eat and digest plants.

Decomposers

◀ **Producers**

In this food chain, salt-marsh plants and algae are the producers.

Food Webs

In an ecosystem, there are many different food chains. The same food source can be part of more than one food chain. Different food chains connect to form a network of feeding relationships called a **food web**. In food chains, the flow of energy happens in one direction. In food webs, the flow of energy branches out in many directions.

In many food webs, producers and consumers can be eaten by more than one kind of organism. Look at Figure 25.6, showing an example of a salt-marsh food web in the winter. The Norway rat, vagrant shrew, song sparrow, and harvest mouse all feed on grasshoppers. The marsh hawk, in turn, feeds on the Norway rat, harvest mouse, and vagrant shrew. On what animals does the short-eared owl feed?

In a food web, there are different feeding levels. In Figure 25.6, the grasshoppers are first-level consumers because they eat only plants. What other animals are first-level consumers? The shrew is a carnivore and eats first-level consumers. The shrew is a second-level consumer. The marsh hawk and short-eared owl are third-level consumers. No animals feed on the hawk and owl. They are the top consumers in the food web.

Figure 25.6
A Salt-Marsh Food Web

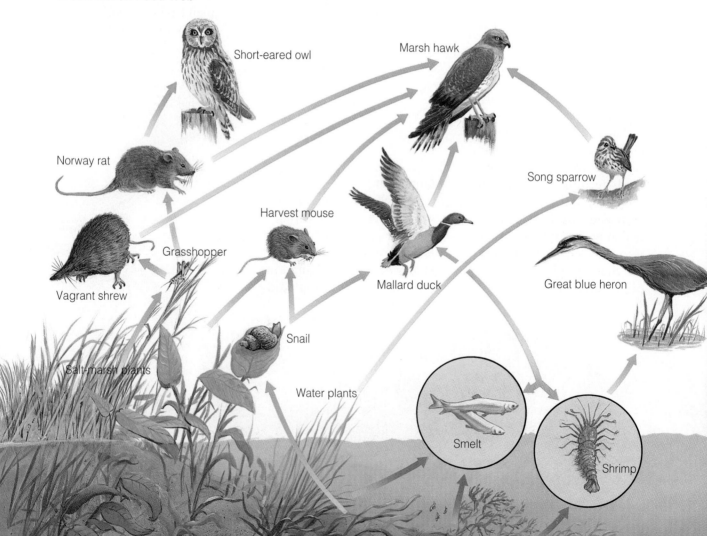

Energy and Energy Pyramids

You have probably heard the word *energy* over and over. But what does it mean? Energy is not an easy word to define because it has many different forms, such as heat, light, sound, water, and wind.

As you know, the sun provides energy for all ecosystems on the earth. You may be surprised to learn that only 1 to 2 percent of the solar energy that reaches the earth is actually used by plants for photosynthesis.

In a food chain, the energy stored in the food is passed along from one organism to the next. An **energy pyramid** is a diagram that shows the amount of energy available at each level of the food chain. However, not all the energy is moved from one link in the chain to the next. Energy is lost at each stage because it is used by the organisms for life processes. In almost all food chains, 10 percent of the energy is transferred at every link.

Look at Figure 25.7. Each level of the pyramid represents the amount of energy stored at that level. At the base of the pyramid are the producers. This is the level where most of the energy is stored. Each level above the producers contains less available food energy than the level below it. The second level represents the first-level consumers. The third level represents the second-level consumers. On the top are the third-level consumers. At this level, the least amount of energy is available because energy has been lost as it passes through each organism. On what level would you place yourself in an energy pyramid?

**Figure 25.7
An Energy Pyramid**

Third-level consumers

Second-level consumers

First-level consumers

Producers

545

Infer Look at the food chain on page 543, the food web on page 544, and the energy pyramid on page 545. Infer how each got its name. What other names can be used to describe food chains, food webs, and energy pyramids?

Science and You *Choose Your Place!*

Most animals and plants can't change their places in a food web. A hawk, for example, will never one day become a first-level consumer and start eating only plants because a hawk is a carnivore. You, however, can change your place. You can choose to be a first-level consumer for a while, then change to a second-level consumer. You can also choose to be a third-level consumer in a food web. You can be any one of these consumers because you can survive on plants or animals, or both. You are an omnivore.

Because you can choose what kind of consumer you would like to be, you can also consider which consumer uses the sun's energy most efficiently. Suppose you could set up your own farm. If you decided to be a second-level consumer and only eat meat, you would need to keep a herd of about seven to ten cattle to support yourself. The cattle, in turn, would need about 5 acres of alfalfa for their feed.

What would happen if you decided to change from a second-level to a first-level consumer? You might, for example, choose to eat only wheat. On this diet, you could support yourself on less than an acre of wheat.

As you can see, if you choose to be a first-level consumer, you use the sun's energy more efficiently than if you are a second-level consumer. However, the disadvantage of eating only one kind of producer, such as wheat, is that wheat can't provide all the proteins you need in your diet. You would have to supplement your diet by eating other producers high in proteins, such as beans and peas.

Check and Explain

1. Identify the producers and consumers in the following food chain: Sun → Wheat → Grasshopper → Field mouse → Snake → Owl

2. How is a food chain different from a food web?

3. **Find Causes** Explain how energy is lost to a community at each level of a food web.

4. **Make a Model** Construct a simple food chain that you would expect to find in a stream community. Use any of the following organisms: frogs, algae, dragonflies, turtles, beetles, bass fish, water lilies.

Activity 25 *How do food chains form a food web?*

Skills Model; Communicate

Task 1 Prelab Prep ✄
1. Collect the following items: 2 large sheets of paper, markers, metric ruler, paste and/or tape, old magazines.
2. Cut one sheet of paper into fourteen 5-cm squares. **CAUTION! Be careful when using scissors.**
3. Study Table 25.1. On each square of paper, write the names of the organisms in the table. On the last square, write *Sun*. These squares are your cards for Task 3.

Task 2 Gathering Data
1. Use reference books to read about the organisms with which you are not familiar. Find out what each organism listed in the table eats.
2. On a piece of paper, use arrows to form as many food chains in the salt-marsh ecosystem as you can.

Task 3 Procedure
1. Refer to your food chains. Use the cards you made to construct a food web. Arrange the cards on a large sheet of paper. *Note: Be sure to include the card labeled* Sun. *Leave a lot of space around each card. Attach your cards.*

2. Refer to your food chains again. Construct a food web by drawing arrows from each organism to all the other organisms that eat it.
3. Label each organism *Producer, First-level Consumer, Second-level Consumer,* or *Third-level Consumer.*

Task 4 Analysis
1. Why is a food web a better model than a food chain of feeding relationships in an ecosystem?
2. Are there any omnivores in your diagram? If so, name them.
3. If you were to remove one of your organisms from the food web, how would other organisms be affected? Explain.
4. Which organisms do you think are the most abundant in the salt-marsh community? The least abundant? Explain your answer.

Task 5 Conclusion
Compare your food web model to other models in the class. Why do ecosystems have a variety of feeding relationships?

Extension
Think of a meal that you've eaten recently. On posterboard, create a food web that shows you as the top consumer for the meal.

Table 25.1 Salt-Marsh Organisms

Producers	First-level Consumers	Second-level Consumers	Third-level Consumers
Water plants	Eel	Billfish	Osprey
Marsh plants	Fluke	Cormorant	Tern
	Mud snail	Merganser	Green heron
	Bay shrimp	Redwing blackbird	
	Cricket		

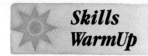
25.3 Cycles in an Ecosystem

Objectives

▶ **Describe** the cycles in nature.

▶ **Explain** the importance of natural cycles to organisms.

▶ **Construct** a model of the water cycle.

Look at the terrarium in Figure 25.8. It is a self-enclosed ecosystem. To keep the terrarium ecosystem working properly, all the biotic and abiotic factors interact in a balanced way. A terrarium is like a small model of the biosphere because the terrarium supplies all the materials the organisms in it need in order to survive.

All organisms need certain substances to live, grow, and reproduce. Many substances, such as water, pass through natural cycles in which they are used and reused. These substances circulate through both living and nonliving things.

Some cycles include mainly nonliving things. For example, forces and pressures within the earth cause rocks to change from one type to another. This process is called the rock cycle. In space, many stars that you see are in different stages of their life cycle. The sun, a medium-sized star, has a life cycle of about 10 billion years. The sun is now about 5 billion years old. At the end of its life cycle, the sun will become a white dwarf.

Figure 25.8 ▶

How is a terrarium like the earth's biosphere?

Figure 25.9 The Water Cycle

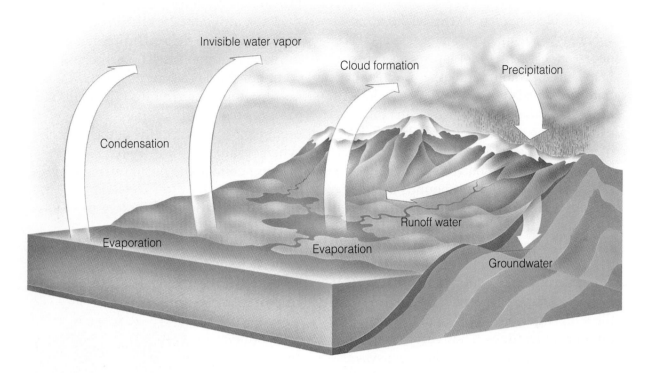

Invisible water vapor

Cloud formation

Precipitation

Condensation

Evaporation

Evaporation

Runoff water

Groundwater

The Water Cycle

All living things need water. Water moves continually throughout the earth by means of the water cycle. Some of the water molecules that once flowed in the Amazon River could fall on you as rain. You also could be drinking some of the water that once existed as snow on the Himalaya Mountains.

Look at Figure 25.9 and follow the pathway of water between the earth and the atmosphere. Energy from the sun changes water from a liquid to a gas through the process of **evaporation**. In its gaseous state, water is called water vapor. Water evaporates from bodies of water, such as oceans, rivers, and lakes. Water also evaporates from soil, plants wet with dew, and even the bodies of animals.

Water vapor is held in the atmosphere. The amount of water vapor the air can hold depends on the air temperature.

When the atmosphere's temperature cools, water vapor changes back to a liquid by the process of **condensation**. The condensed water forms clouds, steam, or fog, and eventually falls back to the earth as **precipitation**. Rain, snow, hail, and sleet are forms of precipitation.

Most precipitation falls back into bodies of water. Some precipitation first strikes land and then flows into bodies of water. Some water droplets that fall on land may soak through the soil and become part of the groundwater. The groundwater may then flow back to the surface as a spring, or it may be pumped to the surface through wells. The water cycle continues when water that has returned to the earth's surface evaporates again.

Plants use water from the ground for life processes. They also release some water into the air. Animals also use water for life processes and release it during respiration and excretion.

The Nitrogen Cycle

Nearly 80 percent of the earth's atmosphere is made up of nitrogen. Nitrogen is a necessary element for organisms because it helps build proteins and other important body chemicals. Although there is a lot of nitrogen in the air, organisms can't directly use it. Nitrogen becomes available after it has been changed into nitrogen compounds.

The process of changing atmospheric nitrogen into usable compounds is called **nitrogen fixation**. Nitrogen fixation is a necessary part of the nitrogen cycle; without it, nitrogen would not be usable to living things. Nitrogen is fixed, or converted, either through the action of lightning or by bacteria. Some of the bacteria live freely in the soil. Other bacteria live in the root nodules of legumes. They carry on most of the nitrogen fixation in land ecosystems. Beans, peas, clover, and soybeans are examples of legumes. When legumes are planted, the bacteria in the nodules provide nitrogen for plant growth.

Look at Figure 25.11. Nitrogen-fixing bacteria change the soil's nitrogen gas into nitrogen compounds. The plants use the compounds to produce proteins. Plants need proteins for growth. When animals eat plants, proteins are passed through the organisms in food chains and food webs. When organisms die or release wastes, bacteria change the proteins to the nitrogen compound ammonia. Bacteria called denitrifying bacteria then break down the ammonia and other nitrogen compounds and convert them into a nitrogen gas.

Figure 25.10 ▲
Bacteria in root nodules provide nitrogen for plant growth.

Figure 25.11   The Nitrogen Cycle

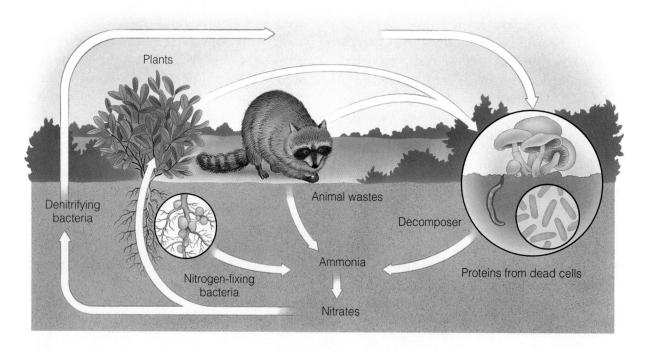

Plants

Denitrifying bacteria

Animal wastes

Decomposer

Nitrogen-fixing bacteria

Ammonia

Proteins from dead cells

Nitrates

Figure 25.12   The Oxygen–Carbon Dioxide Cycle

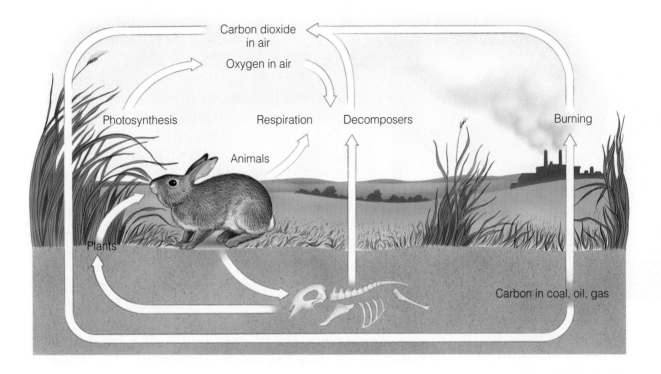

The Oxygen–Carbon Dioxide Cycle

Take a deep breath, then slowly exhale. You have just contributed to the oxygen–carbon dioxide cycle. When you inhaled, you took in air that contained oxygen. What happened when you exhaled? You released carbon dioxide back into the atmosphere.

Look at Figure 25.12. It shows the oxygen–carbon dioxide cycle. During the process of photosynthesis, plants absorb carbon dioxide from the air and release oxygen into the air. Plants are a main source of oxygen in the earth's atmosphere.

There is more than enough oxygen available in land environments. Oxygen becomes scarce at high altitudes. Here the air is thin, so there is less available oxygen. Oxygen is also scarce deep in the ground or in water-soaked soil.

Most organisms use oxygen from the air for the process of respiration. During respiration, food is broken down. Organisms get their energy from respiration and release carbon dioxide in the process.

Another way in which carbon dioxide enters the atmosphere and becomes part of the cycle is through the decay of dead organisms. Dead organisms contain carbon compounds. When decomposers break down the tissues of dead organisms, carbon dioxide is released into the air.

Sometimes the bodies of dead organisms do not decompose. Over thousands of years, the bodies are compressed underground. Millions of years later, the bodies are changed into oil, coal, and gas. People burn these fossil fuels for their energy needs. When they are burned, the fuels release carbon dioxide into the atmosphere.

Science and Society *Global Warming*

Scientists have found that the earth's atmosphere holds nearly 25 percent more carbon dioxide than it did in the early 1900s. The main reason for the buildup is the burning of fossil fuels. The worldwide clearing of forests is also affecting the balance of atmospheric carbon dioxide because the trees use carbon dioxide during photosynthesis. Without trees, carbon dioxide is not recycled, so it stays in the atmosphere.

As carbon dioxide builds up in the air, it acts to trap and keep heat energy in the atmosphere. Although there is disagreement about how much the buildup of heat is actually affecting the earth, some scientists predict that the earth will eventually become much warmer than it is now. The term *global warming* refers to the worldwide warming trend that scientists are currently investigating.

What would happen if the earth's average temperature increased by 3°C? If the earth's temperature rises significantly, the results could be disastrous for living things. Polar glaciers would melt, causing widespread flooding in coastal areas. Climates around the world would change. Many agriculture regions could become too hot and dry to grow crops.

Scientists are currently studying ways to slow down the buildup of carbon dioxide in the atmosphere and reduce the risk of global warming. One way you can help is to recycle newspapers. Recycling will help preserve trees.

Figure 25.13 ▲
During the Gulf War in 1991, the smoke from huge oil fires in Kuwait added carbon dioxide to the atmosphere.

Check and Explain

1. What is a natural cycle?

2. Why are natural cycles important to organisms?

3. **Infer** Some farmers wanted their soil to be richer in nitrogen, but they didn't want to add chemicals. How can they increase the amount of nitrogen in the soil?

4. **Make a Model** Draw a model of the water cycle. Include any or all of the following: plants, trees, animals, clouds, soil, ponds, groundwater, mountains, rain, or snow. Also, label the processes of evaporation, condensation, and precipitation.

25.4 Changes in Ecosystems

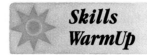
Objectives

▶ **Describe** the stages of succession in nature.

▶ **Explain** how a pioneer community differs from a climax community.

▶ **Predict** how natural disasters can affect an ecosystem.

What changes have occurred in your neighborhood within the past year? You may have noticed that a new house or building was built. You may have noticed that a road was recently paved, or that a new stop sign was placed at a busy intersection.

Ecosystems in nature also change over time. Some changes are hardly noticeable. Other changes have major effects on an ecosystem. In some cases, entire communities within the ecosystem are replaced.

Succession

If you have been to a forest, you may have wondered what the area looked like before the trees and other plants grew. You may be surprised to know that hundreds of years ago, the forest may have been a lake. The communities that once made up the lake ecosystem were gradually replaced by other communities that formed a forest ecosystem. The replacement of one community by another over a period of time is called **succession.** The complete process of succession may take hundreds, even thousands, of years.

In the process of succession, communities will grow and replace one another until a climax community forms. A climax community is a stable, almost permanent community that is not easily replaced by other communities. Once the climax community becomes established, fewer changes occur in the area. However, disturbances such as fire, volcanic eruptions, severe weather, or some human activities can change an ecosystem or destroy a climax community.

On page 554, you can follow the formation of a climax community.

Figure 25.14 ▲
Mt. St. Helens in 1981 (top) and in 1990 (bottom). How has Mt. St. Helens changed? What caused the changes?

Pioneer Community At first, the newly formed lake has no living things. In time, sediments are carried into the lake by rivers that feed it. In the sediment are air-borne spores of algae, bacteria, fungi, and protozoa. These organisms form a pioneer community because they are the first to settle in the area.

Lake Community The algae and other organisms add nutrients, such as carbon, to the lake. The lake can now support small plants. Insects that eat the plants enter the lake ecosystem. A variety of plants eventually grow in and around the lake. Different kinds of animals that eat plants and insects become part of the lake community.

Marsh Ducks, dragonflies, mosquitoes, cattails, raccoons, and frogs are among the many organisms that live and interact in the lake community. As the lake ages, it slowly fills with soil, fallen leaves, and material from dead organisms. As these materials fill up the lake's bottom, it becomes shallower. The lake gradually turns into a marsh.

Climax Community As succession continues, the marsh dries up. Land plants, such as pine trees or oak trees, develop in the area. Over time, the pine or oak trees are replaced by larger trees, such as spruce or birch. The spruce–birch forest and all the populations of plants and animals living in the forest form a stable climax community.

Science and Society *City Succession*

Succession is a natural process; however, succession can also be caused by human actions. When people settle and develop an area, many changes take place within the communities. For example, when a city is built, the natural vegetation in the area is cleared away. Concrete structures and increasing populations of people gradually take over the area. In this process, a new environment is created.

To create a new city environment, the original topsoil is often bulldozed away. Much of the land is then covered with concrete and asphalt. People replace native plants with ornamental plants. When you picture plants in a city, you may think of tree-lined streets, green parks, and planter boxes of flowers. This introduced vegetation helps create the city environment.

Just as the vegetation changes, so does the animal population. A city environment, with its buildings, people, and roadways, is not suited for most native animals, such

Consider This

Should Climax Forests Be Logged?

The logging of trees is a major industry in the United States. Trees provide important products for people. However, the number of trees in the United States is not endless. In fact, the Wilderness Society estimates that 95 percent of the United States' original forests have been logged.

Consider Some Issues Many populations and communities live in forests. The roots of trees help control flooding and prevent landslides. Trees are also important in the oxygen–carbon dioxide cycle. In addition to their role in nature, forests are valued for their beauty.

Trees are considered one of the United States' most valuable natural resources. The wood from trees has provided many products, services, and jobs for people. If logging is stopped, jobs would be lost, and the prices for houses, paper, and furniture would increase.

Think About It Should trees in climax forests be cut down? What might happen to the organisms living in climax forests if logging continues? If forests are no longer logged in the United States, how will this affect people who live in

areas where logging is a major industry?

Write About It Write a paper stating your position for or against the logging of trees in the United States. Write your reasons for choosing your position.

Figure 25.15 ▶

A city is an example of succession caused by people. Why do only certain native animals survive in a city?

as deer, rabbits, and snakes. They cannot survive in a city, so they migrate to more suitable places, or die off. Other animals—that benefit from human activity—move in. For example, pigeons thrive well because there are few predators. There is also a large supply of food from human scraps. Barn swallows, chimney swifts, and house sparrows often make their nests on building eaves and road overpasses. Bird nests and bird feeders placed near homes also extend the habitat range of many species.

Some mammals migrate to city environments. In the city, rats and mice find an abundance of waste food. They can nest in and under buildings. Skunks, possums, and raccoons can adapt to environments where people live.

Check and Explain

1. Briefly explain the process of succession.

2. How is a pioneer community different from a climax community?

3. **Find Causes** Why do you think climax communities are identified by their plants rather than by the animals that live in them?

4. **Predict** A forest was struck by lightning and a large fire resulted. The trees, bushes, and grasses were all burned. Predict how the area will change. What kinds of communities and populations would you expect to find in the area in the future?

Chapter 25 Review

Concept Summary

25.1 Ecosystems and Communities

▶ The biosphere is a zone near the earth's surface that supports all organisms on the earth.

▶ Organisms interact with each other and the environment in an ecosystem.

▶ Ecosystems have biotic and abiotic factors.

▶ Within each ecosystem, each organism has a habitat and a specific niche within its habitat. Adaptations help determine an organism's niche.

25.2 Food and Energy

▶ The food chain shows how food energy moves from one organism to another within an ecosystem.

▶ Organisms have a role in the food chain as producers, consumers, or decom-posers. Food chains connect together to form feeding relationships, or food webs.

▶ Energy pyramids show how much energy is available at each level of the food chain. At each level in a food chain, energy is lost.

25.3 Cycles in an Ecosystem

▶ Natural cycles include the water cycle, the oxygen–carbon dioxide cycle, and the nitrogen cycle. They allow organisms to live, grow, and reproduce.

▶ The water cycle has three stages: precipitation, condensation, and evaporation.

25.4 Changes in Ecosystems

▶ Communities succeed each other, beginning with a pioneer community and ending with a climax community.

Chapter Vocabulary

ecosystem (25.1)	population (25.1)	consumer (25.2)	condensation (25.3)
biotic factor (25.1)	niche (25.1)	food web (25.2)	precipitation (25.3)
abiotic factor (25.1)	food chain (25.2)	energy pyramid (25.2)	nitrogen fixation (25.3)
community (25.1)	producer (25.2)	evaporation (25.3)	succession (25.4)

Check Your Vocabulary

Use the vocabulary words above to complete the following sentences correctly.

1. Plants are ____ because they can fuel their own growth.

2. Rain and snow are forms of ____ .

3. The specific role an organism has in its habitat is called its ____ .

4. The process of changing atmospheric nitrogen into usable compounds is called ____ .

5. A cat eats a sparrow that ate a beetle that ate a blade of grass. The cat is a ____ in the food chain.

6. The replacement of communities over a period of time is called ____ .

Explain the difference between the words in each pair.

7. pioneer community, climax community
8. condensation, evaporation
9. habitat, niche
10. scavenger, decomposer
11. community, population
12. biotic factor, abiotic factor
13. ecosystem, ecology
14. food web, food chain

Chapter 25 Review

Check Your Knowledge

Answer each of the following in complete sentences.

1. What is a habitat?

2. Name three ways a climax community can be destroyed.

3. List three abiotic factors.

4. What is the main source of oxygen in the oxygen–carbon dioxide cycle?

5. List the following in order from smallest to largest: community, population, organism, ecosystem, biosphere.

6. Give one example of a decomposer.

7. What adaptations have helped the heron to establish a niche in the wetlands?

8. Where do the producers in a food chain get their energy?

9. List the stages of the water cycle.

Determine whether each statement is true or false. Write *true* if it is true. If it is false, change the underlined term to make the statement true.

10. <u>Potassium</u> is a necessary element for organisms because it helps build proteins.

11. Most energy is stored at the <u>third level</u> of the energy pyramid.

12. A heron's sharp beak and long legs are <u>adaptations</u>.

13. A rabbit is an example of a <u>producer</u>.

14. Nitrogen is fixed through the action of <u>lightning</u> and bacteria.

15. A <u>pioneer</u> community is a stable, almost permanent community.

16. Clouds, steam, and fog are forms of <u>precipitation</u>.

Check Your Understanding

Apply the concepts you have learned to answer each question.

1. Describe three human activities that might disturb a balanced ecosystem.

2. Describe a city environment. Include biotic and abiotic factors.

3. Design a fish tank. What animals and plants will you include? What abiotic factors will be part of the fish tank? What natural cycles will take place in your fish tank?

4. What specific changes in a field mark the succession of a pioneer community as it eventually changes to a climax community?

5. **Extension** Draw food chains using the following:

   a. corn, human, chicken

   b. beetle, spider, leaf, owl

   Now create an energy pyramid using the items in the food chains above. Identify each organism as a producer or a consumer.

6. **Mystery Photo** The photograph on page 536 shows a bittern, a close relative of the heron. The bittern is difficult to see in the tall marsh reeds because of its coloring and tall, slim shape. Bitterns feed on fish and small animals in the marsh. What kind of consumer is a bittern? How is it adapted to life in a marsh?

7. **Main Ideas** Using the outline on page 536, write the main idea for each section in the chapter.

8. **Application** Identify four factors that could limit the number of flowers growing in a garden. Describe how each factor might limit the population growth.

Develop Your Skills

Use the skills you have developed to complete each activity.

1. **Infer** Create a food web for animals and plants in a mountain environment including: hawk, finch, pine tree, blueberry bush, mountain lion, caterpillar, squirrel, and oak tree.

2. **Interpret Data** The map below shows the population distribution of carp, water bugs, toads, and water-lily plants in a pond.

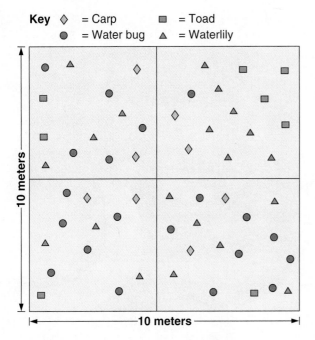

Key ◇ = Carp   ■ = Toad
      ● = Water bug ▲ = Waterlily

a. Which species has the largest population in the community?

b. What factors might influence each species' niche?

3. **Data Bank** Use the information on page 629 to answer the following questions.

What percent of the evaporation entering the water cycle comes from oceans? What percent comes from land?

Make Connections

1. **Link the Concepts** Below is a concept map showing how some of the main concepts in this chapter link together. Only parts of the map are filled in. Copy the map. Using words and ideas from the chapter, complete the map.

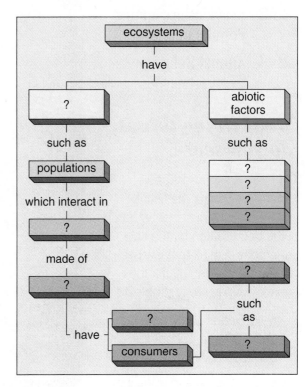

2. **Science and Language Arts** Write a play about the formation of a climax community, beginning with a pioneer community. Include the following elements: lichen, rock, soil, seed, plant, rabbit, fox, rain, and a human. Use additional characters if you need them.

3. **Science and Technology** The main cause of global warming is the burning of fossil fuels for heat, transportation, and power. Research technological advances, including alternative power sources, that may help reduce global warming.

Chapter 26

Interactions Among Organisms

What living things do you see?

66 I see a fish and a sea anemone. I think the fish is either hiding from another fish or is being eaten by the sea anemone. I think they swim and eat together. I think their relationship is pretty simple. 99

Kelly Reed
Supai Middle School
Scottsdale, Arizona

To find out more about the photograph, look on page 576. As you read this chapter, you will learn more about relationships among organisms.

26.1 Changes in Populations

Objectives

▶ **Describe** the factors that affect population growth and size.

▶ **Classify** organisms as predators or prey.

▶ **Communicate** how limiting factors and population density are related.

Skills WarmUp

Predict An area is set aside as a park preserve, and no hunting is allowed in the park. A number of deer are placed in the area. There are plenty of plants to serve as food for the deer population. The herd is healthy and begins to grow faster than expected. Predict what will happen if the deer population continues to increase in the park area.

Picture yourself walking in a dense jungle. How many different kinds of organisms do you see? A jungle has many populations, or groups of similar organisms. Some populations, such as ants, fungi, and ferns, can be very large in number. Other populations, such as jaguars and boa constrictors, have fewer members. Why do population sizes vary among organisms?

Population Size

Population sizes change when new members move into an ecosystem. They decrease when members move out of an ecosystem. The number of births, or birth rate, and the number of deaths, or death rate, also affect a population's size. For example, on an ocean island, few new members enter the isolated populations. Few members leave the island. Therefore, if more births than deaths occur in a population from year to year, the population will increase. If there are more deaths than births, the population will decrease. If the birth rate and death rate are equal, the population remains steady.

Ecologists study the birth rates and death rates of populations so they can measure population growth. They can then predict the future of a population, including whether or not it is in danger of becoming extinct. For example, if the size of the caribou population shown in Figure 26.1 suddenly decreased, ecologists would try to find out the cause. They might find that a certain disease was affecting the herd. Steps could then be taken to ensure the survival of the herd.

Figure 26.1 ▲
The size of this population of caribou is influenced by many factors, including the number of births and deaths.

Population Density

Populations can be the same size, but they may have different densities. The number of individuals in an area is called **population density**. Population density is calculated by dividing the number of organisms in an area by the size of the area in which they live. Suppose 60 ants live in a 4 sq m plot of grass. The population density of the ants would be 15 ants per sq m because 60 ants divided by 4 sq m equals 15. What would the population density be if 100 ants lived in an 8 sq m plot of grass?

Population density can affect the growth rate of a population. For example, if the population density of plant seedlings is too great, there may not be enough water to support the growth and development of all the seedlings. Many will not survive, thereby reducing the size of the population.

Limiting Factors

Certain environmental conditions called **limiting factors** keep a population from increasing in size and help balance ecosystems. Examples of limiting factors are the availability of food, water, and living space, and the spread of disease. Light, temperature, and types of soil are also limiting factors because they help determine the types of organisms that can live in an ecosystem.

Limiting factors are often related to population density. The greater the population density, the greater effect limiting factors have on a population. For example, plants may be a limiting factor to deer living in a forest. If the population of deer is too dense, there may not be enough food for each one. Some deer will not survive, and the population will decrease.

Competition

Populations can grow when their needs are met. But when many populations share an ecosystem, the resources needed by one population may be the same as those needed by other populations. When two or more species in an ecosystem must use the same limited resources, competition occurs.

Living space is a major cause of competition. All populations need a certain amount of living space to find food, to reproduce, and to interact. For example, two species of birds may compete for nesting sites in the same tree.

Because they can move about easily, animals often move to another habitat to avoid competition. Other animals, such as owls and hawks, adapt to the ecosystem by changing their feeding habits. Both owls and hawks feed on some of the same animals. To reduce competition, hawks hunt during the daytime, while owls hunt at night.

Figure 26.2 ▲
These two different species of birds are competing for the same food source.

Predators and Prey

Many interactions among organisms are related to their feeding patterns. For example, some animals obtain food by killing and eating other organisms. Animals that obtain their food in this way are called **predators**. Some common predators are wolves, lions, robins, and flesh-eating sharks. The organisms that are eaten by a predator are called **prey**.

Predator-prey relationships limit population density. In this way, they help maintain balance in an ecosystem. In fact, predators may actually be beneficial to populations of prey animals by removing members who are weak or sick. This allows only the stronger members of the prey population to survive and reproduce. Predator-prey relationships also prevent too large a population of prey organisms from developing. If there are not enough predators and too many prey, the prey population may starve or die of disease.

Look at the graph in Figure 26.3. It shows the changing populations of Canadian lynxes and snowshoe hares over an 80-year period. The lynx is the predator. The hare is the prey. As the number of hares increases, so does the number of lynxes. Then what happens? The increased number of lynxes causes a drop in the hare population. The lynxes then begin to starve to death, which allows the hare population to increase again.

Figure 26.3 ▲
Lynx-Hare Population Cycle

◀ **Figure 26.4**
The predator-prey relationship of the Canadian lynx and snowshoe hare helps balance the sizes of both populations. What other factors might account for the changing population sizes of both animals?

Figure 26.5 ▲
World Population Growth

Science and Society
Human Population Growth

If all the people living on the earth were lined up side by side, they would produce a line longer than the distance from the earth to the moon and back! Although the human population started to grow at a slow rate, it has grown very rapidly in the last two centuries. Today more than five billion people live on the earth.

There are different ways to measure human population growth rates. One way is to find the population's doubling rate, or the length of time it takes for the population to double in size. In 8000 B.C., the doubling rate was 1,500 years. In 1975, the doubling rate was estimated to be 35 years. If this rate is accurate, there could be 10 billion people on the earth by the year 2010.

When the growth pattern for human population is graphed, it produces a J-shaped curve. Look at Figure 26.5. Notice that the curve starts slowly. Then, when the bend

Consider This

Should the World's Population Be Limited?

Can the earth's environment handle as many as 10 billion people in the future? Many people fear that it can't and have suggested that governments impose limits on family sizes. They feel that reducing birth rates would help relieve the strain on the environment.

As shown in the graph at right, if each family in the United States only had two children, instead of three, for two or three generations, the population of the United States would stay at today's level. This concept is called *zero population growth*.

Consider Some Issues Large families can be a source of wealth in some cultures. Young people take care of the old, and young workers strengthen a nation's economy.

Smaller families could have a better standard of living. There would be less disease and hunger. Fewer people would put less strain on the environment.

Think About It How will the earth be affected if its population continues to grow as predicted? How can population growth be controlled? Should governments be involved in determining the sizes of families?

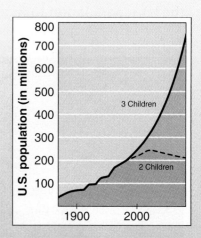

Write About It Your legislator is going to vote on imposing limits on family size. Write a letter telling the legislator how you'd like him or her to vote. Explain your opinions.

◀ **Figure 26.6**
Although there are more than 14,000 people per sq km living in Tokyo, Japan, the population growth rate in Japan is far less than that of developing nations, such as India.

in the J becomes rounded, the line on the graph becomes almost vertical.

Why has the human population grown so rapidly? The steady increase in the human population is partly because humans think of ways to adapt to their surroundings in order to meet their needs. For example, humans can grow food and control some diseases.

Although the human population is increasing, the growth rate varies regionally. For example, the growth rate is much higher in developing regions, such as India, than in industrialized nations, such as Canada. In fact, nine out of ten babies born today are born in developing nations. Unfortunately, many of these nations do not have adequate resources to feed and provide shelter for all these people.

Skills WorkOut

Collect Data The U.S. Census Bureau collects information about the number of people who live in a household. You will be collecting similar data. Find out how many people live in the household of at least ten of your classmates. Include your own household. Graph this data. What is the average number of people in a household?

Check and Explain

1. Name factors that limit a population's size.

2. Owls often kill and eat mice. Which organism is the prey? Which organism is the predator?

3. **Infer** If the number of students in your school doubled, what effect would this have on the resources of your school? Explain.

4. **Communicate** In a population, limiting factors and population density are often related. Explain how. Give examples of limiting factors that may affect the density of a population.

Activity 26 *How do you measure population density?*

Skills Measure; Communicate; Interpret Data; Calculate

Task 1 Prelab Prep
1. Collect the following items: metric ruler, paper, pencil.
2. Study the three patterns of population distribution in Figure 26.7.
3. Review the formula for calculating density:

$$\text{density} = \frac{\text{number of individuals}}{\text{size of area}}$$

Task 2 Data Record
On a separate sheet of paper, copy Table 26.1. Record each population's name in the table.

Task 3 Procedure
1. Calculate and record the area of Figure 26.7.
2. Select one population in Figure 26.7. Count the members present. Record this number in Table 26.1.
3. Calculate the density of that population. Record this number in the table.

Table 26.1 Population Density

Population name	Number of organisms	Density

4. Count the members and calculate the density for the other two populations. Record these numbers.

Task 4 Analysis
1. Compare the distribution patterns of the three populations. Which population has the greatest density?
2. What factors could be responsible for the dif-

Figure 26.7 ▼

18 cm

20 cm

○ Dandelions ■ Clover ▲ Plantains

ferences in the population densities?
3. Name a factor or condition that could change the density of any of the populations.

Task 5 Conclusion
Write a short paragraph describing how measuring a population's density can be used to learn about the needs and characteristics of a population.

Everyday Application
Count the number of people in your classroom. Then measure the area of the classroom. What is its population density? Find the approximate population densities of other occupied rooms in your school, such as the study hall, the gym, or the lunchroom. Make a table listing the densities. How do they compare? How could knowing the population densities of these rooms affect the scheduled classes or lunch periods?

Extension
Find the population density of your state. A local library can supply you with the number of people living in your state and its area. Compare your state's density with that of another state.

26.2 Relationships Among Populations

Skills WarmUp

Infer Think about how organisms relate to each other. For example, a dog scratches its fleas; a bird builds a nest in a tree. List ten organisms. Next to each organism, write about some type of interaction that you think it has with another organism. In each case, describe whether the organisms were helped, harmed, or not at all affected by each other.

Objectives

▶ **Define** symbiosis.

▶ **Compare** and **contrast** the three major kinds of symbiotic relationships among organisms.

▶ **Explain** the helpful and harmful effects of a parasitic relationship.

▶ **Predict** if two different species can develop a symbiotic relationship.

G o back to your imaginary jungle scene and picture many types of animals. Do these animals live alone? Or do they have contact with one another? In most ecosystems, different species of organisms interact with one another. These interactions help populations survive. They also help balance the ecosystems in which they live.

Symbiosis

Few organisms live alone. Populations that live in close physical contact with each other interact in a variety of ways. Many relationships between organisms involve the transfer of energy or food. Some organisms also provide services to each other such as protection, transportation, or support. A relationship between species in which at least one member benefits is called **symbiosis** (SIHM by OH sihs).

An example of a symbiotic relationship can be seen in Figure 26.8. Notice that the cattle egret is living peacefully on top of the cape buffalo. As the cape buffalo moves and grazes, it flushes out insects from the vegetation. This benefits the egret because an egret eats insects. The cape buffalo is not harmed in any way by the relationship.

There are three major types of symbiotic relationships. They are classified according to how one species is affected by the other.

Figure 26.8 ▲
The cape buffalo and the cattle egret have a symbiotic relationship. Which organism benefits from this relationship?

Commensalism   A symbiotic relationship in which one organism benefits while the other organism is unaffected is called commensalism. Trees are often involved in relationships of commensalism. For example, some kinds of birds and squirrels build their nests in trees.

Mutualism   A symbiotic relationship in which both organisms benefit is called mutualism. Organisms that share a mutualistic relationship often give each other protection and food.

An example of commensalism is the relationship between trees and flowers called orchids. The orchids live by attaching to the branches of the tree. The tree is neither benefited nor harmed. However, the orchid benefits because it gains easy access to sunlight. ▼

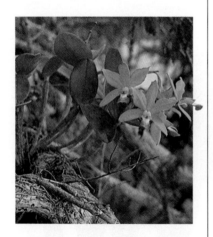

A lichen is an organism ▶ made up of a green alga or a blue-green alga and a fungus. It is an example of mutualism. Together these organisms live as one, often on the surface of rocks. The alga supplies the fungus with sugar, other nutrients, and water. The fungus protects the alga from intense sunlight and temperature extremes. Neither of these organisms could survive in its habitat without the other.

You can also see com- ▶ mensalism in action here, as a whale transports attached barnacles throughout the ocean. Because barnacles can't move on their own, their relationship with whales increases the barnacles' chances of finding food. The whales are not affected by the barnacles.

Parasitism A symbiotic relationship in which one organism benefits and the other is harmed is called parasitism. Parasites are organisms that live on or in another organism. The organism that is harmed by the parasite is called the host. Both plants and animals can act as parasites and as hosts.

A parasite uses its host as a source of food. Usually the parasite does not kill its host. However, the parasite may weaken or sicken the host. Why would the death of the host be a disadvantage to the parasite?

Some parasites live outside the body of the host. Fleas, ticks, lice, and mites are examples of external parasites. Each of these parasites feeds on animals, including humans. Here, you can see a louse, magnified many times, on a human hair. ▼

▲ Mistletoe is a plant that is a parasite of trees. The roots of the mistletoe tap into the tree's tissues to get food and water. The loss of nutrients to the tree can weaken the tree.

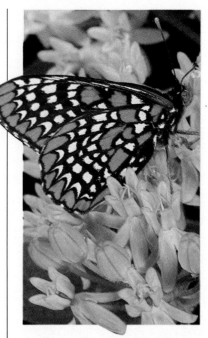

▲ Butterflies get food from the nectar of flowers. As the butterfly feeds, pollen from the flower sticks to the butterfly's body. The butterfly carries the pollen to the next plant it feeds on. In this way, the butterfly helps pollinate the plant, ensuring the survival of the plant species. What kind of symbiotic relationship do the flower and butterfly have?

The ants and acacia trees ▶ in Central and South America have an unusual mutualistic relationship. The ants live on the thorns of the acacia. They also eat food provided by its leaves. The acacia benefits, too. Ants protect their territory by attacking predators that try to eat the acacia. They will even destroy other plants that shade sun from the acacia.

Science and You *Human Symbionts*

Did you know that you are never alone? Living within your body are entire ecosystems of organisms! Some of these organisms form mutualistic relationships with you. Others are parasites that use your body to meet their nutritional needs.

Millions of bacteria make their home in your intestines. The bacteria contribute to your health by making vitamin K, which is necessary for blood clotting. The bacteria also assist in changing foods that enter your intestines so that wastes can be eliminated from your body. Both you and the intestinal bacteria benefit from this association.

You know that not all types of bacteria are helpful to humans. Many parasitic bacteria cause disease. Tuberculosis, for example, is a respiratory disease caused by parasitic bacteria. A person with this disease tires easily, loses weight, and coughs persistently. Today, drugs are used to treat people infected by tuberculosis. Cholera is also a disease caused by parasitic bacteria. The bacteria that cause cholera enter the body in contaminated food or water. Once in the body, the cholera bacteria may cause a person to lose large amounts of fluids needed by the body. With adequate care, most people can recover from cholera.

Check and Explain

1. What is symbiosis? Name and explain the major types of symbiosis.

2. How do symbiotic relationships help keep an ecosystem in balance?

3. **Compare and Contrast** Explain how predator-prey relationships and parasitism are alike but different. Give an example of each.

4. **Predict** In a farm field, soybeans were the only crop that was planted on several acres. A farmer noticed that a fungus was growing all over the soybean fields. Predict what might eventually happen to the soybeans. What could possibly happen to the fungus itself? What kind of symbiotic relationship do the soybeans and fungus have?

26.3 Animal Behavior

Objectives

▶ **Distinguish** between learned behavior and innate behavior.

▶ **Describe** social behavior among organisms.

▶ **Observe** behaviors and **classify** them as innate or learned.

Skills WarmUp

Communicate Think of at least 20 things you have learned since your birth, such as walking or tying your shoe. Make a list, including approximately how long it took you to learn each task. What was the hardest thing to learn? What was the easiest? Compare your list with that of a classmate.

Each year, millions of monarch butterflies travel thousands of miles to Mexico. When it gets very cold, ground squirrels curl up and become inactive. A dog may turn around several times before it lies down. All these actions show ways in which animals respond to their internal or external environments. The way an organism responds to its environment is called behavior.

Innate Behavior

Sea turtles lay their eggs on beaches. Newly hatched turtles immediately run toward the water and begin swimming. Why does this happen? The turtles were not taught this behavior. A behavior that is natural for an organism and does not need to be learned is called an **innate behavior**. Innate behaviors protect an organism and help in its survival.

Innate behaviors are inherited, or genetically passed from parent to offspring. Many innate behaviors are simple. For example, a newborn chick will peck at particles on the ground without ever seeing another chicken perform this behavior. You also have innate behaviors. For example, if something comes close to your eyes, you blink. What other innate behaviors do you have?

Some innate behaviors are complex and involve many responses. For example, some species of birds migrate great distances to warmer places in the fall. Migration is a complex animal behavior that occurs in a repeated pattern. This type of behavior is called cyclic behavior. Cyclic behaviors generally happen as a result of changes in the external environment. Another example of cyclic behavior is hibernation. Hibernation is a state of inactivity that occurs in some animals when outside temperatures are cold. Some mammals and many reptiles and amphibians hibernate.

Figure 26.9 ▲
What makes this newly hatched sea turtle move toward water?

Who Teaches Animals New Behaviors?

Have you ever taught a pet to beg for food, fetch a ball, or perform some other trick? If so, you may have a skill that you can turn into a career. Animal trainers are people who specialize in working with animal behaviors.

Many animal trainers work with animals for entertainment purposes. For example, trainers teach dolphins to perform in amusement parks and aquariums. Animal trainers also teach animals to carry out tasks that help people. These tasks may include offering protection, assisting in daily chores, and guiding or assisting people who are physically challenged.

Animals have been trained to be companions and helpers for people with disabilities. Seeing-eye dogs are often used as guides for blind people. In Thailand, trainers teach macaques, a type of monkey, how to pick and transport coconuts.

Animal trainers must learn about the innate behaviors of animals. Patience, skill, and knowledge about the animals are needed in this career. To obtain more information about this kind of animal training, you might speak with such people

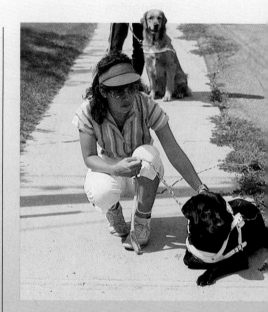

as obedience trainers, veterinarians, or staff who train dogs to work with the blind.

Figure 26.10 ▲
Chimpanzees learn to use sticks to get food that is hard to reach, such as termites living in mounds.

Learned Behavior

Behaviors that are acquired after birth and are a result of changes in experience are called learned behaviors. Since your birth, you have learned many things. You may have learned to ride a bicycle. You have probably learned to solve different kinds of math problems. What other things have you learned?

Animals also learn to respond to certain conditions to produce new behaviors. This helps them survive. Carp that are fed by people will swim to the surface when people are near, even if the people don't have food. Have you seen a dog bark or get excited when a leash is picked up? This, too, is a learned behavior.

Because learned behavior takes a long time to develop, it mainly happens among animals that have long life spans, such as mammals. In addition, learned behavior requires a complex nervous system. So the more advanced an organism's brain, the more it is capable of learning.

Social Behavior

Humans all over the world live in groups called societies. Many animals also form organized societies. Each member in a society has a specialized role or niche. The role may be to protect other members of the society, to get food, or to raise the young. In a society, the cooperative behavior and specific jobs of the members increase the survival chances of the group.

Social behavior is common in many insect groups, such as termites and honeybees. In a termite society, some termites build and repair the nest. Other termites produce a substance that defends the nest. Only the queen can reproduce, but she is dependent on the other members for raising the young. Each member contributes only one service, but all members benefit from each of the tasks in the society. Honeybees have similar tasks in a hive. Look at Figure 26.12. What is the role of a worker bee?

Figure 26.11 ▲
Honeybees form organized societies in hives.

Figure 26.12   A Honeybee Hive

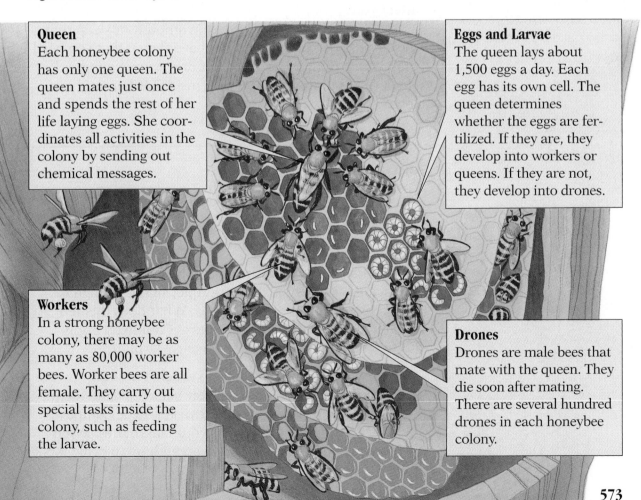

Queen
Each honeybee colony has only one queen. The queen mates just once and spends the rest of her life laying eggs. She coordinates all activities in the colony by sending out chemical messages.

Eggs and Larvae
The queen lays about 1,500 eggs a day. Each egg has its own cell. The queen determines whether the eggs are fertilized. If they are, they develop into workers or queens. If they are not, they develop into drones.

Workers
In a strong honeybee colony, there may be as many as 80,000 worker bees. Worker bees are all female. They carry out special tasks inside the colony, such as feeding the larvae.

Drones
Drones are male bees that mate with the queen. They die soon after mating. There are several hundred drones in each honeybee colony.

573

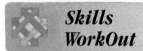

Skills WorkOut

Research Many animals have unique behaviors. Research to find out about some unusual behaviors among animals. You can start by looking in books about birds, bats, insects, and primates, such as baboons. Choose one animal to write about. Write a description of the animal's behavior and present it to the class.

In your lifetime, you will spend about a third of your life asleep. Is that much sleep necessary? Why do you get drowsy at certain times?

Sleep is an example of an innate cyclic behavior. It is controlled by the brain. Many scientists think that a sleep-inducing chemical builds up in your body while you are awake. When the chemical reaches a certain level, you get sleepy.

Why do you need sleep? Scientists are conducting studies to find the answer to this question. Some think that sleep may allow your brain time to process all the information it received during the day. Sleep also allows the body time to rest. For example, during sleep your heart rate and metabolic rate slow down. Your muscles also relax.

When people don't get enough sleep, they often experience difficulty in concentrating. Memory can also be affected. Lack of sleep may interfere with learning ability and coordination. In what ways does lack of sleep affect you?

Of course, people differ in the amount of sleep that they need. For example, studies have shown that you need more sleep than an adult. What does your biological clock tell you about your sleep needs? When and how often are you ready to snooze?

Check and Explain

1. What is a society? Give an example.

2. Describe two actions: one in which you use an innate behavior, and one in which you use a learned behavior.

3. **Generalize** Some animals can be trained to communicate with people. For example, sign language is exchanged with chimpanzees. What does this tell you about the learning process? Could you apply this information to other species? Explain.

4. **Observe** Select one person to watch. Carefully observe five of their actions. Name their behaviors and identify each of them as either innate or learned. Compare your findings with those of your classmates. What does this information tell you about human behaviors?

Chapter 26 Review

Concept Summary

26.1 Changes in Populations
▶ Population sizes vary among organisms. They change with number of births and when new members move into an eco-system. They also change when mem-bers die or move out of an ecosystem.
▶ Limiting factors are environmental conditions that keep a population from increasing in size and help balance ecosystems.
▶ Predators are animals that eat other organisms. The organisms they eat are prey.

26.2 Relationships Among Populations
▶ Symbiosis is a relationship between species in which at least one member benefits.
▶ Commensalism benefits one organism; the other organism is unaffected.

▶ Mutualism benefits both organisms.
▶ Parasitism benefits one organism and harms the other.

26.3 Animal Behavior
▶ Innate behaviors are genetically passed from parent to offspring. Innate behav-iors protect an organism and help it survive.
▶ Learned behaviors are acquired after birth and are a result of changes in experience. Learned behavior usually takes a long time to develop. It mainly happens among organisms with long life spans and complex nervous systems.
▶ Like humans, many animals also form organized societies. Members of soci-eties have special roles and cooperate with each other. Cooperation increases the group's chances for survival.

Chapter Vocabulary

population density (26.1)	predator (26.1)	symbiosis (26.2)	innate behavior (26.3)
limiting factors (26.1)	prey (26.1)		

Check Your Vocabulary

Use the vocabulary words above to com-plete the following sentences correctly.

1. An organism that is eaten by a predator is called ____ .

2. A behavior that is natural for an organ-ism and does not need to be learned is ____ .

3. The number of individuals in an area, or ____ , is calculated by dividing the num-ber of organisms by the size of the area.

4. A relationship between species in which at least one member benefits is called ____ .

5. An animal that obtains its food by killing and eating other organisms is called a ____ .

6. Availability of food, water, and living space, and the spread of disease are examples of ____ .

Identify the word or term in each group that does not belong. Explain why it does not belong.

7. Predator, prey, symbiosis

8. Limiting factors, competition, commensalism

9. Learned behavior, parasitism, symbiosis

10. Population density, limiting factors, cyclic behavior

11. Commensalism, prey, mutualism

Chapter 26 Review

Check Your Knowledge

Answer the following in complete sentences.

1. What kinds of factors might affect the size of a population? List two examples.

2. What are the three types of symbiotic relationships?

3. Is riding a bicycle an innate or learned behavior?

4. How do you calculate population density? Give one example.

5. How do limiting factors affect a population? Give two examples of limiting factors.

6. Describe the relationship between predator and prey. Then give one example of a predator and its prey.

7. What is cyclic behavior? Give one example.

Choose the answer that best completes each sentence.

8. When two or more species in an ecosystem must use the same limited resources, (parasitism, competition, expansion, extinction) occurs.

9. When the growth pattern of the human population is graphed, it produces a (K, M, Z, J) -shaped curve.

10. Predator-prey relationships (limit, increase, exaggerate, prevent) population density.

11. A lichen is an example of (commensalism, mutualism, parasitism, predator-prey relationship).

12. Certain environmental factors called (growth factors, death factors, birth factors, limiting factors) keep a population from increasing and help balance ecosystems.

Check Your Understanding

Apply the concepts you have learned to answer each question.

1. **Extension** What is the population density of 50 ladybugs living in a 100 sq m plot?

2. **Critical Thinking** Robins are predators and worms are prey for robins. Describe what might happen to the population of robins if an area where they hunted for worms was sprayed with pesticides.

3. **Application** List two activities you did today that were innate behaviors. Then list two activities that were learned behaviors.

4. **Mystery Photo** The photo on page 560 shows a clownfish swimming among the tentacles of a sea anemone. While the tentacles of most sea anemones are very poisonous, the clownfish is immune to the sting of most varieties. So the tentacles provide protection for the clownfish, since its predators either avoid the sea anemone or are stopped by its sting. The clownfish drops small pieces of food as it feeds, and the sea anemone absorbs this food. The clownfish may also lure prey into the tentacles so that the sea anemone can feed.

   a. What type of symbiotic relationship do the clownfish and sea anemone have?

   b. How does the clownfish benefit from the relationship? How does the sea anemone benefit?

5. Describe the role of a drone, a worker, and the queen bee in a honeybee hive. What kind of behavior are the honeybees in a hive exhibiting? Explain.

Develop Your Skills

Use the skills you have developed in this chapter to complete each activity.

1. **Interpret Data** The diagram below shows the movement of a paramecium in a petri dish. The geometric shapes are solid objects in the dish.

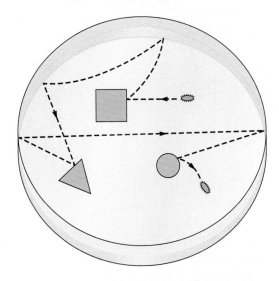

a. How would you describe the paramecium's movement?

b. What does the paramecium do when it encounters an object? Is there a pattern in its behavior?

2. **Data Bank** Use the information on page 626 to answer the following questions.

a. What is the population density of Africa?

b. Which continent has the greatest population density?

c. How much more dense is the population in Asia than in North America?

3. **Make a Model** Create a model of a symbiotic relationship. You may create your own organisms, or use examples of real organisms. Label your model commensalism, parasitism, or mutualism.

Make Connections

1. **Link the Concepts** Below is a concept map showing how some of the main concepts in this chapter link together. Only part of the map is filled in. Copy the map. Using words and ideas from the chapter, finish the map.

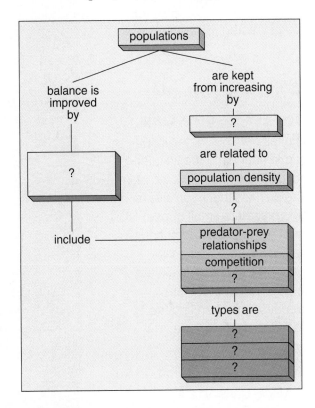

2. **Science and Math** Use the formula for calculating density to find out the population density in a place that you often visit, such as a recreation center.

3. **Science and Society** Human population growth generally varies from country to country. Choose one country in Asia, one country in Europe, and one country in Africa. Find out the growth rate of each country over the past ten years. Infer any factors that might have influenced the differences in growth rates among the countries. Write your findings in a report.

Chapter 27 Climate and Biomes

Chapter Sections

What do you see?

66This picture was taken in the fall because of the inspiring scenery and the wonderful colors of nature. Some of the animals that might live in this place are small gopher snakes, deer, gophers, squirrels, owls, mice, blue jays, and all kinds of birds. This is a good habitat for them because they can find the food they need for the winter.99

Ramón Plancarte
Menlo Oaks School
Menlo Park, California

To find out about the photograph, look on page 598. As you read this chapter, you will learn about climate and biomes.

27.1 Climate

Objectives

▶ **Describe** factors that determine the climate of a biome.

▶ **Explain** how rainfall and temperature affect vegetation.

▶ **Describe** how latitude and altitude determine the characteristics of a biome.

▶ **Interpret data** from a graph of global temperatures.

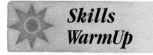
Have you ever wanted to live on a tropical island or a place where it's always cold? You could probably survive in either of these places. People are very adaptable. Look at Figure 27.1. As you can see, people can live in many places, including hot deserts. Not all living things, however, can adapt to environmental conditions as well as people can. For example, orchids are adapted to an environment with lots of rain. They can't survive in a desert environment. Why? Because they can't change the desert environment to meet their needs. Where an organism can live depends on nonliving, or abiotic, factors.

Climate Zones

Weather may vary daily, but from year to year each area has average weather patterns. These patterns are known as **climate**. Climate influences what type of plant life, or vegetation, can live in an area. The vegetation supports specific animal life. So different climates support different living communities.

Ecologists have used patterns of climate, vegetation, and animal life to divide large portions of land and water into **biomes**. Biomes are large communities with similar biotic and abiotic factors. Each biome has a certain climax community of plants and animals. Land biomes include communities such as deserts and forests. There are only two types of water biomes: marine, or ocean, and freshwater.

The different climates in biomes can be classified according to two main factors. One factor is precipitation. Precipitation is moisture in the atmosphere that condenses

Figure 27.1 ▲
How have the humans living here adapted to the hot, dry conditions?

In the warm, tropical climates (between 30°N and 30°S latitude) located around the equator, the average monthly temperature is 18°C. There is little variation between seasons.

In polar climates, (above 60°N and 60°S latitude) there is extreme variation in seasons. The very cold and very short winter days contrast with the mild and endless days of summer.

In the temperate climate zone (between 30° and 60°N and S latitude) of the middle latitudes, there is a noticeable difference between summer and winter. But the temperatures are not extreme. Most of the United States, Canada, and Europe are in the middle latitudes.

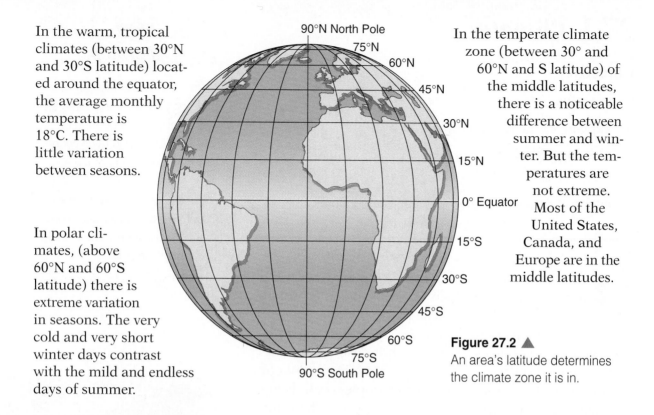

Figure 27.2 ▲
An area's latitude determines the climate zone it is in.

and falls to the earth. Sleet, snow, hail, and rain are forms of precipitation. The other factor is temperature. Each climate has different temperature patterns. Some areas have periods of hot and periods of cold. Others have almost the same temperatures all year.

Different combinations of hot and cold or wet and dry make up different types of climates. In general, there are areas of the earth with particular climates. These are known as climate zones. Find the three major climate zones in Figure 27.2. What are they? What climate zone do you live in?

Each of the climate zones in Figure 27.2 is described by how the seasons vary. The **tropical** climate has warm temperatures year-round. The **polar** climate has a long season of very cold temperatures and a short warm season. The **temperate** climate has a cold season and a warm season of about equal length.

Precipitation

Scientists use rain gauges like the one in Figure 27.3 to measure precipitation in centimeters or inches. The amount of precipitation influences what plants will grow in an area. Most plants have specific water needs. For example, cacti usually grow in dry, desert conditions. The amount of precipitation determines whether grasses, trees, or desert plants will grow in an area.

Different kinds of precipitation also influence vegetation. For example, snow protects plants by providing insulation. Some plants exposed to a cold winter die without insulation. Therefore, certain plants may only be able to survive cold winters where there is snow.

Temperature

While precipitation determines what type of vegetation is in an area, temperature determines what specific plants grow there. For example, a biome may have the right amount of rain to grow grasses. Some grasses can't survive if the temperature falls below freezing. So an area that has below-freezing temperatures will only have certain kinds of grasses.

Two factors influence temperature. One is latitude, or how close an area is to the equator. The other factor is altitude, or how high an area is above sea level.

Latitude One system used to describe a location on the earth's surface is a set of imaginary lines that are parallel to the equator. This system compares locations to the equator. The north-south location of any place on the earth's surface is known as its latitude. Latitude is measured in degrees, and the equator is 0° latitude. Figure 27.2 shows parallel latitude lines. The climate is moderate at 30° north of the equator. What do you think the climate is like 15° south of the equator?

Temperature is influenced by latitude. Areas at or near the equator receive the direct rays of the sun, so they have a warm climate. For example, the Amazon Basin along the equator in South America has a very hot climate. Regions such as northern Canada are far from the equator and are very cold in the winter.

Altitude An area's height above sea level is called altitude. If you climbed Mount McKinley in Alaska, or one of Colorado's Rocky Mountains, you would feel changes in temperature as you climbed to the top. Areas at high altitudes have lower average temperatures than areas at lower altitudes.

Figure 27.3 ▲
Raindrops fall into the open end of a rain gauge. The amount that collects can be measured.

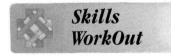

Skills WorkOut

Interpret Data Find latitude and longitude lines on a map or globe. Locate where you live. What are the latitude and longitude? Then find the latitude and longitude of the following cities: Tokyo, Paris, Moscow, Mexico City, Lima, Nairobi, Bombay, and Sydney.

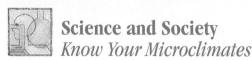

Science and Society
Know Your Microclimates

Figure 27.4 ▲
This area in the foothills of a mountain range receives the right amount of rain for growing pear and apple trees.

You and your neighbor live in the same biome and plant the same kind of grass, but your neighbor's grass is healthier than yours. Why? It might be because of different microclimates.

Microclimates are created by local differences in environmental conditions. The differences can be related to wind currents, hills, bodies of water, or even the shadows of houses. Your grass may be in shadows, preventing it from getting enough light. To grow something in the microclimate in your house's shadow, pick a plant that doesn't need direct sunlight.

Just as you can grow different plants in your yard, farmers can use microclimates to grow different crops. For example, when moist air from the ocean moves over a coastal mountain range, the air rises and cools. The moisture in the air condenses and falls as rain. The farther up the mountain, the greater the amount of rainfall. Pear trees grow best in the wet region partway up the mountain. Apricot trees grow best in the drier region at the base of the mountain.

If a farmer tried to plant the same trees in all of the microclimates, what would happen? Obviously, the crops would not be very successful. As for improving your lawn, maybe it's simply a matter of figuring out the microclimates in your neighborhood.

Check and Explain

1. What is a biome? Give an example.

2. What type of climate would you find near the equator? Explain.

3. **Make a Model** Create a model of a climate. What is the average temperature? How much precipitation is there, and what type is it? What are its latitude and altitude?

4. **Interpret Data** Create a graph of temperatures for City A using the following average temperatures: January, 7°C; March, 11°C; May, 20°C; July, 23°C; September, 24°C; and November, 10°C. Does City A have cold winters? What season is warmest?

Activity 27   *How do different climates compare?*

Skills Make a Graph; Interpret Data; Infer

Task 1   Prelab Prep
Collect the following items: graph paper, calculator, 2 different-colored pencils, ruler.

Task 2   Data Record
1. You will be making 2 graphs. Label one piece of graph paper *Precipitation* and another piece *Temperature.*
2. Select separate colors that will represent the data for City A and City B. Record this legend on each of the graphs.
3. On the horizontal axis of each graph, list the months of the year.
4. Refer to Table 27.1 and write appropriate numbers on the vertical axis for each graph.

Task 3   Procedure
1. On the precipitation graph, plot the precipitation data for City A with the chosen color. Repeat the procedure for City B.
2. On the temperature graph, plot the temperature data in the same manner using the same colors as in the precipitation graph for cities A and B.
3. Calculate the annual precipitation for each city and record this number on the graph.
4. Calculate the annual average temperature for each of the cities and record this number on the graph.

Task 4   Analysis
1. Describe each city's precipitation pattern and temperature pattern. Does City A have a wet season and a dry season? How about City B?
2. Can you infer which form of precipitation occurs in what months for each of the cities?
3. Describe the climate of each city based on the precipitation and temperature data.
4. Are precipitation and temperature data

Table 27.1   Climate Calculations

Month	Precipitation (cm)		Temperature (°C)	
	A	B	A	B
Jan.	1.30	2.3	7.0	1
Feb.	1.30	2.8	10.0	3
March	1.00	5.6	12.5	10
April	0.50	7.9	17.5	15
May	0.50	10.0	22.5	18
June	0.25	13.0	29.0	20
July	1.30	10.0	32.0	20
Aug.	1.30	9.4	30.5	22
Sept.	0.77	8.9	26.5	19
Oct.	0.77	7.0	19.0	16
Nov.	1.00	4.6	12.0	12
Dec.	0.77	3.3	7.0	5

sufficient to identify the type of climate or biome of an area? Why or why not?
5. What kind of vegetation do you think grows around each of the cities?

Task 5   Conclusion
Write a paragraph describing how temperature and precipitation determine climate. How does climate affect the animal and plant life?

Extension
Find out your region's current precipitation and temperature pattern. Determine if there have been any changes in these patterns in the past five years. Make a table listing average temperatures and precipitation over the past five years.

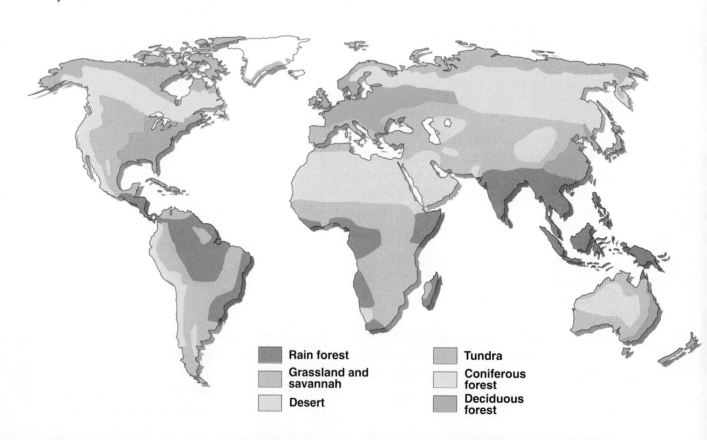

Skills WarmUp

Infer Describe the area that surrounds where you live. Write about each of the following: soil, rainfall, temperature, and kinds of plants. Based on your description, infer what kind of biome you think you live in.

27.2 Land Biomes

Objectives

▶ **List** locations of the land biomes.

▶ **Describe** the major characteristics of the land biomes.

▶ **Make a model** of a biome.

I f you went to a desert in Africa, do you think you would see the same animals and plants as those in a desert in Asia? Probably not. Organisms vary in different areas of the same type of biome. However, the available niches are very similar. The general structure of the communities is also similar.

Figure 27.5 shows the locations of major land biomes. Unlike the borders on the map, biomes don't have sharp boundaries. Each biome blends with the next. On your tour of the following biomes, you'll learn about some adaptations that plants and animals have to live and reproduce in their biomes.

Figure 27.5
Major Land Biomes of the Earth
▼

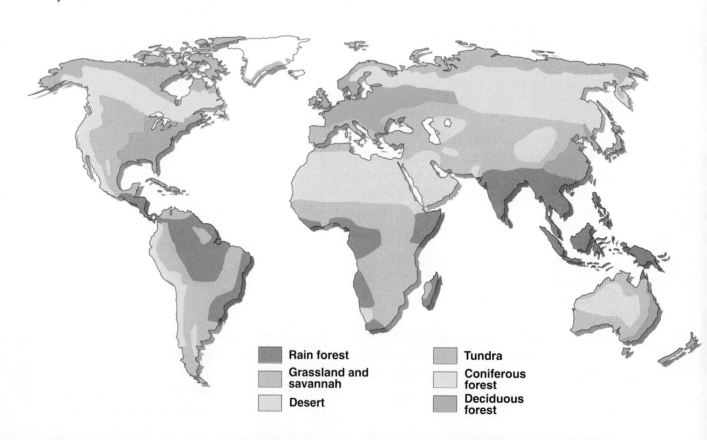

	Rain forest		Tundra
	Grassland and savannah		Coniferous forest
	Desert		Deciduous forest

Tundra

The biome with low average temperatures, little rainfall, and a very short growing season is the **tundra**. Beneath the soil surface in the tundra is a permanently frozen layer of soil known as permafrost. In some areas of the arctic tundra, permafrost can be more than 500 m thick! This layer prevents trees from putting down roots. Only hardy pioneer species and the animals they support can live in the tundra.

The tundra covers about one-tenth of the earth's land surface. Most tundra is near and above the Arctic Circle, but there is also alpine tundra at the tops of mountains.

▲ Many animals in the tundra hibernate or migrate in the winter months. This snowshoe hare is a year-round resident.

Plants in the alpine tundra are low and small. They often grow very slowly to conserve energy. ▼

▲ The caribou is one of the few large animals that live in the North American tundra. Its large body size helps maintain enough heat to survive.

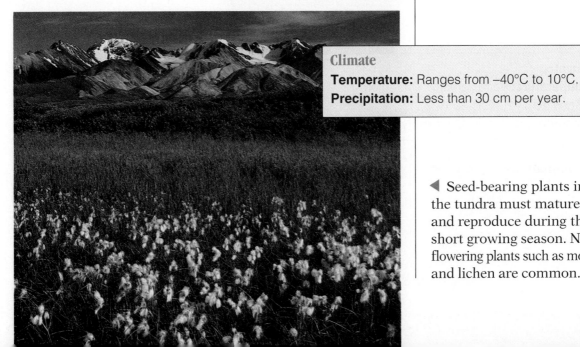

Climate
Temperature: Ranges from –40°C to 10°C.
Precipitation: Less than 30 cm per year.

◀ Seed-bearing plants in the tundra must mature and reproduce during the short growing season. Non-flowering plants such as mosses and lichen are common.

585

Deciduous Forest

Trees that lose their leaves during one season and grow new leaves during another are called **deciduous** (dee SIHJ oo uhs) trees. The biome with deciduous trees, moderate rainfall, six months of mild temperatures, and a cold or dry season is deciduous forest. The soil in deciduous forests is rich in organic material and can hold a lot of water. This means that many plants can live on the forest floor.

Animals and plants live in different layers of the forest. Some live in the treetops, or canopy, while others live on the trees. Deciduous forests are located in parts of North America, South America, Europe, and Asia.

Squirrels, chipmunks, and numerous species of birds inhabit the canopy in the deciduous forest biome. ▼

This raccoon eats ▶ smaller animals and plants. Night vision and feet adapted to climbing or walking the forest floor make it an efficient predator.

▲ The deciduous forest floor supports a variety of fungi and bacteria that help decompose and recycle nutrients.

Climate
Temperature: Varies greatly with region; ranges from −20°C to 30°C.
Precipitation: 50 to 150 cm per year.

Dominant tree species ▶ vary in deciduous forests. In northern areas, beech and maple trees are common. In the south, oak and hickory trees are the dominant species.

Coniferous Forest

The biome with long cold winters of heavy snowfall and three to six months of growing season is the **coniferous** (koh NIHF ur uhs) forest. Coniferous trees, such as spruce, fir, pine, and hemlock, bear their seeds in cones. They do not shed their leaves at one time.

The soil of coniferous forests does not support many decomposers. Smaller animals live in the canopy and trees, while larger animals live on the forest floor. Large areas of Canada and northern Europe have coniferous forests. These forests also occur at high elevations in the western United States and in such states as Maine and Michigan.

Seed-eating birds, such as this evening grosbeak, can find their food in cones. ▼

▲ The porcupine lives on the ground and eats plants. Other plant-eaters include deer, moose, and elk.

Forest predators include the timber wolf, Canadian lynx, grizzly bear, and red fox. The fox is a fast runner, since some of its prey can escape to the trees. ▼

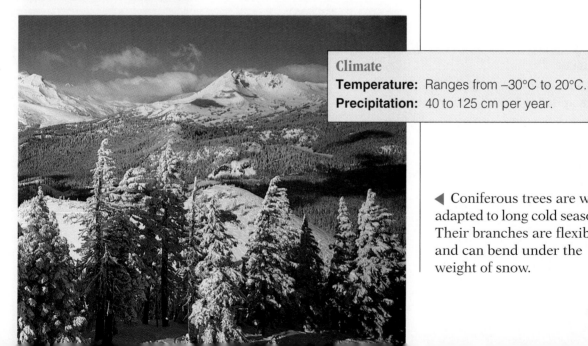

Climate
Temperature: Ranges from –30°C to 20°C.
Precipitation: 40 to 125 cm per year.

◄ Coniferous trees are well adapted to long cold seasons. Their branches are flexible and can bend under the weight of snow.

587

Rain Forest

The biome with heavy rainfall, high humidity, and a warm environment is the tropical rain forest. The soil in the rain forest has little organic matter. The heavy rains wash away most of the nutrients in the soil. But this biome contains the greatest diversity of life. The moisture and warmth create a climate for millions of plant and animal species.

Tropical rain forests are located near the equator in regions of Central and South America, Africa, Australia, and central Asia. There are also rain forests in cool climates in regions that have a lot of rainfall and fog. These forests are called temperate rain forests.

▲ Three-toed sloths use their claws to hang from branches in tropical rain forests. They spend most of their lives in the trees and rarely come down to the ground. They climb high into the canopy of the rain forest. The canopy provides food and a place to sleep.

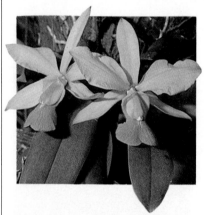

▲ At the tops of the rain forest trees are epiphytes like these orchids. Epiphytes are plants that gather nutrients and water from the air.

There are more different kinds of organisms living in and on a single rain forest tree than in an entire coniferous forest! Many trees grow to more than 45 m high.
▼

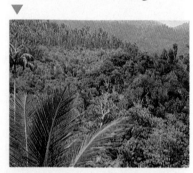

Climate
Temperature: Average is 18°C.
Precipitation: 200 to 500 cm per year.

Along the western coast ▶ of North America there is a temperate rain forest. The conifers here grow much larger than trees in a coniferous forest. Lichens, mosses, and algae grow on nearly every surface.

Grassland

Regions that have hot summers, cold winters, rich soil, and unevenly distributed rainfall support the growth of different species of grasses. Trees can't grow in these areas because there is not enough rain. Biomes that are characterized by grasses are known as **grasslands**.

There are different grasslands all over the world. They include the Great Plains in the United States, the pampas (PAHM puhz) in South America, and the veldt (VEHLT) in South Africa.

Each type of grassland supports different species of grasses and animals. The primary consumers may include birds, mice, rabbits, and gophers. There are also predators, such as coyotes in the United

States and lions in Africa. Grazing animals also live in grasslands, such as these sheep in New Zealand shown below.

Climate
Temperature: –8°C to 28°C.
Precipitation: 25 to 75 cm per year.

Consider This

How Should Rain Forests Be Used?

More than two-thirds of the people on the earth live in countries with tropical rain forests. More than 10 000 sq km of rain forests, per year, are cleared for building materials, to supply wood for fuel, to build new towns, and for other reasons.

Consider Some Issues
People who live near rain forests depend on them for food, water, shelter, and medicines. Farm animals graze on the cleared land. People plant crops that provide food. The forests also provide work for farmers, ranchers, and loggers. As populations increase in these

countries, more and more space and food are needed.

Rain forests are home to more than half of the earth's plants and animals. Habitats are lost when forests are cleared. Rain forests help cycle the earth's available fresh water. The plants in rain forests produce much of the earth's oxygen. Some countries will lose all their tropical rain forests within a few decades if the rate of destruction continues.

Think About It How do you think rain forests should be used? What steps can people take now to save rain forests?

Write About It Write a paper stating your position on rain forest use. Include your reasons for choosing your position.

Desert

Areas that have greater rates of evaporation than rainfall are known as **deserts**. Desert biomes have scarce rainfall, high air pressure, high winds, and poor soils. Heat and water are the main factors that limit life in the desert. Each species of plant and animal has methods of conserving water and staying cool.

Hot deserts are located between latitudes of 20° north and 30° south of the equator. Cold deserts are located near the earth's poles. Currently more than one-third of the earth's land area is desert.

Thorny bushes and cacti are typical desert plants. Cacti have shallow root systems that take up water rapidly when it rains. The lack of leaves decreases water loss from evaporation.
▼

▲ Kangaroo rats, pocket mice, and jackrabbits avoid the heat by remaining in the shade or underground during the day.

Lizards, skinks, and snakes are desert predators. They eat seed-eaters, such as ants, rodents, and birds. They are often light in color so they can stay cool by reflecting sunlight. ▼

Climate
Temperature: Ranges from 5°C to 60°C.
Precipitation: Less than 25 cm per year.

To reproduce, some ▶ desert plants bloom quickly after periods of rainfall. Springtime in the Mojave Desert in California, for example, has a brilliant-colored landscape.

Science and Society *Desertification*

Worldwide, deserts claim more than 70 000 sq km of land per year. Although deserts expand and shrink naturally, human activity can also cause desert expansion, or desertification. Desertification destroys land that can be used for farming or grazing.

One way people cause desertification is through soil erosion. When forests are cut down or lands are overgrazed, the soil can dry out and be blown away. Scientists have calculated that between 1972 and 1981, more than 400 million tons of African soil were blown over the Atlantic Ocean each year.

Some farming practices expose soil. This is what happened in the Great Plains of the United States in the 1930s. Farmers plowed the plains to plant wheat, then high winds carried most of the soil into the air. The dust clouds were estimated to contain 355 million tons of topsoil.

Another farming practice that has led to erosion problems is the slash-and-burn technique. In this process, trees and plants are burned, leaving the soil unprotected. When rain falls on unprotected soil, huge amounts of the soil wash away.

Throughout the world, people are working to stop the spread of deserts. Some people are working to stop deforestation. Others are trying to teach people different ways of managing the land they farm.

Figure 27.6 ▲
When winds carried away its topsoil in the 1930s, this area was named the Dust Bowl.

Check and Explain

1. Describe how the tundra differs from the desert.

2. Name two biomes that you might expect to see if you climbed a very high mountain.

3. **Reason and Conclude** Tropical rain forests contain plants that grow on trees. Give reasons why these plants can survive even though they do not obtain their nutrients from roots in the ground.

4. **Make a Model** Select a biome and design a plant that could survive in that environment. Explain the plant's adaptations to the biome.

Skills WarmUp

Compare Imagine that you just completed training in scuba diving. Describe the kind of water you would swim in if you went scuba diving in ocean water. What would it be like if you then swam in Lake Superior? Describe the similarities and differences of the two bodies of water.

27.3 Water Biomes

Objectives

▶ **Describe** the characteristics of marine and freshwater biomes.

▶ **Identify** adaptations of organisms living in water biomes.

▶ **Compare** and **contrast** two freshwater environments.

Why do you think the earth is often called the water planet? If you said it's because most of the earth is covered with water, you are right. More than 70 percent of the earth's surface is water.

Although most of the earth's water is in the oceans, a small percentage is fresh water. What is the main difference between ocean water and fresh water? The answer is salt. The oceans contain nearly 3.5 percent salt. Fresh water, however, contains less than 0.006 percent salt.

Figure 27.7
Major Zones of the Marine Biome ▼

Littoral Zone

Sublittoral Zone

Jellyfish

Angelfish

Crab

Starfish

Sea horses

Mussels

Sponges

Sea urchin

Sublittoral Zone
From the shore, the land slopes downward and the water becomes much deeper. This area is called the sublittoral zone, or the continental shelf. Many types of organisms live here because there is an abundance of sunlight and nutrients.

Littoral Zone
The place where land and ocean join is called the littoral (LIHT uh ruhl) zone, or seashore. Organisms in this zone must adapt to constant changes caused by the tides. They must also survive temperature changes and the pounding action of waves.

Marine Biome

The ocean environment is called the **marine** biome. Look at the marine biome in Figure 27.7. Marine life varies from the microscopic plankton, which are a food source for many animals, to the giant sperm whale, which grows to more than 15 m long. How many organisms do you recognize?

Marine life is limited by a number of factors. One major factor is salinity, or salt composition. Marine organisms must adapt to the salt in water. They have the ability to remove excess salts.

Water pressure is also a limiting factor. As you go deeper into the ocean, the pressure increases greatly. Some organisms can live only in surface waters, while others can easily dive to great depths.

Light and temperature also limit marine life. These factors vary throughout the ocean. In the deepest parts of the ocean, some organisms have adapted to a very dark and cold environment.

Pelagic Zone

Most of the ocean is in the pelagic (pih LAYJ ihk) zone. Here, sunlight is only visible to a depth of about 200 m. Below 200 m, the ocean becomes very cold and dark. Water pressure increases greatly. Animals that live deep in this zone have special adaptations for survival.

Pelagic Zone

Flying fish

Plankton

Herring

Dolphin

Cod

Sperm whale

200 m

Hammerhead shark

Deep-sea anglerfish

Stingray

Hatchetfish

Viperfish

2000 m

Skills WorkOut

Infer A friend of yours just returned from a vacation and brought you insects for an aquarium. The insects had streamlined bodies and suction-like appendages. Infer if the insects came from a pond, a lake, or a stream. Explain your choice.

Figure 27.8 ▲
What organisms do you think live in this lake?

Figure 27.9
Plants grow in a shallow pond ▶
in Grand Teton National Park.

Freshwater Biomes

Organisms living in freshwater biomes have adaptations for regulating the amount of water in their bodies. A fish's gills remove most excess water. A plant releases water through openings in the undersides of its leaves. Some freshwater organisms adapt to life in running water. Some adapt to life in still water.

Still Water In the still water of lakes and ponds, light penetrates only to a certain depth. Most of the oxygen, too, is at the surface. The surface of a stillwater biome, therefore, is where most photosynthesis occurs. Deeper waters are rich in nutrients because plants and algae do not grow there and use the nutrients.

Organisms in lakes and ponds almost always have a large supply of food. Because still waters have little current, nutrients are not washed away, and plankton can easily grow.

Lakes have life zones that are similar to the marine biome. Fishes that feed on plankton live close to the surface of lakes. Plants with roots, birds, and frogs all live near the shore. In the deeper part of a lake, near the bottom, live worms, bacteria, and fungi.

Running Water Streams and rivers contain running water. Certain factors, such as light, water current, temperature, and the availability of nutrients, determine the kinds of organisms that can live in running water. For example, fishes living in fast-moving streams are strong swimmers. They generally have large fins to guide their movements. Some fishes, such as brook

SkillBuilder *Comparing and Contrasting*

Salt Water Versus Fresh Water

Have you ever spent a long time in the water? What happens to your skin? Does the ocean affect your body differently than a lake? You will be investigating how fresh water and salt water affect organisms. Collect the following items: 8 glass jars, salt, spoon, 2 small equal-sized pieces each of apple and potato, 2 raisins, 2 grapes.

Data Table	Potato	Apple	Grape	Raisin
Before				
Salt prediction				
Salt water				
Fresh prediction				
Fresh water				

1. Fill 8 jars with tap water. Label 4 jars *Salt Water* and 4 jars *Fresh Water*. Put 2 spoonfuls of salt into each of the saltwater jars and stir.

2. Copy the data table to the right. Your version may be larger.

3. Observe the size and texture of each fruit and vegetable. Predict the effects of salt water and fresh water for each. Record your observations and predictions in the table.

4. Place one sample of each fruit and vegetable in a saltwater jar and one sample in a freshwater jar.

5. Observe each of the samples after one hour. Record these observations in your table.

6. What happened to each fruit and vegetable? Why do you think you got those results?

7. Describe the adaptations you think are needed to survive in a saltwater environment.

---

trout, have streamlined bodies that give less resistance to fast currents. Other animals, such as snails, have sticky undersides that help them cling tightly to rocks.

In most fast-moving water, tumbling action and cool water provide much dissolved oxygen. Also, light can reach the bottom. However, little photosynthesis takes place because plants are swept away. So are many nutrients, preventing the growth of plankton. Organisms must feed on insect larvae and on plants and algae that are anchored to the bottom or attached to rocks. Fallen land plants are also a source of food.

In slow-moving streams and rivers, organisms require less oxygen and warmer water. Organic matter is more likely to settle to the bottom. This provides food for scavengers and bottom-feeding organisms, such as tube-dwelling worms, crayfish, and numerous kinds of insects. Such fishes as muskies and pike, as well as turtles, move more easily in streams with a slow current.

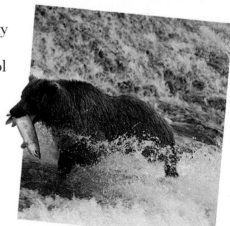

Figure 27.10 ▲
An Alaskan brown bear catches a salmon in a fast-moving stream. What other kinds of organisms live in fast-moving water?

Science and Society
Living by the Yellow River

Rivers are important not only to organisms such as fishes. They are important to people as well. One of the most populated river regions in the world is the Yellow River Valley in China. More than 100 million people live there.

The Yellow River's name comes from its color. The river passes through land areas where the soil erodes rapidly. This erosion fills the river with yellowish sand and silt. Most of the sand flows into the sea. However, the silt builds up in the riverbed. When the riverbed gets very high and a storm comes, the water floods out of the river. The floods are so frequent and disastrous that the river has been nicknamed China's Sorrow.

Why do people live near a river that floods? One major reason is that the silt and water from the river create very fertile cropland. Even in times of drought, the land near the river produces a lot of grain and cotton. The water is also used for water-power stations and industry.

Since 1949, China has invested much money in projects to control the river. These projects include dikes to block overflow and gates to change the water's direction. The government also built a canal called the People's Victory Canal. The canal has provided effective crop irrigation. The efforts to control the river have been successful so far. There have been no serious floods of the Yellow River for more than 40 years.

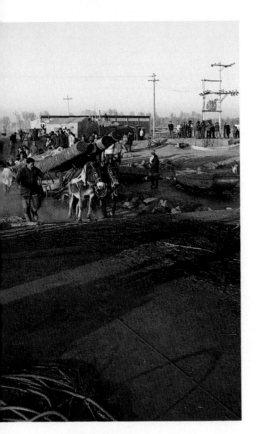

Figure 27.11 ▲
Why do people tend to live along rivers?

Check and Explain

1. Describe three characteristics of the marine biome.

2. If you place an organism that lives in salt water into a freshwater environment, will it survive? Explain.

3. **Reason and Conclude** In the past, garbage was regularly dumped into the oceans and the Great Lakes. If this practice happened in smaller lakes or ponds, what would be the effect on these stillwater systems?

4. **Compare and Contrast** Explain why the food sources for organisms living in ponds differ from the food sources for organisms living in fast-moving streams. How does sunlight affect these two environments?

Chapter 27 Review

Concept Summary

27.1 Climate
▶ Climate is an area's pattern of weather and temperature.
▶ Latitude and altitude influence climates.
▶ Different climates support different vegetation.
▶ A biome is a large land or water area with similar climate, vegetation, and plant and animal life.

27.2 Land Biomes
▶ The earth's major land biomes are tundra, deciduous forest, coniferous forest, tropical rain forest, grassland, and desert.
▶ Land biomes are characterized by climate and dominant plant species.

27.3 Water Biomes
▶ Most of the earth's water is in the marine biome.
▶ The freshwater biome is made up of running water and stillwater environments.
▶ Organisms have special adaptations for the different water biomes.

Chapter Vocabulary

climate (27.1)	polar (27.1)	deciduous (27.2)	desert (27.2)
biome (27.1)	temperate (27.1)	coniferous (27.2)	marine (27.3)
tropical (27.1)	tundra (27.2)	grassland (27.2)	

Check Your Vocabulary

Use the vocabulary words above to complete the following sentences correctly.

1. An area's average rainfall and temperature determine its _____ .
2. A _____ rain forest biome has high rainfall, high humidity, and constant warm temperatures.
3. If you were in a biome with high air pressure, little precipitation, high winds, and poor soil, you'd probably be in a _____ .
4. Trees that lose their leaves in the autumn and grow new ones in the spring are called _____ .
5. You can find permafrost in the _____ biome.
6. The _____ biome is made up of the ocean.
7. Winters are long and cold in the _____ biome.
8. Trees can't grow in the _____ biome.
9. Large regions with distinctive weather, temperature, and plant and animal life are called _____ .
10. Spruce, fir, and pine are examples of _____ trees.
11. The climate of the middle latitudes is _____ .

Explain the difference between the words in each pair.

12. tropical, polar
13. latitude, altitude
14. deciduous forest, coniferous forest
15. littoral zone, sublittoral zone

Write Your Vocabulary

Write sentences using each vocabulary word above. Show that you know what each word means.

Chapter 27 Review

Check Your Knowledge

Answer the following in complete sentences.

1. What are the water biomes? Where do people get most of the water they use, and where is most of the water on the earth located?

2. What are the land biomes?

3. Compare and contrast coniferous and deciduous forests.

4. How is precipitation measured?

5. How is climate influenced by latitude?

6. Explain why most freshwater organisms cannot live in saltwater environments.

7. Explain why most rooted plants cannot survive at the bottom of fast-moving streams.

8. Name and describe the three major climate zones on the earth.

9. Why does precipitation influence the kinds of vegetation that grow in an area?

Determine whether each statement is true or false. Write *true* if it is true. If it is false, change the underlined word to make the statement true.

10. People <u>cannot</u> live in deserts.

11. Water covers more than <u>70</u> percent of the earth.

12. Where there are similar environmental conditions, there are <u>similar</u> biomes.

13. Tundra is one of the <u>largest</u> biomes.

14. Grassland biomes have hot summers, cold winters, and <u>poor</u> soils.

15. An area's height above sea level is called <u>latitude</u>.

Check Your Understanding

Apply the concepts you have learned to answer each question.

1. Describe at least three factors that influence where organisms can live.

2. **Compare and Contrast** Compare the climate and animal and plant species of two different land biomes. Give examples of where each biome is found.

3. Describe the four factors that limit life in the marine biome. Using Figure 27.7 on pages 592 and 593, give examples of how organisms have adapted to each of these factors.

4. **Mystery Photo** The photograph on page 578 was taken during autumn on the upper peninsula of Michigan. The photograph shows a deciduous forest, which supports a wide variety of plant and animal life. What is happening to make the leaves change color? What animals and plants might live in the deciduous forest canopy? What lives on the forest floor?

5. Why do you think some people continue to farm in ways that may cause desertification?

6. **Extension** Create an imaginary land biome. Describe its temperature, precipitation, latitude, and altitude. What kinds of animals and plants live there? How are they adapted to the biome? What will you call your biome? How is it different from others?

7. **Application** Choose the biome in which you would most like to live. Explain the reasons for your choice.

Develop Your Skills

Use the skills you have developed in this chapter to complete each activity.

1. **Interpret Data** The map below shows average yearly temperatures and rainfall across North America.

   a. Using the biome climate information in this chapter, locate where the different biomes are on the map.

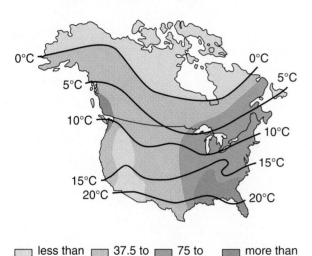

| less than 37.5 cm | 37.5 to 75 cm | 75 to 125 cm | more than 125 cm |

   b. In what biome do you live?

   c. What is the average yearly temperature and rainfall where you live?

2. **Data Bank** Use the information on page 626 to answer the following questions.

   a. If you were at the top of a tall mountain with tundra vegetation, what is the next biome you might expect to encounter as you climbed down the mountain?

   b. Near the equator, what kind of biome is most likely to be found at the lowest altitudes?

3. **Communicate** Make a poster that shows different plants and animals in a particular biome.

Make Connections

1. **Link the Concepts** Below is a concept map showing how some of the main concepts in this chapter link together. Only part of the map is filled in. Copy the map. Using words and ideas you find on the previous page, finish the map.

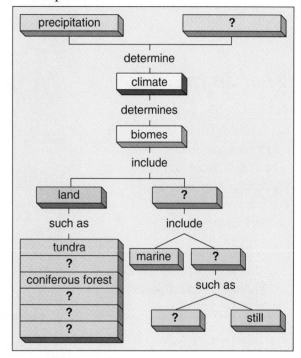

2. **Science and Writing** Write a story about what it would be like to live in a desert or tropical rain forest biome. What is it like for people who really live there? Use the library to find out, and include some real information in your story.

3. **Science and Technology** What products in your life come from the rain forest? Research products from the rain forest.

Chapter 28 Humans and the Environment

What do you see?

❝I see a cornfield. Somebody plowed it. It serves as a food source. It looks like a cornfield because it has yellowish-green and green in a continuous pattern. The yellow looks like corn.❞

Christina Dickson
Barnstable Summer School
Hyannis, Massachusetts

To find out more about the photograph, look on page 620. As you read this chapter, you will learn more about humans and the environment.

28.1 Natural Resources

Objectives

▶ **Distinguish** between renewable and nonrenewable resources.

▶ **Identify** ways that soil and water can be conserved.

▶ **Describe** the changes that may take place when a wild area is taken over for human use.

▶ **Organize** information relating to natural resources and their conservation.

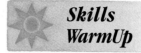

Skills WarmUp

Predict Imagine that you and your classmates will be sent to explore two Pacific islands. The islands are very similar in size, age, and location. But one has a human population and the other does not. Predict what you would expect to see on each island. List ways in which the environment of the populated island has been changed by its human inhabitants.

Have you drunk any water or eaten food today? Have you turned on a light, ridden in a car, or used a computer? When you do any of these things, you are using one or more **natural resources**. Natural resources are materials from the environment that people use to carry on their daily lives.

Every human society that has ever existed has used natural resources. But societies vary in the kinds and amounts of resources they use. People in modern industrial societies use oil, natural gas, and coal for energy. They mine metals for making cans, cars, and many other objects. They use soil for growing food, trees for making paper, and water for keeping their bodies clean. Nearly everything on, above, and below the earth's surface is being used as a natural resource today. And these resources are being used faster than ever before.

Renewable and Nonrenewable Resources

Natural resources can be divided into two types. Resources that can be replaced by natural cycles or processes are called **renewable resources**. For example, when trees are cut for lumber, seedlings can grow up to take their place. Other renewable resources include water and soil. Even though these resources can replace themselves, the cycles that replace them can be destroyed.

Resources that can't be replaced by natural processes are called **nonrenewable resources**. The supplies of nonrenewable resources, such as oil and natural gas, get smaller as people use them.

Figure 28.1 ▲
The photograph shows copper ore being mined. Copper is a nonrenewable resource that is used for many things, including electrical wiring.

Conservation of Resources

Have you ever shut off a light when it was not needed? If so, you were helping conserve the earth's natural resources. To *conserve* means to protect from being lost or reduced. It is the root of the word *conservation*.

Conservation of resources can be accomplished in two major ways. One way is by reducing the amount of natural resources each person uses. This means recycling and cutting down on waste. The second way is by using and managing renewable resources wisely.

Water Conservation

How much water do you think you use each day? If you are typical, you probably use at least 228 liters of water a day. That's enough water to fill several bathtubs. It includes the water used to wash your clothes and dishes, the water you bathe with, and the water you drink.

The 228 liters per person is only a small part of the water used each day in the United States. Factories and power

Figure 28.3 ▲

As you can see in this circle graph, only 3 percent of the earth's water is fresh. People, therefore, must continue to find ways to conserve this valuable resource.

plants use tremendous amounts of water for cooling and other purposes. Farmers use even more, especially in dry climates.

Where does all this water come from? About 75 percent of the water used in the United States comes from rivers and lakes. The other 25 percent comes from ground water. Both of these sources are limited. Look at Figure 28.3. It shows that only a small amount of the water on the earth is fresh water.

In some places, water supplies are still plentiful. In other places, however, there is not nearly enough water to meet the demand. So much water is taken from some rivers and streams that plant life and animal life are threatened. And in some places, ground water is being used faster than it can be replaced. This can cause permanent damage to the underground areas that store water, called aquifers.

A simple way you can help conserve water is by paying attention to your daily use. For example, you can take shorter showers and turn off the faucet while you brush your teeth.

Figure 28.2 ▲

Water is stored in the Roosevelt Dam in Arizona for use in farming, electrical power, and recreation.

Soil Conservation

Soil is one of the most important natural resources as well as the most abused. It is estimated that each year the amount of topsoil blown or washed away would fill a train of freight cars long enough to encircle the earth 138 times! At the same time, much of the soil that is left becomes less fertile. New soil forms naturally but slowly. It can actually take hundreds of years for 20 cm of topsoil to form.

Causes of Soil Loss   In a natural setting, soil, plants, and animals are connected as an ecosystem. The soil and its fertility are renewed by natural cycles. When crops are grown, cycles are disturbed.

Soil often erodes during periods when farmers leave it fallow, with no plants growing in it. The soil surface is exposed to wind and rain. There are no roots to help hold the soil in place.

Growing crops also reduces the soil's fertility. Crops remove large amounts of plant nutrients from the soil, which are then themselves removed. Chemical fertilizers restore these nutrients, but only for a short time. Continued use of chemical fertilizers also reduces the soil's ability to hold moisture and support organisms.

Soil Management   Some farmers prevent soil erosion and loss of fertility by managing their farm fields as ecosystems. In a natural ecosystem, plants die, decompose, and return to the soil as nutrients. Farmers copy this process by plowing back into the soil the parts of crops not harvested or by leaving the remains of the last crop standing.

Another characteristic of a natural ecosystem is that a variety of plants grow in one area. Farmers copy this pattern by growing different kinds of crop plants together in one field. One of these methods is called strip cropping, shown in Figure 28.5. A related method, called crop rotation, is to plant a different crop every year. These methods also help decrease pest damage.

Contour farming of crops can also prevent erosion. Rows or crops are plowed across the slopes of hills rather than up and down the hill.

Figure 28.4 ▲
Terracing is a type of contour farming that slows down the runoff of water and helps keep the soil on hills from being washed away.

Figure 28.5 ▲
Strip cropping is the planting of alternate strips of crops in areas where soil is easily eroded by wind and water.

Land Use

As the human population increases, more and more land is developed to meet human needs. Land is paved over to make highways and parking lots. It is graded to make room for housing developments. In the process, valuable farmland is lost and open space is reduced.

When land is taken over for human use, it is changed dramatically. Natural cycles are modified or destroyed. The number and kinds of species the land will support are reduced. The land is no longer a habitat for most of the plants and animals that once lived there.

Human development also affects the surrounding area and its life. For example, large mammals, such as deer, no longer have space in which to roam. Water becomes polluted. Paved and built-up areas may also change the local climate, raising temperatures or reducing rainfall.

Decisions about how to use land are increasingly more difficult. Voters, elected officials, and planners must choose between uses that may seem equally important. They have to weigh the needs of the present with those of the future.

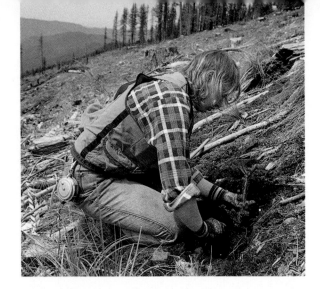

Figure 28.7 ▲
Trees are often replanted after forests are cut down. Here, a technician checks a planted tree seedling.

Forest Management

People use the wood from trees to build houses, to make furniture, to produce paper and cardboard, and to burn as fuel. For thousands of years, people have harvested timber from forests for these purposes. But in the last few hundred years, the demand for wood has grown as rapidly as the population. Huge areas of forest have been cut down as a result. Forests have also been cleared to make room for towns and cities and to provide land for farming.

The environment changes in many ways when forests are cut down. The habitats of many forest-dwelling plants and animals are destroyed. Erosion increases because there are fewer plants to hold the soil in place. Less water is stored in the soil, and the quality of the surface water is reduced.

The forests that are left must be managed very wisely if they are to continue to supply human needs. Forests are not just stands of trees to be harvested. They have value as wilderness, as animal habitat, and as recreation areas.

Figure 28.6 ▲
When housing developments are built, valuable farmland is sometimes lost.

Wildlife Conservation

Many species of animals are endangered, or facing extinction. Some, like the mountain lion, have been hunted for sport or because they are seen as dangerous. Others have been victims of poachers who sell their skins or body parts. African elephants, for example, are hunted for their tusks, which are ivory. But the greatest single threat to most species of wildlife is the destruction of their habitats. Whenever a salt marsh is drained, a river dammed, or a forest cut down, valuable habitats for one or more species are lost forever.

▲ Grizzly bears were once found in most of western North America. Today most grizzly bears live in western Canada and Alaska. The population has dwindled because of loss of habitat and conflict with humans.

In 1948, fewer than 20 whooping cranes were living. Many had been shot by hunters and much of their breeding habitat had been destroyed. Today there are over 150 whooping cranes, but the species remains close to extinction. These birds spend the winter on the coast of Texas. ▼

◀ Pronghorns, or the American antelope, came close to extinction in the 1920s because of habitat loss and hunting. Now, due to herd management, their population has increased greatly.

Blue morpho butterflies live among the trees in the tropical rain forests of Central and South America. As their habitat is logged, their population is threatened. ▼

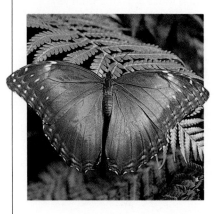

Green sea turtles live in the warm waters of the Indian and Pacific oceans. When they return from the ocean to their nesting grounds, they can be hunted very easily. ▼

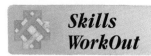
Plant Conservation

Over one-tenth of all the known plant species on the earth are in danger of becoming extinct. Scientists estimate that many thousands of plant species will become extinct before they are even discovered and named. Many of these plants live in tropical rain forests, which are being cleared at a rapid rate. Among these endangered plant species are many with life-saving medicinal qualities. Some may be good sources of food. In addition, many endangered plants may be sources of valuable genetic material because they can contribute important traits to other species of plants.

The extinction of plant species is not just a loss to humans. Plants are primary producers. They are a vital part of the relationships that exist in nature. When plant species are lost, the balance of ecosystems can be upset. As many as 30 other species can depend on one plant for survival.

Career Corner *Agricultural Researcher*

Who Helps Farmers Grow More and Better Food?

Modern agriculture depends on knowledge of soil, climate, insects, chemistry, plant growth and nutrition, plant genetics, and plant diseases. An agricultural researcher may be involved in any one of these areas.

Agricultural researchers work to develop new plant varieties. They help solve soil erosion problems. They study insect life cycles to determine how to control these pests without using dangerous chemical pesticides. Some agricultural researchers experiment with planting different mixtures of crops, or with letting certain weeds grow with crops to attract beneficial insects.

Some agricultural researchers work mostly outdoors, but many spend much of their time in laboratories or offices. However, any new treatments or plant varieties developed in the lab must be tested in the field.

Since food production is a global concern, some agricultural researchers travel to other countries to assist with their agricultural needs. Advances in biotechnology may provide many new opportunities and challenges for people in agricultural research.

Many businesses and government agencies hire agricultural researchers. Some also work at universities. For most jobs, a doctorate degree in a biological science or agronomy is required.

Science and Technology *Alternative Fuels*

In the United States, people depend on natural gas and oil for their energy needs. However, there isn't an infinite supply of these fuels, and they are nonrenewable resources. One day, we may run out of these fuels. Another problem is that they cause pollution.

Today scientists are searching for alternative fuels for people to use. One example is synfuels, or synthetic fuels. Synfuels are liquid and gaseous fuels that are made from oil shale, tar sands, and coal. All three, especially oil shale and tar sands, are found in great quantities in the earth. However, none can be used yet on a large scale. Major obstacles include high production costs, low energy yields, and pollution problems.

Another alternative fuel is hydrogen. Where would hydrogen be obtained? If you said water, you're right. Because there is so much water on the earth, hydrogen use could be a major energy-saving method. It is also a clean fuel. In order to use hydrogen as a fuel, however, it must be isolated from water. One method of obtaining hydrogen is to "split" water molecules into hydrogen and oxygen.

There are already some hydrogen-powered vehicles in cities around the world, but they are mostly experimental models. In order to make hydrogen fuel available to the public, the water-splitting process would have to be set up on a large scale. This would mean building huge hydrogen plants and places for storage.

Figure 28.8 ▲
Synthetic fuels are made in this plant in New Zealand (top). This hydrogen-powered automobile was built in 1992.

Check and Explain

1. Give examples of renewable and nonrenewable resources. Explain how these resources are different.

2. What ecological changes may result when a forest is cleared to make room for a housing development?

3. **Find Causes** How can crop rotation and strip cropping help reduce the damage caused by pests?

4. **Organize Data** Make five columns, and then place the name of an important natural resource at the top of each. Complete the chart by describing the importance of each resource to human society and ways that it can be conserved.

28.2 Energy Resources

Objectives

▶ **Identify** types of renewable and nonrenewable energy sources.

▶ **Compare** and **contrast** alternative energy sources.

▶ **Explain** the importance of energy conservation efforts.

▶ **Make a model** of an energy-efficient house.

I f you have ever experienced a power outage or blackout, you know how much people depend on energy. Energy is required to cook your food, heat and cool the place where you live, warm the water you bathe with, and transport you from home to school. Energy is even needed to make most of the products you use every day. Where does this energy come from? Will there always be enough for everyone?

Fossil Fuels

Most of the energy used in modern industrial societies is provided by coal, oil, and natural gas. These energy sources are known as **fossil fuels**. Fossil fuels were formed from the buried remains of decayed plants and animals that lived hundreds of millions of years ago. These remains were covered with many layers of mud, sand, and rock. Their complex molecules slowly changed into simpler molecules made of chains of carbon. Under certain conditions, the solid fossil fuel, coal, was formed. Under other conditions, either liquid petroleum or natural gas was created.

Because it has taken millions of years for fossil fuels to form, they are nonrenewable. Some day, the earth's supply of fossil fuels will run out. Currently humans are burning fossil fuels so rapidly that this day may not be very far in the future.

To replace fossil fuels, both today and in the future, scientists are working to develop several alternative energy sources. Many of these alternative sources have great advantages over fossil fuels. Most are nonpolluting and based on renewable resources.

Figure 28.9 ▲
Oil is extracted from wells deep in the ground (above) and at offshore sites.

Solar Energy

Did you know that the sunlight striking the earth on a typical summer day may contain twice as much energy as the United States uses in an entire year? The sun's energy is free, nonpolluting, and will not run out for millions of years. Why, then, doesn't everyone just use the sun's energy? The problem is that there are no practical methods of collecting and using it on a large scale. The sun, therefore, isn't yet a practical alternative to fossil fuels.

Energy from the sun is called **solar energy**. One kind of solar energy is the heat produced when sunlight strikes a surface. Figure 28.10 shows a house designed to use the sun's heat energy.

The sun's heat energy can also be collected and stored in devices called solar collectors. Water is passed through dark-colored pipes that absorb the heat energy in sunlight and transfer it to the water. Today over one million homes in the United States use solar collectors as their source of hot water.

Solar energy is also produced with solar cells. They convert sunlight into electricity. If solar cells can be made cheaper and more efficient, they may become important energy sources.

Energy from the sun can also be used indirectly. Plants convert solar energy into plant tissue. When plants and plant products are burned, they release energy that people use. Energy that comes from plants is called **biomass energy**.

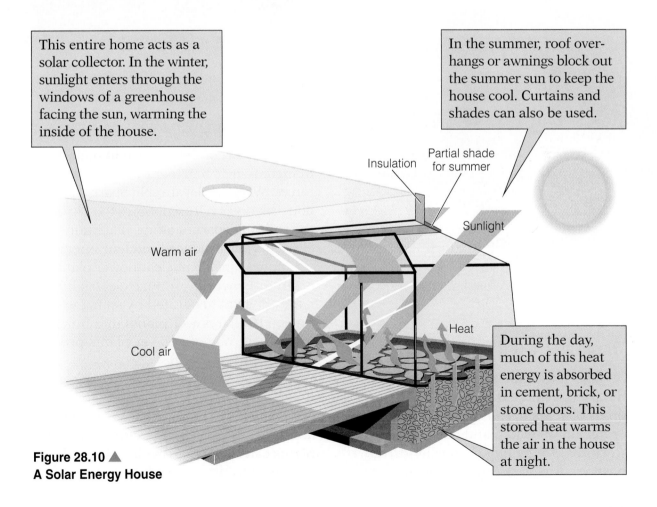

This entire home acts as a solar collector. In the winter, sunlight enters through the windows of a greenhouse facing the sun, warming the inside of the house.

In the summer, roof overhangs or awnings block out the summer sun to keep the house cool. Curtains and shades can also be used.

Insulation

Partial shade for summer

Sunlight

Warm air

Cool air

Heat

During the day, much of this heat energy is absorbed in cement, brick, or stone floors. This stored heat warms the air in the house at night.

Figure 28.10 ▲
A Solar Energy House

Geothermal Energy

Deep below the surface, the earth is very hot. In certain places, the hot interior is close enough to the surface to come in contact with ground water. The water is heated and turned to steam. The steam is released at the surface through hot springs, geysers, and wells. When people use this heat from the earth as an energy source, it is called **geothermal energy**.

In a geothermal power plant, steam from the earth drives turbines that produce electricity. Nothing is burned, so geothermal energy is pollution-free. However, geothermal energy use is limited because not many places on the earth are suitable for producing it.

Figure 28.11 ▲
A geyser in Iceland releases hot water and steam.

Water and Wind Power

One of the oldest sources of energy is the wind. Wind has been used for hundreds of years to sail ships, grind grain crops, pump water, and cut wood at sawmills. Today huge propeller-driven turbines produce electricity. Often many hundreds of wind turbines are set up in areas known as wind farms, as shown in Figure 28.12.

Water has also been a source of power for centuries. Falling water can spin turbines to produce electricity. Energy produced in this way is known as hydropower.

Figure 28.12 ▲
Windmills generate electricity in California.

Nuclear Energy

The nuclei of the atoms that make up matter are held together by very strong forces. When nuclei are split apart, tremendous energy is released. Since the 1950s, the splitting apart of atoms of certain elements has produced **nuclear energy**.

More than 400 nuclear power plants around the world produce electricity from the heat generated by splitting nuclei. Unlike power plants that burn fossil fuels, nuclear power plants produce no air pollution.

However, many people worry about nuclear energy. No safe way has been found to dispose of the dangerous radioactive waste produced. Accidents at the plants can also release radioactive substances into the atmosphere.

Science and You *Turn Off the Lights!*

There are many reasons for each person to cut down on energy use. The United States uses much more than its share of the world's fossil fuels. Fossil fuels also affect the environment. Extracting and transporting them can cause environmental damage, such as oil spills. Processing fossil fuels pollutes the air, and burning them for energy pollutes it even more. Here are some suggestions to help you and your family become more energy efficient.

▶ Turn off lights and appliances when not in use.

▶ Open curtains when you need light during the day.

▶ Close the curtains when the weather is cold.

▶ Dust the light bulbs. Dusty ones waste more energy.

▶ Use fluorescent bulbs instead of incandescent bulbs.

▶ Check for drafts around windows and doors. Fix seals around the windows and doors, if necessary.

▶ Check to see if your water heater is insulated.

▶ If you have a furnace, change the air filter regularly.

▶ Cover pots of boiling water.

▶ Open the refrigerator only when you know what you want from it.

▶ Recycle cans, paper, and plastics.

▶ Encourage others to become more energy efficient.

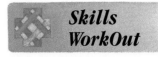

Skills WorkOut

Classify Study the suggestions on this page for becoming more energy efficient. Classify these suggestions into three or more groups. Give each group a name and explain how the items in the group are related.

Check and Explain

1. Give an example of a renewable energy source and explain why it is renewable.

2. Which alternative energy sources would you recommend be developed for wider use? Explain.

3. **Generalize** Explain why energy conservation efforts can improve the quality of life for people and help protect the environment.

4. **Make a Model** Design an energy-efficient house. Make sure it uses the heat and light of the sun wisely. Include ways to get energy from wind, water, biomass, or solar cells.

Communicate You have probably seen in books or magazines how pollution has affected the earth's air, water, or land. Maybe you've even seen pollution in your own neighborhood. Describe your reaction to the pollution.

28.3 Pollution

Objectives

▶ **Describe** some of the harmful effects and sources of air, land, and water pollution.

▶ **Explain** how pollution can be reduced.

▶ **Predict** the condition of the earth's ecosystems ten years from now.

In what ways is the environment around you polluted? Make a list of all the places where you have seen pollution. Pollution is any physical, chemical, or biological change in the environment that is harmful to living organisms. A substance is a pollutant if it makes the environment unfit or undesirable for humans and other organisms.

Air Pollution

Would you choose to eat rotten food or drink waste water? Of course not. But people often have no choice about the quality of air that they breathe. Huge amounts of solids, liquids, and gases are added to the earth's air by humans every day. Many of these materials not only make breathing difficult but cause harm to other living organisms and the environment.

Smog One of the results of air pollution is **smog**. Many cities are covered with a blanket of smog during much of the year. One type of smog results from the burning of oil and coal. It forms when tiny particles and gases from the burning combine with moisture in the air. Particles from the smog cause health problems and reduce visibility.

Areas that have sunny, dry climates and a lot of exhaust from automobiles often have another type of smog. It is called photochemical smog. This smog forms when chemicals from car exhaust react in the presence of sunlight. Ozone and other harmful substances produced in these reactions combine with nitrogen oxides and carbon monoxide from the exhaust. The result is air that is very unhealthy to breathe.

Figure 28.13 ▲
Smog surrounds the city of Denver, Colorado. What causes smog?

Acid Rain The gases produced when fossil fuels are burned can create more than smog. These gases combine with the moisture in clouds to form acidic water droplets. The droplets then fall to the earth as **acid rain**. Acid rain is precipitation with a pH below 5.6.

Acid rain can damage forests and freshwater ecosystems. In many parts of the eastern United States, lakes have become so acidic from acid rain that they can no longer support most forms of life. Acid rain also corrodes buildings, metals, and painted surfaces.

Ozone Depletion At ground level, ozone is a harmful pollutant. In the upper atmosphere, however, ozone forms a layer that protects humans, plants, and animals from the sun's harmful ultraviolet rays. It also helps stabilize the earth's climate.

Recently scientists have detected a thinning of the ozone layer. You can see this in Figure 28.15. It is believed that a number of gases produced by humans are responsible for breaking down this protective layer. Scientists worry that ozone depletion will cause an increase in skin cancer.

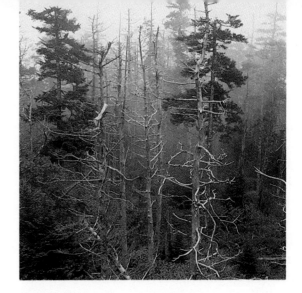

Figure 28.14 ▲
How has acid rain affected this forest?

Greenhouse Effect Greenhouses trap solar energy in the form of heat to help plants grow. Look at Figure 28.16. The earth is like a giant greenhouse because certain gases in the atmosphere trap the sun's heat and keep the earth warm. However, these gases have been building up in the atmosphere for over 100 years because of the burning of fossil fuels. Scientists believe that the increasing levels of these "greenhouse gases" could cause the earth to warm, changing the climate and melting the polar ice caps.

Figure 28.15 ▲
The ozone hole is shown in pink in this satellite map.

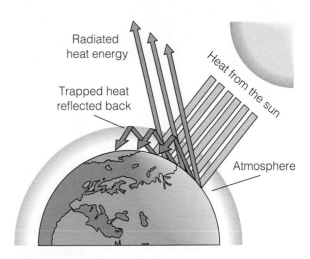

Figure 28.16 ▲
How is the earth like a giant greenhouse?

Land Pollution

Land is polluted by litter, garbage, solid waste, and other substances that humans dispose of. Household garbage is one of the largest sources of land pollution. Every day, each person in the United States throws away an average of 3.6 kg of garbage. Most of this enormous amount of trash ends up in landfills, places where garbage is dumped and then covered with soil. A large amount of garbage never makes it to landfills, instead becoming litter that fouls the landscape.

A more dangerous kind of land pollution can occur when **hazardous wastes** are disposed of. Hazardous wastes are substances that are very harmful to humans and other organisms. They can be radioactive, corrosive, poisonous, or disease-causing. Most hazardous wastes are produced by industry, but the typical household creates hazardous wastes, too.

Until recently, most hazardous wastes were put in barrels or other containers and buried in the ground. But many of the containers have since leaked. As a result, old hazardous waste dumps have become environmental nightmares. In hundreds of places, toxic chemicals from these dumps have seeped into the ground water and threaten to poison drinking water.

◀ Hazardous Wastes

Some companies dispose of their hazardous wastes illegally rather than incur the costs of proper disposal. The photograph shows workers cleaning up hazardous waste barrels left by a paint manufacturer who had gone out of business. Locating the companies who dump illegally is usually difficult, since most abandoned barrels are not labeled with company names.

Solid Wastes ▶

Solid wastes are mainly produced by agriculture, manufacturing, mining, and people's daily lives. Wastes produced by daily life include materials discarded by schools, stores, and homes. In the United States, these wastes are increasing at a rate of 2 to 4 percent a year.

Water Pollution

Is there a stream, river, or lake near where you live? Most likely it is polluted. According to the Environmental Protection Agency, all but a few of the water basins in the United States are polluted.

Water pollution has many sources. Pollutants are sometimes dumped directly into rivers and lakes by factories. Fertilizers and pesticides used by farmers can enter waterways in the runoff from farm fields. Litter, oil, and sewage can flow into rivers from storm drains. Water pollution kills fish and other freshwater organisms. Polluted water can harm people if they drink it or bathe in it.

The slow seepage of pollutants from landfills, toxic waste dumps, and farm fields also pollutes the ground water. These pollutants are often hard to detect because they are tasteless and odorless. Ground water makes up the drinking water supply of many people in the United States.

The pollutants in rivers and streams eventually end up in the earth's oceans. Even though the oceans are very large, they are affected by all the waste that has been dumped into them. One serious pollutant in the oceans is oil. Each year millions of tons of oil are added to the oceans.

◀ **Freshwater Pollution**
Industrial wastes are the major source of pollution in rivers, lakes, and streams. The water cannot break down the polluting substances naturally. The poisonous substances accumulate, killing plants and animals. Here, the wastes from a paper mill have severely polluted a nearby river.

Ocean Pollution ▶
Each year millions of tons of oil are added to the world's oceans. Here, workers begin the huge task of cleaning the Alaskan shoreline in 1989. The oil tanker *Exxon Valdez* had struck a reef. More than 240,000 barrels of oil leaked into the waters, polluting the surrounding shoreline.

Protecting the Earth

There are no easy or quick solutions to environmental problems. Today, however, more and more people and governments are becoming aware of the dangers of polluting the earth. Since 1970, many laws have been passed in the United States to control the amount of pollution produced by factories and automobiles. The Environmental Protection Agency has been created. Endangered species have received legal protection.

People are helping by recycling more paper, bottles, cans, and plastic than ever before. Many people are making their homes energy efficient and cutting down on the use of gasoline by carpooling and bicycling.

But preserving the quality of life on the earth and its ecosystems may require more than small changes in people's lifestyles. Everyone can begin by trying to better understand the complex interactions of living things and the earth's nonliving environment.

Consider This

How Much Should Be Done to Prevent Oil Spills?

People in the United States depend greatly on oil for their energy needs. Oil accounts for nearly half of the total energy consumption in the United States. However, demand for oil has also harmed the environment in a number of ways. One way is by oil tankers. Accidents from these vessels cause serious spills in waters all over the world.

Consider Some Issues   Since the 1970s, the U.S. government has created many new safety standards for oil tankers. Imposing regulations on oil companies is costly, however.

Companies raise prices for fuel to pay for modern equipment. People are then burdened with these rising costs when buying gasoline and paying home heating bills.

Environmentalists argue that the government needs to create even more restrictions that will make oil tankers less likely to accidentally spill oil. They also feel that oil companies need to do a better job of cleaning up the oil spills by spending more money on cleanup efforts.

Think About It   What action should the government take to help prevent oil spills? How will

more restrictions affect people dependent on oil?

Write About It   Write a proposal that describes what you think the government should do about oil spills. Include reasons for your recommendations.

Science and Society *Recycling*

Each day in the United States over 400,000 tons of materials are discarded and dumped. What can be done about all this waste? Recycling is one option. Recycling reduces the amount of waste that goes into landfills, *and* it saves natural resources. For example, 95 percent less energy is needed to make an aluminum can from recycled aluminum than to produce one from aluminum ore.

Fewer pollutants are created when materials are recycled. Producing a new product from raw materials often releases harmful pollutants into the environment. In addition, disposing of the product after it is used can also cause pollution. But if the product is recycled, both kinds of pollution can be eliminated.

In the United States, only about 10 percent of all the waste is recycled. The national goal for recycling is 25 percent. If you think this goal is difficult, consider that some European countries recycle 40 percent or more of their waste. To help increase recycling, many communities have started curbside recycling programs. Cans, bottles, and newspapers are picked up every week. In addition, some states have passed laws requiring deposits on beverage containers. When the containers are returned for recycling, the deposit is returned to the consumer.

Examine how much waste you create in a day. What percentage do you recycle? Does your family and school recycle over 25 percent of its wastes? Does your community have a curbside recycling program? If not, think about how you could help start one. Your actions do make a difference.

Figure 28.17 ▲
These aluminum products will be recycled and used again. How does recycling help the environment?

Check and Explain

1. How does acid rain affect the environment?

2. Describe three sources of water pollution.

3. **Generalize** What is an important action an individual can take to protect the environment?

4. **Predict** Describe what the earth's ecosystems will be like in ten years. What about in 50 years? Give reasons for your prediction.

Activity 28   *How does acid rain affect plants?*

Skills   Observe; Hypothesize; Control Variables

Task 1   Prelab Prep

1. Collect the following items: water, distilled vinegar, graduated cylinder, pH paper, 4 small pots or paper cups, potting soil, 2 leaves each from 3 deciduous trees or shrubs, eyedropper, radish and bean seeds.
2. Make an acidic water solution by mixing 50 mL of vinegar with 150 mL of water in a graduated cylinder. The solution should have a pH of 4.0. Test it.
3. Fill four pots or cups three-quarters full of potting soil.
4. Make the following labels: *Radish—Normal pH*, *Radish—Acidic pH*, *Bean—Normal pH*, and *Bean—Acidic pH*. Attach one label to each pot.
5. For each pair of deciduous leaves, label one *Normal pH* and the other *Acidic pH*.

Task 2   Data Record

On a separate sheet of paper, copy Table 28.1. Use it to record your data and include dates.

Table 28.1   Effects of Acid on Vegetables

	Observations
Radish—Normal pH	
Radish—Acidic pH	
Bean—Normal pH	
Bean—Acidic pH	
Leaf A—Normal pH	
Leaf A—Acidic pH	
Leaf B—Normal pH	
Leaf B—Acidic pH	
Leaf C—Normal pH	
Leaf C—Acidic pH	

Task 3   Procedure

1. Place a few drops of normal water on the surfaces of the deciduous leaves labeled *Normal pH*. Place the same amount of acidic water on the leaves labeled *Acidic pH*.
2. Set aside these leaves for a few minutes. Continue with the second part of the activity. Record your observations later.
3. Plant 5 radish seeds in each radish pot and 5 bean seeds in each bean pot.
4. Wet the soil of each pot with the normal water or the acidic water as shown on the pot's label.
5. Set aside these pots and make daily observations and records of their growth.
6. Observe and record any changes on the surfaces of the deciduous leaves.

Task 4   Analysis

1. Identify the variable in this activity.
2. What effect did the different water samples have on the surfaces of the leaves?
3. What effect did the different water samples have on the seeds' abilities to germinate?
4. Were there differences in the germination and growth patterns of radishes and beans?

Task 5   Conclusion

Write a short summary of how the pH of water affected seed growth and leaf appearance.

Everyday Application

What is the pH of the soil in your yard or on the school grounds? Mix some soil with water and test it with the pH paper. Find out which plants like slightly acidic soil and which do not. Which plants will grow best in your soil?

Extension

Collect water samples from several sites in the area of your school. Test the pH of each sample. Collect rain or snow samples from different areas in the community and test the pH of each.

Chapter 28 Review

Concept Summary

28.1 Natural Resources

▶ Natural resources are materials people take from the environment to meet their needs. Natural resources are either renewable or nonrenewable.

▶ Wise use of water, land, and forests helps conserve these limited resources.

▶ Managing farm fields as ecosystems helps conserve their soil.

▶ Many plant and animal species are endangered because their habitats have been destroyed.

28.2 Energy Resources

▶ Fossil fuels were formed from the remains of organisms that lived long ago. They are the major source of energy in modern industrial societies.

▶ Solar energy, geothermal energy, water power, and wind power are alternative energy sources based on renewable natural resources.

▶ Many people are concerned about the use of nuclear energy because it poses several dangers.

28.3 Pollution

▶ Pollution of the air causes smog, acid rain, and destruction of the ozone layer, which may warm the earth through the greenhouse effect.

▶ Disposal of solid wastes and hazardous wastes can pollute the land. Many sources of chemicals and wastes pollute streams, rivers, lakes, the ocean, and ground water.

▶ Steps are being taken to preserve the earth's ecosystems, but much remains to be done.

Chapter Vocabulary

fossil fuel (28.2)	natural resource (28.1)	nuclear energy (28.2)	geothermal energy (28.2)
acid rain (28.3)	renewable resource (28.1)	solar energy (28.2)	hazardous waste (28.3)
smog (28.3)	biomass energy (28.2)	nonrenewable resource (28.1)	

Check Your Vocabulary

Use the vocabulary words above to complete the following sentences correctly.

1. Automobile exhaust reacts in the air with sunlight to produce a kind of ____ .

2. Energy from the sun is called ____ .

3. Humans use materials from the environment called ____ to meet their needs.

4. Corrosive, poisonous, and radioactive wastes are examples of ____ .

5. No safe way has been found to dispose of the waste produced by ____ .

6. The burning of ____ can cause air pollution.

7. Supplies of a ____ cannot be replaced.

8. Energy that comes from plants is called ____ .

9. Trees, water, and soil are examples of ____ .

10. Freshwater ecosystems and forests are damaged by ____ .

11. In some places, ____ can be produced because superheated ground water rises to the surface.

Write Your Vocabulary

Write sentences using each vocabulary word above. Show that you know what each word means.

Chapter 28 Review

Check Your Knowledge

Answer the following in complete sentences.

1. What are two ways of using energy from the sun?

2. Describe one source of water pollution. What effect might this pollutant have on the environment?

3. What are fossil fuels? Are they renewable or nonrenewable?

4. How is a forest ecosystem affected when its trees are cut down?

5. What is the main cause of the extinction of plant and animal species?

Choose the answer that best completes each sentence.

6. Many (nonrenewable, polluting, alternative, expensive) energy sources are being developed to replace fossil fuels.

7. Pollutants dumped into rivers and streams eventually find their way to (the ocean, the atmosphere, groundwater supplies, Chicago).

8. The average temperature of the earth's atmosphere may rise as a result of (the greenhouse effect, water pollution, strip cropping, nuclear energy).

9. Some endangered plants in tropical rain forests may be sources of (ozone, fossil fuel, hazardous waste, medicine).

10. A geothermal power plant uses water heated by (fossil fuels, heat energy inside the earth, volcanoes, the greenhouse effect) to produce electricity.

11. Humans are using (fewer, different, more, better) natural resources than they did 100 years ago.

Check Your Understanding

Apply the concepts you have learned to answer each question.

1. **Application** If you were lost in a wilderness area, what natural resources might you use to survive? Where would you look for them?

2. Each of the following is designed to conserve what natural resource?

   a. recycling soft drink cans

   b. reusing paper bags

   c. a protected wilderness area

   d. low-flush toilets

3. **Compare and Contrast** As energy sources, how are fossil fuels and the sun different? Are they similar in any way?

4. **Mystery Photo** The photograph on page 600 shows crops that have been planted along level lines that follow the contour of the land, called contour farming. What would happen if this land were farmed without using contour farming methods?

5. **Extension** Make a list of ten things that you can do to help protect the earth's ecosystems. Explain the purpose of each action.

6. **Predict** In what ways would the global environment benefit if fossil fuels were replaced as a source of energy?

7. **Infer** Which of the alternative energy sources you learned about in this chapter could be used by people to supply their own energy needs? Which require large-scale development by industry or government?

8. If you lived far from any cities, would you be safe from water and air pollution? Explain your answer.

Develop Your Skills

Use the skills you have developed in this chapter to complete each activity.

1. **Interpret Data** The bar graph below shows the average amount of garbage produced per person each year in the United States.

a. About how much garbage did each person produce during 1980?

b. During what five-year period did the amount per person increase the most?

c. How much garbage do you predict the average person will produce in 1995? What factors should you take into account in making this prediction?

2. **Calculate** A leaky faucet drips 47 times per minute. If you fix it, how much water do you save every hour? Every day? In a whole year?

3. **Data Bank** Use the information on page 631 to answer the following questions.

a. What type of fuel provided most of the energy used in the United States in 1850? In 1920? In 1980?

b. Between 1900 and 1970, by approximately how many times did the United States increase its energy use?

Make Connections

1. **Link the Concepts** Construct a concept map to show how the following concepts from this chapter link together: fossil fuels, energy, smog, nonrenewable resources, acid rain, solar energy, greenhouse effect, geothermal energy, wind power.

2. **Science and Conservation** Find out what endangered plant and animal species live in your state. Choose one, and research where it lives and why it is endangered. Then outline a plan for protecting it.

3. **Science and Technology** Contact your local sewage treatment plant. Find out how sewage is treated in your community to make it safer for the environment.

4. **Science and Social Studies** Many communities are working to reduce the use of automobiles in order to save energy and cut down on air pollution. Investigate what is being done in your area to encourage bicycling, carpooling, and the use of mass transit. Then write a report on alternative transportation, including your ideas for what should be done and why.

5. **Science and You** Contact your nearest recycling center to find out how it works. What materials does it accept? Then ask where these materials are sent to be recycled. What are the glass bottles you recycle made into? What do recycled plastic containers become? Make a poster that shows the information you uncover.

Science and Literature Connection

There was a certain chief in a certain village. He had many slaves. Whatever he wanted to be done, he ordered it. If it was a wise thing he wanted, his various counselors said to him: "Yes, it is good." If it was not a wise thing, they said, just the same, "Yes, it is good," because if they disagreed with him he grew angry, saying, "What! Do you say the chief doesn't know what he is doing?" But the lowest of his counselors never said yes or no. If the chief asked him about a certain thing he would think for a while and then reply: "All things are linked."

It happened one time that the chief could not sleep at night because of the croaking of frogs in the marshes. Night after night he could not sleep, and decided at last that the frogs would have to be exterminated. He told his counselors what he intended to do. One by one, as usual, they applauded him, saying, "Yes, it is good." Only the lowest of the counselors did not speak. The chief said: "You, counselor, have you no tongue in your mouth?" The man thought for a while, then he said: "O chief, all things are linked." The chief thought: "This man knows nothing else to say."

"All Things Are Linked"

This story comes from the Lega people of Zaire and appears in the book The Crest and the Hide *by Harold Courlander.*

The chief sent his slaves out to exterminate the frogs in the marsh. They killed frogs until no more frogs remained. They returned, saying, "Sir, the frogs are done with." That night the chief slept well, and he slept well for many nights thereafter. He was pleased with life.

But in the marshes, the mosquitoes began to rise in swarms because there were no frogs to eat their larvae. They came into the village. They came into the chief's house and bit him. They made his life a misery. The people of the village suffered. So the chief ordered his slaves to go out and kill mosquitoes. The slaves went out, they tried, but the mosquitoes were too numerous. They continued to plague the village. The chief called his counselors. He scolded them, saying, "When I asked you about killing the frogs, you answered, 'It is good.' Why did you not say, 'If the frogs are killed the mosquitoes will multiply?' Only one of you said something for me to think about. He said, 'All things are linked,' but I did not understand his words."

The mosquito hordes made life unlivable. People left their houses and fields and went away. They went to distant places, cleared new fields, and began living again. The old village became deserted except for the chief and his family. Finally, the chief, too, took his family and went away.

Because of what happened there came to be a saying:

"'Yes, it is good' caused a village to become deserted."

Skills in Science

Reading Skills in Science

1. **Drawing Conclusions** What did the counselor mean when he said "All things are linked"?

2. **Find Context Clues** The story identifies part of a food chain. What might the other organisms in the food chain be?

3. **Predict** What do you think happened to the population of consumers that fed on frogs?

Writing Skills in Science

1. **Infer** Suppose you lived in the village depicted in this story. Write a diary entry that describes how the extermination of frogs affected daily life in your village.

2. **Reason and Conclude** Imagine you are one of the chief's counselors. Rather than agree with his decision to exterminate the frogs, you offer him an alternative way of handling the situation. Write a new ending to the story describing your plan, the reasons you give the chief to follow your plan, and his reaction to it.

Activities

Collect Data In a library, research two different pests that are controlled by pesticides. Who are the people who want to control the pests? Why do they want to use pesticides? What are the negative effects of the pesticides? Is there another way to control the pests that you think is better?

Communicate Use reference books to identify at least two different food chains that involve both mosquitoes and frogs. Design a chart illustrating your findings.

Where to Read More

A Caribou Alphabet by Mary Beth Owens. Brunswick, Maine: Dog Ear Press, 1988. The interdependence of animals and nature is explored in this text, which was originally inspired by a project to ward off extinction of the caribou.

The Pied Piper of Hamlin by Mercer Mayer. New York: Macmillan Publishing, 1987. A colorfully illustrated contemporary retelling of this famous tale, which explores the problems of solid waste disposal, disease, and environmental relationships.

Data Bank

Planetary Statistics

Name	Distance from Sun (millions of km)	Diameter (km)	Gases in Atmosphere
Mercury	58	4 880	None
Venus	108	12 104	Carbon dioxide
Earth	150	12 756	Nitrogen, oxygen
Mars	228	6 794	Carbon dioxide, nitrogen, oxygen
Jupiter	778	142 796	Helium, hydrogen
Saturn	1 427	120 660	Helium, hydrogen
Uranus	2 870	50 800	Helium, hydrogen, methane
Neptune	4 496	48 600	Helium, hydrogen, methane
Pluto	5 900	about 3 000	Methane

Essential Nutrients in Plants

Element	Form Available	% of Dry Weight
Oxygen	O_2, H_2O	45.0
Carbon	CO_2	45.0
Hydrogen	H_2O	6.0
Nitrogen	NO_3^-, NH_4^+	1.5
Potassium	K^+	1.0
Calcium	Ca^{2+}	0.5
Magnesium	Mg^{2+}	0.2
Phosphorus	$H_2PO_4^-$, HPO_4^-	0.2
Sulfur	SO_4^-	0.1

Results of Mendel's Crosses of Peas

Cross	First Generation	Second Generation
Round X wrinkled seeds	All round	5474 round, 1850 wrinkled
Yellow X green seeds	All yellow	6022 yellow, 2001 green
Colored X white seed coats	All colored	705 colored, 224 white
Smooth X pinched pods	All smooth	802 smooth, 229 pinched
Green X yellow pods	All green	428 green, 152 yellow
Side X end flowers	All side	651 side, 207 end
Tall X short stems	All tall	787 tall, 277 short

Relative Sizes of Organisms

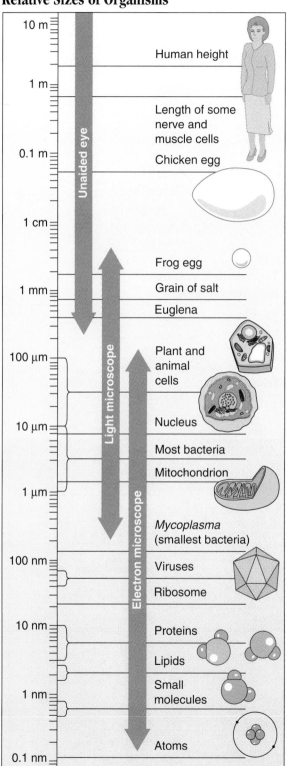

10 m	Human height
1 m	Length of some nerve and muscle cells
0.1 m	Chicken egg
1 cm	
	Frog egg
1 mm	Grain of salt
	Euglena
100 μm	Plant and animal cells
10 μm	Nucleus
	Most bacteria
	Mitochondrion
1 μm	
	Mycoplasma (smallest bacteria)
100 nm	Viruses
	Ribosome
10 nm	Proteins
	Lipids
1 nm	Small molecules
	Atoms
0.1 nm	

Unaided eye

Light microscope

Electron microscope

World Crop Production in Millions (metric tons)

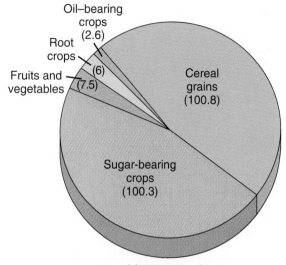

Oil–bearing crops (2.6)
Root crops (6)
Fruits and vegetables (7.5)
Cereal grains (100.8)
Sugar-bearing crops (100.3)

Average Life Spans

Species	Years
Mayfly	1 day
Mouse	2-3
Trout	5-10
Squirrel	11
Rabbit	12
Sheep	10-15
Cat, Dog	13-17
Rattlesnake	18
Owl	24
Lion	25
Horse	30
Hippopotamus	40
Pelican	45
Ostrich	50
Alligator	55
African elephant	60
Macaw	63
Dolphin	65
Raven	69
Rhinoceros	70
Man, Woman (USA)	68, 76
Tortoise	100

Human Bones by Region

Region of Skeleton	Number of Bones
Head	29
Torso	51
Arms and legs	20
Hands	54
Feet	52
Total	**206**

Cell Numbers and Life Spans

Cell Type	Number of Cells	Average Life Span
Red blood cell	4-6 million (per mm^3 of blood)	100 to 120 days
Brain cells	30 billion	Up to 100 years
Skin cells	6.5 million (per sq cm of skin)	Hours to days
White blood cells	4 000–11 000 (per mm^3 of blood)	A few hours to 9 days, depending on type

Population Density of the Continents (1991)

Asia	190 persons per sq. mi. (73 per km^2)
Europe	172 persons per sq. mi. (66 per km^2)
Africa	57 persons per sq. mi. (22 per km^2)
North America	46 persons per sq. mi. (18 per km^2)
South America	44 persons per sq. mi. (17 per km^2)
Australia	6 persons per sq. mi. (2 per km^2)

Vegetation Variations near the Equator

Tundra

Coniferous forest

Deciduous forest

Tropical rain forest

High

Altitude

Low

Tallest Tree Species

| California redwood 113 m | Douglas fir 93 m | Noble fir 85 m | Giant sequoia 84 m | Ponderosa pine 72 m | Cedar 67 m | Sitka spruce 66 m |

Oxygen Requirements for Activities

Activity	Oxygen used per hour (L)
Baseball	70
Basketball	90
Bicycling	55
Dancing	100
Football	110
Jogging	120
Playing piano	35
Sitting	25
Sleeping	14
Soccer	115
Swimming	120
Tennis	96
Walking	60

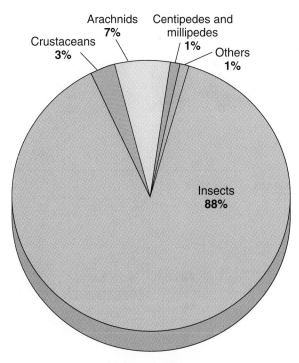

Relative Number of Species in the Major Arthropod Classes

Effects of Blood Alcohol Concentration (BAC) on the Body*

Number of Drinks	BAC	Effects
	.02–.03	Slight relaxation and mood change
	.05–.06	Relaxation and warmth; some loss of coordination
	.08–.10	Increased loss of coordination; slightly impaired balance, vision, speech, and hearing
	.10–.13	Coordination and balance increasingly difficult; lack of judgment
	.13–.16	Mental and physical abilities impaired; slurred speech; blurred vision; lack of motor skills
	.16–.19	Loss of motor control; assistance required for moving about; mental confusion
	.19–.23	Severe intoxication; little mind and body control
	.22–.26	Unconscious; near coma state

*Figures based on body weight of 100 to 120 lbs, and drinks consumed in the span of 1 hour.

Relationships Among Carnivora

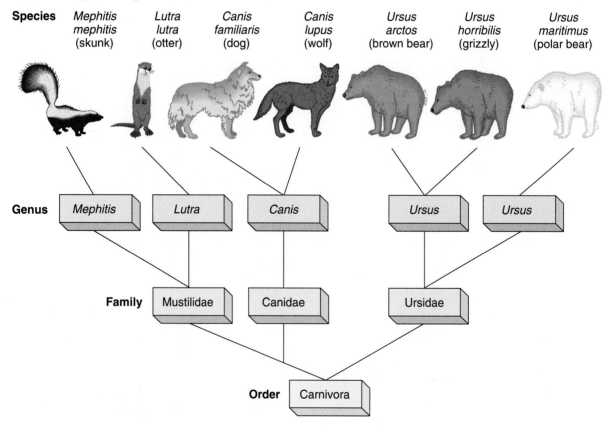

Global Cycling of Water

Process	Annual % leaving atmosphere	Annual % into atmosphere
Evaporation from land	N/A	16
Precipitation over land	30	N/A
Surface runoff	N/A	7
Precipitation over ocean	84	N/A
Evaporation from ocean	N/A	84

Invertebrates I Species Numbers (approximate)

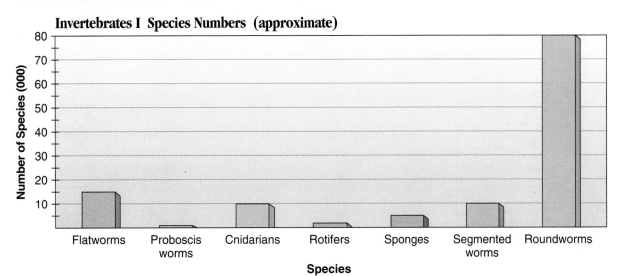

Cancer Risk Factors

Type of Cancer	Risk Factors	Warning Signals
Breast cancer	Over age 50, first child born after age 30, personal or family history of breast cancer, never had children	Breast lumps, swelling, thickening; nipple discharge, pain, tenderness, scaliness
Uterine cancer	Early age at first intercourse, multiple sex partners, late menopause, history of infertility, failure of ovulation, and combination of diabetes, obesity, and high blood pressure	Unusual vaginal bleeding or discharge
Lung cancer	Heavy cigarette smoking, history of smoking 20 years or more, exposure to certain industrial substances, such as asbestos	Persistent cough, spitting blood, chest pain
Oral cancer	Heavy drinking and smoking, use of chewing tobacco	Sore lips, tongue, mouth, or throat that bleeds easily and does not heal; lump or thickening; difficulty chewing, swallowing
Skin cancer	Excessive exposure to the sun, fair complexion, occupational exposure to coal tar, radium, arsenic compounds, pitch and creosete	Unusual skin conditions, especially size or color changes of a mole or a darkly pigmented growth or spot

Evolution of Mammals (millions of years ago)

PALEOZOIC ERA	570	Cambrian period	Trilobites become abundant.
	505	Ordovician period	Corals, brachiopods, nautiloids, and graptolites are common.
	438	Silurian period	Fish with jaws appear. Sea scorpions present.
	408	Devonian period	Fish become abundant. The first amphibians appear.
	360	Mississippian period	The first reptiles and first winged insects appear. Amphibians become abundant.
	320	Pennsylvanian period	
	286	Permian period	Insects become diverse. Reptiles begin to take over the land.
MESOZOIC ERA	245	Triassic period	The first mammals appear. Reptiles are abundant.
	208	Jurassic period	The first birds appear. Dinosaurs dominate.
	144	Cretaceous period	Mammals and birds begin to diversify. Dinosaurs become less common and finally die out.
CENOZOIC ERA	66	Palaeocene epoch	The first primates appear. Mammals rapidly diversify, but are still unlike those alive today.
	58	Eocene epoch	Bats and early horses appear.
	37	Oligocene epoch	The first mastodons appear, and many relatives of the rhino.
	24	Miocene epoch	Apes present. More modern plant-feeding mammals become abundant.
	5	Pliocene epoch	The first hominids evolve.
	1.6	Pleistocene epoch	Ice Age mammals abundant as the ice caps advance and retreat.
	0.01	Holocene epoch	Modern mammals. Humans increase on all continents.

Data Bank

Large Reptile Size Comparison

1-3 m   Giant tortoise

2m   Leatherback sea turtle

3m   Komodo dragon

1m   Grass snake

2m   Rattlesnake

6m   Crocodile

5.5m   King cobra

9m   Anaconda

10m   Reticulated python

Energy Use in the United States by Type of Fuel

Y-axis: Quads (quadrillion British Thermal Units)
X-axis: Years

Labels: Nuclear energy; Hydropower, geothermal, and other; Natural gas; Oil; Wood; Coal

Glossary

A simple, phonetic spelling is given for words in this book that may be unfamiliar or hard to pronounce.

Stressed syllables are printed in capital letters. Sometimes a word has two stressed syllables. The syllable with the primary stress is printed in full capitals. The syllable with the secondary stress is printed in small capitals.

Example: *Chromosome* is pronounced KROH muh zohm.

Most of the time, the phonetic spelling can be interpreted without referring to the key. The key to the right gives the pronunciations for letters that are commonly used for more than one sound.

Pronunciation Key

a	cat	ih	pin
ah	hot	oh	grow
ai	care	oo	rule, music
ah	all	ow	now
ay	say, age	oy	voice
ee	meet	u	put
eh	let	uh	sun, about
eye	ice or by	ur	term

 abdomen   In arthropods and vertebrates, the part of the body containing many of the animal's organs. (p. 325)

abiotic factor   The nonliving part of an ecosystem, such as air, soil, and water. (p. 538)

acid rain   Highly acidic droplets formed when gases produced by the burning of fossil fuels combine with moisture in the clouds. (p. 613)

active immunity   Body's production of its own antibodies for a particular pathogen. (p. 526)

adaptation   A change in character or structure that helps an organism live and reproduce successfully in its environment. (pp. 39, 139)

addiction   Physical and/or psychological dependence on a drug or other substance or behavior, usually including an overwhelming urge to continue or increase the use or the behavior. (p. 499)

aerobe   (AIR ohb) A microorganism that requires oxygen to live and grow, such as an aerobic bacterium. (p. 201)

alcoholism   The disease of alcohol addiction. (p. 503)

algae   (AL jee) A type of protist, single-celled or many-celled, containing chlorophyll and having no true root, stem, or leaf, such as seaweed. Singular: alga. (p. 211)

alveoli   (al VEE uh LY) Tiny air sacs in the lungs at the end of the bronchioles. (p. 431)

ameba   (uh MEE buh) Single-celled microorganism that uses pseudopods for moving and engulfing food. (p. 214)

amino acid   Simple molecule containing carbon, oxygen, hydrogen, and nitrogen; the building block of protein molecules. (pp. 64, 488)

anaerobe   (AN ur OHB) A microorganism that does not require oxygen to live and grow, such as an anaerobic bacterium. (p. 201)

angiosperm   (AN jee oh SPURM) A flowering plant that produces seeds enclosed in a fruit or pod. (p. 239)

animals   Many-celled organisms consisting of complex cells, having membrane-bound nuclei and organelles, that can move, eat, and usually reproduce sexually. (p. 181)

antenna   (an TEHN uh) One of a pair of appendages extending from the head of certain arthropods, used for balancing and sensing. (p. 328)

anther   (AN thur) A saclike part of a flower's stamen that produces pollen grains. (p. 281)

antibiotic   A chemical that inhibits or stops bacterial growth, such as penicillin; used to treat infectious diseases. (p. 527)

antibody   A specially-shaped molecule that is part of the immune system; interacts with and neutralizes a particular pathogen. (p. 518)

arachnid   (uh RAK nihd) Arthropods, such as spiders, ticks, and scorpions, that generally have two main body regions. (p. 327)

artery   A blood vessel that transports blood from the heart to organs and muscles. (p. 422)

arthropod   (AR throh pahd) An invertebrate with jointed appendages and segmented body, such as a spider, insect, or lobster. (p. 325)

asexual reproduction   Reproduction in which a single individual copies its genetic material. (p. 145)

atmosphere   An envelope of gases that extends approximately 700 km above the surface of the earth. (p. 34)

atom The building block of an element; atoms combine with other atoms to form a molecule. (p. 53)

B **bacilli** (buh SIHL EYE) Rod-shaped bacteria. (p. 201)

bilateral symmetry Characteristic of certain animals, such as humans and insects, in which the body has two similar sections. (p. 300)

binary fission The process of asexual reproduction in protists and most protozoans in which the cell of the organism divides into two identical cells. (p. 202)

biomass energy Energy that is released when plants and plant products are burned. (p. 609)

biome A large community of plants and animals whose makeup is determined by soil and climate. (p. 579)

biosphere A life-supporting zone extending from the earth's crust into the atmosphere. (pp. 31, 537)

biotic factor The living part of an ecosystem. (p. 538)

bivalve (BY valv) A mollusk with two shells hinged together, such as a clam or oyster. (p. 323)

bronchi (BRAHN kee) The two main branches of the trachea that lead into the lungs. (p. 430)

bryophyte A type of nonvascular plant, such as mosses and liverworts, that grows only in moist environments. (p. 256)

budding A type of asexual reproduction in which a new individual develops from an outgrowth on the parent. (p. 224)

C **Calvin cycle** The second stage of photosynthesis, in which chemical reactions produce glucose and other simple sugars. (p. 244)

cambium (KAM bee uhm) Growth tissue in a plant that makes up new xylem and phloem cells. (p. 276)

cancer A body disorder in which abnormally rapid cell reproduction causes a tissue to grow and spread. (p. 522)

capillary The smallest blood vessel in the body, where the exchange of oxygen and wastes between blood cells and the surrounding tissue occurs. (p. 422)

capsid A protein coat that makes up most of a virus and gives the virus shape. (p. 195)

carbohydrate An organic compound made of carbon, hydrogen, and oxygen, such as sugar, starch, and cellulose. (p. 487)

carcinogen A substance that causes cancer, such as some chemicals, radiation, and some viruses. (p. 523)

cardiac muscle (KAR dee ak) The striated, involuntary muscle of the heart. (p. 403)

cartilage (KART uhl ihj) Strong, flexible tissue in the skeletal system of vertebrates; also forms the skeleton in cartilaginous fishes. (pp. 349, 396)

cast A fossil formed by minerals in water that build up in a mold. (p. 163)

cell Basic unit of a living organism that can perform all the processes associated with life. (pp. 37, 75)

cell division The process in which one cell divides to produce two identical cells. (p. 103)

cell membrane The thin structure, made mostly of proteins and lipids, that encloses the cytoplasm and nucleus of plant and animal cells. (p. 79)

cell wall The stiff structure outside the cell membrane in a plant; provides support for the cell. (p. 79)

centriole A Structure in the cytoplasm that duplicates during interphase and forms the spindle. (p. 103)

cephalopod (SEF uh loh pahd) A mollusk with a distinct head and a foot divided into tentacles, such as a squid or octopus. (p. 323)

cerebrum (SUR uh bruhm) Part of the brain in vertebrates where higher brain functions occur. (p. 378)

chemical change Change in the chemical identity of a substance. (p. 59)

chemical digestion Chemical changes that take place when nutrients in food are broken down into simpler molecules that dissolve in water. (p. 415)

chemical equation Symbols and formulas that represent a chemical reaction. (p. 60)

chemical formula A combination of chemical symbols that represent a compound. (p. 55)

chemical symbol The shorthand name of an element, consisting of either a single capital letter or a capital and lowercase letter. (p. 55)

chlorophyll Green pigment in plants that captures the sun's energy for photosynthesis. (p. 83)

chloroplast An organelle in plant cells that contains chlorophyll. (p. 83)

cholesterol (kuh LEHS tuh ROHL) A fatty substance found in all animal tissues. (p. 488)

chromosome (KROH muh ZOHM) A threadlike strand in the nucleus that controls cell activity and carries genetic material to pass traits to offspring. (p. 104)

cilia (SIHL ee uh) Tiny, hairlike structures that facilitate movement in protozoans and small worms; also move fluid in animals with greater specialization, as in the human trachea. (pp. 215, 430)

class A division of a phylum. (p. 177)

climate Average weather patterns from year to year. (p. 579)

climax community Stable, permanent ecosystem. (p. 554)

cnidarian (ny DAIR ee uhn) An invertebrate, usually marine, with a body cavity and stinging cells, such as a jellyfish or a sea anemone; also called coelenterate. (p. 305)

cocci (KAHK sy) Round or egg-shaped bacteria. (p. 201)

cochlea (KAHK lee uh) The spiral-shaped, fluid-filled structure of the inner ear. (p. 452)

coefficient The number that shows how many molecules or atoms of a substance are involved in a chemical equation. (p. 60)

coelom (SEE luhm) The fluid-filled body cavity in some animals, providing space for organ systems. (p. 313)

community Two or more groups of different organisms that live and interact in the same area. (p. 538)

compact bone The dense, smooth outer layer of bone. (p. 395)

competition Struggle among living things for the proper amount of water, food, and living space. (p. 44)

compound A substance made of more than one kind of element. Most compounds are made of molecules. (p. 54)

condensation The process in which a gas changes phase to a liquid. (p. 549)

coniferous (koh NIHF ur uhs) Referring to trees that bear their seeds in cones and do not shed their leaves at one time. (p. 587)

conifer Most common living gymnosperm, with needle-shaped leaves and seeds produced in cones. (p. 262)

conserve To protect from being lost, reduced, or damaged; to save. (p. 602)

constant A factor that is kept the same in a controlled experiment. (p. 7)

consumer An organism that eats other living things. (p. 542)

controlled experiment Experiment with two test groups: an experimental group and a control. (p. 7)

crustacean (kruhs TAY shun) An arthropod, such as a lobster or crab, with a hard outer shell and specialized appendages. (p. 328)

cubic meter The amount of space occupied by a cube: 1 m X 1 m X 1 m; abbreviated m3. (p. 14)

cytoplasm A jellylike substance that makes up all the living material in a cell except the nucleus. (p. 81)

 data Information from which conclusions can be made. (p. 3)

deciduous (dee SIHJ oo uhs) Referring to trees that lose their leaves annually. (p. 586)

decomposer An organism, such as a fungus or bacterium, that feeds on and breaks down dead plants and animals. (pp. 203, 542)

density Measure of how much matter exists in a given volume; density = mass/volume. (p. 15)

depressant Drug that relaxes the central nervous system, causing the heart rate to slow and blood pressure to fall. (p. 500)

dermis Lower layer of skin, beneath the epidermis. (p. 408)

desalination (dee sal ih NAY shun) Process by which salt is removed from ocean water. (p. 45)

desert A biome that receives less than 25 cm of rainfall per year and has a greater rate of evaporation than rainfall. (p. 590)

diatomic molecule A molecule made of two chemically bonded atoms. (p. 55)

dicot (DY kaht) A variety of angiosperm whose seeds have two cotyledons; examples are maple trees and tomatoes. (p. 273)

diffusion (dih FYOO zhuhn) Movement of a substance from an area of high concentration to an area of low concentration. (p. 93)

digestion The process of breaking down food into simpler forms the body can use. (p. 415)

diversity The variety of life. (p. 140)

dominant gene Strong form of a gene, which is expressed even if a recessive gene is present. (p. 113)

duodenum (DOO oh DEE nuhm) First section of the small intestine. (p. 417)

E **eardrum** The round, thinly stretched membrane that vibrates when struck by sound waves. (p. 452)

echinoderm (ee KY noh DURM) An invertebrate with radial symmetry that lives in the ocean, such as a sand dollar or sea star. (p. 337)

ecosystem Area in which living things interact with each other and the environment. (p. 538)

ectotherm (EHK toh THURM) An animal, such as a reptile or fish, whose body temperature varies according to the external temperature; often called cold-blooded. (p. 346) Adjective form: *ectothermic.* (p. 43)

element A form of matter that cannot be changed into simpler substances by any chemical process or by heating. Elements exist in nature as solids, liquids, or gases. (p. 53)

endocrine gland A ductless gland that releases hormones directly into the bloodstream. (p. 458)

endoplasmic reticulum (ehn duh PLAZ mihk rih TIHK yuh luhm) An organelle that transports materials throughout a cell. (p. 82)

endoskeleton (ehn doh SKEL uh tuhn) The skeleton inside the body. The backbone is the central part of an endoskeleton. (pp. 345, 393)

endospore A bacterium with a thick protective wall. (p. 202)

endotherm (EHN doh THURM) An animal, such as a dog, bird, or human, capable of maintaining a stable body temperature regardless of surroundings. (p. 345) Adjective form: *endothermic.* (p. 43)

energy pyramid A diagram showing the amount of energy available at each level of a food chain. (p. 545)

epidermis (EHP uh DUR mihs) The outer layer of protective cells in plants and animals. (pp. 276, 408)

era The largest division of the earth's history. The Precambrian, Paleozoic, Mesozoic, and Cenozoic eras are measured in millions of years. (p. 158)

esophagus (ih SAHF uh guhs) Muscular tube extending from the mouth to the stomach through which food travels. (p. 416)

eukaryote (yoo KAIR ee OHT) An organism with complex cells, having nuclei, mitochondria, and other organelles. (p. 211)

evaporation The process by which heat energy changes a liquid to a gas. (p. 549)

evolution The concept originated by Charles Darwin, explaining that organisms are the products of historical change and that new species gradually developed from previous ones. (p. 149)

exoskeleton The hard outer support structure of an arthropod. (p. 325)

extensor A muscle that straightens a joint. (p. 404)

extinct Referring to forms of life that have died out. (p. 162)

family A division of an order. (p. 177)

feces (FEE seez) Semisolid wastes that form in digestive organs. (p. 418)

fermentation An anaerobic process in which cells break down sugar or starch into carbon dioxide, either alcohol or lactic acid, and a small amount of ATP. (p. 100)

fertilization The process in which an egg cell and a sperm cell unite to form one cell called a zygote. (p. 469)

fetus The unborn young of an animal while still in the uterus. The human embryo is called a fetus after the eighth week of pregnancy. (p. 474)

fiber Indigestible substances in plant cell walls that help move food quickly through the intestine. (p. 489)

filter feeding The method of feeding used by certain animals, such as sponges, in which food is removed from water passing through the animal's body. (p. 302)

flagellum (fluh JEHL uhm) A whiplike structure of some cells and single-celled organisms that allows movement. (p. 200)

flagellate (FLA juh LAYT) Protozoan that uses a flagellum to move. (p. 215)

flatworm A worm with a flattened shape. (p. 311)

flexor A muscle that bends a joint. (p. 404)

food chain A sequence of organisms through which food energy passes. (p. 542)

food web A network of relationships in which the flow of energy branches out in many directions. (p. 544)

fossil Remains or traces of an organism that lived in the past. (p. 162)

fossil fuel An energy source formed from the buried remains of decayed plants and animals that lived hundreds of millions of years ago. (p. 608)

fossil record Record of life on earth provided by fossils. (p. 162)

fungus (FUHN guhs) An organism with a membrane-bound nucleus and organelles. Most fungi are many-celled; examples are mushrooms. (pp. 180, 222)

gamete (GAM eet) In organisms that reproduce sexually, one of the sex cells that unites with another to form a zygote. (p. 114)

gametophyte (guh MEET uh fyt) A generation of a plant that produces gametes and reproduces sexually. (p. 254)

gastropod (GAS troh PAHD) A mollusk that glides along on a foot underneath its body, such as a snail or slug. (p. 322)

gene A unit of genetic material that determines a trait. (p. 113)

genetics The study of heredity. (p. 111)

genotype (JEHN oh TYP) Gene combination that determines phenotype. (p. 113)

genus A division of a family. (p. 177)

geologic time The time scale of the history of the earth and its life. (p. 158)

geothermal energy (jee oh THUR muhl) Energy that comes from heat from the earth's hot interior. (p. 610)

gill An organ that removes dissolved oxygen from water. (p. 348)

Golgi body (GOHL jee) An organelle that manufactures and moves materials within a cell. (p. 83)

grassland A biome that is characterized by grasses, having hot summers, cold winters, rich soil, and unevenly distributed rainfall. (p. 589)

gymnosperm (JIHM noh SPURM) A plant that produces naked seeds not enclosed in fruit, such as a pine, spruce, or cedar. (p. 239)

H **habitat** The area or place where an organism naturally lives in an ecosystem. (pp. 139, 305, 539)

hair follicle (FAHL ih kuhl) A structure in the dermis; each one grows a single hair. (p. 408)

hallucinogen (huh LOO sih nuh juhn) A drug or other substance that causes hallucinations, or dreamlike "trips," in which a person sees, hears, smells, or feels things that do not exist. (p. 501)

hazardous waste Waste substances that are very harmful to humans and other organisms. (p. 614)

heredity The passing of traits from parents to offspring. (p. 111)

holdfast The rootlike structure in brown and red algae that anchors the alga to a stable surface. (p. 219)

homeostasis Ability of an organism to keep conditions inside its body the same even though conditions in the environment may change. (pp. 43, 79)

hominid (HAHM uh nihd) The primate ancestor of modern humans. (p. 168)

hormone (HOR mohn) A chemical secretion made in endocrine glands that regulates a certain body function. (p. 458)

host A living thing another organism lives on or in for protection or nourishment. (p. 196)

hybrid An organism that has two different genes for a trait. (p. 113)

hydroponics (HY droh PAHN ihks) Method of growing plants without soil. (p. 242)

hyphae (HY fee) Branching, threadlike filaments that form the bodies of many-celled fungi. (p. 222)

I **immune system** The complex set of cells and tissues that makes up the body's natural defenses, which attack invading pathogens and prevent them from growing inside the body. (p. 514)

impermeable Referring to a membrane through which substances can not pass. (p. 95)

incomplete dominance A condition that results when genes produce a trait somewhere in between the traits of the parents. (p. 116)

incubate To keep an egg, or other object, in an environment suitable for hatching or development. (p. 373)

infectious disease A disease that can be transmitted between people by harmful organisms. (p. 511)

ingest To take in food from the environment. (p. 299)

innate behavior Behavior that is natural for an organism and does not need to be learned. (p. 571)

inorganic compound A compound that usually does not contain carbon. (p. 64)

inorganic nutrient A substance the body needs, such as water or a mineral, that does not come from a living thing. (p. 490)

invertebrate An animal without a backbone. (p. 301)

iris The round, colored disk surrounding the pupil that controls how much light enters the eye by changing the size of the pupil. (p. 451)

J **joint** A place where two or more bones meet. (p. 397)

K **kilogram** Basic unit of mass; abbreviated kg. (p. 15)

kingdom One of the five major divisions into which all living things can be classified. (p. 176)

L **labor** The process of human childbirth, especially the muscle contractions that push a baby out of the uterus and through the vagina. (p. 475)

lactic acid   A chemical that builds up in muscles during anaerobic reactions. (p. 406)

larva   (LAHR vuh) The early stage of an organism's development which changes structurally when the organism becomes an adult; plural: larvae. (p. 303)

lens   A piece of glass that can bend light in some way to make an object look smaller, larger, closer, or farther away. (p. 21)

ligament   Stretchable connective tissue that joins bones and reinforces movable joints. (p. 397)

limiting factor   An environmental condition that keeps a population from increasing, such as the availability of food, water, and living space, and the spread of disease. (p. 562)

lipid   (LIH pihd) A type of organic compound that is insoluble in water, such as fat and oil. (p. 488)

liter   A metric unit of volume; abbreviated L. (p. 14)

littoral zone   (LIHT uh ruhl) The place where land and ocean meet; also called the seashore. (p. 592)

liverwort   A bryophyte with either flat, leaflike structures, or a body divided into rounded sections, or lobes. (p. 257)

lysosome   An organelle that breaks down food molecules, waste products, and old cells. (p. 83)

M **mandible**   (MAN duh buhl) A jawlike appendage in arthropods used for chewing and crushing food; the lower jaw of invertebrates. (p. 328)

marine   Referring to the ocean. (p. 593)

marsupial   (mar SOO pee uhl) A mammal with a pouch in which the young complete their development. (p. 381)

mass   A scientific measurement for the amount of matter that an object contains. (p. 14)

matter   Anything that takes up space and has mass. (p. 51)

mechanical digestion   Physical changes that take place as food is broken down into smaller pieces. (p. 415)

medusa   (muh DOO suh) Body form of cnidarians that is free-swimming. (p. 305)

meiosis   (my OH sihs) Cell division that produces gametes or spores having one set of unpaired chromosomes. (p. 118)

melanin   (MEHL uh nihn) The dark pigment in skin, hair, and parts of the eye that partially determines the color. (p. 410)

meniscus   (mih NIHS kuhs) Curved surface of a liquid in a graduated cylinder. (p. 14)

menstruation   (MEHN STRAY shun) The flow of blood and tissue from the uterine lining out of the body when a human egg is not fertilized; also, the period of time when this flow occurs. (p. 470)

metabolism   The continual chemical and physical processes that balance the production, consumption, and storage of energy in an organism. (p. 37)

metamorphosis   (MEHT uh MOR fuh sihs) The process of development in which a young organism undergoes changes in appearance to become an adult. (pp. 333, 355)

meter   Basic SI unit of length; abbreviated m. (p. 13)

microscope   An instrument with one or more lenses that makes very small objects appear larger so they can be seen and studied. (p. 21)

migrate   To move to a different place for a certain part of every year, or simply to move from one place to another. (p. 372)

mitochondrion   (myt uh KAHN dree uhn) An organelle that produces energy in the cell. (p. 82)

mitosis   (my TOH sihs) The process by which a cell nucleus divides into two identical nuclei. (p. 103)

mixture   A substance with two or more components that are not combined chemically. (p. 58)

mold   A fossil impression left in rock by the hard parts of an organism. (p. 163)

molecule   The smallest part of a compound that has all the properties of the compound; two or more atoms chemically bonded. (p. 54)

mollusk   MAHL uhsk) An invertebrate with a soft, unsegmented body, such as an oyster, snail, or octopus; many are covered with hard shells. (p. 321)

moneran   A simple organism with no membrane-bound nuclei or organelles; occurs as a single cell or in colonies; examples are bacterium and blue-green bacterium. (pp. 180, 200)

monocot   (MAHN oh KAHT) A variety of angiosperm whose seeds have only one cotyledon; examples are corn and tulips. (p. 273)

monotreme   (MAHN oh TREEM) An egg-laying mammal, such as a platypus, with two unique characteristics: hair and mammary glands. (p. 380)

moss   A bryophyte with tiny green leaflike structures arranged in a spiral on a short stalk. (p. 256)

motor neuron   A specialized nerve cell that carries an impulse from the central nervous system to voluntary muscles, causing the muscles to contract. (p. 447)

mutation A change in DNA or chromosomes; can occur in body cells and sex cells. Most mutations are not harmful. (p. 124)

N **narcotic** A drug that numbs or takes away feelings and is often addictive. (p. 501)

natural resource Material from the environment that people use to carry on their daily lives. (p. 601)

natural selection The process by which organisms that are best adapted to their environment survive and reproduce, passing their traits on to their offspring. (p. 150)

nephron (NEHF rahn) One of many tiny structures in the kidney that filter blood. (p. 436)

neuron (NOO rahn) A nerve cell; receives and sends electrical and chemical messages. (p. 445)

niche (nihch) The specific role of an organism in its habitat. (p. 539)

nicotine The mild stimulant in tobacco. (p. 500)

nitrogen fixation The bacterial conversion of atmospheric nitrogen to usable compounds. (p. 550)

nonrenewable resource A natural resource, such as oil or natural gas, that cannot be replaced by natural processes. (p. 601)

nonvascular plant (NAHN VAS kyuh lur) A plant that lacks the specialized tissues to transport water, such as a moss. (p. 238)

nuclear energy Energy released by either the splitting apart or the joining together of atoms of certain elements. (p. 610)

nuclear membrane A thin layer that separates the nucleus from the rest of the cell. (p. 80)

nucleic acid A combination of proteins and carbohydrates that controls all cell activities and carries reproduction instructions; examples are DNA and RNA. (p. 65)

nucleus The control center for most of a cell's activities. (p. 80)

nutrient A substance needed by an organism to live and grow. (p. 415)

nymph (NIHMF) A stage in certain insect metamorphosis, such as that of a grasshopper, in which the organism looks like an adult but has no wings and cannot reproduce. (p. 333)

O **oral groove** A channel in a paramecium's body that is lined with cilia; food particles are swept down the oral groove into the mouth. (p. 215)

order A division of a class. (p. 177)

organ A group of tissues that work to perform a special function. (p. 87)

organ system A group of organs working together. (p. 87)

organelle A tiny part of a cell having a special form and function; organelles carry out all life processes. (p. 81)

organic compounds A carbon compound that occurs naturally in the bodies, products, and remains of living things. (p. 64)

organic nutrient An essential compound found in living things; examples are carbohydrates, fats and oils, proteins, vitamins, and fiber. (p. 487)

organism The highest level of cell organization. All organisms carry out life processes. (p. 87)

osmosis (ahz MOH sihs) Diffusion of water or other solvent through a membrane. (p. 94)

ovary (OH vuh ree) The female sex gland, which produces egg cells and, in vertebrates, sex hormones. (p. 469)

oviduct (OH vi duhkt) The tube through which egg cells travel from ovary to uterus. (p. 469)

P **passive immunity** Temporary immunity to a disease, gained when a person is injected with antibodies produced by a donor. (p. 526)

pathogen A microorganism that causes an infectious disease. (p. 511)

pelagic zone (pih LAYJ ihk) Part of the ocean beyond the sublittoral zone, where water is deeper than 200 m. (p. 593)

penis The male external sex organ, through which semen and, in mammals, urine flows out of the body. (p. 468)

peristalsis (PEHR uh STAHL sihs) Rhythmic contraction and relaxation of smooth muscles that pushes food through the digestive tract. (p. 416)

permeable Referring to a membrane through which substances diffuse freely. (p. 95)

pharynx (FAR ihnks) The funnel that leads from the nose and mouth to the windpipe and esophogus. (p. 430)

phase Property of matter; the three phases of matter are solid, liquid, and gas. (p. 52)

phenotype (FEE noh TYP) A trait that an organism actually shows. (p. 113)

phloem (FLOH ehm) A set of linked cells inside the vascular tissue of a plant that serves as the distribution path for glucose and nutrients. (p. 275)

photosynthesis (foh toh SIHN theh sihs) The process by which plants use energy from sunlight and raw materials from air and water to make glucose to obtain energy. (pp. 97, 243)

phylum (FY luhm) The largest group in the animal kingdom, or a subdivision in the plant kingdom. (p. 176)

physical change The change in a substance's physical properties, but not in its chemical identity. (p. 58)

physical property A characteristic of matter that can be observed or measured without changing the make-up of the object. (p. 51)

pioneer community A community of the first organisms to settle in an area. (p. 554)

pistil The female reproductive part of a flowering plant. (p. 281)

placenta (pluh SEHN tuh) An organ in most mammals that connects the fetus to the uterus of the mother, through which nutrients and waste products are exchanged. (p. 381)

placental mammal A mammal whose young develop in the mother's uterus, attached by a placenta. (p. 381)

plant A many-celled organism with cell walls that makes glucose by photosynthesis and does not move voluntarily. (p. 181)

polar climate A climate with a long cold season and a short warm season. (p. 580)

pollen Dustlike particles that are protective carrying cases for the sperm cells of gymnosperms. (p. 262)

pollination The transfer of pollen, containing the male gametophyte, to the pistil, containing the female gametophyte. (p. 263)

polyp (PAHL ihp) Body form of cnidarians that is usually attached to a stable surface. (p. 305)

population A group of individuals of the same species living in a particular area. (pp. 150, 539)

population density The number of individuals in an area, calculated by dividing the number of organisms in a certain area by the area's size. (p. 562)

precipitation Moisture in the atmosphere that condenses and falls to the earth as sleet, snow, hail, or rain. (p. 549)

predator An animal that obtains its food by killing and eating other organisms. (p. 563)

prey An organism that is hunted or eaten by predators. (p. 563)

primate A member of a group of mammals that includes humans. Primates appeared more than 65 million years ago. (p. 167)

producer An organism that can make its own food. (p. 542)

product A substance produced by a chemical reaction. (p. 60)

protein A large, complex molecule made of amino acids. (p. 488)

protist (PROHT ihst) A member of the kingdom Protista, most of which are single-celled organisms, with complex cells and membrane-bound nuclei and organelles, that reproduce by cell division and may make or eat food. (p. 181)

protozoan (PROH tuh ZOH uhn) A single-celled, animal-like organism belonging to the kingdom Protista. (p. 211)

pseudopodium (soo duh POH dee uhm) A temporary footlike projection of cell matter that facilitates protozoan movement and ingestion. (p. 214)

pupa (PYOO puh) The stage of metamorphosis in which an insect is often surrounded by a cocoon and many changes occur. (p. 333)

pupil The opening in the choroid layer at the front of the eye. (p. 451)

R **radial symmetry** A characteristic of certain animals, such as cnidarians, in which the body is organized around the center. (p. 300)

radioactive dating A method of determining an object's age based on known decay rates of radioactive elements. (p. 161)

reactant Raw material in a chemical reaction. (p. 60)

recessive gene The weak form of a gene, which is not expressed when the dominant form is also present. (p. 113)

renewable resource A natural resource, such as trees or soil, that can be replaced by natural cycles or processes. (p. 601)

replication The copying process in which new DNA is created. (p. 123)

reproduction The process by which organisms produce more organisms like themselves. (p. 38)

respiration The process by which a cell breaks down glucose into carbon dioxide and water. (p. 99)

response A reaction to a stimulus. (p. 38)

retina (REHT ih nuh) The light-sensitive layer that lines the back and sides of the inner eye. (p. 451)

rhizoid (RY zoyd) The rootlike structure of bryophytes. (p. 256)

ribosome An organelle that produces protein for the cell. (p. 82)

roundworm A worm with a round shape and a one-way digestive tube with two openings. (p. 312)

S **sarcodine** (SAR kuh deen) Type of protozoan, including the ameba, that moves using pseudopodia. (p. 214)

scrotum (SKROHT uhm) A sac that protects the testes in most male mammals. (p. 468)

sedimentary rock Rock formed from layered sediments that pile up and squeeze together, offering clues to the earth's past. (p. 160)

segmented worm A worm whose body is divided into small segments or units. (p. 313)

selectively permeable Referring to a membrane through which only some materials may pass. (p. 95)

semen (SEE muhn) The fluid mixture of sperm cells and accompanying secretions produced by male animals. (p. 468)

sensory neuron A nerve cell that carries impulses from other neurons to the spinal cord. (p. 447)

sepal (SEE puhl) A specialized structure at the base of a flower that encloses or protects the flower as it develops. (p. 281)

sex-linked trait A trait whose genes are located on the sex chromosomes. (p. 119)

sexual reproduction Reproduction through the union of a male and a female gamete, each contributing genetic material to the offspring. (p. 145)

simple sugar A substance in living things, such as glucose, that provides food for energy. (p. 65)

skeletal muscle A type of muscle attached to bones by tendons, allowing movement at the joints. (p. 403)

smog Air pollution caused by automobile exhaust, burning coal, or by other means, resulting in air that is unhealthy to breathe. (p. 612)

smooth muscle A type of muscle that makes up the walls of most internal organs. (p. 403)

solar energy Energy from the sun. (p. 609)

solution A type of mixture in which one substance is evenly mixed with another substance. (p. 59)

specialized Referring to a cell, tissue, or other unit that has certain characteristics in order to perform a particular function. (p. 86)

species The basic unit of classification, the division of a genus, made of very similar organisms that are able to mate and reproduce offspring of the same type. (pp. 142, 177)

spinal cord Nerve fibers extending from the base of the brain down the back. (p. 444)

spirilla (spy RIHL uh) Spiral-shaped bacteria. (p. 201)

spongy bone Soft, lightweight bone that contains red marrow. (p. 395)

spore A reproductive cell produced by sporozoans. (pp. 216, 254)

sporophyte (SPOH roh FYT) A plant that reproduces nonsexually by spores. (p. 254)

sporozoa (SPOH roh ZOH uh) A group of parasitic protozoan living in the bodies of another animals; produces spores, from which new sporozoans grow. (p. 216)

stamen (STAY muhn) The male reproductive part of a flower. (p. 281)

stigma The part of a flower's pistil that collects pollen. (p. 281)

stimulant A substance that stimulates the nervous system, raises blood pressure, and makes the heart beat faster. (p. 500)

stimulus A change that occurs in the environment, such as sound, light, or odor, that may affect an organism's behavior. (p.38)

stomate (STOH mayt) An opening in a plant surface through which gases are exchanged. (p. 244)

stress Emotional or mental strain or imbalance. (p. 496)

sublittoral zone (SUHB LIHT uh ruhl zohn) Part of the ocean near the littoral zone, where the water is less than 200 m deep, and the bottom slopes gradually; also called the continental shelf. (p. 592)

subscript The number written below the line in a chemical formula, that indicates the number of atoms in a molecule. (p. 55)

succession The replacement of one community by another over a period of time. (p. 553)

symbiosis (SIHM by OH sihs) The relationship between species that live together, in which at least one member benefits. (p. 567)

synapse (SIHN aps) The space between neurons. Electrical impulses must be chemically transmitted across the synapse. (p. 445)

synthetic polymer A giant molecule made of many smaller molecules that does not occur naturally, such as plastics and nylon. (p. 62)

T

taxonomy The science of classifying living things. (p. 175)

temperate climate A climate with a cold season and warm season of nearly equal lengths. (p. 580)

tendon A connective tissue that joins muscle and bone. (p. 397)

testes (TEHS teez) Male sex glands that produce male hormones and sperm. (p. 468)

thorax The part of an arthropod's body where legs are attached; in some vertebrates, the part of the body between the neck and the abdomen. (p. 325)

tissue A group of specialized cells in plants and animals that are organized to perform a certain function. (p. 86)

tolerance The body's adjustment to a drug, so that more and more must be used to obtain the same effects, possibly resulting in addiction. (p. 499)

trace element An element occurring in only a very small quantity in a certain substance. (p. 57)

trachea (TRAY kee uh) In most land vertebrates, the windpipe, leading from the larynx to the bronchi. In insects, the tubules that conduct air from the exterior. (p. 430)

transpiration A plant's loss of water through the stomates of the leaves. (p. 275)

tropical climate A warm climate with little variation in temperature during the year; most tropical climates have a lot of rainfall. (p. 580)

tropism (TROH PIHZ uhm) In plants, movement or turning in response to an external stimulus, such as light or gravity. (p. 287)

tundra The vast, treeless plains of arctic and subarctic regions. (p. 585)

U

umbilical cord A soft rope of blood vessels that connects the embryo to the placenta, through which materials are exchanged between mother and embryo. (p. 474)

ureter A tube through which urine passes from the kidney to the urinary bladder or cloaca. (p. 436)

urethra A tube through which urine passes from the bladder to the outside of the body. (p. 436)

uterus (YOOT uhr uhs) A hollow, muscular organ in female mammals where a zygote embeds and develops into a baby. (p. 469)

V

vaccine A medicine that produces immunity to a disease without causing the disease;

contains weakened or dead pathogens, which induce the production of antibodies. (p. 525)

vacuole (VAK yoo ohl) An organelle that stores water, food, and wastes in a cell and helps get rid of wastes. (p. 83)

vagina (vuh JY nuh) A canal in female mammals extending from the cervix to the outside of the body; receives the penis during sexual intercourse. (p. 469)

variable The factor that is changed in a controlled experiment. (p. 7)

variation A difference within a species. (p. 144)

vascular plant (VAS kyuh lur) A plant, such as a flowering plant, having tissues with tubelike structures that transport water and other materials. (p. 238)

vegetative propagation (prahp uh GAY shun) A method of producing genetically identical plants from pieces of stems or leaves. (p. 284)

vein A blood vessel that carries blood to the heart. (p. 422)

vertebra (VUR tuh BRUH) One of the small bones that make up the backbone. (p. 393)

vertebrate (VUR tuh briht) An animal with a backbone. (p. 301)

villi (VIHL eye) Tiny, fingerlike projections that line the small intestine and absorb nutrients from food. (p. 418)

virus A piece of hereditary material with a coat of protein. (p. 195)

vitamin An organic nutrient that helps regulate the chemical reactions that convert food into energy and living tissue. (p. 489)

volume The amount of space that something occupies. (p. 14)

X

X chromosome The longer sex chromosome. Females have two X chromosomes; males have one X chromosome and one Y chromosome. (p. 119)

xylem (ZY luhm) A set of linked cells inside the vascular tissue of a plant that forms a pipeline for water and minerals. (p. 275)

Y

Y chromosome The shorter sex chromosome. Males have one X chromosome and one Y chromosome. (p. 119)

Z

zygote A cell formed by the union of two sets of genes when a male and female gamete unite; a fertilized egg. (p. 145)

Index

Acknowledgments

Photographs

Title page i-CR David M. Phillips/Visuals Unlimited; i-R M. Austerman/Animals, Animals; i-L Norm Thomas/Photo Researchers; i-CL Zig Leszczynski/Animals, Animals

Contents iii-T Roger Ressmeyer/Starlight; iii-BR Zig Leszczynski/Animals, Animals; iii-BC Zig Leszczynski/ Animals, Animals; iv-R Biofotos Associates/Science Source/Photo Researchers; iv-L Photo Researchers; v-B Eric Gave/Phototake; v-T Ken Karp*; vi-C Alford W. Cooper/ Photo Researchers; vi-BL Gareth Hopson*; vii-BC Brian Parker/Tom Stack & Associates; vii-BR David Scharf/Peter Arnold, Inc.; vii-T Paul Skelcher/Rainbow; vii-C Runk-Schoenberger/Grant Heilman Photography; viii-BR Breck P. Kent/Animals, Animals; viii-BL Runk-Schoenberger/Grant Heilman Photography; viii-BC Science Photo Library/Science Source/Photo Researchers; ix-T David Scharf/Peter Arnold, Inc.; ix-BR Dennis Kunkel/CNRI/Phototake; ix-BL Manfred Kage/ Peter Arnold, Inc.; ix-BC Dennis Kenkel/CNRI/Phototake; x-T Fritz Polking/Peter Arnold, Inc.; x-B Grant Heilman/Grant Heilman Photography; xi-TL Calvin Larsen/Photo Researchers; xi-BL Gary Braasch; xi-BR NASA

Unit 1 xviii Gareth Hopson*; xviii-1 Will & Deni McIntyre/ Photo Researchers;

Chapter 1 2 David Scharf/Peter Arnold, Inc.; 3B John Colwell/ Grant Heilman Photography; 3T Craig Newbauer/Peter Arnold, Inc.; 4 Richard Shiell/Earth Scenes; 5 Larry Brownstein/The Stock Shop; 11B Livestock; 11T Ron Colby/Fran Heyl Associates; 13 Ken Karp*; 14B Yoav/Phototake; 14C Ken Karp*; 15 Ken Karp*; 16 Ken Karp*; 17 Ken Karp*; 21 Phillip A. Harrington/Fran Heyl Associates; 24B Argon Dyelaser/ Denny Studios/TheStock Shop; 24C CNRI/Science Photo Library/Custom Medical Stock Photo; 24T Secchi, Lecaque, Roussel, Uclaf,CNRI/ Science Photo Library/Photo Researchers; 25 Roger Ressmeyer/Starlight

Chapter 2 30 Photo Researchers; 35 NASA; 36 Zig Leszczynski/Animals, Animals; 37B Eric V.Grave/Photo Researchers; 37T Rod Planck/Photo Researchers; 38 Gregory G. Dimijian, M.D./Photo Researchers; 39 Leonard Lee Rue III/Photo Researchers;40 Stephen J. Krasemann/ DRK Photos;41 Zig Leszczynski/Animals, Animals;44 Livestock; 45 Grant Heilman/Grant Heilman Photography

Chapter 3 50 Frans Lanting/Minden Pictures;51 NASA;56 The Bettmann Archive; 57L Lawrence Migdale*; 57R The Stock Shop;58 Tom Till/DRK Photos; 59B Martha Cooper/Peter Arnold, Inc.; 59T Brian Lovett/The Stock Shop; 62 Lawrence Migdale*; 64 Fred Bavendam/Peter Arnold, Inc.; 65 Renee Lynn*; 70-71 Gary Braasch/Woodfin Camp & Associates; 70B Gerard Lacz/Peter Arnold, Inc.; 70T Gareth Hopson*

Unit 2 72 Hans Reinhard/Bruce Coleman Inc.; 72-73 Jim Foster/The Stock Market

Chapter 4 74 Manfred Kage/Peter Arnold, Inc.; 75 The Bettmann Archive; 76 The Bettmann Archive; 77 Courtesy Cornell University; 78L Manfred Kage/Peter Arnold, Inc.; 78R E.R. Degginger/Animals, Animals; 81 K. Love/Custom Medical Stock Photo; 82B Photo Researchers; 82T Science Photo Library/Photo Researchers; 83L James Dennis/CNRI/ Phototake; 83R J. L. Carson/Custom Medical StockPhoto; 84 Nubar Alexanian/Woodfin Camp & Associates; 86C Don Fawcett/Visuals Unlimited; 88 Martin/Potker/Phototake

Chapter 5 92 Science Photo Library/ Photo Researchers; 93B Ken Karp*; 93C Ken Karp*; 93T Ken Karp*; 96 Peter Menzel; 97 Gary Braasch/Woodfin Camp & Associates, Inc.; 100 Barbara Pfeffer/ Peter Arnold, Inc.; 101 David Burnett/Contact Press Images/Woodfin Camp & Associates, Inc.; 104B John D. Cunningham/Visuals Unlimited; 104T Eric Grave/Phototake; 105B John D. Cunningham/Visuals Unlimited; 105C John D. Cunningham/Visuals Unlimited; 105T Eric Grave/Phototake; 106 J. L. Carson/Custom Medical Stock Photo

Chapter 6 110 Heather Angel/Biofotos; 111 Bob Daemmrich/Stock, Boston; 116 Dan Clark/Grant Heilman Photography; 117 Biofotos Associates/Science Source/Photo Researchers; 119 CNRI/Phototake; 120 Richard Hutchings/ Science Source/Photo Researchers; 120R CNRI/Science Photo Library/ Photo Researchers; 126 Bob Daemmrich/Stock, Boston; 127B Jacana/Scientific Control/Photo Researchers; 127T Frank Siteman/Stock, Boston; 128B Keith V. Wood; 128TR Grant Heilman/Grant Heilman Photography; 130 Peter Menzel; 134-135 Art Wolfe; 134TC Stan Osolinski/Oxford Scientific Films/Earth Scenes

Unit 3 136 Norman Owen Tomalin/Bruce Coleman Inc.; 136-137 Jeff Foott/Bruce Coleman Inc.

Chapter 7 138 M. P. Kahl/Photo Researchers; 139B Anup & Manoj Shah/Animals, Animals; 139T Walter E. Harvey/Photo Researchers; 140BC Stephen P. Parker/Photo Researchers; 140BL Warren Garst/Tom Stack & Associates; 140BR John R. MacGregor/Peter Arnold; 140TC Calvin Larsen/Photo Researchers; 140TL Grant Heilman/Grant Heilman Photography; 140TR G. C. Kelley/Tom Stack & Associates; 141L Tom McHugh/Photo Researchers; 141R Tom McHugh/ Photo Researchers; 142 John Cancalosi/Stock, Boston; 144 Karen Tweedy-Holmes/Animals, Animals; 145R Eric Grave/ Phototake; 145L Roger Wilmshurst/Bruce Coleman Inc.; 148 The Granger Collection; 150 Mark Stouffer/Animals, Animals; 150R David M. Phillips/Visuals Unlimited; 151 Nuridsany & Perennou/Photo Researchers;152B J. Cancalosi/Stock, Boston; 152T Ken Cole/Animals, Animals

Chapter 8 156 J. Koivula/Photo Researchers; 160 D. & J. Heaton/Stock, Boston; 162 Gerd Ludwig/Woodfin Camp & Associates; 163B Fred Bavendam/Peter Arnold; 167 Larry Tackett/Tom Stack & Associates; 168BR UPI/Bettmann; 168TL Cleveland Museum of Natural History

Chapter 9 174 Norbert Wu; 175B Breck P. Kent/ Animals, Animals; 175C Jacana Scientific Control/Photo Researchers; 175T Charles Palek/Animals, Animals; 177 Jim Brandenburg/ Minden Pictures; 179 Ken Karp*; 180L Rod Planck/Tom Stack & Associates; 181 Michael Abbey/Photo Researchers; 183 Michael Giannechini/Photo Researchers; 184 Lynn

Funkhouser/Peter Arnold, Inc.; 185L Doug Wechsler/Animals, Animals; 185R Ken Karp*; 190-191 Stephen Frink/AllStock; 190BL Fred McConnaughey/Photo Researchers; 190BR M. Doolittle/Rainbow; 190CR Ralph Oberlander/Stock, Boston; 190T Nuridsany et Perennou/Photo Researchers; 190TR L. West/Photo Researchers; 191 Phil Dotson/Photo Researchers

Unit 4 192 Runk-Schoenberger/Grant Heilman Photography; 192-193 Doug Wechsler/Earth Scenes

Chapter 10 194 Dr. Tony Brain & David Parker/Science Photo Library/Custom Medical Stock Photo; 197 Custom Medical Stock Photo; 198BL Science Photo Library/Photo Researchers; 198BR CNRI/Science Photo Library/Photo Researchers; 198CL P. Hawtin, University of Southhampton/ Science Photo Library/Photo Researchers; 198CR Photo Researchers; 201C David M. Phillips/Visuals Unlimited; 201L David Scharf/Peter Arnold, Inc.; 201R David M. Rollins/Visuals Unlimited; 203L Pat Miller/The Stock Shop; 203R Inga Spence/LiveStock; 204 Thomas Hovland/Grant Heilman Photography

Chapter 11 210 Dr. Paul A. Zahl/Photo Researchers; 211 Pat & Tom Leeson/Photo Researchers; 212 Manfred Kage/Peter Arnold, Inc.; 212C Eric Grave/Photo Researchers; 212T Fred Bavendam/Peter Arnold, Inc.; 213L W. H. Hodge/Peter Arnold, Inc.; 213R Lawrence Migdale*; 214B Eric Gave/ Phototake; 215B Michael Abbey/Photo Researchers; 215T Eric Grave/Photo Researchers; 216 Holt Studios Ltd./Animals, Animals; 217A M.I. Walker/Science Source/Photo Researchers; 217B Biofoto Associates/Science Source/Photo Researchers; 218BL E. R. Degginger/Animals, Animals; 218CL E. R. Degginger/Animals, Animals; 218TR Peter Parks/Oxford Scientific Films/Animals, Animals; 219C Manfred Kage/Peter Arnold, Inc.; 219L Dan McCoy/Rainbow; 219R Runk-Schoenberger/Grant Heilman Photography; 220B Greg Vaughn/Tom Stack & Associates; 220T Brian Parker/Tom Stack & Associates; 221 Runk-Schoenberger/Grant Heilman Photography; 222 S. Rannels/Grant Heilman Photography; 224B Dr. Paul Zahl/Photo Researchers; 224TL Ralph C. Eagle/Photo Researchers; 225B Frans Lanting/Minden Pictures; 225T Ted Streshinsky/Photo 20-20; 226 David M. Dennis/Tom Stack & Associates; 227 Dr. Jeremy Burgess/ Science Photo Library/Custom Medical Stock Photo; 232-233 Renee Lynn*

Unit 5 234 Charles Krebs/The Stock Market; 234-235 Richard R. Hansen/Photo Researchers

Chapter 12 236 Rod Planck/Photo Researchers; 237B Owen Franken/Stock, Boston; 237T Norm Thomas/Photo Researchers; 238B John Gerlach/Earth Scenes; 238C Runk-Schoenberger/ Grant Heilman Photography; 239BL Ed Reschke/Peter Arnold, Inc.; 239BR Coco McCoy/Rainbow; 239TC F. Gohier/Photo Researchers; 239TL Doug Wechsler/Earth Scenes; 239TR Thomas Kitchin/Tom Stack & Associates; 240BL Frans Lanting/Minden Pictures; 240BR L. L. T. Rhodes/Earth Scenes; 240C Dallas & John Heaton/The Stock Shop; 240T Greg Vaughn/Tom Stack & Associates; 241TL Patti Murray/ Earth Scenes; 241TR Michael Fogden/Earth Scenes; 242 Catherine Ursillo/Photo Researchers; 246B Fred Bavendam/ Peter Arnold, Inc.; 246T Stephen R. Swinburne/Stock, Boston; 247 Christiana Dittmann/Rainbow

Chapter 13 252 Matt Meadows/Peter Arnold; 253 Greg Vaughn/Tom Stack & Associates; 255B Sinclair Stammers/ Science Photo Library/Photo Researchers; 255T Breck P.

Kent/Earth Scenes; 256 C.W. Perkins/Earth Scenes; 257B Gary Braasch/Woodfin Camp & Associates; 257T Runk-Schoenberger/Grant Heilman Photography; 258 Addison Geary/Stock, Boston; 260 Ed Reschke/Peter Arnold, Inc.; 261 Runk-Schoenberger/Grant Heilman Photography; 262BL Patti Murray/Earth Scenes; 262C Patti Murray/Earth Scenes; 262R Zig Leszczynski/Earth Scenes; 262TL Grant Heilman/ Grant Heilman Photography; 263 Runk-Schoenberger/Grant Heilman Photography; 264B Sinclair Stammers/Science Photo Library/ Photo Researchers; 264T J. & L. Weber/Peter Arnold, Inc.; 265L John Blaustein/Woodfin Camp & Associates; 265R Ted Streshinsky/Photo 20-20

Chapter 14 270 D. Cavagnaro/DRK Photos; 271B G. I. Bernard/Earth Scenes; 271T G. I. Bernard/Earth Scenes; 272 Peter Arnold, Inc.; 274 M. J. Balick/Peter Arnold, Inc.; 277C Lynwood M. Chace/Photo Researchers; 277L Jeff Foott/Tom Stack & Associates; 277R Don & Pat Valenti/Tom Stack & Associates; 278BC Manfred Kage/Peter Arnold, Inc.; 278CL Breck P. Kent/Earth Scenes; 278L W. H. Hodge/Peter Arnold, Inc.; 278T Z. Leszczynski/Earth Scenes; 280 Renee Lynn*; 282 Renee Lynn*; 282TL Jeff Lepore/Photo Researchers; 283CL Runk-Schoenberger/Grant Heilman Photography; 283CR Runk-Schoenberger/Grant Heilman Photography; 283L Runk-Schoenberger/Grant Heilman Photography; 283R Runk-Schoenberger/Grant Heilman Photography; 284B Nick Pavloff*; 284T Steve Maines/Stock, Boston; 285C David Scharf/Peter Arnold, Inc.; 285T Grant Heilman/Grant Heilman Photography; 287B Runk-Schoenberger/Grant Heilman Photography; 287T Runk-Schoenberger/Grant Heilman Photography; 288C Richard Shiell/Earth Scenes; 288T Fletcher & Baylis/Photo Researchers; 289 Peter Menzel; 290 Alford W. Cooper/Photo Researchers; 294-295 Renee Lynn*; 294BL Renee Lynn*; 294R Renee Lynn*; 294TC Renee Lynn*; 295 Jerry Jacka Photography

Unit 6: 296 M. P. Kahi/DRK Photos; 296-297 Art Wolfe

Chapter 15 298 S. Summerhays/Biofotos; 299 Anne Wertheim/Animals, Animals; 302T J. Selig/Photo 20-20; 304T Charles Hornbrook Photo Co.; 304CL Gareth Hopson*; 307BL Dave B. Fleetham/Tom Stack & Associates; 307BR Fred Bavendam/Peter Arnold, Inc.; 307C Ed Robinson/Tom Stack & Associates; 307TL Denise Tackett/Tom Stack & Associates; 307TR Runk-Schoenberger/Grant Heilman Photography; 309 Kevin Schafer/Tom Stack & Associates; 310 Runk-Schoenberger/Grant Heilman Photography; 311 Ed Reschke/Peter Arnold, Inc.; 312B Cubberly/Phototake; 314A David M. Dennis/Tom Stack & Associates; 315 J. H. Robinson/Photo Researchers

Chapter 16 320 E. R. Degginger/Animals, Animals; 321B W. Gregory Brown/Animals, Animals; 321T Neil G. McDaniel/ Photo Researchers; 322B Runk-Schoenberger/Grant Heilman Photography; 323T Ed Robinson/Tom Stack & Associates; 324B Runk-Schoenberger/Grant Heilman Photography; 324T Takeshi Takahara/Photo Researchers; 326R Breck P. Kent/ Animals, Animals; 326L David Scharf/Peter Arnold, Inc.; 327BC Kevin Schafer; 327BL Paul Skelcher/Rainbow; 327BR Mary Clay/Tom Stack & Associates; 328L Runk-Schoenberger/ Grant Heilman Photography; 328T George H. Harrison/Grant Heilman Photography; 329B Doug Wechsler/Animals, Animals; 329T Klaus Uhlenhut/Animals, Animals; 330 Richard Kolar/ Animals, Animals; 332 Billy Jones/Photo Researchers; 334B A. Griffiths Belt/Woodfin Camp & Associates; 334T Stanley Breeden/DRK Photos; 335 Mark Moffett/Minden Pictures; 337

E. R. Degginger/Animals, Animals; 338BR Fred Bavendam/ Peter Arnold, Inc.; 338C Denise Tackett/Tom Stack & Associates; 338TL Dave B. Fleetham/Tom Stack & Associates; 338TR Chuck Nicklin/ Nicklin & Associates; 339 Zig Leszczynski/Animals, Animals; 340 John Cancalosi/Tom Stack & Associates

Chapter 17 344 Gerard Lacz/Peter Arnold, Inc.; 345 G. I. Bernard/Oxford Scientific Films/Animals, Animals; 348 Larry Lipsky/Tom Stack & Associates; 349B Kelvin Aitken/Peter Arnold, Inc.; 349L Runk-Schoenberger/Grant Heilman Photography; 349R Andrew J. Martinez/Photo Researchers; 350 Tom McHugh/Photo Researchers; 351 Zig Leszczynski/ Animals, Animals; 352 Jim Brandenburg/Minden Pictures; 353 Tom McHugh/Photo Researchers; 354B Barry L. Runk/ Grant Heilman Photography; 354T David M. Dennis/Tom Stack & Associates; 355 Zig Leszczynski/Animals, Animals; 356 Zig Leszczynski/Animals, Animals; 357 Joe McDonald/ Tom Stack & Associates; 359C Zig Leszczynski/Animals, Animals; 359L Don & Ester Phillips/Tom Stack & Associates; 359R Zig Leszczynski/Animals, Animals; 360B Lawrence Migdale*; 360C Brian Parker/Tom Stack & Associates; 360T Stephen J. Krasemann/Peter Arnold, Inc.; 361 David M. Dennis/Tom Stack & Associates

Chapter 18 366 Frans Lanting/Minden Pictures; 367 Mangelsen/Peter Arnold, Inc.; 368 AP/Wide World Photos, Inc.; 368BL Perry D. Slocum/Animals, Animals; 369BR Carl R. Sams II/Peter Arnold, Inc.; 369C John R. MacGregor/Peter Arnold, Inc.; 369TL Jeff Lepore/Photo Researchers; 369TR Tom McHugh/Photo Researchers; 373 Hal H. Harrison/Grant Heilman Photography; 374 Galen Rowell/Mountain Light; 377C Brian Parker/Tom Stack & Associates; 377L Gunter Ziesler/Peter Arnold, Inc.; 377R Stephen Dalton/Oxford Scientific Films/ Animals, Animals; 378 Matt Meadows/Peter Arnold, Inc.; 379B Fred Bavendam/Peter Arnold, Inc.; 379C Renee Lynn/Photo Researchers; 379T Steve Kaufman/Peter Arnold, Inc.; 380 Tom McHugh/Photo Researchers; 381 John Cancalosi/Peter Arnold, Inc.; 382BL Francois Gohier/Photo Researchers; 382BR Cris Crowley/Tom Stack & Associates; 382C J. R. McGregor/Peter Arnold, Inc.; 382TR Judd Cooney/ Phototake; 383BL Mickey Gibson/Animals, Animals; 383BR Frans Lanting/Minden Pictures; 383C Fritz Polking/Peter Arnold, Inc.; 383TL M. Austerman/Animals, Animals; 383TR Gerard Lacz/Peter Arnold, Inc.; 384 Lawrence Migdale*; 388-389 Renee Lynn*

Unit 7 390 CNRI/Science Photo Library/Photo Researchers; 390-391 Michel Tcherevkoff/The Image Bank

Chapter 19 392 Pix Elation/Fran Heyl Associates; 395 Breck P. Kent/Animals, Animals; 397L Biophoto Associates/Science Source/Photo Researchers; 397R Biophoto Associates/ Science Source/Photo Researchers; 399 Nicholas Secor/ Medichrome Div./The Stock Shop; 402B Biophoto Associates/ Photo Researchers; 402L M. I. Walker/Science Source/Photo Researchers; 402T Michael Abbey/Photo Researchers; 403 Lawrence Migdale*; 406 Focus on Sports; 407 Biophoto Associates/Science Source/Photo Researchers

Chapter 20 414 Dennis Kunkel/CNRI/Phototake; 418 Electra/ Phototake; 424C Runk-Schoenberger/Grant Heilman Photography; 424L Dennis Kunkel/CNRI/Phototake; 424R Lennart Nilsson/Boehringer Ingelheim International GmbH; 427 Lennart Nilsson/The Incredible Machine; 428 Lori

Adamski Peek/Tony Stone Worldwide; 432 Jose Fernandez/ Woodfin Camp & Associates; 433 Day Williams/Photo Researchers; 435 Lennart Nilsson/The Incredible Machine; 437 Tom Raymond/Medichrome Div./The Stock Shop, Inc.

Chapter 21 442 Secchi-Lecaque/Roussel-Oclaf/CNRI/ Science Photo Library/Photo Researchers; 443 Lawrence Migdale*; 445 Ed Reschke/Peter Arnold, Inc.; 447 Lawrence Migdale*; 448 Tim Davis*; 449 Science Photo Library/ Science Source/Photo Researchers; 450 Tony Savino/The Image Works; 451 Manfred Kage/Peter Arnold, Inc.; 452 Patricia Barber, RBP/Custom Medical Stock Photo; 453 Lennart Nilsson, 'BEHOLD MAN', Little Brown and Company

Chapter 22 466 Howard Sochurek/Medical Images Inc.; 467 Dan McCoy/Rainbow; 473 David Scharf/Peter Arnold, Inc.; 474C Lennart Nilsson, 'A CHILD IS BORN', Dell Publishing Company; 474R Fran Heyl Associates; 474C Lennart Nilsson, 'A CHILD IS BORN', Dell Publishing Company; 475C Lennart Nilsson, 'A CHILD IS BORN', Dell Publishing Company; 475L Lennart Nilsson, 'A CHILD IS BORN', Dell Publishing Company; 475R Penny Gentieu/Black Star; 476 The National Foundation, March of Dimes; 477 Richard Hirneisen/ Medichrome Div./The Stock Shop; 478 Anthony Bannister/ Earth Scenes; 479B Peter Menzel; 479T Lowell Georgia/ Photo Researchers; 480L Susan Kuklin/Photo Researchers; 480R Susan Kuklin/Photo Researchers; 481C Nathan Benn/Woodfin Camp & Associates; 481T Frank Siteman/Stock, Boston

Chapter 23 486 D. Cavagnaro/DRK Photos; 487 Jim Brandenburg/Minden Pictures; 488 Renee Lynn*; 489 Renee Lynn*; 492C C. J. Collins/Photo Researchers; 492T D. & J. Heaton/The Stock Shop; 494 Mickey Pfleger/Photo 20-20; 496L Bob Daemmrich/Stock, Boston; 496R Joseph Lynch/ Medical Images Inc.; 497 Roberto Soncin Gerometta/Photo 20-20; 498 Harry J. Przekop, Jr./Medichrome Div./The Stock Shop Inc.; 500 Gareth Hopson*; 500L Owen Franken/ Stock, Boston; 501L E. R. Degginger/Earth Scenes; 501R Deni Bown/Oxford Scientific Films/Earth Scenes; 502B Coco McCoy/Rainbow; 502T Laura Dwight/Peter Arnold, Inc.; 506 Yoav Levy/Phototake

Chapter 24 510 Lennart Nilsson, Boehringer, Ingelheim International GmbH; 511 Yoav Levy/Phototake; 512 Lennart Nilsson, Boehringer, Ingelheim International GmbH; 513BR Ken Karp*; 513C Renee Lynn*; 513L Kent Wood/Photo Researchers; 513TR Bernard Furnival/Fran Heyl Associates; 514 Alon Reininger/Woodfin Camp & Associates; 515 Dr. Durland Fish/Fran Heyl Associates; 516 Bob Daemmrich/ Stock, Boston; 517 Manfred Kage/Peter Arnold, Inc.; 521B Bill Longcore/Photo Researchers; 521T Dennis Kunkel/CNRI/ Phototake; 522L Dan McCoy/Rainbow; 522R Electra/CNRI/ Phototake; 523B Matt Meadows/Peter Arnold, Inc.; 523T Geoff Tompkinson/Science Photo Library/Photo Researchers; 524B Dennis Kunkel/CNRI/Phototake; 524T David Scharf/ Peter Arnold, Inc.; 525 Carl Purcell/Photo Researchers; 526 Barbara Alper/Stock, Boston; 527 Jim Brandenburg/Minden Pictures; 528 David M. Dennis/Tom Stack & Associates; 532 Dennis Kunkel/CNRI/Phototake; 532-533 Biophoto Associates/ Photo Researchers; 533BL Dennis Kunkel/CNRI/Phototake; 533TL Dennis Kunkel/CNRI/Phototake; 533TR Institut Pasteur/ CNRI/Phototake

Unit 8 534 Larry Lipsky/Tom Stack & Associates; 534-535 Tom Stack & Associates

Chapter 25 536 Stephen J.Krasemann/Peter Arnold, Inc.; 537 NASA; 540 Richard R. Hansen/Photo Researchers; 541 Arthur Gloor/Earth Scenes; 542 Grant Heilman/Grant Heilman Photography; 548 Wayland Lee*; 550 Runk-Schoenberger/Grant Heilman Photography; 552 Compoint/Sygma; 553B Gary Braasch; 553T Gary Braasch; 555 Harvey Lloyd/Peter Arnold, Inc.; 556 Mike Yamashita/Woodfin Camp & Associates

Chapter 26 560 William Townsend/Photo Researchers; 561 Michio Hoshino/Minden Pictures; 562 Francois Gohier/Photo Researchers; 563 Tom & Pat Leeson/DRK Photos; 565 Timothy Eagan/Woodfin Camp & Associates; 567 Fritz Polking/Peter Arnold, Inc.; 568BR F. Gohier/Photo Researchers; 568L Francois Gohier/Photo Researchers; 568TR Ira Kirschenbaum/Stock, Boston; 569BR Patti Murray/Animals, Animals; 569C Charlie Ott/Photo Researchers; 569L CNRI/Science Photo Library/ Photo Researchers; 569TR Robert A. Luback/Animals, Animals; 571 Frans Lanting/Minden Pictures; 572B Warren & Genny Garst/Tom Stack & Associates; 572T C. Prescott-Allen/ Animals, Animals; 573 Grant Heilman/Grant Heilman Photography

Chapter 27 578 John Gerlach/Earth Scenes; 579 Robert Caputo/Stock, Boston; 581 Stephen Frisch*; 582 John Marshall/AllStock; 585BL W. Perry Conway/Tom Stack & Associates; 585C Jack Stein Grove/Tom Stack & Associates; 585TL Len Rue, Jr./Stock, Boston; 585TR Johnny Johnson/Animals, Animals; 586B John Lemker/Earth Scenes; 586C Robert Winslow/Tom Stack & Associates; 586TL Stanley Breeden/DRK Photos; 586TR Rod Planck/Tom Stack & Associates; 587B Bob Pool/Tom Stack & Associates; 587TC Grant Heilman/Grant Heilman Photography; 587TL Stephen J. Krasemann/Peter Arnold, Inc.; 587TR Tom & Pat Leeson/Photo Researchers; 588B Alan Pitcairn/Grant Heilman Photography; 588C Luiz Claudio Marigo/Peter Arnold, Inc.; 588TL Warren Garst/Tom Stack & Associates; 588TR Kimball Derrick/Rainbow; 589B John Cancalosi/Stock, Boston; 589T Eastcott/Momatiuk/Woodfin Camp &Associates; 590BR Jeff Foott/Tom Stack & Associates; 590L Christine M. Douglas/Photo Researchers; 590TC John Cancalosi/Stock, Boston; 590TR E. R. Degginger/Animals, Animals; 591 Arthur Rothstein/The Bettmann Archive; 594B Jack Wilburn/Earth Scenes; 594TL Greg Gawlowski/Photo 20-20; 595 Leo Keeler/Animals, Animals; 596 Delta Willis/Bruce Coleman Inc.

Chapter 28 600 Woodward Payne/Photo 20-20; 601 Adam Woolfitt/Woodfin Camp & Associates; 602 Richard Kolar/Earth Scenes; 603B J. Howard/Stock, Boston; 603T Ian Lloyd/Black Star; 604B Francois Gohier/Photo Researchers; 604T Greg Vaughn/Tom Stack & Associates; 605BL Leonard Lee Rue III/Photo Researchers; 605BR Frans Lanting/Minden Pictures; 605C Cary Wolinsky/Stock, Boston; 605TL S. J. Krasemann/Peter Arnold, Inc.; 605TR Lawrence Migdale/Stock, Boston; 606 Nick Pavloff*; 607C Mazda; 607T John Marmaras/Woodfin Camp & Associates; 608 Jon Brenneis/Photo 20-20; 610L Simon Fraser/Science Photo Library/Photo Researchers; 610R Giorgio Sclarandis/Black Star; 612 Tom Stack/Tom Stack & Associates; 613B NASA; 613T Breck P. Kent/Earth Scenes; 614B Bruce M. Wellman/Stock, Boston; 614C Holt Confer/Grant Heilman Photography; 615B E. Adams/Sygma; 615C, Grant Heilman/Grant Heilman Photography; 616 Mark N. Boulton/Photo Researchers; 617 Phil Degginger/Bruce Coleman Inc.; 622-623 Thomas Bachand*

*Photographed expressly for Addison-Wesley Publishing Company, Inc.

Illustrations

Raychel Ciemma
pgs. 393, 395, 397, 401, 408

Elizabeth Morales-Denney
pgs. 158 -159, 163, 164, 165, 169, 238 -239, 243, 244, 245a

Carlyn Iverson
pgs. 4, 7, 8, 9, 22, 23, 26, 52, 53, 54, 55, 60, 446, 447, 448, 454, 456, 459, 468, 469, 470

Mapping Specialists
pgs. 32-33, 157, 580, 584

Barbara Massey
pgs. 112, 113, 118, 123, 302, 303, 322, 323, 325, 328, 331

Michael Maydak
pgs. 42-43, 134, 135, 232, 233, 345, 346, 351, 354, 355, 358, 370-371, 372, 373, 376, 388-389, 538-539, 543, 544, 545, 554

Barbara Melodia
All reflective artwork for unit and chapter openers, half-page activity bars, chapter review bars, icons for WarmUp, WorkOut, and STS feature.

Precision Graphics
pgs. 18, 19, 29, 49, 63, 69, 94, 103, 109, 114, 115a, 119, 124, 129, 133, 142, 155, 173, 189, 209, 231, 245b, 251, 269, 288, 293, 319, 343, 362, 365, 387, 413, 424, 441, 461, 465, 485, 493, 509, 531, 559, 563, 564, 566, 577, 599, 602, 603, 613, 621, 624, 625, 626, 627, 628, 629, 630, 631

Rolin Graphics
pgs. 79, 80, 82, 83, 86, 87, 214, 215, 218, 223, 224, 225, 305, 306, 308, 311, 312, 313, 504

Margo Stahl-Pronk
pgs. 273, 275, 276, 279, 281, 282, 286, 287, 327, 332, 333, 339, 394, 398, 402, 404-405, 592-593

Carla Simmons
pgs. 176, 180-181, 186, 254, 256, 259, 260, 263, 300, 573

Nadine Sokol
pgs. 195, 196, 200, 202, 416, 417, 422, 423, 436

Sarah Woodward
pgs. 38, 39, 95, 98, 104-105, 141, 143, 149, 415, 418, 421, 425, 429, 430, 431, 444, 445, 451, 452, 453, 518, 540, 549, 550, 551

Science and Literature Credits

Unit 1 From *The Gorilla Signs Love* by Barbara Brenner. Copyright ©1984 by Barbara Brenner. By permission of Lothrop, Lee & Shepard Books, a division of William Morrow & Co., Inc.

Unit 2 From *The Plant People* by Dale Carlson, Franklin Watts, 1977. Copyright ©1977 by Dale Carlson. Used with permission of Franklin Watts, Inc., NY.

Unit 3   Reprinted with the permission of Atheneum Publishers, an imprint of Macmillan Publishing Company, from *In the Night, Still Dark* by Richard Lewis. Text copyright ©1988 by Richard Lewis. "The Weasel" from *Consider the Lemming* by Jeanne and William Steig. Verse copyright ©1988 by Jeanne Steig. Reprinted by permission of Farrar, Straus & Giroux.

Unit 4   "The Great Mushroom Mistake" from *Uninvited Ghosts and Other Stories* by Penelope Lively. Copyright ©1974, 1977, 1981, 1984 by Penelope Lively. Used by permission of Dutton Children's Books, a division of Penguin Books USA Inc.

Unit 5   "Songs in the Garden of the House God," from *Journal of American Folklore*, Vol. 7, 1894, pp. 187–193, reprinted in *In the Trail of the Wind*, John Bierhorst, ed., Farrar, Straus & Giroux, 1971.

Unit 6   "The Cloud Spinner" is adapted from "The Spider Weaver," *Japanese Children's Favorite Stories*, edited by Florence Sakade. Used by permission of Charles E. Tuttle Co., Inc. of Tokyo, Japan.

Unit 7   From *Fantastic Voyage* by Isaac Asimov, ©1966 Bantam Books. Based on the screenplay by Harry Kleiner from the original story by Otto Klement and Jay Lewis Bixby.

Unit 8   "All Things Are Linked" reprinted by permission of Coward, McCann & Geoghegan from *The Crest and the Hide* by Harold Courlander, text copyright ©1982 by Harold Courlander.